Nathaniel Hawthorne and his Wife

JULIAN HAWTHORNE

Nathaniel Hawthorne and his wife, J. Hawthorne
Jazzybee Verlag Jürgen Beck
86450 Altenmünster, Loschberg 9
Deutschland

ISBN: 9783849671839

www.jazzybee-verlag.de
admin@jazzybee-verlag.de

Printed by Createspace, North Charleston, SC, USA

CONTENTS:

- Preface To The Original Edition. ... 1
- Volume 1 ... 2
  - Chapter 1 - Ancestral Matters ... 2
  - Chapter 2 - Sophia Amelia Peabody ... 18
  - Chapter 3 - Boyhood and Bachelorhood (Part 1) ... 35
  - Chapter 4 - Boyhood and Bachelorhood (Part 2) ... 55
  - Chapter 5 - Courtship ... 75
  - Chapter 6 - The Old Manse ... 102
  - Chapter 7 - Salem ... 127
  - Chapter 8 - Lenox ... 149
  - Chapter 9 - Concord ... 181
  - Chapter 9 - Notes for Stories and Essays ... 202
- Volume 2 ... 209
  - Chapter 1 - First Months in England ... 209
  - Chapter 2 - From the Lakes to London ... 225
  - Chapter 3 - Mrs. Blodgett's, Lisbon, and London ... 239
  - Chapter 4 - Eighteen Months Before Rome ... 252
  - Chapter 5 - Donati's Comet ... 270
  - Chapter 6 - Rome to England ... 283
  - Chapter 7 - The Marble Faun ... 297
  - Chapter 8 - The Wayside and the War ... 308
  - Chapter 9 - The Beginning of the End ... 323
  - Chapter 10 - Conclusion ... 337
- Appendix ... 354

PREFACE TO THE ORIGINAL EDITION.

THIS biography will not be found to err on the side of reticence. The compiler has given everything that the most liberal construction of his obligation could demand. The closet, to be sure, had no skeleton in it; there was nothing to be hidden. What should be published and what withheld, became, therefore, a matter of taste rather than of discretion; and though a right selection under the former condition may be more difficult than under the latter, its importance is less.

I have allowed the subjects of the biography, and their friends, to speak for themselves whenever possible; and, fortunately, they have done so very largely. My own share in the matter has been chiefly confined to effecting a running connection between the component parts. I have not cared to comment or to apologize, nor have I been concerned to announce or confirm any theory. This book is a simple record of lives; and whatever else the reader wishes to find in it must be contributed by himself. I will only remark that if true love and married happiness should ever be in need of vindication, ample material for that purpose may be found in these volumes.

Of Hawthorne as an author I have had little or nothing to say: literary criticism had no place in my present design. His writings are a subject by themselves; they are open to the world, and the world during the past thirty or forty years has been discussing them,--not to much purpose as a rule. Originality remains a mystery for generations.

I have received assistance, in the shape of letters and other material, from various friends, to whom I gratefully acknowledge my indebtedness. Mr. Henry Bright (whose death occurred as the last pages of the book were writing) sent me valuable notes of Hawthorne's English experiences; and Miss E. P. Peabody has afforded me help which could scarcely have been dispensed with. Mr. Richard Manning, of Salem, in addition to other courtesies, has allowed the portrait of Hawthorne, in his possession, to be etched by Mr. Schoff. And in this connection I cannot refrain from saying that Mr. Schoff's success in all the six likenesses which illustrate these volumes has been quite exceptional. As likenesses they could not be better; and they are their own evidence of their artistic merit.

JULIAN HAWTHORNE.
NEW York, July, 1884

VOLUME 1
CHAPTER 1 - ANCESTRAL MATTERS

THE forefathers of a distinguished man (especially in this country) are not of much practical use to him. What he is, outweighs what they can contribute. Instead of their augmenting his dignity, his own proper lustre is reflected back on them; and such interest as we take in them is for his sake. For his distinction--so far as it may have any relation to them at all--seems to be the culmination or flower of their prevailing traits and tendencies, added to that personal and forming quality in him, without which no mere accumulation even of the best material would be of avail. How much the material in question may amount to, and of how great importance it may be as a factor in the individual's character, is, indeed, still undetermined. It is not necessary, here, to enter upon a discussion of the merits of the theory of Heredity; but we may, perhaps, assume that faults and frailties are more readily and persistently reproduced than virtues,--since the former belong to a man's nature, as distinguished from that self-effected modification of his nature, which we call *character*. A tendency to drunkenness, for example, or to pocket-picking, is more easily traced in a man's ancestry than a tendency to love one's neighbor as one's self, or to feel as charitably disposed towards those who injure us as towards those who injure our enemies. In other words, nature is passive, and character is active; and activity is more apt than passivity to be original, or peculiar.

It might seem an ungracious task, however, to analyze this great reservoir of ancestry with a view to reveal the imperfections of an individual. If a man contrives to get through life respectably and honorably, why ferret out the weaknesses which he strove to conceal? Would not vice be encouraged by the knowledge that even the greatest figures of history partook of its infirmity? The present writer, for his own part, confesses to feeling no sympathy with those who answer these questions in the affirmative. If it be true that human nature is evil, we shall gain nothing by blinking the fact. If the truth be humiliating, so much the wholesomer for us who are humiliated; the complacency born of ignorance of--and still more of ignoring--that which exists, can have in it no health or permanence. Sooner or later it will be overthrown, and then, the greater the security has been, the more disastrous will be the catastrophe. We are too apt to forget that intellectual eminence can exist side by side with moral frailty or depravity; and we are prone to infer that because a man does right, he has felt no temptation to do wrong. But, in reality, the beauty, the pathos, and the power of the spectacle of humanity lies in the fact that it is a spectacle of a mortal struggle between two eternal forces,--a struggle more or less stubbornly and conspicuously maintained, but common and inevitable to every one of us. The greatest men, so far as we know anything about them, have not been those who were virtuous without effort. Ever since Christ was tempted in the wilderness, and prayed that the cup might pass from him, and accused God of forsaking him, character has been, not innate, but the issue of this endless conflict between the desire of good and the tendency to evil; and its strength has been in proportion to the weight of the tendency as well as to the intensity of the desire. Indeed, the desire can be intense only in so far as the tendency is weighty. The imminence of peril creates the faculty to analyze and overcome it. If Christ was greater than other men, it was not because he did right more easily than they, but, on the contrary, because he resisted in his own person the tendencies to evil of the whole human race. Good men are not monsters: they know, better than others, what it means to be human. no doubt, we seldom have an opportunity to perceive the painful and laboring steps by which goodness or greatness is achieved; only the result comes into our range of vision. The reason is, that strength is silent and calm, and has the reserve and humility of a conqueror who knows the cost of victory, and how precarious and incomplete all victory is. It cannot talk about itself; it cannot find anything in itself worth talking about. Looking at itself from within, as it were, it sees only its negative aspect. None the less it is well for outsiders to investigate the processes of the growth and development of heroes, not in order to console ourselves for our shortcomings, but to gain encouragement from the discovery that human weakness is the very essence and occasion of human strength.

Now, as regards the subject of this biography,--a man whose personal weight and influence was strongly impressed upon all who knew him, and whose private moral life was as free from degradation as his writings are,--there is no reason to doubt that he inherited, or at all events possessed in himself a full share of the faults and foibles of mankind in general. He was, moreover, hampered by certain inconveniences or misfortunes incident to the period and society in which he was placed,--such as Puritanism, Calvinism, narrow social and moral prejudices, the tyranny of local traditions and precedents, and very limited pecuniary resources. Furthermore, he was brought up (as will appear later on) under what might be considered special disadvantages. His mother, a woman of fine gifts but of extreme sensibility, lost her husband in her twenty-eighth year; and, from an exaggerated, almost Hindoo-like construction of the law of seclusion which the public taste of that day imposed upon widows, she withdrew entirely from society, and permitted the habit of solitude to grow upon her to such a degree that she actually remained a strict hermit to the end of her long life, or for more than forty years after Captain Hawthorne's death. Such behavior on the mother's part could not fail to have its effect on the children. They had no opportunity to know what social intercourse meant; their peculiarities and eccentricities were at least negatively encouraged; they grew to regard themselves as something apart from the general world. It is saying much for the sanity and healthfulness of the minds of these three children, that their loneliness distorted their judgment, their perception of the relations of things, so little as it did. Elizabeth, the eldest, had, indeed, an understanding in many respects as commanding and penetrating as that of her famous brother; a cold, clear, dispassionate common-sense, softened by a touch of humor such as few women possess. "The only thing I fear," her brother said once, "is the ridicule of Elizabeth." As for Louisa, the youngest of the three, she was more commonplace than any of them; a pleasant, refined, sensible, feminine personage. with considerable innate sociability of temperament.

Nathaniel, two years younger than Elizabeth and four years older than Louisa, had the advantage, in the first place, of being a boy. He could go out in the streets, play with other boys, fight with them. make friends with them. He was distinguished by a cool and discriminating judgment, with a perception of the ludicrous which, especially in his earlier years, manifested itself in a disposition to satire. Being more than a match, intellectually, for the boys of his own age with whom he came in contact, he had a certain ascendency over them, which could be enforced, at need, by his personal strength and pugnacity. He was daring, but never reckless; he did not confound courage with foolhardiness. These characteristics could hardly have failed to inspire in him a fair degree of self-complacency, which would probably continue until the deeper thoughts which succeed those of boyhood made him look more broadly, and therefore more humbly, upon the relations of things and men. But, at all events, he had a better chance than his sisters to escape from the pensive gloom of his mother's mode of existence into the daylight and breeze of common life. Her solitary habits, however, affected and stimulated his imagination, which was further nourished by the tales of the War of 1812 and of the Revolution related to him by his elders, and by the traditions of the witchcraft period,--in all of which episodes his own forefathers had borne a part; and his mother, who, in spite of her unworldliness, had some wise views as to education, gave him books to read of romance, poetry, and allegory, which largely aided to develop the ideal side of his mind. Too much weight can hardly be given to the value of this imaginative training in a boy who united a high and sensitive organization to robust bodily powers. It provided him with a world apart from the material world, in which he could find employment and exercise for all those vague energies and speculations of an active and investigating temperament, which has not yet acquired the knowledge and experience necessary to a discrimination between the sound and the unsound. If all imaginative resources had been closed to him, the impulse to live throughout the range of his capacities would doubtless have led him into mischief which could not afterwards have been repaired.

Such, slightly indicated, were some of the conditions under which Nathaniel Hawthorne began to live. But before proceeding further with his personal history, it may be useful to take a glance at the leading facts of his family annals, from the time of the landing in New England of the first emigrant, onwards. In so doing, the reader will be left to draw his own conclusions as to how much light, if any, the deeds and characters of his ancestors cast upon their descendant. The writer's province will be simply to present, without garbling or reservation, whatever may seem likely to illustrate the matter. In such an investigation nothing beyond plausible inference is possible; and of inferences, however plausible, it is my purpose, in this work, uniformly to decline the responsibility.

The family seat of the Hawthornes, at the time of the first emigration, is supposed to have been in Wiltshire. The father of the first emigrant was born about 1570, and was married near the beginning of the seventeenth century. The issue of this marriage was four children,--Robert, the eldest, who remained in England; William, the second son, born in 1607, who was the emigrant; a daughter, Elizabeth; and John, the youngest, who followed William to New England after an interval of some years, and died there in 1676, leaving behind him four sons and four daughters, from whom are probably descended the Hathornes and Hathorns whose names occasionally appear in newspapers and elsewhere, but concerning whom I am able to give no further information. I append, however, an extract from a letter written to Una Hawthorne by her aunt, the Miss Elizabeth Hawthorne already mentioned, which touches the subject. The suggestion as to the Welsh origin of the family is a novel one. The coat-of-arms, and Nathaniel Hawthorne's impression that the name "Hawthorne" was a translation of "de l'Aubépine," indicate a French descent.

"Mrs. Forrester was a Storey, and her husband, John Forrester, was a son of Rachel Hathorne, my father's sister. Mrs. Forrester likes to talk of the ancestral glories of the Hawthorne family. Several years ago she brought a copy of our coat-of-arms, drawn by one of her daughters. She had made researches in heraldry, but she could not tell what some figures upon it were. Nobody could, from that drawing. But our coat is the one attributed in the 'White Old Maid' to some great family: 'Azure, a lion's head erased, between three fleurs-de-lis.'

"I never heard of the English 'Admiral Hawthorne' you mention, living at Boulogne. In the Court-guide I find a Mr. George Hawthorne, wine-merchant, Bristol,--perhaps this gentleman's father. There are not a few who write themselves 'Hathorn,' but none of them, so far as I know, are in positions that make it desirable to claim kinship with them. They may be of the same blue blood, but we have a right to ignore them. That, I suppose, is the way every family, however lofty, maintains its superiority. Your father told me that he believed there were not many of the English nobility better born than ourselves. Mrs. Anne Savage told me that her mother, who was a Hawthorne, was convinced that we were of Welsh origin. She also said that she believed that Upham, in his 'History of Witchcraft,' had purposely and maliciously belittled John Hathorne, the witch judge. It is very possible; for Dr. Wheatland, who has investigated our history, thinks him an eminent man, in talent and weight of character not inferior to his father, William. William Hathorne came over with Winthrop, and first settled in Dorchester. I never heard of any insanity in the family. We are a remarkably 'hard-headed' race, not easily excited, not apt to be carried away by any impulse. The witch's curse is not our only inheritance from our ancestors; we have also an unblemished name, and the best brains in the world."

William Hawthorne, or Hathorne (the spelling was either way, but the pronunciation the same in both), was a passenger on board the "Arbella," and disembarked in Boston, in 1630, when he was twenty-three years of age. While still a resident of Dorchester, and before he had entered upon his thirtieth year, he twice acted as Representative; and after his removal to Salem, in 1637, he filled the position of Speaker during seven or eight years. His parliamentary activity seems to have been suspended for one year,--1643,--but in 1644 he was again Speaker and Deputy, and remained so until 1661, when he was fifty-four years old. Some echoes of his eloquence have come down to posterity; and it must have been of a sturdy and trenchant sort, to hold the ears of Puritan law-givers so long. Unquestionably, this William Hawthorne was a man of restless energy, as well as unusual powers of mind. He put his vigorous hand to every improvement and enterprise that was going forward in the new settlement; he cleared the woods, he fought the Indians and treated with them, he laid plans for the creation of a great Fur Company, he led adventurous expeditions into the untrodden wilderness,--the latest being made in his seventieth year, along with Captains Sill and Waldron; and in the same year, in his capacity as Magistrate, he caused the execution of one John Flint, for the crime of shooting an Indian. Justice, with him, does not seem to have been tempered with mercy. Quakers received the lash at his command, and itinerant preachers and vagabonds were happy if they escaped with the stocks or the pillory. He was Commissioner of Marriages in 1657; in 1681, a gray-headed old man, he led the opposition against Randolph. It was in this year, moreover, that he died, full of years and honors; for his life had been as successful as it was vigorous and versatile. There was scarcely any field of activity open to him, in which he had not exerted himself. Even religion received the benefit of his zeal and eloquence, as may appear from this passage in a letter written by Miss Elizabeth Hawthorne to her brother: "Perhaps you never heard that our earliest peculiar ancestor, whose remembrance you have made permanent in the Introduction to the 'Scarlet Letter,' preached, besides all his other great doings. Mr. Taylor, the minister at Manchester, a man addicted to antiquarian pursuits, called to ask me if I knew anything about it. He said he thought it possible I might have paid some attention to my ancestry, and told me that this old Major, with about a dozen others, whose names he mentioned, used to go by turns to Manchester to preach. He had the information from Mr. Felt,"--who, it may be observed, was the author of "The Annals of Salem," a painstaking work containing much curious information about the respectable old town and its inhabitants.

But the chief testimony in support of Major Hawthorne's claims to statesmanship and a prominent position among his fellow-colonists, is the document which he wrote under an assumed name, to Mr. Secretary Morrice, in the year 1666, at the age of fifty-nine. One cannot read it, and note the turns of argument and expression, without feeling that he has gained some insight into the character of its author. It is subtle, ingenious, politic, and audacious; indicating a keen understanding of human nature on the writer's part, as well as a wise and comprehensive grasp of the whole situation as between the Colonists and the King. The occasional ambiguity of the language calls to mind the speech which Scott puts into the mouth of Oliver Cromwell, in one of his romances; it seems to be an intentional ambiguity, as of an intrepid and resolute man, who yet prefers to resort to cunning and policy rather than to open defiance, when the former may gain his end. What Secretary Morrice thought of this communication is not known; but, at all events, Governor Bellingham and Major Hawthorne did not go to London at the King's command. Miss Hawthorne, in writing of this document, says:--

"Mr. Palfrey told Mr. Hawthorne that he felt certain the memorable letter referring to the order from England for Governor Bellingham and Major William Hathorne to repair thither, 'was written by our aforesaid ancestor.' 'The letter,' he adds, 'was a very bold and able one, controverting the propriety of the measure above indicated.' It was a greater honor to defy a king than to receive from him such nobility as so many great families owed to Charles Second. I cannot remember the time when I had not heard that the King sent for our forefather, William Hathorne to come to England, and that he refused to go. And I have always been pleased when monarchs have met with opposition."

The document is endorsed in Nathaniel Hawthorne's handwriting as follows: "Copy of a letter, supposed to have been written by Major William Hawthorne, of Massachusetts, defending that Colony against the accusations of the Commission of Charles II., and excusing the General Court for declining to send over Governor Bellingham and himself, in compliance with the King's orders. (From the State Paper Office, London. Rec'd July 24, 1856.)"

I give it below in full, with the alteration only of the spelling.

Account Of the Massachusetts Transaction.

From the MASSACHUSETTS COLONY IN NEW ENGLAND, October 26th, 1666.

SECRETARY MORRICE, RIGHT HONORABLE: That good character from sundry hands received of you, doth embolden to give you the trouble of these following lines, although not so meetly digested and disposed of as becomes your dignity and honor, yet hoping it may be a service to his Majesty, I shall venture the bearing of your just censure for my folly and ignorance, being here resident for some years past, and diligently observing the guise and temper of all sorts of people, I shall briefly give you this following account. And whereas, by a copy of a signification that came to your hands of the Governor and Magistrates of this place (as I am informed) referring to their actings with the Commissioners sent over to them by his Majesty the last year, they are charged with denying his Majesty's jurisdiction over them, the account of their actings with the said Commission being by the General Court at large sent over to England, and (as it is here said) lies on file with my Lord Chancellor, I shall not now insist on the particulars thereof; yet this I assuredly know, that the Commission had more kindness and respect shown them by the people and Government of this place, than from any other,--nay, I may truly say than from all the rest of his Majesty's Colonies in New England. This Colony being for their entertainment, and raising of soldiers for their assistance in reducing the Manhattoes, at a very considerable charge, and, would Colonel Cartwright speak his conscience, he very well knows it was the countenance this Colony gave them, and the assistance of their messengers in treating with the Dutch, that did greatly alleviate that undertaking. And as to that charge of denying the King his jurisdiction over them, I shall briefly acquaint your Honour with the more general answer of the people thereto, viz.: They thus say, that they left their native Country and dear relations there, not with any dislike of his Majesty then reigning, or of monarchical power, for they esteem it the best of Governments, and the laws of the land they highly honor and esteem; but it was, that they might, without offence to any, worship the Lord according to His own institutions, not being able to bear the yoke imposed upon them by the then prevailing Hierarchy. For the orderly effecting whereof, they obtained of the King's Majesty a Royal Charter for this place, his Majesty therein giving them liberty to transplant themselves, families, and substance, and, for their encouragement in their undertaking, gave them full power to elect all their own officers for rule and Government, from the least to the greatest; to make their own laws not repugnant to the laws of England, and absolute power of ruling and governing all the people of this place and all this, with sundry other immunities and privileges to them granted, is confirmed to them and their heirs forever, under the Broad Seal of England. In confidence whereof, they hither came to a waste and howling wilderness, where they have conflicted with difficulties and sorrows of all sorts, they finding both the French and Dutch nations possessed North and South of their Patent bounds, and with whom they had some scuffling at their first entrance on this place. And the wild natives, whom they found to be very numerous, being for some time pricks in their sides, and thorns in their eyes, and when weak, made a prey of their lives and estates, sundry of them losing their dear relations; to this very day the salvage tortures and cruelties that sundry of them suffered, being cruelly murdered, not being forgotten by the survivors. The extremity of summer heat and winter cold and barrenness of the land discouraging some others, causing them to repent their design and desert the place. And those that remained, having, by the Blessing of God on their indefatigable labors, accompanied with many wants and straits, wrestled through the difficulties of their first plantings, and here sown the seeds of man and beast, so that now they are grown up to a considerable body of people and some small beginnings of a Common Weal, and all this at their own proper charges, not one penny being disbursed out of his Majesty's Exchequer. Now, thus they reason with themselves, viz.: That whiles they own his Majesty's charter which comprehends the conditions on which they transplanted themselves, they cannot justly be charged with denying his jurisdiction over them, for thereby they acknowledge themselves to be his Majesty's liege subjects; their power of Government, executive and legislative, proceeding from, and is according with, his Majesty's appointment, and all Courts of Justice constituted by his authority and appointment; their writs and processes of law going forth in his Majesty's name. Now, while they thus act, they apprehend they cannot justly be charged with denying his authority and jurisdiction over them. And in case they may not be confident in their Royal Grant, so orderly obtained, so long enjoyed and often confirmed, they apprehend they can have no certainty of their lives, estates, houses, and lands, and much less of that liberty which hitherto they have had in the free passage of the Gospel, far dearer to them than all their other comforts, whether natural or civil; they well knowing that if the wall of the civil government be pulled down, the wild boar will soon destroy the Lord's vineyard, and that it is impossible for them to keep the Waters of the Sanctuary, when that Venice glass which holds them is broken in pieces; there not wanting many sectaries and profane persons that are sprung up among themselves, who do long for such an opportunity. And whereas they are charged with denying his Majesty's jurisdiction, because they refuse to submit to the mandates of his Commission, requiring the General Court of this Colony to answer at their tribunal,--to this they answer as followeth, viz.: That the Commissioners by interpreting of and acting upon color of their Commission contrary to the Charter granted by his Majesty, as it was a great abuse of his Majesty's power granted unto them, so also an injury to his subjects, thereby violating their liberty, and was repugnant to the instructions given them by his Majesty, to the due observance of which the power granted them by their Commission is expressly limited, and had the people here submitted to them therein, they had destroyed themselves by their voluntary acting to the utter ruin of their Government and liberties, so legally secured to them by Charter, confirmed by his Majesty's letters, and indemnified by that power of the said Commissioners by his Majesty's special instructions given, as above said; all which will fully appear, reference to the said Commission and their instructions from his Majesty being had and perused. This people here planted, having purchased their liberty at so dear a rate, and being in so orderly a way removed from their native Country, thereby losing the benefit of those privileges in the Parliament of England, and laws under which they and their fathers were born, all that they crave of his Majesty is, that they may stand among the rest of his Majesty's dominions and plantations as the shrub among the cedars, growing upon their own root, and not be forced to be the slaves of rulers imposed upon them contrary to the rule of their Charter. Honored Sir, I may not further enlarge, lest I should too much abuse your patience, but the truth is, it is great pity that so hopeful a plantation should he now lost through the malice of those whose design it is to beget a misunderstanding in his Majesty of this people. It is in his Majesty's power easily to crush them by the breath of his nostrils; their best weapons are prayers and tears; they are afraid to multiply their supplications to his Majesty, lest they should thereby further provoke; their hope is in God, who hath the hearts of Kings in His hand. They have long been laboring how they might express their duty of good affection and loyalty to his

Majesty, at last have ordered a present of masts of large dimensions, such as no other of his Majesty's dominions can produce, to be presented to his Majesty; they are not without hope of a favorable acceptance, which will be to their souls as a cloud of latter rain. This I clearly see, that the body of the people have a higher esteem of their liberties, sacred and civil, than of their lives; they will know they are such twins as God and not nature have joined together; and are resolved to bury their estates and liberties in the same grave. Should the Lord be pleased to move the heart of the King (of His gracious disposition and clemency) to smile upon them and speak comfortably to them, as I have reason to be confident his Majesty hath no subjects more faithful to him in all his dominions, so he will still gain more and more of their hearts and affections towards him. And this poor Colony, if it may be accounted any small addition to his Majesty's dominions, by the blessing of God upon their endeavors will be daily increased, and his Majesty's interest here by them maintained, to the great advance of his Majesty's customs) which have already by that Colony been considerably augmented; the whole product of their manufacture by land and trading by sea being so improved, as that it is constantly returned to England. Whereas, on the other hand, should the malicious accusations of their adversaries prevail with his Majesty to impose hard measure upon them, as their dwellings are not desirable for luxurious minds, so they would not be long inhabited by them, the country being large and wide. And what great pity is it, that a hopeful plantation, so suddenly raised without any expense to his Majesty, should now be made a prey to foreign enemies; the French waiting for such an opportunity, and are much fleshed by their prevailing in Christopher's Island: and the French King (as is here reported by some Rochellers) designing to secure those parts of America for himself; and for that purpose, in '65, as also this last summer, hath sent sundry ships with soldiers to a considerable number, that he may thereby strengthen his interest here; who, arriving in Canada, from thence the last winter took the advantage of the frost, and travelled across the great lake, quite across the Massachusetts patent, as far as Fort Albany, formerly in the possession of the Dutch, and now under his Highness the Duke of York. The more particular account whereof I doubt not but his Highness have received from Colonel Nicols. It is credibly reported by the Indians that about seven hundred Frenchmen are building and fortifying on this side the lake, above our plantations, and have already built two Forts, intending there to settle some plantations of their own; their further design being to the people here unknown. The English of this colony in their frontier towns, more remote from Boston, have already been so alarmed by reports of neighboring Indians, so as that they were forced to stand upon their watch this last summer, although disabled from giving them any offence by reason of their great distance from these parts, and the unpassableness through the country for any considerable force, as also want of powder and ammunition; and how acceptable will it be to French and Dutch to see this people frowned on by their King, your Honor may easily judge. The thoughts whereof I do undoubtedly believe would be an utter abhorrency to all, good and bad. But what extremity may force them to, that God only knows, who is wonderful in counsel and mighty in working, whose thoughts are not as man's, and His counsel only shall stand.

The present of masts above mentioned, containing two great ones, now aboard Captain Pierce, fitting to accommodate the building another "Prince Royal," and a shipload containing twenty-eight large masts, prepared for his Majesty's service against next year,--may I tell you with what difficulty this small business of masts is by the poor planters here effected; for (although some few merchants and traders among them have acquired to themselves considerable estates) yet I can assure you for the generality of the people 't is all (if not more than all) that they can do, by hard labor and great prudence in the improvement of the summer season, to get bread and clothing for their necessary supply and relief in the winter season. True it is, every man generally hath a little house and small . . . parcel in dimension from twenty-six to thirty-eight inches, which they have now bargained for, that they may be . parcel of land with some few cattle; but all will not purchase five pounds' worth of clothing in England. And, for sundry years past, God hath much frowned on their crops, so that for attaining this small present for his Majesty they are forced to take up money at interest, and for the payment thereof particular persons stand obliged; yet may it find acceptance with his Majesty, they will be more refreshed at the news thereof than at the reaping of a plentiful harvest. Honored Sir, my interest is only to inform, assuring you these foregoing lines are words of truth, and such as I shall not be ashamed of, when I shall stand before the Judgment seat of Him who judgeth not by the seeing of the eye (as to the verity thereof, I mean).

There came to the hands of the Governor and General Court here assembled this winter, a writing, being a copy of a signification from his Majesty requiring the Governor and some others to appear in England. But the very truth is, the Governor is an ancient gentleman near eighty years old, and is attended with many infirmities of age, as stone-colic, deafness, etc., so that to have exposed him to such an undertaking had been extreme cruelty. And for the further alleviating, please to be informed that the writing which came to their hands was neither original nor duplicate, but only a copy without any seal or notification that his Majesty had appointed the exhibition thereof to the Colony. Also the answer of the General Court to the mandates of the Commissioner by them denied to be observed, being fully and at large sent over last year, and is on file as they are informed, and no particulars nominated to which they are to answer. All these aforesaid considerations put together, the General Court and people here do generally hope that the King's Majesty will favorably interpret them herein.

Honored Sir, how can your unfeigned loyalty to his Majesty better appear than by your love to the peace of his subjects wherever scattered, although in the remotest of his dominions? I need not tell your Honor the meaning of these lines; what you do for the interest of God's people, God Himself will own, and Jesus Christ His Son will own you for it, when He shall appear in all His glory with his saints and holy angels to judge the world. If in your wisdom you shall perceive it will do no good to this people your declaring the contents hereof, I do humbly for Christ's sake beg that favor of your Honor that it may not be improved to any provocation; this being privately done by my own hand, without the privity of the authority or advice of any other person whatsoever; against whom, whiles I have been here resident, I see no just grounds of complaint.

The truth is, the acting of the late Commissioner in this place, putting the spurs too hard to the horses sides, before they were got into the saddle; and there being added thereto the vigorous dealing of Lord Willoughby on Barbadoes Island, so uncivilly and inhumanely carrying it towards sundry gentlemen of his Council, and cruelly towards all sorts, have greatly alarmed the people here, making the name of a Commission odious to them. And whereas the Commissioners have informed his Majesty that the obstruction given them here was by the Magistrates and leading men and not by the people, your Honor may easily take a demonstration of the falseness thereof. The Government being popular, and election of all public officers, Governor and Magistrates, being annually made by the people, were they divertly minded from their rulers, they have advantage enough to attain their desires.

And had the Governor and all the leading men of the Colony adhered to the Commissioners' mandates, the people were so resolved, that they would, for the generality of them (some discontents, Quakers, and others excepted), have utterly protested against their concession.

Honored Sir, I take leave, and am

Your humble servant,

SAMUEL NADHORTH.

This must suffice for this notable old statesman, warrior, and priest, whose steel head-piece, bluff uncompromising visage, and resolute figure seem to stand forth quite distinctly through the mists of two hundred and fifty years. His successor was his son John, the fifth of eight children, who lived to enjoy the sinister renown of having, in his capacity of Judge, examined and condemned to death certain persons accused of witchcraft,--one of whom, according to tradition, invoked a heavy curse upon him and upon his children's children. In the book of Court records of that period, under date of the 24th of March, 1691, there is entered a transcript of the examination of "Rebekah Nurse, at Salem village," from which I extract the following dialogue between John Hathorne, Rebekah, and others:--

"Mr. Hathorne.--'What do you say?' (speaking to one afflicted.) 'Have you seen this woman hurt you?'

"'Yes, she beat me this morning.'

"'Abigail, have you been hurt by this woman?'

"Ann Putnam in a grievous fit cried out that she hurt her.

"Mr. H.--'Goody Nurse, here are now Ann Putnam, the child, and Abigail Williams complains of your hurting them. What do you say to it?'

"Nurse.--'I can say before my Eternal Father I am innocent, and God will clear my innocency.'

"Mr. H.--'You do know whether you are guilty, and have familiarity with the Devil; and now when you are here present to see such a thing as these testify,--a black man whispering in your ear, and devils about you,--what do you say to it?'

"N.--'It is all false. I am clear.'

"Mr. H.--'Is it not an unaccountable thing, that when you are examined, these persons are afflicted?'

"N.--'I have got nobody to look to but God.'"

This passage in the Judge's career has thrown the rest of his life into the shade; but he was almost as able a man as his father, if less active and versatile. He began with being Representative; during the witchcraft cases he was "Assistant Judge," Jonathan Curwin being with him on the bench; ten years later; he was made Judge of the Supreme Court, and held that position until within two years of his death, which happened in 1717, in his seventy-seventh year. He also bore the title of Colonel, which was not, perhaps, a dignity so easily won then as now. In his will he describes himself as simply a "merchant." His brother William was a sea-captain, and the Judge probably invested a large part of his capital in commercial enterprises. He seems to have been an austere, painstaking, conscientious man, liable to become the victim of lamentable prejudices and delusions, but capable, also, of bitterly repenting his errors. He was a narrower man than his father, but probably a more punctiliously righteous person, according to the Puritan code of morality. He ended a poorer man than he began,--the witch's curse having taken effect on the worldly prosperity of the family. The site of the present town of Raymond, in Maine, once belonged to the Hathornes; but the title-deeds were in some unaccountable way lost, and were not recovered until the lapse of time had rendered the claim obsolete. Something similar to this is related of the Pyncheon family, in the "House of the Seven Gables." The Judge married Ruth, the daughter of Lieutenant George Gardner, and had by her six children, the eldest of whom seems to have died abroad, as may be gathered, along with other details of the testator's history, from his will, which is here subjoined:--

In the name of God Amen. I, John Hathorne of Salem in the County of Essex in New England, Merchant, being weak and infirm of Body but of perfect mind and Memory, do make and ordain this my last Will and Testament, hereby revoking all former Wills by me at any time heretofore made.

Impis: I Resign my Soul to God that gave it, and my Body to the Earth to be decently buried at the Discretion of my Executors hereafter named: and for my Worldly Estate that God hath given me, I Dispose thereof as followeth.

Item. I will that all my just Debts and funeral charges be paid and discharged by my Executors, and particularly that they pay to the Orders of Mr. Nathaniel Higginson late of London, Merchant, deceased, the sum of Fifty-three pounds Seventeen shillings, which the said Higginson furnished my Son John Hathorne with and paid for his Sickness and Funeral; and that my son Ebenezer be paid for Money he lent me and that I had out of his Estate in my hands, about four hundred pounds (viz.) so much as may be due to him as pr. account. And that my son Joseph be paid the sum of twenty-five pounds which I had of him towards repairing the house, and twenty-four pounds more which I had of him.

Item.. I give to my Grandson John Hathorne, the Son of my Son Nathl. Hathorne Decd., if he live to the age of twenty-one years, the sum of twenty-five pounds to be paid by my Executors in passable money of New England or Province Bills of Credit.

I give to my Daughter Ruth, the Wife of James Ticknam (sic), the sum of ten pounds besides what I have already given her.

I give to Anne Foster, that lived with me many years and was a faithful servant, the sum of five pounds in passable Money or Bills of Credit; and also I give her the great Rugg she made for me.

Item. I give to the poor of this [Parish] the sum of five pounds to be distributed by my executors.

I give to my three sons, Ebenezer, Joseph, and Benjamin, all the Remainder of my Estate both Real and Personal, whatsoever and wheresoever it may be, to be equally divided betwixt them, to be to them and their Heirs forever.

Lastly I appoint and Constitute my Sons Ebenezer and Joseph Hathorne Executors of this my last will and Testament. But in case I should die when they are both at Sea, then I Desire and appoint Captain William Bowditch Executor in trust, and Direct about my funeral, and to take care of the Improvement of my Estate until one of my forenamed Executors shall return home.

In Testimony and Confirmation of what is above written I have hereunto set my Hand and Seal this second day of February, anno Domini 1716.

Signed, Sealed, published and declared in presence of
STEPHEN SEWALL,
WALTER PRICE,
BENJA. PICKMAN.
JOHN HATHORNE. SEAL.
Executed before Judge John Appleton Esq. June 27: 1717.

It was the Judge's third son, Joseph, born in 1691 who was destined to carry on the family name. John had died early, as aforesaid, and Ebenezer appears to have fallen a victim to the small-pox in 1717; at all events, he has the credit of having brought the disease into Salem in that year. Of the other children, nothing important is known. Joseph was a quiet, home-keeping personage; he did not share the general family craving for a seafaring life, but established himself upon a farm in Salem township, and, having taken to wife a daughter of Captain William Bowditch, he passed the better part of his threescore years and twelve in agricultural pursuits, and acquired the nickname of "Farmer Joseph." His ambition was towards crops and cattle, instead of towards war, statesmanship, and adventure; and inasmuch as less is known of him than of any of his predecessors or descendants, it is fair to assume that his existence was peaceful and happy. He was blessed with five sons and two daughters, all of whom, save one,--Joseph,--lived to be married. The fifth son, born in 1731, was named Daniel; and he, in addition to the distinction of being the great-grandfather of Nathaniel Hawthorne, made a figure in the war of the Revolution. He had been bred to the sea, and his operations against the British were conducted upon that element; at one time he was commander of a privateer, the "Fair America," which was the occasion of more or less inconvenience to English vessels, and the exploits of which were celebrated in a quaint ballad, written, apparently, by some poet who had found his way into the crew. "Bold Daniel," as he was called, was probably rather a wild fellow in his youth. A miniature of him, preserved in the family (and of which an engraving is here given), shows him to have been a robust man, of fair, sanguine complexion, with strong, sharply cut features, and large blue eyes. The expression of his ruddy countenance is open and pleasant; but one sees that he was of a temperament easily moved to wrath or passion. A romantic and rather strange story is connected with his younger days, which, although the *dénouement* of it occurred more than sixty years after his death, may be inserted here. In the year 1858 Nathaniel Hawthorne was living with his family in the Villa Montauto, just outside the walls of Florence. Among his near neighbors during that summer--the summer of Donati's comet--were Mr. and Mrs. Robert Browning; and they were often visitors at Montauto. Mrs. Browning was at that time deeply interested in spiritualism; and in the course of some discussions on the subject, it was accidentally discovered that the governess in Mr. Hawthorne's family, a young American lady of great attainments and lovely character, was a medium,--the manifestation of her capacities in this direction being by writing. If she held a pencil over a sheet of paper for a minute or so, her hand would seem to be seized, or inspired with motion, and words, sentences, or pages would be written down, sometimes rapidly, sometimes slowly, and in various totally dissimilar styles of handwriting, none of which bore any resemblance to the lady's own. She herself had no belief in the spiritual source of the phenomenon; she ascribed it to some obscure and morbid action of the minds of the spectators upon her own mind; and the process was so distasteful to her, that, after experimenting a week or two, the matter was finally abandoned, with the cordial concurrence of Mr. Hawthorne and Mr. Browning, who had both abominated it from the beginning. The medium used to say that she never knew beforehand what the communication was going to be, but that, if she fixed her attention upon what was going forward, she could generally tell each word just before it was written down. The names which were signed to the communications were limited in number, and almost all of them belonged to deceased friends of one or other of the persons present. It was soon possible to distinguish each of the visitors, the moment he or she began to write (through the medium), by the character of the chirography, the style of thought and expression, and even the peculiar physical movement by which the writing was effected.

One day, in the midst of some heavenly-minded disquisition from the dead mother of one of the onlookers, the medium's hand seemed to be suddenly arrested, as by a violent though invisible grasp, and, after a few vague dashes of the pencil, the name of "Mary Rondel" was written across the paper in large, bold characters. Nothing followed the name, which was unknown to every one present; and at last somebody put the question, who Mary Rondel was? Hereupon the medium's hand was again seized as before, and some sentences were rapidly dashed off to the effect that Mary Rondel had no rest, and demanded the sympathy of Nathaniel Hawthorne. Subsequent inquiries elicited from Mary Rondel the information that she had been, in her lifetime, connected in some way with the Hawthorne family; that she had died in Boston about a hundred years previous, and that nothing could give her any relief but Nathaniel Hawthorne's sympathy. Mr. Hawthorne was amused, and perhaps somewhat impressed, by this reiterated and vehement appeal, and assured Mary Rondel that although, so far as he could remember, he had never heard of her before, she was welcome to as much of his sympathy as she could avail herself of.

From this time forth, Mary Rondel, violent, headstrong, often ungrammatical, and uniformly eccentric in her spelling, was the chief figure among the communicants from the other world. She would descend upon the circle like a whirlwind, at the most unexpected moments, put all the other spirits unceremoniously to flight, and insist upon regaling her audience with a greater or less number of her hurried, confused, and often obscure utterances. But the burden of them all was, that at last, after her long century of weary wandering, she was to find some relief and consolation in the sympathy of Nathaniel Hawthorne. The other spirits resented Mary's intrusion, and would denounce her as a disorderly, mischievous person, in whom it was impossible to place confidence, inasmuch as she was an inveterate liar, and, in general, no better than she should be. Nevertheless, and whatever the frailty of her moral character,--which, indeed, she never attempted to defend,--there was something so genuine, so human, and so pathetically forlorn about poor Mary Rondel, that nobody could help regarding her with a certain compassionate kindliness. Liar though she doubtless was, she produced a more real and consistent impression upon her mortal audience than did any of her disembodied associates; and though she was often unruly and troublesome, and occasionally even deficient in propriety, we forgave her for the sake of the strong infusion of human nature which characterized her even in her spiritual state.

Before long, however, the seances were discontinued, as above stated. Mr. Hawthorne moved his family to Rome, where other interests soon put Mary Rondel and the rest of her tribe out of their heads. In 1859 Hawthorne returned to England, whence, after a year's sojourn, he sailed for America; and there, in 1864, he died. The governess (whose acquaintance, by the way, we had made for the first time in 1857) had left us while we were still in England, to marry the man to whom she had been for several years betrothed. All this while, Mary Rondel's name had not been mentioned, and she was practically forgotten. But after Nathaniel Hawthorne's death his son came into possession of a number of letters, documents, manuscripts, books, and other remains, some of which had all along been in possession of the family, while others were forwarded to him by near relatives in Salem and elsewhere. Among these was a large, old-fashioned folio volume, bound in brown leather, and much defaced in binding and paper by the assiduous perusal of half a dozen generations. It was a copy of an early edition of Sir Philip Sidney's "Arcadia," and had been brought to New England for Major William Hathorne, whose autograph appeared upon the margin of one or two pages. In turning over these venerable leaves, brown with age and immemorial thumb-marks, there appeared, written in faded ink, the name of Mary Rondel; and opposite to it, in the same chirography, that of Daniel Hathorne. This unexpected discovery interested the finder not a little; and his interest was increased when, on coming to the latter part of the volume, which is mainly taken up with love-sonnets and other amatory versification, he found certain verses underlined, or surrounded by a wavy mark in ink, together with such inscriptions (also in bold Daniel's handwriting) as "Lucke upon this as if I my on self spacke it," "Pray mistris read this," and so forth. Two of the verses thus indicated contained fond allusions to fair hair and blue eyes; the tenor of the lines was warm, though not unduly so; and in one instance, where the poem comprises the appeal of the lover to his beloved, and her answer to him, certain passages of the latter were also marked out, as if the lady upon whom Daniel had centred his affections had taken this method of replying to his solicitations. Upon the whole, it seemed reasonable to infer that two young people, who had conceived a fancy for each other, had been in a position to peruse Sir Philip's romance at or about the same time, and that they had adopted this rather shy and retiring device to make each other aware of their sentiments. Conceiving that some information on the subject might be forthcoming from certain elder connections of the family, resident in Salem, application was made to them, but without saying anything about the spiritualistic communications in Florence. The following facts were elicited: that, in 1755 or thereabouts, when Daniel was over twenty-one years old, he fell in love with a young woman named Mary Rondel, who lived in Boston. She returned his love; but, somehow or other, the affair ended unhappily, and Mary soon after died. No more than this was known; but this was enough to complete a singular and unaccountable story. Mr. Hawthorne may have been acquainted with it when he was a young man; but he could not have read the "Arcadia" for twenty years previous to the Florentine episode, and it is impossible to suppose that there was any collusion between him and the medium on that occasion. The name of Mary Rondel is not a common one; the present writer does not recollect ever to have met with it, except in this instance. But, at all events, these are the facts, and the reader is free to deal with them according to the best of his belief or incredulity.

Bold Daniel, in due course of time, wedded Rachel Phelps, and they had seven children; the witch's curse seeming to take no effect upon the prosperity of the Hawthorne marriages as regarded offspring. The first son, Daniel, died in infancy; the first daughter, Sarah, was married to John Crowninshield; the fourth daughter, Ruth, died an old maid in 1847; Rachel, the fifth daughter, became the wife of Simon Forrester; and Nathaniel, the third son, who was born in 1775, married, about the beginning of this century, Elizabeth Clarke Manning, a beautiful and highly gifted young lady, five years his junior. Nathaniel was a silent, reserved, severe man, of an athletic and rather slender build, and habitually of a rather melancholy cast of thought; but the marriage was a very happy one. It did not last long; he was a captain in the merchant marine, and in 1808, while at Surinam, he died of yellow fever, at the age of thirty-three. His wife had previously given birth to the three children already mentioned, one of whom was Nathaniel Hawthorne the romancer.

Madame Hawthorne came of a family who seem to have been as reserved and peculiar in their own way as the Hawthornes were in theirs; they possessed more than the Hawthorne sensibility, without sharing the latter's Puritan sternness and bodily strength. They were descendants of the stout-hearted widow of Richard Manning, of St. Petrox Parish, Dartmouth, England, who sailed for the New World with her seven children—four sons and three daughters—in the ship "Hannah and Elizabeth," in 1679. Her son Thomas married a Miss Mary Giddings, and had six children; of whom the fifth, John (whose twin brother Joseph died a bachelor at the age of eighty-one), more than maintained the matrimonial average of the family, by becoming the husband of three wives in succession: Jane Bradstreet being the first, Elizabeth Wallis the second, and Ruth Potter the third. Only the last marriage, however, was fruitful; it produced six children. The youngest son, Richard, born in 1775, married, at the age of twenty-one, Miss Miriam Lord, of Salem, and had by her nine children, of whom Elizabeth Clarke was the third. Robert, born in 1784, was the uncle who paid Hawthorne's way through college; and it was he who built the house in Raymond, which afterwards passed into the hands of his brother Richard. William Manning, born in 1778, employed Hawthorne as his private secretary, in the latter's boyhood; and this good gentleman continued to be alive down to 1864, when he expired at the age of eighty-six. A similar, or even greater, age was attained by Mr. John Dike, who married the fourth daughter, Priscilla Miriam; and the younger generation of the family are at this day respected citizens of the town in which they and their forefathers have lived for more than two hundred years.

This much must suffice concerning the ancestry of Nathaniel Hawthorne; and certainly it amounts to little more than an outline. But, for manifest reasons it is difficult to obtain vivid and lifelike portraits of persons who have so seldom been in contact with the historical events of their time, and whose characters, therefore, have not developed in the daylight of public recognition. They kept their own counsel, and it is now too late to question them. Miss Elizabeth P. Peabody, the sister-in-law of Nathaniel Hawthorne, writes of them that they "were unsocial in their temper, and the family ran down in the course of the two centuries, in fortune and manners and culture. But Mr. Hathorne of Herbert Street was a gentleman whom I knew, and who was an exception. He was a neighbor of ours in 1819, and I have dined at his table. He died without children, before I knew your father, who told me he never knew personally any of the name. You alone bear up the name, I think."

This Hathorne of Herbert Street was probably Nathaniel Hawthorne's uncle Daniel,--the second son of that name born to Daniel the Privateersman. His birth took place in 1768, and he lived to be about sixty years old. Another relative, Ebenezer Hathorne, mentioned in the "American Note-Books," must have belonged to a collateral branch of the family, since there is no Ebenezer in the direct line of descent later than 1725.

CHAPTER 2 - SOPHIA AMELIA PEABODY

THE life of a man happily married cannot fail to be influenced by the character and conduct of his wife. Especially will this be the case when the man is of a highly organized and sensitive temperament, and most of all, perhaps, when his professional pursuits are sedentary. and imaginative rather than active and practical. Nathaniel Hawthorne was particularly susceptible to influences of this kind; and all the available evidence goes to show that the most fortunate event of his life was, probably, his marriage with Sophia Peabody. To attempt to explain and describe his career without taking this event into consideration would, therefore, be like trying to imagine a sun without heat, or a day without a sun. Nothing seems less likely than that he would have accomplished his work in literature independently of her sympathy and companionship. Not that she afforded him any direct and literal assistance in the composition of his books and stories; her gifts were wholly unsuited to such employment, and no one apprehended more keenly than she the solitariness and uniqueness of his genius, insomuch that she would have deemed it something not far removed from profanation to have offered to advise or sway him in regard to his literary productions. She believed in his inspiration; and her office was to promote, so far as in her lay, the favorableness of the conditions under which it should manifest itself. As food and repose nourish and refresh the body, so did she refresh and nourish her husband's mind and heart. Her feminine intuition corresponded to his masculine insight; she felt the truth that he saw; and his recognition of this pure faculty in her, and his reverence for it, endowed his perception with that tender humanity in which otherwise it might have been deficient. Her lofty and assured ideals kept him to a belief in the reality and veracity of his own. In the warmth and light of such companionship as hers, he could not fall into the coldness and gloom of a selfish intellectual habit. She revived his confidence and courage by the touch of her gentle humor and cheerfulness; before her unshakable hopefulness and serenity, his constitutional tendency to ill-foreboding and discouragement vanished away. Nor was she of less value to him on the merely intellectual side. Her mental faculties were finely balanced and of great capacity; her taste was by nature highly refined, and was rendered exquisitely so by cultivation. Her learning and accomplishments were rare and varied, and yet she was always childlike in her modesty and simplicity. She read Latin, Greek, and Hebrew: she was familiar with history; and in drawing, painting, and sculpture she showed a loving talent not far removed from original genius. Thus she was able to meet at all points her husband's meditative and theoretic needs with substantial and practical gratification. Awaking to her, he found in her the softened and humanized realization of his dreams. In all this she acted less of defined purpose than unconsciously and instinctively, following the natural promptings of her heart as moulded and enlightened by her love. What she did was done so well, because she could not do otherwise. Her husband appreciated her, but she had no appreciation of herself. She only felt what a privilege it was to love and minister to such a man, and to be loved by him. For he was not, as so many men are, a merely passive and complacent absorber of all this devotion. What she gave, he returned; she never touched him without a response; she never called to him without an echo. He never became so familiar with her ministrations, unceasing though these were, as to accept them as a matter of course. The springs of gratitude and recognition could not run dry in him; his wife always remained to him a sort of mystery of goodness and helpfulless. He protected her, championed her, and cherished her in all ways that a man may a woman; but, half playfully and all earnestly, he avouched her superiority over himself, and, in a certain class of questions relating to practical morality and domestic expediency, he always deferred to and availed himself of her judgment and counsel. This was no make-believe or hollow humility on his part; he believed, and was delighted to believe, in the higher purity and (as it were) angelic wisdom of her feminine nature; and if he ever ascribed wisdom to himself, it was on the ground that he accepted her views upon all matters as to which mere worldly experience and sagacity were uncertain guides. In comparing himself with her (supposing him to have done such a thing), he would leave entirely out of account his vast intellectual power and capacity. Intellect, in his opinion, was but an accident of organization or inheritance, aud could be almost entirely divorced from purity and elevation of character,--upon the basis of which only could a man's value as a creature of God be finally estimated. He deemed the cultivation and improvement of the intellect to be mainly selfish and instinctive; whereas goodness of character was the result of a purely Christian and regenerated effort. From this point of view, Hawthorne's attitude towards his wife becomes natural and comprehensible enough; and no doubt, as some writer has suggested, no one but he knew how great was his debt to her.

When I said that the life of Hawthorne could not be understood apart from that of his wife, I might have added that without her assistance it could not have been written. In fact, the almost continuous story of their married life is contained in her letters aud journals. While she was still a child, she acquired the habit of keeping a journal of her daily existence,--her doings, her seeings, and her thoughts; and during her visits of a week or a month at a time to friends in the vicinity of Salem, she wrote long letters home to her mother. After her marriage, these letters to her mother constitute a nearly uninterrupted narrative of the quiet but beautiful and profound experiences of her domestic career. No part of this narrative is without a value, literary as well as human,--for Mrs. Hawthorne had an unusual gift of expression, in writing as well as in conversation,--but only a small part of it can be brought within the limits of this volume. Enough, however, will be shown to furnish an adequate impression both of the writer and of what she wrote about. Her mother's share in the correspondence is also full of temptations to the biographer; but the extracts from it have been made mainly with an eye to the outward events which they help to explain, and only incidentally to the traits of character and morality which they illustrate. Taken altogether, the letters contain, in addition to their private interest, the revelation of a remarkable and perhaps unique state of society. Plain living and high thinking can seldom have been more fully united and exemplified than in certain circles of Boston and Salem during the first thirty or forty years of this century. The seed of democracy was bearing its first and (so far) its sweetest and most delicate fruit. Men and women of high refinement, education, and sensibilities thought it no derogation, not only to work for their living, but to tend a counter, sweep a room, or labor in the field. Religious feeling was deep and earnest, owing in part to the recent schism between the severe and the liberal interpretations of Christian destiny and obligations; and the development of commerce and other material interests had not more than foreshadowed its present proportions, nor distracted people's attention from less practical matters. Such a state of things can hardly he reproduced, and, in our brief annals, possesses some historic value.

Sophia Peabody was descended from an ancient and honorable stock. The American Peabodies are the posterity of a certain Francis Peabody, who came to this country in 1640. He was a North-of-England man,--a Yorkshireman. Whether he was married iu England or in New England, and whether his children were all born before his emigration or otherwise, we are not informed. But we know that he became the father of ten children, born somewhere; and the stock flourished exceedingly. For nearly a hundred years there were ten children in each generation in the line of direct descent, not to mention the offspring of the collateral sons and daughters, which accounts for the large number of persons now bearing the name of Peabody in New England. Dr. Andrew Peabody, who has for so many years preached to the students of Harvard College, and Mr. George Peabody, the millionnaire and philanthropist, sprung from this root. Dr. Nathaniel Peabody, the father of Sophia, practised dentistry in Salem and Boston, and was a man of much activity of nature, and versatility. He married Elizabeth Palmer, a granddaughter of General Palmer of the Revolutionary Army, who had married Miss Elizabeth Hunt of Watertown, Massachusetts.

Tradition relates that the Peabody clan were descendants of no less a personage than Boadicea, Queen of the Britons. After her death, her son fled to the Welsh mountains, where he and his posterity for many hundred years bore the title of Pe-boadie, which, being interpreted, means Men of the Peak (*Pe,* peak, or hill; *Boadie,* man). Among the distinguished offshoots of this race was Owen Glendower, who was wont, according to Shakspeare, to call spirits from the vasty deep. After Sophia Peabody was married and had children of her own, she often used to amuse them with these and similar wondrous tales of their maternal lineage, which had just sufficient possibility of truth in them to render them captivating to a child's imagination. There was no definite reason why Boadicea should not have been their indefinitely great-grandmother; and therefore it was their pleasure to regard her in that pious light, and somewhat to resent Hotspur's unsympathetic attitude towards Mr. Glendower's supernatural feats.

Mrs. Hawthorne was connected with the Hunts of Watertown through her mother, in the manner following: John Hunt, of Watertown, was the only son of Samuel Hunt, of Boston, and Mary Langdon. He graduated from Harvard College in 1734, and four years later married Ruth Fessenden. He had been designed for the ministry; but inherited property and left the pulpit. He was a very popular man, and his wife was a beauty; they kept open house for the American officers during the Revolution. The marriage was blessed by many children. One of the sons (Samuel) was master of the Boston Latin School for thirty-six-years. The youngest, Thomas, left college and joined the army at the time of the battle of Bunker Hill. One of the daughters, named Elizabeth, married Joseph B. Palmer, whose father was General Palmer of the Revolutionary army. Their daughter, also named Elizabeth, a gentle, ladylike person, highly cultivated, a student, and a most estimable character, married Dr. Nathaniel Peabody, of Salem, and thus became the mother of Sophia Amelia Peabody, the wife of Nathaniel Hawthorne. The Hunts were Tory cavaliers in England, and the first emigrant was a refugee from Marston Moor. Leigh Hunt is said to have been of this same stock; but I do not know that there is any confirmation of the saying.

Dr. Peabody had three daughters and three sons; of the latter, only one lived to maturity. The eldest daughter, Miss Elizabeth Palmer Peabody, is still in the vigor of an honored and useful old age, as is, likewise, the second daughter, Mary, who became the wife of Horace Mann. Sophia, the youngest, born in 1809, on the 21st of September, died at the age of sixty years. She inherited, however, the full strength of the family constitution. She is said to have been a fine and healthy baby; but her teething was difficult, and, by way of relieving her, she was incontinently dosed with drugs, from the harmful effects of which she never recovered, and which subjected her, among other things, to an acute nervous headache, which lasted uninterruptedly from her twelfth to her thirty-first year, and, of course, shortened her life by an unknown quantity. It is very possible, on the other hand, that both her character and her mind may have been materially uplifted, enlightened, and enlarged by this long and fierce discipline of her youth. There is no doubt that such was her own view of the matter. The pain was of such a nature as to sharpen rather than obscure her mental faculties; and in process of time she was enabled in a manner to stand apart from it (as to her spiritual part) and study its significance and effect upon herself. The wisdom and resignation she drew from it were worth many years of ordinary experience to her, and the lesson was probably of a kind peculiarly adapted to her temperament. For she was a child of frolicsome spirits, inclined to playful mischief, high-strung, quick-witted, and quick-tempered. She was enthusiastic, prone to extremes, and to make sweeping judgments of people and things, founded upon intuitive impressions. Her mind was independent and intrepid; she was high-spirited, generous without limit, and, above all, profound and vital in her affections. For a nature like this, what better training and restraining power could be devised than pain? It controlled her without making her feel that her liberty was invaded; it withdrew her into a region apart, where much that would have grieved and shocked her was necessarily unknown. Constantly reminding her of the sensitiveness of her own feelings, it made her tender and thoughtful of the feelings of others; and it stimulated the tenderness and love of all with whom she came in contact. In proportion as it made her physical world a torture and a weariness, it illuminated and beautified the world of her spirit. It taught her endurance, charity, self-restraint, and brought her acquainted with the extent and wealth of her internal resources. In respect of innocence, simplicity, and ideal beliefs, it kept her a child all her life long; it drew around her, as it were, an enchanted circle, across which no evil thing could come. She was disciplined and instructed by pain, as others are by sin and its consequences; and thus she could become strong and yet remain without stain. What seems more remarkable is, that all her suffering never tempted her, even for a moment, into a self-pitying or morbid frame of mind. She was always happy, and fertile in strength and encouragement for others; her voice was joyful music, and her smile a delicate sunshine. Natures apparently far sturdier and ruder than hers depended upon her, almost abjectly, for support. She was a blessing and an illumination wherever she went; and no one ever knew her without receiving from her far more than could be given in return. Her pure confidence created what it trusted in. He who writes this is not well disposed to eulogy; but he asserts less than he knows. In person she was small, graceful, active, and beautifully formed. Her face was so alive and translucent with lovely expressions that it was hard to determine whether or not it were physically lovely; but I incline to think that a mathematical survey would have pronounced her features plain; only, no mathematical survey could have taken cognizance of her smile. Her head was nobly shaped; her forehead high and symmetrically arched; her eyebrows strongly marked; her eyes, gray, soft, and full of gentle light; her mouth and chin at once tender, winning, and resolute. Beautiful or not, I have never seen a woman whose countenance better rewarded contemplation.

Sometimes, at her children's solicitation, she would tell them anecdotes of "when I was a little girl;" and many of these are remembered. One dream she was fond of relating was of a dark cloud, which suddenly arose in the west and obscured the celestial tints of a splendid sunset. But while she was deploring this eclipse, and the cloud spread wider and gloomier, all at once it underwent a glorious transformation; for it consisted of countless myriads of birds, which by one movement turned their rainbow-colored breasts to the sun, and burst into a rejoicing chorus of heavenly song. This dream was doubtless interpreted symbolically by the dreamer; and the truth which it symbolized was always among the firmest articles of her faith. Illustrative of her mischievous tendency was the story of how she cured her sister Lizzie of biting her finger tips while reading or studying. It seems that various expedients had been tried to break the young student of this habit; among others, that of obliging her to wear gloves: but her preoccupation was so great that nothing availed with her; and when she could do nothing else, she would roll up bits of paper, or anything else that happened to be within reach, and put them in her mouth. Noticing this, Sophia one day went out in the garden and gathered a quantity of the herb known as bitter-sweet, which has a most disheartening flavor. This she rolled up in a number of little bunches, and quietly substituted them for the scraps of paper upon which her sister was feeding. The result appears to have fulfilled her most sanguine expectations; Lizzie remembered the bitter-sweet, and never again was guilty of the objectionable practice.

But instead of multiplying these anecdotes, there shall here be inserted some reminiscences of her earliest years, expressed in her own language. They were written in 1859, shortly before leaving England for America, and were designed, of course, solely to afford entertainment to her children. Only a beginning was made; after a few pages the narrative breaks off, and was never resumed. Enough is given, however, to justify a regret that there is no more for, as the writer warmed to her work, it would evidently have increased in minuteness and suggestiveness. The full names of the *dramatis personae* are not given, nor are they important to the matter in hand.

"When I was four or five years old, I was sent away, for the first time, from home and from my mother, to visit my grandmamma. My mother was the tenderest and loveliest mother in the world, and I do not understand how I could have borne to be separated from her for a day. The journey I entirely forget, and also my arrival; but after I was there, I remember a scene in the sunny courtyard as plainly as if it were yesterday. I was playing with two tiny puppies, belonging to my aunt Alice, and I was endeavoring to take up one of them in my small, in-adequate hands. It struggled vigorously and squealed, and was so hard and fat, I could not get a firm hold of it; so I dropped it on the pavement, which caused it to squeal louder than before.

Hereupon, out rushed my aunt, and violently shook me by the arm, uttering some severe words, that have entirely gone out of my mind. She was tall, stately, and handsome, and very terrible in her wrath. I felt like a criminal; and as it had never yet occurred to me that a grown person could do wrong, but that only children were naughty, I took the scolding, and the earthquake my aunt made of my little body, as a proper penalty for some fault which she saw, though I did not. I only intended to caress her unmanageable pet, not to hurt it; but innocence is unconscious, and not quick to defend itself. I was forbidden ever to touch the dogs again, and was sent into the house out of the bright sunshine. I can see now, as then, that bright sunshine, as it flooded the grass and shrubbery; the clear, fresh appearance of every object, as if lately washed and then arrayed in gold; the great trees, spreading forth innumerable branches, with leaves glistening and fluttering in the wind. I forget how I found my way to my grandmother's room upstairs; but I was soon looking out of her window into a street. I saw, sitting on a doorstep directly opposite, a beggar-girl; and when she caught sight of me, she clenched her fist and uttered a sentence which I never forgot, though I did not in the least comprehend it. 'I 'll maul you!' said the beggar-girl, with a scowling, spiteful face. I gazed at her in terror, feeling scarcely safe, though within four walls and half-way to the sky--as it seemed to me. I was convinced that she would have me at last, and that no power could prevent it; but I did not appeal to grandmamma for aid, nor utter a word of my awful fate to any one. Children seldom communicate their deepest feelings or greatest troubles to those around them. What tragedies are often enacted in their poor little hearts, without even the mother's suspecting it! It may, perhaps, partly be caused by their small vocabulary; and, besides, they are seldom individually conscious, but take it for granted that their own experience is that of all other children. How can a child of three years old find language to express its inward emotions? A child's dim sense of almightiness in events that happen, overpowers its faculty of representation. My aunt Alice's anger was, to my mind, a very insignificant matter beside this peril; and as I fixed my eyes intently upon the girl, I recognized with dismay the fearful creature who had once met me when I had escaped out of the garden-gate at home, and was taking my first independent stroll. No nurse nor servant was near me on that happy day. It was glorious. My steps were winged, and there seemed more space on every side than I had heretofore supposed the world contained. The sense of freedom from all shackles was intoxicating. I had on no hat, no out-door dress, no gloves. What exquisite fun I really think every child that is born ought to have the happiness of running away once in their lives at least. I went up a street that gradually ascended, till, at the summit, I believed I stood at the top of the earth. But, alas! at that acme of success my joy ended; for there I was suddenly confronted by this beggar-girl,-- the first ragged, begrimed human being I had ever seen. She seized my wrist and said, 'Make me a curtsy!' All the blood in my veins tingled with indignation: *'No, I will not!'* I said. How I got away, and home again, I cannot tell; but as I did not obey the insolent command, I constantly expected revenge in some form, and yet never told my mother anything about it. A short time after the grievous encounter, my hobgoblin passed along when I was standing at the door, and muttered threats, and frowned; and now here she was again, so far from where I first met her, evidently come for me, and I should fall into her hands and be *mauled!* What was that? Something, doubtless, unspeakably dreadful. The new, strange word cast an indefinite horror over the process to which I was to be subjected. Where could the creature have got the expression? I have never heard it since, I believe. Neither did I ever see or hear the beggar-girl again in all my life.

"Other memories of that visit to my grandmamma are neither rich nor sweet, but so indelibly engraven on my memory that I can discern them well. My aunt Alice had two sisters, who were unkind and tyrannical to such a degree that she seemed quite angelic in comparison with them. My uncle George was my mamma's beloved brother, and radiant with benevolence and all the gracious amenities. I did not think, however, of taking refuge in him, or even of speaking to him. He came into view, sometimes, like a gleam of sunshine, and passed away I knew not whither,--a kind of inaccessible blessing, or, rather, an unavailable one to me. I perceive now that he was the only amiable individual in the house. The favorite pastime of my aunts Emily and Matilda was to torment me; and whenever they could take me captive, I was led off for cruel sport. The mischievous gleam of their dark eyes, and the wonderful rivulets of dark curls flowing over their crimson cheeks, are painted on my inner tablets in fixed colors. Sometimes they opened a great book (which I now fear was the Bible) and commanded me to read a lesson. If I miscalled the letters in trying to spell the words, they shouted in derision. My sensitiveness doubtless incited them to ingenious devices to mortify and frighten me. One day they asked me if I would like to see the most beautiful of gardens, blooming with the sweetest, gayest flowers; and when I gratefully and joyfully assented, trusting them with-out misgiving, they opened a door and gave me a sudden push, which sent me falling down several steps into utter darkness. Another time they took me into a courtyard full of turkeys, and drove the creatures, gobbling like so many fiends, towards me. I expected to be devoured at once, and my distress was immeasurable; and the enjoyment of the young ladies was complete. Their mocking laughter made me feel ashamed of being miserable. My loving mamma, in the unknown distance, seemed a Heaven to which I should return at last; but there was nothing like her here, except perhaps the visionary uncle George.

"Grandmamma was a severe disciplinarian. I was always sent to bed at six o'clock, without liberty of appeal in any case; and this was right and proper enough. But I was put into an upper room, alone in the dark, and left out of reach of help, as I supposed, from any human being. It was my first trial of darkness and loneliness; for my blessed mother never inflicted needless misery on her children. Every night I lay in terror at street noises as long as I was awake. I am not aware of having derived any benefit from that Spartan severity, and I have always been careful that my children should have the light and society they desired in their tender age. At table, food was sometimes given me which I did not fancy; and I was sternly told that I must eat and drink whatever was placed before me, or go without any food at all. In consequence of this absurd decree, I hate even now some of those things that were forced upon me then. A sense of injustice turned my stomach. On one memorable occasion I utterly refused a saucer of chocolate prepared for me, and so stoutly set my will against it, that in all the rest of my life I have not been able to tolerate the taste of chocolate.

"I was subjected to grandmamma's unenlightened religious zeal, and taken to church elaborately dressed in very tight frocks, and made to sit still; and after infinite weariness in the long church service, I was led into the sacristy, and, with other unfortunate babies, tortured with catechism, of which I understood not a word. I see myself sitting on a high bench, my feet dangling uncomfortably in the air, while I was put to the question; and I pity me very much. Grown people forget that the Lord has said, 'I will have mercy and not sacrifice.'

"I remember one more circumstance of this unhappy visit. My aunt Alice had a large party, an afternoon party,--and I was arrayed carefully for the occasion. Oh, shall I ever forget the torture of the little satin boots and of the pantalets, to which I was doomed, besides the utter general sense of discomfort and bondage! I was fetched into the salon, where the bevy of fine ladies were sitting, in clouds of white muslin and bright silks,--to be passed round like a toy, as one of the entertainments, I suppose. But being in great bodily pain from my dress, as soon as I was released from their caresses, I escaped, and darted up the staircase, and fled into a room where I thought I should be undisturbed. There I untied the cruel strings that fastened the pantalets round my ankles, and somehow managed to pull them wholly off, though I could do nothing with the dainty little boots. However, glad to be released so far, I gayly returned to the drawing-room. Alas for it! My aunt Alice was immediately down upon me, like a broad-winged vulture on an innocent dove. I see her white robe swirling about her as she swooped me up, and consigned me to a servant, to be put to bed in the middle of the afternoon. I dare say there was a bright scarlet line round my wretched little ankles, where the strings had cut into the tender flesh. I wonder I do not remember the relief of being freed from boots and frock; but that solace has passed into oblivion, and the memory of the pain alone survives.

"The time at last arrived for me to go home. I can recall no joy at the announcement or at the preparations for the return, and probably I was told nothing about it. The idea of giving me pleasure seemed to enter none of their heads or hearts. But I found myself in a carriage, on a wide seat,--so wide that my two feet were in plain sight, horizontally stuck out before me, at the edge of the cushion. By my side sat a stately gentleman, who was very grave and silent; and I looked up at him with awe. It was my uncle Edward; and, with the enthusiastic delight in perfect form that was born in me, I gazed at the noble outline of his face, the finely chiselled profile, so haughty and so delicate. I adored him because he was handsome, though he did not speak to me or seem aware of my presence. When the carriage stopped at a hotel for refreshment and rest, I was lifted out by a servant as black as ebony, and deposited on a sofa in the parlor, where cake and wine were placed on the table. I was well content with the golden cake so politely offered me by my uncle, as if I were a grown-up lady; but when he put a glass of wine into my hand, I did not drink, and was inclined to rebel. His commanding eye was upon me, however, so that I tried to taste it; but, choking and shuddering being the only consequence of my efforts, he kindly smiled and took it away, saying, 'You do not like wine, then?' These were the only words spoken during the whole journey; and I had no more voice to answer him than if I had been dumb. I wonder where children's voices go to, when reverence and love fill their hearts? They are often scolded for not speaking, when it is physically and morally impossible for them to do so. I had worshipped my uncle for his beauty, and now his gentleness made me love him with all the ardor of my nature. A smile and a kind word cause little loss to the giver, but what riches they often are to the recipient! My uncle's smile was pleasanter to me than the sunshine; and the next thing I remember is being perfectly happy with my mother."

The relations of Sophia Peabody and her mother were always of the tenderest and most intimate description; and one of the former's letters, written towards the close of the latter's life, bears eloquent and moving testimony to this fact. The two were in all respects worthy of each other. The three sons of the family--Wellington, George, and Nathaniel--were, like other boys, the occasion sometimes of anxiety and sometimes of pride to their parents and sisters. Wellington was a high-spirited youth, impulsive, a favorite among his fellows, at once generous and selfish, with a warm and affectionate heart. He was difficult to manage and control; and the severe, old-fashioned discipline to which his father subjected him seems to have done him little good. He and his brothers attended the Salem Latin School, and Wellington somewhat forfeited his father's confidence by his escapades. He was afterwards sent to college; but, in spite of his fine abilities, he was unable to complete his course there. It then became a problem what to do for him. He went to sea for a time; but in a few years he repented of his boyish follies, and went to the South to pursue a business career. Here however, just as his promise was becoming performance, he was attacked by yellow fever, and died. George, of a more sedate and solid character, had meanwhile been serving his apprenticeship at business, and was following it up with every prospect of success. He was an athletic and handsome youth, with a fine aquiline profile, and great charm of character and manner. About 1836 or 1837 he took part in a foot-race from Boston to Roxbury, in which he came in first, but at the cost of a strain which, though it was thought little of at first, ultimately cost him his life, by consumption of the spinal marrow; he died, after a long and wearying illness, patiently and heroically borne, in 1839. Nathaniel, the third son, with many fine gifts and an almost excessive conscientiousness, had not the qualities which command success. He married comparatively young, and adopted the calling of a homoeopathic pharmacist, and enjoyed the reputation of making the purest medicines in Boston. He died but a year or two since, leaving a widow and two daughters.

The foregoing information will put the reader in a position to understand what follows. Miss E. P. Peabody has kindly contributed the ensuing *resume* of the family annals up to about 1835:--

"The religious controversies that ended in changing all the old Puritan churches of Boston and Salem from Calvinism to Liberal and Unitarian Christianity, were raging in 1818, and divided all families. Some of our relatives became Calvinists; our own family, and especially our mother, who was very devout, remained Liberal. Sophia was an instance, if ever there was one in the world, of a child growing up full of the idea of God and the perfect man Jesus, and of the possibility as well as duty (but rather privilege than duty) of growing up innocent and forever improving, with the simple creed that everything that can happen to a human being is either for enjoyment in the present or instruction for the future; and that even our faults, and all our sufferings from others' faults, are means of development into new forms of good and beauty.

"When I was sixteen and Sophia eleven, I took my school in Lancaster in the house; and Mary and Sophia were among my scholars. They never went to any other school. I taught history as a chief study,--the History of the United States,--not in textbooks, but Miss Hannah Adams's History of New England, and Rollins's Ancient History, and Plutarch's Lives. Sophia was intensely interested, and liked to have in the recitations the part of comparing the heroes, that occurs in Plutarch, and summing up their heroic deeds, as occurs constantly in Rollins; and I remember with what enthusiasm she would do this. I remember she would give me accounts of a volume of Fawcett's sermons, which she read with great delight, 'not because it was Sunday,' I remember her saying, 'but because they were beautiful and sublime.'

"When the family went to Salem in 1828, they lived in a house near the water at the end of Court Street, and had to suffer many hardships. We had formerly, in 1812 and thereafter, lived in Union Street, very near Herbert Street. Sophia had been a very sick child on account of teething, and was made a life-long invalid by the heroic system of medicine which was then in vogue. After moving into this Court Street house, her headaches increased, and she became unable to bear the noise of knives and forks, and was obliged to take her food upstairs, and also often had to retreat in the evening when her three brothers were at home. They went to the Salem Latin School, and had terrible lessons under old Eames, who was a most severe master, flogging for mistakes in recitation; so that Mary, and Sophia when she could, would have them learn all their lessons perfectly and say them in the evening, so as to prevent those cruel punishments. M. Louvoisier, a Frenchman, taught Sophia French; he was a wonderful teacher, and required enormous study and writing of French, and carried her all through the classic facts of France, and much of the literature besides. In addition to this, and in spite of her suffering, she studied Italian, and, for the sake of learning to draw, she undertook to teach a little class of children in Miss Davis's school. Her drawing was so perfect that it looked like a model. But the exertion was too much for her, and she was thrown into a sickness from which she never rose into the possibility of so much exertion again; and a slight accident disabled her band, so that she could not draw. Shortly afterwards, she was invited down to Hallowell, to the Gardiners', whom she interested immensely. It was her first visit into the world, and her last for a long time; for she went home and grew worse.

"We afterwards moved to Boston; and the Boston physicians, one after another, tried their hands at curing her, and she went through courses of their poisons, each one bringing her to death's door, and leaving her less able to cope with the pain they did not reach. But the endurance of her physical constitution defied all the poisons of the *materia medica*,--mercury, arsenic, opium, hyoscyamus, and all. Her last allopathic physician was Dr. Walter Channing, who limited himself to fighting the pain without attempting a radical cure. He was a delightful friend; and during the four years she remained in Boston she enjoyed the *élite* of Boston society, who admired and loved her for the exquisite character she showed, and her unvarying sweetness. All these years her mother was her devoted nurse,--watching in the entries that no door should be shut hard, and so forth. Sophia was never without pain; but there were times when it was not so extreme but that she could read. She read Degerando, and translated it for me to read to my pupils; and Plato. Sometimes my scholars (I kept my school in the house) would go up to see her in her room; and the necessity of their keeping still so as not to disturb her was my means of governing my school, for they all spontaneously governed themselves for Sophia's sake. I never knew any human creature who had such sovereign power over everybody--grown or child--that came into her sweet and gracious presence. Her brothers reverenced and idolized her. She was for some years the single influence that tamed Ellery Channing.

"In 1830, when she was living on hyoscyamus, which did her less harm than any other drug, she was able to come downstairs occasionally and into the schoolroom on drawing-days; and one day--it was four years after the practice in drawing above-mentioned, during which time she had not touched a pencil--she undertook to copy a little pastoral landscape. After this she did a good deal of drawing. Then the painter Doughty came to Boston, and opened a school of painting. He gave the lessons by making his pupils look on while he was painting; and then they would take canvases and, in his absence, imitate what they had seen him do; and then he would come and paint some more on his picture: but he never explained anything, or answered questions. It occurred to me that Doughty might come and paint a picture in her sight, and I brought this about. She would lie on the bed, and he had his easel close by. Every day, in the interval of his lessons, she would imitate on another canvas what he had done. And her copy of his landscape was even better than the original, so that when they were displayed side by side, everybody guessed her copy to be the one that Doughty painted. She then, by herself, copied one of Salmon's sea-pieces perfectly, and did two or three pieces by coloring copies which she made from uncolored engravings. Then I succeeded in borrowing a highly finished landscape of Allston's, which she copied so perfectly that, being framed alike, when the two pictures were seen together, even Franklin Dexter did not at once know which was which. She sold all her pictures at good prices.

"At the end of our Boston residence, Sophia went to Lowell on a visit to her friends, Mr. and Mrs. Sam. Haven. She had been very much cast down at the idea of leaving Boston and all her interesting life there ; but it was a transient mood: she always met every event with victorious faith. After the Havens she visited Mrs. Rice's, where she painted a number of other pictures. While there, Mr. Allston, who had heard of her successful copy of his picture, went to see her, and began to speak of her going to Europe and devoting herself to art. She told him she was an invalid; and he then said that she ought to copy only masterpieces,--nothing second-rate. She said she had tried to get his Spanish Maiden to copy; but Mr. Clarke, its owner, had told her that Allston exacted a promise from those who purchased his pictures, never to permit them to be copied. At this Allston flushed with indignation, and said gentlemen had no right to make him partner of their meanness. He should be proud to have her copy everything he had painted, and he claimed no right over his pictures after he had sold them.

"Returning to Salem, Sophia was the sunshine in our house. Our mother was likewise in much better health than she had heretofore been, and this made Sophia very happy. In 1832 she and Mary went to Cuba; but it was not until the following August that the heat even of the tropics gave Sophia her first relief from the pain that, during twelve years, had never remitted entirely for one hour. They returned in the spring of 1835, but had a long, terrible voyage of storms and cold, which undid the good she had obtained and brought back her headaches."

In order that the reader may realize a little more clearly the nature of the family relations, and the manner in which the members of it regarded one another, I append passages from three letters written to Sophia by her mother during the year 1827-28.

MY DEAR SOPHIA,--We think that your stay at your aunt Tyler's must not exceed six weeks. She is kind, hospitable, and likes to see you enjoy yourself; but you have not health enough to make yourself useful in the family or in the school; and, besides, I must acknowledge that the kind and cheering tones of your voice and your mirth-inspiring laugh and affectionate smile would be cordials to me. As Nat expressively has it, "We feel desolate." You will have many delightful scenes to reflect upon, and many pleasant events to amuse and instruct your brothers with. You may make a visit of a week in Lancaster, if you leave Brattleborough seasonably; and that will lessen the fatigue of your journey home. The high state of excitement you are in is not exactly the thing for your head. I am delighted to see you alive to the simple pleasures of nature. That heart must be the least corrupt that can enjoy them most; but you enjoy too fervently for your strength. Come home now, and live awhile upon the past. Something, ere many months, must be planned out for your future support. To be independent, so far as money is concerned, of every one, is very desirable; of love and kind offices you may receive and give as liberally as you please. Do not let any considerations induce you to exceed much the time mentioned.

WELL, darling of my heart, how are you? Well enough to enjoy the delightful friends who have called you to their fireside? I want you to be happy, but I want you to find happiness a *sober certainty;* that is, I want you to remember that the millennium is not yet,--that the very best among us are fallible, very fallible beings. Admire and love with the whole warmth of your nature, but let the eye of prudence keep strict watch; hide it in the depths of your heart, lest the evil-minded call it suspicion, but never let it go from you. It will preserve you from bitter heartaches, for it will tell you that you must be prepared to meet, to guard against, and to forgive errors, nay, even faults, in the highest and noblest characters. It will tell you that the most disinterested are sometimes selfish, and suffer themselves to enjoy the present without reflecting whether or not evil may result to those they most value, from this selfish indulgence. It will tell you that the love which settles down on the household circle, though more quiet, is deeper, steadier, more efficient, than any other love. Sickness never wearies it; it forgives waywardness; it hopes all things;--I had almost said that *crime,* even, only draws the wanderer closer to hearts that watched over the days of innocence,--and I may say it, for so it would he with me. But to preach a sermon was not my intention; though when I think of your vivid imagination, your confiding affection, your admiration of excellence, and your instinctive shrinking from the idea that those you love, and who really have such claims upon your love, can err in judgment, can misinterpret your high-minded and pure actions, looks, and words,--when I think of your sensitive nature, your shattered nerves, your precarious health,--can I do less than long, by precept upon precept, by caution upon caution, to try to induce you to arm yourself at all points against disappointment, or, rather, to prevent disappointment by thinking more soberly of the good among us, by remembering that as yet there are no unmixed characters on earth? I never shall forget the heartache I one day had, when Elizabeth came from Squire Savage's, whither she had gone with a heart glowing, to seek sympathy on some subject, and met a cold reception, that sent her home bathed in tears. I would shield you from this by telling you that every individual has absorbing interests known to no other mind, and, without the least abatement of affection, may be unprepared to meet your affectionate greetings with sympathy. You have experienced this, for I have seen your lip quiver at this apparent coldness in not very intimate friends (Mr. Gardner, for instance). Since you are thus constituted, and since you have no physical strength, gird up the loins of your mind,--be strong in faith,--be candid,--anchor your soul on domestic love, at the same time that you open your warm, affectionate heart to receive the kindness and love of the excellent of the earth, to whom your kindred nature attaches you; never forgetting that they may speak harshly, look coldly, censure what you do with the purest intentions, and yet have a deep and strong affection for you, and even admiration. Such is man, and must be, while we all do and say wrong and ill-judged things. . .

MY DARLING,--How can I, how can any of us, be grateful enough for the peace of mind, the just views, the exalted feelings, with which you are blessed! If anything could be added to the high and holy motives for perseverance in duty, it would be the power given to you thus to support years of pain. My beloved child, your mother feels it all deeply; and, as the still more afflicted Mrs. Prescott said to me a few days since, " we live for our dear invalids; our happiness is to devote time and talents for their comfort."

Dear Wellington, my heart aches for him. But God is his Father too; and it may be, indeed it *must* be, that all will tend to his perfection at last. If he were callous, if he cared not for the good or ill opinion of his friends, I should despair. But while I see him so sensitive, while I see the tears flow at the idea that his father and sisters have no confidence in him, I hope all things. Cannot you write to your father, and state the expediency of expressing more hope of Wellington's future conduct? His last interview with him was painful,--he again told him that he expected he would be expelled from college. The poor boy felt heart-stricken. I doubt not your father's motives, but I know he has no knowledge of human nature; and if Wellington is not better managed, he will be driven from society, or, what is still worse, seek happiness away from home, in reckless dissipation. It is almost cruel to trouble your poor head by such a request; but really, dear, I believe you may be an instrument of much good, and that will reward you. Wellington was nurtured in the most agonized period of my life; and I solemnly believe that the state of the mother's mind, while nursing, has an essential effect on the character of the child. Elizabeth has the firmest constitution; and she was born and nursed while my heart was at rest, and my hopes *all* of happiness.

YOUR MOTHER.

The visit to Cuba, referred to in Miss E. P. Peabody's communication, was the occasion of a series of letters which were afterwards bound together in a manuscript volume, and which give a vivid and delightful picture of life on a plantation there fifty years ago. Justice could hardly be done to these letters by quotations, however, and they are too voluminous to be printed here entire. The Cuban experiences, as related by Mrs. Hawthorne, were of inexhaustible interest to her children; she had the faculty of seizing upon the picturesque or humorous side of an occurrence, and bringing it memorably before the mind. The voyage was made in a small sailing-vessel, and lasted some weeks. Miss Sophia was at first a victim to seasickness, but felt better as long as she could remain in sight of the horizon line; and she was therefore furnished with a sort of bed on the deck, where she lay whenever the weather permitted. One day, when she was feeling very badly, she told the captain that she thought, if a rope could be made fast to the mainmast, and the other end placed in her hands, so that she could raise herself up by it, she would be cured. The captain laughed at this novel prescription; but, being an amiable gentleman, and very courteous to ladies, he consented to let the experiment be tried. It was done accordingly; Miss Sophia raised herself from her sick-bed, and, to every one's surprise, never afterwards suffered from the malady. The captain declared that he would henceforth recommend the rope's end to all his patients but whether its exhibition was attended with the same good results in other cases, I know not.

There was a sow on board the vessel, and during the voyage she gave birth to a litter. Among the passengers was a stout French lady, much addicted to gormandizing; and she pursued the captain with persistent entreaties to have "yon leetle pig" for dinner. At length he consented, and, much to her delight, one of the infant swine was killed and roasted. She appeared at the dinner-table attired in a rich silk dress, in honor of the occasion; the captain sat at the head of the table, and her place was at his right hand. It happened that a stiff breeze had arisen, and the ship was pitching very heavily. As the captain raised the carving-knife to begin upon the pig, the latter, impelled by a sudden lurch of the vessel, rose lightly from its dish, and, all streaming with gravy as it was, alighted plump in the French lady's silken lap. She screamed; and the captain, laying down his knife, said gravely, with a courteous wave of the hand, "Madame, you have your leetle pig!" And it is on record that she devoured the whole of it, but never asked for another.

Arrived at the plantation, Miss Sophia was able to indulge to her heart's content in her favorite exercise of horseback-riding. The time for her excursions was in the early dawn, while the sun was still below, or only just above, the cloudless tropical horizon. She rode down long avenues of orange-trees, plucking and eating the fruit as she passed beneath. In Cuba, only the sunny side of the orange is eaten, the rest is thrown away; and even the negroes will not deign to pick up the fruit that has fallen from the branches. Ladies in Cuba ride--or, at that epoch, they rode--in a saddle something like a basket; it was very easy, and admitted of their standing up in it, if necessary, but, on the other hand, it allowed them comparatively little firmness of seat. One morning Miss Sophia had sallied forth as usual, on a horse which she especially affected,--a noble and beautiful animal, but extremely sensitive. At length she came to an orange-tree where there was a particularly fine orange, hanging from a lofty bough. She reined in her horse, and, finding it impossible to reach the orange as she sat, she stood up in the basket and grasped the bough. At that moment the horse, whether startled at something or unmindful of the situation, moved gently forward, leaving his rider, like some strange fruit, suspended in the air. Having placed her in this predicament, he turned his head and contemplated her with a most sympathetic and compassionate expression, as if he would have given worlds to relieve her from her embarrassment, but was at a loss how to do so. After hanging as long as was reasonable, she was forced to drop a considerable distance to the ground; and I forget how the adventure ended, but I think a servant came up and reinstated her in the saddle.

One evening, when a number of ladies and gentlemen were assembled in the drawing-room of the planter (Mr. Morrell), one of the ladies expressed a desire to see a scorpion. Mr. Morrell sent one of his slaves to bring one in a bucket. The slave in question had been chastised, by his master's orders, some time before, and seems to have harbored resentment. At all events, he came hack with his bucket brimming full of live scorpions, and turned them out upon the polished floor. Hereupon ensued much outcry and consternation, and climbing upon chairs and sofas; and luckily no one was hurt,--except the slave, who caught another whipping. But he probably laid it to the account of profit and loss, and was sullenly content.

This, however, must be the limit of the Cuban reminiscences, which would make a delightful little volume by themselves. The concluding pages of this chapter shall be devoted to extracts from a journal written in the autumn of 1830 (two years previous to the above tropical experiences), at a country retreat near Salem. It is good reading in itself, and exhibits much of the writer's character and mental habits, though out of the sixty or more pages only some half-dozen are given. The Havens referred to, were a Mr. Samuel Haven, a Salem lawyer and his young wife,--intimate and dear friends of Miss Sophia and her family.

"The Lord is in His holy temple
Let the earth keep silence before Him."
HABAKKUK.

DEDHAM, *August to October,* 1830. --Here I am in the holy country, alone with the trees and birds,--my first retreat into solitude. The day has been perfectly beautiful; and my ride out was delightful, save and except the grasp of the iron hand upon my poor brain, which was more excruciating than almost ever. It is not any better yet, but I hope to-morrow for relief in a degree. I have been reading a part of Addison's critique upon Milton to-day, and since have endeavored to master two or three of Degerando's first chapters. I feel quite independent of all things when I am reading this book. The Havens drove over to see me, and to make sure that I was comfortable in my new abode; and while they were here, I made a discovery that turned my heart quite over. It was, of the River! --the merest glimpse, but still a glimpse; and now I am satisfied with my view. I have hill, vale, forest, plain, almost mountain, and River,--a sweep of sky and earth. . . My landlady came up after tea, and indulged her Yankee curiosity by finding out where I lived, how many sisters I had, etc. I cannot sympathize with such idle curiosity, but I answered her questions. Then there was an amusing little incident under my window. I heard a boy's voice saying, "Give me every one of those peaches, or go into the house, - one or t' other, come!" The other boy began to cry, "Cry yourself to death, if you 're mind to; but give me those peaches, or go into the house." "I don't want to go into the house," stammered the other; "I got some on t' other side,--all them in my hat, I got t' other side." "Come," replied the first, "you need n't lie so, you must give me the peaches, and mind and not steal." The other cried the more violently. "Cry away,--but be quiet: I must have them." Here the little thief proceeded to empty his pockets of dozens of stolen peaches, crying, and insisting all the while that he got those in his hat "on t'other side." The first boy begged him not to lie so, and kept his hand extended for the fruit. He emptied his pockets, and then began upon his hat very reluctantly. The first boy softened as he came to the last, and told him he might "keep those." Another little urchin was present at the scene, and every time the culprit said he got those in his hat "on t' other side," he exclaimed, "Well, that's all the same,--it's stealing just as much, ain't it, Joe?"

Last night I jumped up once or twice to see how the moonlight went on, for it looked too spiritually fair to leave. I dreamed that George Villiers, Duke of Buckingham, stabbed me in the bosom; and I awoke with a tremendous start, and trembled for an hour. It was because I had been reading Shakspeare, I suppose. The moon rose, and conquered the clouds, and became again enveloped, but tingeing them so magically that you could hardly wish her free. Once the queen became embedded in a mass of fleecy clouds, and around her spread the brightest halo of a pale crimson, softened gradually into white; and the heavens seemed wrinkled,-- furrowed. In the east rose fiery Mars, uncommonly red and large, because, I suppose, France is going to declare war; and a snowy wreath of mist told where Wiggam Pond wound itself among the meadows. This morning the world is full of wind; and I have been reading the Bible and Fénelon. I cannot understand the Lesser Prophets, and do believe they are translated very unintelligibly.

Rain and clouds. I read Degerando, Feénelon, St Luke and Isaiah, Young, the Spectator, and Shakspeare's "Comedy of Errors," "Taming of the Shrew," "All's Well that Ends Well," and "Love's Labor's Lost," besides doing some sewing, to-day. No Havens came. .

"Clouds, and ever-during dark." Last night, mid. night, I was wakened by a tremendous crash of thunder; and I went to sleep again to dream of all kinds of horrors. But at two o'clock this afternoon, ye Powers, what did I see? A blue space in the heavens! Even so. My heart gave such a bound towards it, that I verily thought it had forever left my body desolate. About five came Samuel Haven; and while he was here, the Sun's most excellent Majesty actually threw out a glance of fire over the hills and vales, and the clouds began to wear marvellous beauty. And how nature did rejoice from the past deluge! One cannot but sympathize with such visible delight, - audible, too. Oh, how much I do enjoy here! . . .

A day without a cloud! The dewy freshness and life of this sweet prospect were reviving. My whole inward being was in a wilderness of melody as I gazed. I fed upon the air. But let me tell of the sun-rising. When I first opened my eyes, I found the eastern and northern horizon blushing deeply at the coming glory. Just above the soft orange and celestial green lay a long, heavy cloud, which I knew would become illuminated very soon. I had a short nap between, and dreamed of watching a sunrise, and that the sky was covered with clouds shaped like coffins! When I awoke, I could not help shouting. That dun mass was a magnificent pile of wrought gold and amethyst, fretted, quivering, gorgeous. The east looked like a wreck of precious stones, only the dyes were not of earth. Below, deep orange and that tender green melted into one another; just above, rolled out this dazzling fold of unimaginable glory, and, higher still, floated soft fleecy clouds in the pale, infinite azure. Not the slightest shroud of mist lay upon anything. As soon as the Sun's crowned head rose up (and I watched it rise), it seemed as if myriads of diamonds were at that moment flung upon the earth, for the dew-drops each reflected the smile of the mighty Alchemist. Truly he turns everything into gold!

My pain clung to me like a faithful friend; but I made up my mind to walk to Havenwood and surprise them all. So, at one, I began my journey. I felt so grand and elated, as I found myself actually on the way, that I could not help laughing to myself. I went quite fast, because it was cool, and, slyly entering the avenue gate, burst upon the family, all unforeseen. They were duly astonished, and seemed glad to see me. . . . I have been reading Combe; I admire the book exceedingly, and feel very much inclined to believe in Phrenology Just before five, the beauty of the scene outdoors so worked upon me that, unwilling as my body was, Ideality led me out. I went to my noble wood, where the shadows were overwhelmingly beautiful. At a corner of the road I found a cedar that had been felled, and I stopped and sung a requiem over it after this fashion, "It is a shame--abominable--wicked!" I came home and read Combe, and manufactured a terrific headache; and just then Lydia came in, and her hurried manner so completed the discumgarigumfrigation of my wits that she said I looked perfectly crazy, and so I felt. She wanted me to come the next day and see old Mr. and Mrs. Howes; and at the appointed time we walked to their most picturesque and convenient cottage. They are two patriarchs, of unsullied simplicity and purity. We found them in the midst of exquisite neatness. The old man, originally tall, was now bowed and thin, obliged to walk with crutches, his venerable head nearly bald, only a few gray locks lying on his shoulders; his face was placid as an infant's. He was dressed in primitive style,--small-clothes and buckled shoes,--with perfect nicety. But the old lady called upon my admiration, as well as respect and love. There was an ease, dignity, and graciousness in her air and manner that might become a queen. The majesty of spotless virtue gave it to her. Her large eyes were full and tender and bright, and her whole countenance had an open, beaming expression or benevolence and sweetness which melted my whole heart. They both and she especially were once remarkable for personal beauty. Hers must have been captivating, since age and the smallpox have not obliterated it; but nothing could obliterate such a divine expression,--for what is it but the soul looking out of its prison-house? How my heart bows down before the virtuous old and the innocent young! There is a sympathy in the emotions. She is very lame, but there is nothing infirm or feeble in her appearance. Her strong and sweet spirit sits enthroned above decay. When we left them, I instinctively went to the old man and took his hand, feeling as if I had always known him; and he gently pressed it with a smile and a broken "Good-by,--I hope ye'll get better." "God bless you!" was on my lips, but unuttered. I took her hand, and she cordially shook mine, and said with such grace and so affectionately that she hoped I should be benefited by the country, that I was in a confusion of the purest pleasure. I left them with a lesson learned that I shall not soon forget,--a good lesson to be learned on my birthday. .

In the evening we all went over to see the new Court House by moonlight. Just as we were near it, I called to Kate to tell her of a little circumstance about Dr. Boyle, when Sam said he was immediately behind us My very heart stopped beating; and I felt at once all my wrongfulness, my want of thought and delicacy and consideration. All my happiness faded, and tears thronged to my eyes, remorse to my heart. But I believe Sam was mistaken, and that it was Judge Ware instead of Dr. Boyle. This comforted me only as it spared *him*. My trouble was the same. O Heaven! how hard it is to follow the straight and narrow way that leads to Life Eternal! I never can forget this warning.

. . . Sam Haven told us to-day about a Mr. Lovering, a most singular being. He thought it was of great importance to REFLECT, and so set about systematically to cultivate his reflection; and whenever the simplest question was proffered to him, he would immediately wrinkle his brow and screw up his eyes and shake his head, in the agony of exercising his whole powers of reflection. I have written a long letter to Miss Loring this evening, with the moon all the while in my face. This is revelry!

CHAPTER 3 - BOYHOOD AND BACHELORHOOD (PART 1)

A CERTAIN mystery invests the early life of Nathaniel Hawthorne. There is a difficulty in reconciling the outward calm and uneveutfulness of his young manhood with the presence of those qualities which are known to have been in him. It is not his literary or imaginative qualities that are now referred to; he found sufficient outlet for them. But here was a young man, brimming over with physical health and strength; endowed (by nature, at all events) with a strong social instinct; with a mind daring, penetrating, and independent; possessing a face and figure of striking beauty and manly grace; gifted with a stubborn will, and prone, upon occasion, to outbursts of appalling wrath; in a word, a man fitted in every way to win and use the world, to have his own way, to live throughout the full extent of his keen senses and great faculties; and yet we find this young engine of all possibilities and energies content (so far as appears) to sit quietly down in a meditative solitude, and spend all those years when a man's blood runs warmest in his veins in musing over the theories and symbols of life, and in writing cool and subtle little parables apposite to his meditations. Had he been a fanatic or an enthusiast; had he been snatched into the current of some narrow and overpowering preoccupation, whose interests filled each day, to the exclusion of all other thoughts and interests; had he been a meagre and pallid anatomy of overwrought brain and nerves,--such behavior would have been more intelligible. But he was many-sided, unimpulsive, clear-headed; he had the deliberation and leisureliness of a well-balanced intellect; he was the slave of no theory and of no emotion; he always knew, so to speak, where he was and what he was about. His forefathers, whatever their less obvious qualities may have been, were at all events enterprising, active, practical men, stern and courageous, accustomed to deal with and control lawless and rugged characters; they were sea-captains, farmers, soldiers, magistrates; and, in whatever capacity, they were used to see their own will prevail, and to be answerable to no man. True, they were Puritans, and doubtless were more or less under dominion to the terrible Puritan conscience; but it is hardly reasonable to suppose that this was the only one of their traits which they bequeathed to their successor. On the contrary, one would incline to think that this legacy, in its transmission to a legatee of such enlightened and unprejudiced understanding, would have been relieved of its peculiarly virulent and tyrannical character, and become an object rather of intellectual or imaginative curiosity than of moral awe. The fact that it figures largely in Hawthorne's stories certainly can scarcely be said to weaken this hypothesis; the pleasurable exercise of the imagination lies in its relieving us from the pressure of our realities, not in repeating and dallying with them. Upon the whole, therefore, there is no ground for assuming that, leaving out of the question the personal or original genius of Nathaniel Hawthorne, he was not in all other respects quite as much of a human being, in the widest sense of the term, as old Major William himself, or Bold Daniel either. How then, is his extraordinary undemonstrativeness to be accounted for?

This problem has perplexed all who have had anything to say about the great New England romancer. The most common escape has lain in the direction of constructing an imaginary Hawthorne from what was assumed to be the internal evidence of his writings,--a sort of morbid, timid, milk-and-water Frankenstein, who was drawn on by a grisly fascination to discuss fearful conceptions, and was in a chronic state of being frightened almost into hysterics by the chimeras of his own fancy. His aversion from bores and ignorant or uncongenial intrusion was magnified into a superhuman and monstrous shyness; in the earlier part of his literary career, opinion was divided as to whether he were a young lady of a sentimental and moralizing turn of mind, or a venerable and bloodless sage, with dim eyes, thin white hair, and an excess of spirituality. Some of these sagacious guesses came to the ears of the broad-shouldered and ruddy-checked young man, and he smiles over them inthe preface to the "Twice-Told Tales," and was tempted, as he intimates, to "fill up so amiable an outline, and to act in consonance with the character assigned to him; nor, even now, could he forfeit it without a few tears of tender sensibility." Later, he was suspected of being identical with the ineffective, inquisitive, and cynical poet, Miles Coverdale, in "The Blithedale Romance;" and, for aught I know, of being Arthur Dimmesdale, or Roger Chillingworth, or Clifford, or the Spectre of the Catacombs itself. But this is not the way to get at the individuality of a truly imaginative writer; and, latterly, the concoctions of the deductive philosophers have begun to have less weight.

Meanwhile, however, another school of Hawthorne analysts has sprung up, with great hopes of success. These are persons, some of whom were acquaintances of Hawthorne during his bachelor days and for a time afterwards, and who maintain that he not only possessed broad and even low human sympathies and tendencies, but that he was by no means proof against temptation, and that it was only by the kind precaution and charitable silence of his friends that his dissolute excesses have remained so long concealed. Singularly enough, it is as a tippler that the author of "The Scarlet Letter" most frequently makes his appearance in the narratives of these expositors; he was the victim of an insatiable appetite for gin, brandy, and rum, and if a bottle of wine were put on the table, he could hardly maintain a decent self-restraint. So probable in themselves and so industriously circulated were these stories, that, when the present writer was in London, three or four years ago, Mr. Francis Bennoch, the gentleman to whom the "English Note-Books" were dedicated by Mrs. Hawthorne, related to him the following anecdote: At a dinner at which Mr. Bennoch had been present, some time before, a gentleman had got up to make some remarks, in the course of which he referred to Nathaniel Hawthorne. He spoke of him as having been, during his residence in England, a confirmed inebriate, mentioned a special occasion on which he had publicly disgraced himself at an English table, and wound up with the information that his death had been brought about by a drunken spree on which he and Franklin Pierce had gone off together. When this historian had resumed his seat, Mr. Bennoch rose and spoke nearly as follows:

"I was the friend of Nathaniel Hawthorne during many years; I knew him intimately: no man knew him better. I was his constant companion on his English excursions and during his visits to London. I have seen him in all kinds of circumstances, in all sorts of moods, in all sorts of company; and I wish to say, to the gentleman who has just sat down, and to you all, that, often as I have seen Nathaniel Hawthorne drink wine, and though he had a head of iron, I have never known him to take more than the two or three glasses which every Englishman drinks with his dinner. I have never known him to be, and I know I am saying the truth when I say that he never was, under the influence of liquor. I myself was present on the occasion to which the gentleman has alluded, and I sat beside Nathaniel Hawthorne; and I am happy to tell you that then, as at all other times, where all were sober, he was the soberest of all. And in conclusion I will say, that the statement which the gentleman has just made to you, and which I am willing to believe he merely repeated upon hearsay, is a lie from beginning to end. Whoever repeats it, tells a lie; and whoever repeats it after hearing what I have said, tells a lie knowing it to be such."

This terse little speech embodies nearly all there is to be said on this subject. Mr. Hawthorne never was a teetotaler, any more than he was an abolitionist or a thug; but he was invariably temperate. During his lifetime he smoked something like half a dozen boxes of cigars, and drank as much wine and spirits as would naturally accompany that amount of tobacco. Months and sometimes years would pass without his either drinking or smoking at all; but when he would resume those practices, it was not to "make up for lost time,"--his moderation was not influenced by his abstention. Though very tolerant of excesses in others, he never permitted them in himself; and his conduct in this respect was the result not more of moral prejudice than of temperamental aversion. He would have been sober if he had had no morality. At one time, in his younger days, he was accustomed to sup frequently at a friend's table, where the lady of the house made very excellent tea, which the guest was very fond of. One evening, in sending down to replenish his cup, she remarked, "Now, Mr. Hawthorne, I am going to play Mrs. Thrale to your Johnson. I know you are a slave to my tea." Mr. Hawthorne made no reply, but contented himself with mentally noting that he had been guilty of a personal indulgence; and during five years, dating from that evening, he never touched another cup of tea. Every aspect of his life reflects the same principle; he could not endure the thought of being in the thraldom of any selfish or sensuous habit. Nevertheless, there is one other remark to make before this matter is laid aside.

I have just said that he was very tolerant of excesses in others; and herein, if anywhere, he would be open to blame. The commandment, "Judge not," cannot be held to excuse a man for toleration which amounts to passive encouragement of vice. Now Hawthorne, both by nature and by training, was of a disposition to throw himself imaginatively into the shoes (as the phrase is) of whatever person happened to be his companion. For the time being, he would seem to take their point of view and to speak their language; it was the result partly of a subtle sympathy and partly of a cold intellectual insight, which led him half consciously to reflect what he so clearly perceived. Thus, if he chatted with a group of rude sea-captains in the smoking-room of Mrs. Blodgett's boarding-house, or joined a knot of boon companions in a Boston bar-room, or talked metaphysics with Herman Melville on the hills of Berkshire, he would aim to appear in each instance a man like as they were; he would have the air of being interested in their interests and viewing life by their standards. Of course, this was only apparent; the real man stood aloof and observant, and only showed himself as he was, in case of his prerogatives being invaded, or his actual liberty of thought and action being in any way infringed upon. But the consequence may sometimes have been that people were misled as to his absolute attitude. Seeing his congenial aspect towards their little round of habits and beliefs, they would leap to the conclusion that he was no more and no less than one of themselves; whereas they formed but a tiny arc in the great circle of his comprehension. This does not seem quite fair; there is a cold touch in it; it has a look of amusing one's self at others' expense or profiting by their follies. The drunkard who complains that his companion allows him to get drunk, but empties his own glass over his shoulder, generally finds some sympathy for his complaint. Literally, as well as figuratively, it might have been said that Hawthorne should "drink square," or keep out of the way. There is nothing, however, to prevent the most contracted mind from perceiving that to be a student of human nature is not the same as to be a spy upon it. Nor can Hawthorne be charged with deception,--with pretending to be that which he was not. "I have no love of secrecy," he has written in his journal (1843). "I am glad to think that God sees through my heart; and if any angel has power to penetrate into it, he is welcome to know everything that is there. Yes, and so may any mortal who is capable of full sympathy, and therefore worthy to come into my depths. But be must find his own way there. I can neither guide nor enlighten him. . . . I sympathize with them, not they with me." Here lies the gist of the matter. Hawthorne always gave as much as he could to his companions; but it was not within the possibilities of his temperament for him to give them much more than they gave him. He could not force his depths to be visible to them; and if they could not see into them, they must perforce limit themselves. to the outward aspect. But because they could not sympathize with him, he was not to preclude himself from sympathizing with them. He was powerless to reveal himself fully, save in fit company; and such company, for him, was very rare. There were not more than two or three persons in the world to whom he could disclose himself freely; though there may have been scarcely any to whom he could not have made a partial (and therefore, doubtless, misleading) disclosure. It only remains to add that what was true of his personal conversation was also true of his letters. He involuntarily addressed each one of his companions in a different vein and style. If a man was pinnacled high in the intense inane, and could not extricate himself from that position, then Hawthorne would gravely descant to him upon his intense inanities; or if a poor creature were unable to comprehend anything higher than gin and politics, then would gin and politics constitute the argument of Hawthorne's epistles to him. All this, it must be understood, was apart from the demands and obligations of personal friendship, as to which no one was ever more stanch and trustworthy than Hawthorne. But he had his own views regarding the manner in which people should be interfered with, even for their own salvation, and regarding the extent to which such interference was justifiable.

But if the Hawthorne problem can be solved neither by rarefying him into a metaphysical abstraction nor by condensing him into a gross sensualist, what is to be done with him? By what means, through what experience, did he acquire that air and manner of a man of the world, which so early invested both his writings and his personality, and which to the world always remained so impenetrable? In what struggle, catastrophe, or abyss did those powerful energies which his nature contained achieve quiescence and composure? What victory or what loss endowed him with that even mood of humorous gravity, that low, melodious, masculine speech, that calm and commanding bearing? Whence came that veiled strength of character that so impressed and magnetized all with whom he came in contact? Was all this the mere consequence of a day-to-day growth and development, and was his profound insight into the structure and frailties of the human heart purchased at no more poignant cost than that of a succession of meditative and secluded years? "I used to think," he writes, "that I could imagine all feelings, all passions, and states of the heart and mind," which is as much as to say that he thought he could make imagination do the work of experience. Again: "Living in solitude till the fulness of time was come, I still kept the dew of my youth and the freshness of my heart," which indicates that his experience, if he had any, was not of a kind to destroy his self-respect or discourage his faith in virtue. "Had I sooner made my escape into the world, I should have grown hard and rough, and been covered with earthly dust, and my heart might have become callous by rude encounters with the multitude." These, certainly, are the words of a man who had no stain, at any rate, upon his conscience. But there are other channels, besides that of the personal conscience, through which a shock or an impression may be conveyed which shall color and mould the whole after-existence.

The truth is, that hunters on this sort of trails are apt to miss their way by being too violent and, so to say, palpable in their expectations. A profound and exceptional nature does not meet with vulgar mishaps; and, on the other hand, it may be reached by influences that would be scarcely noticed by persons of a coarser texture. In Nathaniel Hawthorne the sentiment of reverence was very highly developed, and I do not know that too much weight can be given to this fact. It is the mark of a fine and lofty organization, and enables its possessor to apprehend, to suffer, and to enjoy things which are above the sphere of other people. It exalts and refines his power of discrimination between right and wrong. It lays him open to mortal injuries, and, in compensation, it enriches him with exquisite benefits. It opens his eyes to what is above him, and thereby deepens his comprehension of what is around him and at his feet. Reverence, combined with imagination, and vivified by that faculty of divining God's meaning, which belongs to genius,--this equipment is, of itself, enough to educate a man in all the wisdom of the world, as well as in much that appertains to a higher region. And it is evident that, with a character thus equipped, a relatively small shock to the sensibilities may produce a remarkably strong effect.

Before entering more minutely into this matter, let us review the available facts concerning Nathaniel Hawthorne's boyhood,--which cannot be said to amount to much. A composition, in the form of a diary, has indeed been brought to light, which purports to have been written by him while living in Raymond, Maine. But, with deference to the contrary opinion of those who are worth listening to on the subject, the present writer has been unable to find in this "diary', any trustworthy evidence, either external or internal, of its being anything else than a rather clumsy and leaky fabrication. Assuming it to be genuine, however, it seems singularly destitute of biographical value; and, at all events, it shall not here be inflicted upon the reader. It may be doubted whether Shakspeare, or even Solomon, at twelve years of age, could have been a seriously interesting subject of study. Babies are interesting and instructive in a high degree, because they are as yet impersonal or un-self-conscious; but a half-grown boy is a morally amphibious creature, who, so far as he has attained individuality, is disagreeable, and, so far as he has not attained it, is superfluous. The boy Hawthorne's achievements as a newspaper editor are also of slight significance, despite the fact that he afterwards grew to be an author. Many boys who grew up to be horse-car conductors or members of the Legislature have edited better newspapers at the same age. What is most noticeable in his juvenile days is, one would say, the wholesome absence of any premonitions of what he was afterwards to become. He was, so far as any one could see, nothing more than a healthy, handsome, intelligent, mischievous boy, who deserved some credit for not letting himself be seriously spoilt by the admiration of his mother and sisters. The only trustworthy autobiographical fragment of his, known to be extant, is comprised in the following few paragraphs which he wrote out for his friend Stoddard, who was compiling an "article" on him for the "National Review," 1853. It contains little that is new; but it is always worth while to listen to Hawthorne's own words on even the most familiar subject.

"I was born in the town of Salem, Massachusetts, in a house built by my grandfather, who was a maritime personage. The old household estate was in another part of the town, and had descended in the family ever since the settlement of the country; but this old man of the sea exchanged it for a lot of land situated near the wharves, and convenient to his business, where he built the house (which is still standing), and laid out a garden, where I rolled on a grass-plot under an apple-tree, and picked abundant currants. This grandfather (about whom there is a ballad in Griswold's 'Curiosities of American Literature') died long before I was born. One of the peculiarities of my boyhood was a grievous disinclination to go to school, and (Providence favoring me in this natural repugnance) I never did go half as much as other boys, partly owing to delicate health (which I made the most of for the purpose), and partly because, much of the time, there were no schools within reach.

"When I was eight or nine years old, my mother, with her three children, took up her residence on the banks of the Sebago Lake, in Maine, where the family owned a large tract of land; and here I ran quite wild, and would, I doubt not, have willingly run wild till this time, fishing all day long, or shooting with an old fowling-piece; but reading a good deal, too, on the rainy days, especially in Shakspeare and 'The Pilgrim's Progress,' and any poetry or light books within my reach. Those were delightful days; for that part of the country was wild then, with only scattered clearings, and nine tenths of it primeval woods. But by and by my good mother began to think it was necessary for her boy to do something else; so I was sent back to Salem, where a private instructor fitted me for college. I was educated (as the phrase is) at Bowdoin College. I was an idle student, negligent of college rules and the Procrustean details of academic life, rather choosing to nurse my own fancies than to dig into Greek roots and be numbered among the learned Thebans.

"It was my fortune or misfortune, just as you please, to have some slender means of supporting myself; and so, on leaving college, in 1825, instead of immediately studying a profession, I sat myself down to consider what pursuit in life I was best fit for. My mother had now returned, and taken up her abode in her deceased father's house, a tall, ugly, old, grayish building (it is now the residence of half a dozen Irish families), in which I had a room. And year after year I kept on considering what I was fit for, and time and my destiny decided that I was to be the writer that I am. I had always a natural tendency (it appears to have been on the paternal side) toward seclusion; and this I now indulged to the utmost, so, that, for months together, I scarcely held human intercourse outside of my own family; seldom going out except at twilight, or only to take the nearest way to the most convenient solitude, which was oftenest the seashore, the rocks and beaches in that vicinity being as fine as any in New England. Once a year, or thereabouts, I used to make an excursion of a few weeks, in which I enjoyed as much of life as other people do in the whole year's round. Having spent so much of my boyhood and youth away from my native place,

I had very few acquaintances in Salem, and during the nine or ten years that I spent there, in this solitary way, I doubt whether so much as twenty people in the town were aware of my existence.

"Meanwhile, strange as it may seem, I had lived a very tolerable life, always seemed cheerful, and enjoyed the very best bodily health. I had read endlessly all sorts of good and good-for-nothing books, and, in the dearth of other employment, had early begun to scribble sketches and stories, most of which I burned. Some, however, got into the magazines and annuals; but, being anonymous or under different signatures, they did not soon have the effect of concentrating any attention upon the author. Still, they did bring me into contact with certain individuals. Mr. S. C. Goodrich (a gentleman of many excellent qualities, although a publisher) took a very kindly interest in me, and employed my pen for 'The Token,' an annual. Old copies of 'The Token' may still be found in antique boudoirs and on the dusty shelves of street bookstalls. It was the first and probably the best--it could not possibly be the worst--annual ever issued in this country. It was a sort of hot-house, where native flowers were made to bloom like exotics.

"From the press of Munroe & Co., Boston, in the year 1837, appeared 'Twice-Told Tales.' Though not widely successful in their day and generation, they had the effect of making me known in my own immediate vicinity; insomuch that, however reluctantly, I was compelled to come out of my owl's nest and lionize in a small way. Thus I was gradually drawn somewhat into the world, and became pretty much like other people. My long seclusion had not made me melancholy or misanthropic, nor wholly unfitted me for the bustle of life; and perhaps it was the kind of discipline which my idiosyncrasy demanded, and chance and my own instincts, operating together, had caused me to do what was fittest."

Mr. Hawthorne's sister Elizabeth, who has been already quoted, gives other details in letters written to her niece in the year after Hawthorne's death (1865 or thereabouts). Extracts from these letters are appended.

"Your father was born in 1804, on the 4th of July, in the chamber over the little parlor in the house in Union Street, which then belonged to my grandmother Hathorne, who lived in one part of it. There we lived until 1808, when my father died, at Surinam. I remember that one morning my mother called my brother into her room, next to the one where we slept, and told him that his father was dead. He left very little property, and my grandfather Manning took us home. All through our childhood we were indulged in all convenient ways, and were under very little control except that of circumstances. There were aunts and uncles, and they were all as fond of your father and as careful of his welfare as if he had been their own child. He was both beautiful and bright, and perhaps his training was as good as any other could have been. We were the victims of no educational pedantry. We always had plenty of books, and our minds and sensibilities were not unduly stimulated. If he had been educated for a genius, it would have injured him excessively. He developed himself. I think mental superiority in parents is seldom beneficial to children. Shrewdness and good-nature are all that is requisite. The Maker of the child will train it better than human wisdom could do. Your father was very fond of animals, especially kittens; yet he sometimes teased them, as boys will. He once seized a kitten and tossed it over a fence; and when he was told that she would never like him again, he said, 'Oh, she'll think it was William!' William was a little boy who played with him. He never wanted money, except to spend; and once, in the country, where there were no shops, he refused to take some that was offered to him, because he could not spend it immediately. Another time, old Mr. Forrester offered him a five-dollar bill, which he also refused; which was uncivil, for Mr. Forrester always noticed him very kindly when he met him. At Raymond, in Maine, my grandfather owned a great deal of wild land. Part of the time we were at a farmhouse belonging to the family, as boarders, for there was a tenant on the farm; at other times we stayed at our uncle's. It was close to the great Sebago Lake, now a well-known place. We enjoyed it exceedingly, especially your father and I. At the time our father died, Uncle Manning had assumed the entire charge of my brother's education, sending him to the best schools and to college. It was much more expensive than it would be to do the same things now, because the public schools were not good then, and of course he never went to them. Your father was lame a long time from an injury received while playing bat-and-ball. His foot pined away, and was considerably smaller than the other. He had every doctor that could be heard of; among the rest, your grandfather Peabody. But it was 'Dr. Time' who at last cured him. I remember he used to lie upon the floor and read, and that he went upon two crutches. Everybody thought that, if he lived, he would be always lame. Mr. Joseph E. Worcester, the author of the Dictionary, who at one time taught a school in Salem, to which your father went, was very kind to him; he came every evening to hear him repeat his lessons. It was during this long lameness that he acquired his habit of constant reading. Undoubtedly he would have wanted many of the qualities which distinguished him in after life, if his genius had not been thus shielded in childhood.

"He did not, in general, profess much love for flowers,--less than be felt, no doubt. Once, when he expected to leave Salem soon, he told us, on his return from a walk, that he had switched off the heads of all the columbines he passed, as he never meant and never wished to see their successors again. But, as it happened, he did not go away, and visited the same spots for several years after that."

Mr. Hawthorne has told his son many of his boyish experiences on the great Sebago Lake: how he used to skate there in winter, and how, one day, he followed for a great distance, armed with his fowling-piece, the tracks of a black bear, but without being able to overtake him. He was a good deal of a sportsman, and had all the fishing and hunting he wanted; but be was more fond of the idea or sentiment of the thing than of the actuality of it, and often forbore to pull the trigger, and threw back the fish that he drew from the river or lake. Not only he, but his mother and sisters likewise, appear to have enjoyed this half-wild Raymond life very much; nevertheless, as Miss Elizabeth Hawthorne writes, "by some fatality we all seemed to be brought back to Salem, in spite of our intentions and even resolutions." Hawthorne was in Raymond even less than the rest of the family; in 1818 he was at school in Salem, and only made them occasional visits. By 1820 they were all in Salem together; and now, having attained his seventeenth year, he began to make experiments in verse. "Except letters," says his sister, "I do not remember any prose writings of his till a much later period. I send you one of his poems, composed at the age of sixteen, which I found among some old papers. These verses have not much merit; they were written merely for amusement, and perhaps for the pleasure of seeing them in print,--for some like this he sent to a Boston newspaper." The poem, which has no title, is as follows:--

I.
The moon is bright in that chamber fair,
And the trembling starlight enters there
With a soft and quiet gleam;
The wind sighs through the trees around,
And the leaves send forth a gentle sound,
Like the voices of a dream.

II.
He has laid his weary limbs to sleep;
But the dead around their vigil keep,
And the living may not rest.
There is a form on that chamber floor
Of beauty which should bloom no more,--
A fair, yet fearful guest!

III.
The breath of morn has cooled his brow,
And that shadowy form has vanished now,
Yet he lingers round the spot;
For the pale, cold beauty of that face,
And that form of more than earthly grace,
May be no more forgot.

IV.
There is a grave by yon aged oak,
But the moss-grown burial-stone is broke
That told how beauty faded;
But the sods are fresh o'er another head,
For the lover of that maiden dead
By the same tree is shaded.

There is an agreeable ghastliness in this conception of a young man dying for love of a ghost, who had been a ghost since some generations before he was born; and though the form of versification and the vein of sentiment is hackneyed enough, there is considerable felicity and severity in the choice of words. At the same time the composition helps us to see that its author never could have been a genuine poet. Had Poe, at the same age, treated such a subject, he would have thrown his whole heart and earnestness into it, and would have produced something, by hook or by crook, that must have held a place in literature. Hawthorne, on the other hand, cannot regard the matter seriously; he knows he is only in jest, and is merly concerned not to be vapid or verbose. He always thoroughly enjoyed and appreciated. good poetry; but the idea of being a poet himself was something he could scarcely contemplate with a grave countenance. Possibly his insensibility to music--he was wont to declare that he never could distinguish between "Yankee Doodle" and "Hail Columbia "--may have had something to do with it; the lilt and jingle of measured feet and rhymes were not reconcilable, to his mind, with the sobriety of earnest utterance. If he had anything important to say, it must be said, not sung. Yet he read Scott's Poems to his children; and with the keenest relish of their rhythm and melody, the beauty of which was enhanced by his delivery.

Be that as it may, his letters of this period are much more entertaining and characteristic than his poetry; there was always a touch about them that prompts one to say, "There is the man!" Among the various scraps of browned and fragile paper which have been wafted down to us from his youthful days, is one sibylline leaf, containing scarce twoscore words, but full of pith and inscrutable suggestiveness. Who was the Ass? what was the Book? and did Aunt Mary ever get possession of the Secret? Here is the communication, which, on the evidence of the handwriting, may have been written about Hawthorne's eighteenth year.

"That Ass brought the book, and gave it directly to your aunt Mary. I hope you were wise enough to pretend to know nothing of the matter, if she has said anything to you about it.

"NATH. HAWTHORNE."

The handwriting is particularly legible, and the word "Ass" is engrossed with special care, significant of cordial emphasis. Of all asses who ever put their blundering hoofs into other people's pies, this ass was evidently the most utterly and irritably asinine. Impressive, likewise, is the bold and immoral exhortation to hypocrisy with which the missive concludes. Little did poor Aunt Mary suspect what a mine of dark dissimulation was yawning beneath her virtuous feet.

The six following letters belong to the period preceding and following Hawthorne's entrance into Bowdoin College, and convey further enlightenment as to what sort of a youth he was.

SALEM, Tuesday, Sept. 28, 1819.

DEAR SISTER,--We are all well, and hope you are the same. I do not know what to do with myself here. I shall never be contented here, I am sure. I now go to a five-dollar school,--I, that have been to a ten-dollar one. "O Lucifer, son of the morning, how art thou fallen!" I wish I was but in Raymond, and I should be happy. But "'t was light that ne'er shall shine again on life's dull stream." I have read "Waverley," "The Mysteries of Udolpho," "The Adventures of Ferdinand Count Fathom," "Roderick Random," and the first volume of "The Arabian Nights."

> Oh, earthly pomp is but a dream,
> And like a meteor's short-lived gleam;
> And all the sons of glory soon
> Will rest beneath the mould'ring stone.
> And Genius is a star whose light
> Is soon to sink in endless night,
> And heavenly beauty's angel form
> Will bend like flower in winter's storm.

Though those are my rhymes, yet they are not exactly my thoughts. I am full of scraps of poetry; can't keep it out of my brain.

> I saw where in the lowly grave
> Departed Genius lay;
> And mournful yew-trees o'er it wave,
> To hide it from the day.

I could vomit up a dozen pages more if I were a mind to turn over.
> Oh, do not bid me part from thee,
> For I will leave thee never.
> Although thou throw'st thy scorn on me,
> Yet I will love forever.
> There is no heart within my breast,
> For it has flown away,
> And till I knew it was thy guest,
> I sought it night and day.

Tell Ebe she's not the only one of the family whose works have appeared in the papers. The knowledge I have of your honor and good sense, Louisa, gives me full confidence that you will not show this letter to anybody. You may to mother, though. My respects to Mr. and Mrs. Howe.

I remain

Your humble servant and affectionate brother,

N. H.

Yours to uncle received.

SALEM, March 13, 1821.

DEAR MOTHER,--Yours of the ---- was received. I am much flattered by your being so solicitous for me to write, and shall be much more so if you can read what I write, as I have a wretched pen. Mr, Manning is in great affliction concerning that naughty little watch, and Louisa and I are in like dolorous condition. I think it would he advisable to advertise him in the Portland papers. How many honors are heaped upon Uncle Richard! He will soon have as many titles as a Spanish Don. I am proud of being related to so distinguished a personage. What has become of Elizabeth? Does she never intend to notice me again? I shall begin to think she has eloped with some of those "gay deceivers" who abound in Raymond, if she does not give me some proof to the contrary. I dreamed the other night that I was walking by the Sebago; and when I awoke was so angry at finding it all a delusion, that I gave Uncle Robert (who sleeps with me) a most horrible kick. I don't read so much now as I did, because I am more taken up in studying. I am quite reconciled to going to college, since I am to spend the vacations with you. Yet four years of the best part of my life is a great deal to throw away. I have not yet concluded what profession I shall have. The being a minister is of course out of the question. I should not think that even you could desire me to choose so dull a way of life. Oh, no, mother, I was not born to vegetate forever in one place, and to live and die as calm and tranquil as--a puddle of water. As to lawyers, there are so many of them already that one half of them (upon a moderate calculation) are in a state of actual starvation. A physician, then, seems to be "Hobson's choice;" but yet I should not like to live by the diseases and infirmities of my fellow-creatures. And it would weigh very heavily on my conscience, in the course of my practice, if I should chance to send any unlucky patient "ad inferum," which being interpreted is, " to the realms below." Oh that I was rich enough to live without a profession! What do you think of my becoming an author, and relying for support upon my pen? Indeed, I think the illegibility of my handwriting is very author-like. How proud you would feel to see my works praised by the reviewers, as equal to the proudest productions of the scribbling sons of John Bull. But authors are always poor devils, and therefore Satan may take them. I am in the same predicament as the honest gentleman in "Espriella's Letters,"--

"I am an Englishman, and naked I stand here, A-musing in my mind what garment I shall wear."

But as the mail closes soon, I must stop the career of my pen. I will only inform you that I now write no poetry, or anything else. I hope that either Elizabeth or you will write to me next week.

I remain
Your affectionate son,
NATHL. HATHORNE
Do not show this letter.

BRUNSWICK, April 14, 1822.

MY DEAR SISTER, I received your letter of April 10, and also one which was dated the 20th of March. How it could have been so long on the road, I cannot conceive. I hope you will excuse my neglect in writing to mother and you so seldom; but still I believe there is but one letter due from me to you, as I wrote about the middle of March. My health during this term has been as good as usual, except that I am sometimes afflicted with the Sunday sickness; and as that happens to be the case to-day, I employ my time in writing to you. My occupations this term have been much the same as they were last, except that I have, in a great measure, discontinued the practice of playing cards. One of the students has been suspended, lately, for this offence, and two of our class have been fined. I narrowly escaped detection myself, and mean for the future to he more careful.

I believe our loss by the fire is or will be nearly made up. I sustained no damage by it, except having my coat torn; but it luckily happened to be my old one. The repairs on the building are begun, and will probably he finished by next Commencement. I suppose Uncle Robert has arrived at Raymond. I think I shall not want my pantaloons this term, the end of which is only three weeks from Wednesday. I look forward with great pleasure to the vacation, though it is so short that I shall scarcely have time to get home. A great part of the students intend to remain here.

I have some cash at present, but was much in want of it the first part of the term. I suppose you have heard that a letter containing money which Uncle Robert sent me some time ago, was lost. I have since received some by Joseph McKean. Excuse my bad writing.

I remain
Your affectionate brother,
NATH. HATHORNE.
You need not show this.

BRUNSWICK, May 4, 1823.

MY DEAR SISTER, I received your letter, and was very glad of it, for they are "like angel visits, few and far between." However, to say the truth, I believe I have not much right to complain of the dilatory nature of our correspondence.

I am happy to hear that Uncle Robert has arrived safe, and was pleased with his journey. I should have thought a longer stay would have been necessary to make observations sufficient for a reasonable book of travels, which I presume it is his intention to publish.

The bundle of books which you mention, I saw, with my own eyes, put into the desk where all orders for Sawin are deposited. As it was a stormy day, Sawin did not come himself, but sent a boy.

There is in the medical class a certain Dr. Ward, of Salem, where he intends to settle, after taking his degree of M.D., which will be given him this term. I shall give him a letter of introduction to you when be returns to Salem, which be intends in about a fortnight. He is the best scholar among the medicals, and I hope you will use your influence to get him into practice.

I am invited by several of the students to pass the vacation with them. I believe I shall go to Augusta, if mother and Uncle R. have no objections. The stage fare will be about five dollars, and I should like about ten dollars as spending money, as I am going to the house of an Honorable. As Mr. McKean is sick, I think the money had better be directed to me than to him. The term ends in a fortnight from Wednesday next.

I wish to receive instructions about my thin clothes, whether I am to get them made here or have them sent down to me. I have but one good pair of pantaloons, the others being in rather a dilapidated condition.

If I had time, I would tell you a mighty story, how some of the students hung Parson Mead in effigy, and how one of them was suspended. Mother need not be frightened, as I was not engaged in it. Give my love to all and sundry.

Your affectionate brother,
N. HATHORNE

BRUNSWICK, 1823.
...I have been introduced to Gardiner Kellog. A few weeks ago, as I was entering the door of the college, somebody took hold of my cloak and said that "Kellog wished the honor of Mr. Hathorne's acquaintance." I looked round, and beheld a great, tall, awkward booby, frightened to death at his own boldness, and grinning horribly a ghastly smile. I saw his confusion, and with that condescending affability which is one among my many excellences, I took him by the hand, expressed my pleasure at the meeting, and inquired after his sister and friends. After he had replied to these queries as well as his proper sense of my superiority would admit, I desired to see him at my room as soon as convenient, and left him. This interesting interview took place before numerous spectators, who were assembled round the door of the college. He has since been at my room several times, and is very much pleased (how should it be otherwise?) with my company. I am, however, very much displeased with him for one thing. I bad comfortably composed myself to sleep on Saturday afternoon, when I was awakened by a tremendous knocking at the door, which continued about ten minutes. I made no answer, but swore internally the most horrible oaths. At last, the gentleman's knuckles being probably worn out, he retired; and upon looking out of the window, I discovered that my pestilent visitor was Mr. Kellog. I could not get asleep again that afternoon.

I made a very splendid appearance in the chapel last Friday evening, before a crowded audience. I would send you a printed list of the performances if it were not for the postage.

BRUNSWICK, Aug. 11, 1824.

MY DEAR LOUISA,--I have just received your letter, and you will no doubt wonder at my punctuality in answering it. The occasion of this miracle is, that I am in a terrible hurry to get home, and your assistance is necessary for that purpose. In the first place, I will offer a few reasons why it is expedient for me to return to Salem immediately, and then proceed to show you how your little self can be instrumental in effecting this purpose.

Firstly, I have no clothes in which I can make a decent appearance, as the weather in this part of the world is much too cold for me to wear my thin clothes often, and I shall therefore be compelled to stay at home from meeting all the rest of the term, and perhaps to lie in bed the whole of the time. In this case my fines would amount to an enormous sum.

Secondly, if I remain in Brunswick much longer, I shall spend all my money; for, though I am extremely prudent, I always feel uneasy when I have any cash in my pocket. I do not feel at all inclined to spend another vacation in Brunswick; but if I stay much longer, I shall inevitably be compelled to, for want of means to get home.

Thirdly, our senior examination is now over, and many of our class have gone home. The studies are now of little importance, and I could obtain leave of absence much easier than at any other time.

Fourthly, it is so long since I saw the land of my birth that I am almost dead of homesickness, and am apprehensive of serious injury to my health if I am not soon removed from this place.

Fifthly, the students have now but little to do, and mischief, you know, is the constant companion of idleness. The latter part of the term preceding Commencement is invariably spent in dissipation, and I am afraid that my stay here will have an ill effect upon my moral character, which would be a cause of great grief to mother and you.

I think that by the preceding arguments I bave clearly shown that it is very improper for me to remain longer in Brunswick; and we will now consider the means of my deliverance. In order to effect this, you must write me a letter, stating that mother is desirous for me to return home, and assigning some reason for it. The letter must be such a one as is proper to be read by the president, to whom it will be necessary to show it. You must write immediately upon the receipt of this, and I shall receive your letter on Monday; I shall start the next morning, and be in Salem on Wednesday. You can easily think of a good excuse. Almost any one will do. I beseech you not to neglect it; and if mother has any objections, your eloquence will easily persuade her to consent. I can get no good by remaining here, and earnestly desire to be at home.

If you are at a loss for an excuse, say that mother is out of health; or that Uncle R. is going a journey on account of his health, and wishes me to attend him; or that Elizabeth is on a visit at some distant place, and wishes me to come and bring her home or that George Archer has just arrived from sea, and is to sail again immediately, and wishes to see me before he goes; or that some of my relations are to die or be married, and my presence is necessary on the occasion. And lastly, if none of these excuses will suit you, and you can think of no other, write and order me to come home without any. If you do not, I shall certainly forge a letter, for I *will* be at home within a week. Write the very day that you receive this. If Elizabeth were at home, she would be at no loss for a good excuse. If you will do what I tell you, I shall be

Your affectionate brother,
NATH. HAWTHORNE.

My want of decent clothes will prevent my calling at Mrs. Sutton's. Write immediately, write immediately, write immediately.

Haste, haste, post-haste, ride and run, until these shall be delivered. You must and shall and will do as I desire. If you can think of a true excuse, send it; if not, any other will answer the same purpose. If I do not get a letter by Monday, or Tuesday at farthest, I will leave Brunswick without liberty.

BRUNSWICK, Nov. 26, 1824.

MY DEAR AUNT,--Elizabeth has informed me that you wish me to write to you, and as I am always ready to oblige, I shall endeavor to find materials for a letter. There is so little variety at college that you will not expect much news, or if you do, you will be disappointed. If my letter should happen to be very short, you will excuse it, as I attend to my studies so diligently that I have not much time to write.

A missionary society has lately been formed in college, under the auspices of a gentleman from Andover; but it does not meet with much encouragement: only twenty-two of the students have joined it, and most of them are supported by the Education Society, so that they have not much to give. I suppose you would be glad to hear that I am a member; but my regard to truth compels me to confess that I am not.

There is a considerable revival of religion in this town, and those adjoining, but unfortunately it has not yet extended to the college. The students have generally been very steady and regular this term, but religion is less regarded than could be desired. This is owing in part to the unpopularity of Mr. Mead, whom the students dislike so much that they will attend to none of his exhortations. I sincerely sympathize with Uncle Robert, and the family, in the pleasure they must feel at the approaching event. I wish that it were possible for me to be present in order that I might learn how to conduct myself when marriage shall be my fate. I console myself with the hope that you, at least, will not neglect to give me an invitation to your wedding, which I should not be surprised to hear announced. Elizabeth says that you are very deeply in love with Mr. Upham. Is the passion reciprocal?

The weather has lately been very cold, and there is now snow enough to make some sleighing. I keep excellent fires, and do not stir from them unless when it is absolutely necessary. I wish that I could be at home to Thanksgiving, as I really think that your puddings and pies and turkeys are superior to anybody's else. But the term does not close till about the first of January. I can think of nothing else that would be interesting to you, and as it is now nearly recitation time, I must conclude. I shall expect a letter from you very soon, otherwise I shall not write again.

Your affectionate nephew,
N. HATHORNE.

BRUNSWICK, April 21, 1825

MY DEAR SISTER,--I have been negligent about answering your letter, but you know my habits too well to be at all concerned at it. Nothing of any importance has taken place lately; my health has been very good, and I have neither been suspended nor expelled.

The term, I believe, will close about three weeks from the present time. I feel extremely anxious to see you all; and unless the government should compel me to stay in Brunswick during the vacation (of which there is little danger), I shall certainly return home. Mr. Leach was extremely anxious that I should accompany him on a visit to Raymond this spring; but I think I shall decline the honor.

I hope mother's health continues to improve, and that I shall find her as well as ever, when I return. You ought to give me a more particular account of yourselves and all that concerns you) as) though it might appear trifling to others, it would be interesting to me. I suppose Louisa has by this time returned from Newburyport, and gives herself the airs of a travelled lady.

I betook myself to scribbling poetry as soon as I heard of Lucy's album, and, after much labor, produced four lines, which I immediately burnt. I fear I shall he unable to write anything worthy of the immortality of such a record.

I have been thinking all the term of writing to Uncle William, according to his request, and shall expect a good scolding when I return, for neglecting it. I believe I promised to write to him, but promises are not always performed. He is so engaged in business, however, that he will never think of it.

I have scarcely any money, and wish to have fifteen dollars sent me in about a fortnight. I am not sure whether the term ends in three or in four weeks. If it is more than three, I will write after receiving the money. I have nothing more to write, excepting my respects to family and friends.

I am,

NATH. HAWTHORNE.

A boy's college life is often, in some respects, an epitome of his after life in the world. In the one place, as in the other, his character and tastes betray themselves; he selects the associates who are congenial to his nature, and finds his level among them. Nathaniel Hawthorne's academic career shows him to have been independent, self-contained, and disposed to follow his own humor and judgment, without undue reference to the desires or regulations of the college faculty. His friends were men who afterwards attained a more or less distinguished position in the world,--Franklin Pierce, Horatio Bridge, and Longfellow. He evinced no unnatural and feverish thirst for college honors, and never troubled himself to sit up all night studying, with a wet towel round his head and a cup of coffee at his elbow; but neither did he see fit to go to the other extreme. He assimilated the knowledge that he cared for with extreme ease, and took just enough of the rest to get along with; in this respect, as in most others, displaying a delectable maturity of judgment and imperturbable common-sense. He perceived that the value of college to a man--or, at any rate, to him--was not so much in the special things that were taught as in the general acquaintance it brought about with the various branches of learning; and still more, in the enlargement which it incidentally gives to one's understanding of foreign things and persons. At no time during his residence at Bowdoin did he have the reputation of being a recluse, or exclusive; it was his purpose and practice to he like his fellows, and (barring certain private and temperamental reservations) to do as they did. He steered equally clear of the Scylla of prigdom, and the Charybdis of recklessness; in a word, he had the mental and moral strength to be precisely his natural and unforced self. Within certain limits he was facile, easy-going, convivial; but beyond those limits he was no more to be moved than the Rock of Gibraltar or the North Pole. He played cards, had "wines" in his room, and went off fishing and sheeting with Bridge when the faculty thought he was at his books; but he maintained without effort his place in the recitation room, and never defrauded the college government of any duty which he thought they had a right to claim from him. His personal influence over his college friends was great; and he never abused it or employed it for unworthy ends.

He was the handsomest young man of his day, in that part of the world. Such is the report of those who knew him; and there is a miniature of him, taken some years later, which bears out the report. He was five feet ten and a half inches in height, broad-shouldered, but of a light, athletic bulld, not weighing more than one hundred and fifty pounds. His limbs were beautifully formed, and the moulding of his neck and throat was as fine as anything in antique sculpture. His hair, which bad a long, curving wave in it, approached blackness in color; his head was large and grandly developed; his eyebrows were dark and heavy, with a superb arch and space beneath. His nose was straight, but the contour of his chin was Roman. He never wore a beard, and was without a mustache until his fifty-fifth year. His eyes were large, dark blue, brilliant, and full of varied expression. Bayard Taylor used to say that they were the only eyes he had ever known flash fire. Charles Reade, in a letter written in 1876, declared that he had never before seen such eyes as Hawthorne's, in a human head. When he went to London, persons whose recollections reached back through a generation or so, used to compare his glance to that of Robert Burns. While he was yet in college, an old gypsy woman, meeting him suddenly in a woodland path, gazed at him and asked, "Are you a man or an angel?" His complexion was delicate and transparent, rather dark than light, with a ruddy tinge in the cheeks. The skin of his face was always very sensitive, and a cold raw wind caused him actual pain. His hands were large and muscular, the palm broad, with a full curve of the outer margin; the fingers smooth, but neither square nor pointed; the thumb long and powerful. His feet were slender and sinewy, and he had a long, elastic gait, accompanied by a certain sidewise swinging of the shoulders. He was a tireless walker, and of great bodily activity; up to the time he was forty years old, he could clear a height of five feet at a standing jump. His voice, which was low and deep in ordinary conversation, had astounding volume when he chose to give full vent to it; with such a voice, and such eyes and presence, he might have quelled a crew of mutinous privateersmen at least as effectively as Bold Daniel, his grandfather: it was not a bellow, but had the searching and electnfying quality of the blast of a trumpet.

During the ensuing summer Mr. Dike, his uncle by marriage, made him a visit at Brunswick, and saw fit, on his return to Salem, to give the young man's mother a somewhat eulogistic account of him. The young man, however, was displeased at being so reported. There was an indolence in his nature, such as, by the mercy of Providence, is not seldom found to mark the early years of those who have some great mission to perform in the world, and who, but for this protecting laziness, would set about the work prematurely, and so bring both it and themselves to ruin.

Nathaniel Hawthorne hated to be told that he was going to be a distinguished man. For, in the first place, it was an invasion of his private freedom thus to hamper and mortgage his right to do as he pleased with himself; and, in the second place, he was secretly conscious that his ideal of ambition was altogether too lofty and refined an affair ever to attain that gross and palpable realization that is commonly the condition of public distinction. He imagined that his own commendation was the only thing worth his striving for; and it took a good many years of lonely and unrecognized labor to deliver him from that persuasion. But although this attitude which he assumed may have been open to the charge of selfishness and indolence, it was more dignified and respectable than that of the man who thirsts for popular applause, and grasps at it pell-mell, before he has gained experience enough to tell black from white. The former is selfish, because it is concerned solely with one's own benefit and enjoyment, apart from any benefit to mankind; and it is indolent, because it involves the necessity only of thinking fine things, and not also of giving them such visible or tangible form that others may see and know them. But the latter attitude is vulgar, because it finds pleasure less in achievement than in recognition. Hawthorne never knew how to be vulgar; and in due time he got the better both of his selfishness and his indolence. Meanwhile, however, he deemed it prudent to affirm that he would "never make a distinguished figure in the world," and that all he hoped or wished was "to plod along with the multitude." That is to say, he was reluctant to commit himself to anything. Nevertheless, here is what his sister writes of him:--

"It was while in college that he formed the design of becoming an author by profession. In a letter to me he says that he had 'made progress on my novel.' I have already told you that he wrote some tales to be called 'Seven Tales of my Native Land,' with the motto from Wordsworth, 'We are Seven.' I read them and liked them. I think they were better than 'Fanshawe.' Mr. Goodrich (Peter Parley) told him afterwards that he thought 'Fanshawe' would have brought him some profit if it had bad an enterprising publisher. These 'Seven Tales' he attempted to publish; but one publisher, after keeping them a long time, returned them with the acknowledgment that he had not read them. It was the summer of 1825 that he showed them to me. One was a tale of witchcraft,--'Alice Doane,' I believe it was called; and another was 'Susan Grey.' There was much more of his peculiar genius in them than in 'Fanshawe.' I recollect that he said, when he was still in hopes to publish them, that he would write a story which would make a smaller book, and get it published immediately if possible, before the arrangements for bringing out the Tales were completed. So he wrote 'Fanshawe' and published it at his own expense, paying $100 for that purpose. There were a few copies sold, and he gave me one; but afterwards he took possession of it, and no doubt burned it. We were enjoined to keep the authorship a profound secret, and of course we did, with one or two exceptions; for we were in those days almost absolutely obedient to him. I do not quite approve of either obedience or concealment. Your father kept his very existence a secret, as far as possible. When it became known to literary men that there was such a person, he had applications to write for annuals and periodicals, etc.; and that is the way, I suppose, that genius is made known to the world in these days. But even then he was not paid punctually, so that he had much to depress his spirits. His habits were as regular as possible. In the evening after tea he went out for about one hour, whatever the weather was; and in winter, after his return, be ate a pint bowl of thick chocolate (not cocoa, but the old-fashioned chocolate) crumbed full of bread: eating never hurt him then, and he liked good things. In summer he ate something equivalent, finishing with fruit in the season of it. In the evening we discussed political affairs, upon which we differed in opinion; he being a Democrat, and I of the opposite party. In reality, his interest in such things was so slight that I think nothing would have kept it alive but my contentious spirit. Sometimes, when he had a book that he particularly liked, he would not talk. He read a great many novels; he made an artistic study of them. There were many very good books of that kind that seem to be forgotten now."

And thus it was that he entered upon that long vigil in the "haunted chamber" of the family mansion in Herbert Street,--the antechamber of his fame. "Sometimes," he writes, in the often-quoted passage, it seemed as if I were already in the grave, with only life enough to be chilled and benumbed. But oftener I was happy,--at least, as happy as I then knew how to be, or was aware of the possibility of being." His melancholy, indeed, belonged rather to his imagination than to his realities; it was the melancholy of a mind conscious of power, but as yet doubtful whether that power could be so used or adjusted as to leave its mark upon mankind. His happiness was the result of good health, freedom from petty annoyances, and the author's inestimable privilege of artistic creation. There may be a revulsion of feeling about the creations, when they have achieved outward embodiment; but so long as the process of production is going on, there is pleasure of a very high and enviable sort.

From the letters belonging to this period, I will give the following, to his sister Louisa: --

SALEM, Nov. 4, 1831.

DEAR L.,--I send Susannah's Gibraltars. There were fourteen of them originally, but I doubt whether there will be quite a dozen when she gets them. Susannah knows well enough that she was the debtor, instead of the creditor, in this business; and if she has any sort of conscience she will send me back some sugar-plums.

I also send the bag of coins. I believe there is a silver threepence among them, which you must take out and bring home, as I cannot put myself to the trouble of looking for it at present. It was a gift to me from the loveliest lady in the land, and it would break my heart to part with it.

I don't understand the hint about the smelling-bottle. I have made all possible inquiries, but neither mother nor Elizabeth recollect to have seen such a thing. I never make use of a smelling-bottle myself, and of course would have no motive for keeping it. I will speak to the town-crier to-morrow.

Mrs. Ede's wedding-cake will be very acceptable, and I wish she had brought it with her when she went through town. I am afraid there is little prospect of my repaying her in kind; but when I join the Shakers, I will send her a great slice of rye-and-Indian bread.

NATH. HAWTHORNE.

P.S. You can't imagine how quiet and comfortable our house has been since you went away.

The paragraph about the silver threepence is worth marking.

Though the coin in question had been given to him by the loveliest lady in the land (whoever she may have been), and though it would have broken his heart to part with it, yet he would not be at the pains to put his hand into the bag to take it out, but devolved that labor upon his sister. This seems to show that the frenzy of amorous passion had not, at the age of twenty-seven, succeeded in making an absolute slave of him. Concerning these "loveliest ladies," his sister Elizabeth has the following remarks to make:--

"About the year 1833, your father, after a sojourn of two or three weeks at Swampscott, came home captivated, in his fanciful way, with a 'mermaid,' as he called her. He would not tell us her name, but said she was of the aristocracy of the village, the keeper of a little shop. She gave him a sugar heart, a pink one, which he kept a great while, and then (how boyish, but how like him!) he ate it. You will find her, I suspect, in 'The Village Uncle.' She is Susan. He said she had a great deal of what the French call *espièlerie*. At that time he had *fancies* like this whenever he went from home."

Susan remains Susan still, and nothing more, to all the world; but I should like to know how she was affected by the description of herself in "The Village Uncle." This is how she appeared when he first caught sight of her:--

"You stood on the little bridge, over the brook, that runs across King's beach into the sea. It was twilight; the waves rolling in, the wind sweeping by, the crimson clouds fading in the west, and the silver moon brightening above the hill; and on the bridge were you, fluttering in the breeze like a sea-bird that might skim away at your pleasure. You seemed a daughter of the viewless wind, a creature of the ocean foam and the crimson light, whose merry life was spent in dancing on the crests of the billows, that threw up their spray to support your footsteps. As I drew nearer, I fancied you akin to tha race of mermaids, and thought how pleasant it would be to dwell with you among the quiet coves, in the shadow of the cliffs, and to roam along secluded beaches of the purest sand, and when our northern shores grew bleak, to haunt the islands, green and lonely, far amid summer seas. And yet it gladdened me, after all this nonsense, to find you nothing but a pretty girl, sadly perplexed with the rude behavior of the wind about your petticoats."

And, upon a further acquaintance, he addresses her thus:--

"At a certain window near the centre of the village, appeared a pretty display of gingerbread men and horses, picture-books and ballads, small fish-hooks, pins, needles, sugar-plums, and brass thimbles,--articles on which the young fishermen used to expend their money from pure gallantry. What a picture was Susan behind the counter! A slender maiden, though the child of rugged parents, she had the slimmest of all waists, brown hair curling on her neck, and a complexion rather pale, except when the sea-breeze flushed it. A few freckles became beauty-spots beneath her eyelids. How was it, Susan, that you always talked and acted so carelessly, yet always for the best, doing whatever was right in your own eyes, and never once doing wrong in mine, nor shocked a taste that had been morbidly sensitive till now? And whence had you that happiest gift, of brightening every topic with an unsought gayety, quiet but irresistible, so that even gloomy spirits felt your sunshine, and did not shrink from it? Nature wrought the charm. She made you a frank, simple, kind-hearted, sensible, and mirthful girl. Obeying nature, you did free things without indelicacy, displayed a maiden's thoughts to every eye, and proved yourself as innocent as naked Eve."

Charming though all this declares her to have been, however, the mermaid was not destined to have any further effect on Hawthorne's destiny than to inspire him to write this delicately conceived and gracefully expressed sketch of her.

CHAPTER 4 - BOYHOOD AND BACHELORHOOD (PART 2)

BEFORE going further, it will be necessary to examine the epistolary records which cover the period (between 1830 and 1837) during which Hawthorne began to become known as a man of letters. There are numerous communications from Goodrich and other publishers, and from Hawthorne's college friends, Horace Bridge, Franklin Pierce, and Cilley. They have reference to his early contributions to the "Token," the "Knickerbocker," and other periodicals; to his connection with the "Boston Bewick Company's Magazine" (which became insolvent), to a scheme of joining a South Polar expedition in the capacity of historian, and various incidental matters. The letters sufficiently explain themselves, and will be given in the order of their dates, without further comment.

HARTFORD, CONN., Jan. 19, 1830.

DEAR SIR,--I brought the MSS. which you sent me to this place, where I am spending a few weeks. I have read them with great pleasure. "The Gentle Boy" and "My Uncle Molineaux" I liked particularly; about "Alice Doane" I should be more doubtful as to the public approbation. On my return to Boston in April, I will use my influence to induce a publisher to take hold of the work, who will give it a fair chance of success. Had "Fanshawe" been in the hands of more extensive dealers, I do believe it would have paid you a profit. As a practical evidence of my opinion of the uncommon merit of these tales, I offer you $35 for the privilege of inserting "The Gentle Boy" in the "Token," and you shall be at liberty to publish it with your collection, provided it does not appear before the publication of the "Token." In this case I shall return "Roger Malvin's BuriaL" I will retain the MS. till your reply, which please address to this place.

Respectfully, S. G. GOODRICH.

BOSTON, May 31, 1831.

DEAR SIR,--I have made very liberal use of the privilege you gave me as to the insertion of your pieces in the "Token." I have already inserted four of them; namely, "The Wives of the Dead," "Roger Malvin's Burial," "Major Molineaux," and "The Gentle Boy." As they are anonymous, no objection arises from having so many pages by one author, particularly as they are as good, if not better, than anything else I get. My estimate of the pieces is sufficiently evinced by the use I have made of them, and I cannot doubt that the public will coincide with me.

Yours respectfully,
S. G. GOODRICH

NEW YORK, Jan. 4, 1836.
NATHANIEL HAWTHORNE, Esq.

MY DEAR SIR,--I have only to-day found time to thank you for your truly beautiful article, "The Fountain of Youth," in the current number of the "Knickerbocker." I have rarely read anything which delighted me more. The style is excellent, and the *keeping* of the whole excellent. We should be glad to hear from you as often as your leisure will permit you to write; and you will please inform "Clark and Edson" when you desire the *quid pro quo.*

Among our contributions for next month will be a poem of forty stanzas by Robert Southey, that will make you laugh, I think; and other articles by Professor

Wolff of Jena University, Mr. Galt, and Wordsworth. If you have a paper by you that we might have for the February number, it would appear among foreign and exotic plants of a good order.

Very truly, and with high regard,
S. GAYLORD CLARK.

HAVANNAH, Feb. 20, 1836.

DEAR HAWTHORNE,--It is now ten days since I received your letter in the country near Matanzas. Nothing has given me so much pleasure for many a day as the intelligence concerning your late engagement in active and responsible business. I have always known that whenever you should exert your self in earnest, that you could command respectability and independence and fame. As for your present situation, I do not regard it so much in itself--though it seems tolerably good to begin with--as I do for its being the introduction to other and better employment. Besides, it is no small point gained to get you out of Salem. Independently of the fact about "the prophet," etc., there is a peculiar dulness about Salem,--a heavy atmosphere which no literary man can breathe. You are now fairly embarked with the other literary men, and if you can't sail with any other, I'll be d----d. I hope you will write for the "New York Mirror." It has a great circulation, and its editor is a man of influence and standing in the literary world, although in my judgment he is not very deep. His good opinion will be of service to you. I am writing with my coat and hat off, doors and windows open, and mosquitoes biting my feet. My letter is neither long nor neat; such as it is, though, it is probably worth the postage.

With best wishes for your success and happiness, I am
Yours truly, HORACE BRIDGE.

WASHINGTON, March 5, 1836.

DEAR HAWTHORNE,--I could make a very tolerable apology for this long delay in answering your letter, but as they are usually unsatisfactory, as they sometimes are insincere, we will if you please dispense with them altogether. I was, as you supposed, trying to effect a negotiation with Blair at the time your letter was received; but I doubt whether I should have succeeded in accomplishing anything that would have been either agreeable or advantageous to you. And I congratulate you sincerely upon your installation in the editorial chair of the "American Magazine." I hope you will find your situation both pleasant and profitable. I wish you to enter my name as a subscriber to the magazine. Where do you board, and where is your office? I may be at Boston in three or four weeks, and I shall have no time to search out locations. If you do not write to me soon, Hath, I will never write a puff of the "American Magazine," or say a clever thing of its editor.

Ever and faithfully your friend,
FRANK PIERCE.

AUGUSTA, May 14, 1836.

AM I not virtuous to-day? have I not refused an invitation to play cards with some friends, thereby compelling them to play each *per se?* This shows what a good effect your letter had upon my morals. But, after all, the worst accusation I can make against myself is that I have no settled plan of existence, even now, at the age of thirty. Meantime I keep my heart as warm and kindly as possible, and am happy enough in the friendship of a goodly number of warm and indulgent friends.

I have read the April number of your journal, and like it well. The other, which you say is best, has not come yet. There must be a great deal of labor necessary to conduct it, and I rejoice that you bear it so well. I fear that you may tire of your present situation too soon; but I think there is no danger of your wanting literary employment long in future. You are in for it, and are known. Goodrich has opened a heavy fire upon P. Benjamin, I see. I am glad that it is not you, and yet I should like to see you thoroughly angry and pouring it into that same fellow. I find that the Mill Dam is going on famously. From present appearances I shall be obliged to invest some twenty thousand dollars. You must publish an article descriptive of this work, when it is finished.

I shall try your advice with regard to the women some time when I am away from here, though I shall make a poor hand of it most certainly. I sometimes think seriously of matrimony for ten minutes together, and should perhaps perpetrate it if I did not like myself too well. My morals have improved exceedingly in the past year; your advice in a former letter was very efficient in this improvement, and Helen J-----'s fate has confirmed me. I take advice from you kindly. It seems divested of the presumption and intermeddling spirit with which advice is usually tinctured. I am a vain man, and a proud one; and I would spurn with scorn the interference of any one whom I suspected of giving me advice with any other than the most friendly feelings. But when I am sure of the purity and kindness of motive that dictates the advice of a real friend, I can and do feel grateful. But a little wickedness will not hurt one, especially if the sinner be of a retiring disposition. It stirs one up. and makes him like the rest of the world.

And now good-by to you till we meet, which I trust will be soon. By the way, I wish you would inquire of Earle, the tailor, if he has sent my clothes. I want them very much.

Yours truly,
HORACE BRIDGE.

BOSTON, June 3, 1836.
Mr. HAWTHORNE.

DEAR Sir,--Yours of this date is at hand. In answer to your wish that the Company would pay you some money soon, I would say it is impossible to do so just now, as the Company have made an assignment of their property to Mr. Samuel Blake, Esq., for the benefit of their creditors. They were compelled to this course by the tightness of the money market, and losses which they had sustained. We would like to have you, when in the city, sign the assignment. We shall continue the magazine to the end of the volume. Your bills from the 27th May will be settled by the assignee promptly.

Yours respectfully,
GEORGE A. CURTIS,
For Samuel Blake, assignee of B. Bewick Co.

BOSTON, Sept. 23, 1836.

DEAR SIR,--Your letter and the two folios of Universal History were received some days ago. I like the History pretty well,--I shall make it do,--I have requested Mr. Curtis to make you the earliest possible remittance. The "Token" is out; the publisher owes you $108 for what you have written,--shall it be sent to you? I shall want three or four sketches from you for the next volume, if you can finish them.

Yours, S. G. GOODRICH.

N. HAWTHORNE, Esq., Salem, Mass.

AUGUSTA, Sept. 25, 1836.

DEAR HATHORNE,--The "Token" is out, and I suppose you are getting your book ready for publication. What is the plan of operations? who the publishers, and when the time that you will be known by name as well as your writings are? I hope to God that you will put your name upon the title-page, and come before the world at once and on your own responsibility. You could not fail to make a noise and an honorable name, and something besides.

I've been thinking how singularly you stand among the writers of the day; known by name to very few, and yet your writings admired more than any others with which they are ushered forth. One reason of this is that you scatter your strength by fighting under various banners. In the same book you appear as the author of "The Gentle Boy," the author of "The Wedding Knell," "Sights from a Steeple," and, besides, throw out two or three articles with no allusion to the author, as in the case of "David Snow," and "The Prophetic Pictures," which I take to be yours. Your articles in the last "Token" alone are enough to give you a respectable name, if you were known as their author. But you must be aware of the necessity of coming out as you are, and have probably made some arrangements about the matter. I thought of writing a notice of the "Token;" and naming you as the author of several articles, with some candid remarks upon your merits as a writer. Would you have any objection to this? If not, I will do it.

I went to Boston this week, and saw Mrs. Fessenden, who told me that you were in Salem and had been since last winter; that you had taken your farewell in the last number of the magazine (which by the way does not come to me), and that the magazine had been sold out to some one who is to edit it. Who is it? Write me soon if it will not interfere with your book that is to come out. Don't flinch, nor delay to publish. Should there be any trouble in a pecuniary way with the publishers, let me know, and I can and will raise the needful with great pleasure.

Your friend,
H. BRIDGE.

AUGUSTA, Oct. 16, 1886.

DEAR HATH,--I have a thousand things to say to you, but can't say more than a hundredth part of them. You have the blues again. Don't give up to them, for God's sake and your own and mine and everybody's. Brighter days will come, and that within six months. It is lucky you didn't quarrel with Goodrich, he being a practical man who can serve you.

I should have been rejoiced to have been at Fresh Pond with you and Frank Pierce, and think I should have done honor to the good cheer. He is an honorable man, that Frank, and of kind feelings; and I rejoice that he likes me.

By all means cultivate the "Knickerbocker;" and I should think it good policy to write for the "New York Mirror," though it is rather of the namby-pamby order. See what I have written for the "Boston Post," and tell me is it best to send it: "It is a singular fact that of the few American writers by profession, one of the very best is a gentleman whose name has never yet been made public, though his writings are extensively and favorably known. We refer to Nathaniel Hawthorne, Esq., of Salem, the author of 'The Gentle Boy,' 'The Gray Champion,' etc., etc., all productions of high merit, which have appeared in the annuals and magazines of the last three or four years. Liberally educated, but bred to no profession, he has devoted himself exclusively to literary pursuits, with an ardor and success which will ere long give him a high place among the scholars of this country. His style is classical and pure; his imagination exceedingly delicate and fanciful, and through all his writings there runs a vein of sweetest poetry. Perhaps we have no writer so deeply imbued with the early literature of America, or who can so well portray the times and manners of the Puritans. Hitherto, Mr. Hawthorne has published no work of magnitude; but it is to be hoped that one who has shown such unequivocal evidence of talent will soon give to the world some production which shall place him in a higher rank than can be attained by one whose efforts are confined to the sphere of magazines and annuals." This is not satisfactory by any means, and yet it may answer the purpose of attracting attention to your book when it comes out. It is not what I wish it was, nor can I make it so.

Yours ever, H. BRIDGE.

NEW YORK, Oct. 17, 1836.

DEAR SIR,--In the midst of the "tempest and I may say whirlwind" of avocations, I have only time to say that I shall be glad to hear from you as soon as you can, agreeably to yourself, favor us with anything from your pen, and that I shall never heed postage in your case. In all cases, therefore, please send communications by mail.

Very truly, etc.,
S. GAYLORD CLARK.
NATH. HAWTHORNE, Esq.

AUGUSTA, Oct. 22, 1836.

DEAR HATH,--I have just received your last, and do not like its tone at all. There is a kind of desperate coolness in it that seems dangerous. I fear that you are too good a subject for suicide, and that some day you will end your mortal woes on your own responsibility. However, I wish you to refrain till next Thursday, when I shall be in Boston, *Deo volente*. I am not in a very good mood myself just now, and am certainly unfit to write or think. Be sure and come to meet me in Boston.

Yours truly, H. BRIDGE.

BOSTON, Nov. 7, 1836.

DEAR SIR,--I have seen Mr. Howes, who says he can give a definite answer Saturday. When I get it, I will communicate it to you. *He seems pretty confident that he shall make the arrangement with a man who has capital, and will edit the book.* I think your selection of the tales nearly right. Suppose you say, for title, "The Gray Champion, and other Tales, by N. H."

Yours truly, S. G. GOODRICH.

N. HAWTHORNE, Esq.

AUGUSTA, Nov. 17, 1886.

DEAR HATH,--Have you obtained the magazine again? How does the book come on? I am anxious to see the effect it will produce, though nothing doubting of its success. I fear you will hurt your self by puffing Goodrich *undeservedly*,--for there is no doubt in my mind of his selfishness in regard to your work and yourself. I am perfectly aware that he has taken a good deal of interest in you, but when did he ever do anything for you without a *quid pro quo?* The magazine was given to you for $100 less than it should have been. The "Token" was saved by your writing. What compensation you received I do not know,--probably the same with the others. And now he proposes to publish your book because he thinks it will be honorable and lucrative to he your publisher now and hereafter, and perhaps because he dares not lose your aid in the "Token." Unless you are already committed, do not mar the prospects of your *first* book by hoisting Goodrich into favor.

On the " 15th November, 1836," I opened the package so long since sealed, and forthwith notified Cilley that he had lost the bet, sending him also a copy of it, and of the agreement to pay within a month. I think you will hear from him soon, and that he will pay promptly. He is a candidate for Congress, and would not like his Democratic friends at the seat of governinent to think him dishonorable. By all means accept the wine if he sends it. He is able to pay, and would have exacted it if you had lost. I think the odds were decidedly against you. It is doubtful whether to rejoice or be sad at the result. Anyhow, I hope to taste the liquor.

Yours ever, H. BRIDGE.

THOMASTON, Nov. 17, 1836

FRIEND HATHORNE,--I have this day received a letter from our classmate, Horace Bridge, containing copies of a matrimonial wager made by us and left with him twelve years ago last Monday. "Tempus fugit." Now to the question. Have I won or lost? Are you single or double ? Were you, on the fourteenth day of November last past, and to the uttermost limits of said day, double or single? or hast thou, since the day and date above-named, ever tasted the bliss of double-trouble blessedness? Please answer truly and 'pon honor, as you love "the best old Madeira wine." I see, by the articles signed and scaled, that one month's grace is allowed the loser.

Bridge informs me that "you are about to publish a book, and are coming into repute as a writer very fast." I am gratified to hear it; but just now it would have pleased me more to have heard that you were about to become the author and father of a legitimate and well-begotten boy than book. What! suffer twelve years to pass away, and no wife, no children, to soothe your care, make you happy, and call you blessed. Why, in that time I have begotten sons and daughters to the number of half a dozen, more or less; though I mourn that some of them are not. Peace be with them!

Now you are indeed a writer of great repute, and soon to be the author of a book. I did not mistake your vein in that particular, if I did in the line matrimonial. Damn that barrel of old Madeira: who cares if I have lost it! If only you and Frank Pierce and Joe Drummer and Sam Boyd and Bridge and Bill Hale were together with me, we would have a regular drunk, as my chum in college used to call it, on that same barrel of wine.

What sort of a book have you written, Hath? I hope and pray it is nothing like the damned ranting stuff of John Neal, which you, while at Brunswick, relished so highly. Send me a copy, and I'll review it for you. If I can't make a book, my partisan friends call me good at a political harangue or stump speech. Don't turn up your aristocratic nose, for it is a pathway to fame and honor, as well as the course you have marked out, and attended with more stimulus, noise, and clatter, if not *eclat*, than that of a book author and writer for immortality, who bides himself from his own generation in a study or garret, and neglects in the spring-time of life to plant and maintain that posterity to which he looks for praise and commendation.

Don't fail to send me your hook, on pain of my not paying the barrel of wine. Is it a novel or poem?--has it a moral or religious tendency? If not, Cheever will be down upon it in the "Review." I have no doubt it will be good. but I assure you I'll find fault with it if I can.

I am, dear sir, very truly
Your obedient servant,
JONATHAN CILLEY.
Mr. NATH. HATHORNE.

BOSTON, Dec. 12, 1836.
DEAR SIR,--Owing to peculiar circumstances, we shall not be able to engage a good printer on your book till next week. I thought it best to drop you a line to this effect, that you might not think it unreasonably delayed or neglected.

Yours truly,
J. B. RUSSELL.
N. HAWTHORNE, Esq.

BOSTON, Dec. 13, 1836.
DEAR SIR,--I will with pleasure supply the copies of the "Token" for the edition of the Tales. I believe the work is to go forward next week.

If you are disposed to write a volume of six hundred small 12mo pages on the manner, customs, and civilities of all countries,--for $300, I could probably arrange it with you. I should want a mere compilation from books that I would furnish. It might be commenced immediately. Let me know your views. It would go in old Parley's name.

Yours in haste,
S. G. GOODRICH.

AUGUSTA, Dec. 25, 1836.

DEAR HAWTHORNE,--On this Christmas day and Sunday I am writing up my letters. Yours comes first. I am sorry that you didn't get the magazine; because you wanted it, not that I think it very important to you. You will have the more time for your book. I rejoice that you have determined to leave Goodrich to his fate. I do not like him. Whether your book will sell extensively may be doubtful, but that is of small importance in the first book you publish. At all events, keep up your spirits till the result is ascertained; and my word for it, there is more honor and emolument in store for you from your writings than you imagine. The bane of your life has been self-distrust. This has kept you back for many years, which, if you had improved by publishing, would have long ago given you what you must now wait a short time for. It may be for the best, but I doubt it.

I have been trying to think what you are so miserable for. Although you have not much property, you have good health and powers of writing, which have made and can still make you independent. Suppose you get but $300 per annum for your writings. You can with economy live upon that, though it would he a d----d tight squeeze. You have no family dependent on you, and why should you "borrow trouble"? This is taking the worst view of your case that it can possibly bear. It seems to me that you never look at the bright side with any hope or confidence. It is not the philosophy to make one happy. I expect next summer to be full of money, a part of which shall be heartily at your service if it comes. I doubt whether you ever get your wine from Cilley. His inquiring of you whether he had really lost the bet is suspicious; and he has written me in a manner inconsistent with an intention of paying promptly; and if a bet grows old it grows cold. He wished me to propose to you to have it paid at Brunswick next Commencement, and to have as many of our classmates as could be mustered to drink it. Though a bet of wine, it does not seem to me like a bet of a bottle or a gallon even, which are to be drunk by all concerned. A bet of a barrel can only be intended for the individual's use who wins. It may be Cilley's idea to pay over the balance after taking a strong pull at it; if so, it is well enough. But still it should be tendered within the month. Cilley says to me that if you answer his interrogatories satisfactorily, he shall hand over the barrel of old Madeira.

And so Frank Pierce is elected Senator. There is an instance of what a man can do for himself by trying. With no very remarkable talents, he, at the age of thirty-four, fills one of the highest stations in the nation. He is a good fellow, and I rejoice at his success. He can do something for you perhaps. The inclination he certainly has. Have you heard from him lately?

H. BRIDGE.

AUGUSTA, Feb. 1, 1837.

DEAR HAWTHORNE,--The Legislature is here in session. I have not met Cilley yet, but probably shall in a week or two, his election coming on again February 6; and of course he will come here immediately after. The probability is that he will be successful this third time.

So your book is in press, and will soon be out. Thank God that the plunge will be made at last. I am sure it will be for good. It is a good omen that you and Park Benjamin are reconciled, though I should fear to trust him or Goodrich, particularly the last. I believe them both selfish and unscrupulous.

I coincide perfectly with you touching the disparity of profit between a writer's labor and a publisher's. It *is* hard that you should do so much and receive so little for the "Token." You say an editorship would save you. I tell you that within six months you may have an editorship in any magazine in the country if you wish it. I wish to God that I could impart to you a little of my own brass. You would dash into the contest of literary men, and do honor to yourself and country in a short time. But you never will have confidence enough in your self, though you will have fame. You must send Frank Pierce a copy of your book by mail. He will have no postage to pay, and will be gratified. Frank's whole energies have been exerted for years in building up himself and with surprising success. Hence he has not been able to think or act for others, as be would have done had he been less engrossed with self. And yet I do not think him a selfish man. He has been. in a measure, driven forward by circumstances, and obliged to obey his destiny. He will be a good friend to you.

By next fall you and I will both have settled our destiny in no small degree. Write soon.

Yours truly, HORACE.

BOSTON, Feb. 9, 1837.

MY DEAR SIR,--If you have any articles written for the "Token," I should be glad to get them soon, as I am about putting the work into the hands of the printers. The "Twice-Told Tales" will be ready for the public eye in about ten days. It will be a handsome book,--as to the interior, I know it will take.

Yours, S. G. GOODRICH.
N. HAWTHORNE, Esq., Salem.

BOSTON, March 4, 1837.

DEAR SIR,--We shall publish your book next Monday. I am directing the presentation copies, as you directed, and have sent you twelve herewith, all which shall be charged at *cost*.

In haste, yours truly,
J. B. RUSSELL.
N. HAWTHORNE, Esq.

BOSTON, March 17, 1887.

DEAR SIR,--I have sent all the copies of your book as you desired. It may he gratifying to you to know that, in addition to the favorable opinions expressed by the newspapers, your book is spoken of in the highest terms by discriminating gentlemen here and at Cambridge.

Yours truly, J. B. RUSSELL.

AUGUSTA, March 19, 1837.

DEAR HATH,--The "Twice-Told Tales," came yesterday, to my especial joy. The appearance of the book is decidedly good. The name is excellent. I have begun to write a notice which shall be published as soon as our booksellers here receive any copies. One of them ordered a dozen on my recommendation. Has Goodrich kept his faith with you, and done everything to promote the success of the book which is usual in such cases? I have never read "The Gentle Boy" till to-day, when it had the credit of making me blubber a dozen times at least during the two readings which I have given it. I like it very much, and think it better than any other in the book. "Little Annie's Ramble" is also new to me, and very pleasant. It must be that you had some particular child in your mind's eye, and perhaps did actually take the walk. How was it? *Have* you a smile that is more winning to children than other men's? I don't remember to have heard you say anything about your partiality for children.

It is not unlikely that the "Mirror" man may, upon reading your book, try to engage your services as editor, unless the "Mirror" clique should have some interest in keeping you back, such as the glorification of Willis. Two Nats cannot have their reflections in one Mirror, perhaps. Your first name bids fair to stand high in the literary catalogue. There is yourself, Willis, and Nat Deering,--which idea shall be wrought into a puff of you, under the heading of "The Three Nats," which title will probably take enough to cause its republication.

As for me, I shall probably go to New York for several weeks, if my "Mill Dam" continues to look as well as it does now. Though I have forty or fifty thousand at stake, I do not sleep the worse for it. If I lose, I shall try for the appointment of Purser in the Navy, and with a good chance of success. This is a profound secret at present. Good times for both of us are coming. You have broken the ice; the ice can't break me.

Your ancient friend, HORACE.

AUGUSTA, March 26, 1837.

DEAR HATH,--I am delighted to hear that you are likely to succeed in your wishes regarding the South Sea, and would to God that I could go with you, ruined or not Maybe I may, yet. I forwarded a copy of your book to Cilley, telling him that his assistance would be needed to get your situation. What is the situation you want? I only wait to know this before procuring some letters for you. I think I can do something with men of influence in this State, and perhaps in yours also. For instance, j am well acquainted with George Bancroft. Hodgson, our Land Agent, goes to-morrow to New Hampshire and will see Pierce; and if you will give Pierce a hint, the thing may be managed easily. I will answer for the whole Maine delegation. But, after all, it will still be very doubtful if you succeed. Therefore do not set your heart too thoroughly upon it.

You seem to think that Pierce and I had some mutual understanding upon this subject; but I assure you that not a syllable has passed between us about it. Your book will do good, if the papers are cold about it. Most of the coldness is due to the fact that the stories are "Twice-Told;" and this I know from remarks of some of my friends, who declined buying because the book was not original! But your fame here has become respectable, and I derive some credit from being your friend.

Is it true that the man who was appointed Historian is sick and likely to resign? I hope so.

Yours ever, H. BRIDGE.

HILLSBORO, March 28, 1837.

DEAR HATHORNE,--Yours of the 22d inst., with the enclosure, came this morning, and you will learn from the copy herewith enclosed what disposition I propose to make of the latter. You will perhaps be surprised that I seem to depend so much on Reynolds. I think my letter in this respect is judicious; the reasons I will explain to you when we meet. I presume he will induce Camberling to write a letter to the President and enclose the articles, which I now forward to him. I have taken the liberty further to presume that it is important to you, on account of other arrangements, to know as soon as practicable what is to be the issue of this project. I shall now remain quiet until I hear from Reynolds; then communicate with you and take our measures accordingly. Should anything, in the present posture of affairs, occur to you as important, not contained in my letter, I will supply its deficiency without delay on being apprised of it. You will receive herewith a copy of so much of my letter to Mr. Reynolds as relates to the subject of your appointment.

In much haste, ever and truly your friend,
FRANK PIERCE.
NATH. HAWTHORNE, Esq., Salem.

(Copy.)
J. N. REYNOLDS, Esq.

DEAR SIR,--Since we parted I have thought much of the subject of our Sabbath evening conversation, and am exceedingly desirous that my friend Hawthorne should accompany you on the South Sea expedition. He is, as I remarked to you, extremely modest, perhaps diffident,--a diffidence, in my judgment, having its origin in a high and honorable pride; but he is a man of decided genius, without any whims or caprices calculated to impair his efficiency or usefulness in any department of literature.

I was with him a day or two in Boston on my way home; and after full consideration, and consultation with a few literary friends, he is disposed to accept a situation, if tendered, though I was unable to inform him precisely what would be the scope and character of his duties, or what the compensation,--it ought to be $1,500 at least. His recent publication ("Twice-Told Tales") has been most favorably noticed by many of the periodicals of the day. I should have sent you a copy of the book, but had no opportunity. Now, how is our object to be attained? What is the precise situation to apply for? To whom should the application be made? To the Secretary of the Navy, or directly to the President? What testimonials with regard to him will be useful, and from whom? These are questions upon which I desire your opinion in order that our efforts may be promptly and efficiently seconded by his friends. I hope you will converse with Messrs. Camberling, Lee, McKean, and Moore upon this subject, if you have a convenient opportunity while in New York. Perhaps you may enlist sufficient interest to address a letter to the President; however, I would indicate no particular course, but leave all to your better discretion. Hawthorne is very desirous of seeing you. Shall you be in Boston before you visit Ohio ? If so, address a letter to him at Salem, stating at what time and where in that city he may expect to meet you. In any event, he will be happy to receive a letter from you on the subject. I hope to hear from you soon, as it is important for my friend, on account of other arrangements, that the probability of his becoming attached to the expedition should be ascertained as soon as practicable. I have before stated that Mr. Hawthorne is not subject to any of those whims and eccentricities which are supposed to characterize men of genius, and which might disqualify him for any solid and steady business; but as the articles I send refer only to his abilities as a romance-writer, it may be proper for me to add that he has been hardly less successful in other departments. He edited for some time the Boston Bewick Company's "Magazine of Useful Knowledge," with great diligence and success,--more, I believe, to the satisfaction of the proprietors and the public than any previous editors. You will perceive that I am in earnest upon this subject; it would be singular if it were otherwise. I know Hawthorne's worth, and am sure you would admire him as a man of genius, and love him as a companion and friend.

AUGUSTA, April 7, 1837.

DEAR HATH,--I wrote George Bancroft, yesterday, in your behalf, requesting a letter to the Secretary of the Navy to be sent under cover to Pierce. I don't know whether he will comply, but I think I tickled him in the right place. He can't well help doing the handsome thing by you. Has any one interested Alexander Everett in your favor? Pierce might get him interested by a word, for he is ambitious of office and honors. Pierce has not as yet written me, nor am I certain that he will. If he has not written Cilley, he ought at once; for Cilley's having been a classmate may have much weight. It looks favorable for you now, but I must say again that it is not good policy to set your heart wholly upon this cast. You may not succeed, and what then? Why, you will be no worse off than now; on the other hand, you will be much better; for having made interest among many of the high officers and high privates in the land, your reputation will be of course extended, and the same men will feel bound to help you again, if called upon. Pierce will not rest until he does something for your permanent benefit. In short, you now stand decidedly higher as a writer than you would have done had not the post you seek been thought of. It is absolute folly to think of despairing, should you fail in this. There is many a good day in store for you yet, if you never go to the South Seas, of which, however, I have little doubt. You must write often to Pierce; every letter will stimulate him to action, whether you push him or not.

Yours truly, HORACE.

BOSTON, April 8, 1837.

DEAR SIR,--The book is selling well, and making its way to the hearts of many. It will prove decidedly successful. I wish you could send me one or two more stories for the "Token" within a week or fortnight. What say you?

Yours, S. G. GOODRICH.

AUGUSTA, April 14, 1837.

DEAR HAWTHORNE--I am rejoiced that you seem to think that the disappointment can be borne, even if you do not succeed in getting the post of Historian, the more because it looks very doubtful to me whether you succeed. The disagreement between Reynolds, who holds your destiny in this respect, and the Secretary will be a hard stumbling-block to get over.

Are you seriously thinking of getting married? If you are, nothing that I could say would avail to deter you. I am in doubt whether you would be more happy in this new mode of life than yon are now. This I am sure of, that unless you are fortunate in your choice, you will be wretched in a tenfold degree. I confess that, personally, I have a strong desire to see you attain a high rank in literature. Hence my preference would be that you should take the voyage *if you can*. And after taking a turn round the world, and establishing a name that will be worth working for, if you choose to marry you can do it with more advantage than now.

I hope Longfellow will review the book, for I think him a man of good taste and kindly feelings. Good-by, and God bless us.

Yours ever, HORACE.

APRIL 19, 1887.

THE editors of the "United States Magazine and Democratic Review," a new literary and political periodical about to be commenced at Washington City, knowing and highly appreciating Mr. Hawthorne's style of writing (as shown in a few sketches and tales that have met their eye, such as "David Snow," "Fancy's Show-Box," etc.), would be happy to receive frequent contributions from him. This magazine is designed to be of the highest rank of magazine literature, taking *ton* of the first class in England for model. The compensation to good writers will be on so liberal a scale as to command the best and most polished exertions of their minds. It is therefore intended that nothing but matter of distinguished excellence shall appear in its pages, and that will be very handsomely remunerated. Many of the finest writers of the country are engaged for contribution, as some will also be from England; and as nothing will be accepted which shall be worth a less price than three dollars per page, in the judgment of the editors, Mr. Hawthorne will perceive the general tone of superiority to the common magazine writing of this country, at which they aim. In many cases they propose to give five dollars per page, depending on the kind and merit of the writing. As this magazine will have a vast circulation throughout the Union, and as it will occupy so elevated a literary rank, it will afford to Mr. Hawthorne what he has not had before, a field for the exercise of his pen, and the acquisition of distinction worthy of the high promise which the editors of the "United States Magazine" see in what he has already written. The first number appearing in July, any communication must be sent in by the end of May. Please address "Langtree and O'Sullivan, Washington City, D. C."

[I must say that the above strikes me as being the most amusing document of this whole batch. The man who wrote it might have been retained as Head Composer of Prospectuses for that famous speculative enterprise in "Martin Chuzzlewit." He was, as a matter of fact, John O'Sullivan, at this time about eight-and-twenty years of age, a cosmopolitan of Irish parentage on his father's side, and one of the most charming companions in the world. He was always full of grand and world-embracing schemes, which seemed to him, and which he made appear to others, vastly practicable and alluring, but which invariably miscarried by reason of some oversight which had escaped notice for the very reason that it was so fundamental a one. He lived in the constant anticipatory enjoyment of more millions than the Adelantado of the Seven Cities ever dreamed of; and yet he was not always able to make his income cover his very modest and economical expenditure. Under disappointments which would have crushed (one might suppose) hope itself, be remained still hopeful and inventive; and it was difficult to resist the contagion of his eloquent infatuation. He and Hawthorne became very dear friends; and he was godfather to Hawthorne's first child.]

BOSTON, April 28, 1837.

DEAR HAWTHORNE,--I saw Goodrich yesterday, and had a long talk about you and your affairs. I like him very much better than before. He told me that the book was successful. It seemed that he was inclined to take too much credit to himself for your present standing, on the ground of having early discovered and brought you forward. But on the whole, I like him much. I have also received a strong letter of recommendation from Pierce in my behalf, accompanied by a kind letter to me, in which he speaks of you in terms of warmest friendship. He says that he has written Reynolds in your behalf, and not yet received an answer. Still, I am glad that you seem more disposed to stay at home than awhile ago, for there is certainly much doubt of your success. What has become of your matrimonial ideas? Are you in a good way to bring this about?

I want you to spend two or three mouths this summer with me in my bachelor lodgings at Augusta. We can be all to ourselves, and I am a famous cooker of breakfast and tea. And then we will make an excursion or two. Think of this seriously, and let me know when I return.

Yours ever, HORACE.

AUGUSTA, May 17, 1837.

DEAR HAWTHORNE,--Have you heard anything more of the Exploring Expedition? It seems to me that your chance of employment is as small almost as mine. I am told that there is to be but one historiographer, and that Colton, the chaplain, has consented to perform that duty. My views of the expedition have been materially changed since I went to Washington. It is predicted by many of the wise ones that it will be a decided failure, and bring ridicule upon those who are connected with it. If so, we had better keep out of it, especially if you can marry a fortune, and I finish my Mill Dam. I wish you would tell me if you were in earnest about marrying. Goodrich told me that the book had sold between six and seven hundred copies already, and received high praise from some of the most eminent literati of Boston and Cambridge. This is an earnest of future eminence that cannot be mistaken. It seems, however, as if all the reviewers in a small way were determined to let you make your own way, without giving the least assistance. Well, let them take that course, and see who will come out brightest. If the "North American" gives a good review of the book, it will be worth the whole of these twopenny critics' praise. Are you writing another book? You ought to follow up so good a beginning, if beginning this may be called. I wish you would come to Augusta and write all summer in my poor domicile. I expect to take my French master into my house, if he will come. God knows whether there will be another opportunity, after this summer, for you and me to be together again. My Mill Dam looks well, in spite of the blue times.

Yours ever,
H. BRIDGE

BOSTON, May 20, 1837.
Mr. NATHANIEL HAWTHORN.

SIR,--Mr. J. L. O'Sullivan, of Washington City, wishes me to ask you if you have received a letter from him. Having sent it by private hand, he is doubtful whether you received it.

Very respectfully yours,
SAMUEL DEXTER.

MAY 24, 1837.

DEAR HAWTHORNE,--I am rejoiced that your last gives reason to expect that you will pay me a visit soon. When you come, make your arrangements so that you can stay two or three months here. I have a great house to myself; and you shall have the run of it. As for old acquaintances, rely upon it they will not trouble you. No one but Eveleth and Bradbury are here. The first is ruined and moping; the other prosperous, but does not darken my doors. We are not friends.

I received a letter two days ago from Pierce, dated May 2d, requesting me to ascertain exactly how matters were relating to the Exploring Expedition. I have written to Pierce advising him to inquire of the Secretary if there is any vacancy, and recommending you for it. It might be well to put your papers on file in his office, in case you are hereafter a candidate for one of the editors of the magazine. It is no use for you to feel blue. I tell you that you will be in a good situation next winter, instead of "under a sod." Pierce is interested for you, and can make some arrangement, I know. An editorship or clerkship at Washington he can and will obtain. So courage, and *au diable* with your sods! I have something to say to you upon marriage, and about Goodrich, and a thousand other things. I shall be inclined to quarrel with you if you do not come, and that would be a serious business for you, for my wrath is dreadful. Good-by till I see you here.

Yours truly,
H. BRIDGE.

P.S. Before I commenced this letter I put three eggs into my teakettle to boil for dinner; and it was not till I had signed my name that the thought of my eggs occurred to me. You see that I must have been interested, and I shall see that the eggs are sufficiently hard.

--The following passage from a letter to Miss E. M. Hawthorne, from Miss E. P. Peabody, belongs to a period a few months subsequent to the above, but has its significance here nevertheless: --

MY DEAR MISS HAWTHORNE,-... I saw how much your brother was suffering on Thursday evening, and am glad you think it was not a trial, but rather the contrary, to hear my *loquaciousness*. I talked because I thought it was better than to seem to claim entertainment from him, whose thoughts must be wandering to the so frightfully bereaved. There seems so little for hope and memory to dwell on in such a case (though I hope everything always from the Revelation of Death), that I thought perhaps it would be better if he could divert himself with the German.. .. Even your brother, studying the *Pattern Student of the World*, may be enabled to take such a view of a literary life as will fill his desire of action, and connect him with society more widely than any particular office under Government could do. If, as you say, he has been so long uneasy - however, perhaps he had better go; only, may he not bind himself *long*, only be free to return to freedom. In general, I think it is better for a man to be harnessed to a draycart to do his part in transporting "the commodity" of the world; for man is weak, and needs labor to tame his passions and train his mind to order and method. But the most perilous season is past for him. If, in the first ten years after leaving college, a man has followed his own fancies, without being driven by the iron whip of duty, and yet has not lost his moral or intellectual dignity, but rather consolidated them, there is good reason for believing that he is one of Nature's ordained priests, who is consecrated to her higher biddings. I see that you both think me rather *enthusiastic;* but I believe I say the truth when I say that I do not often *overrate*, and I feel sure that this brother of yours has been gifted and kept so choice in her secret places by Nature thus far, that he may do a great thing for his country. And let me tell him what a wise man said to me once (that Mr. J. Phillips of whom I once spoke to you): "The perilous time for the *most highly gifted* is not *youth*. The holy sensibilities of genius--for all the sensibilities of genius are holy--keep their possessor *essentially unhurt* as long as animal spirits and the idea of *being young* last; but the perilous season is *middle age*, when a false wisdom tempts them to doubt the divine origin of the dreams of their youth; when the world comes to them, not with the song of the siren, against which all books warn us, but as a wise old man counselling acquiescence in what is below them." I have no idea that any such temptation has come to your brother yet; but no being of a social nature can be entirely beyond the tendency to fall *to the level* of his associates. And I have felt more melancholy still at the thought of his owing anything to the patronage of men of such thoughtless character as has lately been made notorious. And it seems to me they live in too gross a region of selfishness to appreciate the ambrosial moral *aura* which floats around our ARIEL,--the breath that he *respires*. I, too, would have him help govern this great people; but I would have him go to the *fountains* of greatness and power,--the unsoiled souls,--and weave for them his "golden web," as Miss Burley calls it,--it may be the *web of destiny* for this country. In every country *some one man* has done what has saved it. It was one Homer that made Greece, one Numa that made Rome, and one Wordsworth that has created the Poetry of Reflection. How my pen runs on,--but I can write better than I can speak.

Here or hereabouts it was that Hawthorne met with an experience that carried with it serious results. If there be any hidden cause for what seems the premature reserve and gravity of his early manhood, it will not, perhaps, be necessary to look further for it than this. For a man such as he has been shown to be, it was enough; and it might, indeed, have left deep traces upon a nature less sensitive and a conscience less severe than his.

Among the young ladies of good family and Social standing that formed what were then the "best circles of Salem and Boston, there was one who, for convenience sake, shall be designated as Mary. As a child, she had been the victim of an abnormal and almost diseased sensitiveness, which often caused her to behave oddly and unaccountably. A distorted vanity, or craving for admiration, was perhaps at the bottom of this behavior; the child was passionately desirous of producing an impression or a sensation, and indifference or ridicule was an agony to her. The success of her performance was tripped up by the very intensity of her desire, and she had intelligence enough to be keenly aware of her own shortcomings and awkwardness. She was sent to dancing-school, but suffered so much from the real or fancied slights and raillery of her companions, that it was found necessary to take her home again. Later on, a violent ambition to become learned took possession of her; she imagined that she could win by the power of intellect that conspicuousness and homage which were to her as the breath of her life. Her mind, however, was not of the calibre of a De Stael or even of a Margaret Fuller; she was clever, subtle, and cunning, but possessed no real mental weight or solidity. Nor did this yearning after the fruits of wisdom long abide with her; she was now growing out of her hobbledehoyhood, and was developing a certain kind of glancing beauty, slender, piquant, ophidian, Armida-like. Instead of a prophetess or sibyl, she now aimed to become a social enchantress; and everything favored her purpose. She had learnt how to conceal her true feelings and sentiments, or to let only so much of them appear as might enhance the complexity of her fascinations. She had a considerable share of the dramatic instinct,--the art of the actress; and it was her constant delight to devise combinations and surprises wherein, in a manner seemingly the most involuntary and unconscious, she should appear as the centre and culmination of interest. The alertness and rapidity of her mental operations and perceptions enabled her to produce, upon persons whom she wished to dazzle or captivate, an impression not only of intellectual brilliance, but of a strange and flattering sympathy with and understanding of their most intimate prepossessions and aspirations. In this way she secured the regard, confidence, and occasionally the devotion, of persons who were in every high respect her immeasurable superiors. For she was, in reality, a creature of unbounded selfishness, wantonly mischievous, an inveterate and marvellously skilful liar; she was coarse in thought and feeling, and at times seemed to be possessed by a sort of moral insanity, which prompted her to bring about all manner of calamities upon innocent persons, with no other motive than the love of exercising a secret and nefarious power. Thus, on one occasion, a certain very agreeable young lady, a cousin of hers, happened to meet an English nobleman, who fell violently in love with her. She returned his affection, and their marriage was already arranged, when Mary stepped between them, and, by means of a series of anonymous letters, devised with diabolical ingenuity, succeeded in breaking off the match. The nobleman returned to England heart-broken, and remained a bachelor the rest of his life; the cousin, some fifteen years later, made a marriage of friendship with an elderly and unromantic gentleman. As for Mary, she had the benefit of whatever enjoyment is to be derived from the disinterested torture of one's fellow-creatures.

While this notable personage was in the full tide of her social triumph and fascination, a gentleman, whom I will call Louis, and who was on terms of familiar intercourse with her, happened to speak to her of his friend, Nathaniel Hawthorne. The report thus given of the handsome and mysterious young author aroused Mary's curiosity and ambition; she resolved to add him to her museum of victims. At her request, Louis brought him to her house and introduced him. She at once perceived how great his value would be to her, as a testimony to the potency of her enchantments, and set herself to ensnare him. In order to encourage his confidence, she regaled him with long extracts from the most private passages of her own autobiography, all of which were either entirely fictitious, or such bounteous embroideries on the bare basis of reality, as gave to what was mean and sordid an appearance of beauty and a winning charm. Hawthorne, who was himself above all things truthful, and who had never considered the possibility of a lady being a deliberate and gratuitous liar, accepted her confidences with sympathetic interest, and allowed her to decoy him into assuming towards her the attitude of a protecting friend and champion, - the rather, since she assured him that he was the only human being to whom she could reveal the secrets of her inmost soul.

So far all was well; but when it came to taking the next step,--to beguiling him into exchanging confidence for confidence, autobiography for autobiography,-- Armida began to meet with difficulties. Hawthorne intimated to her, in the gentlest and most considerate manner, that it was impossible for him to regard himself as an object of so much interest as to warrant his dissecting himself for her benefit. Mary had the tact not to seem put out by this rebuff, and greatly augmented Hawthorne's kindly feelings towards her by forbearing to urge him any further in this direction. She did not, however, entertain any idea of giving up her purpose. She merely resigned herself to the necessity of changing her mode of attack; and after due meditation she hit upon a scheme which more than sustained her unhallowed reputation for ingenuity. She summoned Hawthorne to a private and mysterious interview, at which, after much artful preface and well-contrived hesitation and agitated reluctance, she at length presented him with the startling information that his friend Louis, presuming upon her innocence and guilelessness, had been guilty of an attempt to practise the basest treachery upon her; and she passionately adjured Hawthorne, as her only confidential and trusted friend and protector, to champion her cause. This story, which was devoid of a vestige of truth, but which was nevertheless so cunningly interwoven with certain circumstances known to her auditor as to appear like truth itself, so kindled Hawthorne's indignation and resentment, that, without pausing to make proper investigations, he forthwith sent Louis a challenge.

Mischief was now afoot; and Mary was charmed at the prospect of seeing two men, who had always been dear and cordial friends, engage in a duel on her account. Fortunately, however, Louis was not such a fool as most young fellows would have been under the circumstances; and he was, moreover, cognizant of instances in which this baleful young personage had played a similar game. Accordingly, instead of at once accepting the challenge, he made himself acquainted with all the details of the matter, and then wrote Hawthorne a frank and generous letter, in which, after fully and punctually explaining to him the ins and outs of the deception which had been practised upon him, and completely establishing his own guiltlessness of the charge against him, he refused the challenge, and claimed the renewal of Hawthorne's friendship.

Hawthorne immediately called upon him, overwhelmed both by the revelation of the woman's falsehood and by his own conduct in so nearly bringing destruction upon a man he loved. He could scarcely bring himself to believe, however, that Mary had knowingly, and with full comprehension of what she was about, contrived a plot of such wanton malice; and perhaps his self-esteem made him reluctant to admit that the tender and confidential conduct she had maintained towards him was nothing more than the selfish artifice of a coquette. Howbeit, Louis left his vanity not a leg to stand upon; and finally, to use the expression of one who was cognizant of these events at the time, Hawthorne went to Mary and "crushed her."

If the matter had ended here, it would have remained in Hawthorne's memory only as a rash and regrettable episode of his impetuous youth, from the worst consequences of which he had been providentially preserved. But it is at this point that the story takes a tragic turn. While the duel was still a topic of conversation among the few of Hawthorne's friends who knew anything about it, one of those friends--Cilley--received the challenge of Graves. Now, Cilley belonged to a knot of young Northern men who had resolved to put down the tyranny of the fire-eating Southerners. Nevertheless, he hesitated some time before accepting this challenge, the subject in dispute being unimportant, and his position with regard to it being such that the "code of honor" did not necessitate a meeting. At length, however, some one said, "If Hawthorne was so ready to fight a duel without stopping to ask questions, you certainly need not hesitate;" for Hawthorne was uniformly quoted by his friends as the trustworthy model of all that becomes a man in matters of honorable and manly behavior. This argument, at all events, put an end to Cilley's doubts; he accepted the challenge, the antagonists met, and Cilley was killed.

When Hawthorne was told of this, he felt as if he were almost as much responsible for his friend's death as was the man who shot him. He said little; but the remorse that came upon him was heavy, and did not pass away. He saw that it was Cilley's high esteem for him which had led him to his fatal decision; and he was made to realize, with unrelenting clearness, how small a part of the consequences of a man's deeds can be monopolized by the man himself. "Had I not aimed at my friend's life," was the burden of his meditation, "this other friend might have been still alive." And if the reproach be deemed fanciful, it would not on that account be easier for Hawthorne to shake off. He had touched hands with crime; and all the rest was but a question of degrees.

In the first volume of "Twice-Told Tales" there is a short story, or "morality," as the author styles it, which, if read in the light of the foregoing narrative, will be found to have a peculiar interest. In it the question is discussed, whether the soul may contract the stains of guilt, in all their depth and flagrancy, from deeds which may have been plotted and resolved upon, but which physically have never had an existence. The conclusion is reached that "it is not until the crime is accomplished, that guilt clinches its gripe upon the guilty heart and claims it for its own. . . . There is no such thing, in man's nature, as a settled and full resolve, either for good or evil, except at the very moment of execution." Nevertheless, "man must not disclaim his brotherhood with the guiltiest, since, though his band be clean, his heart has surely been polluted by the flitting phantoms of iniquity. He must feel that, when he shall knock at the gate of Heaven, no semblance of an unspotted life can entitle him to entrance there. Penitence must kneel, and Mercy come from the footstool of the throne, or that golden gate will never open!"

Those who wish to obtain more than a superficial glimpse into Hawthorne's heart cannot do better than to ponder every part of this little story, which is comprised within scarcely more than a half-dozen pages. It was written about the time of Cilley's unhappy death, and contains more than its due proportion of "sad and awful truths."

I will append here a list of most of Hawthorne's contributions to various periodicals from 1832 to 1838, inclusive.

In the "Token" for 1832 appeared: Wives of the Dead, My Kinsman, Major Molineaux; Roger Malvin's Burial; The Gentle Boy. In the "Token" for 1833, The Seven Vagabonds; Sir William Pepperell; The Canterbury Pilgrims. In the "New England Magazine" for 1834 (vol. vii.), The Story-Teller;--in vol. viii. of the same periodical, Visit to Niagara Falls; Old News; Young Goodman Brown; Ambition's Guest;--in vol. ix., Graves and Goblins; The Old Maid in the Winding-Sheet; Sketches from Memory; The Devil in Manuscript. In the "Token" for 1835, The Mermaid (afterwards called The Viilage Uncle); Alice Doane's Appeal; The Haunted

Mind. In the "American Magazine of Knowledge" (which he edited at this period, 1836-38, and pretty much all of the contents of which be wrote and prepared) will be found the following in particular: The Ontario Steamboat; The Boston Tea Party; Preservation of the Dead; April Fools; Martha's Vineyard; The Duston Family; Nature of Sleep; Bells; etc. In the "Token" for 1837, The Man of Adamant; and in 1838, The Shaker Bridal; Sylph Etheredge; Endicott and his Men; Peter Goldthwaite; Night Thoughts under an Umbrella. In the "Knickerbocker," 1836, Edward Fane's Rosebud; A Bell's Biography. In the "Democratic Review," 1838-39, Memoir of Jonathan Cilley; Toll-Gatherer's Day; Footprints on the Seashore; Snow-Flakes; Chippings with a Chisel; and the four Tales of the Province House.

CHAPTER 5 - COURTSHIP

"IN 1811 and onwards," writes Miss E. P. Peabody,

"when we lived in Herbert Street, Salem, we used to play with the Hawthorne children, who lived in Union Street,--their yard stretching between the two streets. Elizabeth Hawthorne, the eldest of the children, used to do her lessons with me. I vividly remember her; she was a brilliant little girl, and I thought her a great genius. Nathaniel Hawthorne I remember as a broad-shouldered little boy, with clustering locks, springing about the yard. Madame Hawthorne was a recluse, and was not in the habit of receiving her husband's relations, or many of her own; it was considered, at that time, a mark of piety and good taste for a widow to withdraw herself from the world. About 1816 to 1820 the Hawthornes were, most of the time, living in Raymond, Maine, and we lost sight of them. But in the latter year I heard that they had returned to Salem, and that Miss Elizabeth now secluded herself in like manner as her mother did, spending most of her time in reading and in solitary walks. People said it was a love-disappointment; but that was merely hearsay.

"Between 1830 and 1836 some stories in the 'New England Magazine' arrested my attention. I thought they were probably written by some 'new-light' Quaker, who had outgrown his sectarianism; arid I actually wrote (but never sent) a letter to the supposed old man, asking him how he knew that 'sensitive natures are especially apt to be malicious.' It was not until 1837 that I discovered that these stories were the work of Madame Hawthorne's son. It was a difficult matter to establish visiting relations with so eccentric a household; and another year passed away before Mr. Hawthorne and his sisters called on us. It was in the evening. I was alone in the drawing-room; but Sophia, who was still an invalid, was in her chamber. As soon as I could, I ran upstairs to her and said, 'O Sophia, you must get up and dress and come down! The Hawthornes are here, and you never saw anything so splendid as he is,--he is handsomer than Lord Byron!' She laughed, but refused to come, remarking that since he had called once, he would call again. So I went down to them again, and we passed a very pleasant evening. Elizabeth, with her black hair in beautiful natural curls, her bright, rather shy eyes, and a rather excited, frequent, low laugh, looked full of wit and keenness, as if she were experienced in the world; there was not the least bit of sentiment about her, but she was strongly intellectual. There was nothing peculiar about Louisa; she seemed like other people. Mr. Hawthorne was very nicely dressed; but he looked, at first, almost fierce with his determination not to betray his sensitive shyness, which he always recognized as a weakness. But as he became interested in conversation, his nervousness passed away; and the beauty of the outline of his features, the pure complexion, the wonderful eyes, like mountain lakes reflecting the sky,--were quite in keeping with the 'Twice-Told Tales.'

"He did call again, as Sophia had predicted, not long afterwards; and this time she came down, in her simple white wrapper, and sat on the sofa. As I said 'My sister, Sophia,' be rose and looked at her intently,--he did not realize how intently. As we went on talking, she would frequently interpose a remark, in her low, sweet voice. Every time she did so, he would look at her again, with the same piercing, indrawing gaze. I was struck with it, and thought, 'What if he should fall in love with her!' and the thought troubled me; for she had often told me that nothing would ever tempt her to marry, and inflict on a husband the care of an invalid. When Mr. Hawthorne got up to go, he said he should come for me in the evening to call on his sisters, and he added, 'Miss Sophia, won't you come too?' But she replied, 'I never go out in the evening, Mr. Hawthorne.' 'I wish you would!' he said, in a low, urgent tone. But she smiled, and shook her head, and he went away."

It may be remarked here, that Mrs. Hawthorne, in telling her children, many years afterwards, of these first meetings with their father, used to say that his presence, from the very beginning, exercised so strong a magnetic attraction upon her, that instinctively, and in self-defence as it were, she drew back and repelled him. The power which she felt in him alarmed her; she did not understand what it meant, and was only able to feel that she must resist. By degrees, however, her resistance was overcome; and in the end, she realized that they had loved each other at first sight.

"Mr. Hawthorne told me," continues Miss Peabody,

"that his sisters lived so completely out of the world that they hardly knew its customs. 'But my sister Elizabeth is very witty and original, and knows the world, in one sense, remarkably well, seeing that she has learned it only through books. But she stays in her den, and I in mine: I have scarcely seen her in three months. After tea, my mother and Louisa come down and sit with me in the little parlor; but both Elizabeth and my mother take their meals in their rooms, and my mother has eaten alone ever since my father's death.'

"Mr. Hawthorne was never a ready talker; but every word was loaded with significance, and his manner was eminently suggestive, though there was nothing oracular in it. I never saw any one who listened so comprehendingly as he; and he was by nature profoundly social. I was always especially struck by his observations of nature. Nature reappeared in his conversation humanized; and he spoke of the office of nature's forms in building up the individual mind.

"Whenever, after this, he called at our house, he generally saw Sophia. One day she showed him her illustration of 'The Gentle Boy,' saying,' I want to know if this looks like your Ilbrahim?' He sat down and looked at it, and then looked up and said, 'He will never look otherwise to me.' He had remarked to me long before, 'What a peculiar person your sister is!' And again, a year later, he wrote to me, 'She is a flower to be worn in no man's bosom, but was lent from Heaven to show the possibilities of the human soul.' In return, I had talked to him about her freely, and had described to him her rare childhood. I also told him of her chronic headaches, and how the pain did not imbitter or even sadden the unspoiled imagination of her heart. I showed him her letters from Cuba, which we had had bound as a book; and by these means he became quite intimately acquainted with her spirit and inner character.

"When I left Salem to live in West Newton, he saw a great deal of Sophia, who, having grown up with the feeling that she never was to be married, looked upon herself as practically a child; and she would sometimes go over to Madame Hawthorne's, in this way forming an acquaintance with her and with Louisa. It afterwards transpired that Madame Hawthorne became very fond of her. Madame Hawthorne always looked as if she had walked out of an old picture, with her antique costume, and a face of lovely sensibility and great brightness,--for she did not *seem* at all a victim of morbid sensibility, not withstanding her all but Hindoo self-devotion to the manes of her husband. She was a woman of fine understanding and very cultivated mind. But she had very sensitive nerves, and appears not to have been happily affected by her husband's relatives, the Hawthornes being of a very sharp and stern individuality, and oddity of temper. Old Captain Knights had once said to

Mr. Manning, 'I hear your darter is going to marry the son of Captain Hathorne?' 'I believe she is,' replied Mr. Manning. 'I knowed him,' continued Captain Knights,--'I knowed the Captain; and he was the sternest man that ever walked a deck!' Mr. Hawthorne used to say that he inherited the granite that was in this ancestor of his, and which contrasted so strongly with the Manning sensibility. It is such contrasts of parents that bring forth the greatest geniuses,--provided, of course, that they are in some degree harmonized and placed in equipoise by culture."

It was previous to the opening of the acquaintance between the Peabodies and the Hawthornes, that Wellington Peabody, as has already been mentioned, died in New Orleans; and it was at about that time that the second brother, George, returned thence, to die of his lingering disease. His death occurred in 1839; and during the preceding eighteen months he lay on his bed, in the house in Charter Street, Salem (the home of *Dr. Grimshawe*), awaiting the inevitable end with a noble patience, courage, and cheerfulness. Miss Elizabeth Peabody spent the spring and summer of 1838 with her brother Nathaniel, in West Newton, a village near Boston; and this was the occasion of letters (whereof some extracts follow) being written to her by Sophia. Besides the allusions which they contain to well-known persons, and the descriptions of Hawthorne himself, which creep in more often than the writer was probably aware of, they show the growth and advancement of her mind since the period of the Dedham Journal (1830), already given. The extracts close with Hawthorne's starting on the journey to Western Massachusetts, the record of which appears in his published Note-Books,--July 27 to September 24, 1838.

"What a proof of the divinity of our nature is it, that, by merely being true to it, we may attain to all things. It is the simplest and the grandest command uttered by the oracle within, and every human being has capacity enough to obey it. Whenever my wing is ready to droop in endeavoring to reach the upper regions, it immediately grows buoyant again at the thought that I can *every moment* get onward if I remember this. How simple as a unit is the whole problem of life, sometimes, to the mind; and I suppose it is always to the absolutely single-eyed. Oh, let not the light within me be darkness!..

"Last night I was left in darkness,--soft, grateful darkness,--and my meditations turned upon my habit of viewing things through the 'couleur de rose' medium, and I was questioning what the idea of it was,--for since it was *real,* there must be some good explanation of it,--when suddenly, like a night-blooming cereus, my mind opened, and I read in letters of paly golden-green words to this effect: The beautiful and good and true are the only real and abiding things,--the only proper *use* of the soul and nature. Evil and ugliness and falsehood are *abuses,* monstrous and transient. I do not see what is *not,* but what is, through the passing clouds. Therefore, why is not my view more correct than the other?

"All day yesterday, my head raged, and I sat a passive subject for the various corkscrews, borers, pinchers, daggers, squibs, and bombs to effect their will upon it. Always I occupy myself with trying to penetrate the mystery of pain. Towards night my head was relieved, and I seemed let down from a weary height full of points into a quiet green valley, upon velvet turf. It was as if I had fought a fight all day and got through. After tea I lay down; but scarcely touched my cheek to the pillow, when the bell rang, and I was just as sure it was Mr. Hawthorne as if I had seen him. I descended, armed with a blue, odorous violet. Mr. Hawthorne would not take off his coat or stay, because he had the headache and an engagement. He said be had written to you, and that it was a great thing for him to write a letter. He looked very brilliant notwithstanding his headache. I showed him a little temple mosaic I had begun to make, and he thought it very pretty. He said he was going to Boston next week, and should have the little forget-me-not I painted set. Mary invited him to come with his sister on Saturday and read German; but it seems to me he does not want to go on with German. I had a delightful night, and this morning feel quite lark-like, or like John of Bologna's Mercury. Mr. Hawthorne said he wished he could have intercourse with some beautiful children,--beautiful little girls; he did not care for boys. What a beautiful smile he has! You know, in 'Annie's Ramble,' he says that if there is anything he prides himself upon, it is on having a smile that children love. I should think they would, indeed. There is the innocence and purity and frankness of a child's soul in it. I saw him better than I had ever before. He said he had imagined a story, of which the principal incident is my cleaning that picture of Fernandez. To be the means, in any way, of calling forth one of his divine creations, is no small happiness, is it? How I do long to read it! He did not stay more than an hour. Father came in, and he immediately got up and said he must go. He has a celestial expression. It is a manifestation of the divine in human. . .

"I have been reading of the ruins of Persepolis. Shall I ever stand upon the Imperial Palace of Persepolis? Who knows but when I am dried to an atomy like Mrs. Kirkland, I too may go to the East? And when I go, perhaps my husband will not be a paralytic. Oh I forget. I never intend to have a husband. Rather, I should say, I never intend any one shall have me for a wife.

"I read 'Persia' all day yesterday. The account of Zoroaster is deeply interesting. Alas, me how little I know! It will indeed take an Eternity to satisfy this thirst for knowledge. Whenever my mind gets into a bustle about it, this thought of Eternity can alone quiet it. How natural it is for the mind to generalize! It seems to me sometimes as if every material object and every earthly event were only signs of something higher signified; and at such times all particulars are merged into one grand unit. Then I feel as if I could read a minute portion of the universe. How everything hurries into its place the moment we are high enough to catch the central light! All factitious distinctions hide their diminished heads. Conventionalities disappear. I suppose Mr. Emerson holds himself in that lofty region all the time. I wonder not at the sublimity of his aspect, the solemnity of his air. I have read the second volume of Miss Martineau's 'Retrospect.' I admire her picture of Mr. Emerson. I think Mr. Emerson is the greatest man that ever lived. *As a whole* he is satisfactory. Everything has its due with him. In all relations he is noble. He is a unit. His uncommon powers seem used for right purposes. It is often said, 'Oh, such an one must not be expected to do thus and thus,--so gifted!' Such nonsense Mr. Emerson proves it to be, does he not ? Because he is gifted, therefore he cannot be excused from doing everything and being equal to everything. He is indeed a 'Supernal Vision.' For the rest, I think a great deal more fuss is made over Miss Martineau's books than there is any reason for. After all, what great matter is it what she says? She is not the Pope. . . . I have read Carlyle's 'Miscellanies' with deep delight. The complete manner in which he presents a man is wonderful. He is the most impartial of critics, I think, except Mr. Emerson. Every subject interesting to the soul is touched in these essays. Such a reach of thought produced no slight stir within me.

I am rejoiced that Carlyle is coming to America. But I cannot help feeling that Emerson is diviner than he. Mr. Emerson is Pure Tone.

"I have not told you of my Farm. A fortnight ago, mother brought me some Houstonias in their own bit of earth, those meek blue starry flowers which cover our hills and fields all summer. I put them in a glass saucer, with some beautiful moss, and, by degrees, have added violets and a periwinkle and a delicious aromatic lavender. Several blades of grass sprang up, and tiny clover. So you see I have grass for cattle, and herb for the service of man, and flowers to rejoice his heart, all growing and flourishing within my little farm. I am constantly amazed at the unfailing stores of that bit of earth. The Houstonias say as plainly as flowers can speak, 'Be humble and win love;' and if one may infer the importance of the injunction from its repetition, surely the angels never wrote a truth upon this earth so important. . . .

"Live forever, Captain Pillsbury! Even on this earth I would have you live a thousand years. prisons and prisoners have been to me, ever since I could reflect, the subjects of the deepest interest. I always believed in that way of trusting even the greatest criminals. I always believed that *real* confidence and love could win even the hardest heart. Captain Pillsbury *proves* it. I always wished prisoners could be more visited by persons who honor humanity. Our Saviour's command to visit prisoners seems very little regarded. The sick in body obtain more attention and need it less than the sick in soul. One of my dearest visions is getting well enough to go into prisons and tell felons I have sympathy for them, especially women; though I should fear a corrupt woman more than a corrupt man. . . .

"After dinner I was lost in a siesta, when Mr. Hawthorne came. I was provoked that I should have to smooth my hair and dress, while he was being wasted downstairs. He looked extremely handsome, with sufficient sweetness in his face to supply the rest of the world with and still leave the ordinary share to himself. He took from his pocket the 'Forget-me-not,' set in elegant style beneath block crystal, gold all over the back, so that it is enshrined from every possible harm. He said he would leave it for inspection, and I have it on at this moment. 'It is beautiful, isn't it?' he said. He thought it too fine for himself to wear; but I am sure it is as modest as a brooch could be.

"This afternoon I went to the Hawthornes' house in Herbert Street. Louisa came to the door, and took me upstairs. As Elizabeth did not know I was coming, I thought I should not see her. It would be an unprecedented honor if she should come. I asked for her immediately, and Louisa said that she would be there in a few minutes There, now! Am not I a privileged mortal? She received me very affectionately, and seemed very glad to see me; and I all at once fell in love with her. I think her eyes are very beautiful, and I liked the expression of her taper hands. I stayed in the house an hour! I could not get away; she urged me to stay so much, as if she wanted me. She asked whether you were not always cheerful, for you seemed so to her. She spoke of Wordsworth and Coleridge, and surprised me by saying she admired Pope. We talked about the sea, and the winds, and various things. Now, what think you of my triumph? I think I should love her very much. I believe it is extreme sensibility which makes her a hermitess. It was difficult to meet her eyes; and I wanted to, because they are uncommonly beautiful. She said tulips were her favorite flower, and she did not wonder that a thousand pounds had formerly been given for a bulb! So I determined that she should have a gorgeous bunch of them as soon as I could procure any. . . . The next day Mr. Hawthorne came here, and I was glad he seemed a little provoked he was not at home yesterday. He asked for his pin, and when I brought it, said that if 'he did not like it so much he could wear it better.' I inquired whether the story of the picture were written yet, and he replied, 'No, but this week I am going about it.' He had promised to get up at dawn from the 1st May. Mary asked if he had remembered to do so. 'No, I have not,' he said. 'I have not slept well; but I will certainly begin to-morrow morning, if the sun rises, I mean, if it shines,' he added, laughing. . . .

"Our brother George has been very ill all day. This week I have realized his pain as I had not before. It is a new trial to me, and unimagined with all my imagination. I never have thought, you know, that it was any trial to bear my own pain, I could arrange that in the grand economy of events; but I must yet learn to be patient and serene at the sight and consciousness of his. His slow and ever-increasing suffering is an appalling prospect. For myself, after using all human means to be in the best condition of health, I am utterly content if they fail. I am happy because first my heart, and daily, more and more, my reason, assure me that there is a God. But George's pain added to my own weakness seems to obliterate me. The sublimity of his patience and demeanor impresses me more and more. The idea that he may die has not been fully presented to me before. There is something in the family tie that is different from any other. There is no reasoning about it; it *exists*, and that is the whole matter. The void made in my life by Wellington's departure can never be filled till I meet him again. He is a part of my being, and I cannot be complete without him. It seems as if I could not bear another rending; but I know, of course, it would be George's immeasurable gain. I would not withhold him for a moment, yet, with all this, *there is the pang!* It cannot be helped,--it is the way I am made. God knows that my heart says, 'Thy will be done,' and therefore He will forgive the irrepressible sorrow. Remember, when the hour comes, that I do not despond or question or complain, but that I love, and that I am sadly weakened in the organs by which I might manifest repose. My body is one, and my mind is another; and disease has in part destroyed their connection. . . .

"Since the *furor scribendi* has been upon Mr. Hawthorne, we have not seen him. I carried your packet and the flowers there on Saturday. I supposed the flowers were for him; but I received a note from Elizabeth yesterday, in which she says, 'The flowers which E. sent, so sweet and so tastefully arranged' (Mary arranged them), 'I thought would be unworthily bestowed upon my brother, who professes to regard the love of flowers as a feminine taste. So I permitted him to look at them, but considered them as a gift to myself, and beg you to thank her in my name, when you write.' Now, I am a little provoked at this, aren't you? I do not believe he does not care for flowers. Mary has sent him word that he may write for to-morrow's packet, and I hope he will bring a letter for you this evening. . . . He came the next morning for a take-leave call, looking radiant. He said he was not going to tell any one where he should be for the next three months; that he thought he should change his name, so that if he died no one would be able to find his gravestone. He should not tell even his mother where he could be found,--that he intended neither to write to any one nor to be *written to*. He seems determined to be let alone. He said he wished he could read German, but could not take the trouble. It seems he talked a little of me to Miss Rawlins, and paid me a splendid compliment,--that I was the Queen of

Journalizers! I shall ever thank my stars that I have given him so much pleasure. He looked like the sun shining through a silver mist when he turned to say good-by. It is a most wonderful face. Mary asked him to write a journal while he was gone. He at first said he should not write anything, but finally concluded it would suit very well for hints for future stories. I feel as if he were a born brother. I never, hardly, knew a person for whom I had such a full and at the same time perfectly quiet admiration. I do not care about seeing him often; but I delight to remember that he *is,* and that from time to time I shall have intercourse with him. I feel the most entire ease with him, as if I had always known him. He converses a great deal with me when you are not present,--just as he talks more to you when we are not present. He said of Helen Barstow, that he thought she was not natural; but he expressed a sense of her brilliant powers, her wit and acuteness, and then said he thought 'women were always jealous of such a kind of remarkability' (that was his word) 'in their own sex,' and endeavored to deprecate it. I wonder what has given him such a horrid opinion of us women. But enough of Mr. Hawthorne." . . . .

The little episode about the flowers sent to Hawthorne, which his sister Elizabeth quietly appropriated, is amusing; and there can be no doubt that the latter took an unwarrantable and characteristic liberty. No one was more sensible than Hawthorne of the beauty and charm of flowers; but the truth was, that his sister was jealous of any attentions paid to him, and was apt to offer at least a passive resistance to them. Her letter, referred to above, is here subjoined entire.

SALEM, 1838.

MY DEAR MISS SOPHIA,--For many days I have wished to write and tell you how much I regretted not having thanked you immediately for those beautiful tulips; but, as Mary supposed, I was ashamed to appear before you, either in person or by note. I have not seen so great a variety for several years, and I kept them as long as possible, and looked at them almost continually, till, in defiance of my efforts to preserve them, they faded. The flowers which Elizabeth sent, so sweet and so tastefully arranged, I thought would be unworthily bestowed upon my brother, who professes to regard the love of flowers as a feminine taste ; so I permitted him to look at them, but consider them as a gift to myself, and beg you to thank her, in my name, when you write. I hope this warm weather agrees with you, and that next week it will be cool enough for Mary and me to walk. I wished to go this afternoon; but the thermometer stands at 98 degreees in the shade, though it is after four o'clock. I did not know until last evening that your brother wished for Mr. Payne's Letters. I send them now, with the book of fruits, which your mother said she would like to see; and the "Quarterly Review." I do not know whether you can read this scrawl, but I have forgotten how to write.

Believe me yours, E. M. H.

We now come to the critical period of the Hawthorne Romance,--the Romance that he lived, not wrote. In 1837 he had remarked in his journal, "My circumstances cannot long continue as they are and have been;" but herein he referred rather to his worldly condition than to the state of his affections, for he adds that "Bridge, too, stands between high prosperity and utter ruin," and "Fate seems preparing changes for both of us." In fact, Hawthorne felt that he had tried the experiment of seclusion long enough, and that no further benefit was to be expected from it. He was fast growing to be as a shadow, walking in a shadowy world, and losing all sense of reality in either himself or his surroundings. The feeling crops out here and there in his journal:

"A man tries to be happy in love," he writes; "he cannot sincerely give his heart, and the affair seems all a dream. In domestic life, the same; in politics, a seeming patriot;--all seems like a theatre." The work which he had done in literature had not brought him satisfaction; it had failed to put him into vital and tangible relations with the world. He was awakened to the urgent necessity of acting as a man among men, of shouldering in with the crowd, of measuring himself and weighing himself against all comers. Precisely how he was to set about producing this change in his habits and circumstances, he knew not; but rather than not have a change, he would have been willing to become a blacksmith, or push a huckster's hand-cart through the streets. It was the instinctive impulse of a healthy nature to guard against the imminent peril of morbidness. "I want to have something to do with this material world," he said to Miss Peabody. Martin Van Buren was in the Presidential chair at this time, and George Bancroft was Collector at Boston. It came to the ears of the latter gentleman that Nathaniel Hawthorne stood ready to put his hand to any respectable and arduous employment; whereupon Mr. Bancroft got him appointed weigher and gauger in the Boston Custom House. Here was hard work enough to do, and of a kind, too, to afford the strongest possible contrast to his previous existence. It lasted but a couple of years, that is to say, during the remainder of the Democratic regime; but it enabled Hawthorne to realize his ambition of being entitled to call the sons of toil his brethren. And after this spell of rough and grimy work was over, he could take up his pen once more with a new stimulus and appreciation, and with the certainty that mankind was a solid reality and that he himself was not a dream.

And yet the Custom House was only one, and not the most important, of the causes which produced this wholesome state of affairs. Sophia Peabody was Hawthorne's true guardian and recreating angel. The acknowledgment between them of their mutual love took place about the time of the Custom House appointment, and furnished an object and a spur for his labors. A strict secrecy was maintained by them respecting their engagement during nearly the entire three years of its continuance; and the reason of this concealment was a somewhat singular one. Enough has been said about the extreme impressibility of Madame Hawthorne; and it appears that her son was led to imagine that the news of his relations with Miss Sophia would give her a shock that might endanger her life. What, then, was Madame Hawthorne's objection to Miss Sophia supposed to be, since, as has already been shown, she was personally very fond of her? It was owing to what was assumed to be the latter's hopeless state of invalidism. Madame Hawthorne (her son was assured) could never endure the thought of his marrying a woman who was a victim to constant nervous headaches; and were he, nevertheless, to do so, the most lamentable consequences were to be anticipated. Now, any other conceivable obstacle than this would have influenced Hawthorne not a whit; but he was not prepared to face the idea of defying and perhaps "killing" his mother. All this time, be it observed, he and his mother had never exchanged a single word, good or bad, on the subject of Miss Sophia Peabody. This was owing partly to the apprehension on his part as to the issue of such a discussion, and partly to the habit of mutual undemonstrativeness (so to say) which had grown up between them during a lifetime. He had never spoken freely and unrestrainedly to her about any matter which deeply concerned him, nor had she ever invited such a confidence; and this despite the fact that the mother and son entertained a profound love and respect for each other. But for the sort of people who build up these viewless barriers, nothing seems to be so difficult and apparently impossible as to break them down again. Be that as it may, Hawthorne delayed to speak, and thereby laid up for himself a good deal of unnecessary anxiety.

But who put it into his head to think that his mother would adopt this attitude? I fear it must be confessed that the Machiavelli in question was none other than his own sister Elizabeth. This bright-eyed and brilliant little lady saw plainly enough how matters were likely to go between her brother and Miss Sophia, and was resolved to do what she could to prevent it. She was quite sincere, moreover, in her belief that Sophia would never be strong enough properly to fulfil the duties of married life and this added substance to the dislike she felt to the idea of her brother's marrying at all. ("He will never marry," she had once remarked: "he will never do anything; be is an ideal person." The wish was father to the assertion.) But though she thus found herself provided with a good ground for opposing the marriage, she was wise enough to perceive that Hawthorne was not likely to pay much heed to her opposition. The time when brothers are most sensible of their fraternal obligations is not, as a general rule, precisely the time when they are in love. It was necessary, therefore, for Elizabeth to seek some reinforcement. She knew how great was Hawthorne's reverence and tenderness for his mother, and she saw that by simply intimating to him that such and such a possible event would dangerously agitate Madame Hawthorne, she would be enlisting in her cause the very most powerful auxiliary that could have been selected. This, accordingly, she did; and let all indignant lovers do her the justice to believe that, in representing her mother in this light, she was not conscious of unduly emphasizing what might probably turn out to be the truth.

Indeed, Hawthorne himself, and Sophia not less than he, felt the weight of the pathological objection; and Sophia consented to let the engagement continue only upon the stipulation that their marriage was to be strictly contingent upon her own recovery from her twenty years' illness. "If God intends us to marry," she said to him, "He will let me be cured; if not, it will be a sign that it is not best." The likelihood of a cure taking place certainly did not seem great; in fact, it would be little less than a miracle. Miracle or not, however, the cure was actually accomplished; and the lovers were justified in believing that Love himself was the physician. When Sophia Peabody became Sophia Hawthorne, in 1842, she was, for the first time since her infancy, in perfect health; nor did she ever afterwards relapse into her previous condition of invalidism. Meanwhile, however, there was a period of suspense to be lived through. There is reason to believe, on the other hand, that the secrecy which was now, perforce, a condition of their communion, may not have been without its charm. Elizabeth and Louisa may probably have suspected that their brother's apparent acquiescence in the general opinion as to Sophia's unmarriageableness was apparent only; but they could not do more than they had done. Hawthorne had taken up his residence in Boston, in order to attend to his business, and saw them not oftener than once a fortnight; and it may easily be imagined that, on those occasions, Miss Peabody was not the subject of conversation. They at all events, would not venture to introduce a subject on which he chose to be silent. But the lovers, aided by Miss E. P. Peabody, maintained a constant correspondence by letter; they enjoyed occasional walks and talks together; and when, after George Peabody's death, the Peabodies moved to Boston, and lived at No. 13 West Street, the two were able to have almost daily interviews. It is likely, therefore, that the course of their love was only just not smooth enough to keep them constantly mindful of its sweetness.

In 1841, Hawthorne (not much to his regret, evidently) was turned out of office by the Whig administrahon, and resolved to try what virtue there might be, for him and his future wife, in the experiment of Brook Farm. The subject of this Community has been so exhaustively and exhaustingly canvassed of late, and it seems to be intrinsically so barren of interest and edification, save only for the eminent names that were at first connected with it, that the present writer has pleasure in passing over it without further remark. The chief advantage it brought to Hawthorne was, that it taught him how to plant corn and squashes, and to buy and sell at the produce market; and that it provided him with an invaluable background for his "Blithedale Romance," written about ten years afterwards. He did his share of the farm work like a man,--indeed, with the vigor and fidelity of two or three men,--and he was elected to certain responsible offices in the board of management. Meantime he was able to do very little writing; though the "True Stories" were on the stocks at this time, and Miss Sophia was drawing illustrations for some of them. His pecuniary prospects were not reassuring; for he had sunk most of his Custom House savings in the Community, and his publishers seem to have betrayed an illiberal tendency happily unknown in that guild at the present day. But rents were low in New England forty years ago, and domestic life could be managed at little cost. Hawthorne, at all events, was not the man to wait until he was a millionnaire before he began to be happy. He married in the summer of 1842, and took up his first abode in Concord. His wife, as has been said, had got rid of her infirmities; and the family opposition which he had dreaded had melted away at the first touch. For when it became necessary to acquaint his mother with his matrimonial intentions, she received the intelligence not only without agitation, but with a sympathetic cordiality that not a little amazed her son. "What you tell me is not a surprise to me," she said; "I already knew it." "How long have you known it?" he demanded. "Almost ever since you knew it yourself," was her reply; "and Sophia Peabody is the wife of all others whom I would have chosen for you." The moral of this anecdote is obvious. As for the wicked sisters, Elizabeth and Louisa, they seem altogether to have failed to maintain the consistency of their role. They shamelessly rejoiced in their brother's happiness, and loved his wife quite as much as if they had never cherished any dark designs against the alliance.

The foregoing narrative owes its existence chiefly to the necessity of making the following batch of letters intelligible. They are Hawthorne's love-letters, or so much of them as may properly be made public. Some of the elements of greatest beauty in them are necessarily suppressed; but, after all excisions, they are beautiful enough. The pure, spontaneous style in which they are expressed; their tone, at once tender, playful, and profound; and the testimony they bear to the possibility of a passion not less delicate and magnanimous than it was ardent,--these qualities are not without value and significance in times like ours. The single-hearted love and reverence which marks these letters, written before marriage, are, moreover, just as conspicuous in every letter that Hawthorne wrote to his wife, up to the end of their wedded existence on earth. No cloud or change ever passed over their affection, even for a moment but every succeeding year found their union more exquisitely complete.

BOSTON, April 17, 1839.

MY DEAREST,--I feel pretty secure against intruders, for the bad weather will defend me from foreign Invasion; and as to Cousin Haley, he and I had a bitter political dispute last evening, at the close of which he went to bed in high dudgeon, and probably will not speak to me these three days. Thus you perceive that strife and wrangling, as well as eastwinds and rain, are the methods of a kind Providence to promote my comfort,--which would not have been so well secured in any other way. Six or seven hours of cheerful solitude! But I will not be alone. J invite your spirit to be with me,--at any hour and as many hours as you please,--but especially at the twilight hour, before I light my lamp. I bid you at that particular time, because I can see visions more vividly in the dusky glow of firelight than either by daylight or lamplight. Come, and let me renew my spell against headache and other direful effects of the east-wind. How I wish I could give you a portion of my insensibility! and yet I should be almost afraid of some radical transformation, were I to produce a change in that respect. If you cannot grow plump and rosy and tough and vigorous without being changed into another nature, then I do think, for this short life, you had better remain just what you are. Yes; but you will be the same to me, because we have met in Eternity, and there our intimacy was formed. So get well as soon as you possibly can, and I shall never doubt that you are the same Sophie who have so often leaned upon my arm and needed its superfluous strength. I never, till now, had a friend who could give me repose; all have disturbed me, and, whether for pleasure or pain, it was still disturbance. But peace overflows from your heart into mine. Then I feel that there is a Now, and that Now must be always calm and happy, and that sorrow and evil are but phantoms that seem to flit across it.

You must never expect to see my sister Elizabeth in the daytime, unless by previous appointment or when she goes to walk. So unaccustomed am I to daylight interviews with her, that I never imagine her in sunshine; and I really doubt whether her faculties of life and intellect begin to be exercised till dusk, unless on extraordinary occasions. Their noon is at midnight. I wish you could walk with her; but you must not, because she is indefatigable, and always wants to walk half round the world when once she is out of doors.

When this week's first letter came, I held it a long time in my band, marvelling at the superscription. How did you contrive to write it? Several times since I have pored over it, to discover how much of yourself mingled with my share of it; and certainly there is grace flung over the fac-simile, which never was seen in my harsh, uncouth autograph, and yet none of the strength is lost. You are wonderful.

What a beautiful day! and I had a double enjoyment of it--for your sake and my own. I have been to walk, this afternoon, to Bunker's Hill and the Navy Yard, and am tired, because I had not your arm to support me.

God keep you from east-winds and every other evil.

Your own friend, N. H.

MAY 26.

. . . .It is very singular (but I do not suppose I can express it) that, while I love you so dearly, and while I am so conscious of the deep union of our spirits, still I have an awe of you that I never felt for anybody else. Awe is not the word, either, because it might imply something stern in you; whereas--but you must make it out for yourself. I do wish I could put this into words,--not so much for your satisfaction (because I believe you will understand) as for my own. I suppose I should have pretty much the same feeling if an angel were to come from Heaven and be my dearest friend,--only the angel could not have the tenderest of human natures too, the sense of which is mingled with this sentiment. Perhaps it is because, in meeting you, I really meet a spirit, whereas the obstructions of earth have prevented such a meeting in every other case. But I leave the mystery here. Some time or other it may be made plainer to me. But methinks it converts my love into religion. And then it is singular, too, that this awe (or whatever it be) does not prevent me from feeling that it is I who have the charge of you. And will not you rebel? Oh, no; because I possess the power to guide only so far as I love you. My love gives me the right, and your love consents to it.

Since writing the above, I have been asleep; and I dreamed that I had been sleeping a whole year in the open air, and that while I slept, the grass grew around me. It seemed, in my dream, that the bed-clothes were spread beneath me; and when I awoke (in my dream) I snatched them up, and the earth under them looked black, as if it had been burnt,--a square place, exactly the size of the bed-clothes. Yet there were grass and herbage scattered over this burnt space, looking as fresh and bright and dewy as if the summer rain and the summer sun had been cherishing them all the time. Interpret this for me; but do not draw any sombre omens from it. What is signified by my nap of a whole year (it made me grieve to think that I had lost so much of eternity? --and what was the fire that blasted the spot of earth which I occupied, while the grass flourished all around? --and what comfort am I to draw from the fresh herbage amid the burnt space ? But it is a silly dream, and you cannot expound any sense out of it.

BOSTON, Monday eve, July 15, 1839.

MY DEAREST,--Your letter was brought to me at East Cambridge, this afternoon; otherwise I know not when I should have received it, for I am so busy that I know not whether I shall be at the Custom House these two or three days. I put it in my pocket, and did not read it till just now, when I could be quiet in my own chamber; for I always feel as if your letters were too sacred to be read in the midst of people, and (you will smile) I never read them without first washing my hands.

And so you have been ill, and I cannot take care of you. Oh, my dearest, do let our love be powerful enough to make you well. I will have faith in its efficacy,--not that it will work an immediate miracle, but it shall make you so well at heart that you cannot possibly be ill in the body. Partake of my health and strength, my beloved. Are they not your own, as well as mine? Yes,--and your illness is mine as well as yours; and, with all the pain it gives me, the whole world should not buy my right to share in it.

My dearest, I will not be much troubled, since you tell me (and your word is always truth) that there is no need. But, oh, be careful of yourself, remembering how much earthly happiness depends on your health. Be tranquil,--let me be your Peace, as you are mine. Do not write to me, unless your heart be unquiet, and you think that you can quiet it by writing. May God bless you!

NOVEMBER 15, 1839.

DEAREST,--Your yesterday's letter was received, and gave me comfort; yet, oh, be prepared for the worst,--if that may be called worst which is in truth best for all, and, more than all, for George. I cannot help trembling for you, dearest. God bless you and keep you!

NOVEMBER 29.

DEAREST,--I pray you, for some little time to come, not to muse too much upon your brother, even though such musings should be untinged with gloom and should appear to make you happier. In the eternity where he now dwells, it has doubtless become of no importance to himself whether he died yesterday or a thousand years ago. He is already at home in the Celestial city,--more at home than ever he was in his mother's house. Then let us leave him there for the present; and if the shadows and images of this fleeting time should interpose between us and him, let us not seek to drive them away, for they are sent of God. By and by it will be good and profitable to commune with your brother's spirit; but so soon after his release from mortal infirmity, it seems even ungenerous towards himself to call him back by yearnings of the heart and too vivid picturings of what he was.

DECEMBER 5.

DEAREST,--I wish I had the gift of making rhymes, for methinks there is poetry in my head and heart since I have been in love with you. You are a Poem. Of what sort, then? Epic? Mercy on me, no A sonnet? No; for that is too labored and artificial. You are a sort of sweet, simple, gay, pathetic ballad, which Nature is singing, sometimes with tears, sometimes with smiles, and sometimes with intermingled smiles and tears.

DECEMBER 31, 1839.

BEST BELOVED,--I send you some allumettes wherewith to kindle the taper. There are very few, but my second finger could no longer perform extra duty. These will serve till the wounded one be healed, however. How beautiful is it to provide even this slightest convenience for you, dearest! I cannot tell you how much I love you, in this backhanded style. My love is not in this attitude,--it rather bends forward to meet you.

What a year has this been to us! My definition of Beauty is, that it is love, and therefore includes both truth and good. But those only who love as we do can feel the significance and force of this.

My ideas will not flow in these crooked strokes. God be with you. I am very well, and have walked far in Danvers this cold morning. I am full of the glory of the day. God bless you this night of the old year. It has proved the year of our nativity. Has not the old earth passed away from us?--are not all things new?

YOUR SOPHIE.

--The above letter is the only surviving one of those which Sophia Peabody wrote in answer to Hawthorne's. It will be remembered that in the "American Note-Books" he says that, before going to England, he burned "great heaps of old letters and other papers. . . . Among them were hundreds of Sophia's letters. The world has no more such, and now they are all dust and ashes." This letter was written with the left hand,

and has a backward inclination, very different from the usual graceful flow of her chirography.

JANUARY 1, 1840

BELOVED, My heart was exceedingly touched by that little back-handed note, and likewise by the bundle of allumettes. Nurse that finger well, dearest; for no small portion of my comfort and cheeriness of heart depends upon that beloved finger. If it he not well within a few days, do not be surprised if I send down the best surgeon in Boston to effect its speedy cure.

I have a mind, some day, to send you a journal of all my doings and sufferings, my whole external life, from the time I awake at dawn till I close my eyes at night. What a dry, dull history would it be! But then, apart from this, I would write another journal, of my inward life throughout the self-same day,--my fits of pleasant thought, and those likewise which are shadowed by passing clouds,--the desires of my heart towards you, - my pictures of what we are to enjoy together. Nobody would think that the same man could live two such different lives simultaneously. But then the grosser life is a dream, and the spiritual life is a reality.

Dearest, I wish you would make out a list of books that you would like to be in our library; for I intend, whenever the cash and the opportunity occur together, to buy enough to fill up our new bookcase, and I want to feel that I am buying them for both of us. The bookcase will hold about two hundred volumes ; but we will collect it in small lots, and then we shall prize every volume, and receive a separate pleasure from the acquisition of it.

JANUARY 3, 1840.

. . . You cannot think how much delight those pictures you are painting are going to give me. I never owned a picture in my life ; yet pictures have been among the earthly possessions (and they are spiritual possessions too) which I most coveted. They will be incomparably more precious to me than all the productions of all the painters since Apelles. When we live in our own house, we will paint pictures together,--that is, our minds and hearts shall unite to form the conception, to which your hand shall give external existence. I have often felt that I could be a painter, only I am sure that I could never handle a brush; now you will show me the images of my inward life, beautified and etherealized by the mixture of your own spirit. I think I shall get these two pictures put into mahogany frames, because they will harmonize better with the furniture of our parlor than gilt frames would.

How strange that such a flower as our affection should have blossomed amid snow and wintry winds,--accompaniments which no poet or novelist, that I know of, has ever introduced into a love-tale. Nothing like our story was ever written, or ever will be; but if it could be told, methinks it would be such as the angels might take delight to hear. . . .

JANUARY 24.

. . . .I came home as soon as I possibly could, and there was the package! I actually trembled as I undid it, so eager was I to behold them. There was never anything so lovely and precious in this world! They are perfect. So soon as the dust and smoke of my fire had evaporated, I put them on the mantelpiece, and sat a long time before them, painting a fac-simile of them in my heart, in whose most sacred chamber they shall keep a place forever and ever. I was not long in finding out the little white figure in the Menaggio. In fact, she was the very first object that my eyes rested on. She came straight to my heart, and yet she remains just where you placed her. If it had not been for your strict injunctions that nothing must touch the pictures, I do believe that my lips would have touched that Sophie, as she stands on the bridge. Do you think the pensive little damsel would have vanished beneath my kiss? What a misfortune would that have been to her poor lover,--to find that he had kissed away his mistress! However, I shall refrain from all endearments, till you tell me they may be hazarded without fear of her taking it in ill part and absenting herself without leave.

My dearest, it is a very noble-looking cavalier with whom Sophie is standing on the bridge. Are you quite sure that he is the right person? Yet I need not ask; for there is Sophie to bear witness to his identity. Yes, it must be my very self: it is not my picture, but the very I; and as my inner self belongs to you, there is no doubt that you have caused my soul to pervade this figure.

I have put the pictures into my bedroom for the present, being afraid to trust them on the mantel-piece; but I cannot help going to feast my eyes upon them, every little while. I have determined not to hang them up now, for fear of the dust and of the fingers of the chambermaid. Whenever I am away, they will be safely locked up. I shall want your express directions as to the height at which they ought to be hung, and the width of the space between them, and other minutest particulars. We will discuss these matters when I come home to you. . . .

FEBRUARY 14.
DEARISSIMA,--I have put the Isola picture on the mantel-piece, and the Menaggio on the opposite wall. I sit before them with something of the quiet and repose which your own beloved presence is wont to impart to me. I gaze at them by all sorts of lights,--daylight, twilight, and candle-light; and when the lamps are extinguished, and before going to bed, I sit looking at these pictures by the flickering firelight. They are truly an infinite enjoyment.

BOSTON, March 15, 1840.
DEAREST,--What an ugly day is this My heart is heavy; or, no, it is not heaviness,--not the heaviness, like a great lump of ice, which I used to feel when I was alone in the world,--but--but -in short, dearest, where you are not, there it is a sort of death,--a death, however, in which there is still hope, and assurance of a joyful life to come. Methinks, if my spirit were not conscious of yours, this dreary snow-storm would chill me to torpor; the warmth of my fireside would be quite powerless to counteract it. Most absolute little Sophie, didst thou expressly command me to go to Father Taylor's church this very Sabbath? Now, it would not be an auspicious day for me to hear the aforesaid Son of Thunder. I have a cold, though, indeed, I fear I have partly conjured it up to serve my naughty purpose. Some sunshiny day, when I am wide awake and warm and genial, I will go and throw myself open to his blessed influence; but now there is only one thing that I feel anywise inclined to do, and that is to go to sleep. But indeed, dearest, I feel somewhat afraid to hear this divine Father Taylor, lest my sympathy with your admiration of him be colder and feebler than you look for. Our souls are in happiest unison, but we must not disquiet ourselves if every

tone be not re-echoed from one to the other,--if every slightest shade be not reflected in the alternate mirror. Our broad and general sympathy is enough to secure our bliss, without our following it into minute details. Will you promise not to be troubled, should I be unable to appreciate the excellence of Father Taylor? Promise me this, and at some auspicious hour, which I trust will soon arrive, Father Taylor shall have an opportunity to make music with my soul. But I forewarn you, dearest, that I am a most unmalleable man; you are not to suppose, because my spirit answers to every touch of yours, that therefore every breeze, or even every whirlwind, can upturn me from my depths. Well, I have said my say in this matter. And now, here are the same snow-flakes in the air that were descending when I began. Would that there were an art of making sunshine! Do you know any such art? Truly you do, and have often thrown a heavenly sunshine round my spirit, when all things else were full of gloom. What a woe, what a cloud, it is, to be away from you!

BOSTON, April 21.

I DO trust, my dearest, that you have been employing this bright day for both of us; for I have spent it in my dungeon, and the only light that broke upon me was when I opened your letter. I am sometimes driven to wish that you and I could mount upon a cloud (as we used to fancy in those heavenly walks of ours), and be borne quite out of sight and hearing of all the world; for now all the people in the world seem to come between us. How happy were Adam and Eve! There was no third person to come between them, and all the infinity around them only served to press their hearts closer together. We love one another as well as they; but there is no silent and lovely garden of Eden for us. Will you sail away with me to discover some summer island? Do you not think that God has reserved one for us, ever since the beginning of the world? Foolish that I am to raise a question of it, since we have found such an Eden--such an island sacred to us two--whenever we have been together! Then, we are the Adam and Eve of a virgin earth. Now, good-by; for voices are babbling around me, and I should not wonder if you were to hear the echo of them while you read this letter.

APRIL 22.

I HAVE met with an immense misfortune. Do you sympathize from the bottom of your heart? Would you take it upon yourself, if possible? Yes, I know you would, even without asking the nature of it; and, truth to tell, I would be selfish enough to wish that you might share it with me. Now art thou all in a fever of anxiety? Shall I tell thee? No--yes; I will. I have received an invitation to a party at General McNeil's next Friday evening. Why will not people let poor persecuted me alone? What possible good can it do for me to thrust my coal-begrimed visage and salt-befrosted locks into good society? What claim have I to be there,--a humble measurer, a subordinate Custom House officer, as I am? I cannot go; I will not go. I intend to pass that evening with you,--that is, in musing and dreaming of you; and moreover, considering that we love each other, methinks it is an exceeding breach of etiquette that you were not invited! How strange it is, tender and fragile little Sophie, that your protection should have become absolutely necessary to such a great, rough, burly, broad-shouldered personage as I! I need your support as much as you need mine.

JUNE 2.

MY DEAREST,--I know not what counsel to give you about calling on my sisters, and therefore must leave the matter to your own exquisite sense of what is right and delicate. We will talk it over at an early opportunity. I think I can partly understand why they feel cool towards you; but it is for nothing in yourself personally, nor from any unkindness towards you, whom everybody must feel to be the lovablest being in the world. But there are some untoward circumstances. Nevertheless, I have faith that all will he well, and that they will receive Sophia Hawthorne into their heart of hearts. So let us wait patiently on Providence, as we always have, and see what time will bring forth. And, my dearest, whenever you feel disquieted about things of this sort,--if ever that he the case,--speak freely to me; for these are matters in which words may be of use, because they concern the relations between ourselves and others.

I have bought a very good edition of Milton (his poetry) in two octavo volumes, and I saw a huge new London volume of his prose works; but it seemed to me that there was but a small portion of it that you and I would ever care to read; so I left it on the shelf. I have bought some lithographic prints at another store, which I mean to send you, that you may show them to me the next afternoon you permit me to spend with you. You are not to expect anything very splendid; for I did not enter the auction room till a large part of the collection was sold, so that my choice was limited. Perhaps there are one or two not altogether unworthy to be put on the walls of our sanctuary; but this I leave to your finer judgment. I would you could peep into my room and see your own pictures. There is no telling how much brighter and cheerfuller the parlor looks now, whenever I enter it.

Belovedest, I love thee very especially much to-day. Rut it is now breakfast-time, and I have an appetite. What did you eat for breakfast?--but I know well enough that you never eat anything but bread and milk and chickens. Do you love pigeons in a pie? I am fonder of Dove than any thing else,--it is my heart's food and sole sustenance.

God bless us. YOUR OWN.

JUNE 22, 1840.

BELOVEDEST, what a letter! Never was so much beauty poured out of any heart before; and to read it over and over is like bathing my brow in a fresh fountain, and drinking draughts that renew the life within me. Nature is kind and motherly to you, and takes you into her inmost heart and cherishes you there, because you look on her with holy and loving eyes. How can you say that I have ever written anything beautiful, being yourself so potent to reproduce whatever is loveliest? If I did not know that you loved me, I should even be ashamed before you. Worthy of you I am not; but you will make me so, for there will be time or eternity enough for your blessed influence to work on me. Would that we could build our cottage this very summer, amid these scenes of Concord which you describe. My heart thirsts and languishes to be there, away from the hot sun, and the coal-dust, and the steaming docks, and the thick-pated, stubborn, contentious men, with whom I brawl from morning till night, and all the weary toil that quite engrosses me, and yet occupies only a small part of niy being, which I did not know existed before I became a measurer. I do think I should sink down quite disheartened and inanimate if you were not happy, and gathering from earth and sky enjoyment for both of us; but this makes me feel that my real, innermost soul is apart from all these unlovely circumstances, and that it has not ceased to exist, as I might sometimes suspect, but is nourished and kept alive through you. You know not what comfort I have in thinking of you amid those beautiful scenes and amid those sympathizing hearts. If you are well and happy, if your step is light and joyous there, and your cheek is becoming rosier, and if your heart makes pleasant music, then is it not better for you to stay there a little longer? And if better for you, is it not so for me likewise? Now, I do not press you to stay, but leave it all to your wisdom; and if you feel it is now time to come home, then let it be so.

    I meant to have written to you yesterday; but, dearest, on that day Hillard and I took a walk into the country. We set out over the Western Avenue, a dreary, fierce-sunshiny, irksome route; but after journeying four or five miles, we came to some of the loveliest rural scenery--yes, the very loveliest--that ever I saw in my life. The first part of the road was like the life of toil and weariness that I am now leading; the latter part was like the life that we will lead hereafter. Would that I had your pen, and I would give you pictures of beauty to match your own; but I should only mar my remembrance of them by the attempt. Not a beautiful scene did I behold, but I imaged you in the midst of it;--you were with me in all the walk, and when I sighed it was for you, and when I smiled it was for you, and when I trusted in future happiness it was for you; and if I did not doubt and fear, it was altogether because of you. What else than happiness can God intend for you? and if your happiness, then mine also. On our return we stopped at Braman's swimming-baths, and plunged in, and washed away all stains of earth and became new creatures. I am not entirely satisfied with any more contracted bath than the illimitable ocean; and to plunge into it is the next thing to soaring into the sky.

    This morning I rose early, to finish measuring a load of coal; which being accomplished, and Colonel Hall perceiving that my energies were somewhat exhausted by the heat and by much brawling with the coal-people, did send me home immediately for dinner. So then I took a nap, with a volume of Spenser in my hand, and, awaking at four, I re-re-re-perused your letter, and sat down to pour myself out to thee; and in so doing, dearest, I have had great comfort. I must not forget to thank Mr. Emerson for his invitation to Concord, but really it will not be in my power to accept it. Now, good-by. You have our whole treasure of happiness in your keeping. Keep it safe, and add to it continually. God bless you.

    BOSTON, July 10, 1840.
    DEAREST,--My days have been so busy and my evenings so invaded with visitants, that I have not had a moment's time to talk with you. Scarcely till this morning have I been able to read your letter quietly. Night before last came Mr. Jones Very; and you know he is somewhat unconscionable as to the length of his calls. The next afternoon came Mr. Hillard's London brother, and wasted my precious hours with a dull talk of nothing; and in the evening I was sorely tried with Mr. Conolly, and a Cambridge law-student, who came to do homage to my literary renown. So you were put aside for these idle people. I do wish the blockheads, and all other blockheads in this world, could comprehend how inestimable are the quiet hours of a busy man, especially when that man has no native impulse to keep him busy, but is

continually forced to battle with his own nature, which yearns for seclusion (the solitude of a united two) and freedom to think and dream and feel.

Well, dearest, I am in perfect health this morning, and good spirits; and much do I rejoice that you are so soon to be near me. But do not you make yourself ill in the bustle of removing; for I think that there is nothing more trying, even to a robust frame and rugged spirit, than the disturbance of such an occasion. Now, good-by.

YOUR OWN DE l'AUBÉPINE.

BOSTON, October, 1840.

. . . . Sometimes, during my solitary life in our old Salem house, it seemed to me as if I had only life enough to know that I was not alive; for I had no wife then to keep my heart warm. But, at length, you were revealed to me, in the shadow of a seclusion as deep as my own. I drew nearer and nearer to you, and opened my heart to you, and you came to me, and will remain forever, keeping my heart warm and renewing my life with your own. You only have taught me that I have a heart,--you only have thrown a light, deep downward and upward, into my soul. You only have revealed me to myself; for without your aid my best knowledge of myself would have been merely to know my own shadow,--to watch it flickering on the wall, and mistake its fantasies for my own real actions. Do you comprehend what you have done for me? And is it not a somewhat fearful thought, that a few slight circumstances might have prevented us from meeting, and then I should have returned to my solitude, sooner or later (probably now, when I have thrown down my burden of coal and salt), and never should have been created at all! But this is an idle speculation. If the whole world had stood between us, we must have met; if we had been born in different ages, we could not have been sundered!

When we shall be endowed with spiritual bodies, I think they will be so constituted that we may send thoughts and feelings any distance, in no time at all, and transfuse them warm and fresh into the consciousness of those we love. Oh, what happiness it would be, at this moment, if I could be conscious of some purer feeling, some more delicate sentiment, some lovelier fantasy, than could possibly have had its birth in my own nature, and therefore be aware that you were thinking through my mind and feeling through my heart! Perhaps you possess this power already.

SALEM, Nov. 27, 1840.

DEAREST,--I pity you now; for I apprehend that by this time you have got my dullest of old books to read. And how many pages can you read without falling asleep? Well is it for you that you have adopted the practice of extending yourself on the sofa while at your studies; for now I need be under no apprehension of your sinking out of a chair. I would, for your sake, tbat you could find something laudable in this awful little volume, because you would like to tell me that I have done well. Dearest, I am utterly ashamed of my handwriting. I wonder how you can anywise tolerate what is so ungraceful. being yourself all grace. But I think I seldom write so shamefully as in this epistle.

Whenever I return to Salem, I feel how dark my life would be without the light that you shed upon it,--how cold, without the warmth of your love. Sitting in this chamber, where my youth wasted itself in vain, I can partly estimate the change that has been wrought. It seems as if the better part of me had been born since then. I had walked those many years in darkness, and might so have walked through life, with only a dreamy notion that there was any light in the universe, if you had not kissed my eyelids and given me to see. You, dearest, have always been positively happy. Not so I,--I have only not been miserable. Then which of us has gained the most? I, assuredly! When a beam of heavenly sunshine incorporates itself with a dark cloud, is not the cloud benefited more than the sunshine? Nothing at all has happened to me since I left you. It puzzles me to conceive how you meet with so many more events than I. You will have a volume to tell me, when we meet, and you will pour your beloved voice into my ears in a long stream; at length you will pause and say, "But what has your life been?" and then will stupid I look back upon what I call my life, for three or four days past, and behold, a blank! You live ten times as much as I, because your spirit takes so much more note of things.

I am enduring my banishment here as best I may methinks, all enormous sinners should be sent on pilgrimage to Salem, and compelled to spend a length of time there, proportioned to the enormity of their offences. Such punishment would be suited to crimes that do not quite deserve hanging, yet are too aggravated for the State's Prison. Oh, naughty I! If it be a punishment, I deserve to suffer a life-long infliction of it, were it only for slandering my native town so vilely. But any place is strange and lonesome to me where you are not; and where you are, any place will be home. I ought to love Salem better than I do; for the people have always had a pretty generous faith in me, ever since they knew me at all. I fear I must be undeserving of their praise, else I should never get it. What an ungrateful blockhead am I!

Now I think of it, it does not please you to hear me spoken slightingly of. Well, then you should not have loved such a vulnerable person. But, to your comfort be it said, some people have a much more exalted opinion of me than I have. The Rev. Mr. Gannet delivered a lecture, at the Lyceum here, the other evening, in which he introduced an enormous eulogium on whom do you think? Why, on my respectable self! Thereupon all the audience gave a loud hiss! Now is my mild little Sophie exceedingly enraged, and will plot some mischief and all involving calamity against the Salem people. Well, then, they did not actually hiss at the praises bestowed on me,--the more geese they!

God bless you, you sinless Eve!

SALEM, Jan. 13, 1841.
OH, beloved, what a weary week is this Never did I experience the like. Will you know my face when we meet again? Are you much changed by the flight of years, my poor little Sophie? Is your hair turned gray? Do you wear a day-cap as well as a night-cap? How long since did you begin to wear spectacles? Perhaps you will not like to have me see you, now that time has done his worst to mar your beauty; but fear not, for what I have loved and admired in you is eternal. I shall look through the envious mist of age, and discern your immortal grace, as perfectly as in the light of Paradise. As for me, I am grown quite bald and gray, and have very deep wrinkles across my brow, and crowsfeet and furrows all over my face. My eyesight fails me, so that I can only read the largest print in the broadest day light; but it is a singular circumstance that I make out to decipher the pygmy characters of your epistles, even

by the faintest twilight. The secret is, that they are characters of light to me, so that I could undoubtedly read them in midnight darkness. . . .

--At this point, chronologically if not sentimentally, comes in the following letter from Hawthorne to his sister Louisa, with three from her to him. If they interrupt for a few moments the flow of lovers' talk, they do so in a pleasant fashion, and incidentally afford a glimpse worth having of the way these invisible and problematical Hawthornes felt towards one another.

BROOK FARM, WEST ROXBURY, May 8, 1841.
As the weather precludes all possibility of ploughing, hoeing, sowing, and other such operations, I bethink me that you may have no objections to bear something of my whereabout and whatabout. You are to know, then, that I took up my abode here on the 12th ultimo, in the midst of a snow-storm, which kept us all idle for a day or two. At the first glimpse of fair weather, Mr, Ripley summoned us into the cow-yard, and introduced me to an instrument with four prongs, commonly entitled a dung-fork. With this tool I have already assisted to load twenty or thirty carts of manure, and shall take part in loading nearly three hundred more. Besides, I have planted potatoes and pease, cut straw and hay for the cattle, and done various other mighty works: This very morning I milked three cows, and I milk two or three every night and morning. The weather has been so unfavorable that we have worked comparatively little in the fields; but, nevertheless, I have gained strength wonderfully, --grown quite a giant, in fact,--and can do a day's work without the slightest inconvenience. In short, I am transformed into a complete farmer.

This is one of the most beautiful places I ever saw in my life, and as secluded as if it were a hundred miles from any city or village. There are woods, in which we can ramble all day without meeting anybody or scarcely seeing a house. Our house stands apart from the main road, so that we are not troubled even with passengers looking at us. Once in a while we have a transcendental visitor, such as Mr. Alcott; but generally we pass whole days without seeing a single face, save those of the brethren. The whole fraternity eat together; and such a delectable way of life has never been seen on earth since the days of the early Christians. We get up at half-past four, breakfast at half-past six, dine at half-past twelve, and go to bed at nine.

The thin frock which you made for me is considered a most splendid article, and I should not wonder if it were to become the summer uniform of the Community. I have a thick frock, likewise; but it is rather deficient in grace, though extremely warm and comfortable. I wear a tremendous pair of cowhide hoots, with soles two inches thick,--of course, when I come to see you I shall wear my farmer's dress.

We shall be very much occupied during most of this month, ploughing and planting; so that I doubt whether you will see me for two or three weeks. You have the portrait by this time, I suppose; so you can very well dispense with the original. When you write to me (which I beg you will do soon), direct your letter to West Roxbury, as there are two post-offices in the town. I would write more) but William Mien is going to the village, and must have this letter. So good-by.
NATH. HAWTHORNE, *Ploughman*

SALEM, May 10, 1841.

MY DEAR BROTHER,--I am very glad you did bethink yourself that we might want to hear from you; for we had looked for you so long in vain, that we were very impatient to know in wbat quarter of the world you had bestowed yourself What a delightful beginning of your farmer's life that snowstorm was! I could not help thinking all day how dreary it must look to you. You do give a wonderful account of your works. Elizabeth does not seem to have entire faith in it, it passes her comprehension; she says she knows you will spoil the cows if you attempt to milk them, and she thinks William Allen will have the hardest time of all, it being his province to direct you. What an event it will be when the potatoes you have planted come up I should like to see you at work; what a figure you must cut after a day's ploughing, or labor in the barnyard! Your carpet will suffer this summer if you tread upon it with your cowhide boots. Do not work too hard; I have more faith in your working than Elizabeth has, and I am afraid you will take it too hard. Mother groans over it, and wishes you would come home. The portrait came home a fortnight ago, and gives great delight. Mother says it is perfect; and if she is satisfied with the likeness, it must be good. The color is a little too high, to be sure; but perhaps it is a modest blush at the compliments which are paid you to your face. Mrs. Cleveland says it is bewitching, and Miss Carlton says it only wants to speak. Elizabeth says it is excellent. It has one advantage over the original,--I can make it go with me where I choose! But good as it is, it does not by any means supply the place of the original, and you are not to think that you can stay away any longer than before we had it. If you only knew how we anticipated your coming home, and how impatient we are when you do not come at the usual time, you would not think you could be spared. It is a comfort to look at the picture, to be sure; but I am tempted to speak to it sometimes, and it answers never a word; and when mother looks at it, she takes up a lamentation because you stay away so long and work so hard. I wonder if they would not take me into the Community for a week this summer. I should like to get into the country and ramble in the woods. I won't work much, though; neither, I hope, will you when the hot weather comes,--which does not seem likely to be very soon. Do you see the newspapers, so as to know what is going on among the world's people? What a sweep there is among your old friends at the Custom House!

You do not tell us what you eat. I should like to know what your farmer's fare is. What a loaded table you must want, so many of you, after a hard day's work! I should think you would bring us home a box of butter, if your dairy-woman is very nice. Do you know, when Sunday comes now, I think among so many ministers you might have preaching! Shall not you be at home by next Friday,--the National Fast? It is five weeks to-morrow since you went away, and we do so want to see you. I am glad your frock gives satisfaction; I suppose that is your Sunday dress. You can wear that when you are at home; but Beelzebub begs that you will leave your thick boots behind you, as her nerves are somewhat delicate and she could not bear them. She came into the room the other night, and looked all round for you, and uplifted her voice. She will not take the least notice of the picture; she wants the real, not the imitation. She is rather conceited just now, as she has been told that there is a canary bird named for her, which has added to her vanity. I have written a very long letter; but if it continues to rain, you will have time to read it. If you do not come home this week, do write,--but do come.

Your affectionate sister,
M. L. HAWTHORNE.

SALEM, June 11, 1841.
DEAR NATTY,--We received your letter, and were very glad to hear from you, although we should have been much better pleased to have had you come yourself. I had not written before, because we had been looking for you every day; and we do most seriously object to your staying away from home so long. Do you know that it was nine weeks last Tuesday since you left home? --a great deal too long. I do not see how you manage to work this hot weather without your thin clothes; and I do not like your working so hard at all. I am sure it cannot be good for your health to work from half-past four till seven; and I cannot bear to think that this hot sun is beating upon your head. You could but work hard if you could do nothing else; as it is, you can do a great deal better. What is the use of burning your brains out in the sun, when you can do anything better with them? Ebe says she thought you were only to work three hours a day for your board, and she cannot understand your keeping at it all day.

I am bent upon coming up to see you this summer. Do not you remember how you and I used to go a-fishing together in Raymond? Your mention of wild-flowers and pickerel has given me a longing for the woods and waters again; and I want to wander about as I used to in old times; and I mean to come! Who are the four young ladies who give you so much trouble? They ought to work as well as you. I should think so much company would hinder you very much. I only wish you were near enough to Salem to be visited. Elizabeth Cleveland says she saw Mr. George Bradford in Lowell last winter, and he told her he was going to be associated with you; but they say his mind misgave him terribly when the time came for him to go to Roxbury, and whether to take such a desperate step or not, he could not tell. Mrs. Cleveland saw a young lady who had seen you in your *frock,* and they told her you carried milk into Boston every morning; so she says she stared at every milk-cart she met to see if the milkman resembled the *picture,* but she was disappointed in her hopes of seeing you. I hope you were dressed in your best frock at the *fete* in Brook Farm. I should think your clothes were in a very dilapidated condition by this time, and I am glad of it; for then you will have to come home. We have sent that frock-coat to be dyed, and it is to be done to-morrow; your stocks are in progress, and mother is this afternoon putting buttons on your thin pantaloons, of which you have three pairs, which you must want very much. I wish you had said if you wanted any more of those working-shirts; they are pretty thick for this weather. Mother apostrophizes your picture because you do not come home. Elizabeth walked over to Marblehead the other day, and got plenty of violets and columbines. I went to Harmony Grove last week; it looked pretty enough. We saw in the Boston Post a notice of that article of yours, and part of it was copied into the "Gazette." If you have the magazine do bring it home with you, that we may see the whole article. I shall he g]ad when you renew your acquaintance with the person therein mentioned, and recommend you to do it speedily. Mother says she shall look for you sometime tomorrow; if you do not come then, do not defer it longer than next week We do want to see you, and you must not stay any longer; only think, it is more than two months since you went away, and my patience is exhausted. Beelzebub is very well, but she had the misfortune to set herself on fire the other day, which improves her beauty by contrast. She wants one of those partridges you tell of. I am writing in your chamber. Do come very soon.

Your affectionate sister,
M. L. HAWTHORNE.

SALEM, Aug. 3, 1841.
DEAR NATTY,--I have waited for a letter from you till I am tired and cannot wait any longer. And I have been to the post-office and received the same answer so often, that I am ashamed to go any more. What do you mean by such conduct, neither coming, nor writing to us? It is six weeks to-day since you left us, and in all that time we have heard nothing from you. We do not like it at all. It was a great deal better, and, I am sure, a great deal pleasanter and happier, when you came home once a fortnight at least; that was quite long enough to stay away. Mother is very vehement about it. I take for granted you would like to hear from us; we are all pretty well. Susan Giddings says they frequently heard from you by way of Mr. Farley, whose sister-in-law lives in the house with them, and to whom he writes frequently. She was very much amazed at the idea of your working so hard. By the way, I hope you do not work very hard this hot weather. I have been troubled about it when the sun was so hot that I could not step out of doors. How did you get through haying? I was glad to hear of your going to Plymouth, because it seemed as if your *hurry* was over. Elizabeth walked to Marblehead the other day. Poor Beelzebub is very unfortunate: she has been lame this three weeks; whether it is the gout, or a sprain, or fighting, we cannot tell; but she bobbles on three legs in a most pitiable manner, though I suppose you might be wicked enough to laugh at her. I doubt very much if she ever walks on four legs again. Mr. George Bradford, one of your *brethren,* has paid a visit in Lowell, where I understand his *hands* excited great wonderment. I can imagine how they looked, having seen yours. Healy Barstow has been walking round town this week, dressed in a black velvet coat, looking very much like a *play-actor.* It is said that you are to do the travelling in Europe for the Community. Mrs. Sparks is boarding at Nahant for her health. I hope you will come home *very* soon; we do want to see you. You do not know how long it seems since you went away. But if you are not coming *immediately,* you must write and let us hear from you at least. Mother takes up such a lamentation for you, and then she scolds about you; and Beelzebub comes into the room and hops round it, looking for you; and Ebe is troubled about your working; so you must pacify us all. If you write, say if you want any clothes got ready.

Your affectionate sister,
M. L. HAWTHORNE.

--Here ends Miss Louisa's contribution, and Hawthorne resumes. It is probably not necessary to remark that Beelzebub, in this connection, signifies only the family cat; but it may be as well to explain that "Ebe" stands for Miss Elizabeth. When Hawthorne was a baby, the sound he made in attempting to pronounce his sister's name is represented by these letters; and it became her family appellation. Hawthorne's children, in after years, always spoke of Miss Elizabeth Hawthorne as "Aunt Ebe."

BROOK FARM, Aug. 12, 1841.

DEAREST UNUTTERABLY,--Mrs. Ripley is going to Boston to Miss Slade's wedding, so I sit down to write a word to you, not knowing whither to direct it. My heart searches for you, but wanders about vaguely and is strangely dissatisfied. Where are you? I would that I were with you. It seems as if all evil things had more power over you when I am away. Then you are exposed to noxious winds and to pestilence and to death-like weariness; and, moreover, nobody knows how to take care of you but I. Everybody else thinks it of importance that you should paint and sculpture; but it would be no trouble to me if you should never touch clay or canvas again. It is not what you do, but what you are, that I concern myself about. And if your mighty works are to be wrought only by the anguish of your head, and weariness of your frame, and sinking of your heart, then I do never desire to see another. And this should be the feeling of all your friends. Especially ought it to be yours, for my sake. . . .

BROOK FARM, Aug. 22, 1841.

. . . .When am I to see you again? The first of September comes a week from Tuesday next; but I think I shall compel it to begin on Sunday. Will you consent? Then, on Saturday afternoon, I will come to you, and remain in the city till Monday. Thence I shall go to Salem, and spend a week there, longer or shorter according to the intensity of the occasion for my presence. I do long to see our mother and sisters; and I should not wonder if they felt some slight desire to see me. I received a letter from Louisa a week or two since, scolding me most pathetically for my long absence. Indeed, I have been rather naughty in this respect; but I knew that it would be unsatisfactory to them and myself if I came only for a single day, and that has been the largest space that I could command. . . .

SALEM, Sept. 3, 1841.

. . . .You do not expect a letter from me; and yet, perhaps, you will not be absolutely displeased should one come to you to-morrow. At all events, I feel moved to write, though the haze and sleepiness which always settles upon me here, will be perceptible in every line. But what a letter you wrote to me--it is like one angel writing to another angel. But alas, the letter has miscarried, and has been delivered to a most unworthy mortal. Now will you exclaim against my naughtiness And indeed I am very naughty. Well, then, the letter was meant for me, and could not possibly belong to any other being, mortal or immortal. I will trust that your idea of me is truer than my own consciousness of myself.

I have been out only once, in the daytime, since my arrival. How immediately and irrecoverably (if you did not keep me out of the abyss) should I relapse into the way of life in which I spent my youth! If it were not for you, this present world would see no more of me forever. The sunshine would never fall on me, no more than on a ghost. Once in a while people might discern my figure gliding stealthily through the dim evening,--that would be all. I should be only a shadow of the night; it is you that give me reality, and make all things real for me. If, in the interval since I quitted this lonely old chamber, I had found no woman (and you were the only possible one) to impart reality and significance to life, I should have come back hither ere now, with a feeling that all was a dream and a mockery. Do you rejoice that you have saved me from such a fate? Yes; it is a miracle worthy even of you, to have converted a life of shadows into the deepest truth by your magic touch.

BOSTON, May 27, 1842.

DEAREST HEART,--Your letter to my sisters was most beautiful,--sweet, gentle, and magnanimous; such as no one but you could have written. If they do not love you, it must be because they have no hearts to love with,--and even if this were the case, I should not despair of your planting the seeds of hearts in their bosoms. They will love you, all in good time, dearest; and we will be very happy. I am so at this moment. I see more to admire and love in you every day of my life, and shall see more and more as long as I live, else it will be because my own nature retrogrades, instead of advancing. But you will make me better and better, till I am worthy to be your husband.

Three evenings without a glimpse of you; and I know not whether I am to come at six or seven o'clock, or scarcely, indeed, whether I am to come at all. But, unless you order me to the contrary, I shall come at seven o'clock. I saw Mr. Emerson at the Atheneum yesterday, and he tells me that our garden, etc., make progress. Would that we were there!

YOURS.

SALEM, June 9, 1842

DEAREST,--Scarcely had I arrived here, when our mother came out of her chamber, looking better and more cheerful than I have seen her this some time, and inquired about your health and well-being. Very kindly, too. Then was my heart much lightened; for I know that almost every agitating circumstance of her life had hitherto cost her a fit of sickness, and I knew not but it might be so now. Foolish me, to doubt that my mother's love could be wise, like all other genuine love And foolish again, to have doubted your instinct,--whom, henceforth (if never before) I take for my unerring guide and counsellor in all matters of the heart and soul. Yet if, sometimes, I should perversely follow my own follies, do not you be discouraged. I shall always acknowledge your superior wisdom in the end. Now, I am happier than my naughtiness deserves. It seems that our mother had seen how things were, a long time ago; at first her heart was troubled, because she knew that much of outward as well as inward fitness was requisite to secure our peace; but, gradually and quietly, God has taught her that all is good, and so we shall have her fullest blessing and concurrence. My sisters, too, begin to sympathize as they ought; and all is well. God be praised I thank Him on my knees, and pray Him to make me worthy of the happiness you bring me.

Time and space, and all other finite obstructions, are fast flitting away from between us. We can already measure the interval by days and hours. What happiness! and what awe is intermingled with it--no fear nor doubt, but a holy awe, as when an immortal spirit is drawing near to the gates of Heaven. I cannot tell what I feel, but you know it all.

I shall be with you on Friday at seven o'clock. I have no more words, but a heart full of love.

YOUR OWN.

SALEM, June 20, 1842.

TRUE AND HONORABLE,--You have not been out of my mind a moment since I saw you last,--and never will you be, so long as we exist. Can you say as much? Dearest, do you know that there are but ten days more in this blessed month of June? And do you remember what is to happen within those ten days? Poor little Sophie. Now you begin to tremble and shrink back, and fear that you have acted too rashly in this matter. Now you say to yourself, "Oh that I could prevail upon this wretched person to allow me a month or two longer to make up my mind; for, after all, he is but an acquaintance of yesterday, and unwise am I to give up father, mother, and sisters for the sake of such a questionable stranger!" Ah, it is too late! Nothing can part us now; for God himself hath ordained that we shall be one. So nothing remains, but to reconcile yourself to your destiny. Year by year we shall grow closer to each other; and a thousand ages hence, we shall be only in the honeymoon of our marriage. But I cannot write to you. The time for that species of communion is past.

DEAREST,--Your sister Mary told me that it was her opinion you and I should not be married for a week longer. I had hoped, as you know, for an earlier day; but I cannot help feeling that Mary is on the safe and reasonable side, and should you feel that this postponement is advisable, you will find me patient beyond what you think me capable of. I will even be happy, if you will only keep your heart and mind at peace. I will go to Concord tomorrow or next day, and see about our affairs there.

P.S. I love you! I love you! I love you!

P.S. 2. Do you love me at all?

On the 9th of July, 1842, the marriage took place at the house of Dr. Peabody, No. 13 West Street, Boston. The ceremony was performed by Rev. James Freeman Clarke, who, by a singular chance, never afterwards met Mr. and Mrs. Hawthorne until, on the 23d of May, 1864, he preached the funeral sermon, at Concord church, over Mr. Hawthorne's dead body. The spectators of the wedding were very few; but, such as they were, they looked on with loving and praying hearts. The imagination lingers over this scene, with its simplicity, its deep but happy emotion, its faith, its promise, and its courage. The future that lay before the married lovers had in it its full proportion of joy, of sorrow, of honor, and of loss; but there was, in the chapter of their life which had just closed, an ethereal bloom of loveliness which can come but once even to the pure in heart, and which to many comes not at all.

CHAPTER 6 - THE OLD MANSE

IN the preceding chapters little space has been given to discussion of the merely literary aspect and details of Hawthorne's life. A good deal might have been said about his early successes and disappointments in this direction: how hard he worked for publishers who paid him only with promises; how the "Athenaeum" and Mr. Longfellow praised him; how Poe criticised him; how the "Church Review" attacked him; and more to the same effect, with the writer's meditations and comments thereupon. But such matters appertain less to the biographer than to the bibliographer. They give no solidity or form to our conception of the man. Hawthorne's works are published to the world, and any one may read them, and derive from them whatever literary or moral culture he may be susceptible of. But any attempt to make the works throw light upon their author is certain to miscarry, unless the student be previously impregnated with a very distinct and unmistakable conception of that author's human and natural (as distinct from his merely imaginative and artistic) personality. The books may add depth and minuteness to this conception, when once it has been attained, but they cannot be depended on to create it beforehand. Accordingly, it is the biographer's business, so far as his abilities and materials allow, to confine himself to putting the reader in possession of this human aspect of his subject, and to let the rest take care, in great measure, of itself. In other words, he must do for the reader only so much as the reader cannot do for himself. To do more would be superfluous, if not presumptuous. Few men, who have made literature the business of their lives, have been less dependent than Hawthorne upon literature for a character. If he had never written a line, he would still have possessed, as a human being, scarcely less interest and importance than he does now. Those who were most intimate with him not only found in him all the promise of his works, but they found enough more to put the works quite in the background. His literary phase seemed a phase only, and not the largest or most characteristic. In the same way, when he was a consul at Liverpool, nobody could have been a better consul than he; but when you came into his presence, the consul was lost sight of and the man shone out. Some men are swallowed up by their profession, so that nothing is left of them but the profession in human form. But, for men like Hawthorne, the profession is but a means of activity; they use it, and are not used by it. Hawthorne's son remembers that, twenty or thirty years ago, it seemed to him rather a regrettable thing that his father had written books. Why write books? He was a very good and satisfactory father without that. When, afterwards, he read the books, they struck him as being but a somewhat imperfect reflection of certain regions of his father's mind with which he had become otherwise familiar.

In the pages which are to follow, the same general aim and principle as heretofore will control the biographer in his selection and treatment of materials; but the character of the materials themselves undergoes a certain modification. A domestic career has been begun; there is a wife to be loved and to love, and there are children to be born and raised. The narrative moves more slowly as to time; it is more circumstantial and homogeneous; it is, for some years, rather contemplative than active. We feel that stories are being written, up there in the little study; we catch echoes, now and then, of the world's appreciation of them; but we are not called upon to give special heed to these matters. For there are the river, and the woods, and Sleepy Hollow; and the Old Manse itself, with its orchard, its avenue, and its vegetable garden; and Mr. Emerson passes by, with a sunbeam in his face; and Margaret Fuller receives rather independent treatment; and those odd young men, Ellery Channing and Henry Thoreau, make themselves agreeable or otherwise, as the case may be. The man has reached a region of repose, -temporary repose only, and complete merely on the side of the higher nature; for there are *res angustoe domi* to be dealt with, and other half-comical, half-serious difficulties to be overcome. Much of the history of this sojourn in the Old Manse has already been made public in the "Note-Books," and in the preface to the "Mosses;" but a note slightly more personal remains to be struck. In preparing Hawthorne's literary remains for the press, his wife labored under the embarrassment of being herself the constant theme of his journalizings, and the subject of his most loving observation and reflection; and the omission of this entire element from the record left a very perceptible gap. Even now the omission can be only partially repaired; but the additions, so far as they go, are full of significance and charm. The married lovers during several years were in the habit of a more or less continuous diary of their daily experiences, in which first one and then the other would hold the pen, in lovely strophe and antistrophe; and there is, moreover, that unfailing History of Happiness (as it might well be called),--the letters of Mrs. Hawthorne to her mother. In the present chapter, for reasons of clearness and convenience, a strict chronological sequence will occasionally be departed from disconnected references to the same subject will be brought together, and other slight liberties be taken with some of the more arbitrary arrangements of time. And perhaps we could not begin better than with this eloquent epithalamion--if such a title may be given to a retrospective essay, written after the death of both Hawthorne and his wife--by the latter's sister, Miss E. P. Peabody:--

"The mental idiosyncrasies of Hawthorne and his wife were in singular contrast,--a contrast which made their union more beautiful and complete. Her ministration was done as delicately as Ariel's 'spiriting,' as was needful with respect to an individuality so rare and alive as Hawthorne's, and a habit so reserved. He was not morbid or gloomy in nature; his peculiar form of shyness was rather the result of the outward circumstance that he belonged to a family which had done nothing (as the mother and sisters of a man generally do) to put him into easy relations with society,--into which, indeed, he never had any natural introduction until it was in some degree made by his wife, whose nature was very social. But they were thirty-two and thirty-eight years old, respectively, before they were married, and Sophia thought it too late to attempt to break up his secluded habits entirely. His reserved manners had come to be a barrier against intrusion, and she felt that the work he had to do for mankind was too important for him to waste any time and undergo any unnecessary suffering in reforming his social habits. In the hermitage made for him by his extreme sensibility, he was not in the dark, but saw clearly out of it, as if he walked among men with an invisible cap on his head. She guarded his solitude, perhaps with a needless extreme of care; but it was not in order to keep him selfishly to herself,--it was to keep him for the human race, to whose highest needs she thought he could minister by his art, if not interrupted in his artistic studies of men in their most profound relations to one another and to nature. She never had any jealousy of his study and books, as wives of many artists and authors have had. She delighted in the wide relations he held with the human race. There never was a love which was at the same time more intense and complete and personally unselfish. It is true, the bounty of his love for her could not but disarm, by rendering unnecessary, all disposition to exaction on her part. She protected him by her womanly tact and sympathy; he protected her by his manly tenderness, ever on the watch to ward off from her the hurts to which she was liable from those moral shocks given by the selfishness and cruelty she could never learn to expect from human beings. For though Sophia had the strength of a martyr under the infliction of those wounds which necessarily come to individuals by the providential vicissitudes of life, there was one kind of thing she could not bear, and that was, moral evil. Every cloud brought over her horizon by the hand of God had for her a silvery lining; but human unkindness, dishonor, falsehood, agonized and stunned her,--as, in 'The Marble Faun' the crime of Miriam and Donatello stunned and agonized Hilda. And it was this very characteristic of hers that was her supreme charm to Hawthorne's imagination. He reverenced it, and almost seemed to doubt whether his own power to gaze steadily at the evils of human character, and analyze them, and see their bounds, were really wisdom, or a defect of moral sensibility. Their mutual affection was truly a moral reverence for each other, that enlarges one's idea of what is in man; for it was without weakness, and enabled her to give him up without a murmur when, as she herself said, he came to need so much finer conditions than she could command for him; and thus it was that, as she herself also said in the supreme hour of her bereavement, 'Love abolished Death.'

"Before they met, they were already 'two self-sufficing worlds;' and this gave the peculiar dignity, without taking away the tender freshness, of their union,--for it was first love for both of them, though the flower bloomed on the summit of the mountain of their life, and not in the early morning; and it was therefore, perhaps, that it was amaranthine in its nature. As was said by a writer in the 'Tribune,' at the time of Mrs. Hawthorne's death, 'the world owes to this woman more than any one but Hawthorne knew;' but it will know better as he is better and better understood by the advancing thought of the English and American mind."

--Happiness is not especially articulate until one becomes a little accustomed to it; but no words are more weighted with tender and pathetic meaning than those of a mother who feels the loss of a favorite child; nor is any ingenuity more touching than that with which she endeavors to disguise her heartache, lest it cast a shadow upon the child's sunshine. The subjoined extracts from some of Mrs. Peabody's letters to her daughter have a beautiful and simple wistfulness that renders them valuable to literature as well as to this biography. The first is dated within six days after the wedding.

DEAR SOPHIE,--I could fill sheets with what my heart is full of, on several subjects; but I am more and more convinced that this world is not the place to pour out the soul without reserve. In a higher and a better, to know even as we are known will be a part of heaven, to our disciplined race. Here the noblest and best feelings are misunderstood, and our safety consists in forbearing to say--certainly to *write* - what it is our highest merit to feel. . . .

I never doubted that you would be most happy in the connection you have formed; you are kindred spirits, and it must be so; yet it was delightful to read such an outpouring of entire felicity. Yet, however happy you may be in each other, you will feel a void, if the enlarged circle of love is not occupied with objects worthy to be there. True love increases our capability of loving our fellow-beings, and, in the hour of sickness and worldly perplexity, the face of a friend is like a ray from heaven.

Probably I shall often mention things which have already occurred to your own mind; but you must bear it, dear. Old housekeepers are apt to imagine they know a great deal; but after forty years' experience I find many new things may be learned; and so you must not wonder if my letters are often garnished with homely but very important hints upon family matters.

You need give no injunctions, dear, to any of the dear ones I am with. Their care of me is only greater than I wish. To be useful while I live, is my effort; to have health and strength for it, is my prayer. When any one reflects how much I have been with you for thirty years, how fully we shared each other's thoughts, how soothing in every trial was your bright smile and ready sympathy, such an one will give me credit for behaving heroically, as well as gratefully for the blessings left. My hours are fully occupied; I housekeep, paint, sew, study German, read, and give no room for useless regrets and still more useless anxieties. We are all religiously doing all we can, for ourselves and others. . . .

--The privacy of the Old Manse was at first but little invaded, and only by friends who bestowed something almost as good as solitude. Nevertheless, Mr. and Mrs. Hawthorne had not been many days settled in their dwelling, when a project was mooted to engraft upon their felicity that of another newly married couple,--Mr. and Mrs. Ellery Channing. Ellery's wife was the sister of Margaret Fuller; and the latter took upon herself the office of suggesting the plan to the Hawthornes; and it was to Mrs. Hawthorne that she addressed herself. Mrs. Hawthorne suppressed her own feelings in the matter (whatever they may have been) and referred the responsibility of decision to her husband. He, doubtless, perceived in her a secret repugnance to the idea, and shared that sentiment; and so far all was easy enough. But it was necessary for him to write a letter to Margaret refusing her proposal; and here was an embarrassment. Miss Fuller was a very clever woman, and most people stood in some awe of her. The fact that she was somewhat deficient in tact would increase the difficulty of dealing with her successfully. Furthermore, her proposal had been made in a spirit of benevolence to both the parties involved in it, and the rejection of it must therefore be made as considerate as it was explicit. Finally (and foremost probably, in Hawthorne's estimation), it was desirable to relieve his wife from any suspicion of bearing an active part in the conclusion arrived at, and to indicate unmistakably that the entire odium of it--if there were any rested upon his own shoulders. It will be seen, therefore, that Hawthorne was here afforded an unusually promising opportunity of making mortal enemies of three worthy persons; and to emerge from the scrape with credit to himself and without offence to them, would be a feat worthy of a practised diplomatist and man of the world. His management of the problem was as follows:--

CONCORD, Aug. 28, 1842.

DEAR MARGARET,--Sophia has told me of her conversation with you, about our receiving Mr. Ellery Channing and your sister as inmates of our household. I found that my wife's ideas were not altogether unfavorable to the plan,--which, together with your own implicit opinion in its favor, has led me to consider it with a good deal of attention; and my conclusion is, that the comfort of both parties would be put in great jeopardy. In saying this, I would not be understood to mean anything against the social qualities of Mr. and Mrs. Channing,--my objection being wholly independent of such considerations. Had it been proposed to Adam and Eve to receive two angels into their Paradise, as *boarders,* I doubt whether they would have been altogether pleased to consent. Certain I am, that, whatever might be the tact and the sympathies of the heavenly guests, the boundless freedom of Paradise would at once have become finite and limited by their presence. The host and hostess would no longer have lived their own natural life, but would have had a constant reference to the two angels; and thus the whole four would have been involved in an unnatural relation,--which the whole system of boarding out essentially and inevitably is.

One of my strongest objections is, the weight of domestic care which would be thrown upon Sophia's shoulders by the proposed arrangement. She is so little acquainted with it, that she cannot estimate how much she would have to bear. I do not fear any burthen that may accrue from our own exclusive relations because skill and strength will come with the natural necessity; but I should not feel myself justified in adding one scruple to the weight. I wish to remove everything that may impede her full growth and development,--which in her case, it seems to me, is not to be brought about by care and toil, but by perfect repose and happiness. Perhaps she ought not to have any earthly care whatever,--certainly none that is not wholly pervaded with love, as a cloud is with warm light. Besides, she has many visions of great deeds to be wrought on canvas and in marble during the coming autumn and winter; and none of these can be accomplished unless she can retain quite as much freedom from household drudgery as she enjoys at present. In short, it is my faith and religion not wilfully to mix her up with any earthly annoyance.

You will not consider it impertinent if I express an opinion about the most advisable course for your young relatives, should they retain their purpose of boarding out. I think that they ought not to seek for delicacy of character and nice tact and sensitive feelings in their hosts. In such a relation as they propose, those characteristics should never exist on more than one side; nor should there be any idea of personal friendship, where the real condition of the bond is to supply food and lodging for a pecuniary compensation. They will be able to keep their own delicacy and sensitiveness much more inviolate, if they make themselves inmates of the rudest farmer's household in Concord, where there will be no nice sensibillty to manage, and where their own feelings will be no more susceptible of damage from the farmer's family than from the cattle in the barnyard. There will be a freedom in this sort of life, which is not otherwise attainable, except under a roof of their own. They can then say explicitly what they want, and can battle for it, if necessary, and such a contest would leave no wound on either side. Now, when four sensitive people were living together, united by any tie save that of entire affection and confidence, it would take but a trifle to render their whole common life diseased and intolerable.

I have thought, indeed, of receiving a personal friend, and a man of delicacy, into my household, and have taken a step towards that object. But in doing so, I was influenced far less by what Mr. Bradford is, than by what he is not; or rather, his negative qualities seem to take away his personality, and leave his excellent characteristics to be fully and fearlessly enjoyed. I doubt whether he be not precisely the rarest man in the world. And, after all, I have had some misgivings as to the wisdom of my proposal to him.

This epistle has grown to greater length than I expected, and yet it is but a very imperfect expression of my ideas upon the subject. Sophia wished me to write; and as it was myself that made the objections, it seemed no more than just that I should assume the office of stating them to you. There is nobody to whom I would more willingly speak my mind, because I can be certain of being thoroughly understood. I would say more,--but here is the bottom of the page.

Sincerely your friend,
NATH. HAWTHORNE,

This finished the episode; Miss Fuller, if she felt any dissatisfaction, not thinking it advisable to express any, and the Channings resigning themselves to finding quarters elsewhere. But Miss Fuller was at this time in her apogee, and had to be doing something; and accordingly, during the ensuing year, she produced a book in which the never-to-be-exhausted theme of Woman's Rights was touched upon. The book made the rounds of the transcendental circle, and was sufficiently discussed; and doubtless there are disciples of this renowned woman now living who could quote pages of it. But married women, who had in their husbands their ideal of marital virtue, and whose domestic affairs sufficiently occupied them, were not likely to be cordial supporters of such doctrines as the book enunciated. Mrs. Hawthorne and her mother, in letters which happen to be written on the same day, expressed themselves on the subject as follows. I give passages from the former's epistle first.

Mr. Emerson's review of Carlyle in the 'Dial' is noble, is it not? What a cordial joy it must be to Carlyle to find in another such worthy appreciation of his best purposes. In all his writings I have been mainly impressed with his pure humanity, which has made me love the man and listen reverently to all he utters,--though in chaotic phrase, like rattling thunder echoed among ragged hills. If ever a mortal had a high aim, it is certainly he. What do you think of the speech which Queen Margaret Fuller has made from the throne? It seems to me that if she were married truly, she would no longer be puzzled about the rights of woman. This is the revelation of woman's true destiny and place, which never can be *imagined* by those who do not experience the relation. In perfect, high union there is no question of supremacy. Souls are equal in love and intelligent, and all things take their proper places as inevitably as the stars their orbits. Had there never been false and profane marriages, there would not only be no commotion about woman's rights, hut it would be Heaven here at once. Even before I was married, however, I could never feel the slightest interest in this movement. It then seemed to me that each woman could make her own sphere quietly, and also it was always a shock to me to have women mount the rostrum. Home, I think, is the great arena for women, and there, I am sure, she can wield a power which no king or conqueror can cope with. I do not believe any man who ever knew one noble woman would ever speak as if she were an inferior in any sense: it is the fault of ignoble women that there is any such opinion in the world."

Mrs. Peabody writes from very much the same standpoint:--

"Margaret Fuller's book has made a breeze, I assure you. Seems to me I could have written on the very same subjects, and set forth as strongly what rights yet belonged to woman which were not granted her, and yet have used language less offensive to delicacy, and put in clearer view the only source (vital religion) from which her true position in society can be estimated. A consistent Christian woman will be exactly what Margaret would have woman to be; and a consistently religious man would readily award to her every rightful advantage. I believe that woman must wait till the lion shall lie down with the lamb, before she can hope to be the friend and companion of man. He has the physical power, as well as conventional, to treat her like a play thing or a slave, and will exercise that power till his own soul is elevated to the standard set up by Him who spake as never man spoke. I think Margaret is too personal. It is always painful to me to hear persons dwell on what they have done and thought,--it is taxing human sympathy too heavily. It is still worse in a book designed for the public. The style, too, is very bad. How is it that one who talks so admirably should write so obscurely? The book has great faults, I think,--even the look of absolute irreligion,--yet it is full of noble thoughts and high aspirations. I wish it may do good; but I believe little that is high and ennobling can have other foundation than genuine Christianity."

I find no further allusion to Margaret in any of the American letters or journals; but fifteen years afterwards, when she was dead, and Hawthorne was in Rome, he came across some facts regarding her marriage which led him into the following interesting and not too eulogistic analysis of her character and career.

Extract from Roman Journal.

Mr. Mozier knew Margaret well, she having been an inmate of his during a part of his residence in Italy. . . .He says that the Ossoli family, though technically noble, is really of no rank whatever; the elder brother, with the title of Marquis, being at this very time a working bricklayer, and the sisters walking the streets without bonnets,--that is, being in the station of peasant-girls. Ossoli himself, to the best of his belief, was -----'s servant, or had something to do with the care of -----'s apartments. He was the handsomest man that Mr. Mozier ever saw, but entirely ignorant, even of his own language; scarcely able to read at all; destitute of manners,--in short, half an idiot, and without any pretension to be a gentleman. At Margaret's request, Mr. Mozier had taken him into his studio, with a view to ascertain whether he were capable of instruction in sculpture; but after four months' labor, Ossoli produced a thing intended to be a copy of a human foot, but the great toe was on the wrong side. He could not possibly have had the least appreciation of Margaret; and the wonder is, what attraction she found in this boor, this man without the intellectual spark, she that had always shown such a cruel and bitter scorn of intellectual deficiency. As from her towards him, I do not understand what feeling there could have been; as from him towards her I can understand as little, for she had not the charm of womanhood. But she was a person anxious to try all things, and fill up her experience in all directions; she had a strong and coarse nature, which she had done her utmost to refine, with infinite pains; but of course it could only be superficially changed. The solution of the riddle lies in this direction; nor does one's conscience revolt at the idea of thus solving it; for (at least, this is my own experience) Margaret has not left in the hearts and minds of those who knew her any deep witness of her integrity and purity. She was a great humbug,--of course, with much talent and much moral reality, or else she could never have been so great a humbug. But she had stuck herself full of borrowed qualities, which she chose to provide herself with, but which had no root in her. Mr. Mozier added that Margaret had quite lost all power of literary production before she left Rome, though occasionally the charm and power of her conversation would reappear. To his certain knowledge, she had no important manuscripts with her when she sailed (she having shown him all she had, with a view to his procuring their publication in America), and the "History of the Roman Revolution," about which there was so much lamentation, in the belief that it had been lost with her, never had existence. Thus there appears to have been a total collapse in poor Margaret, morally and intellectually; and, tragic as her catastrophe was, Providence was, after all, kind in putting her and her clownish husband and their child on board that fated ship. There never was such a tragedy as her whole story,-- the sadder and sterner, because so much of the ridiculous was mixed up with it, and because she could bear anything better than to he ridiculous. It was such an awful joke, that she should have resolved--in all sincerity, no doubt--to make herself the greatest, wisest, best woman of the age. And to that end she set to work on her strong, heavy, unpliable, and, in many respects, defective and evil nature, and adorned it with a mosaic of admirable qualities, such as she chose to possess; putting in here a splendid talent and there a moral excellence, and polishing each separate piece, and the whole together, till it seemed to shine afar and dazzle all who saw it. She took credit to herself for having been her own Redeemer, if not her own Creator; and, indeed, she was far more a work of art than any of Mozier's statues. But she was not working on an inanimate substance, like marble or clay; there was something within her that she could not possibly come at, to re-create or refine it; and, by and by, this rude old potency bestirred itself and undid all her labor in the twinkling of an eye. On the whole, I do not know but I like her the better for it; because she proved herself a very woman after all) and fell as the weakest of her sisters might.

During the greater part of the time that the Hawthornes were living in Concord) Dr. and Mrs. Peabody remained in their house in West Street, Boston; and the outward circumstances of their existence lacked a good deal of being luxurious. Though advanced in years, they were obliged to work for their daily bread; and it was only within a short distance of the close of their lives that they were able to enjoy even a partial and comparative repose. For several years they placed their main dependence upon what they called "the book-room,"--a combination of a circulating library and a book-shop,--which they fitted up on the ground floor of their house. This business was under the especial charge of Mrs. Peabody; and, though always an invalid, she gave, as might have been expected, a good account of her stewardship. She also contrived to do occasional work in the way of making translations of famous European books, which yielded some profit, though almost infinitesimal according to present standards. Meanwhile, those instincts of hospitality and philanthropy, which still characterize in undiminished degree the surviving members of Dr. Peabody's family, induced them to take under their protection all such persons as were content to live upon them without making any return for their entertainment; so that the house got the name of being a sort of hospital for incapables. Through it all, Mrs. Peabody maintained her cheerfulness and religious serenity. For reasons indicated above, I have collected in this place extracts from her letters written to her daughter during the nine years following the latter's marriage.

MY DEAR SOPHIA,--I think of you continually, but know that you have a guardian beyond price, who cares for you always. Your wood-pile will diminish rapidly this month. Do not be anxious on our account. God takes care of us: we are neither lazy nor extravagant; we are honest, and faithfully employ the talents given us, and I believe we shall not be left to beg our bread. I have finished transcribing

"Hermann and Dorothea" literally, and perhaps may, some future time, put it into purer English. It is beautiful. It is well that, as we must earn our bread by the sweat of our brows, there are some labors which occupy the mind profitably and keep it from preying on itself, as well as others which give vigor to physical existence by furnishing wholesome exercise in the open air. Now, traffic of any kind has neither of these advantages, and yet it must be attended to, and often by these who are worthy of better things. This seems to be an evil, but who knows but high moral results may flow from this most unattractive stream of human action? In one way I am sure good may come of it,--we may conquer by proper effort many of our worst propensities, and resolve to be high-minded, just, and generous, even in selling a book. Hard study is a blessing to me in many ways, and I feel indebted to it more than I can well explain, since I must be shut up in brick walls. How you must enjoy your woods and rivers and birds and flowers in the summer, and in winter even the pure snow. We shall be able to economize more than ever the coming year, because we have less time than ever to be lavish of hospitality. It has become an imperative duty for us no longer, as heretofore, to invite almost strangers to stay day after day and week after week. My feelings would impel me to say to all the good and to all the unfortunate, Come and find an asylum here. But, to be just before you are generous, I consider almost equal to the command, Do unto others as you would that others should do unto you."

YOUR MOTHER.

MY DEAREST,--I have a thousand things to say, which are silly perhaps, but mothers cannot always be wise. When I gave you up, my sweetest confidante, my ever lovely and cheering companion, I set myself aside and thought only of the repose, the fulness of bliss, that awaited you under the protection and in possession of the confiding love of so rare a being as Nathaniel Hawthorne. Still, my heart was at times rebellious, and sunk full low when I entered the rooms so long consecrated to you; and I had to reason with myself and say, "I have not lost her, but have gained a noble son, and we can meet often." I suppose you and yours will be flying to another hemisphere some of these years; but unless it be to recruit health, I must hope you will find charms enough in sober New England, where native Apollos and Platos spring up in your every-day walk.

"I am strong in hope that my day of usefulness will be protracted till some of our bairns can do as dear Wellington used to say he hoped to,--place me in an easy-chair at a comfortable fireside, to knit stockings, read, and write. Why not hope this, as well as torment one's self with fears of being a burden to any one? The idle and the vicious may be burdens; but the mother and father who have done their duty, have a claim to the kind offices of the beings to whom their lives have been devoted. Is it not so? Oh, dear, what a vexation--grief, I may say--is this want of Gold! Mr. Hawthorne, who is writing to make the world better, ought to see all that is doing in the world. He ought to mingle as much as possible with the human beings he is doing so much to cultivate and refine. . . . I was glad indeed to hear that your husband was better; but have you not influence enough to induce him to be more saving of his mental treasures? The whole country as well as his family possess that in him which cannot be replaced. This is simple truth, and he ought to listen and take heed. . . . If your husband knew the man about whom we wish him to use his powerful pens he would feel a holy joy in tracing the character of the incorruptible patriot, the ardent lover of freedom, the unwearied doer of public duties, the devoted husband and father, the indulgent master, the saint-like follower of his Divine Teacher, of whose spirit be was full. I never think of my grandfather Palmer without enthusiasm,--I should be ashamed of myself if I could. It is so rare to find a consistent Christian, that we ought to rejoice and be exceeding glad when we know that such a one has lived. By writing this sketch, the knowledge of your husband's inimitable style of composition will be more widely diffused, and he will confer a lasting obligation on all who love the memory of those who struggled for the birthright of man! . . .

"Mrs. Alcott has just come in to tell us about her house in Concord. It is at the entrance of a wood, two miles in a direct line to the river. She would enjoy Mr. Hawthorne's having it more than she can express; thinks the house would be forever honored; and, though she might never be so happy as to bear him speak, if she could sometimes see his inexpressibly sweet smile, it would be an enhancement of the value of her property only to be realized by those who know him. Thus she! . .

"Mr. Phillips, on reading 'The Procession of Life,' which calls forth praise everywhere, said that for the first time he comprehended the superior character of the writer, that he thought it a great production, and that he wished for a personal acquaintance. You know he is not a man who speaks unadvisedly, but is one on whom the purity, the high moral tone, the exquisite humor, of Mr. Hawthorne's style would have full effect. But what crude ideas some people have about talents, and genius, and taste, and love of literature! They cannot conceive them to be united with the every-day duties of life.

"I think 'The Celestial Railroad' capital. How skilfully he introduces the droppings of the sanctuary into everything he writes, without preaching or distraction! And what a sweet tale that of 'The Widows'! Who but Nathaniel Hawthorne could have written it? Who but he would have left the scenes of restored happiness to each individual reader? No language can do justice to the reality in such a case. Most sincerely do I wish that no thought of the body, wherewithal it may be fed and clothed, should ever stop the flight of such a mind into the region of the infinite. Still, we do not know what the effect of wealth and leisure might be. .

There is also the subjoined allusion to Fourier, to which is added Mrs. Hawthorne's reply:--

BOSTON, March 28, 1845.

The French have been and are still corrupt, and have lost all true ideas relative to woman. There is a sad tendency to the same evil among us. Why does not some *undoubted* man translate Fourier? Can the heavenly-minded W. H. Channing admire and follow an author whose books are undermining the very foundations of social order? Swedenborg, you know, has been misunderstood, and his doctrine corrupted. It is possible it may be so with Fourier's. This subject is often discussed in the book-room, and it is strange to me that among learned men, who are interested about public morals and our civil institutions, no one should take the trouble to read what Charles Fourier wrote. Time will prove, I trust; but many a young mind may be ruined first. I used to wish that I could take all my little ones and shelter them in some nook where God and trees and flowers should be all in all to them. But such feelings were momentary. It was not for this we were created. We must do our Father's work,--we must gird on His armor and fight with the spirit of Evil. Ours must not be negative virtue; therefore our darlings must do as we have done. We cannot hope to win an immortal crown merely by biding ourselves in a hermitage, where no temptations assail, where no virtue can be tested. All the tenderest parent can do is to watch, pray for, guide, and guard the immortals intrusted to them, and trust in God for the rest Is it not so, darling? But I must not preach. My vocation--now, at least--is buying and selling. . .

APRIL 6, 1845.
It was not a translation of Fourier that I read, but the original text,--the fourth volume; and though it was so abominable, immoral, irreligious, and void of all delicate sentiment, yet George Bradford says it is not so bad as some other volumes. Fourier wrote just after the Revolution; and this may account somewhat for the monstrous system he proposes, because then the people worshipped a naked woman as the Goddess of Reason. But I think that the terrific delirium that prevailed then with regard to all virtue and decency can alone account for the entrance of such ideas into Fourier's mind. It is very plain, from all I read (a small part), that he had entirely lost his moral sense. To make as much money and luxury and enjoyment out of man's lowest passions as possible, this is the aim and end of his system! To restrain, to deny, is not suggested, except, alas! that too great indulgence would lessen the riches, luxury, and enjoyment.

This is the highest motive presented for not being inordinately profligate. My husband read the whole volume, and was thoroughly disgusted. As to Mr. Theodore Parker, I think he is only a scholar, bold and unscrupulous, without originality. It seems to me that the moment any person thinks he is particularly original, and the private possessor of truth, he becomes one-sided and a monomaniac. No one can dam up the mighty flowing stream and secure private privileges upon it. It will be sure to break away the impertinent obstructions and ruin the property. . .

The last quotation from Mrs. Peabody's letters which I shall make in this chapter, speaks of the death of the painter Allston, who, it will be remembered, had taken an interest in Mrs. Hawthorne's (then Sophia Peabody's) artistic capacities.

"Mr. Allston is dead. What a light is extinguished! He had a party of friends who were to stay all night. At half-past ten, he took a most affectionate leave of each, and Mrs. Allston went upstairs with her guests to see them arranged for the night. Mr. Allston went into his little room, where he always had a small fire to warm his feet before going to bed, and to which he always retired, probably for devotion. After the guests were attended to, Mrs. Allston came down to see how Mr. Allston felt, for he had complained during the evening of a pain in his chest. He appeared to be asleep in his chair. She went to him, and found that the pure spirit had departed. He was dead. There could have been no struggle. He looked tranquil."

We may now take up the regular series of Mrs. Hawthorne's letters to her mother, up to the close of the Old Manse period. It would be a pity to encumber them with comment, and they need little if any explanation. They begin in October, 1842.

". . . Mr. Hawthorne's abomination of visiting still holds strong, be it to see no matter what angel. But he is very hospitable, and receives strangers with great loveliness and graciousness. Mr. Emerson says his way is regal, like a prince or general, even when at table he hands the bread. Elizabeth Hoar remarked that though his shyness was very evident, yet she liked his manner, because he always faced the occasion like a man, when it came to the point. Of what moment will it be, a thousand years hence, whether he saw this or that person? If he had the gift of speech like some others--Mr. Emerson, for instance--it would be different, but he was not born to mix in general society. His vocation is to observe and not to be observed. Mr. Emerson delights in him; he talks to him all the time, and Mr. Hawthorne looks answers. He seems to fascinate Mr. Emerson. Whenever he comes to see him, he takes him away, so that no one may interrupt him in his close and dead-set attack upon his ear. Miss Hoar says that persons about Mr. Emerson so generally echo him, that it is refreshing to him to find this perfect individual, all himself and nobody else.

"He loves power as little as any mortal I ever knew; and it is never a question of private will between us, but of absolute right. His conscience is too fine and high to permit him to be arbitrary. His will is strong, but not to govern others. He is so simple, so transparent, so just, so tender, so magnanimous, that my highest instinct could only correspond with his will. I never knew such delicacy of nature. His panoply of reserve is a providential shield and breastplate. I can testify to it now as I could not before. He is completely pure from earthliness. He is under the dominion of his intellect and sentiments. Was ever such a union of power and gentleness, softness and spirit, passion and reason? I think it must be partly smiles of angels that make the air and light so pleasant here. My dearest Love waits upon God like a child. . . ."

APRIL 20, 1843.

DEAREST MOTHER,--. . Sunday afternoon the birds were sweetly mad, and the lovely rage of song drove them hither and thither, and swelled their breasts amain. It was nothing less than a tornado of fine music. I kept saying, "Yes, yes, yes, I know it, dear little maniacs! I know there never was such an air, such a day, such a sky, such a God! I know it,--I know it!" But they would not be pacified. Their throats must have been made of fine gold, or they would have been rent with such rapture-quakes. Mary Bryan, our cook, was wild with joy. She had not heard any birds sing since she came from dear Ireland. "Oh, gracious! isn't it delicious, Mrs. Hawthorne? It revives my hort entirely!" I went into the orchard, and found my dear husband's window was open; so I called to him, on the strength of the loveliness, though against rules. His noble head appeared at once; and a new sun, and dearer, shone out of his eyes on me. But he could not come then, because the Muse had caught him in a golden net. At the end of Sunday evening came Ellery Channing, who was very pleasant, and looked brighter than he did last summer. We invited him to dine next day. It was dark and rainy; but he came, and stayed in the house with us till after tea, and was very interesting.

Mr. Hawthorne received a letter from James Lowell this week, in which was a proposal from Mr. Poe that he should write for his new magazine, and' also be engraved to adorn the first number! . . .

DECEMBER 27, 1843.

We had a most enchanting time during Mary the cook's holiday sojourn in Boston. We remained in our bower undisturbed by mortal creature. Mr. Hawthorne took the new phasis of housekeeper, and, with that marvellous power of adaptation to circumstances that he possesses, made everything go easily and well. He rose betimes in the mornings, and kindled fires in the kitchen and breakfast-room, and by the time I came down, the tea-kettle boiled, and potatoes were baked and rice cooked, and my lord sat with a book, superintending. Just imagine that superb head peeping at the rice or examining the potatoes with the air and port of a monarch! And that angelico riso on his face, lifting him clean out of culinary scenes into the arc of the gods. It was a magnificent comedy to watch him, so ready and willing to do these things to save me an effort, and at the same time so superior to it all, and heroical in aspect,--so unconsonant to what was about him. I have a new sense of his universal power from this novel phasis of his life. It seems as if there were no side of action to which he is not equal,--at home among the stars, and, for my sake, patient and effective over a cooking-stove.

Our breakfast was late, because we concluded to have only breakfast and dinner. After breakfast, I put the beloved study into very nice order, and, after establishing him in it, proceeded to make smooth all things below. When I had come to the end of my labors, my dear lord insisted upon my sitting with him; so I sat by him and sewed, while he wrote, with now and then a little discourse; and this was very enchanting. At about one, we walked to the village; after three, we dined. On Christmas day we had a truly Paradisiacal dinner of preserved quince and apple, dates, and bread and cheese, and milk. The washing of dishes took place in the mornings; so we had our beautiful long evenings from four o'clock to ten. At sunset he would go out to exercise on his wood-pile. We had no visitors except a moment's call from good Mrs. Prescott.

FEBRUARY 4, 1844.

In the papers it is said that there has not been so cold a January for a hundred years I think we are miracles to have survived that fortnight in this house. Were we not so well acclimated, we should probably have become pillars of ice. As it was, our thoughts began to hang in icicles, and my powers of endurance were frozen solid. Mary the cook, while washing in a cloud of steam, put her hand to her head, and found her hair all rough and stiff with hoar frost,--frozen steam! In her extreme desperation at the cold, she began to sing, and sang as loud as she could for several days. I walked out with my husband every day, and braved the enemy. But, oh, our noses! I shall certainly make muffs for them if any more such days come. But on the first of February there was 30-degree increase of temperature, which thawed our minds and made all things seem practicable. A flock of crows, whose throats had thawed, poured out a torrent of caws, as if they had been nearly choked by withholding them so long.

My husband has been reading aloud to me, afternoons and evenings, Macaulay's "Miscellanies," since he finished Shakspeare. Macaulay is very acute, a good hater, a sensible admirer, and one of the best simile-makers I know. His style is perfectly clear, though by no means perfect. His humor makes his grave topics shine quite pleasantly, but we do not always agree with his dicta.

I suspect that Mary's baby must have opened its mouth the moment it was born, and pronounced a School Report; for its mother's brain has had no other permanent idea in it for the last year. It will be a little incarnation of education systems, a human school.

The "Mary" here alluded to is Mrs. Hawthorne's sister, who married Horace Mann. She entered so unreservedly into her husband's educational schemes, that the above sally of imagination might not seem altogether beyond bounds.

On March 3, 1844, Mrs. Hawthorne's first child, Una, was born; and here is George S. Hillard's letter of congratulation upon that event:--

DEAR HAWTHORNE,--I heard yesterday, with great joy, of the happiness which has come upon your house and heart. I think you will now agree with me that the first child is the greatest event in life. Nothing else approaches it in its influences upon the mind and character. May God give you all the sweetness of my cup and none of its bitterness! As to the name of Una, I hardly know what to say. At first it struck me not quite agreeably, but on thinking more of it I like it better. The great objection to names of that class is that they are too imaginative. They are to be rather kept and hallowed in the holy crypts of the mind, than brought into the garish light of common day. If your little girl could pass her life in playing upon a green lawn, with a snow-white lamb, with a blue ribbon round its neck, all things would be in a "concatenation accordingly;" but imagine Sophia saying, "Una, my love, I am ashamed to see you with so dirty a face," or, "Una, my dear, you should not sit down to dinner without your apron." Think of all this, before you finally decide.

The Longfellows are very well and happy, and you will be glad to learn that there is a bud of unexpanded joy in store for them which will one day ripen and expand into such another perfect flower of bliss as now blooms upon your hearth. God bless the poets, and keep up their line to the end of time; for you are a poet and a true one, though not wearing the garb of verse. My love to Sophia, who I am sure is wearing meekly and gently her crown of motherhood.

Are you writing for Graham now?

Ever yours,

GEO. S. HILLARD.

The mother does not seem to have shared their friend's misgivings as to the prudence of challenging comparison with Spenser's heroine.

APRIL 4, 1844.

MY DEAREST MOTHER,--*I have no time*,--as you may imagine. I am baby's tire-woman, handmaiden, and tender, as well as nursing mother. My husband relieves me with her constantly, and gets her to sleep beautifully. I look upon him with wonder and admiration. He is with me all the time when he is not writing or exercising. I do not think I shall have any guests this spring and summer, for I cannot leave Baby a minute to enact hostess it is a sweet duty which must take precedence of all others.

Wednesday.--Dearest mother, little Una sleeps.

Thursday.--Dearest mother, yesterday little Una *waked* also, and I had to go to her. But she sleeps again this morning. She smiles and smiles and smiles, and makes grave remarks in a dovelike voice. Her eyelashes are longer every morning, and bid fair to be, as Cornelia said Mr. Hawthorne's were, "a mile long and curled up at the end." Her mouth is sweetly curved, and, as Mary the cook prettily says, "it has so many lovely *stirs* in it." Her hands and fingers--ye stars and gods! This is all as true and as much a fact as that twice three is six. Every morning when I wake and find the darling lying there, or hear the sound of her soft breathing, I am filled with joy and wonder and awe. God be praised for all the influences and teachings and inward inclinings that have kept for me upon the fruit of life the down and bloom. Thanks to you, blessed mother, for your lofty purity and delicacy of nature; to my father, who caused me to grow up with the idea that guilelessness and uprightness were matters of course in grownup gentlemen; to Elizabeth, who was to my childhood and first consciousness the synonym of goodness. Never can I forget to thank God for His beneficence.

Father [Dr. Peabody] has done everything for us. He has fixed my chamber-bell, mended the bellows, mended the rocking-chair,--that unfortunate arm, which was forever coming off. One day Mr. Hawthorne took hold of it, to draw it towards him; and as the crazy old arm came off in his hand, he threw himself into a despairing attitude, and exclaimed, " Oh, I will flee my country!" It was indescribably witty; I laughed and laughed. Well, father has split all the wood, taken down the partition in the kitchen, pasted all the torn paper on the walls, picked up the dead branches on the avenue, mended baby's carriage, mended the garden gate,--in short, I cannot tell you what he has not done, besides tending Una beautifully and making my fire in the mornings.

". . . Una observes all the busts and pictures, and Papa says he is going to publish her observations on art in one volume octavo next spring. She knows Endymion by name, and points to him if he is mentioned; and she talks a great deal about Michael Angelo's frescos of the Sibyls and Prophets, which are upon the walls of the dining-room. At the dinner-table she converses about Leonardo da Vinci's Madonna of the Bas Relief, which hangs over the fire-place. She now waves her hand in farewell with marvellous grace."

"Una, some time ago, began to say 'Adam!' a great deal; and lately she has taken to omitting the first syllable. She will take a book which I have given her for a plaything, and sit down and begin 'Dam--dam--dam,' often in dulcet tones, and then again as loudly and emphatically as if she were firing a cannon. I always say 'Adam' to remind her of her original pronunciation. I am anxious to enlarge her vocabulary, that she may have some variety of language in which to express her mind. But no words can express the comicality of hearing this baby utter that naughty word with those sweet little lips, and with such energy, and sometimes so aptly."

". . .Thank you for my sun-bonnet. My husband laughed greatly at the depth of it, and says that if I should wear it to the village, the ruffle would be there as soon as I turned out of our avenue; and he asked if he might walk before me in the hot summer days, so as to be benefited by the shade of the front part. He says he has not the smallest idea of my face at the end of the scoop,--it is entirely too far off."

MAY, 1845.

. . .The other day, when my husband saw me contemplating an appalling vacuum in his dressing-gown, he said he was "a man of the largest rents in the country, and it was strange he had not more ready money." Our rents are certainly not to he computed; for everything seems now to be wearing out all at once, and I expect the dogs will begin to bark soon, according to the inspired dictum of Mother Goose. But, somehow or other, I do not care much, because we are so happy. We

"Sail away

Into the region of exceeding Day,"

and the shell of life is not of much consequence. Had my husband been dealt justly by in the matter of his emoluments, there would not have been even this shadow upon the blessedness of our condition. But Horatio Bridge and Franklin Pierce came yesterday, and gave us solid hope. I had never seen Mr. Pierce before. As the two gentlemen came up the avenue, I immediately recognized the fine, elastic figure of the "Admiral." When he saw me, he took off his hat and waved it in the air, in a sort of playful triumph, and his white teeth shone out in a smile. I raised the sash, and he introduced "Mr. Pierce." I saw at a glance that he was a person of delicacy and refinement. Mr. Hawthorne was in the shed, hewing wood. Mr. Bridge caught a glimpse of him, and began a sort of waltz towards him. Mr. Pierce followed; and when they reappeared, Mr. Pierce's arm was encircling my husband's old blue frock. How his friends do love him! Mr. Bridge was perfectly wild with spirits. He danced and gesticulated and opened his round eyes like an owl. He kissed Una so vehemently that she drew back in majestic displeasure, for she is very fastidious about giving or receiving kisses. They all went away soon to spend the evening and talk of business. My impression is very strong of Mr. Pierce's loveliness and truth of character and natural refinement. My husband says Mr. Pierce's affection for and reliance upon him are perhaps greater than any other person's. He called him "Nathaniel," and spoke to him and looked at him with peculiar tenderness.

Mr. Bridge, on another occasion, had happened to call at the Old Manse when both Mrs. Hawthorne and Una were ill; and he took his departure after leaving the following playfully ironic note, in pencil, on the drawing-room table:--

"Mr. Bridge presents his compliments and his condolence to Mrs. Hawthorne, and begs to assure her that, out of the friendship he bears her, he can never presume to approach again a house where his presence is heralded by the sickness of the mistress. Mr. B. is unwilling that disease shall be any longer considered as his own premonitory symptom, and with sincere reluctance will henceforth deprive himself of a friendly intercourse in Concord, which, though promising great pleasure to him, brings only pain to his friend.

"Little Una, too, seems to have entered into an alliance with the weird sisters to keep the intruder off, and, though famed for her gentleness and amiability, cries at the very sight of her father's friend. Truly Mr. B. is a persecuted man; but he feared this would be the result of Hawthorne's marriage, as it was intimated in a former letter.

"What queer expedients Mrs. H. resorts to for driving off her husband's bachelor friends! A suspicious man would think that the lady was shamming, and that the child had been pinched by its father. But Mr. B. does not allow himself to entertain, much less to intimate, such an idea.

"Mr. B. closes with the hope that Mrs. H. will speedily recover her health; and, to promote that desirable object, he will leave by the earliest conveyance.

"THE MANSE, Jan. 5, 1845."

--In this year James Russell Lowell was married; and Mrs. Lowell wrote, from their home in Philadelphia, the letter which will be found below:--

PHILADELPHIA, Jan. 16, 1845.

MY DEAR SOPHIA,--I wished to write to you before I left home; but, in the hurry of those last hours, I had no time, and, instead of delicate sentiments, could only send you gross plum-cake, which I must hope you received.

We are most delightfully situated here in every respect, surrounded with kind and sympathizing friends, yet allowed by them to be as quiet and retired as we choose; but it is always a pleasure to know you can have society if you wish for it, by walking a few steps beyond your own door.

We live in a little chamber on the third story, quite low enough to be an attic, so that we feel classical in our environment; and we have one of the sweetest and most motherly of Quaker women to anticipate all our wants, and make us comfortable outwardly as we are blest inwardly. James's prospects are as good as an author's *ought* to be, and I begin to fear we shall not have the satisfaction of being so *very* poor after all. But we are, in spite of this disappointment of our expectations, the happiest of mortals or spirits, and cling to the skirts of every passing hour, although we know the next will bring us still more joy.

How is the lovely Una? I heard, before I left home, that she was sunning Boston with her presence, but I was not able to go to enjoy her bounty. James desires his love to Mr. Hawthorne and yourself, and sends a kiss to Una, for whom he conceived quite a passion when he saw her in Concord. I shall not ask you to write, for I know how much your time must be occupied. But I will ask you to bear sometimes in your heart the memory of

Your most happy and affectionate
MARIA LOWELL

--Also belonging to this period is a letter from Hawthorne's friend (and Una's godfather), John L. O'Sullivan. It refers to various projects for Hawthorne's political advancement, which, however, came to nothing at the time.

NEW YORK, March 21, 1845.

MY DEAR HAWTHORNE,--I have written to Bancroft again about the Salem P.O., though I do not believe Brown will be removed. Bancroft spoke of him as an excellent and unexceptionable man. I did not speak of the other places you named at Salem, because you say the emoluments are small. I named the following consulships,--Marseilles, Genoa, and Gibraltar. What would you say to go out as a consul to China with A. H. Everett? It seems to me that in your place I should like it; and the trade opening there would give, I should suppose, excellent opportunity for doing a business which would soon result in fortune. I have no doubt Una would be delighted to play with the Chinese pigtails for a few years, on such a condition. If the idea smiles at all to you, I will make more particular inquiries about its worth, and, if satisfactory, will apply for it, if neither of the others above-named is accessible. At any rate, something satisfactory shall be done for you. For the purpose of presenting you more advantageously, I have got Duyckinck to write an article about you in the April Democratic; and what is more, I want you to consent to sit for a daguerreotype, that I may take your head off in it. Or, if Sophia prefers, could not she make a drawing based on a daguerreotype? By manufacturing you thus into a Personage, I want to raise your mark higher in Polk's appreciation. The Boston Naval Office was forestalled,-Parmenter's appointment coming out immediately after. Bancroft suggested a clerkship only *en attendant* for the Smithsonian Librarianship. You underrate his disposition in the matter. I have received "P.'s Correspondence," though not till long after its date, owing to my absence. I will send you the money for it in a few days.

Your friend ever faithfully,

JOHN L. O'SULLIVAN.

--It had now become necessary to give up the Old Manse, and seek another home in Salem, Mr. Ripley resuming possession of the former abode.

SEPTEMBER 7, 1845.

MY BEST MOTHER,--My husband is writing, and I cannot now ask him about your suggestion for the transfer of our furniture. But he has said he could do everything there is to be done, and I think he could, with instructions; but it is rather hard for him to fasten his thoughts upon a dish, so as to dispose of it in the best manner, because that is not the tendency of his fancies. Nevertheless, he can by violent wrenching twist his imagination round a plate with the finest results. Dear mother, I assure you it is neither heroism nor virtue of any kind for me to be beyond measure thankful and blest to find shelter anywhere with my husband. Unceiled rafters and walls, and a pine table, chair, and bed would be far preferable with him, to an Albambra without him even for a few months. He and Una are my perpetual Paradise; and I besieged Heaven with prayers that we might not find it our duty to separate, whatever privations we must outwardly suffer in consequence of remaining together. Heaven has answered my prayers most bounteously. My first idea was that we would take the old kitchen in Mr. Manning's house, because I thought he would not ask so much for that as for the parlor; but Louisa says now that he would ask as much for the kitchen as for the parlor; so we will have the parlor. So now I shall have a very nice chamber, upon whose walls I can hang Holy Families, and upon the floor can put a pretty carpet. The three years we have spent here will always be to me a blessed memory because here all my dreams became realities. I have got gradually weaned from it, however, by the perplexities that have vexed my husband the last year, and made the place painful to him. If such an involved state of things had come upon him through any fault or oversight on his own part there would have been a solid though grim satisfaction in meeting it. But it was only through too great a trust in the honor and truth of others. There is owing to him, from Mr. Ripley and others, more than thrice money enough to pay all his debts; and he was confident that when be came to a pinch like this, it would not be withheld from him. It is wholly new to him to be in debt, and he cannot "whistle for it," as Mr. Emerson advised him to do, telling him that everybody was in debt, and that they were all worse than he was. His soul is too fresh with Heaven to take the world's point of view about anything. I regret this difficulty only for him; for in high prosperity I never should have experienced the fine temper of his honor, perhaps. But, the darker the shadow behind him, the more dazzlingly is his figure drawn to my sight. I must esteem myself happiest of women, whether I wear tow or velvet, or live in a log-cabin or in a palace. "Them is my sentiments!" . .

While his wife had thus been keeping up her version of the family records, Hawthorne, in addition to writing the "Mosses," had occasionally varied this imaginative work by a few pages of journal. Some of these pages have already seen the light in the published "Note-Books;" many are not to be published; there remain a few letters, and detached observations upon his wife, and upon some of the celebrities of Concord with whom he was brought in contact. The letters were written to his wife either while he was visiting his mother and sisters in Salem, or while she was with her mother in Boston. The journal extracts cover the first year of marriage, beginning in the summer of 1842.

". . Having made up my bunch of flowers, I return home with them to my wife, of whom what is loveliest among them are to me the imperfect emblems. My imagination twines her and the flowers into one wreath; and when I offer them to her, it seems as if I were introducing her to beings that have somewhat of her own nature in them. 'My lily, here are your sisters; cherish them'--this is what my fancy says, while my heart smiles, and rejoices at the conceit. Then my dearest wife rejoices in the flowers, and hastens to give them water, and arranges them so beautifully that they are glad to have been gathered, from the muddy bottom of the river, and its wet, tangled margin,--from among plants of evil smell and uncouth aspect, where the slimy eel and the frog and the black mud-turtle hide themselves,-- glad of being rescued from this unworthy life, and made the ornaments of our parlor. What more could the loveliest of flowers desire? It is its earthly triumph, which it will remember with joy when it blooms in the Paradise of flowers. . . . The chief event of the afternoon, and the happiest one of the day, is our walk. She must describe these walks; for where she and I have enjoyed anything together, I always deem my pen unworthy and inadequate to record it."

"My wife is, in the strictest sense, my sole companion, and I need no other; there is no vacancy in my mind, any more than in my heart. In truth, I have spent so many years in total seclusion from all human society, that it is no wonder if now I feel all my desires satisfied by this sole intercourse. But she has come to me from the midst of many friends and a large circle of acquaintance; yet she lives from day to day in this solitude, seeing nobody but myself and our Molly, while the snow of our avenue is untrodden for weeks by any footstep save mine; yet she is always cheerful. Thank God that I suffice for her boundless heart!"

". . . Dear little wife, after finishing my record in the journal, I sat a long time in grandmother's chair, thinking of many things; but the thought of thee, the great thought of thee, was among all other thoughts, like the pervading sunshine falling through the boughs and branches of a tree and tingeing every separate leaf And surely thou shouldst not have deserted me without manufacturing a sufficient quantity of sunshine to last until thy return. Art thou not ashamed?"

"Methinks my little wife is twin-sister to the Spring; so they should greet one another tenderly,--for they both are fresh and dewy, both full of hope and cheerfulness; both have bird-voices, always singing out of their hearts; both are sometimes overcast with flitting mists, which only make the flowers bloom brighter; and both have power to renew and re-create the weary spirit. I have married the Spring! I am husband to the month of May!"

"About nine o'clock (Sunday) Hillard and I set out on a walk to Walden Pond, calling by the way at Mr. Emerson's to obtain his guidance or directions. He, from a scruple of his external conscience, detained us till after the people had got into church, and then he accompanied us in his own illustrious person. We turned aside a little from our way to visit Mr. Hosmer, a yeoman, of whose homely and self-acquired wisdom Mr. Emerson has a very high opinion. He had a free flow of talk, and not much diffidence about his own opinions. . . . I was not impressed with any remarkable originality in his views, but they were sensible and characteristic. Methought, however, the good yeoman was not quite so natural as he may have been at an earlier period. The simplicity of his character has probably suffered by his detecting the impression he makes on those around him. There is a circle, I suppose, who look up to him as an oracle; and so he inevitably assumes the oracular manner, and speaks as if truth and wisdom were uttering themselves by his voice. Mr. Emerson has risked the doing him much mischief by putting him in print,--a trial which few persons can sustain without losing their unconsciousness. But, after all, a man gifted with thought and expression, whatever his rank in life and his mode of uttering himself, whether by pen or tongue, cannot he expected to go through the world without finding himself out; and as all such self-discoveries are partial and imperfect, they do more harm than good to the character. Mr. Hosmer is more natural than ninety-nine men out of a hundred, and is certainly a man of intellectual and moral substance. It would be amusing to draw a parallel between him and his admirer, Mr. Emerson, the mystic, stretching his hand out of cloud-land in vain search for something real; and the man of sturdy sense, all whose ideas seem to be dug out of his mind, hard and substantial, as he digs potatoes, carrots, beets, and turnips out of the earth. Mr. Emerson is a great searcher for facts, but they seem to melt away and become unsubstantial in his grasp."

"I find that my respect for clerical people, as such, and my faith in the utility of their office, decrease daily. We certainly do need a new Revelation, a new system; for there seems to be no life in the old one."

"Mr. Thoreau dined with us. He is a singular character,--a young man with much of wild, original nature still remaining in him; and so far as he is sophisticated, it is in a way and method of his own. He is as ugly as sin, long-nosed, queer-mouthed, and with uncouth and somewhat rustic, though courteous manners, corresponding very well with such an exterior. But his ugliness is of an honest and agreeable fashion, and becomes him much better than beauty. He was educated, I believe, at Cambridge, and formerly kept school in the town; but, for two or three years back, he has repudiated all regular modes of getting a living, and seems inclined to live a sort of Indian life,--I mean, as respects the absence of any systematic effort for a livelihood. He has been for some time an inmate of Mr. Emerson's family, and, in requital, he labors in the garden, and performs such other offices as may suit him, being entertained by Mr. Emerson for the sake of what true manhood may be in him. He says that Ellery Channing is coming back to Concord, and that he (Mr. Thoreau) has concluded a bargain in his behalf for the hire of a small house, with land, at $56 per year. I am rather glad than otherwise; but Ellery, so far as he has been developed to my observation, is but an imperfect substitute for Mr. Thoreau. Mr. Emerson, by the way, seems to have suffered some inconvenience from his experience of Mr. Thoreau as an inmate. It may well be that such a sturdy, uncompromising person is fitter to meet occasionally in the open air, than to have as a permanent guest at table and fireside. He is to leave Concord, and it is well on his own account; for, morally and intellectually, he does not seem to have found the guiding clew."

"Ellery Channing is one of those queer and clever young men, whom Mr. Emerson (that everlasting rejecter of all that is, and seeker for he knows not what) is continually picking up by way of a genius. Ellery, it appears looks upon his own verses as too sacred to be sold for money. Prose he will sell to the highest bidder; but measured feet and jingling lines are not to be exchanged for gold,--which, indeed, is not very likely to be offered for them."

--These two letters were both written from Salem:
MARCH 12, 1843.

DEAR WIFE,--I found our mother tolerably well; and Louisa, I think, in especial good condition for her; and Elizabeth comfortable, only not quite thawed. They speak of you and us with an evident sense that we are very happy indeed; and I can see that they are convinced of my having found the very little wife that God meant for me. I obey your injunctions, as well as I can, in my deportment towards them; and though mild and amiable manners are foreign to my nature, still I get along pretty well for a new beginner. In short, they seem content with your husband, and I am very certain of their respect and affection for his wife.

Take care of thy little self, I tell thee. I praise Heaven for this snow and "slosh," because it will prevent thee from scampering all about the city, as otherwise thou wouldst infallibly have done. Lie abed late, sleep during the day, go to bed seasonably, refuse to see thy best friend if either flesh or blood be sensible of the slightest repugnance, drive all trouble from thy mind, and, above all things, think continually what an admirable husband thou hast!

Mr. Upham, it is said, has resigned his pastorship. When he returned from Concord he told the most pitiable stories about our poverty and misery, so as almost to make it appear that we were suffering for food. Everybody that speaks to me seems tacitly to take it for granted that we are in a very desperate condition, and that a government office is the only alternative of the almshouse. I care not for the reputation of being wealthier than I am; but we never have been quite paupers, and need not have been represented as such.

Now, good-by. I thank God above all things that thou art my wife. Nobody but we ever knew what it is to be married. If other people knew it, this dull old earth would have a perpetual glory round about it.

--Hawthorne's debts, at this most impoverished period of his life, were of a ridiculously small amount,--not more than a popular magazine writer of the present day could work off by a few days' labor. But magazine prices were not at that time what they are now; and it was by no means unusual for contributors (and especially for Hawthorne) to be left without any remuneration whatever. Indeed, had this not been the case, the butcher and the grocer who had Nathaniel Hawthorne's name upon their books would never have had to wait for their money; for he never spent until after he had earned. However, these indispensable personages were all enabled to receipt their bills before their customer left Concord; and so everybody was made happy.

His next visit to his mother's home was made in the winter of 1844.

SALEM, Dec. 20, 1844.

SWEETEST PHOEBE,--It will be a week to-morrow since I left you. Our mother and sisters were rejoiced to see me, and wish me to stay here till after Christmas, which I think is next Wednesday; but I care little for festivals. My only festival is when I have you. But I suppose we shall not get home before the last of next week. If I had not known it before, I should have been taught by this separation that the only real life is to be with you, and to share all things, good or evil, with you. The time spent away from you is unsubstantial,--there is nothing in it; and yet it has done me good, in making me more conscious of this truth.

Give Una a kiss, and her father's blessing. She is very famous in Salem. We miss you and her greatly here in Castle Dismal. Louisa complains of the silence of the house; and not all their innumerable cats avail to comfort them in the least. When

Una and three or four or five other children are grown up and married off, you will have a little leisure, and may paint that Grecian picture which used to haunt your fancy. But then our grandchildren--Una's children and those of the others--will be coming upon the stage. In short, after a woman has become a mother, she may find rest in heaven, but nowhere else. I have been much affected by a little shoe of Una's, which I found on the floor. Does she walk well yet?

YOUR HUSBAND.

--There has been a good deal of speculation as to the precise nature of the episode which Hawthorne used, nine years later, to give color to the culminating scene of the "Blithedale" tragedy. I therefore print the record of it here, as it stands in his journal; and it shall conclude this chapter. The date, it will be noticed, is that of the first anniversary of his marriage.

"On the night of July 9, 1843, a search for the dead body of a drowned girl. She was about nineteen years old; a girl of education and refinement, but depressed and miserable for want of sympathy,--her family being an affectionate one, but uncultivated, and incapable of responding to her demands. She was of a melancholic temperament, accustomed to solitary walks in the woods. At this time she had the superintendence of one of the district schools, comprising sixty scholars, particularly difficult of management. Well, Ellery Channing knocked at the door, between nine and ten in the evening, in order to get my boat to go in search of the girl's drowned body. He took the oars, and I the paddle, and we went rapidly down the river, until, a good distance below the bridge, we saw lights on the bank, and the dim figures of a number of people waiting for us. Her bonnet and shoes had already been found on this spot, and her handkerchief, I believe, on the edge of the water; so that the body was probably at no great distance, unless the current (which is gentle and almost imperceptible) had swept her down.

"We took in General Buttrick, and a young man in a blue frock, and commenced the search; the General and the other man having long poles, with hooks at the end, and Ellery a hay-rake, while I steered the boat. It was a very eligible place to drown one's self. On the verge of the river there were water-weeds; but after a few steps the bank goes off very abruptly, and the water speedily becomes fifteen or twenty feet deep. It must be one of the deepest spots in the whole river; and, holding a lantern over it, it was black as midnight, smooth, impenetrable, and keeping its secrets from the eye as perfectly as mid-ocean would. We caused the boat to float once or twice past the spot where the bonnet, etc., had been found, carefully searching the bottom at different distances from the shore, but for a considerable time without success. Once or twice the pole or the rake caught in bunches of water-weed, which in the starlight looked like garments; and once Ellery and the General struck some substance at the bottom, which they at first mistook for the body, but it was probably a sod that had rolled in from the bank. All this time, the persons on the bank were anxiously waiting, and sometimes giving us their advice to search higher or lower, or at such and such a point. I now paddled the boat again past the point where she was supposed to have entered the river, and then turned it, so as to let it float broadside downwards, about midway from bank to bank. The young fellow in the blue frock sat on the next seat to me, plying his long pole.

"We had drifted a little distance below the group of men on the bank, when the fellow gave a sudden start. 'What's this?' cried he. I felt in a moment what it was; and I suppose the same electric shock went through everybody in the boat. 'Yes; I've got her!' said he; and, heaving up his pole with difficulty, there was an appearance of light garments on the surface of the water. He made a strong effort, and brought so much of the body above the surface that there could be no doubt about it. He drew her towards the boat, grasped her arm or hand, and I steered the boat to the bank, all the while looking at the dead girl, whose limbs were swaying in the water, close at the boat's side. The fellow evidently had the same sort of feeling in his success as if he had caught a particularly fine fish, though mingled, no doubt, with horror. For my own part, I felt my voice tremble a little, when I spoke, at the first shock of the discovery, and at seeing the body come to the surface, dimly, in the starlight. When close to the bank, some of the men stepped into the water and drew out the body; and then, by their lanterns, I could see how rigid it was. There was nothing flexible about it; she did not droop over the arms of those who supported her, with her hair hanging down, as a painter would have represented her, but was all as stiff as marble. And it was evident that her wet garments covered limbs perfectly inflexible. They took her out of the water and deposited her under an oak-tree; and by the time we had got ashore, they were examining her by the light of two or three lanterns.

"I never saw or imagined a spectacle of such perfect horror. The rigidity, above spoken of, was dreadful to behold. Her arms had stiffened in the act of struggling, and were bent before her, with the hands clenched. She was the very image of a death-agony; and when the men tried to compose her figure, her arms would still return to that same position; indeed, it was almost impossible to force them out of it for an instant. One of the men put his foot upon her arm, for the purpose of reducing it by her side; but in a moment it rose again. The lower part of the body had stiffened into a more quiet attitude; the legs were slightly bent, and the feet close together. But that rigidity--it is impossible to express the effect of it; it seemed as if she would keep the same position in the grave, and that her skeleton would keep it too, and that when she rose at the Day of Judgment, it would be in the same attitude.

"As soon as she was taken out of the water, the blood began to stream from her nose. Something seemed to have injured the eye; perhaps it was the pole when it first struck the body. The complexion was a dark red, almost purple; the hands were white, with the same rigidity in their clench as in all the rest of the body. Two of the men got water and began to wash away the blood from her face; but it flowed and flowed, and continued to flow; and an old carpenter, who seemed to be skilful in such matters, said that this was always the case, and that she would continue to 'purge,' as he called it, until her burial, I believe. He said, too, that the body would swell, by morning, so that nobody would know her. Let it take what change it might, it could scarcely look more horrible than it did now, in its rigidity; certainly she did not look as if she had gotten grace in the world whither she had precipitated herself but rather, her stiffened death-agony was an emblem of inflexible judgment pronounced upon her. If she could have foreseen, while she stood, at five o'clock that morning, on the bank of the river, how her maiden corpse would have looked, eighteen hours afterwards, and how coarse men would strive with hand and foot to reduce it to a decent aspect, and all in vain,--it would surely have saved her from the deed. So horribly did she look, that a middle-aged man, David Buttrick, absolutely fainted away, and was found lying on the grass at a little distance, perfectly insensible. It required much rubbing of hands and limbs to restore him.

"Meantime General Buttrick had gone to give notice to the family that the body was found; and others had gone in search of rails, to make a bier. Another boat now arrived, and added two or three more horror-struck spectators. There was a dog with them, who looked at the body; as it seemed to me, with pretty much the same feelings as the rest of us,--horror and curiosity. A young brother of the deceased, apparently about twelve or fourteen years old, had been on the spot from the beginning. He seemed not much moved, externally; but answered questions about his sister, and the number of the brothers and sisters (ten in all, with composure. No doubt, however, he was stunned and bewildered by the scene,--to see his sister lying there, in such terrific guise, at midnight, under an oak, on the verge of the black river, with strangers clustering about her, holding their lanterns over her face; and that old carpenter washing the blood away, which still flowed forth, though from a frozen fountain. Never was there a wilder scene. All the while, we were talking about the circumstances, and about an inquest, and whether or no it were necessary, and of how many it should consist; and the old carpenter was talking of dead people, and how he would as lief handle them as living ones.

"By this time two rails bad been procured, across which were laid some boards or broken oars from the bottom of the boat; and the body, being wrapt in an old quilt, was laid upon this rude bier. All of us took part in bearing the corpse or in steadying it. From the bank of the river to her father's house was nearly half a mile of pasture-ground, on the ascent of a hill; and our burden grew very heavy before we reached the door. What a midnight procession it was! How strange and fearful it would have seemed if it could have been foretold, a day before-hand, that I should help carry a dead body along that track! At last we reached the door, where appeared an old gray-haired man, holding a light; he said nothing, seemed calm, and after the body was laid upon a large table, in what seemed to be the kitchen, the old man disappeared. This was the grandfather. Good Mrs. Pratt was in the room, having been sent for to assist in laying out the body, but she seemed wholly at a loss how to proceed; and no wonder,--for it was an absurd idea to think of composing that rigidly distorted figure into the decent quiet of the coffin. A Mrs. Lee had likewise been summoned, and shortly appeared,--a withered, skin-and-bone-looking woman; but she too, though a woman of skill, was in despair at the job, and confessed her ignorance how to set about it. Whether the poor girl did finally get laid out, I know not; but can scarcely think it possible. I have since been told that on stripping the body they found a strong cord wound round the waist and drawn tight,--for what purpose is impossible to guess.

" 'Ah, poor child!'--that was the exclamation of an elderly man, as he helped draw her out of the water. I suppose one friend would have saved her; but she died for want of sympathy,--a severe penalty for having cultivated and refined herself out of the sphere of her natural connections.

"She is said to have gone down to the river at five in the morning, and to have been seen walking to and fro on the bank, so late as seven,--there being all that space of final struggle with her misery. She left a diary, which is said to exhibit (as her whole life did) many high and remarkable traits. The idea of suicide was not a new one with her; she had before attempted it, walking up to her chin in the water, but coming back again, in compassion to the agony of a sister who stood on the bank. She appears to have been religious and of a high morality.

"The reason, probably, that the body remained so near the spot where she drowned herself, was that it had sunk to the bottom of perhaps the deepest spot in the river, and so was out of the action of the current."

CHAPTER 7 - SALEM

FOUR years in his native town of Salem succeeded Hawthorne's four years' residence in Concord. The period is externally definable as that in which he held the post of Surveyor in the Salem Custom House, and wrote "The Scarlet Letter." In its more interior aspect it was a season of ripened manhood, of domestic happiness and sorrow, of the bringing-up of children, of the broadening and deepening of character. The country was exchanged for the town; and something symbolical, perhaps, may be divined in the change. The man was made to feel, more intimately than heretofore, the strength and beauty of human sympathies; and the lovely experience of married happiness which he enjoyed, raised him to a moral standpoint from which he was enabled clearly to discern and state the nature and consequences of unfaithfulness, which form the theme of his memorable romance.

The Hawthornes occupied, in succession, three houses during their Salem residence. The first was the old family mansion in Herbert Street, where they had for fellow-inmates Madame Hawthorne and the two sisters, Elizabeth and Louisa. This proved inconvenient; and they afterwards rented, for a short time, a house in Chestnut Street. Their third and final abode was in Mall Street; and here there was room enough for the accommodation of Hawthorne's mother and sisters in a separate part of the house, so that the two families were enabled to carry on their respective existences with no further contact than might be voluntary on their part. It was in this house that Madame Hawthorne died; and not long after that event, Hawthorne, no longer one of the obscurest men of letters in America, but the author of one of America's most famous novels, removed to Lenox, in the county of Berkshire, Massachusetts.

The Salem letters and journals which constitute the bulk of this chapter are full of references to Hawthorne's children,--to the daughter, Una, born in Concord, and to the son, Julian, who came into the world two years later. Some of these references the biographer has thought fit to retain. A human being before he or she becomes a self-conscious individual possesses a certain charm which every humane person acknowledges, for the very reason that it is a natural and spontaneous charm, instead of being the result of character. There is something universal in it; the doings and sayings of a child, so far as they are childlike, are the doings and sayings of all children. The consideration which has weight in the present instance, however, is by no means the value to the biography of the children themselves. That could, at best, be but very small; it would be limited to such reflection of the parents' characteristics as might be perceived or imagined in the offspring. But the attitude of the father and mother towards their children, the manner of their dealings with them, and the calling-forth in the former of traits and phases of nature and character which are manifested only in response to the children's demand,--these are considerations which no biographer can afford to neglect; on the contrary, he may deem himself fortunate when he finds such material at hand. Moreover, Nathaniel Hawthorne and his wife so merged their own personal aims and desires in the welfare and interests of their children, that it would be impossible to give an intelligible picture of their domestic career, were the children to be blotted out of it.

The writer offers this explanation less out of a desire to shield his own modesty than in order to protect the vicarious delicacy and fastidiousness of a certain class of readers; and, in the hope that his attempt has not been unsuccessful, will proceed with his narrative.

Early in the new year Mrs. Hawthorne wrote to her mother:--

SALEM, HERBERT ST., January, 1846.

. . Una's force is immense. I am glad to see such will, since there is also a fund of loveliness. No one, I think, has a right to break the will of a child, but God; and if the child is taught to submit to Him through love, all other submission will follow with heavenly effect upon the character. God never drives even the most desperate sinner, but only invites or suggests through the events of His providence. I remember my own wilfulness, and how I used to think, when quite a child, that God was gentle and never frowned upon me, and that I would try more and more to be gentle to everybody in gratitude to Him, though they were not gentle to me. Una has her father's loveliness of nature, added to what little I possessed; and so I hope her task will be less difficult.

I have made my husband a new writing-gown,--one of those palm-leaf Moscow robes,--his old one being a honeycomb of holes. He looks regal in it. Purple and fine linen become him so much that I cannot bear to see him tattered and torn. And now I have almost arranged his wardrobe for a year to come, so that he can begin all over new again. He never lets me get tired. He arrests me the moment before I do too much, and he is then immitigable; and I cannot obtain grace to sew even an inch more, even if an inch more would finish my work. I have such rich experience of his wisdom in these things, that whatever may be the inconvenience, I gratefully submit.

We have not yet made any arrangements for the summer. On many accounts it would be inconvenient to remain in this house. Madame Hawthorne and Louisa are too much out of health to take care of a child, and I do not like to have Una in the constant presence of unhealthy persons. We have never let her go into Madame Hawthorne's mysterious chamber since November, partly on this account, and partly because it is so much colder than the nursery, and has no carpet on it. We cannot go to Boston to live, for it would not suit my husband's arrangements, and I would rather live in a tub than where he is not.

--One of the present biographer's earliest recollections is of his father's palm-leaf dressing-gown, and of the latter's habit of wiping his pen upon the red flannel lining of it. At length his wife made a cloth pen-wiper in the form of a butterfly, and surreptitiously sewed it on in the blackest centre of the ink-stains, much to Mr. Hawthorne's gratification and amusement. Here is another letter, bearing date March 22, 1846:--

DEAREST MOTHER,--I am glad you approve of our plan of a temporary residence in Boston. There is only one solitary drawback, and this is the occasional absence of my husband, should he enter his official station before we return to Salem. But he will only be absent in the morning, so that I shall see him as much as now. As for Una, she will throw a light on the sunshine for you this summer. Every day she has greater command of expression. Of late, a nice sense of propriety has found utterance in her. Last evening, after I had been picking down the wick of a lighted lamp, she said with the most tender and protecting air, "Has oo burned oosef, mamma? Oo must take tare and not burn oosef, betause it is not proper to burn oosef." At table she says, "A little water, if oo please, papa; and be tareful not spill, betause it is not proper to spill water on the tloth, papa."

--The appointment to the "official station" came the next day.

MARCH 23.

THIS morning we had authentic intelligence that my husband is nominated, by the President himself, for Surveyor of the Custom House. It is now certain, and so I tell it to you. Governor Fairfield wrote the letter himself. The salary is twelve hundred dollars.

Will you ask father to go to Earle's and order for Mr. Hawthorne a suit of clothes: the coat to be of broadcloth, of six or seven dollars a yard; the pantaloons of kerseymere or broadcloth of quality to correspond; and the vest of satin,--all to be black?

--An inscrutable destiny had decreed that Mr. Hawthorne's next child should be born in Boston, and accordingly the summer and autumn of this year were spent in a house in Carver Street in that city. Afterwards the family went back to Salem, and lived awhile in the Chestnut Street dwelling. Towards the beginning of the winter Mrs. Hawthorne wrote:--

SALEM, Nov. 17, 1846.

My husband sees the actual bearings of things with wonderful precision, though some would suppose him "of imagination all compact." But those of whom Shakspeare spoke were probably as many-sided as Mr. Hawthorne; for people who fail in imagination are apologies for men, like the poor wronged horses with side-blinders. If I had a hundred thousand of the dead Dudley L. Pickman's fifteen hundred thousand dollars, I would do several things for my friends. But instead of a hundred thousand dollars, we shall not have a cent over our expenses this year, both because we had to spend more in Boston, and because Custom House fees have been unusually small this summer, and government is abominably remiss in paying the "constructed fees" due the officers.

As to Baby, his cheeks, eyes, and limbs affirm enormous well-being. He weighs twenty-three pounds, which is within two pounds of Una's weight when she was eighteen months old,--and he is not quite five months old. His mighty physique is not all fat, but he is modelled on a great plan in respect to his frame. Una looks like a fairy golden-hair beside him: she is opaline in lustre and delicacy.

I wish you would tell Mr. Cheney that Mr. Hawthorne was never so handsome as now, and he must come directly and draw him.

Yesterday we went to Mrs. Forrester's to see an old book once belonging to our distinguished ancestor William Hathorne, 1634. Rachel Forrester is making out a genealogical tree of the Hawthorne race. In the evening my husband and I spent an hour and a half at Mr. Howes', with Mr. Emerson while Louisa Hawthorne and Dora kept watch here. It is the first time we have spent the evening out since Una was born. . . .

--Here is a passage which throws light upon Mr. Hawthorne's taste in the matter of female attire:--

APRIL 23, 1847.

The dark purple mousseline which I wore in Boston I have had to give up; for my husband all at once protested that he could not see me in it any longer, and that he hated it beyond all endurance. He begged me to give it to Dora and to pay her for accepting it! Dora made it, you know, and admired it exceedingly, and needed it very much, and was made quite happy by possessing it. I only regret it because a certain beloved Fairy sent it to me from Fairy Land; but this is a secret, and you must not ask me any questions about it. Mr. Hawthorne does not like to see me wear dark materials, and he is truly contented only when I shine in silk.

We have not a house yet. That house in Bridge Street is unattainable. We may have to stay here during the summer, after all. Birds do visit our trees in Chestnut Street, and Una talks incessantly about flowers, birds, and fields. She is a perfect little Idyl of the Spring,--a Pastoral Song.

--The new house was not discovered until six or seven months later; but its suitableness, when found, seems to have compensated for the delay. The mention of the study (in Mrs. Hawthorne's subjoined description of it) suggests the remark that Hawthorne did a good deal of literary work in Salem in addition to "The Scarlet Letter." It was in the Mall Street house that "The Snow Image" and some of the other tales included in the volume bearing that title, were written. Still, the productiveness of these years is not to be compared with that of the period following the publication of his first great Romance.

SALEM, Sept. 10, 1847.

How glad you will be, dear mother, to hear that we are to have the Mall Street house, and for $200! We shall move this month, and Una will have the splendid October to live out of doors on a smiling earth. There could not be anything more convenient for us in almost all respects. The middle parlor I am going to live in, because it will save going up and down stairs, both for me and my handmaiden, who will be close at hand in her kitchen across the entry; and because it will save much wood to have no separate nursery, and because there is no other room for a nursery unless I take the drawing-room or the guest-chamber in the third story. The little room next the parlor will hold all the rubbish of a nursery, so that I can keep the parlor very nice, - and this parlor overlooks the yard and garden, so that I can watch Una all the time she is out of doors. Our chamber is to be the room I have named the drawing-room, because it will be so mightily convenient to have all on one floor. The house is single in depth, and so we shall bask in sunshine all the winter. The children will have a grand race-course on rainy days from the end of the chamber to the end of the pantry. My husband's study will be high from all noise, and it will be to me a Paradise of Peace to think of him alone and still, yet within my reach. He has now lived in the nursery a year without a chance for one hour's uninterrupted musing, and without his desk being once opened! He--the heaven-gifted Seer--to spend his life between the Custom House and the nursery! I want him to be with me, not because he must be, but only when he is just in the mood for all the scenes of Babydom. In the evening he is always mine, for then he never wishes to write.

By this arrangement I expect to have a very easy time, and also to have some TIME. Our drawing-room will be above the chamber; but it will be, at present, unfurnished, because we have nothing to put into it, and cannot now afford to buy any furniture. I wish we could chance to get furniture as cheaply as Mary did at some auction, yet so pretty and new. But we cannot get any now.

It will be very pleasant to have Madame Hawthorne in the house. Her suite of rooms is wholly distinct from ours, so that we shall only meet when we choose to do so. There are very few people in the world whom I should like or would consent to have in the house even in this way; but Madame Hawthorne is so uninterfering, of so much delicacy, that I shall never know she is near excepting when I wish it; and she has so much kindness and sense and spirit that she will be a great resource in emergencies. Elizabeth is an invisible entity. I have seen her but once in two years; and Louisa never intrudes. Being responsible persons, also, I can leave one of the children with them, when I take the other out to walk; and it is barely possible that I may take a real walk with my husband again while in the body, and leave both children at home with an easy mind. It is no small satisfaction to know that Mrs. Hawthorne's remainder of life will be glorified by the presence of these children and of her own son. I am so glad to win her out of that Castle Dismal, and from the mysterious chamber into which no mortal ever peeped, till Una was born, and Julian,--for they alone have entered the *penetralia*. Into that chamber the sun never shines. Into these rooms in Mall Street it blazes without stint. . .

SOPHIA.

--In picturesque contrast with the matter-of-fact conditions of existence in the old New England town, is the following picture of Italy, from the pen of George William Curtis, which had reached them during the summer, and which is too pleasant and characteristic to be omitted.

SALERNO, May 4, 1847.

MY DEAR FRIEND,--Yesterday I went to Paestum, and had a Grecian day. When I am at beautiful places here in Italy, I am attended by troops of invisible friends, and all day yesterday I was thinking of you; so while the Mediterranean rolls and plunges under my window in this little town below Naples, I can look upon the dim, dark line, fancy you upon the other shore, and send this shout across, which, in telling you of the rare delight which I experienced yesterday, will tell you how constantly you are remembered in a country which is only more beautiful with every new day.

I left Naples with Burril and two other young artists last Friday, for an excursion of some two or three weeks among the mountains upon the seashore, where Salvator Rosa studied, and in whose magnificent heights and ravines and arching rocks, through which the sea sleeps far away, the eye constantly detects the kindred of the bold landscapes it has admired of that most picturesque of picture-makers. Intricate mountain paths wind over these ravines, in whose bases, as at home, foam and gurgle silver swift streams, and whose opening vista is broad and calm upon steep pointed hills, whose highest summits are square with convents and castles. Along these paths creep the dark-haired, gypsy-like women, bearing burdens upon their heads, so heavy that I cannot lift them. These weights must injure the brain, so that whole races deteriorate. The toiling processions pause at the small square stone shrines of the Madonna; and some lay a few flowers gathered from the mountain-side before the mild-featured portrait of the Virgin, others fall upon their knees and say an *Ave Maria;* the men raise their hats as they pass, and the half-conscious expression of reliance upon and relations with an unseen beauty and bounty is very beautiful. The Italians are too poetic a people to acknowledge or enjoy a religion which is not altogether picturesque and impressive to the imagination. And how much the Catholic Church is so, one does not realize until he sits here in the very spray of the fountain.

The mountains are a continual succession of nests, like those in Northwestern Massachusetts, and the town where we were lies on a plain as fertile as the Connecticut banks, with a green of spring more lustrous and intense than we see in New England. From the little town of Cava we came here on Sunday morning, riding upon a road which is scooped out of a mountain which slopes into the sea,--for the whole coast here is of that character. All day Sunday I loitered along the shore; and at daybreak yesterday morning we were off for Paestum, which is some twenty-five miles south of Salerno. We drove over a wide plain between the mountains and the sea, which as we came into Calabria was very gloomy and dreary. At first there were a few vineyards, arranged differently from those in Tuscany. There the vines are trained over short yawning-boughed trees; here they are festooned in long garlands from tree to tree. We reached Paestum about nine o'clock. It was one of the oldest Italian cities known to history. Augustus visited its remains as antiquities; and the three temples were long forgotten, buried alive in the desolation of the country, until they were discovered, a century since, by a young Neapolitan artist. They are near the great road and in plain sight; but the people around are so miserably ignorant and wretched, that they would be as much interested and surprised by the mountains or the sea as by structures which seemed coeval and of equal majesty with them. The ancient town was always unhealthy. Its walls were but two and a half miles in circumference; and of the whole city only three temples, an arched gateway, a few rods of grass-grown wall, and some fragments of stone called an amphitheatre, alone remain. But the temples are the oldest and most perfect ruins in Europe. Two of them stand side by side, the other an eighth of a mile distant. The middle one is called of Neptune, under whose protection the city is supposed to have been, and whose Grecian name it bore,--Poseidon. The two others are called of Ceres, and a Basilica. The temple and the arch are in the grandest and simplest and purest taste; I have never before seen buildings which stood in a proper breadth and grandeur of space. The sea lies a mile away over the plain; on the other side are stern mountains, their bases smoothly green with the rounding tufts of olive groves. The plain in many parts is uninhabitable from the stagnant waters which breed the most deadly miasmas. Yet it is matted around the temples with the rankest luxuriance of weeds and plants, which lace and choke each other, covered with the most profuse variety of deeply colored flowers. Everywhere it is desolate and sad. A young man who had been there for a few days gave me mournful accounts of the poverty and misery of the people, who are all beggars, and who contract horrible diseases from the famine and malaria. In early June the proprietors who own the land retire to the mountains for the summer, leaving those who cannot afford to go to the mercy of the deadly atmosphere and the most griping want. All the children came begging, with prematurely old faces, heavy, sick eyes, and an unnatural prominence of the stomach which was horrible. Two little girls moaned to me, one of whom had only a battered nightgown and a heavy woollen wrapper to protect her head and body from the sun, which yesterday, in the first days of May, was very intense. I saw several children eating a root which looked and smelt like a rank weed; and I realized the misery of Ireland, except that there are thousands, and here a few dozens. Droves of cattle and flocks of sheep and goats passed silently and heavily by, followed by the taciturn, wondering peasant, who stopped and looked curiously upon the strangers; and in the late afternoon an old beggar sat under the arch of the gateway, and displayed a picture of the Blessed Mary, in whose name he gasped for charity.

We lingered the whole day among the ruins, in the temples, or lying a little way from them on beds of the most honey-breathed clover, which made the air sweet enough for all the gorgeous blossoms that hung and nodded among it. I have never seen any building so exquisite as the Temple of Neptune. It is like a strain of music; and the satisfaction in looking upon it was complete and rapturous, like that of seeing finest flowers and pictures and sunsets and fruits and statues. It stands so firm and free in the air, an unimpaired witness of the Grecian grandeur in art. I have not seen anything that inspired in me more reverence for human genius; and I could well fancy that Time would not prey upon a form so delicately perfect, which draws upon the flowery plain, midway between the mountains and the sea, lines as aerial as their own. It defies Nature and her withering years. Birds were singing in and around it, and wheeling above it in long sweeping lines, which seemed transfixed in the temple's flowing grace. We must feel that the Greeks are yet our masters in those arts and aims which are still the best; and could you have seen that temple in the sunny silence of the fresh May morning, I am sure that you would have thrilled with the consciousness that your ideas of Grecian grace and culture were buds only, when measured by this flower.

Paestum was famous in history and poetry for its roses, and I plucked a few buds, which I hope will be well enough preserved for me to offer Mrs. Hawthorne when I return to America. But how return from a life which is so constantly new and charming? I left Rome three weeks since, only comforted because I promised myself to return, and found Naples sunny and sauntering, quite as beautiful although so different,--having no association to interest, but spacious and sunny, with an unending series of pictures upon its bay; for the bay of Naples is as beautiful as its fame. Its lines are long and grand,--mountain and sea lines; and you have lived too long upon the seashore not to know that it is dower enough for any situation. Naples is a lazy Italian Paris upon these sunny shores. There is a great appearance of business, but it is only the bustle of laziness riding to its enjoyment. Upon the shore the streets are wide, and the Royal Villa or Promenade stretches for half a mile upon the water, tastefully and carefully arranged, with fine copies of the noblest statues so placed under trees and among flowers that their beauty is greater, and art is dignified by their harmonious blending with the line of the waves and clouds and trees. Handsome women and children walk and play among the trees, and it is by far the finest public walk I have seen in Italy.

During the last part of my Roman residence I became much acquainted with and fascinated by a boy of some nine or ten years, named John Risley, who is an American, and who, with his father and younger brother, has acquired great fame in Europe as a gymnast. They play at all the great theatres; and while I have often seen wonderful feats of strength and skill, I have never seen any human motion, not excepting Fanny Ellsler's dancing, so flowingly graceful as this boy's. I went constantly to see them, particularly him, in Rome, and could not resist knowing him. We walked a great deal together. I saw him constantly, and found him noble and affectionate, with all the elements of the finest manly character. Whether he will be such a man as he is boy, I doubt; for his father, although a perfect physical man, is not refined or gentle, and necessarily has a great influence upon my boy. During the time, too, I felt the full fascination of the heads of Antinous in the Vatican, and realized the pure deep love he could have inspired. I speak of Risler because they return to America during the summer, and after one tour through the United States will retire from the stage; and I hoped that Una might be old enough to realize her fairy love in his beautiful motions. Margaret Fuller reached Rome about a fortnight before I left. She seems well, and it was very pleasant to hear her stories of the famous men she has seen in France and England,--because I see no men and she sees them always so well. I liked her more than I ever did. I hope to find her on my return to Rome, if Southern Italy does not charm us too long. Cranch, also, I left in Rome. Did you know that he is a father of a month's standing, and that his son bears my name? Mr. Emerson's poems have reached these benighted shores; but I find that he has published all the best, except the "Threnody." Ellery Channing's I have not seen. In the dearth of newspapers I gradually drift away from all knowledge of what is going on in the book way at home; but beyond the confines of newspaper reading lie many good things. On Vesuvius I saw the grandest daybreak and sunrise. I go on no mountain-tops now without remembering Wachusett. Pompeii, too, is unspeakably solemn and imposing. We think at home that we know something of these things, but it is only the imagination of mountain prospects from the valley below. Ascend into this Italian heaven, and you shall find all shackles of men and customs fall away like clouds at sunrise. The want of the public opinion which is the safeguard at home is the security of satisfaction here.

Give much love to Mrs. Hawthorne and Una.

G. W. CURTIS.

NATH. HAWTHORNE, Esq., Salem, Mass.

--Life now went on smoothly for a time, from a worldly as well as from a spiritual point of view. The Surveyor's salary was sufficient unto the day, if not unto the future; and the surroundings were congenial. Change of air is uniformly beneficial; and, after a season in the rarefied atmosphere of Emerson and Margaret Fuller, it was wholesome to seek temporary relaxation on the levels of ordinary humanity. Mrs. Hawthorne writes (November, 1847):

My husband began retiring to his study on the 1st of November, and writes every afternoon. Have you seen the most exquisite of reviews upon 'Evangeline,' very short, but containing all? Evangeline is certainly the highest production of Mr. Longfellow.

Julian was seventeen months old yesterday, and walked to the Common on his little feet, with Dora, while Una had gone to walk with her father. They met, and I went to the gate and saw them returning together, Julian taking hold of his father's and Una's hands, and Una shining with joy at taking the first walk with Julian. Oh, am I not happy? I am, I am!' as the Peri sang when she opened Heaven's gate with a tear; (my husband says, 'That is, she tore it open!') Julian idolizes his father, and will not come to me when he is in the room. Una is full of surprising stories. The other day she told one about a little girl who was naughtier and naughtier, and finally, as a culmination of wickedness, 'struck God'.' I could not help thinking how many people 'struck God.'

"We have been surprised by a visit from Ellery Channing. He stayed but two hours, and was as entertaining and inexplicable as ever, making himself welcome by his wonderful smile. He said that Mr. Emerson had become a man of the world more, and that he was not so easy of access as formerly."

--About this time the family journal, begun in Concord, seems to have turned up again; but its pages are now devoted almost exclusively to chronicling the exploits of the two children. Hawthorne himself, quite as often as his wife, acted the part of reporter; and it would be instructive to contrast the style and the quality of the insight of the two observers. The mother sees goodness and divinity shining through everywhere; the father's attitude is deductive and moralizing. After following them through all the vicissitudes of a day, for example, there comes this passage:--

"SALEM, *1/4 of 8 o'clock, March,* 1848.--I have just been for a walk round Buffum's corner, and returning, after some half an hour's absence, find Una and Julian gone to bed. Thus ends the day of these two children,--one of them four years old, the other some months less than two. But the days and the years melt away so rapidly that I hardly know whether they are still little children at their parents' knees, or already a maiden and a youth, a woman and a man. This present life has hardly substance and tangibility enough to be the image of eternity. The future too soon becomes the present, which, before we can grasp it, looks back upon us as the past. It must, I think, be only the image of an image. Our next state of existence, we may hope, will be more real,--that is to say, it may be only one remove from a reality. But, as yet, we dwell in the shadow cast by time, which is itself the shadow cast by eternity."

--During the ensuing summer Mrs. Hawthorne made a visit of a few weeks to her mother in Boston, taking the children with her; and while she was away, her husband wrote her the two following letters:--

SALEM, SURVEYOR'S OFFICE, June 19, 1848.

ONLY BELOVEDEST,--I received thy letter, and was as much refreshed by it as if it had been a draught of ice-water,--a rather inapt comparison, by the way. Thou canst not imagine how lonely our house is. I wish, some time or other, thou wouldest let me take the two children and go away for a few days, and thou remain behind. Otherwise thou canst have no idea of what it is. And after all, there is a strange bliss in being made sensible of the happiness of my customary life by this blank interval.

Tell my little daughter Una that her dolly, since her departure, has been blooming like a rose,--such an intense bloom, indeed, that I rather suspected her of making free with a brandy-bottle. On taxing her with it, however, she showed no signs of guilt or confusion, and I trust it was owing merely to the hot weather. The color has now subsided into quite a moderate tint, and she looks splendidly at a proper distance, though, on close inspection, her skin appears rather coarse. She has contracted an unfortunate habit of squinting, and her mouth, I am sorry to say, is somewhat askew. I shall take her to task on these matters, and hope to produce a reformation. Should I fail, thou must take her in hand. Give Una a kiss, and tell her I love her dearly.

THINE OWNEST HUSBAND.

SALEM, July 5, 1848.

UNSPEAKABLY BELOVEDEST,--Thy letter has just been handed to me. It was most comfortable to me, because it gives such a picture of thy life with the children. I could see the whole family of my heart before my eyes, and could hear you all talking together.

I went to town, and got home here between eleven and twelve o'clock at night. I went into the little room to put on my linen coat, and, on my return to the sitting-room, behold! a stranger there,--whom dost thou think it might be? --it was my sister Elizabeth! I did not wish to risk frightening her away by anything like an exhibition of wonder; and so we greeted each other kindly and cordially, but with no more *empressement* than if we were constantly in the habit of meeting. It being so late, and I so tired, we did not have much talk then; but she said she meant to go to walk this afternoon, and asked me to go with her, which I promised to do. Perhaps she will now make it her habit to come down and see us occasionally in the evening.

The other night, I dreamt that I was at Newton, in a room with thee and with several other people and thou tookst occasion to announce that thou hadst now ceased to be my wife, and hadst taken another husband. Thou madest this intelligence known with such perfect composure and *sang-froid,--* not particularly addressing me, but the company generally,--that it benumbed my thoughts and feelings, so that I had nothing to say. But, hereupon, some woman who was there present, informed the company that, in this state of affairs, having ceased to be thy husband, I had become hers, and, turning to me, very coolly inquired whether she or I should write to inform my mother of the new arrangement How the children were to be divided, I know not. I only know that my heart suddenly broke loose, and I began to expostulate with thee in an infinite agony, in the midst of which I awoke. But the sense of unspeakable injury and outrage hung about me for a long time, and even yet it has not quite departed. Thou shouldst not behave so when thou comest to me in dreams.

Oh, Phoebe, I want thee much. Thou aft the only person in the world that ever was necessary to me. Other people have occasionally been more or less agreeable; but I think I was always more at ease alone than in anybody's company, till I knew thee. And now I am only myself when thou art within my reach. Thou art an unspeakably beloved woman. How couldst thou inflict such frozen agony upon me in that dream?

If I write any more, it would only be to express more lovings and longings; and as they are impossible to express, I may as well close.

THY HUSBAND.

--There is a tradition in the family that the extraordinary seclusion of "Aunt Ebe," mentioned above, was due to the following grievous misunderstanding. Una had been in the habit of passing an hour or two of each day in her aunt's room, the child being a great favorite with that lady. On one occasion, however, when her mother was about sending her up as usual, Una said, "I don't want to go to Aunt Ebe any more!" "Why not?" her mother inquired. "Because," Una replied, "Aunt Ebe makes me naughty. She gives me candy; and when I tell her you don't let me have candy, she says, 'Oh, never mind; your mother will never know!" This alarming report led to investigations and inquiries, the upshot of which was a suspension of Una's visits, and the total disappearance from mortal view of Aunt Ebe. In process of time, however, the breach was happily mended, as we have seen.

The next letter is to Una from her father, containing more news of the dolly previously mentioned. It should, perhaps, he explained that the splendor of dolly's complexion, and the other modifications in her physiognomy, were the result of Mr. Hawthorne's practices upon her with his wife's palette and brushes. He often used to amuse himself and the children by painting little faces for them; and it was always his way to make the cheeks of these visages as ruddy as vermilion would allow.

SALEM, June 7, 1848.

MY DEAR LITTLE UNA,--I have been very much pleased with the letters which you have sent me: and I am glad to find that you do not forget me, for I think of you a great deal. I bring home a great many beautiful flowers,--roses and poppies and lilies and bluebells and pinks and many more besides, -but it makes me feel sad to think that my little Una cannot see them. Your dolly wants to see you very much. She sits up in my study all day long and has nobody to talk with. I try to make her as comfortable as I can, but she does not seem to be in very good spirits. She has been quite good, and has grown very pretty, since you went away. Aunt Louisa and Dora are going to make her a new gown and a new bonnet.

I hope you are a good little girl, and are kind to your little brother, and Horace, and Georgie, and the baby. You must not trouble mamma but must do all you can to help her.

Dora wishes to see you very much. So do Grandmamma and Aunt Ebe and Aunt Louisa. Aunt Ebe and I went to walk together, a day or two ago, and the rain came and wet us a little.

Do not you wish to come home and see me? I think we shall be very happy when you come, for I am sure you will be a good little girl. Good-by.

YOUR AFFECTIONATE FATHER

--The summer and autumn passed away without incident; but there is a dim impression on the mind of one of the children of having heard a story read to him about a certain miraculous snow image, which he was, for a long time, firmly convinced that he and his sister had made in their own yard. Be that as it may, the subjoined letter shows that Hawthorne was at work about something; and "The Snow Image" was among the results of his labor. It was first published in a "Memorial Volume " to Mrs. Osgood, and afterwards, I believe, was issued by itself with colored illustrations. "Elizabeth's Book," spoken of below, was brought out the next year, under the title of "Aesthetic Papers." The article finally contributed to it by Hawthorne was that called "Main Street." The story alluded to in the first paragraph of his letter was probably "Ethan Brand." It was too lurid for Miss Peabody's aestheticism.

SALEM, December, 1848.

MY DEAR MOTHER,--I shall send with this letter my husband's article for Elizabeth's book. What is the name of the book? My husband says that if this paper will not suit the book, he will make some other use of it if you will send it back. He wishes the note at the end of the manuscript to be placed at the beginning of the printed text as a preface; and he thinks it had better be upon a separate fore-leaf. It is a tremendous truth, written, as he often writes truth, with characters of fire, upon an infinite gloom,--softened so as not wholly to terrify, by divine touches of beauty,--revealing pictures of nature, and also the tender spirit of a child.

What good news from France! What a pleasant surprise it must have been to that worthy Monsieur who was imprisoned for a political offence and condemned to be executed, to find himself all at once made Governor! There seems to be a fine fresh ail in France just now, and I hope it will extend through the atmosphere of Europe. It is a great day when kings are, after all, found to be nothing but helpless men as soon as the people feel them to be so; and it is very pretty when the people do not hurt the kings, but merely make them run. Since Prince Metternich has resigned, I conceive that monarchy is in its decline.

Julian rides very far on his hobby-horse,--round the whole earth,--and then dismounts, loaded down with superb presents for us all,--for his father, golden books, golden pens, golden horses, and all appropriate gifts for a scholar and a gentleman; for me, golden work-baskets, golden needles, and such things. In these golden dreams he reminds me of my brother Wellington, who used to pour golden showers upon his friends. He goes to Boston a great deal to see you; but I suppose you do not often perceive him.

--I find this allusion to "Main Street" and to the "Aesthetic" volume in a letter from Mrs. Peabody to her daughter:--

BOSTON, 1849.

MY DEAR Sophy,--In our "Evening Traveller" is a very excellent notice of Elizabeth's book by the editor. Speaking of "Main Street," he says: "No one but Hawthorne could have written it. It is perfectly graphic. If there were an artist of genius enough to transfer it to canvas, it would make a panorama of inestimable worth." Miss Lucy Osgood gave an oration about it in our book-room yesterday, in her usual emphatic manner, declaring she never was so charmed. We have good hope that the book will sell, and those who have it are already expressing a wish to have another. One gentleman has subscribed for three numbers of the next volume. If this edition all sells, she will make $400 clear.

--The time was now approaching when a bit of shrewd political manoeuvring on the part of persons professing to be his friends was to oust Hawthorne from the Surveyorship, and bring forth "The Scarlet Letter." Meanwhile, from the pages of the family journal, I extract the following curious study of the children,--one out of many which he wrote there.

SALEM, *January,* 1849.--It is one of Una's characteristics never to shut the door. Yet this does not seem exactly to indicate a loose, harum-scarum disposition; for I think she is rather troubled by any want of regularity in matters about her. She sometimes puts the room in order, and sets things to rights, very effectively. When she leaves anything loose, it is owing to a hasty, headlong mood, intent upon the end, and rushing at once towards it. It is Julian's characteristic, on the other hand, *always* to shut the door, whatever hurry he may be in. It does not seem to interfere with the settled purpose wherewith he pursues his object, although, indeed, he is not so strenuous in his purposes as Una; and it seems to cost him little or no sacrifice of feeling to give them up. "Well," he says benignly, after being reasoned or remonstrated with, and turns joyfully to something else. Nevertheless, he is patient of difficulties, and unweariable in his efforts to accomplish his enterprises,--as, for instance, in building a house of blocks, where he renews the structure again and again, however often it may tumble down, only smiling at each new catastrophe; when Una would have blazed up in a passion, and tossed her building materials to the other side of the room. Her mother thinks that her not shutting the door is owing to laziness. She *has* a great fund of laziness, like most people who move with an impetus.

Her beauty is the most flitting, transitory, most uncertain and unaccountable affair, that ever had a real existence; it beams out when nobody expects it; it has mysteriously passed away when you think yourself sure of it. If you glance sideways at her, you perhaps think it is illuminating her face, but, turning full round to enjoy it, it is gone again. When really visible, it is rare and precious as the vision of an angel. It is a transfiguration,--a grace, delicacy, or ethereal fineness,--which at once, in my secret soul, makes me give up all severe opinions that I may have begun to form about her. It is but fair to conclude that on these occasions we see her real soul.

When she seems less lovely, we merely see something external. But, in truth, one manifestation belongs to her as much as another; for, before the establishment of principles, what is character but the series and succession of moods?

The sentiment of a picture, tale, or poem is seldom lost upon her; and when her feelings are thus interested, she will not hear to have them interfered with by any ludicrous remark or other discordance. Yet she has, often, a rhinoceros-armor against sentiment or tenderness; you would think she were marble or adamant. It seems to me that, like many sensitive people, her sensibilities are more readily awakened by fiction than realities.

Julian and Una are now running to and fro across the room. There never was a gait more expressive of childish force and physical well-being than his; no faintness, weakness, weariness, about it. Una has vigor, too, but it is extremely dependent on the state of her spirits or her nerves; and unless her mind be right, she will be tired, perhaps, the moment she is out of bed; or, if there is anything to excite her, she may be in the highest physical force after all the toils of a weary day. Julian's vigor is, in a much greater degree, what is natural and proper to his body. . . .

--In the "English Note-Books," in 1855, Hawthorne wrote that he was much moved while reading the manuscript of "The Scarlet Letter" to his wife. "But I was then," he adds, "in a very nervous state, having gone through a great diversity and severity of emotion, while writing it." In fact, several calamities befell at this time, as if in sinister atonement for the quiet felicity of so many years. First of all, came his unexpected official decapitation, and the consequent necessity of concentrating his whole imaginative energy upon his new book,- the success of which, of course, he was very far from anticipating. The obligation to write for one's bread is (for a sensitively organized man, with a family dependent upon him) likely to be productive of considerable anxiety of mind; but these conditions were not, it appears, severe enough by themselves for the birth of "The Scarlet Letter." Midway in its composition, Madame Hawthorne was taken dangerously ill,--she was above seventy years of age,--and, after a struggle of a few weeks, she died. Domestic embarrassments, arising from insufficient pecuniary means, followed; and in the autumn the entire household was prostrated by illness, Mr. Hawthorne's disease being an almost intolerable attack of earache, lasting without intermission for several days, during which he was obliged to take the whole charge of the children. Matters might have become still worse, had not Miss E. P. Peabody chanced to hear of the family's condition; when she immediately, at no small personal loss and inconvenience, hastened to the scene of disaster, and by her exertions succeeded in substantially alleviating it. Such were the straits and turmoils amidst which the most terse and concentrated Romance of that generation was conceived and written; but, despite all hindrances, moral and physical, it was in the printer's hands within six months from the time of its commencement.

Regarding the political intrigue which turned Hawthorne out of his position, it is not necessary to say much. A Mr. Upham, whose name has already appeared in these pages, and some other persons who had always avowed the utmost friendly solicitude for Hawthorne, drew up a petition praying that a certain individual be appointed to a certain office, namely, the Salem Surveyorship; and to this petition they obtained the signatures of a number of men of Hawthorne's own party, by the simple device of suppressing the fact that Hawthorne was himself the incumbent of the

Surveyorship in question. When the truth came out, they protected themselves by casting reflections upon Hawthorne's political and even upon his private character. One may smile, now, at the final issue of all these evilly meant designs; but it is none the less refreshing to read such a letter as this which Dr. Peabody wrote on the subject:--

BOSTON, June 12, 1849.

DEAR SOPHIE,--Yours announcing a startling disclosure was received to-day about ten o'clock. I was truly astonished. About the close of the session of our Legislature, I was at the State House, and fell in with Mr. Upham. I asked him if he thought Hawthorne would be turned out. He was quite cosey, and said he thought nothing would be done about it. In looking back upon the interview, I now have an impression revived that there was a sort of mystification in his manner. But what I now write for is to suggest that nothing should be done hastily. That is, I would collect all the evidence I could about the document signed and sent on. If possible, I would get the document, or get some one in Washington to procure it or inquire about it and see it, so that he could make affidavit. After getting all the testimony, and finding out all the names upon the paper, I would, if the case will authorize it, commence a suit for damages. A false statement which deprives a man of his living is a libel and an actionable offence. If I did not do that, I would make the welkin ring, and expose all the names connected with the affair. Mr. Hawthorne can defy the world to prove that he ever wrote a political article: if I have a right impression, he can defy them to prove that he ever cast a political vote; perhaps he has not voted in any case. He will find Whigs enough to enlist in his cause, and it will be nuts to politicians on his side to make capital out of it. I should like to have Mr. Upham asked if he prays nowadays, and what sort of a prayer he made after he put his name to that document. I should like to ask him if he ever heard of the Ninth Commandment. Tell Mr. Hawthorne to be busy, but not to fire till he gets his battery well manned and charged, and then he will make a Buena Vista conquest.

With remembrances as due,

Your father, N. P.

--Six weeks later, Mrs. Peabody discourses on the same subject in this manner:--

BOSTON, July 28, 1849.

MY DEAR SOPHY,--I hope a letter will come to-day; I want to know how Madame Hawthorne is. I feel as if her illness is of a kind to cause much alarm. If you should leave Salem, I hope you will find some cottage not far from Boston; for, charming as are sheltering trees and verdant fields, a literary man has a wider scope for the exercise, or rather for profit from the exercise, of his mind in the city than in the country.

Miss Burley has just returned from Salem. She was very desirous that your husband should come out with the whole truth, at all risks and notwithstanding all delicacies. She said she believed that it was better for all, even for the criminals, that there should be no hushings-up. We told her that we believed Mr. Hawthorne would appeal in behalf of his character next winter. She was earnest to know if something could not be done by him earlier. She said she never knew such things delayed without becoming more complicated and giving rise to more difficulties. Mr. Upham might get possessed of political power which he had no moral right to have. Mr. Everett ought to be undeceived. Since Mr. Hawthorne had publicly denied the first charges, which were of things morally innocent, this acquiescence under more grave charges might seem, to people at a distance, to imply confession. Mr. Hawthorne's reputation belonged to his country, and ought not to be allowed to rest under any imputation. Reputation was a subtle good, which did not bear bad breath. You will know Miss Burley's warm-hearted interest in all that concerns you; but your husband will act according to his own sense of right; and there certainly was much weight in what he said of the danger in which some of his friends in office would be involved, by coming forward in his cause, if he acted immediately relative to his removal. You know in whom you trust, and will, I doubt not, be guided by His wisdom and goodness....

--In spite of Miss Burley, Hawthorne refused to enter upon a vindication of his private character; on the contrary, he treated with imperturbable indifference, not to say levity, all efforts to arouse him on that score, both at this epoch and in similar cases afterwards. Sometimes he would put off his advisers with grotesque threats of the revenge he proposed to take upon his enemies; but the hardest blow he ever actually dealt, in this kind, was to introduce one of them as the leading character in a certain Romance of his. There he stands for all time,--subtle, smooth, cruel, unscrupulous; perfectly recognizable to all who knew his real character, but so modified as to outward guise that no one who had met him merely as an acquaintance would ever suspect his identity.

On the day he received the news of his discharge, Hawthorne came home several hours earlier than usual; and when his wife expressed pleasure and surprise at his prompt reappearance, he called her attention to the fact that he had left his head behind him. "Oh, then," exclaimed Mrs. Hawthorne, buoyantly, "you can write your book!" for Hawthorne had been bemoaning himself, for some time back, at not having leisure to write down a story that had long been weighing on his mind. He smiled, and remarked that it would be agreeable to know where their bread and rice were to come from while the story was writing. But his wife was equal to the occasion. Hawthorne had been in the habit of giving her, out of his salary, a weekly sum for household expenses; and out of this she had every week contrived secretly to save something, until now there was quite a large pile of gold in the drawer of her desk. This drawer she forthwith with elation opened, and triumphantly displayed to him the unsuspected treasure. So he began "The Scarlet Letter" that afternoon; and blessed his stars, no doubt, for sending him such a wife.

In July, Madame Hawthorne fell ill, and her symptoms were such as to cause serious anxiety. Her daughters were neither of them available as nurses, and the duty of attending on her devolved, therefore, exclusively on Mrs. Hawthorne. To her husband, consequently, was left the charge of the two children. As the latter required constant supervision, the Romance had to be practically discontinued for the time. Day after day, throughout the hot and sunny summer weather, Hawthorne sat in the nursery, or stationed himself at the window overlooking the yard, and watched them play and prattle before him; settling their little disputes, sympathizing with their little squabbles, listening to their voices, their laughter, and their tears; while, all the time, in the chamber above, his mother lay upon what all knew to be her death-bed. And upon that dark background of emotion the airy and careless gambols of the children showed like a bright, fantastic embroidery; strangely contrasted, and yet more strangely harmonious, for the reigning motive of all their various games was the reproduction, in fun and frolic, of the tragedy enacting upstairs. The anguish and the mirth of life have seldom been more strikingly intertwined together.

At length, when the hour of his mother's departure was evidently near at hand, he sought to relieve the dreary pain of suspense by having recourse to the old family journal. Here he wrote down, from hour to hour, the features of the scene that passed before him. In all his writings there is, perhaps, no passage more impressive than this which follows; so simple is it--so spontaneous, so tragic. And there is nothing, certainly, which casts so searching a light upon the inner region of his nature.

July 29, 1849, Sunday, half-past nine o'clock, A. M.--A beautiful, fresh summer morning! All my Journals of the children, hitherto, have been written at fireside seasons, when their daily life was spent within doors. Now it is a time of open doors and windows, when they run in and out at will, and their voices are heard in the sunshine, like the song of birds. Our metes and bounds are rather narrow; but still there is fair room for them to play under the elms, the pear-tree, and the two or three plum-trees that overshadow our brick avenue and little grass-plot. There is air, too, as good almost as country air, from across the North River; and so our little people flourish in the unrestrained freedom which they enjoy within these limits. They are inactive hardly for a moment throughout the day, living a life as full of motion as the summer insects, who are compelled to crowd their whole existence into this one season.

This morning, however, my journal begins with trouble; for Una is shut up in the drawing-room, and crying bitterly for her mamma, who is compelled to be in grandmamma's sick-chamber. Julian looks very sad and dolorous, and puckers up his little face, in sympathy with his sister's outcries; and, being himself on the point of bursting into tears, I tell him to go to the drawing-room door and release Una from her imprisonment. So he departs on his mission, and forthwith returns, leading Una by the hand, with the tears all over her discolored face, but in peaceful mood. I kiss her forehead, and the sun shines out again, with a bright rainbow in the sky.

By and by, however, she begins to make complaint about her hair, which has not been combed this morning, everybody being busy with grandmamma. At last comes in Dora, and takes her into the little room, where I hear her busily prattling about various matters while Dora combs her hair. Julian, who has been sitting on the floor, playing a sort of tune by pulling a string across a bar of iron, gets up and runs into the little room to talk with Dora and Una. His mother making a momentary flitting appearance, he requests to go up and see grandmamma with her; being refused, he asks for a kiss, and, while receiving it, still offers up a gentle and mournful petition to be allowed to go with his mother. As this cannot be, he remains behind, with a most woful countenance and some few quiet tears. The shower, however, is averted by Dora's telling him a story, while she continues to dress Una's hair. Julian has too much tenderness, love, and sensibility in his nature; he needs to be hardened and tempered. I would not take a particle of the love out of him; but methinks it is highly desirable that some sterner quality should be interfused throughout the softness of his heart, else in course of time, the hard intercourse of the world, and the many knocks and bruises he will receive, will cause a morbid crust of callousness to grow over his heart; so that, for at least a portion of his life, he will have less sympathy and love for his fellow-beings than those who began life with a much smaller portion. After a lapse of years, indeed, if he have native vigor enough, there may be a second growth of love and benevolence; but the first crop, with its wild luxuriance, stands a good chance of being blighted.

"Well, father!" cries Una, coming out of the little room with her hair nicely combed, and looking into the glass with an approving glance. This is not one of her beautiful days, nevertheless; but it is highly possible that some evanescent and intangible cause may, at any moment, make her look lovely, for such changes come and go as unaccountably as the changes of aspect caused by the atmosphere in mountain scenery. A queer comparison, however,--a family of mountains on one side and Una's little phiz on the other.

Una is describing graudmamma's sickness to Julian. "Oh, you don't know how sick she is, Julian; she is sick as I was when I had scarlet fever in Boston." What a contrast between that childish disease and these last heavy throbbings--this funeral march--of my mother's heart! Death is never beautiful but in children. How strange! For them Nature breaks her promise, violates her pledge, and like a pettish child, destroys her own prettiest play-things; whereas the death of old age is the consummation of life, and yet there is so much gloom and ambiguity about it that it opens no vista for us into Heaven. But we seem to see the flight of a dead child upward, like a butterfly's.

Julian has been dressed for a walk; and, surmounted by a very broad-brimmed straw hat, which makes him look not unlike a mushroom, goes off with Dora, while Una stands with her feet on the cross-pieces of the gate to watch their departure. She is infinitely adventurous, and spends much of her time, in this summer weather, hanging on that gate, and peeping forth into the great, unknown world that lies beyond. Ever and anon, without giving us the slightest notice, she is apt to take a flight into the said unknown; and when we go to seek her, we find her surrounded by a knot of children, with whom she has made acquaintance, and who gaze at her with a kind of wonder, recognizing that she is not altogether like themselves.

She has been up to see her grandmamma, and spent a good while in the chamber, fanning the flies from grandmamma's face. She describes grandmamma's sickness to Julian, while he rides on his hobby-horse. "It would be very painful for little Julian to see," she says to him, "for she is very sick indeed, and sometimes she almost cries; but she is very patient with her sickness." "Why, Una," answers Julian, "if I were to go to her, I would stroke her, and she would be very quiet."

Julian assumes the character of mamma, and addresses Una as Julian; and talks very pathetically about how he should feel "if little Julian were to faint away and go to God." In the midst of this scene they are both suddenly transformed into two other characters,--Una into a lady, and Julian into a "coacher," or hackman; then for a fitful moment or two they become themselves again. If their outward shapes corresponded with their imaginations, they would shift to and fro between one semblance and another, faster than even Proteus did. They live themselves into everything that passes under their notice, thereby showing what strong impressions are made on their young and fresh susceptibilities.

Half-past two, P. M.--They are playing with a hen,--a black crested hen, which very often comes into the yard. Of all playthings, a living plaything is infinitely the most interesting to a child. A kitten, a horse, a spider, a toad, a caterpillar, an ant, a fly,-- anything that can move of its own motion,--immediately has a hold on their sympathies. The dread of creeping things appears not to be a native instinct; for these children allow caterpillars to crawl on their naked flesh without any repugnance. Julian has obtained possession of the hen, and seems almost in the mind to put her into the street, but cannot prevail with himself so to do. However, he permits Una to put her through the fence, and they both stand looking at the hen, who chases an insect in the sunny street. Scarcely has she gone, when Julian opens the gate, runs in pursuit, and comes back triumphantly with the abominable fowl in his arms. Again the hen is gone; and Julian stands bemoaning himself at the gate; and both children hang on the gate, looking abroad, and themselves having somewhat the aspect of two birds in a cage. They come back and sit down on the door-step, and Una comforts Julian at great length for the loss of the hen, concluding as follows: "So now little Julian should not cry for the hen, when he has so many good things that God gives him."

At about five o'clock I went to my mother's chamber, and was shocked to see such an alteration since my last visit. I love my mother; but there has been, ever since boyhood, a sort of coldness of intercourse between us, such as is apt to come between persons of strong feelings if they are not managed rightly. I did not expect to be much moved at the time, that is to say, not to feel any overpowering emotion struggling just then,--though I knew that I should deeply remember and regret her. Mrs. Dike was in the chamber; Louisa pointed to a chair near the bed, but I was moved to kneel down close by my mother, and take her hand. She knew me, but could only murmur a few indistinct words; among which I understood an injunction to take care of my sisters. Mrs. Dike left the chamber, and then I found the tears slowly gathering in my eyes. I tried to keep them down, but it would not be; I kept filling up, till, for a few moments, I shook with sobs.

For a long time I knelt there, holding her hand; and surely it is the darkest hour I ever lived. Afterwards I stood by the open window and looked through the crevice of the curtain. The shouts, laughter, and cries of the two children had come up into the chamber from the open air, making a strange contrast with the death-bed scene. And now, through the crevice of the curtain, I saw my little Una of the golden locks, looking very beautiful, and so full of spirit and life that she was life itself. And then I looked at my poor dying mother, and seemed to see the whole of human existence at once, standing in the dusty midst of it. Oh, what a mockery, if what I saw were all,--let the interval between extreme youth and dying age be filled up with what happiness it might! But God would not have made the close so dark and wretched, if there were nothing beyond; for then it would have been a fiend that created us and measured out our existence, and not God. It would be something beyond wrong, it would be insult, to be thrust out of life and annihilated in this miserable way. So, out of the very bitterness of death, I gather the sweet assurance of a better state of being.

At one moment little Una's voice came up, very clear and distinct, into the chamber,--"Yes, she is going to die." I wish she had said, "Going to God," which is her idea and usual expression of death; it would have been so hopeful and comforting, uttered in that bright young voice. She must have been repeating or enforcing the words of some elder person who had just spoken.

July 30, half-past ten o'clock.--Another bright forenoon, warmer than yesterday, with flies buzzing through the sunny air. Mother still lives, but is gradually growing weaker, and appears to be scarcely sensible. Una takes a strong interest in poor mother's condition, and can hardly be kept out of the chamber,--endeavoring to thrust herself in at the door whenever it is opened, and continually teasing me to be permitted to go up. This is partly intense curiosity of her active mind; partly, I suppose, natural affection. I know not what she supposes to be the final result to which grandmamma is approaching. She talks of her being soon to go to God, and probably thinks that she will be taken away bodily. Would to God it were to be so! Faith and trust would be far easier than they are now. But, to return to Una, there is something that almost frightens me about the child,--I know not whether elfish or angelic, but, at all events, supernatural. She steps so boldly into the midst of everything, shrinks from nothing, has such a comprehension of everything, seems at times to have but little delicacy, and anon shows that she possesses the finest essence of it,--now so hard, now so tender; now so perfectly unreasonable, soon again so wise. In short, I now and then catch an aspect of her in which I cannot believe her to be my own human child, but a spirit strangely mingled with good and evil, haunting the house wnere I dwell. The little boy is always the same child, and never varies in his relation to me.

Three o'clock, P. M.--Julian is now lying on his couch in the character of sick grandmamma, while Una waits on him as Mrs. Dike. She prompts him in the performance, showing a quite perfect knowledge of how it should all be: "Now, stretch out your hands to be held." "Will you have some of this jelly?" Julian starts up to take the imaginary jelly. "No; grandmamma lies still." He smacks his lips. "You must not move your lips so hard." "Do you think Una had better come up?" "No." "You feel so, don't you?" His round curly head and rosy face, with a twinkling smile upon it, do not look the character very well. Now Una is transformed into grandmamma, and Julian is mamma, taking care of her. She groans, and speaks with difficulty, and moves herself feebly and wearisomely; then lies perfectly still, as if in an insensible state; then rouses herself and calls for wine; then lies down on her back with clasped hands; then puts them to her head. It recalls the scene of yesterday to me with frightful distinctness; and out of the midst of it little Una looks at me with a smile of glee. Again, Julian assumes the character. "You're dying now," says Una ; "so you must lie still." "I shall walk, if I 'm dying," answers Julian; whereupon he gets up and stumps about the room with heavy steps. Meantime Una lies down on the couch, and is again grandmamma, stretching out her hand in search of some tender grasp, to assure herself that she is still on the hither side of the grave. All of a sudden, Julian is Dr. Pearson, and Una is apparently mamma, receiving him, and making excuses for not ushering him into the sick-chamber. Here ensues a long talk about the patient's condition and symptoms. Una tells the doctor plainly that she thinks we had better have Dr. Cummins; whereupon Dr. Pearson replies, "We can't have any more talking; I must go." The next instant Una transforms him into Dr. Cummins, --one of the greatest miracles that was ever performed, this instantaneous conversion from allopathy to homoeopathy.

--Here the record stops. Madame Hawthorne's death occurred the next day; and we can only conjecture what may have been the thoughts and the emotions which visited Hawthorne's soul in the interval. His wife wrote on the 1st of August to Mrs. Peabody, announcing the death; and the sentence in which she alludes to her husband is the only direct testimony as to his condition.

WEDNESDAY, Aug. 1, 1849.

MY DEAREST MOTHER,--Mrs. Hawthorne died yesterday afternoon, after four or five days of pain, relieved by intervals of unconsciousness. I am weary, weary, weary, heart and head. I have watched through all the days (not nights), keeping off flies, holding her in my arms as she sat up for breath, and sympathizing far too deeply and vividly with her children and with herself to escape unscathed. My husband came near a brain fever, after seeing her for an hour; and while all our hearts were aching with sorrow and care, Mrs. ----- has been like some marble-souled fiend. But of that I cannot speak now or perhaps ever. I hope GOD will forgive her, but I do not see how He can! Elizabeth and Louisa are desolate beyond all words. We all have lost an angel of excellence, and in mind and person an angel,--oh, such a loss! She looks so heavenly sweet, calm, happy, peaceful, that I cannot see death in her now; I only *hear* death as I stand over her,--for what else can such silence be?

At the last she had no suffering,--for eight hours no suffering,--but gradually faded as day fades; no difference momentarily, but hourly a change. I thought I could not stay through the final hour, but found myself courageous for Louisa's and Elizabeth's sakes; and her disinterested, devoted life exhaled in a sigh, exquisitely painful to hear when we knew it was the last sigh,--but to her not painful.

I am too tired to rest yet.

SOPHIA.

The funeral takes place to-morrow at four o'clock.

--Arrangements were now made looking towards a removal from Salem to the fresh air and surroundings of Berkshire, where Hawthorne might finish his Romance at a distance from the house now gloomy with sad associations. As it turned out, however, this change was not effected until the spring of the following year, after "The Scarlet Letter" was an accomplished fact. A month after Madame Hawthorne's departure, Mrs. Hawthorne was able to write cheerfully as follows:--

SALEM, Sept. 2, 1849.

We are all very well and in brave spirits. The prospect of "mountaneous air" (as a gentleman here called it the other day) already vivifies our blood. To give up the ocean caused rather a stifling sensation; but I have become used to the idea of mountains now,--the next best breath. I think it probable that Louisa and Elizabeth Hawthorne will remain in Salem at least till summer of next year, and this would simplify our life very much in the first struggle for bread; for they cannot help us possibly,--we only must help them. Louisa is not in strong health enough to do anything, and it would be a pain to me to see her making any efforts; and Elizabeth is not available for every-day purposes of pot-hooks and trammels, spits and flat-irons. I intend to paint at least three hours a day, while my husband takes cognizance of the children; as he will not write more than nine hours out of the twelve, and his study can be my studio as well.

Mr. O'Sullivan sent us $100 of his debt the other day, and we have access to another hundred if we want it before we earn it. So do not be anxious for us in a pecuniary way. Mr. Hawthorne writes *immensely*. I am almost frightened about it. But he is well now, and looks very shining.

The children have been acting Flaxman's outlines. The other day Una happened to hurt Julian unintentionally; he cried out, and she threw herself on her knees before him as he sat on the sofa, and in a tragic and sounding tone exclaimed, "'T is not unknown to thee, Royal Apollo, that I have done no deed of base injustice!" I had no idea she so well comprehended that scene.

I am glad you like "The Great Stone Face." Mr. Hawthorne says he is rather ashamed of the mechanical structure of the story, the moral being so plain and manifest. He seemed dissatisfied with it as a work of art. But some persons would prefer it precisely on account of its evident design. And Ernest is a divine creation,--so grand, so comprehensive, and so simple. . . .

--It is curious to note how (in pursuance of the proverb), when things had reached their worst, they began to mend, in all directions at once. Here is what was doubtless a gratifying letter from Hillard, written a month or two before "The Scarlet Letter" was heard of:--

BOSTON, Jan. 17, 1850.

MY DEAR HAWTHORNE,--It occurred to me and some other of your friends that, in consideration of the events of the last year, you might at this time be in need of a little pecuniary aid. I have therefore collected, from some of those who admire your genius and respect your character, the enclosed sum of money, which I send you with my warmest wishes for your health and happiness. I know the sensitive edge of your temperament; but do not speak or think of obligation. It is only paying, in a very imperfect measure, the debt we owe you for what you have done for American Literature. Could you know the readiness with which every one to whom I applied contributed to this little offering, and could you have heard the warm expressions with which some accompanied their gift, you would have felt that the bread you had cast upon the waters had indeed come back to you.

Let no shadow of despondency, my dear friend, steal over you. Your friends do not and will not forget you. You shall be protected against "eating cares," which, I take it, mean cares lest we should not have enough to eat.

My check, you perceive, is made payable to your order. You must therefore endorse it. I presume that you can get it cashed at some of the Salem banks. With my affectionate remembrances to your wife,

Ever faithfully yours,

GEO. S. HILLARD.

--And here is another note, not less agreeable and characteristic, from the poet Whittier:--

AMESBURY, Feb. 22, 1850.

N. HAWTHORNE, ESQ.

DEAR FRIEND,--I have just learned with regret and surprise that no remittance has been sent thee for thy admirable story in the "Era." Dr. B. wrote me, in receipt of it months ago, that he had directed his agent in Boston to pay thee.

The pecuniary affairs of the "Era" are in the hands of Dr. B.; but I was unwilling to leave the matter unadjusted, and hasten to forward the amount. It is, I feel, an inadequate compensation.

I am glad to hear of thy forthcoming book. It is spoken of highly by the publishers. God bless and prosper thee!

Truly thy friend,

JOHN G. WHITTIER

--The Salem period closes with this foreglimpse, in a letter from Mrs. Hawthorne, of a visit from Miss Bremer, who was at that time in America:--

"I heard of a charming prospect about seeing Miss Bremer, from Lydia Chase. I am sure I should feel honored by a visit from her. She will not mind a ragged carpet, a nursery parlor, and all the inevitable inconveniences of our present *ménage*. I am sure the children would be drawn to her. Lydia said she was to dine with her, and come and make us a call in the afternoon. We cannot give her a room, just now, to be comfortable in; but to have a call from her would be delightful."

CHAPTER 8 - LENOX

BIDDING good-by forever to literary obscurity and to Salem, Hawthorne now turned his face towards the mountains. The preceding nine months had told upon his health and spirits; and, had "The Scarlet Letter" not achieved so fair a success, he might have been long recovering his normal frame of mind. But the broad murmur of popular applause, coming to his unaccustomed ears from all parts of his native country, and rolling in across the sea from academic England, gave him the spiritual refreshment born of the assurance that our fellow-creatures think well of the work we have striven to make good. Such assurance is essential, sooner or later, to soundness and serenity of mind. No man can attain secure repose and happiness who has never found that what moves and interests him has power over others likewise. Sooner or later he will begin to doubt either his own sanity or that of all the rest of the world.

But, for Hawthorne, "The Scarlet Letter" permanently disposed of this danger. It dealt with a subject of universal interest in such a way as to command universal sympathy From the time that it was published, Hawthorne became a sort of Mecca of pilgrims with Christian's burden upon their backs. Secret criminals of all kinds came to him for counsel and relief. The letters he received from spiritual invalids would have made a strange collection. Some of them he showed to his wife; but most of them he withheld even from her, and all of them he destroyed. Had such a pilgrimage occurred before he wrote his great Romance, one might have thought that he had availed himself therein of the material thus afforded him. But such practical knowledge of the hidden places of the human heart comes only to those who have proved their right to it by independent spiritual intuition. Greatness is the only magnet of the materials upon which greatness is based.

Although, therefore, Hawthorne was below his usual mark of vigor when he came to Lenox, there was an inner satisfaction at his heart which would surely make him well again. In fact, the two or three years which lay next before him comprised his period of greatest literary activity. During those years he produced five books, four of which, at least, were masterpieces in their several ways. His mental faculties never reached a higher state of efficiency than at this epoch, when he had just passed his forty-first year; though, on the other hand, his physical energies perhaps never fully recovered from the shock and strain of that last year of Salem. In after life he was more easily affected than before by external accidents and circumstances, such as weather, fatigue, noise, climate; the boundless elasticity of youth was gone. He still, however, retained a solid basis of health and muscular strength up to the time of his daughter's nearly fatal illness in Rome, in 1858. His daughter recovered; but her illness proved fatal, in the end, to him. His countenance, like his mind, sent forth a mellower but graver light than that of youth; and there was a melancholy cadence in the tones of his voice,--the melancholy of a strong, composed, but no longer buoyant spirit.

"The Scarlet Letter" had been published by the firm of Ticknor & Co. Wiley and Putnam had failed some time before, and George Putnam (a relative of Mrs. Hawthorne) had made the best reparation in his power for the small sum owing to Hawthorne, by disposing of the stock and plates of such of his works as were in the firm's possession, to the above-named publishers. The book enjoyed the distinction of stimulating the thieving propensities of several English booksellers; and Henry

Chorley, of the "Athenæum," was as much pleased with it as if he had manufactured its author himself. Hawthorne did not, at first, think so well of the book as of his subsequent ones; or rather, to use his own words, he did not think it a book natural for him to write. But there is reason to believe that, towards the end of his life, he modified this opinion. What the work lacked in breadth and variety, was more than compensated in other ways. As has been already intimated, it produced its effect even upon its own author, when the latter first read the manuscript to his wife. It may be as well, however, in this place, to correct an error into which a biographer of Hawthorne has fallen, in one of the three painstaking treatises upon his subject which he has thus far published. It is there stated that when Mrs. Hawthorne asked her husband (before the book was concluded) how it was going to end, he answered that he did not know. The idea of a man who could conceive "The Scarlet Letter;" being undecided, up to the last moment, as to whether or not Hester and Arthur Dimmesdale were going to elope together, is, when one comes to consider it, not a little startling and suggestive. Why should he have been at the pains of writing the story, had he contemplated the possibility of the alternative catastrophe? The anecdote, nevertheless, is true enough, save and except in one important particular; and that is, that it has been connected with the wrong story. The facts are as follows. When Hawthorne was writing "Rappaccini's Daughter," in the "Old Manse," he read the as yet unfinished manuscript to his wife. "But how is it to end?" she asked him, when he laid down the paper; "is Beatrice to be a demon or an angel?" "I have no idea!" was Hawthorne's reply, spoken with some emotion. In this case, however, as will appear upon reflection, no artistic necessity was involved. Whether the heroine turned out good or evil, the moral of the tale would remain substantially the same; and, moreover, it was a question open to discussion, especially to one of Hawthorne's quality of mind, whether the poison which had permeated the girl's physical system might not but be symbol of a still more terrible poison in her soul. He finally chose the brighter alternative; but there may still be a difference of opinion as to whether, from the merely artistic standpoint, the story loses or gains thereby.

It is scarcely worth while, as a general thing, to correct errors like the above, however constantly they may occur; and I have made an exception of this instance only because the mistake cast a doubt upon Hawthorne's possession of the intelligence of an average human being. Mr. George William Curtis has doubtless been surprised to find himself figuring as Hawthorne's companion in the adventure with the drowned girl in Concord River; the fact being, according to Hawthorne's own account, given above, that Ellery Channing was the person who called him up on that occasion. But it might just as well have been Mr. Curtis, as far as Hawthorne or the drowned girl is concerned; and, for aught I care, posterity may decide that it was. The night was dark; and the point is of no consequence.

The little red house which Hawthorne occupied while in Lenox is said to be still standing. It afforded better accommodation than one would have supposed from its outside, and it commanded a view of mountain, lake, and valley that might have made good many deficiencies. Attached to it, moreover, was a large two-storied hen-coop, populous with hens--an inexhaustible resource to the children. The hens all had their proper names, and were tamer than the pig in an Irish cabin. There were cows in the neighboring farmyard; and a barn with a hay-loft, which trenched very closely upon the delights of Paradise. Then there was the long declivity towards Tanglewood and the lake; and in winter, Hawthorne and the children used to seat themselves one behind another upon the big sled, and go down in headlong career through the snow-drifts,--as is related, in the "Wonder Book," of Eustace Bright and his little people. Even the incident of the collision with the stump, hidden beneath the snow, actually happened precisely as set down in the book, as well as many other humorous and delightful episodes. A little way up the road lived Mr. and Mrs. Tappan, the owners of the little red house, and its next-door neighbors; in the other direction, at a greater distance, was the abode of Luther Butler, who supplied the family with milk, and who, in the mind of one of Hawthorne's children, was for several years identified with the personage who threw his inkstand at the Devil and founded the Lutheran heresy. In Pittsfield, a few miles away, dwelt Herman Melville; Mr. G. P. R. James (not by any means the father of the present novelist, as has been rashly affirmed by an annotator) had a residence in the vicinity; and Fanny Kemble often rode up to the door on her strong black horse, and conversed, in heroic phrases, with the inmates of the red house. On one occasion she asked the smallest of the party whether he would like to have a ride; and, on his answering emphatically in the affirmative, she swung him up astride the pommel of her saddle, and galloped off with him. The wild delight of that gallop will never be forgotten by him who experienced it. On their return, Fanny reined in her steed with one hand, and, grasping her cavalier with the other, held him out at arm's length, exclaiming, "Take your boy!--Julian the Apostate!" Soon after their arrival at their new quarters, Mrs. Hawthorne wrote to her mother as follows:--

". . . .We had begun to be really homesick after such a long overturn of our penates, and I felt that I should never do anything and never feel rested till we were in our own house; and Mr. Hawthorne was so perfectly weary and worn with waiting for a place to be, to think, and to write in, that at last he gave up entirely and was so indisposed that I was quite distressed. He took cold because so harassed in spirit; and this cold, together with brain-work and disquiet, made a tolerable nervous fever. His eyes looked like two immense spheres of troubled light; his face was wan and shadowy, and he was wholly uncomfortable. He is now better, but not so vigorous yet as in former days, before the last year began. Still, he is reviving fast, and I expect soon to see him as in Concord. Mr. Tappan kept remarking that he enjoyed very much Mr. Hawthorne's illness, and finally rendered his reason. It was that he had conceived that Mr. Hawthorne could not be affected by mortal evils. He was glad to find him mortal in some respects. For several days the wounded Bird of Jove remained caged upstairs, and Mr. Tappan and two men took the opportunity to plough up the land on both sides of our house for us. This was an unexpected benefit, and it was no empty favor."

The summer was not Hawthorne's favorite season for writing, and it was not until the end of August that he had sufficiently digested the plan of "The House of the Seven Gables " to begin upon it. The witch element in this romance necessitated the scene being laid in Salem, though the "Custom House" sketch which had prefaced his former work was not taken in good part by some persons whose existence, save for that reminder thereof, would long ago have passed from human memory. Not all his fellow-incumbents, however, maintained a hostile attitude towards him, as may appear from this letter written by one of the personages mentioned in the essay in question, under the title of the Naval Officer.

SALEM, March 23, 1850.

MY DEAR HAWTHORNE,--I feel an inexplainable delicacy in addressing you, for I am altogether incapable of describing the sensations which seem to sway and control me in connection with my subject. I have just concluded the reading of "The Scarlet Letter," and am perfectly spellbound in view of the finy true and vivid picture of human life which is presented in its pages. I can no more tell you of the mighty influence this romance produced on me, than a child can explain a flash of lightning. I can only estimate the power and beauty of the production by its effect on my imperfect and humble powers of judgment. I have never throughout my life been so highly excited in reading a book, as this afternoon by "The Scarlet Letter." My mind has been taken captive, and carried through its scenes, as though I actually lived in its time and participated in its events. I should not have told you of this but that I thought it might possibly give you some little satisfaction. However this may be, I know you will accept this tribute in the spirit that has dictated it,--that of the sincerest friendship and good-will.

I have spent many hours in your society, probably for the first and only time on this side the grave. May Heaven bless you wherever fate or choice may lead you, and may your children and your children's children be blessed, and share the fame your townsmen may deny to you. But what matters it what Salem may do?--the world and all time must feel the power of your mighty and mysterious genius. I do not speak to flatter. I hate flattery and hypocrisy as I do the pains of hell. Write me, if you feel like it: I should be very highly pleased to have a line from you. I thank you for your notice of me in your introduction, although in so close proximity to "Joe." The "Old Inspector" was faithfully portrayed, and, as I understand, the galled jade winces and wishes he was young for your sake!

Yours truly,

JOHN D. HOWARD.

---It will be more to the present purpose, however, to consider the following description of their home and mode of life, furnished to her mother by Mrs. Hawthorne--

LENOX, June 23, 1850.

MY DEAREST MOTHER,--I absolutely long to tell you more of our life. We are so beautifully arranged (excepting the guest-chamber), and we seem to have such a large house *inside*, though outside the little reddest thing looks like the smallest of ten-feet houses. Mr. Hawthorne says it looks like the Scarlet Letter. Enter our old black tumble-down gate,--no matter for that,--and you behold a nice yard, with an oval grass-plot and a gravel walk all round the borders, a flower-bed, some rose-bushes, a raspberry-bush, and I believe a syringa, and also a few tiger-lilies; quite a fine bunch of peonies, a stately double rose-columbine, which grows in memory of Elizabeth, because her favorite flower; and one beautiful Balsam Fir tree, of perfect pyramidal form, and full of a thousand melodies. We have planted flowers, besides; but they are slow to grow. All these will bloom in memory of Mary Mann. The front door is wide open. Enter and welcome. Here sits our little Julian on the floor, making a ship out of a cane, a cannon, and a piece of stick,--"a ship," he says, "in which we are all to go to England to destroy the land" (meaning to discover), for he is a new Columbus. At a mahogany stand sits your daughter, scribbling this history. Round this pretty little hall stand four cane-bottomed chairs, my flower-table, which survived transportation,--Julian's wee centre-table, and, at the fireplace, father's beautiful blind-fireboard. On the tiny mantelpiece reposes the porcelain lion and lamb, and a vase filled with lovely flowers. On the floor is the purple and gold-colored carpet, on the walls a buff paper; over the mantel hangs the divine Madonna del Pesce. Over the flower-table I have put Crawford's sculpture, "Glory to God in the Highest." Generally the little chairs are in this room, in which the children sit while I read about Christ, in the morning. And this reminds me of an occurrence which I meant to tell you. One day they asked me to read about Christ. Una got up out of her chair for something, and Julian took possession. Una complained very much. Her father said, "What did Christ say?--if a man take your cloak, give him your coat also. Do you know what he meant?" Una responded with an inward voice, "Yes, I know." She soon rose and gave Julian the chair, which he received with a radiant smile, having caught light from the radiance of the angel now descended, but immediately resigned again, feeling that he too must act well in such a presence. Do you think no glory was added to the sunshine by this scene, so trivial in appearance, but so universal in its influence? These children are wonderful revealers of truth and beauty. In everything of worth that I read them, they cause me somehow to comprehend it better.

On the right-hand side of the hall is a door. Will you enter the drawing-room? Between the front windows stands the beautiful antique ottoman, the monument of Elizabeth's loving-kindness, covered with woven flowers. In the corner at that side stands crosswise the fairy tea-table,--a Hawthorne heirloom,--and on an embroidered mat upon it lies my pretty white greyhound. In the other corner, on the same side, stands Apollo, whose head I have tied on! Diagonally opposite Apollo stands the ancient carved chair, with its tapestry of roses. Opposite the ottoman is the card-table, with the alabaster vase, and over the vase hangs Correggio's Madonna. Raphael's Transfiguration is over the ottoman. Opposite the door you have entered stands the centre-table; on it are books, the beautiful India box, and the superb India punch-bowl and pitcher, which Mr. Hawthorne's father had made in India for himself. In another corner stands the ancient Manning chair with its worked cover. The scarlet-tipped chair wanders about the room. The black haircloth rocking-chair was much abused in moving, and one of the rockers is off. It has not yet been mended; and when it is mended, the hall is to be its place. Over the centre-table hangs Endymion, and over the fireplace, Leonardo da Vinci's Madonna au Bas-relief. You cannot think how pretty the room looks, though with such a low stud that I have to get acclimated to it, and still fear to be crushed.

Opposite the ottoman is another door. Entrez, Madame ma mère, s'il vous plaît. This is the dining-room, covered with nice straw-carpet. Between the windows looking upon the lake hangs the great looking-glass, over the Pembroke dining-table. On the right, against the wall of the staircase, stands the bookcase, surmounted with the bronzed vase. Mahogany chairs stand round about. Here is a door leading into the bath-room. On one wall are nailed up the "Petit Soldat Orphelin," and the two pictures of Psyche about to bathe and about to be dressed. On another, stretches out the magnificent Tuba-Rheda. On the other side of the stairway another door leads into our charming little boudoir. The window commands the lake and the rich interval of meadow, with its beautiful groups of trees, and beyond, the mountains. Opposite the window is the couch, covered with red patch. Over the couch I have nailed Claude's landscape of the Golden Calf, of which I mended the torn corner, and it looks very handsomely with the soiled margin cut off. Opposite the door, over the small centre-table, hangs Salvator Rosa's Forest, in a fine light; on each side of it the lovely Comos, and over it, Loch Lomond,--all making a beautiful pyramid. Opposite these are book-shelves, with books fit to take up in such a room. Under the shelves stands the great portfolio. On the shelves is the Caryatid, and upon a bracket in one corner, Antinous. Sit down upon the couch, and you will see such a landscape out of the window as will charm perpetually; for the motion of light and shadow among the mountains and on the lake varies the scene all the time. The summer hazes are of exquisite beauty. Sometimes clouds hang low upon the mountain-sides in beautiful shapes. Next summer we intend to have a flower-garden beneath the window of the boudoir, and there we mean to plant only fragrant flowers, which will send up an incense of sweet odors in the evening. Will you go upstairs? The old Brussels stair-carpet looks quite respectably. On the wall at the head of the stairs I have nailed Michael Angelo's frescos of prophets and sibyls, joining all together and making a covering for the wall. On the right is Mr. Hawthorne's study, which can boast of nothing but his presence in the morning and the picture out of window in the evening. It has in it his secretary, my long ottoman, re-covered with red, and the antique centre-table, which lost one foot on its journey from Salem to Lenox. It stands quite even without its foot, and so remains for the present. Now please to step across into our golden chamber. The golden couch is so absurdly huge in the low, shelving chamber, that it looks more as if it could hold the room than the room it. But with the new straw-carpet, and the bright tint of the furniture, and the lovely outlines and snowy counterpane, and the perennial picture of lake and mountain, and the soon-to-be-hung-up snowy full muslin curtains, it makes a pretty show. My looking-glass squeezes just in between the windows. Along the entry is the red straw-carpet to the guest-chamber. Come along it, dear mother, father, brother, sisters; but do not look into the guest-chamber, with its very ugly bare floor, full of knots, and its bedstead full of confusion, but pass by and go into the little lady Una's chamber. On the left, as you enter, stands her bed, covered with a white counterpane. Upon the wall opposite her eyes I have put one of Raphael's angels, a head large as life, and beneath it that pretty engraving of Dawn. Near the window is a superb tree in lithograph.

I began this letter in the morning, and it is now between seven and eight. The children have been long abed, so that you can see in Una's little room the little mistress of it in happy sleep.

I suppose father would like to hear about our household economy. We give only three cents a quart for the best of milk, and we have it of Luther Butler. Butter is fourteen cents a pound, and eggs eleven and twelve cents a dozen; potatoes, very good ones, two shillings a bushel. The most superb buckwheat at half the price we gave at the East, sixty-two cents for twenty-four pounds; wood, three and four dollars a cord; charcoal, eight cents a bushel; veal, six cents a pound; mutton, five cents; beef, nine cents.

Monday P.M.--This is one of Berkshire's golden afternoons, with the most invigorating air. We have been having a splendid hen-coop patched up, being nothing less than the shed attached to the house. On the front of this shed Justus Wetmore Barnes nailed slats in a rude style enough, with so little idea of beauty that Mr.

Hawthorne says he shall put a placard up, signifying that it is not his work. The shed is in two stories, with an opening between; so the hens will have sumptuous accommodation. Mr. Hawthorne will grow corn for them.

SOPHIA.

---Her letters at this time were frequent and full. Here is one of her glowing eulogiums on her husband:--

.... Mr. Hawthorne said this morning that he should like a study with a soft, thick Turkey carpet upon the floor, and hung round with full crimson curtains so as to hide all rectangles. I hope to see the day when he shall have such a study. But it will not be while it would demand the slightest extravagance, because he is as severe as a stoic about all personal comforts, and never in his life allowed himself a luxury. It is exactly upon him, therefore, that I would like to shower luxuries, because he has such a spiritual taste for beauty. It is both wonderful and admirable to see how his taste for splendor and perfection is not the slightest temptation to him; how wholly independent he is of what he would like, all things being equal. Beauty and the love of it, in him, are the true culmination of the good and true, and there is no beauty to him without these bases. He has perfect dominion over himself in every respect, so that to do the highest, wisest, loveliest thing is not the least effort to him, any more than it is to a baby to be innocent. It is his spontaneous act, and a baby is not more unconscious in its innocence. I never knew such loftiness, so simply borne. I have never known him to stoop from it in the most trivial household matter, any more than in a larger or more public one. If the Hours make out to reach him in his high sphere, their wings are very strong. But I have never thought of him as in time, and so the Hours have nothing to do with him. Happy, happiest is the wife, who can bear such and so sincere testimony to her husband after eight years' intimate union. Such a person can never lose the prestige which commands and fascinates. I cannot possibly conceive of my happiness, but, in a blissful kind of confusion, live on. If I can only be so great, so high, so noble, so sweet, as he in any phase of my being, I shall be glad. I am not deluded nor mistaken, as the angels know now, and as all my friends will know, in open vision!

The other afternoon at the lake, when papa was lying his length along beneath the trees, Una and Julian were playing about, and presently Una said, "Take care, Julian; do not run upon papa's head. His is a real head, for it is full of thought." "Yes," responded Julian, with the unconscious wisdom of four years old, "it is thought that makes his head." We found a lovely new place that day. We found Indian council-chambers, boudoirs, and cabinets in the wood, and a high, dignified bank on the edge of the lake; and as we sat above, and were confined to a small view of the really tumultuous waves, we could easily imagine ourselves at Lake Superior. The children talked about the echo, and one of them finally settled the subject by remarking, "God says the echo." How children--all children not crushed by artifice resolve everything with the great, innate, all-satisfying idea of God!

A Mr. Ehninger, a young artist, has been here, who has made an illustration of "The Scarlet Letter." He was once a fashionable youth of New York, but discovered in himself a taste for art; he has been in Europe and studied design very faithfully, and is soon to return to perfect himself in color. He has been an ardent admirer of Mr. Hawthorne's books, and has made several designs in iUustration of them. The "Scarlet Letter" illustration was very remarkable--It is very large. It is the first scene of Hester coming out of the prison door. The figure of Hester is very majestic, noble, and stately, with a face of proud, marble beauty. On one side is a group of old women, whose faces are relieved by the sweet apparition of a child standing just at Hester's feet. On the other side are the officers. The drawing is not finished, but is full of beauty, power, and expression as far as it goes. When I first conducted Mr. Ehninger to our house, I said, "Here is our little red shanty." "The Temple of Art and the Muses!" enthusiastically exclaimed he, lifting his hat. It is certainly very pretty to see homage rendered to one's husband for immortal endowments.

SOPHIA.

---And here is a description of a typical day during their first winter:--

This superb winter's morning, when to live seems joy enough; even the hens are in such an animated state of spirits that Una keeps running in with eggs! There have been no winter horrors of great cold and storm here, as we were led to expect; when we look back, we find that opaline mists on the mountains are our strongest impression of the scene out of doors. The children have lived upon the blue nectared air all winter, and papa said the other day he did not believe there were two other children in New England who had had such uninterrupted health and freedom from colds. Such clear, unclouded eyes, such superb cheeks, as come in and out of the icy atmosphere! such relish for dry bread, such dewy sleep, such joyful uprisings, such merry gambols under pails of cold water! They wake at dawn. From the guest-chamber comes the powerful voice, 'I want to get up!' From a more distant room, 'Bon-jour, mamma! bon-jour, papa!' whereupon papa rises and makes a fire in the bath-room, when down rush the two birds.

In two minutes more they lift up dripping from a flood of fresh water; saying, 'Oh, how nice!' and 'How I am refreshing!' Then comes the vigorous rubbing before the warm fire, and the dressing, and then the leaping, running, springing about the room. Mamma seizes Julian (for Una attends to her own toilet) to brush his wet hair; but it is hard enough to keep him still, for who can hold a fountain! When all is done, papa goes out to feed the hens. After breakfast be disappears in his study, mamma sits down to her work-basket, and the children generally go out; or sometimes they sit side by side while I give them oral lessons in French, arithmetic, history, and geography. At noon papa descends from his study, instead of at night; and this causes great rejoicing throughout his kingdom. We sit down to dine (the children to sup) in a golden glow of sun-setting; and after this ceremony is always my particular hour for reading aloud to the children. About six they go to bed, each in a separate chamber, very happy, full of messages of love, respects, and thanks! and then they fall asleep, and we hear no more of them till the next dawn. Now follows our long, beautiful evening, which we richly enjoy. My husband has read aloud to me ever since he finished his book. 'David Copperfield' he has read. I never heard such reading. It is better than any acting or opera. Now he reads De Quincey. I don't know whether I told you that I bought some black velvet and put a new cover on my brother George's desk, and Kitty scrubbed all the brass bright, and I made the mahogany clean of ink and polished it, so that it looks very handsomely; and it was upon this desk that Mr. Hawthorne wrote 'The House of the Seven Gables'. . . .

--Herman Melville ("Omoo," as they called him, in allusion to one of his early romances) soon became familiar and welcome there; and, not seldom, strange visitors made their appearance, to pay homage to the Romancer's genius and to stare at him, at all of whom Mrs. Hawthorne looked in turn, with a penetrating and amused glance; as, for example,--

". . . .This morning 'Mr. Omoo' arrived; and soon after I went to the door to a knock, and there stood a clerical-looking gentleman, with white cravat and dark eyes. and very dainty in his fingers. He asked for Mr. Hawthorne,--said he did not know him, but had taken the liberty to introduce himself. I took him into the boudoir, where Mr. Melville was. He then said he had a lady in the carriage who would very much like to come in, but did not, because she did not know there was a *Mrs.* Hawthorne. Mr. Hawthorne and I went out, therefore, and escorted her in. She was a New York lady, rather handsome, with yet a hard, pitiless face. The children did not like her. It was diverting to me to see how the Professor (as she called the Reverend gentleman) and she herself devoured my husband with their eyes, as if they were determined to take a picture of him away with them. When Julian appeared, the lady made no hesitation in taking him by the hand and calling him 'Superb' right to his face; and then she remarked that he was 'the image of his father' (*seriatim*, '*You* are superb, Mr. Hawthorne'!). They did not stay very long; and after they went away, Mr. Melville was very agreeable. . .

---As throwing light upon her own character, and also because it is desirable to preserve, as much as possible, the continuity of her letters, I insert here two more of Mrs. Hawthorne's most characteristic epistles.

MY DEAREST MOTHER,--Your birthday approaches. The prospects of all seem brightening in the way of externals, and I love to think of you sitting quietly in your great chair, and brooding over our joys, and good hopes, and successes. I trust you realize the blessing you have been to us, in the way of high principle and sentiment, and lofty purity of heart, and elegance of taste,--to say nothing of a motherly tenderness which has never been surpassed in God's universe, and seldom equalled. To me especially this unspeakable tenderness has been a guard-angelic. In earliest childhood I remember some portions of my life only in moments when, at some crisis of excitement or trouble, you said to me softly, "My love." The tone, the words, used to pour balm and coinfort over my whole being. *Then* I did not know how to thank you; but now I know well enough, and I remember it when my child is in the same mood, and I also say to her "My love!" and with the same effect. Alas for those who counsel sternness and severity instead of love towards their young children! How little they are like God, how much they are like Solomon, whom I really believe many persons prefer to imitate, and think they do well. Infinite patience, infinite tenderness, infinite magnanimity, No less will do, and we must practise them as far as finite power will allow. Above all, no parent should feel a pride or power. This, I doubt not, is the great stumbling-block, and it should never be indulged. From this comes the sharp rebuke, the cruel blow, the anger. A tender sorrow, a most sympathizing regret, alone should appear at the transgression of a child, who comes into the world with an involuntary inheritance of centuries of fallen Adams to struggle with. Yet how immitigable is the judgment and treatment of these little misdemeanors often! When my children disobey, I am not personally aggrieved, and they see it, and find therefore that it is a disinterested desire that they should do right that induces me to insist. There is all the difference in the world between indulgence and tenderness. If the child never sees any acceptance of wrong-doing, but unalterably a horror and deep grief at it, certainly love and forgiveness can do no harm. In you I always felt there was sorrow for anything amiss I did; and very, very early I perceived that the influence of that silent regret was far more powerful with me than any rebuke of any other person. And how forever sweet it is to me to think that I imagined being a mother was synonymous with being disinterested. Silently, unawares almost to myself, but very consciously now, I remember quite small evidences of this: at table, wbat an impression of elegance and spirituality you made upon my mind, by never being preoccupied with your own plate and food, so that I used to think *mothers* lived without eating as well as without sleeping. I saw you were taken up with supplying others with what they wished for, before they had time to find out themselves. "What elegant manners!" I used to feel, and so resolved to do so too. There was a beautiful ideal in your mind; I saw it; *that* was my mother! . . . .

-- The "Elizabeth" in the next passage is, of course, Miss E. P. Peabody.

". . . .Who, I pray, is D. C.? Is he one of the many lame, halt, forlorn, poverty-stricken mortals, whom you and Elizabeth, in the infinite scope of your pity, sympathy, and hospitality, take in from the highways, because they have no other roof to cover them?--because you are so rich, and have so much leisure, and so much room, and so much linen and sumptuous fare, to bestow? I think that if you are obliged to leave your great menagerie, general hospital, Universal Sun, and final depot, then this dismal world, with its throngs of miserable ones, had better strike sail in the vast sea of space and sink, to rise no more, into some horrid vaouum. I declare, if all the nations of the earth--of each of which Elizabeth has certainly befriended and aided in sore distress one representative at least--do not come to kneel, like Flaxman's 'Aria,' and devoutly thank her; with tears of gratitude, I shall think there is no grace in Christendom. As I sit and look on these mountains, so grand and flowing in the illimitable, aerial blue, beyond and over, I seem to realize with peculiar force that bountiful, fathomless heart of Elizabeth, forever disappointed, but forever believing; sorely rebuffed, yet never bitter; robbed day by day, yet giving again from an endless store; more sweet, more tender, more serene, as the hours pass over her, though they may drop gall instead of flowers upon this unguarded heart. . .

--"The House of the Seven Gables" was written in about five months, which indicates pretty close application, even leaving out of account its extraordinary excellence as an achievement of thought and art; but Hawthorne himself seems to have considered that he worked rather slowly. While he was engaged upon it, Mr. Emerson wrote to him in behalf of a new magazine which was in contemplation.

CONCORD, December, 1850.

MY DEAR HAWTHORNE,--Mr. George Bradburn, better known, I think, in the sectarian and agitation than in the literary world, desires to try his luck in solving that impossible problem of a New England magazine. As I was known to be vulnerable, that is, credulous, on that side, I was attacked lately by Hildreth (of U. S. History) and urged to engage in it. I told him to go to Lowell, who had been for a year meditating the like project; that I wished a magazine, but would not think of an experiment and a failure; that if he would assure himself, before he began, of the co-operation of Hawthorne, Cabot, Thoreau, Lowell, Parker, Holmes, and whatever is as good,--if there be as good,--he should be sure of me. So I promised nothing. A few days ago (having heard nothing further for three weeks), I had a letter from Theodore Parker desiring me to write to you and ask your interest and co-operation in Mr. Bradburn's magazine, and to assure you that all articles are to be paid for. So I hope, since they proceed so gently, you will not be taught to deny them, but will let them lay siege to your heart with their soft approaches. A good magazine we have not in America, and we are all its friends beforehand. If they win you, I shall think a great point is gained.

Yours affectionately,
R. W. EMERSON.

--But Hawthorne, having once experienced the scope and freedom of the novel, had ceased to measure himself out in the short lengths of magazine stories; the rather as his experience of that sort of publication had not been, from the pecuniary point of view, very felicitous. He stuck to his Romance, accordingly; and presently his wife was able to write:--

JANUARY 27, 1851.

"The House of the Seven Gables" was finished yesterday. Mr. Hawthorne read me the close, last evening. There is unspeakable grace and beauty in the conclusion, throwing back upon the sterner tragedy of the commencement an ethereal light, and a dear home-loveliness and satisfaction. How you will enjoy the book,--its depth of wisdom, its high tone, the flowers of Paradise scattered over all the dark places, the sweet wall-flower scent of Phoebe's character, the wonderful pathos and charm of old Uncle Venner. I only wish you could have heard the Poet sing his own song, as I did; but yet the book needs no adventitious aid,--it makes its own music, for I read it all over again to myself yesterday, except the last three chapters.

--And three weeks later--

FEBRUARY 12, 1851.

Mr. Hawthorne goes to the village for his proofs. They began to come last Saturday; and when he finds one or more, he remains at the post-office and corrects them, and puts them directly back into the mail. The book is stereotyped, and the printers are going on very fast. The publishers wish to get it out by March. They say they have already orders from all parts for it. . . .

--In fact, the demand was large; and good reports of the book soon began to come in from all quarters. A review, somewhat extravagant in its terms, was published in the "Literary World," and was enclosed to Hawthorne by Longfellow in this cordial note:--

NAHANT.

MY DEAR HAWTHORNE,--I suppose some other friend has already sent you the enclosed notice of yourself and your writings; but it is good enough to have two copies of it. I have rarely seen a more appreciating and sympathizing critic; and though I do not endorse all he says about others, I do endorse all he says about you.

I hear that you are delightfully situated in Berkshire. I hope you are as fully aware of your own happiness, and are enjoying the liberty and air of the mountains, as we are those of the seaside.

A letter from you would be very welcome; a visit, still more so. With kind remembrances to you and your wife from me and mine,

Ever truly,
H. W. L.

--Something of the character of this notice may be gathered from the following passage in a letter of Mrs. Peabody's:--

". . . .I carried the 'Literary World' to Aunt Rawlins. She agreed in the main with the reviewer; but thought he had injured the subject by saying too much. 'No man of common-sense,' she said, 'would seriously name Mr. Hawthorne, deserving as he is of respect and admiration, in the same day with Shakspeare. Shakspeare! the greatest man that ever lived; great in every way,--in science, in knowledge art of human nature, in poetic fire, in historic knowledge, in taste, in imagination, to compare any one to Shakspeare argues ignorance, and only injures the friend he is attempting to serve.' So said that lady."

--It is certainly not necessary to the vindication of Hawthorne's fame to bracket him with Shakspeare; and to the man himself the idea must have appeared too absurdly monstrous to be understood otherwise than as covert satire, or at least as the ravings of well-meaning imbecility. Shakspeare might not have been able to treat the subjects which Hawthorne treated, with more insight and power than he; but, on the other hand, it is certain that Hawthorne could not, under any circumstances, have written a page of any one of Shakspeare's better-known plays. Such comparisons, however, are not worth the ink that traces them. The single pure ray of the American Romancer's genius is just as precious, in itself, as any one of the thousand-hued emanations of the great Poet of the world; for both are truth.

A far more sagacious and poignant discussion of the subject was contributed by Herman Melville in a letter; part of which has already appeared in print.

PITTSFIELD, Wednesday morning.

MY DEAR HAWTHORNE,--Concerning the young gentleman's shoes, I desire to say that a pair to fit him, of the desired pattern, cannot be had in all Pittsfield,--a fact which sadly impairs that metropolitan pride I formerly took in the capital of Berkshire. Henceforth Pittsfield must hide its head. However, if a pair of *bootees* will at all answer, Pittsfield will be very happy to provide them. Pray mention all this to Mrs. Hawthorne, and command me.

"The House of the Seven Gables: A Romance. By Nathaniel Hawthorne. One vol. 16mo, pp. 344." The contents of this book do not belie its rich, clustering, romantic title. With great enjoyment we spent almost an hour in each separate gable. This book is like a fine old chamber, abundantly, but still judiciously, furnished with precisely that sort of furniture best fitted to furnish it. There are rich hangings, wherein are braided scenes from tragedies! There is old china with rare devices, set out on the carved buffet; there are long and indolent lounges to throw yourself upon; there is an admirable sideboard, plentifully stored with good viands; there is a smell as of old wine in the pantry; and finally, in one corner, there is a dark little black-letter volume in golden clasps, entitled "Hawthorne: A Problem." It has delighted us; it has piqued a re-perusal; it has robbed us of a day, and made us a present of a whole year of thoughtfulness; it has bred great exhilaration and exultation with the remembrance that the architect of the Gables resides only six miles of, and not three thousand miles away, in England, say. We think the book, for pleasantness of running interest, surpasses the other works of the author. The curtains are more drawn; the sun comes in more; genialities peep out more. Were we to particularize what most struck us in the deeper passages, we would point out the scene where Clifford, for a moment, would fain throw himself forth from the window to join the procession; or the scene where the judge is left seated in his ancestral chair. Clifford is full of an awful truth throughout. He is conceived in the finest, truest spirit. He is no caricature.

He is Clifford. And here we would say that, did circumstances permit, we should like nothing better than to devote an elaborate and careful paper to the full consideration and analysis of the purport and significance of what so strongly characterizes all of this author's writings. There is a certain tragic phase of humanity which, in our opinion, was never more powerfully embodied than by Hawthorne. We mean the tragedies of human thought in its own unbiassed, native, and profounder workings. We think that into no recorded mind has the intense feeling of the usable truth ever entered more deeply than into this man's. By usable truth, we mean the apprehension of the absolute condition of present things as they strike the eye of the man who fears them not, though they do their worst to him,--the man who, like Russia or the British Empire, declares himself a sovereign nature (in himself) amid the powers of heaven, hell, and earth. He may perish; but so long as he exists he insists upon treating with all Powers upon an equal basis. If any of those other Powers choose to withhold certain secrets, let them; that does not impair my sovereignty in myself; that does not make me tributary. And perhaps, after all, there is no secret. We incline to think that the Problem of the Universe is like the Freemason's mighty secret, so terrible to all children. It turns out, at last, to consist in a triangle, a mallet, and an apron, nothing more! We incline to think that God cannot explain His own secrets, and that He would like a little information upon certain points Himself. We mortals astonish Him as much as He us. But it is this *Being* of the matter; there lies the knot with which we choke ourselves. As soon as you say *Me,* a *God,* a *Nature,* so soon you jump off from your stool and hang from the beam. Yes, that word is the hangman. Take God out of the dictionary, and you would have Him in the street.

There is the grand truth about Nathaniel Hawthorne. He says NO! in thunder; but the Devil himself cannot make him say *yes.* For all men who say *yes,* lie; and all men who say *no,*--why, they are in the happy condition of judicious, unincumbered travellers in Europe; they cross the frontiers into Eternity with nothing but a carpet-bag,--that is to say, the Ego. Whereas those yes-gentry, they travel with heaps of baggage, and, damn them! they will never get through the Custom House. What's the reason, Mr. Hawthorne, that in the last stages of metaphysics a fellow always falls to swearing so? I could rip an hour. You see, I began with a little criticism extracted for your benefit from the "Pittsfield Secret Review," and here I have landed in Africa.

Walk down one of these mornings and see me. No nonsense; come. Remember me to Mrs. Hawthorne and the children.

H. MELVILLE.

P.S. The marriage of Phoebe with the daguerreotypist is a fine stroke, because of his turning out to he a *Maule*. If you pass Hepzibah's cent-shop, buy me a Jim Crow (fresh) and send it to me by Ned Higgins.

---Meanwhile Hawthorne had been writing as follows to his sister Elizabeth:--

LENOX, March 11, 1851.

DEAR E.,--I wish you or Louisa would write to us once in a while, without waiting for regular responses on our part. Sophia is busy from morning till night, and I myself am so much occupied with pen and ink that I hate the thought of writing except from necessity. My book will be out about the 20th instant, and I have directed two copies to be sent to the care of Mr. Dike. You can dispose of them both as you like; but I should think it best to let him have one. The book, I think, has more merit than "The Scarlet Letter;" but it will hardly make so much noise as that. All the copies to which I am entitled (only six) of the new edition of "Twice-Told Tales" have been sent here. If possible, I will keep one for you till I come to Salem, or till Louisa or you come here. At any rate, I will bring you a proof copy of the portrait, which is finely engraved. I am terribly bothered with literary people, who send me their books and expect mine in return.

I trust that you have been at work on the translation of Cervantes' Tales. It appears to me that there can be hardly any doubt of success and profit from it.

It is my purpose to come to Boston (and of course to Salem) some time in June. Until then, I cannot possibly leave home, as our cottage is very lonely, and it would not he safe to go without leaving somebody here to take care of the family. So I mean to take advantage, for that purpose, of a projected visit from Dr. Peabody. We have spent a very pleasant winter; and upon the whole, I think that the best time for living in the country is the winter. I hope that one of you two will come to see us, after my return. The children would be delighted, and it would afford Sophia great pleasure.

Write me what you think of "The House of the Seven Gables."

Yours affectionately, N. H.

-- In the spring of the year, James Russell Lowell sent this careful and cordial definition of his views upon the subject:--

CAMBRIDGE, April 24, 1851.

MY DEAR HAWTHORNE,--I have been so delighted with "The House of the Seven Gables" that I cannot help sitting down to tell you so. I thought I could not forgive you if you wrote anything better than "The Scarlet Letter;" but I cannot help believing it a great triumph that you should have been able to deepen and widen the impression made by such a book as that. It seems to me that the "House" is the most valuable contribution to New England history that has been made. It is with the highest art that you have typified (in the revived likeness of Judge Pyncheon to his ancestor the Colonel) that intimate relationship between the Present and the Past in the way of ancestry and descent, which historians so carefully overlook. Yesterday is commonly looked upon and written about as of no kin to To-day, though the one is legitimate child of the other, and has its veins filled with the same blood. And the chapter about Alice and the Carpenter,--Salem, which would not even allow you so much as Scotland gave Burns, will build you a monument yet for having shown that she did not hang her witches for nothing. I suppose the true office of the historian is to reconcile the present with the past.

I think you hardly do justice (in your preface to "Twice-Told Tales") to your early reception. The augury of a man's popularity ought to be looked for in the intensity and not the vulgarity of his appreciation. However, I shall take to myself a dividend of the blessing you vouchsafe to the earlier acolytes; for I became a disciple in my eighteenth year, which, as Mabel says of day before yesterday, is "Oh, *e-e-ever* so long ago!"

"The House of the Seven Gables" (or "Gabbles," as a foreign friend of mine calls it, converting it into a kind of new tower of Babel) is, I suppose, the old Curwin House in Salem. If so, I flatter myself with a vague sort of ancestral credit in the book, and brag everywhere of my descent from the widow of the very Curwin who built it (I believe), and whose (the widow's) maiden name was Hathorne.

Waiting for the next, I remain
As ever your sincere friend,
J. R. LOWELL.

--The hypothesis as to the identity of the Curwin House with that of the Seven Gables brings to mind a controversy as stale as Egyptian mummy and as interminable as breathing. Did, or did not, the House of the Seven Gables have a prototype? Were, or were not, Zenobia and Margaret Fuller one and the same person? For my part, I should be loath to deprive of any part of their chosen occupation the worthy people who prosecute such inquiries; and although I am in possession of indubitable evidence on both of the above points (as well as on a dozen other and similar ones), the promulgation of which would forever set all conceivable doubts at rest, I shall, for that very reason, forbear to say one word on either side. Let the controversy go on, and the innocent controversialists be happy.

Sometimes letters came to Hawthorne from persons entirely unknown to him, save for that one utterance of gratitude and appreciation; and such letters have a value to an author as great sometimes, in its way, as the applause of friends and rivals. There is more likelihood of sincerity, and less of self-interest, in the former case than in the latter, always provided, of course, that the unknown admirer does not betray a desire for an "autograph." Out of many tributes of this kind I select the following:--

HARTFORD, CONN., April 10, 1851.

MR. HAWTHORNE,--An invalid, I dare address you; for I say, though my dearest author in the world is very wise, he will not disdain my heartfelt, grateful words. As a sick child will be petted, so, nothing fearing, I write to you; for indeed I must tell you how much I thank you--no, that I cannot; yet you have afforded so many pleasant hours to me, one wee one among the thousands. All the long afternoon with grim Cousin Hepzibah and sunshiny Phoebe in the dark gabled house I have been so happy (Phoebe, so like my best friend Genie!), have quite forgotten pain; and though mother says, "Your cheeks are flushed, put away the book!" it is all for pure, deep joy, I am sure. May that joy you give to every one return to you fourfold! May God bless you forever and ever!

Ever your humble, loving admirer,
SALLIE LITCHFIELD.

--This is rather sickly-sentimental, and it is more than easy to laugh at it; but Hawthorne would have worked just as hard, and been just as glad, to give genuine pleasure to Sallie Litchfield as to Lowell, Melville, or Emerson,--the last of whom, by the way, was never able to complete the perusal of any of Hawthorne's stories.

In May, 1851, Mrs. Hawthorne's second daughter was born; and about a month before that event she wrote as follows to her mother:--

LENOX, April 13, 1851.

MY DEAREST MOTHER,--The precious words I received from you last evening went to my inmost heart, and I must answer them. How much in little you say! I am so glad you feel serenely about my little "flower," for it was a very great grievance to me not to tell you of such an expected happiness; but I did not want you to be anxious, and I thought it would save your fear if I should not let you know anything till I could write you that I had multiplied my powers of loving you by a whole new soul in a new form. I am in perfect health, and, now that you are recovering from your attack, again in perfect happiness. After such a winter and spring as I have passed, of tranquil and complete joy, with mountain air and outlines to live upon, I do not see how this new Hawthorne-bud can be otherwise than a lovely and glad existence.

Your child, SOPHIA.

--The birth of the new baby, and other matters, are touched upon in this letter from Hawthorne to his sister Louisa.

LENOX, May 20, 1851.

DEAR L.,--You have another niece. She made her appearance this morning at about three o'clock, and is a very promising child, kicking valiantly and crying most obstreperously. Her hair, I understand, is very much the tinge of Una's. Sophia is quite comfortable, and everything is going on well.

Judging by your long silence, you will not take much interest in the intelligence, nor in anything else which concerns us. I should really like to hear from you once or twice in the course of a twelve-month. Dr. Peabody (who is now here) says that you called in West Street, some time ago; this is our latest news of you. How did you like "The House of the Seven Gables"? Not so well as "The Scarlet Letter," I judge, from your saying nothing about it. I receive very complimentary letters from poets and prosers, and adoring ones from young ladies; and I have almost a challenge from a gentleman who complains of me for introducing his grandfather, Judge Pyncheon. It seems there was really a Pyncheon family formerly resident in Salem, and one of them bore the title of Judge, and was a Tory at the time of the Revolution,--with which facts I was entirely unacquainted. I pacified the gentleman by a letter. Have you seen a horrible wood engraving of me which, with as horrible a biography, has been circulating in the magazines and newspapers?

I am a little worn down with constant work (for I cannot afford any idle time now), but am pretty well, and expect to be greatly refreshed by my visit to the sea.

Affectionately,

NATH. HAWTHORNE.

P.S. Ticknor & Co. want to publish a volume of my tales and sketches not hitherto collected. If you have any, or can obtain them, pray do so. Can you make me a black silk stock, to be ready when I come? To whom is Dora married, and how is she making out?

--After finishing "The House of the Seven Gables," Hawthorne allowed himself a vacation of about four months; and there is every reason to suppose that he enjoyed it. He had recovered his health, he had done his work, he was famous, and the region in which he dwelt was beautiful and inspiriting. At all events, he made those spring days memorable to his children. He made them boats to sail on the lake, and kites to fly in the air; he took them fishing and flower-gathering, and tried (unsuccessfully for the present) to teach them swimming. Mr. Melville used to ride or drive up, in the evenings, with his great dog, and the children used to ride on the dog's back. In short, the place was made a paradise for the small people. In the previous autumn, and still more in the succeeding one, they all went nutting, and filled a certain disused oven in the house with such bags upon bags of nuts as not a hundred children could have devoured during the ensuing winter. The children's father displayed extraordinary activity and energy on these nutting expeditions; standing on the ground at the foot of a tall walnut-tree, he would bid them turn their backs and cover their eyes with their hands; then they would hear, for a few seconds, a sound of rustling and scrambling, and, immediately after, a shout, whereupon they would uncover their eyes and gaze upwards; and lo there was their father--who but an instant before, as it seemed, had been beside them--swaying and soaring high aloft on the topmost branches, a delightful mystery and miracle. And then down would rattle showers of ripe nuts, which the children would diligently pick up, and stuff into their capacious bags. It was all a splendid holiday; and they cannot remember when their father was not their playmate, or when they ever desired or imagined any other playmate than he. Nevertheless, he must sometimes have benefited other people with his companionship, unless he invariably refused invitations like this:--

DEAR MR. HAWTHORNE,--I write you a few lines in case I should not find you at home to-day, in order to ask you to come over on Tuesday next with your two young people. We are going to have a little haymaking after the olden fashion, and a syllabub under the cow; hoping not to be disturbed by any of your grim old Puritans, as were the poor folks of Merrymount. By the way, you do not do yourself justice at all in your preface to the "Twice-Told Tales,"--but more on that subject anon from

Yours truly,

G. P. R. JAMES.

--But it was with Herman Melville that Hawthorne held the most familiar intercourse at this time, both personally and by letter. Subjoined are two characteristic disquisitions by the author of "Moby Dick;" but Hawthorne's answers, if he wrote any, were unfortunately destroyed some years ago.

PITTSFIELD, June 29, 1851.

MY DEAR HAWTHORNE,--The clear air and open window invite me to write to you. For some time past I have been so busy with a thousand things that I have almost forgotten when I wrote you last, and whether I received an answer. This most persuasive season has now for weeks recalled me from certain crotchety and over-doleful chimeras, the like of which men like you and me, and some others, forming a chain of God's posts round the world, must be content to encounter now and then, and fight them the best way we can. But come they will,--for in the boundless, trackless, but still glorious wild wilderness through which these outposts run, the Indians do sorely abound, as well as the insignificant but still stinging mosquitoes. Since you have been here, I have been building some shanties of houses (connected with the old one) and likewise some shanties of chapters and essays. I have been ploughing and sowing and raising and printing and praying, and now begin to come out upon a less bristling time, and to enjoy the calm prospect of things from a fair piazza at the north of the old farmhouse here.

Not entirely yet, though, am I without something to be urgent with. The "Whale" is only half through the press; for, wearied with the long delays of the printers, and disgusted with the heat and dust of the Babylonish brick-kiln of New York, I came back to the country to feel the grass, and end the book reclining on it, if I may. I am sure you will pardon this speaking all about myself; for if I may so much on that head, be sure all the rest of the world are thinking about themselves ten times as much. Let us speak, though we show all our faults and weaknesses,--for it is a sign of strength to be weak, to know it, and out with it; not in set way and ostentatiously, though, but incidentally and without premeditation. But I am falling into my old foible,--preaching. I am busy, but shall not be very long. Come and spend a day here, if you can and want to; if not, stay in Lenox, and God give you long life. When I am quite free of my present engagements, I am going to treat myself to a ride and a visit to you. Have ready a bottle of brandy, because I always feel like drinking that heroic drink when we talk ontological heroics together. This is rather a crazy letter in some respects, I apprehend. If so, ascribe it to the intoxicating effects of the latter end of June operating upon a very susceptible and peradventure feeble temperament. Shall I send you a fin of the "Whale" by way of a specimen mouthful? The tail is not yet cooked, though the hell-fire in which the whole book is broiled might not unreasonably have cooked it ere this. This is the book's motto (the secret one), *Ego non baptiso te in nomine*--but make out the rest yourself.

H. M.

MY DEAR HAWTHORNE,--I should have been rumbling down to you in my pine-board chariot a long time ago, were it not that for some weeks past I have been more busy than you can well imagine,--out of doors,--building and patching and tinkering away in all directions. Besides, I had my crops to get in,--corn and potatoes (I hope to show you some famous ones by and by),--and many other things to attend to, all accumulating upon this one particular season. I work myself; and at night my bodily sensations are akin to those I have so often felt before, when a hired man, doing my day's work from sun to sun. But I mean to continue visiting you until you tell me that my visits are both supererogatory and superfluous. With no son of man do I stand upon any etiquette or ceremony, except the Christian ones of charity and honesty. I am told, my fellow-man, that there is an aristocracy of the brain. Some men have boldly advocated and asserted it: Schiller seems to have done so, though I don't know much about him. At any rate, it is true that there have been those who, while earnest in behalf of political equality, still accept the intellectual estates. And I can well perceive, I think, how a man of superior mind can, by its intense cultivation, bring himself, as it were, into a certain spontaneous aristocracy of feeling,--exceedingly nice and fastidious,--similar to that which, in an English Howard, conveys a torpedo-fish thrill at the slightest contact with a social plebeian. So, when you see or hear of my ruthless democracy on all sides, you may possibly feel a touch of a shrink, or something of that sort. It is but nature to be shy of a mortal who boldly declares that a thief in jail is as honorable a personage as Gen. George Washington. This is ludicrous. But Truth is the silliest thing under the sun. Try to get a living by the Truth--and go to the Soup Societies. Heavens! Let any clergyman try to preach the Truth from its very stronghold, the pulpit, and they would ride him out of his church on his own pulpit bannister. It can hardly be doubted that all Reformers are bottomed upon the truth, more or less; and to the world at large are not reformers almost universally laughing-stocks? Why so? Truth is ridiculous to men. Thus easily in my room here do I, conceited and garrulous, revere the test of my Lord Shaftesbury.

It seems an inconsistency to assert unconditional democracy in all things, and yet confess a dislike to all mankind--in the mass. But not so.--But it's an endless sermon,--no more of it. I began by saying that the reason I have not been to Lenox is this,--in the evening I feel completely done up, as the phrase is, and incapable of the long jolting to get to your house and back. In a week or so, I go to New York, to bury myself in a third-story room, and work and slave on my "Whale" while it is driving through the press. *That* is the only way I can finish it now,--I am so pulled hither and thither by circumstances. The calm, the coolness, the silent grass-growing mood in which a man *ought* always to compose,--that, I fear, can seldom be mine. Dollars damn me; and the malicious Devil is forever grinning in upon me, holding the door ajar. My dear Sir, a presentiment is on me,--I shall at last be worn out and perish, like an old nutmeg-grater, grated to pieces by the constant attrition of the wood, that is, the nutmeg. What I feel most moved to write, that is banned,--it will not pay. Yet, altogether, write the *other* way I cannot. So the product is a final hash, and all my books are botches. I'm rather sore, perhaps, in this letter; but see my hand!--four blisters on this palm, made by bees and hammers within the last few days. It is a rainy morning; so I am indoors, and all work suspended. I feel cheerfully disposed, and therefore I write a little bluely. Would the Gin were here! If ever, my dear Hawthorne, in the eternal times that are to come, you and I shall sit down in Paradise, in some little shady corner by ourselves; and if we shall by any means be able to smuggle a basket of champagne there (I won't believe in a Temperance Heaven), and if we shall then cross our celestial legs in the celestial grass that is forever tropical, and strike our glasses and our heads together, till both musically ring in concert,--then, O my dear fellow-mortal, how shall we pleasantly discourse of all the things manifold which now so distress us,--when all the earth shall be but a reminiscence, yea, its final dissolution an antiquity. Then shall songs be composed as when wars are over; humorous, comic songs,--" Oh, when I lived in that queer little hole called the world," or, "Oh, when I toiled and sweated below," or, "Oh, when I knocked and was knocked in the fight"--yes, let us look forward to such things. Let us swear that, though now we sweat, yet it is because of the dry heat which is indispensable to the nourishment of the vine which is to bear the grapes that are to glve us the champagne hereafter.

But I was talking about the "Whale." As the fishermen say, "he's in his flurry" when I left him some three weeks ago. I'm going to take him by his jaw, however, before long, and finish him up in some fashion or other. What's the use of elaborating what, in its very essence, is so short-lived as a modern book? Though I wrote the Gospels in this century, I should die in the gutter. --I talk all about myself; and this is selfishness and egotism. Granted. But how help it? I am writing to you; I know little about you, but something about myself. So I write about myself;-- at least, to you. Don't trouble yourself; though, about writing; and don't trouble yourself about visiting; and when you do visit, don't trouble yourself about talking. I will do all the writing and visiting and talking myself.--By the way, in the last "Dollar Magazine" I read "The Unpardonable Sin." He was a sad fellow, that Ethan Brand. I have no doubt you are by this time responsible for many a shake and tremor of the tribe of "general readers." It is a frightful poetical creed that the cultivation of the brain eats out the heart. But it's my *prose* opinion that in most cases, in those men who have fine brains and work them well, the heart extends down to hams. And though you smoke them with the fire of tribulation, yet, like veritable hams, the head only gives the richer and the better flavor. I stand for the heart. To the dogs with the head! I had rather be a fool with a heart, than Jupiter Olympus with his head. The reason the mass of men fear God, and *at bottom dislike* Him, is because they rather distrust His heart, and fancy Him all brain like a watch. (You perceive I employ a capital initial in the pronoun referring to the Deity; don't you think there is a slight dash of flunkeyism in that usage?) Another thing. I was in New York for four-and-twenty hours the other day, and saw a portrait of N. H. And I have seen and heard many flattering (in a publisher's point of view) allusions to the "Seven Gables." And I have seen "Tales," and "A New Volume" announced, by N. H. So upon the whole, I say to myself; this N. H. is in the ascendant. My dear Sir, they begin to patronize. All Fame is patronage. Let me be infamous: there is no patronage in *that*. What "reputation" H. M. has is horrible. Think of it! To go down to posterity is bad enough, any way; but to go down as a "man who lived among the cannibals"! When I speak of posterity, in reference to myself; I only mean the babies who will probably be born in the moment immediately ensuing upon my giving up the ghost. I shall go down to some of them, in all likelihood. "Typee" will be given to them, perhaps, with their gingerbread. I have come to regard this matter of Fame as the most transparent of all vanities. I read Solomon more and more, and every time see deeper and deeper and unspeakable meanings in him. I did not think of Fame, a year ago, as I do now. My development has been all within a few years past. I am like one of those seeds taken out of the Egyptian Pyramids, which, after being three thousand years a seed and nothing but a seed, being planted in English soil, it developed itself; grew to greenness, and then fell to mould. So I. Until I was twenty-five, I had no development at all. From my twenty-fifth year I date my life. Three weeks have scarcely passed, at any time between then and now, that I have not unfolded within myself. But I feel that I am now come to the inmost leaf of the bulb, and that shortly the flower must fall to the mould. It seems to me now that Solomon was the truest man who ever spoke, and yet that he a little *managed* the truth with a view to popular conservatism; or else there have been many corruptions and interpolations of the text.--In reading some of Goethe's sayings, so worshipped by his votaries, I came across this, *"Live in the all."* That is to say, your separate identity is but a wretched one,--good; but get out of yourself, spread and expand yourself, and bring to yourself the tinglings of life that are felt in the flowers and the woods, that are felt in the planets Saturn and Venus, and the Fixed Stars. What nonsense! Here is a fellow with a raging toothache. "My dear boy," Goethe says to him, you are sorely afflicted with that tooth; but you must *live in the all,* and then you will be happy!" As with all great genius, there is an immense deal of flummery in Goethe, and in proportion to my own contact with him, a monstrous deal of it in me.

    H. MELVILLE.

    P. S. "Amen!" saith Hawthorne.

    N. B. This "all" feeling, though, there is some truth in. You must often have felt it, lying on the grass on a warm summer's day. Your legs seem to send out shoots into the earth. Your hair feels like leaves upon your head. This is the *all* feeling. But what plays the mischief with the truth is that men will insist upon the universal application of a temporary feeling or opinion.

    P.S. You must not fail to admire my discretion in paying the postage on this letter.

--Mr. Melville was probably quite as entertaining and somewhat less abstruse, when his communications were by word of mouth. Mrs. Hawthorne used to tell of one evening when he came in, and presently began to relate the story of a fight which he had seen on an island in the Pacific, between some savages, and of the prodigies of valor one of them performed with a heavy club. The narrative was extremely graphic; and when Melville had gone, and Mr. and Mrs. Hawthorne were talking over his visit, the latter said, "Where is that club with which Mr. Melville was laying about him so?" Mr. Hawthorne thought he must have taken it with him; Mrs. Hawthorne thought he had put it in the corner; but it was not to be found. The next time Melville came, they asked him about it; whereupon it appeared that the club was still in the Pacific island, if it were anywhere.

In June, Hawthorne began the "Wonder-Book," which is less known than it ought to be; for in simplicity and eloquence of style, and in lovely wealth of fancy and imagination, it is equal to anything he produced. Before the book was in the printer's hands, the children could repeat the greater part of it by heart, from hearing it read so often,--as had before been the case with "The Snow Image,"--and even now, entire passages linger in their memory. It was written rapidly, and with great enjoyment on the author's part; being the only book he ever published which has not a gloomy page in it, though even here--in "The Chimæra," for example--there are the springs of quiet tears. But the humor, throughout, is exquisite; and though the sentiment often mounts to heaven, like Bellerophon's winged steed, it never outsoars the comprehension of the simplest child. The book was finished in the first week of July, 1851; and Hawthorne again wrote to Louisa as follows:--

LENOX, July 10, 1851.

DEAR L.,--If you have any of the magazine articles, mentioned in my last, I wish you would have them sent to B., as he is going to send a package to me within a week or two. The cravat, if ready, might be sent too; but perhaps it would be better to keep it till I come, for fear of its being jammed.

I have been too busy, lately, to write. The truth is, the pen is so constantly in my fingers that I abominate the sight of it. I have written a book for children, two or three hundred pages long, since the first of June. Sophia is likewise too busy to write even to her own family. By the by, it was not she, but myself, who wrote to Mrs. Foote.

Sophia will probably go to West Newton in the course of two or three weeks (some time in August, at all events) to see her mother. She will take the baby and Una, and leave Julian here under my charge. If you want to see the baby before next year, you must make arrangements to do it then. The Boston establishment is broken up, so that you cannot see her there; and unless Miss Rawlins Pickman should ask her to Salem, I see no way but for you to go to West Newton. You can get out there and back any hour in the day.

The baby flourishes, and seems to be the brightest and strongest baby we have had. She grows prettier, but cannot be called absolutely beautiful. Her hair, I think, is a more decided red than Una's. As for Una, she is as wild as a colt, and freckled and tanned so that you would hardly know her. Julian has grown enormous, but otherwise looks pretty much the same as he used to do.

Three or four editions of my two romances have been published in London at prices varying from one shilling to five shillings. Mrs. Kemble writes that it has produced a greater sensation than any book since "Jane Eyre," and advises that I take out my copyrights there.

I think we shall remove to Mrs. Kemble's cottage in the course of the autumn; for this is certainly the most inconvenient and wretched little hovel that I ever put my head in. Mrs. Kemble's has not more rooms, but they are larger, and perfectly convenient. She offers it to me, ready furnished, for the same price that I pay here.

Last year she offered it for nothing, but I declined the terms. I shall regret the prospect from the windows of this house (for it is the most beautiful in Berkshire), but nothing else.

I have received a letter from Elizabeth (a good while ago, however), and should have answered it if I had had time. Send this to her. I want much to see her, and talk over her plans and prospects, and should come eastwards for that purpose, if for nothing else. Possibly I may come immediately after Sophia's return; but I rather think I may put it off till after our removal.

Affectionately,

N. H.

P.S. If the articles are in magazines or volumes, you had better cut them out, in order to get them within smaller compass. I do not intend to publish anything from the "American Magazine."

N. H.

--Mrs. Hawthorne and her two daughters now set forth on their journey to their relatives in the East, leaving Hawthorne and his son, and the old negro cook, Mrs. Peters,--a stern and incorruptible African, and a housekeeper by the wrath of God,--to get along together for three weeks, as best they might. It must have been weary work, sometimes, for Hawthorne, though for the little boy it was one uninterrupted succession of halcyon days. A detailed narrative of their adventures was written, day by day, by the father, and would make a volume of upwards of a hundred pages,--as unique and quaint a little history as was ever seen. I have brought together a few representative extracts, taken from here and there.

Twenty Days with Julian and Bunny.

LENOX, *July* 28, 1851. --At seven o'clock, A. M., wife, Una, and Rosebud took their departure, leaving Julian and me, and Mrs. Peters (the colored lady who does our cooking for us), and Bunny, the rabbit, in possession of the Red Shanty. Bunny does not turn out to be a very interesting companion, and makes me more trouble than he is worth. There ought to be two rabbits, in order to bring out each other's remarkable qualities, if any there be. Undoubtedly, they have the least feature and characteristic prominence of any creature that God has made. With no playfulness, as silent as a fish, inactive, Bunny's life passes between a torpid half-slumber, and the nibbling of clover-tops, lettuce, plantain leaves, pig-weed, and crumbs of bread. Sometimes, indeed, he is seized with a little impulse of friskiness; but it does not appear to be sportive, but nervous. Bunny has a singular countenance, like somebody's I have seen, but whose, I forget. It is rather imposing and aristocratic, at a cursory glance; but, examining it more closely, it is found to be laughably vague. I am strongly tempted of the Evil One to murder him privately; and I wish with all my heart that Mrs. Peters would drown him.

Julian had a great resource in my jack-knife, which, being fortunately as dull as a hoe, I have given him to whittle with. So he made what he called a boat, and covered the floor of the boudoir with chips, twice over; and finds such inexhaustible amusement, that I think it would be cheaply bought with the loss of one or two of his fingers. . .

29th.--A cool, breezy morning, with sunshine glimpsing through sullen clouds, which seemed to hang low, and rest on the ridges of the hills that border the valley. After breakfast, we took Bunny out of doors, and put him down on the grass. Bunny appears to most advantage out of doors. His most interesting trait is the apprehensiveness of his nature, it is as quick and as continually in movement as an aspen leaf. The least noise startles him, and you may see his emotion in the movement of his ears; he starts, and scrambles into his little house, but in a moment peeps forth again and begins nibbling the grass and weeds,--again to be startled and as quickly reassured. Sometimes he sets out on a nimble little run, for no reason, but just as a dry leaf is blown along by a puff of wind. I do not think that these fears are any considerable torment to Bunny; it is his nature to live in the midst of them, and to intermingle them, as a sort of piquant sauce, with every morsel he eats. It is what redeems his life from dulness and stagnation. Bunny appears to be uneasy in broad and open sunshine; it is his impulse to seek shadow,--the shadow of a tuft of bushes, or Julian's shadow, or mine. He seemed to think himself rather too conspicuous--so important a personage as he is--in the breadth of the yard, and took various opportunities to creep into Julian's lap. At last, the northwest wind being cool to-day, and especially so when one of the thousand watery clouds intercepts the sun, we all three came in. This is a horrible, horrible, most hor-ri-ble climate; one knows not, for ten minutes together, whether he is too cool or too warm; but he is always one or the other, and the constant result is a miserable disturbance of the system. I detest it! I detest it!! I detest it!!! I hate Berkshire with my whole soul, and would joyfully see its mountains laid flat. Be it recorded that here, where I hoped for perfect health, I have for tbe first time been made sensible that I cannot with impunity encounter Nature in all her moods. . . .

After dinner (roast lamb for me and boiled rice for Julian), we walked down to the lake. On our way, we waged war with the thistles, which represented many-headed hydras and dragons, and on tall mulleins, which passed for giants. One of these latter offered such sturdy resistance, that my stick was broken in the encounter; and so I cut it off of a length suitable to Julian, who thereupon expressed an odd entanglement of sorrow for my loss and joy for his own gain. As I lay on my back, looking upwards through the branches of the trees, Julian spent nearly a quarter of an hour, I should think, beating down a single great mullein-stalk. He certainly does evince a persevering purpose, sometimes. We strolled through the woods, among the tall pillars of those primeval pines, and thence home along the margin of a swamp, in which I gathered a sheaf of cat-tails. The heavy masses of cloud, lumbering about the sky, threw deep black shadows on the sunny hillsides, so that the contrast between the heat and the coolness of the day was thus visibly expressed. The atmosphere was particularly transparent as if all the haze was collected into these dense clouds. Distant objects appeared with great distinctness; and the Taconic range of hills was a dark blue substance,--not cloud-like, as it often is. The sun smiled with mellow breadth across the rippling lake, rippling with the northwestern breeze. Julian was never out of spirits, and is certainly as happy as the day is long. He is happy enough by himself; and when I sympathize, or partake in his play, it is almost too much, and he nearly explodes with laughter and delight.

Little Marshall Butler has been to inquire whether "the bird" has come yet. I have seldom suffered more from the presence of any individual than from that of this odious little urchin. Julian took no more notice of him than if he had not been present, but went on with his talk and occupations, displaying an equanimity which I could not but envy. He absolutely ignores him; no practised man of the world could do it better, or half so well. After forging about the room and examining the playthings, Marshall took himself off. . . .

30*th*. Bunny has grown quite familiar, and comes hopping to meet us, whenever we enter the room, and stands on his hind legs to see whether we have anything for him. Julian has changed his name (which was Spring) to Hindlegs. One finds himself getting rather attached to the gentle little beast, especially when he shows confidence and makes himself at home. . .

We walked to the village for the mail, and on our way back we met a wagon in which sat Mr. G. P. R. James, his wife and daughter, who had just left their cards at our house. Here ensued a talk, quite pleasant and friendly. He is certainly an excellent man; and his wife is a plain, good, friendly, kind-hearted woman, and his daughter a nice girl. Mr. James spoke of "The House of the Seven Gables" and of "Twice-Told Tales," and then branched off upon English literature generally.

Proceeding homeward, we were overtaken by a cavalier on horseback, who saluted me in Spanish, to which I replied by touching my hat. But, the cavalier renewing his salutation, I regarded him more attentively, and saw that it was Herman Melville! So we all went homeward together, talking as we went. Soon Mr. Melville alighted, and put Julian in the saddle; and the little man was highly pleased, and sat on the horse with the freedom and fearlessness of an old equestrian, and had a ride of at least a mile homeward. I asked Mrs. Peters to make some tea for Herman Melville, and so she did; and after supper I put Julian to bed, and Melville and I had a talk about time and eternity, things of this world and of the next, and books, and publishers, and all possible and impossible matters, that lasted pretty deep into the night. At last he rose, and saddled his horse and rode off to his own domicile, and I went to bed. . . .

I forgot to say that before supper Mr. Tappan came in, with three or four volumes of Fourier's works, which I wished to borrow, with a view to my next romance [Blithedale]. . . .

31*st*.--Bunny ate a leaf of mint to-day, seemingly with great relish. It makes me smile to see how he invariably comes galloping to meet me, whenever I open the door, making sure that there is something in store for him, and smelling eagerly to find out what it is. He eats enormously, and I think has grown considerably broader than when he came hither. The mystery that broods about him--the lack of any method of communicating with this voiceless creature--heightens the interest. Then he is naturally so full of little alarms, that it is pleasant to find him free of them as to Julian and myself.

In the morning, for the first time since some immemorial date, it was really quite pleasant; not a cloud to be seen, except a few white and bright streaks, far off to the southward. Monument Mountain, however, had a fleece of sun-brightened mist, entirely covering it, except its western summit, which emerged. There were also mists along its western side, hovering on the tree-tops; and portions of the same mist had flitted upwards, and become real clouds in the sky. These vapors were rapidly passing away, and by the time we had done our errand (to Luther Butler's for the milk) they had wholly disappeared. . . .

I have sent Bunny over to Mr. Tappan's, in the hope that they may adopt him, as the excellent little animal, for whom I have a great regard, is not exactly suited to be an occupant of our sitting-room. He has, however, very pleasant little ways, and a character well worth studying. He has grown quite familiar with us, and seems to show a fondness for our society, and would always seat himself near us, and was attentive to all our motions. He has too, I think, a great deal of curiosity, and an investigating disposition, and is very observant of what is going on around him. I do not know any other beast, and few human beings, who, always present, and thrusting his little paw into all the business of the day, could at the same time be so perfectly unobtrusive. What a pity that he could not put himself under some restraint and rule as to certain matters!

August 5. --For several days past I have been out of order with a cold, but it seems now to have passed away. As I was sitting in the boudoir this morning, Mrs. Peters came in, and said that a lady wished to see me. The visitor was a lady, rather young, and quite comely, with pleasant and intelligent eyes, in a pretty Quaker dress. She offered me her hand, and spoke with much simplicity, but yet in a ladylike way, of her interest in my works, and of Lowell, Whittier, James, Melville, the scenery, and of various other matters. Her manners were very agreeable; the Quaker simplicity and the little touch of Quaker phraseology gave piquancy to her refinement and air of society. She had a pleasant smile, and eyes that readily responded to one's thought, so that it was not difficult to talk with her; a singular, but yet a gentle freedom in expressing her own opinions; an entire absence of affectation; and, on the whole, it was the only pleasant visit I ever experienced in my capacity as author. She did not bore me with laudations of my own writings, but merely said that there are some authors with whom we feel ourselves privileged to become acquainted, by the nature of our sympathy with their writings, or something to that effect.

All this time Julian was climbing into my lap and off again. She smiled on him, and inquired whether he looked like his mother, remarking that he had no resemblance to myself. Finally she rose to depart, and I ushered her to the gate, where, as she took leave, she told me her name,--Elizabeth Lloyd,--and, bidding me farewell, she went on her way, and I saw her no more. . . .

It has been quite showery this afternoon; and across our valley, from east to west, there was a heavy canopy of clouds, almost resting on the hills on either side. It did not extend southward so far as Monument Mountain, which lay in sunshine, and with a sunny cloud midway on its bosom; and from the midst of our storm, beneath our black roof of clouds, we looked out upon this bright scene, where the people were enjoying beautiful weather. The clouds hung so low over us, that it was like being in a tent, the entrance of which was drawn up, permitting us to see the sunny landscape. This lasted for several minutes; but at last the shower stretched southward, and quite snatched away Monument Mountain, and made it invisible. Now it is mistily reappearing.

Julian has got rid of the afternoon in a miscellaneous manner; making a whip, and a bow-and-arrow, and playing Jackstraws with himself as an antagonist. It was less than an hour, I think, after dinner, when he began to bellow for something to eat, although he dined abundantly on rice and string-beans. I allowed him a slice of bread in the middle of the afternoon; and an hour afterwards, be began to bellow at the full stretch of his lungs for more, and beat me terribly because I refused it. He is really as strong as a little giant. He asked me just now, "What are sensible questions?"--I suppose with a view to asking me some.

After a most outrageous resistance, the old gentleman was put to bed at seven o'clock. I ought to mention that Mrs. Peters is quite attentive to him, in her grim way. To-day, for instance, we found two ribbons on his straw hat, which must have been of her sewing on. She encourages no familiarity on his part, nor is he in the least drawn towards her; nor, on the other hand, does he exactly seem to stand in awe; but he recognizes that there is to be no communication beyond the inevitable,--and, with that understanding, she awards him all substantial kindness. . . .

August 8. --To-day, Herman Melville and the two Duyckincks came in a barouche, and we all went to visit the Shaker establishment at Hancock. I don't know what Julian expected to see,--some strange sort of quadruped or other, I suppose,--and probably he was a little disappointed when I pointed out an old man in a gown and a gray, broad-brimmed hat, as a Shaker. The old man was one of the Fathers and rulers of the community, and under his guidance we visited the principal dwelling-house of the Village. It was a large brick edifice, with admirably contrived arrangements, floors and walls of polished woods, and everything so neat that it was a pain and constraint to look at it; especially as it did not imply any real delicacy or moral nicety in the occupants of the house. There were spittoons (bearing no appearance of ever being used, it is true) at equal distances up and down the broad entries. The sleeping-apartments of the two sexes had an entry between them, on one side of which hung the hats of the men, on the other side the bonnets of the women. In each chamber were two particularly narrow beds, hardly wide enough for one sleeper, but in each of which, the old Elder told us, two persons slept. There were no bathing or washing conveniences in the chambers; but in the entry there was a sink and washboard, where all their attempts at purification were to be performed. This fact shows that all their miserable pretence of cleanliness and neatness is the thinnest superficiality, and that the Shakers are, and must needs be, an unwashed set. And then their utter and systematic lack of privacy is hateful to think of. The sooner the sect is extinct the better, I think.

In the great house we saw an old woman--a round, fat, cheerful little old sister--and two girls, from nine to twelve years old; these looked at us and at Julian with great curiosity, though slyly and with side glances. At the doors of other dwellings we saw women sewing and otherwise at work; and there seemed to be a kind of comfort among them, but of no higher kind than is enjoyed by their beasts of burden. Also, the women were mostly pale, and none of the men had a jolly aspect. They are certainly the most singular and bedevilled set of people that ever existed in a civilized land.

Coming home, we mistook our way, and the drive was by far the most picturesque I have seen in Berkshire. On one height, just before sunset, we had a view for miles and miles around, with the Catskills blue and far on the horizon. Then the road ran along the verge of a deep gulf;--deep, deep, deep, and filled with foliage of trees that could not half reach up to us; and on the other side of the chasm uprose a mountainous precipice; but there were occasional openings through the forest, as we drove along, showing the low country at the base of the mountain. I had no idea that there was such a region within a few miles of us.

By and by, Monument Mountain and Rattlesnake Hill became visible, and we found we were approaching Lenox from the west, and must pass through the village in order to reach home. I got out at the post-office, and received a letter from

Phoebe. By the time we were out of the village, it was beyond twilight: indeed, but for the full moon, it would have been quite dark. The little man behaved himself still like an old traveller; but sometimes he looked round at me from the front seat, and smiled at me with a peculiar expression, and put back his hand to touch me. It was a method of establishing sympathy in what doubtless appeared to him the wildest and unprecedentedest series of adventures that had ever befallen mortal travellers. Anon, we drew up at the little gate of the old red house. . . .

August 9. --We arose at about seven. I felt the better for the expedition; and, asking Julian whether he had a good time, he answered with great enthusiasm in the affirmative, and that he wanted to go again, and that he loved Mr. Melville as well as me and as mamma and as Una.

The rain was pouring down, and from all the hillsides mists were steaming up, and Monument Mountain seemed to be enveloped as if in the smoke of a great battle. During one of the heaviest showers of the day there was a succession of thundering knocks at the front door. On opening it, there was a young man on the doorstep, and a carriage at the gate, and Mr. James thrusting his head out of the carriage window, and beseeching shelter from the storm! So here was an invasion. Mr. and Mrs. James, their eldest son, their daughter, their little son Charles, their maid-servant, and their coachman;--not that the coachman came in; and as for the maid, she stayed in the hall. Dear me! where was Phoebe in this time of need? All taken aback as I was, I made the best of it. Julian helped me somewhat, but not much. Little Charley is a few months younger than he, and between them they at least furnished subject for remark. Mrs. James, luckily, happened to be very much afraid of thunder and lightning; and as these were loud and sharp, she might be considered *hors de combat*. The son, who seemed to be about twenty, and the daughter, of seventeen or eighteen, took the part of saying nothing, which I suppose is the English fashion as regards such striplings. So Mr. James was the only one to whom it was necessary to talk, and we got along tolerably well. He said that this was his birthday, and that he was keeping it by a pleasure-excursion, and that therefore the rain was a matter of course. We talked of periodicals, English and American, and of the Puritans, about whom we agreed pretty well in our opinions; and Mr. James told how he had recently been thrown out of his wagon, and how the horse ran away with Mrs. James; and we talked about green lizards and red ones. And Mr. James told Julian how, when he was a child, he had twelve owls at the same time; and, at another time, a raven, who used to steal silver spoons and money. He also mentioned a squirrel, and several other pets; and Julian laughed most obstreperously.

As to little Charles, he was much interested with Bunny (who has been returned to us from the Tappans' somewhat the worse for wear), and likewise with the rocking-horse, which luckily happened to be in the sitting-room. He examined the horse most critically, and finally got upon his back, but did not show himself quite so good a rider as Julian. Our old boy hardly said a word. Finally the shower passed over, and the invaders passed away; and I do hope that on the next occasion of the kind my wife will be there to see. . . .

August 14.--Going on our usual milky way this morning, we saw a dim rainbow. I fear, from subsequent and present appearances, that it was prophetic of bad weather for the day. At breakfast, Julian observed some cake which Mrs. Peters had set on the table for me; whereupon he became discontented with his own breakfast, and wanted something different from the ordinary bread and milk. I told him that his bread had yeast in it; and he forthwith began to eat it with a great appetite, and thought it better than any he ever tasted. . . .

In the afternoon, Julian insisted that we should go down to the lake; so away we went, and he was in the highest possible exhilaration, absolutely tumbling down with laughter, once or twice, on small cause. On reaching the lake, he sobered himself; and began to angle, with his customary beanpole and bent pin, and with all the staidness of an ancient fisherman. By this time it clouded over, and the lake looked wild and angry, with the gusts that swept across it. . . . On our way home, we seated ourselves on some logs, and the old boy said that one of these logs was Giant Despair, and that the old giant was dead; and he dug a shallow hole, which he said should be the giant's grave. I objected that it was not half large enough; but he informed me that Giant Despair grew very small, the moment he was dead. . . . It was nearly five when we reached home, and within an hour, surely, or very little more, Phoebe cannot fail to shine upon us. It seems absolutely an age since she departed. I think I hear the sound of wheels now. It was not she.

Eight, P. M.--Inconceivable to tell, she did not come! I set out for the post-office; it was a clear and beautiful sunset, with a brisk, Septemberish temperature. To my further astoundment, I found no letter; so that I conclude she must, after all, have intended to come to-day. It may be that there was a decided rain, this morning, in the region round about Boston, and that this prevented her setting out. . . .

August 15. --We did not get up till seven this morning. It was very clear, and of autumnal freshness, with a breeze from the northwest. On our walk this morning, we met three ladies on horseback; and the little man asked me whether I thought the ladies pretty, and said that he did not. They really were rather pretty, in my opinion; but I suspect that their appearance on horseback did not suit his taste; and I agree with him that a woman is a disagreeable spectacle in such an attitude. But the old boy is very critical in matters of beauty; although I think the real ground of his censures lies in some wrong done to his sense of propriety and fitness. For instance, he denied that the Quaker lady who called on me was pretty; and it turned out that he did not like the unaccustomed fashion of her dress, and her thees and thous.

Bunny is evidently out of order. He appeared to be indisposed yesterday, and is still more evidently so to-day. He has just had a shivering fit. Julian thinks he has the scarlet fever; that being the only disease with which he was ever conversant.

Mr. Ward has just been here, expecting to find Phoebe had arrived yesterday. This heightens the mystery. Elizabeth wrote me that he would escort her on Wednesday. He was prevented from coming on that day, but supposed she would have come on Thursday. Where can she be? . . . .

I put Julian to bed, and went to the village. Still no letter from Sophie. I think she must have been under some mistake as to Mr. Ward's movements, and has waited in expectation of his escort. I spent the evening reading newspapers. To bed, disconsolate, a little before ten.

August 16. --On entering the bathing-room this morning, I peeped into Bunny's cage, with something like a foreboding of what had happened; and, sure enough, there lay the poor little beast, stark and stiff. That shivering fit, yesterday, had a very fatal aspect in my eyes. I have no idea what was his disorder; his symptoms had been a disinclination, for the last two days, to move or eat. Julian seems to be interested and excited by the event, rather than afflicted. He imputed it, as he does all other mishaps, to the agency of Giant Despair; and as we were going for the milk, he declared it was the wickedest thing the giant ever did. . . . After breakfast, we dug a hole, and we planted poor Bunny in the garden. Julian said, "Perhaps to-morrow there will be a tree of Bunnies, and they will hang all over it by their ears." I have before this observed that children have an odd propensity to treat death as a joke, though rather nervously. He has laughed a good deal about Bunny's exit.

We went to the lake, in accordance with the old boy's wish; he had taken with him the little vessel that his Uncle Nat had made for him long ago, and which, since yesterday, has been his favorite plaything. He launched it upon the lake, and it looked very like a real sloop, tossing up and down on the swelling waves. I believe he would contentedly have spent a hundred years or so, with no other amusement than this. I meanwhile took the "National Era" from my pocket, and gave it a pretty attentive perusal. I have before now experienced that the best way to get a vivid impression and feeling of a landscape is to sit down before it and read, or become otherwise absorbed in thought; for then, when your eyes happen to be attracted towards the landscape, you seem to catch Nature at unawares, and see her before she has time to change her aspect. The effect lasts but for a single instant, and passes away almost as soon as you are conscious of it; but it is real for that moment. It is as if you could overhear and understand what the trees are whispering to one another; as if you caught a glimpse of a face unveiled, which veils itself from every wilful glance. The mystery is revealed, and, after a breath or two, becomes just as great a mystery as before. I caught one such glimpse, this forenoon, though not so perfectly as sometimes. It was half past twelve when we got back. . . .

If Phoebe does not come to-day--well, I don't know what I shall do. It is nearly six by the clock, and they do not come! Surely, they must, must, must be here to-night!

Within a quarter of an hour after writing the above, they have come,--all well! Thank God!

--The "Wonder-Book" having been put forth, embellished with some wonderful illustrations, amusing to Hawthorne, but perplexing to his children, to whom the text had suggested marvels quite different from those of the artist, this work having been disposed of; nothing but a few months intervened between the author and his third great Romance of "Hollingsworth," or, as he finally resolved to call it, "The Blithedale Romance." Meanwhile, however, he removed from Lenox, and took a house within a few miles of Boston.

In fact, after freeing himself from Salem, Hawthorne never found any permanent rest anywhere. He soon wearied of any particular locality. A novelist would say that he inherited the roving disposition of his seafaring ancestors. Partly necessity or convenience, but partly, also, his own will, drove him from place to place; always wishing to settle down finally, but never lighting upon the fitting spot. In America he moved from place to place and longed for England. In England he travelled constantly and looked forward to France and Italy. In Paris, Rome, and Florence his affections reverted to England once more; but, having returned thither, he made it but a stepping-stone to America. Finding himself at length in Concord, he enlarged and refitted the house he had previously bought there, and tried to think that he was content to spend in it the remainder of his days. No sooner had he come to this determination, however, than memories of England possessed him more and more; he mused about it, wrote about it, and, till near the end, cherished a secret hope that some happy freak of destiny might lead him there again. And when it became evident that destiny forbade such hopes, he made ready for the longest journey of all. It was the only one to the goal of which he could look forward with assured confidence.

On the 21st of November, 1851, the family, with their trunks, got into a large farmer's wagon, and were driven to Pittsfield, leaving the little red house empty behind them. It was a bleak day; and one of the party remembers that the five cats which had been fellow inmates for many months, divining by some inscrutable instinct that this departure was final, and not merely a picnic or a visit, evacuated the premises in a body, and scampered after the wagon for about quarter of a mile. This brought them to the ridge of a hill, from which the road descended rapidly; and upon this ridge the five cats seated themselves in a row, and stared despairingly after the rapidly receding vehicle. There they remained, in motionless protest, outlined against the sky, until distance blotted them from sight. A snow-storm presently arose; and whether the five cats returned to the deserted house, or perished in the fury of the elements, or resumed their vain pursuit of the wagon, can never be revealed. As for the family, it reached West Newton that same evening.

A more dismal and unlovely little suburb than West Newton was in the winter of 1851 could not exist outside of New England. It stood upon a low rise of land, shelving down to a railway, along which smoky trains screeched and rumbled from morning till night. One of these trains had its smoke-stack bound about with gayly colored bunting, for it was carrying Louis Kossuth from New York to Boston. A few days afterwards, one of the children remembers being in a large hall, full of ladies and gentlemen; and the child's mother said, "Here comes Kossuth!" The child had a card in its hand, on which it had printed with a pencil, "God bless you, Kossuth!" and as the slender, dark, bearded gentleman drew near, bowing and smiling, this document was presented to him. It was a tremendous moment in the experience of the child, if not of the Hungarian patriot, who, however, accepted the testimonial very graciously.

Lenox was one of those places where a man might be supposed to write because the beauty around him wooed him to expression. West Newton was a place where the omnipresent ugliness compels a man to write in self-defence. Lenox drew forth "The House of the Seven Gables," and in West Newton "The Blithedale Romance" was composed; from which data the curious in such matters may conclude which kind of environment is the more favorable to the artist. The book was produced somewhere between the first of December and the last of April of the next year, when the snow was lying a foot deep on the ground. West Newton is not far from West Roxbury, where Brook Farm was situated; and it is possible that Hawthorne may have revisited the place in his walks, in order to refresh his memory as to the locality of his story; though I should be inclined to think that he would carefully avoid thus running the risk of disturbing the artistic atmosphere which had softened his ten years' recollection of the spot.

But this chapter has grown to such length that any remarks upon "Blithedale" must be deferred to the next. West Newton, it may be remarked, was only used as a temporary dwelling-place while something better was being looked for; and it was upon Concord that Hawthorne finally fixed his hopes. He made inquiries of, among other persons, Ellery Channing, as to what prospect there was of getting a house there; and Ellery invited him to come and talk it over, as may be gathered from the following whimsical letters:--

CONCORD, Dec. 13, 1851.

MY DEAR HAWTHORNE,--I am glad you have shortened your longitude, and evacuated that devilish institution of Spitzbergen,--that ice-plant of Sedgwicks, etc. Good God! to live permanently in Iceland! I know nothing of West Newton, and do not wish to know any more; but it is further south than the other,--a great advantage,--and you can sell Old Boreas, lusty railer, etc.

I write to say that I have now a room at your command, where perhaps you might make yourself comfortable for a few days. Nobody at home but myself; and a prospect of strong waters. It is so damned near where you live that perhaps you would like to leave home,--always a devilish bore to me, at any rate. I have got a good cook, and some wood; and you can have whole days, as I never dine before five. There is only this, my dear fellow; and if you will come, please let me know *instanter,* as next week is the week I shall be ready for you.

Emerson is gone, and nobody here to bore you. The skating is damned good.

Ever yours, W. E. C.

N. B. Pipes and old tobac no end.

--Hawthorne replied that his literary employments and domestic affairs would not allow him to avail himself of Ellery's pipes and Mr. Emerson's absence; whereupon the eccentric poet entered into a more detailed discussion of the situation.

CONCORD, Friday, Dec. 17, 1851.

DEAR HAWTHORNE,--Your letter, received to-night, got carried to hell before it got here, and the Prince of Darkness interpolated a polite refusal to my lively invitation. Now, by dint of swearing at the cook, damning the butcher; breaking all the temperance laws of the State, and exerting ourselves, I doubt not I might have passed a profitable week, to me.

But as you are sweating Romances, and have got that execrable bore, a small family, it is all right. I am glad *now* you did not come. I was afraid you would be disappointed if you had.

For my own part, I would infinitely rather settle on the icy peak of Mt. Ararat than in this village. It is absolutely the worst spot in the world. There are so many things against it, that it would be useless to enumerate the first. Among others, day before yesterday, at six A. M., the thermometer was ten degrees below nothing. This is enough.

A good climate is a prime consideration to me. Think of the climate of Venice, of Fie-all, of Cuba, of Malaga,--the last best. I have been within about six miles of the last city; behind it rise majestic *Sierras,* before it glitters and dreams the blue Mediterranean, and the thermometer stands at 75 degrees the year round. O God! what a contrast to this d---d place!

I have never lived in Alcott's place; but I judge the thermometer there goes as low as anywhere else in this country. Of course, that place you were at was colder.

How would it do to have a house at Este, or on the Gulf of Spezzia, as Shelley of drowned memory did? The rents are low, and living is cheap. Shelley made good weather, by the aid of Byron, Hunt, Trelawney, Williams, and others. I fancy it would not do to go alone among the peasantry; and you might retire from the Domzilla with a knife in your guts.

Mr. Lowell, whom I did not know, is somewhere in that ilk, and Mr. Story, etc. But they keep at Rome or Florence; and the climate of Rome, though mild, is aguish. So it is, absolutely, *in* Venice.

Self-exiled, etc., how would this seem? The American stamp is pretty strong on you, and could you feel at ease in European circumstances? I disliked Europe, alone, beyond description. You are such a domestic affair, you would feel snug with your family, etc.

What do you think of California? Good climate, but lots of blacklegs. I think a villa among the Euganean Hills would be as good as anything. But it requires a coal-hod of tin to make it work. Byron's income was about $20,000 a year.

Affectionately yours,
W. E. C.

--As there was no immediate prospect of realizing the Gulf of Spezzia, or even California, Hawthorne finally decided to buy Mr. Alcott's honse in Concord, together with the twenty acres or thereabouts of arable and wooded land belonging to it. But he wisely waited until June before entering on possession of it; for there are days in that month when the climate of Concord seems almost as Paradisiacal as that of Malaga or the Euganean Hills.

CHAPTER 9 - CONCORD

WHEN Hawthorne went to Lenox, after Madame Hawthorne's death, the household in Mall Street was, of course, broken up; and his two sisters, Elizabeth and Louisa, were established, the latter with her relatives in Salem, the former in lodgings in a farmer's family on the sea-coast not far from Salem, where she lived, in perfect contentment, for more than thirty years, a life the solitude of which would have killed most women in as many days. Beyond the members of the farmer's family (who could be her associates only in the most literal sense) she very seldom saw or communicated with any one. She got up at noon every day, walked or read till two in the morning, and then all was darkness and silence till noon again. Her health was always perfect, both of mind and body; and she not only kept abreast of all that was going on in the great world, but was to the end of her life a keen and sagacious critic of American and European public men and politics. I mention this because, from the purely intellectual point of view, she bore a very striking resemblance to her brother; and this resemblance will be made to appear more fully in a subsequent portion of the present work. Before Hawthorne left Berkshire, his sister Louisa had spoken of Elizabeth in the letter which follows:--

SALEM, August, 1850.

DEAR SOPHIA, . . Elizabeth is very pleasantly situated in Manchester. We searched the country round for her, but did not find just the right place till five or six weeks ago. She has a large room, with a good bathing-room, and a very large closet all to herself; two of her windows look to the ocean, and one to a wooded hill. It is very retired, and but a short distance to the beach. They are good and kind people, and the living is very good. You seem in great admiration at Elizabeth's sitting at the table with the family, and ascribe it to Mrs. Dike's persuasion. But it was not even necessary to request it; Elizabeth did it as a matter of course. What should you say to see her go to church? She actually did go several times while she was here. I was afraid she would forget herself and speak at meeting, but she only made up a face at me when I looked at her.

I suppose you know that Mr. Upham is nominated for Congress in the place of Mr. King. The papers are full of his praises, and speak of his public services and private virtues as if such things were! I suppose he will be elected. Give my love to Nathaniel. If he only did know how I want to see him, but it is not to be told how much! How does he look now? I suppose the children are tanned brown: how does it become them? Do you think you shall come to Boston in the autumn? I want to hear from you exceedingly, and hope you will find or make time to write to me very soon. Good-by.

Yours ever,
M. L. HAWTHORNE.

And Elizabeth herself wrote, some time afterwards:--

MONTSERRAT, May 3.

DEAR BROTHER,--Your letter gave me an unexpected pleasure, for I really had but little hope of ever hearing from you again. I wish I could see the children, especially Una; I cannot bear the idea of their ceasing to be children before I see them. Why cannot you bring Una with you? I thank you for your invitation, but I do not like to go further from home than I can walk.

I have read "The House of the Seven Gables," as everybody else has, with great delight. People who abjure, upon principle, all other works of fiction, make an exception of yours. I cannot tell whether I prefer it to "The Scarlet Letter," and there is no need of drawing a comparison. The chapter entitled "Governor Pyncheon" seems to me unequalled, in its way, by anything I can remember; and little Pearl, too, is unique,--perfectly natural, but unlike any other child, unless it be Una. Louisa says that Judge Pyncheon is supposed to be Mr. Upham. I do not know Mr. Upham, but I imagined him to be a much more insignificant person,--less weighty in every sense. There may be some points of resemblance, such as the warm smiles, and the incident of the daguerreotype bringing out the evil traits of his character, and his boasts of the great influence he had exerted for Clifford's release. The greatest charm of both books, for me, is the perfect ease and freedom with which they seem to be written; it is evident that you stand in no awe of the public, but rather bid it defiance, which it is well for all authors, and all other men, to do.

I stayed in Manchester from July to November, at a place called Kettle Cove. It is a spot of peculiar charactenstics. Few people are born there, and few die; and they enjoy uninterrupted health. The very old go off from a sense of propriety, to make room for those who have a right to their places. They are more susceptible of enjoyment than any people I have ever met with; they wander about in the woods, and pick berries, and fish, and congregate together to eat chowders in the open air, on the grass,--old men and women seventy and eighty years of age, and those of all intermediate ages down to two or three. I never knew before how much beauty and variety a mist, brightened by sunshine, can impart to a landscape. The hills and the houses at a distance look as if they were based on air. There is a house in the Cove which I think would have suited you; you certainly must have been happier near the sea. I would never go out of the sound of its roar if I could help it.

There are many advantages in my present position at Montserrat. I can lose myself in the woods by only crossing the road, and the air is very pure and exhilarating, and the sea but a mile distant. I have been very busy about "Cervantes's Tales." I want to consult you about what I think a few necessary alterations, when you come.

Yours, E. M. H.

--Near the beginning of 1852 Hawthorne sent a presentation copy of the "Seven Gables" to Washington Irving, who acknowledged the gift in this amusingly courteous little note:--

MY DEAR SIR,--Accept my most cordial thanks for the little volume you have had the kindness to send me. I prize it as the right hand of fellowship extended to me by one whose friendship I am proud and happy to make, and whose writings I have regarded with admiration as among the very best that have ever issued from the American press.

Hoping that we may have many occasions hereafter of cultivating the friendly intercourse which you have so frankly commenced, I remain, with great regard,

Your truly obliged
WASHINGTON IRVING.

Meanwhile one of his English admirers had thus returned the compliment on Irving's behalf, as it were:--

LONDON, Nov. 6, 1851.

DEAR SIR,--I have ventured to send you a little book of mine, principally because it is a pleasure to me to do so, a little perhaps in the hope of pleasing you. Being desirous of drawing closer the acquaintance which I some time ago formed with you, through the medium of Mrs. Butler, afterwards through your books, I can hit upon no better method than this that I have adopted. It is a long way to send such a trifle; but I foresee that you have more than even the author's good-nature, and will accept graciously my little venture.

Your two last books have become very popular here. For my own part, I have read them with great pleasure; and you will not be displeased, I think, when I tell you that whilst I was reading your last book ("The House with the Seven Gables"), the turn of the thought or phrase often brought my old friend Charles Lamb to my recollection.

I entertain the old belief that one may know a good deal of an author (independently of his genius or capacity, I mean) from his works. And if you or Mr. Longfellow should assert that you are not the men that you really are, why, I shall turn a deaf ear to the averment, and put you both to the proof.

Farewell, my dear sir. I wish you all possible success in the world of letters, where you already look so long-lived and robust, and in all other worlds and circles where you desire to be held in affection or respect.

Believe me to be your very sincere

B. W. PROCTER

--Not many months afterwards, Miss Bötta wrote to him, regarding a German translation of his works, in these terms:--

DRESDEN, STRUVE ST., July 7, 1852.

DEAR SIR,--A countryman of yours, Mr. Motley, has given me your address so far that I hope this letter will reach you. Since the appearance of "The Scarlet Letter" in England, your name has become familiar even to Germany; two translations appeared of it, but written by people who write by the hour for their bread, and could not pay any attention to the style. The purport of this letter is to ask you whether you will kindly send us what you have written before "The Scarlet Letter." An author who will be one of us, we must know from the beginning of his career, to follow him step by step, and see the phases of his mind. You therefore would truly oblige me by collecting what you think will form in future times the complete edition of your works, and forward them to my publisher,--the Chevalier Dunker, in Berlin. And next to this, I should be glad to have the proof sheets of your next work, to prevent the professional translators from making a job of it. You write as if you wrote for Germany. The equality before the law--the moral law as well as the juridical--is the great wish of the women of my country; and you have illustrated this point with the skill of an artist, and a deep knowledge of man's secret motives and feelings. We know "The House of the Seven Gables," which is a lesson to family pride,--a frailty which must lie deep in human nature, since you have been able to trace it even in a free country. What it is with us, with our old aristocracy,--penniless beggars with long names,--you scarcely can imagine. Nevertheless, such a picture as you have drawn is a useful lesson, and will do good here if known in the right quarter. This is unfortunately not now the case, and it is the fault of the translators. Your passages are long, you do not write a racy style to carry on the reader, and in bad language it is impossible to get on with it. Instead of curtailing, they have spun out the matter, and made two volumes of one; and the consequence is that the second remains unread. We must prevent this for the future. Those who read English are enchanted with it; but their number is not large, and ladies are almost alone proficient in foreign languages, and at the same time ladies have no position in Germany.

Believe me that I truly appreciate your great talent, and sincerely wish that we might come to a sort of fusion, and longed-for Literature of the World.

With great regard,
AMELIE BÖTTA.

---"The Blithedale Romance" was especially fortunate in eliciting cordial letters of appreciation from the author's friends, some of which are subjoined. The first is from Mr. Pike, an old Salem friend of Hawthorne, and a man of remarkable depth of mind and tenderness of nature. He probably knew Hawthorne more intimately than any other man did; for he had the faculty of calling forth whatever was best and profoundest in him. He was the son of a carpenter, self-educated, and at one time filled a government office in Salem. In religious belief he was a Swedenborgian. Personally, he was barely of the average height, broad-shouldered, strongly built, with gray hair and a short grizzled beard; his eyes were dark, with a peculiar warm glow; his expression grave, gentle, and winning, and his voice low and deep. There was something of the softer side of Hollingsworth in him. Here is his letter:--

SALEM, July 18, 1852.

DEAR HAWTHORNE,--I want to come and see you, and shall tell no one that I am going, nor, when I return, that I have been. I have read your "Blithedale Romance." It is more like "The Scarlet Letter" than "The House of the Seven Gables." In this book, as in "The Scarlet Letter," you probe deeply,--you go down among the moody silences of the heart, and open those depths whence come motives that give complexion to actions, and make in men what are called states of mind; being conditions of mind which cannot be removed either by our own reasoning or by the reasonings of others. Almost all the novel-writers I have read, although truthful to nature, go through only some of the strata; but you are the only one who breaks through the hard-pan,--who accounts for that class of actions and manifestations in men so inexplicable as to call forth the exclamation, "How strangely that man acts what a fool he is!" and the like. You explain, also, why the utterers of such exclamations, when circumstances have brought them to do the very things they once wondered at in others, feel that they themselves are acting rationally and consistently. Love is undoubtedly the deepest, profoundest, of the deep things of man, having its origin in the depths of depths,--the inmost of all the emotions that ever manifest themselves on the surface. Yet writers seldom penetrate very far below the outward appearance, or show its workings in a way to account for its strange phases and fancies. They say two young people fall in love, and then expend their whole talents in describing the disasters that attended them, and how many acts of heroism they performed before accomplishing a marriage union. My mother had a deep idea in her mind when, in talking of incongruous unions, she would say, "It requires deep thinking to account for fancy." In "Blithedale," as in "The Scarlet Letter," you show how such things take place, and open the silent, unseen, internal elements which first set the machinery in motion, which works out results so strange to those who penetrate only to a certain depth in the soul. And I intend this remark to apply not only to love, but to other subjects and persons described in these volumes. I sometimes wish I had the pen of some, for I should like to lay open to the world my idea of love, clear to my own mind, but difficult to communicate,--its profoundness, its elements; how 't is a part of every man and woman; how all other loves, affections, benevolences, aspirations, gratitudes, are from this same fountain; receiving its character, quality, and modification as it passes through the different avenues from the fountain to its object; and how the presence of each object calls forth through its proper channel the love appropriate to itself, as food in the stomach invites the gastric juices proper to itself; how men and women are not perfect without a true spiritual union with the opposite sexes; how the divine nature, ever seeking to come down in forms, cannot do so in making man alone or woman alone, but, whenever it ultimates itself in humanity, a man and a woman is made,--made to be one, and would, in an unperverted state, find each other and remain united forever. But this is not what I intended to write about,--'t was "Blithedale." In "Blithedale" you dig an Artesian well down among the questionings. I was reminded of an Artesian well opened by my neighbor, who, after boring through various strata of earth and several fresh springs, found clear, cold sea-water at the depth of two hundred feet, which came bubbling to the surface from beneath the whole. How little we on the upper crust imagined that, far in the depths, was a stream which received its origin, quality, and character from the mighty ocean,--or fancied that, ere the stream we saw pouring forth could be exhausted, the vast world of waters must be dried up! But so it is; and the motive powers, like pearls, shine far down in the deep waters, and we fail to see them. You show us that such depths exist, and how they operate through the different departments, till they reach the outward and become visible actions. Thus the strange acts of men are in perfect consistency with the individual self, the profound self. How admirably you explore those lurking-places! I think "Blithedale" more profound in maxims than any work of yours. They will be quoted in the future as texts. You hit off the follies and errors of man with a quick humor, as no other man does. I cannot describe your humor, but I can feel and enjoy it. This peculiarity of your writings I always thought wonderful, but "Blithedale" I think excels the others in this particular. It is sudden, bright, but not flashy,--bright enough to make us feel our frailties and weaknesses, yet not so painfully that we hesitate to open our eyes and look again. You make us think the more and resolve the better, because the smart is not so sharp that we have to stop thinking to rub the wound. The best way I can describe it is to say that it opens and shuts just like heat lightning.

Tell your children that I have been thinking of them ever since I sat down to write.

Your friend truly, WM. B. PIKE.

--Another characteristic letter is from George Hillard:--

BOSTON, July 27, 1852.

MY DEAR HAWTHORNE,--You have written another book full of beauty and power, which I read with great interest and vivid excitement. I hate the habit of comparing one work of an author with another, and never do so in my own mind. Many of your readers go off in this impertinent way, at the first, and insist upon drawing parallels between "The Blithedale Romance" and "The Scarlet Letter" or "The House of the Seven Gables." I do not walk in that way. It is enough for me that you have put another rose into your chaplet, and I will not ask whether it outblooms or outswells its sister flowers. Zenobia is a splendid creature, and I wish there were more such rich and ripe women about. I wish, too, you could have wound up your story without killing her, or that at least you had given her a drier and handsomer death. Priscilla is an exquisite sketch. I don't know whether you have quite explained Hollingsworth's power over two such diverse natures. Your views about reform and reformers and spiritual rappings are such as I heartily approve. Reformers need the enchantment of distance. Your sketches of things visible, detached observations, and style generally, are exquisite as ever. May you live a thousand years, and write a book every year!

Yours ever, GEO. S. HILLARD.

--Mrs. Peabody, in a letter to her daughter, mentions both the "Seven Gables" and "Blithedale."

BOSTON.

. . . .You remember that when I was ill in Boston and needed watchers, I had "The House of the Seven Gables" read to me five times, with increasing interest. Recently I have read it again, and find that till now I never realized its wonderful beauty and power. What a vast amount of thought it has, inducing lofty thoughts and high aspirations,--the utterance of a pure and elevated soul, replete at the same time with an enchanting playfulness of fancy, which forces a smile amidst tears of admiration and deep and touching pathos! How natural, circumstanced as she was, are the feelings and actions of good old Hepzibah, who was noble, with all her errors. What a character is Phoebe! and how exquisitely blended in her are the usefulness and the tenderness and refinement and poetry of a Christian woman! Your husband's books should not be read merely, but, like the Book of books, be studied.

"I have also been re-reading "Blithedale." I wonder that I could overlook, even at a first reading, the exquisite instruction it conveys. The real philanthropist, the practical reformer, the friend of his race, must be encouraged in his glorious course by reading this book a second time; and the Hollingsworths, the Zenobias, the Fauntleroys, will read with awe the fate that awaits selfishness and abused privileges.

--After finishing "Blithedale," Hawthorne had at first intended writing another romance,--this time, as he said, on some theme more cheerful than heretofore; but he failed to find the mood or the opportunity, and the project lapsed (as it turned out) forever. Instead of it, however, he produced--in compliance with many entreaties from young people, and also, no doubt, because he enjoyed the work--a second volume of "Wonder" stories, under the title of "Tanglewood Tales." I append a specimen of the numberless letters from children, urging him to this congenial task:--

BOSTON, Dec. 14, 1851.

MY DEAR MR. HAWTHORNE,--I was so much delighted with that Wonder-Book that I wish you would write another like it. I hope you are having a pleasant time at Lenox. I like the story of the Chimæra, and so I did like the other stories. I saw a good portrait of Jenny Lind, which Mrs. Ward brought to this house the other day; but I did not hear her sing, because the tickets cost so much.

Your affectionate friend,
CHARLES S. BOWDITCH.

P. S. Please direct the answer to J. J. Bowditch.

--The Wayside, in which the "Tanglewood Tales" and the Life of Pierce were written, is by this time tolerably familiar to sentimental pilgrims, not to speak of the many printed descriptions which have brought it before the mental eyes of those who are content to take their sentiment at second hand. There is, however, and probably there will always exist, in the public mind, a belief that the Wayside and the Old Manse are one and the same building; and such persons as have ventured to inhabit the former edifice since Hawthorne's death have often found it difficult or impossible to convince investigating travellers to the contrary. Nor is it easy to overstate the indignation and resentment of these same travellers, when an attempt is made to insinuate the idea that the house may even now be a private dwelling, not at all hours of the day and night open to the inquisitive presence of strangers. Be that as it may, a distance of about two miles separates the Wayside from the Old Manse, the latter being situated on the banks of the river, while the former is on the Boston highway, three quarters of a mile beyond the home of Mr. Emerson. Originally it was a small oblong structure, containing only four or five rooms; a mere box with a roof on it, like so many other houses built in New England a hundred and fifty years ago. When Mr. Alcott took possession of it, he put a gabled dormer window in front, over the entrance, and added a wing to each side of the building; and these wings were rendered picturesque by galleries--or "piazzas," as we call them--supported by rustic pillars, across the front. The barn was separate from the house, and stood against the hill on the spectator's left. Hawthorne made no alterations during his first occupancy; but when he returned from England in 1860, he moved the barn to the other side of the house, and connected it with the wing on that side, added another story to the other wing, built in two large rooms behind, and surmounted the whole with the "tower," in the top of which is the study where "Our Old Home" was written. It was all painted a warm buff color, and looks to-day almost precisely as it did then. The hill and the surrounding grounds are, however, somewhat more thickly wooded than in those days; and the old picket fence and thickset hedge, which in some measure protected it from the road, have disappeared.

Though never so secluded as the Old Manse, it was enough so for practical purposes; and by ascending the hill, Hawthorne could withdraw himself from approach as completely as if he were in the primeval forests of Maine. Along the ridge of this hill, which ran parallel with the road, it was his custom to walk several hours each day, until a narrow path, between two and three hundred yards in length, was worn there by his footsteps; and traces of it are still visible. But more will be said of the Wayside in the second volume of this work; meanwhile let this suffice.

It had been arranged that Miss Louisa Hawthorne was to make a visit at her brother's new home during the summer of 1852. She was a lady of sociable and gentle disposition, and a great favorite with the children, as well as with Mr. and Mrs Hawthorne. She had never enjoyed robust health, however, and had therefore been prevented from mingling, as much as she would otherwise have done, with the friends who loved her and whom she loved. But now that Hawthorne had a home of his own, it was hoped that she might finally be enabled to take up her permanent residence there. She was expected to arrive about the first of July, but was prevented, as the following letter shows, by the illness of a relative. The "Cardinal" and the "Chancellor" were two friends of Hawthorne, whom it was the family custom to designate by these titles. The latter dignitary was Mr. David Roberts.

SALEM, July 1, 1852.

MY DEAR BROTHER,--Mrs. Manning is very ill, and I must put off coming to you till next week. I am glad you like your house, and that you seem at last to be settled. I heard of you in Boston, two or three weeks ago, buying carpets. I should have been afraid to trust you. The day I went to Boston I encountered the Cardinal and the Chancellor in the depot. The latter detained me to recount the glorious career which was before you in the diplomatic line, if General Pierce should be elected; and he stopped me in the street the next day to repeat the list of offices. I remember being Minister to Russia was one of them. I, not by any means thinking office the most direct path to glory for you, very coolly told him I hoped you would have nothing to do with it. I believe he thought I was very ridiculous. The Cardinal desired that you might be told that he went for General Pierce. I don't know where he will go next! He wished very much to see you, and will meet you in Boston any day you may appoint. The Democratic party must flourish if it has many more such converts.

Yours affectionately, M. L. H

--When Mrs. Manning recovered, which was in the course of a week, Louisa further postponed her visit in order to accompany another relative to Saratoga. Here she remained two weeks, and then set out for New York by way of the Hudson. The steamer on which she embarked was the "Henry Clay," which, it will be remembered, was burned when within a short distance of its destination, on the 27th of July. The news was soon published in New England; but it was not until the third day that Hawthorne learned that Louisa had been among the passengers; and the letter which his wife wrote, a few hours later, to her mother, bears traces of the agitation which the intelligence had caused.

CONCORD, Friday morning, July 30, 1852.

MY DEAREST MOTHER,--This morning we received the shocking intelligence that Louisa Hawthorne was lost in the destruction of the steamer "Henry Clay" on the Hudson, on Wednesday afternoon, July 27. She has been at Saratoga Springs and with Mr. Dike for a fortnight, and was returning by way of New York, and we expected her here for a long visit. It is difficult to realize such a sudden disaster. The news came in an appalling way. I was at the toilet-table in my chamber, before seven o'clock, when the railroad coach drove up. I was astonished to see Mr. Pike get out. He left us on Monday morning,--two days ago. It struck to my heart that he had come to inform us of some accident. I knew how impossible it was for him to leave his affairs. I called from the window, "Welcome, Mr. Pike!" He glanced up, but did not see me nor smile. I said, "Go to the western piazza, for the front door is locked." I continued to dress my hair, and it was a considerable time before I went down. When I did, there was no Mr. Pike. "Where is Mr. Pike?--I must then have seen his spirit," said I. But upon going to the piazza, there he stood unaccountably, without endeavoring to enter. Mr. Hawthorne opened the door with the strange feeling that he should grasp a hand of air. I was by his side. Mr. Pike, without a smile, deeply flushed, seemed even then not in his former body. "Your sister Louisa is dead!" I thought he meant that his own sister was dead, for she also is called Louisa. "What! Louisa?" I asked. "Yes." "What was the matter?" "She was drowned." "Where?" "On the Hudson, in the 'Henry Clay'!" He then came in, and my husband shut himself in his study.

We were about sitting down to breakfast. We sat down. Una was in the bathroom; I went to tell her. This upset me completely. I began to weep. By and by Mr. Pike got up from the breakfast-table, and said that unless he could do something for us, he must immediately return, and he went out. At last, my mind left the terrible contemplation of Louisa's last agony and fright, and imaged her supremely happy with her mother in another world. For she was always inconsolable for her mother, and never could be really happy away from her. So I burst out, "Oh, I have thought of something beautiful, something that will really comfort us!" Una's face lightened, but Julian could not pay heed. But I bent over him and said, "Aunt Louisa is with her mother, and is happy to be with her. Let us think of her spirit in another world." A smile shone in his eyes for a moment, but another flood of tears immediately followed. All at once he got up and went to the study,--he had the intention of consoling his father with that idea; but his father had gone on the hill.

Mr. Hawthorne will ask his sister Elizabeth to come here, to change the scene. It is an unmitigated loss to Elizabeth. Tell my sister Elizabeth not to stop here as she had intended. Mr. Pike said that Mrs. Dike was almost distracted,--he never saw any body so distressed. The news came by telegraph,--"Maria is lost." Mr. Pike brought us the paper. Good-by.

Your affectionate child, SOPHIA.

--The present writer remembers that morning, with its bright sunshine and its gloom and terror; Mr. Hawthorne stauding erect at one side of the room, with his hands behind him, in his customary attitude, but with an expression of darkness and suffering on his face such as his children had never seen there before. Mr. Pike sat at the breakfast-table; but no one could eat anything, and no one spoke. After a while Mr. Hawthorne went out, and was seen no more that day. It was a blow that struck him to the heart; but he could never relieve himself with words. Louisa's body was recovered a few days later; for she had leapt into the river, preferring that mode of death to the fire.

A week or two afterwards, Mrs. Peabody wrote the letter given below. Hawthorne had been contemplating a visit to the Isles of Shoals in the autumn, and he carried out his intention in the ensuing September. The allusion to "Blithedale" should, chronologically, precede that quoted above.

AUGUST 9, 1852.

MY BELOVED ONES,--Have your high and just views of the dealings of our Heavenly Father soothed the anguish nature must endure for a while under such a shock as you have received? Does Mr. Hawthorne mean to go to the seashore, or has this affliction changed his purpose? It would be best to go, if he can. His soul would then be filled with the glories of that Nature whose favored child he is. His perfect clearness of vision, his mildness, his calmness, his true strength and greatness, render him the ready recipient of all that magnificent scenery conveys to the soul. He is one of the few who can not only look at things, but into and through them. The world has great claims on one who can do so much towards raising the mind from stupid materialism to translucent wonder.

We are all reading "Blithedale." I am interested to see how differently it affects different minds. Some say (Mary, for one), "It is the greatest book Hawthorne has written." Another says, "I do not understand it;" another, "There is no interest in it to me;" another exclaims, "Was ever anything so exquisite!" I have not seen any review of it yet. I hope a reviewer will arise for the task who has soul; who can see the true philanthropist, the real reformer, piercing with a seer's eye all the vain efforts hitherto made to form associations that will really elevate the characters and better the worldly condition of men,--one who has power to realize why all such associations to ameliorate the condition of the laborer have hitherto failed. At Brook Farm, as elsewhere, they did not begin right. Many persons were huddled together there, with all their passions in full vigor; selfishness, covetousness, pride, love of dress, of approbation, of admiration, of flattery, operated on one and all. Petty jealousies rankled in hearts that ought to have throbbed only with love to God and man. How could such incongruous elements amalgamate and produce a genuine Brotherhood? Our associations carry in their very midst the causes of decay.

YOUR MOTHER.

---It was either during this month of August or in the early part of the preceding July, that Hawthorne first met the poet, R. H. Stoddard. Mr. Stoddard made two visits to him before his departure from America, and has written the following account of his impressions:--

"I saw Hawthorne first in the summer of 1852, just after he became possessor of the Wayside. When I was introduced to him, he greeted me warmly, and, throwing open the door of the library, invited me to make myself at home, while he transacted some business with Whipple in the next room. Presently he rejoined me, and we ascended the hill behind the house and sat down in the old rustic summer-house. Here he began to talk with me, mostly about myself and the verses I had written, which, I was surprised to learn, he had read carefully. He mentioned, in particular, an architectural fancy I had thrown up, and compared it with his own little box of a house.

"'If I could build like you,' he said, 'I would have a castle in the air, too.'

"'Give me the Wayside,' I replied, 'and you shall have all the air-castles I can build.'

"He recalled a short memoir of my humble self, and the portrait that accompanied it, and was pleased to observe that I was neither so old nor so ill-looking as this portrait had led him to expect. As we rambled and talked, my heart went out towards this famous man, who did not look down upon me, as he well might have done, but took me up to himself as an equal and a friend. I see him now as I saw him then, a strong, broad-shouldered man, with dark iron-gray hair, a grave but kindly face, and the most wonderful eyes in the world, searching as lightning and unfathomable as night.

"The following winter I visited him again, to talk over a Custom House appointment I hoped to secure. When I reached Concord, the ground was covered with snow; it was freezing in the shade and thawing in the sun. We dined, and after dinner we retired to the study, where he brought out some strong cigars, and we smoked vigorously. Custom House matters were scarcely touched upon; and I was not sorry, for they were not half so interesting to me as the discursive talk of Hawthorne. He manifested a good deal of curiosity in regard to some old Brook Farmers, whom I knew in a literary way; and he listened to my impressions of the individuality of each with a twinkle in his eye; and I can see now that he was amused by my outspoken detestation of certain literary Philistines. He was outspoken, too; for he told me plainly that a volume of fairy-stories I had just published was not simple enough for the young. I could not but agree with him, for by this time I wished sincerely I had let the wee folk alone. We fell to talking about the sea, and the influence it had upon childhood; and other personal matters which I have forgotten. What impressed me most at the time was not the drift of the conversation, but the gracious manner of Hawthorne. He expressed the warmest interest in my affairs, and a willingness to serve me in every possible way. In a word, he was the soul of kindness, and when I forget him I shall have forgotten everything else.

"I have preserved but one of Hawthorne's letters written at this period. It is dated 'Concord, March 16, 1853.'

"DEAR STODDARD,--I beg your pardon for not writing before; but I have been very busy, and not particularly well. I enclose a letter from Atherton. Roll up and pile up as much of a snowball as you can, in the way of political interest; for there never was a fiercer time than this, among the office-seekers. You had better make your point in the Custom House at New York, if possible; for, from what I can learn, there will be a poor chance of clerkships in Washington.

"Atherton is a man of rather cold exterior, but has a good heart,--at least, for a politician of a quarter of a century's standing. If it be certain that he cannot help you, he will probably tell you so. Perhaps it would be as well for you to apply for some place that has a literary fragrance about it,--Librarian to some Department, the office which Lanman held. I don't know whether there is any other such office. Are you fond of brandy? Your strength of head (which you tell me you possess) may stand you in good stead at Washington; for most of these public men are inveterate guzzlers, and love a man that can stand up to them in that particular. It would never do to let them see you corned, however. But I must leave you to find your own way among them. If you have never associated with them heretofore, you will find them a new class; and very unlike poets.

"I have finished the 'Tanglewood Tales,' and they will make a volume about the size of the 'Wonder-Book,' consisting of six myths,--the Minotaur, the Golden Fleece, the story of Proserpine, etc., etc., etc., done up in excellent style, purified from all moral stains, re-created as good as new, or better, and fully equal, in their own way, to Mother Goose. I never did anything else so well as these old baby stories. In haste,

"Truly yours,
"NATH. HAWTHORNE.

"P.S. When applying for office, if you are conscious of any deficiencies (moral, intellectual, or educational, or whatever else), keep them to yourself, and let those find them out whose business it may be. For example, supposing the office of Translator to the State Department to be tendered you, accept it boldly, without hinting that your acquaintance with foreign languages may not be the most familiar. If this unimportant fact be discovered afterwards, you can be transferred to some more suitable post. The business is, to establish yourself, somehow and anywhere.

"I have had as many office-seekers knocking at my door, for three months past, as if I were a prime minister; so that I have made a good many scientific observations in respect to them. The words that Bradamante (I think it was) read in the Enchanted Hall are, and ought to be, their motto,--'Be bold, be bold, and evermore be bold.'

But over one door she read, 'Be not too bold.' A subtile boldness, with a veil of modesty over it, is what is needed."

--It was during August and the first part of September of this year that Hawthorne wrote the biography of Pierce, at the latter's request. Pierce and he had been faithful friends since their college days; Hawthorne admired and respected, as well as loved, the future President, and never, to the end of his life, found any cause to alter his sentiments towards him. But though he was glad, from a personal point of view, to give his friend whatever assistance he might in consummating his career, nevertheless, as he wrote to Bridge, Pierce had now "reached that altitude where a man careful of his personal dignity will begin to think of cutting his acquaintance." In other words, he foresaw that he would be accused of acting the part of a vulgar office-seeker,--of aiding Pierce only in order that Pierce might be the better able to aid him, and of apostatizing from his real political convictions in order to put money in his purse. It is true that he might have avoided the worst part of this reproach by declining the office which Pierce afterwards tendered to him; but, as it happened, he did not decline, but accepted it. We are forced to conclude, therefore, that he either bartered truth and honor for a few thousand dollars and a glimpse of Europe; or else that, being conscious of his own honesty and rectitude of purpose, he regarded with his customary indifference the angry accusations of his opponents. As for the present biographer, his only care will be to afford each reader the fullest liberty to decide the matter according to his private prejudices and prepossessions. Argument on such a subject is futile.

Mrs. Hawthorne wrote to her mother, on the completion of the book, as follows:--

CONCORD, Sept. 10, 1852.

I have just now finished reading the little biography, which I did not see in manuscript. It is as serene and peaceful as a dream by a river; and such another testimony to the character of a Presidential candidate was, I suspect, never before thrown upon the fierce arena of political warfare. Many a foot and hoof may trample on it; but many persons will preserve it for its beauty. Its perfect truth and sincerity are evident within it; as no instrument could wrench out of Mr. Hawthorne a word that he did not know to be true in spirit and in letter, so also no fear of whatsoever the world may attribute to him as motive would weigh a feather in his estimation. He does the thing he finds right, and lets the consequences fly.

How grand and dignified is Mr. Sumner's speech, and what a complete rendering of the subject!

--Miss Elizabeth Hawthorne, although, as we have seen, she was opposed to her brother in politics, seems to have accepted the "Life" with equanimity. This is her letter:--

SALEM, Sept. 23, 1852.

DEAR BROTHER,--You will be surprised to see that this is dated at Salem; but I knew that I must come here again, though I was glad to get away for a little while. I wish to hear from you about the business that we spoke of. I wish to do everything that must be done, while I am here now, and I should be glad never to see the place again. In Beverly I can do exactly as I choose, and even appear to be what I am, in a great degree. They are sensible and liberal-minded people, though not much cultivated.

Mr. Dike has bought your Life of Pierce, but he will not be convinced that you have told the precise truth. I assure him that it is just what I have always heard you say. The "Puritan Recorder" eulogizes the book, for you are a favorite with the Orthodox, and especially with the clergy; and for that reason I think you should judge more charitably of them. Vanity seems to me to be their besetting sin.

The "Gazette" calls the book "an honest biography," but says the subject of it "has never risen above respectable mediocrity." The "Register" calls it your "new Romance." People are talking about something that Mr. Pike is asserted to have said derogatory to General Pierce; perhaps you have heard of it. Uncle William thinks he was unguarded in some expressions in David Roberts's office, where he is in the habit of going, and that his words have been misinterpreted and misrepresented. I thought he was too experienced a politician to be guilty of any imprudence in speech.

Yours, E. M. H.

I hope you and Una will come to Montserrat. I am sure she would enjoy it. Besides the variety of colors in the woods, the barberry bushes, of which you have none, are now more beautiful than vineyards, as I can testify, for I see abundance of grapes here. If yon will send me the Life of Pierce, I could distribute some copies there, perhaps, with advantage.

--While the "Life" was doing its work, were it more or less, Hawthorne and Pierce made their expedition to the Isles of Shoals, where they spent about a fortnight; and Hawthorne's journal of the visit will be found in the first volume of the "American Note-Books." On Hawthorne's return, the quiet life at the Wayside was resumed; and Mrs. Hawthorne has left this picture of one of those lovely autumnal days:--

CONCORD, OCt. 5, 1852.

On the 1st of October we all (except Rosebud) took a walk. We mounted our hill, and "thorough bush, thorough brier," till we came out in Peter's Path, beyond the Old Manse. All that ground is consecrated to me by unspeakable happiness; yet not nearly so great happiness as I now have, for I am ten years happier in time, and an uncounted degree happier in kind. I know my husband ten years better, and I have not arrived at the end; for he is still an enchanting mystery, beyond the region I have discovered and made my own. Also, I know partly how happy I am, which I did not well comprehend ten years ago. We went up the bare hill opposite the Old Manse, and I descended on the other side, so I could look up the avenue, and see our first home for the first time in seven years. It was a very still day. The sun did not shine; but it was warm, and the sky was not sombre. As I stood there and mused, the silence was profound. Not a human being was visible in the beloved old house, or around it. Wachusett was a pale blue outline on the horizon. The river gleamed like glass here and there in the plain, slumbering and shining and reflecting the beauty on its banks. We returned through Sleepy Hollow, and walked along a stately, broad path, which we used to say should be the chariot-road to our castle, which we would build on the hill to which it leads. The trees have grown very much in seven years, and conceal the Hollow. From this we followed a wood-path which I remembered as very enchanting nine years ago, with its deep wooded dells on each side. We sat down in a sheltered spot for some time, and in the silence we heard the hum and sharp tone of summer insects; and the crows sailed above, crying, "Caw! caw!" A few trees had taken prismatic hues as if for particular ornament to the scene, and there was a group of low sumach which had turned a rich crimson color, and Julian wanted to take the whole of it along with him.

--The hill in Sleepy Hollow on which "our castle" was to stand is now the site of Hawthorne's grave; and the "chariot-road" was the path up which his funeral procession mounted.

It was a period of repose and comfort. The relaxing atmosphere of Concord had not yet begun to have its effect on Hawthorne, though he felt it sensibly enough on his return from England. The town stands on low meadow-land,--so low that it is said the bottom of Walden Pond (which is one hundred feet deep) is on a higher level than the top of any building in the village, though the village and the pond are but two miles apart. I will not, however, vouch for the accuracy of this measurement. At any rate, the air in autumn and winter is crisp and invigorating; in summer only, does it subdue the energies. Hawthorne and his children spent much time in exploring the woods and fields in the neighborhood. Walden Pond was at that time as secluded as the legendary lake of the "Great Carbuncle;" and the splendor of the autumn foliage, reflected in its still surface, might have been mistaken for the royal glow of that famous gem itself. Thoreau's hut was still standing on a level, pine-encircled spot, near the margin. When the snows began to fall, there was superb coasting to be had down the sides of the many small hills near the Wayside; and the children, with their father's assistance, rolled up a snowball so large and solid that it remained on the front lawn, an imposing object, all winter, and was only subdued by the soaking. spring rains. Mr. Ephraim Bull, the inventor of the Concord grape, was a next-door neighbor; and his original and virile character had a great attraction for Hawthorne, insomuch that they had much pleasant converse together. When the weather did not admit of excursions, there was always good entertainment within doors; and the new little sister, who had lately made her appearance, was better than the best of playthings to her brother and sister. She had always been regarded by them in the light of a special providence. Her mother has this mention of her in a letter to Mrs. Peabody:--

DECEMBER, 1852.

Our little Rosebud is only a comfort and joy from morning till night, and her rosy cheeks and clear blue eyes are very pleasant to see. She is very facetious, and makes and takes jokes with perfect understanding, looking sidelong, or from beneath her hair, with the drollest expression. Her hair is curling up behind, and I suppose will grow in waving curls, as Una's did. She is the very little blue-eyed daughter I prayed for, in every respect exact, except that I thought of yellow hair. I do not know whether she has the philosophic temperament of the other children; but she has vivid perceptions, and sees things picturesquely. When she looks at a picture, she acts it at once, if there are living beings in it. She has an air of command which is very funny.

--The only literary work of this epoch was the completion of the "Tanglewood Tales" volume, which had been relinquished in order to write the Life of Pierce. The stories appeared without the introductions and after-pieces which had been so agreeable a feature of the "Wonder-Book," and for which method of presenting a tale Hawthorne seems to have always had a liking; it was in such a setting, for example, that he had intended to frame the "Seven Tales of my Native Land." But either he thought a repetition undesirable, or else the idea had not satisfied his taste as well as he had expected. The stories themselves, however, were as good as the others, or perhaps better than they; and it is a pity that none of them bave ever been fittingly illustrated. Hawthorne has been especially unfortunate in his artists; and never more so than in the latest specimens of work in this kind which have been published. Yet no books are more stimulating than his to the artistic sense.

One of the best comments which this series of fairy stories elicited came from the pen of Mr. Robert Carter, a man of rare sagacity and wide learning and, in later years, editor of "Appleton's Journal." His letter is well worth reading:--

CAMBRIDGE, MASS., Feb. 10, 1853.

MY DEAR SIR,--At the time of publication, a copy of the "Wonder-Book" was sent to me as editor of the "Commonwealth." It got mislaid until last New Year's day, when I found it and took it home for my eldest child, a boy four years old, Master James Lowell Carter. Late in the evening, on lighting my cigar, I thought I would look into the book a little, and master the drift of at least one story, to be ready for my young inquisitor in the morning. A diligent reader of novels for at least a quarter of a century, I scarcely expected to find in a child's book a fresh fountain of new sensations and ideas. But the book threw me into a tamult of delight, almost equal to that of the first perusal of "Robinson Crusoe" or the "Arabian Nights." At two o'clock in the morning, my fire having entirely gone out, I laid down the book, every word read except "The Chimæra," which story I read aloud at breakfast to the immense delight of Master James, and the equal gratification of his mother, who pronounced it the finest poem she had heard for many a day, and thought, if the rest of the tales were as good, the book must be a wonder-book indeed.

Notwithstanding the beauty of many passages and descriptions in the tales and the framework, I do not so much admire the execution as the conception of the book, which seems to me exquisitely felicitous, developing as it does a new use for the apparently effete mythology of the ancients. It is, in fact, the most palpable hit that has been made in literature for many a day, and will mark an era in fiction, as did the translation of the "Arabian Nights." The Mahometan mythology does not excel the classic in romantic machinery, while it is far inferior to it in intellectual and moral interest, and in affinity with our current ideas and literature.

I observe with regret that in your preface you exhibit a doubtful, half-apologetic tone, as if you lacked confidence in your theme and its acceptance with critical readers,--the influence of which want of confidence seems to me perceptible in portions of the book, chiefly in leading you to adopt a lighter style now and then, which jars a little with the general effect,--as if, to forestall laughter, you desired to show that you were only in fun yourself. The intermediate parts--the framework--is exceedingly well written, with some fine Berkshire descriptions. But though the contrast is striking between the Old World tales and the fresh young life of America, I should have liked it better if you had given the tales a Greek setting, and thrown back Eustace Bright and his auditors a couple of thousand years, to a country-seat of Attica, Ionia, or Sicily. As it is, Mr. Pringle and his wife are decided excrescences, who ought to be condemned to the preface, and with them your friends the publisher and artist, who are now sadly out of place. I want to see nothing in the "Wonder-Book" that will not read harmoniously there a thousand years hence, or in any language of the world; for if you continue the book as well as you have begun it (and you ought to do it better), so that the value of quantity will be added to that of quality (for a book of tales must be pretty large to live), it will be read in the future as universally as the "Arabian Nights," and not only by children. An author has a strong temptation to introduce his friends into his pages, but it ought never to be done at a sacrifice of art. You doubtless remember that many of your friends and acquaintances who figured in "The Hall of Fantasy," as it appeared in the "Pioneer," have vanished from that structure in its present razeed condition.

Pardon me if I point out what seems to me another fault in the book. I observe that, for brevity, or from some difficulty in the managing the stories, or from some cause which has not occurred to me, you have omitted to use some of the most striking portions of the myths you have dealt with. For instance, the adventures of Perseus on his return, his Rescue of Andromeda, his petrifaction of Atlas, etc., would have added much to the incident of the story. And in "The Golden Touch," I do not understand why you have changed Bacohus into Mercury, or have omitted the capture of Silenus and his entertainment by Midas, which would have afforded fine material for pleasant and varied treatment. "The Three Golden Apples," likewise, ought not to exhaust the achievements of Hercules, which should rather be woven into a series rivalling those of "Sinbad the Sailor," in length and interest. But enough of fault-finding. My object in writing is merely to assure you that at least one of your readers is convinced that in the "Wonder-Book" you have hit upon the entrance to a golden mine, and that it is worth while to carry on the work with care and system, so as to get the full amount of the treasures; and not from haste or want of plan leave any part unworked or unexhausted.

With high respect, I am very truly yours,
ROBERT CARTER.

--Whether or not Hawthorne ever entertained the intention of following this good advice, circumstances prevented him from doing so; and very possibly he would not have felt disposed to linger in a mine, however golden, from the treasures of which he had already extracted such fair specimens. As long as a subject had freshness, he could enjoy working upon it; but when it came to deliberately overhauling it for money's sake alone, enjoyment and inspiration both grew jaded.

There is reason to suppose, however, that he had a new romance in his mind, and would have written it during this year, but for the appointment to the Liverpool consulship, which came in the spring. There is no means of even conjecturing what this romance would have been; no trace of it remains, either in memoranda, or in the recollections of his friends. The following letter from Herman Melville indicates that he had suggested a story to Hawthorne; but Mr. Melville recently informed the present writer that it was a tragic story, and that Hawthorne had not seemed to take to it. It could not, therefore, have been the "more genial" tale which he spoke of to Bridge.

BOSTON.

MY DEAR HAWTHORNE,--The other day, at Concord, you expressed uncertainty concerning your undertaking the story of Agatha, and, in the end, you urged me to write it. I have decided to do so, and shall begin it immediately upon reaching home; and so far as in me lies, I shall endeavor to do justice to so interesting a story of reality. Will you therefore enclose the whole affair to me; and if anything of your own has occurred to you in your random thinking, won't you note it down for me on the same page with my memorandum? I wish I had come to this determination at Concord, for then we might have more fully and closely talked over the story, and so struck out new light. Make amends for this, though, as much as you conveniently can. With your permission I shall make use of the "Isle of Shoals," as far as the name goes at least. I shall also introduce the old Nantucket seaman, in the way I spoke to you about. I invoke your blessing upon my endeavors; and breathe a fair wind upon me. I greatly enjoyed my visit to you, and hope that you reaped some corresponding pleasure.

H. MELVILLE.

Julian, Una, and Rose,--my salutations to them.

--The cares of office were now to take precedence of literary interests for a time; and the disputes of political partisans made themselves audible even in the retirement of the Wayside, where not Hawthorne, indeed, but his wife, was moved to take a part in the discussion. The two letters from which the following extracts are taken are worth reading, not only for their intrinsic eloquence and earnestness, but as showing how ardently the wife identified herself with her husband, while yet retaining her independent judgment on certain points. The point to which I more particularly allude is Mrs. Hawthorne's estimate of Webster. She could not bring herself quite to believe that he was not as great as he looked; but Hawthorne had formed a somewhat different opinion. This opinion is set forth, by the by, in the story of "The Great Stone Face;" and for convenience, I will here quote the passages in which it is embodied:

"But now, again, there were reports and many paragraphs in the newspapers, affirming that the likeness of the Great Stone Face had appeared upon the broad shoulders of a certain eminent statesman. He, like Mr. Gathergold and Old Blood-and-Thunder, was a native of the valley, but had left it in his early days and taken up the trades of law and politics. Instead of the rich man's wealth and the warrior's sword, he had but a tongue; and it was mightier than both together. So wonderfully eloquent was he, that whatever he might choose to say, his auditors had no choice but to believe him; wrong looked like right, and right like wrong; for when it pleased him, he could make a kind of illuminated fog with his mere breath, and obscure the natural daylight with it. His tongue, indeed, was a magic instrument; sometimes it rumbled like thunder; sometimes it warbled like the sweetest music. It was the blast of war, the song of peace; and it seemed to have a heart in it when there was no such matter. In good truth, he was a wondrous man; and when his tongue had acquired him all other imaginable success, when it had been heard in halls of state and in the courts of princes and potentates, after it had made him known all over the world, even as a voice crying from shore to shore, it finally persuaded his countrymen to select him for the Presidency. . . .

"While his friends were doing their best to make him President, Old Stony Phiz, as he was called, set out on a visit to the valley where he was born. Of course, he had no other object than to shake hands with his fellow-citizens, and neither thought nor cared about any effect which his progress through the country might have upon the election. . . .

"'Here he is, now!' cried those who stood near Ernest. 'There! There! Look at old Stony Phiz, and then at the Old Man of the Mountain, and see if they are not as like as two twin brothers!' . . . .

"Now, it must be owned that, at his first glimpse of the countenance, which was bowing and smiling from the barouche, Ernest did fancy there was a resemblance between it and the old familiar face upon the mountain-side. The brow, with its massive depth and loftiness, and all the other features, indeed, were boldly and strongly hewn, as if in emulation of a more than heroic, of a Titanic model. But the sublimity and stateliness, the grand expression of a divine sympathy, that illuminated the mountain visage, and etherealized its ponderous granite substance into spirit, might here be sought in vain. Something had been originally left out, or had departed. And therefore the marvellously gifted statesman had always a weary gloom in the deep caverns of his eyes, as of a child that has outgrown its playthings, or a man of mighty faculties and little aims, whose life, with all its high performances, was vague and empty, because no high purpose had endowed it with reality. . . . Ernest turned away, melancholy, and almost despondent; for this was the saddest of his disappointments, to behold a man who might have fulfilled the prophecy, and had not willed to do so. . . .

--Such was Hawthorne's reading of the character of Webster. Let us now listen to the judgment of his wife.

" . . .I disagree from the pitilessness and severity of the censure of Webster. Would you resolve the great heart and great mind of Webster into a *speech?* I by no means say that, because Webster was great, he was therefore excusable for any sin. Oh, no! but that the vastness of his mental and physical force made it very difficult for colder-blooded, narrower people to judge him fairly. If Webster acknowledged that he was wrong in making the speech, let not vengeance pursue him farther. I should be grieved to hear that he died of a broken heart, and there is no sign of such a thing in the calm, grand death of which we hear. I have in the course of his life felt the utmost abhorrence of his *habits;* but I am glad that God is his judge on that subject, and not man. No man can be, who could not put himself in Webster's body, with all concomitant circumstances,--and then see what he would do! It blinds me with tears of profoundest sorrow to see that Ambition could make him stoop. He made that fatal mistake which so many make; he did evil that good might come of it,--which is an insult to God. I could by no means say Webster was 'a man consummate,' though, from his power and position, he was designed for that. Such a figure, such an intellect, such a heart, were certainly never combined before to awe the world. But greatness, as I use it and feel it in respect of Webster, is the vast plan of him; the front of Jove,--the regal, commanding air which cleared a path before him,--the voice of thunder and music which revealed the broad caverns of his breast,--the unfathomable eye which no sculptor could render,--all these external signs said, 'Here is a Great Man!' When I was present in court in Concord one day, he came in after the assembly had collected. I shall never forget his entrauce. The throng turned round and saw him, and instinctively every one fell back from the door and left a broad path, up which this native king walked along,--with such a majesty, with such a simple state, that the blood tingled in my veins to see him. This was long before he had fallen politically. 'This man,' I thought, 'has capacity to rule the world.' The idea of greatness is inseparable from him. Was not Lucifer the son of the morning, and the loftiest of the archangels? But he fell,--ambition brought him headlong from the Empyrean. If thunder rolled through the heavens at his fall, could one not have thrilled with a sad and sublime emotion? It will take an æon to compose another such man as Webster. I do not believe so great a man is to be found here or in Europe now. There can be found, perhaps, a high degree of moral greatness and noble capacity; but still, there is not the shadow of such a possible man. I cannot express how little it seems to me to dwell upon his failings. I think it takes Omniscience to judge him fairly. That he had a heart of deep power and love, that his immediate friends worshipped him, and the humblest of them perhaps the most, is a proof of a large kindliness and benignity which was revealed outwardly by what has been called 'the sweet grandeur of his smile.' His whole character as a farmer is very beautiful, and, considering his other aspect, even sublime. Such exact and tender care of his brute possessions, such wisdom, such loving interest in his agricultural pursuits, such a genuine enjoyment of nature,--this was a beautiful phase of the giant man. And the infinite melancholy of his kingly face, the deep beyond deep of gloom that quenched his lightnings, was to me most affecting and awful,--as if he were judging himself continually, and found no rest. It would seem that such a look ought to disarm criticism, and make each man, instead of endeavoring with narrow vision and spiritual pride to pronounce upon him, look into his own heart and find out whether, with far less temptations, at a far less dizzy height,--whether he is spotless of sin before God. It really does seem a pity to lose the image of such a man by such rapidity of condemnation. Does any one admire evil? does any one rejoice in iniquity? does any one commend treason to conscience? No! But let us freely, and with generous awe, admire greatness, and with tenderness, not pride, mourn over a vast soul in eclipse, passing into the unknown world.

--The next extract refers to Pierce. It is certainly worth a man's while, even after he is dead, and no matter how large he may have loomed in the world's eye, to have had a friend and champion such as Sophia Hawthorne.

It hurts me, dear mother, to have you speak of General Pierce as if he were too far below Mr. Hawthorne to have Mr. Hawthorne indebted to him. You judge General Pierce from the newspapers, and the slanders spread abroad by the Whigs to prevent his election. The nation's reply to all slander has been to elect him. If you knew the man as we know him, you would be the first to respect him. Mr. Hawthorne wrote the Biography with the most careful sobriety, because he did not wish to seem eulogistic and extravagant. I wish I could convey to you what I know to be the truth about him. He is an incorruptible patriot, and he loves his country with the purity and devotion of the first of our early Patriots. He will never do anything for effect,--he will do anything, however odious it may appear, that he thinks right, and for enduring good. Ambition has not touched him. The offices which he has filled were brought and laid at his feet, without any interference of his own; and it was also so with regard to his nomination for the Presidency. When he was actually nominated, a profound sadness fell upon him. He is a deeply religious man, and a brave man, not only with the sword of steel, but with the sword of the spirit. He is a man who understands duty; he has a living sense of responsibility to God. He is a man great from the very moral force which Webster lacked. His intellect is keen and rapid,--he seizes points. He sees men, and knows what man is fitted for certain places and emergencies. He is modest and captivating from a natural courtesy and grace of address based upon kindness and generosity of heart. The personal homage and love he commands, the enthusiasm of affection felt for him by his friends, are wonderful. His gentleness is made beautiful by a granite will behind; 'out of the strong comes forth sweetness.' He is a man wholly beyond bribery on any score whatever. As regards the stories of his intemperance, if he ever did in dulge unduly in wine, he is now an uncommonly abstemious man. And it is a singular fact that this particular weakness of indulging in too much stimulants does not debase a noble mind as other vices do. When it rises above it, it rises without the stains left by the other vices. My own experience, in my young girlhood, with the morphine that was given me to stop my headaches, has given me infinite sympathy and charity for persons liable to such a habit. But the greater a man's fault has been, the greater is his triumph if it can be said of him, as it can of General Pierce,--*now* he never is guilty of it.

"As regards the Compromise and the Fugitive Slave Law, it is his opinion that these things must now be allowed for the sake of the slave! One of his most strenuous supporters said that, 'viewed in itself, the Fugitive Slave Law was the most abominable of wrongs;' but that it was the inevitable fruit of the passionate action of the Abolitionists, and, like slavery itself, must for the present be tolerated. And so with the Compromise,--that it is the least of the evils presented. It has been said, as if there were no gainsaying it, that no man but Webster could ever be such a fool as really to believe the Union was in danger. But General Pierce has lately, with solemn emphasis, expressed the same dread; and it certainly seems that the severance of the Union would be the worst thing for the slave. General Pierce's lifelong votes and opinions have been uniformly the same on these matters; so it cannot be said that he advocated the Compromise from an ambitious motive. There are always two sides to every question. Two given men may stand on opposite sides, and each think diametrically contrary to the other, and yet each man have the highest principle and the sincerest love of country. But generally the worst motive possible is ascribed to one or both of them. What would become of the planets without the centrifugal as well as the centripetal forces?

"Mr. Hawthorne did not feel as if he could refuse a boon to an old friend, and one whom he could so safely praise. He knew that it would subject him to abuse, and that the lowest motives would be ascribed to him; but, provided his conscience is clear, he never cares a *sou* what people say. He knew he never should ask for an office; and not one word on the subject has ever passed between General Pierce and Mr. Hawthorne. But if Mr. Hawthorne should see fit to accept an office from General Pierce, and people preferred to ascribe it to a low motive, he would make them welcome to the enjoyment of evil-thinking. He chooses to be free, and not act with reference to any person's lack of generous interpretation. He has no sensibility in that direction, and never defends himself, and never can be prevailed upon to do anything but smile good-naturedly at personal attacks. When the Whigs turned him out and told all manner of falsehoods about him, I saw his temper. It was as unhurt and undisturbed as Prince Arthur's shield beneath the veil. Even good Mr. Howes had tried his best to lash him into anger; but he found it as impossible as to excite the distant stars into war with one another."

--These letters were addressed to Mrs. Hawthorne's mother, and were written a month or two before her husband's appointment was made, and confirmed by the Senate. But in the interval another great sorrow was destined to fall upon the family; Mrs. Peabody was taken unexpectedly ill, and died. Mrs. Hawthorne was unable to be with her; and Miss E. P. Peabody, who attended her throughout, wrote to her sister the next day the following account of the good and pure-minded woman's last moments:--

TUESDAY NIGHT.

So very quietly she passed at last, that it was a quarter of an hour we were in doubt; but she had labored so for breath for eighteen hours, that I have no feeling yet but thankfulness that she went without access of suffering, and that she is above and beyond all suffering, forever and ever. Doubt not she is with you, more intimately than ever; for the spirit must be where the heart's affections are. Her last words about you were when I asked her if you should come again. "Oh, no; don't let her come--don't let her come--oh, no; don't let her come and leave that poor baby!" So characteristic! That was yesterday, and I wrote you last evening. Last night we put her to bed at ten o'clock; and L, as usual, lay down at the head of the bed, and, till two o'clock, she slept more peacefully than for a long while. Then she roused and got up for a short time, but soon wanted the bed; and then she lay in my arms two or three hours, during which time I thought she would go; but at five she wanted to get up, and we put her in the lolling-chair. When she was settled there, and the table and pillow put before her, and she had gone to sleep, father came in, and I left him and Mary with her, and lay down and slept soundly three hours. It was ten o'clock before we put her to bed again; and then Mary or father or Margaret or I had her in our arms all day, till she went. She was strong enough to raise her body and hold up her head till the last; and we changed her position, as she indicated, all the time. At the last moment, Mary was lying at the head of the bed, supporting her, with the intervention of some pillows. I was on the other side of the bed, and father in the rocking-chair. So long a time passed without a sound, that father rose and went to look, and then I; and (as I said) it was quarter of an hour. She breathed very gently the first part of the time. We all felt so thankful when it seemed that she had indeed fled without a sigh, when we had been dreading a final struggle between her tenacious life and the death angel. But, no; her life went out into the free spaces, and here she lies, for I am sitting by her bedside this first night. Mary has gone home; father has gone to bed. We are all at peace--peace--peace. This sentiment in me shuts out all realization that the only being in the wide world whose affection for me knew no limit, has gone out of it. It seems to me that I never shall feel separated. She scarcely spoke but in monosyllables; but these showed she was perfectly sensible. Several times she wanted me to "go to bed," and did not seem to realize that it was the daytime. I think she was perfectly conscious, but I am not sure that she knew that she was dying. I was not sure myself, though I knew she could not live long. I read to her one of David's Psalms of Thanksgiving in the afternoon; I thought it might awaken sweet echoes of association.

My dear Sophia, I hope your heart too will rest in peace upon the thought of the ascended one, ascended, and yet, I dare say, hovering over the beloved ones.

From your affectionate
ELIZABETH.

--Hawthorne's nomination was confirmed on March 26, 1853, and he sailed for Liverpool, in the Cunard steamship "Niagara," Captain Leach, in the latter part of the ensuing June. I do not know that I can close this chapter, and the volume, better than by adding the following notes of ideas and studies for stories, taken from his journals of the five or six preceding years. They are similar in general character to those already familiar to the readers of the published "Note-Books;" but, though fully as suggestive as any of the latter, were not included among them.

CHAPTER 9 - NOTES FOR STORIES AND ESSAYS

A sketch,--the devouring of the old country residences by the overgrown monster of a city. For instance, Mr. Beekman's ancestral residence was originally several miles from the city of New York; but the pavements kept creeping nearer and nearer; till now the house is removed, and a street runs directly through what was once its hall.

An essay on the various kinds of death, together with the just before and just after.

The majesty of death to be exemplified in a beggar, who, after being seen humble and cringing, in the streets of a city, for many years, at length, by some means or other, gets admittance into a rich man's mansion, and there dies,--assuming state, and striking awe into the breasts of those who had looked down upon him.

To write a dream which shall resemble the real course of a dream, with all its inconsistency, its strange transformations, which are all taken as a matter of course; its eccentricities and aimlessness,--with nevertheless a leading idea running through the whole. Up to this old age of the world, no such thing has ever been written.

With an emblematic divining-rod to seek for emblematic gold,--that is, for truth; for what of heaven is left on earth.

The emerging from their lurking-places of evil characters on some occasions suited to them,--they having been quite unknown to the world hitherto. For instance, the French Revolution brought out such wretches.

The advantages of a longer life than is allotted to mortals: the many things that might then be accomplished, to which one lifetime is inadequate, and for which the time spent is therefore lost; a successor being unable to take up the task where we drop it.

George First promised his mistress, the Duchess of Kendal, that, if possible, he would pay her a visit after death. Accordingly, a large raven flew into the window of her villa at Isleworth. She believed it to be his soul, and treated it ever after with all respect and tenderness, till either she or the bird died.

The history of an almshouse in a country village from the era of its foundation downwards,--a record of the remarkable occupants of it, and extracts from the interesting portions of its annals. The rich of one generation might, in the next, seek a home there, either in their own persons or in those of their representatives. Perhaps the son and heir of the founder might have no better refuge. There should be occasional sunshine let into the story; for instance, the good fortune of some nameless infant, educated there, and discovered finally to be the child of wealthy parents.

Great expectations to be entertained, in the allegorical Grub Street, of the appearance of the Great American Writer,--or a search-warrant to be made out to catch a Poet. On the former supposition, he shall be discovered under some most unlikely form--or shall be supposed to have lived and died unrecognized.

An old man to promise a youth a treasure of gold, and to keep his promise by teaching him practically the Golden Rule.

A valuable jewel to be buried in the grave of some beloved person, or thrown over with a corpse at sea, or deposited under the foundation-stone of an edifice, and to be afterwards met with by the former owner in the possession of some one.

In moods of heavy despondency, one feels as if it would be delightful to sink down in some quiet spot, and lie there forever, letting the soil gradually accumulate and form a little hillock over us, and the grass and flowers gather over it. At such times death is too much of an event to be wished for,--we have not spirits to encounter it, but choose to pass out of existence in this sluggish way.

A dream, the other night, that the world had become dissatisfied with the inaccurate manner in which facts are reported, and had employed me, at a salary of a thousand dollars, to relate things of importance exactly as they happen.

A person who has all the qualities of a friend, except that he invariably fails you at a pinch.

To find out all sorts of ridiculous employments for people, who have nothing better to do; as, to comb out cows' tails, shave goats, hoard up the seeds of weeds, etc., etc.

Our most intimate friend is not he to whom we show the worst, but the best of our nature.

Some men have no right to perform great deeds or to think high thoughts; and when they do so, it is a kind of humbug. They had better keep within their own propriety.

A young woman in England poisoned by an East Indian barbed dart, which her brother had brought home as a curiosity.

"He looked as if he had been standing up thirty years against a northeast storm."--Description by Pike of an old mate of a vessel.

Death possesses a good deal of real estate; pleasure-grounds, too.

Words,--so innocent and powerless are they, as standing in a dictionary; how potent for good and evil they become to one who knows how to combine them!

Weight, July 4, 1848, one hundred and seventy eight pounds; greater than at any former period.

A man arriving at the extreme point of old age grows young again at the same pace at which he had grown old,--returning upon his path throughout the whole of life, and thus taking the reverse view of matters. Methinks it would give rise to some odd concatenations.

A story, the principal personage of which shall seem always on the point of entering on the scene, but shall never appear.

The same children who make the snow image shall plant dry sticks, and they shall take root and grow.

A ray of sunshine searching for an old blood-spot through a lonely room.

To contrive a story of a man building a house, and locating it over the pit of Acheron. The fumes of hell shall breathe up from the furnace that warms it, and over which Satan himself shall preside. Devils and damned souls shall continually be rising through the registers. Possibly an angel may now and then peep through the ventilators.

A woman's wedding-ring imbedded into the flesh after years of matrimony. Reminiscences of the slender finger on which it at first slid so easily.

Supposing a man to weigh one hundred and forty pounds when married, and after marriage to increase to two hundred and eighty pounds, then, surely, he is half a bachelor, especially if the union be not a spiritual one.

For a child's story, one of baby's rides in her little carriage, drawn by the other two children.

Miss Rebecca Pennell says that in her childhood she used to see a certain old Orthodox minister, dressed in antique style, with his hair powdered and in a queue, a three-cornered hat, knee-breeches, etc. He looked so much unlike everybody else, that it never occurred to her that he was a man, but some other sort of a contrivance.

A spring in Kentucky,--the water certain death to all drinkers.

A man of coarse, vulgar nature breaks his leg or his neck. What is he then? A vulgar fraction.

"The tea makes that little bit of sun crazy," quoth Julian, the other morning, looking at the quivering on the wall of the reflection of the sunshine from a cup of coffee, whenever the jar of the table shook it.

The sunbeam that comes through a round hole in the shutter of a darkened room, where a dead man sits in solitude.

For a child's story,--imagine all sorts of wonderful playthings.

The wizard, Michael Scott, used to give a feast to his friends, the dishes at which were brought from the kitchens of various princes in Europe, by devils, at his command. "Now we will try a dish from the King of France's kitchen," etc. A modern sketch might take a hint from this, and the dishes be brought from various restaurants.

Annals of a kitchen.

A modern magician to make the semblance of a human being, with two laths for legs, a pumpkin for a head, etc.--of the most modest and meagre materials. Then a tailor helps him to finish his work, and transforms this scarecrow into quite a fashionable figure. At the end of the story, after deceiving the world for a long time, the spell should be broken, and the gay dandy be discovered to be nothing but a suit of clothes, with these few sticks inside of it. All through his seeming existence as a human being, there shall be some characteristics, some tokens, that, to the man of close observation and insight, betray him to be a mere thing of laths and clothes, without heart, soul, or intellect. And so this wretched old thing shall become the symbol of a large class.

An angel comes down from heaven, commissioned to gather up, put into a basket, and carry away, everything good that is not improved by mankind, for whose benefit it was intended. She distributes the articles where they will be appreciated.

The first manufacture of the kind of candy called Gibraltar Rock, for a child's story. To be told in the romantic, mystic, marvellous style.

Corwin is going to Lynn; Oliver proposes to walk thither with him. "No," says Corwin, "I don't want you. You take too long steps; or, if you take short ones, 't is all hypocrisy. And, besides, you keep humming all the time."

Captain Burchmore tells a story of an immense turtle which he saw at sea, on a voyage to Batavia, so long that the lookout at the masthead mistook it for a rock. The ship passed close to him, and he was apparently longer than the long-boat, with a head "bigger than any dog's you ever see," and great prickles on his back a foot long. Aniving at Batavia, he told the story; and an old pilot exclaimed, "What! have you seen Bellysore Tom?" It seems the pilots had been acquainted with this turtle as much as twelve years, and always found him in the same latitude. They never did him any injury, but were accustomed to throw him great pieces of meat, which he received in good part, so that there was a mutual friendship hetween the pilots and Bellysore Torn. Old Lee, in confirmation of the story, affirmed that he had often heard other ship-masters speak of the same monster. But he being a notorious liar, and Captain Burchmore an unconscionable spinner of long yarns and travellers' tales, the evidence is by no means perfect. The pilots estimated his length at not less than twenty feet.

A disquisition, or a discussion between two or more persons, on the manner in which the Wandering Jew has spent his life,--one period, perhaps, in wild carnal debauchery; then trying over and over again to grasp domestic happiness; then a soldier; then a statesman, etc.; at last, realizing some truth.

In the eyes of a young child, or other innocent person, the image of a cherub or angel to be seen peeping out; in those of a vicious person, a devil.

A moral philosopher to buy a slave, or otherwise get possession of a human being, and to use him for the sake of experiment, by trying the operation of a certain vice on him.

The human heart to be allegorized as a cavern; at the entrance there is sunshine, and flowers growing about it. You step within, but a short distance, and find yourself surrounded with a terrible gloom, and monsters of divers kinds; it seems like hell itself. You are bewildered, and wander long without hope. At last, a light strikes upon you. You press towards it, and find yourself in a region that seems, in some sort, to reproduce the flowers and sunny beauty of the entrance,--but all perfect. These are the depths of the heart, or of human nature, bright and beautiful; the gloom and terror may lie deep, but deeper still is this eternal beauty.

An examination of wits and poets at a police-court, and they to be sentenced by the Judge to various penalties or fines, the house of correction, whipping, etc., according to the moral offences of which they were guilty.

To consider a piece of gold as a sort of talisman, or as containing within itself all the forms of enjoyment that it can purchase, so that they might appear, by some fantastical chemical process, as visions.

To typify our mature review of our early prospects and delusions, by representing a person as wandering, in manhood, through and among the various castles in the air that he had raised in his youth, and describing how they look to him,--their dilapidations, etc. Possibly some small portion of these structures may have a certain reality, and suffice him to build a humble dwelling to pass his life in.

The hand of one person may express more than the face of another.

When the heart is full of care, or the mind much occupied, the summer and the sunshine and the moonlight are but a gleam and glimmer,--a vague dream which does not come within us, but only makes itself imperfectly perceptible on the outside of us.

People who write about themselves and their feelings, as Byron did, may be said to serve up their own hearts, duly spiced, and with brain sauce, out of their own heads, as a repast for the public.

Nature sometimes displays a little tenderness for our vanity, but is never careful of our pride. She is willing that we should look foolish in the eyes of the others, but keeps our little nonsensicalities from ourselves.

In a grim, weird story, a figure of a gay, laughing, handsome youth, or a young lady, all at once, in a natural, unconcerned way, takes off its face like a mask, and shows the grinning, bare skeleton face beneath.

To sit down in a solitary place (or a busy and bustling one, if you please) and await such little events as may happen, or observe such noticeable points as the eyes fall upon around you. For instance, I sat down to-day, at about ten o'clock in the forenoon, in Sleepy Hollow,--a shallow space scooped out among the woods, which surround it on all sides, it being pretty nearly circular, or oval, and two or three hundred yards in diameter. The present season, a thriving field of Indian corn, now in its most perfect growth, and tasselled out, occupies nearly half the hollow; and it is like the lap of bounteous Nature, filled with breadstuff. On one verge of the hollow, skirting it, is a terraced pathway, broad enough for a wheel-track, overshadowed with oaks, stretching their long, knotted, rude, rough arms between earth and sky; the gray skeletons, as you look upward, are strikingly prominent amid the green foliage. Likewise there are chestnuts, growing up in a more regular and pyramidal shape; white pines also; and a shrubbery composed of the shoots of all these trees, overspreading and softening the bank on which the parent stems are growing;--these latter being intermingled with coarse grass. Observe the pathway; it is strewn over with little bits of dry twigs and decayed branches, and the brown oak leaves of last year, that have been moistened by snow and rain, and whirled about by winds, since their departed verdure; the needle-like leaves of the pine, that we never noticed in falling,--that fall, yet never leave the tree bare; and with these are pebbles, the remains of what was once a gravelled surface, but which the soil accumulating from the decay of leaves, and washing down from the bank, has now almost covered. The sunshine comes down on the pathway with the bright glow of noon, at certain points; in other places there is a shadow as deep as the glow; but along the greater portion sunshine glimmers through shadow, and shadow effaces sunshine, imaging that pleasant mood of mind where gayety and pensiveness intermingle. A bird is chirping overhead among the branches, but exactly whereabout, you seek in vain to determine; indeed, you hear the rustle of the leaves, as he continually changes his position. A little sparrow now hops into view, alighting on the slenderest twigs, and seemingly delighting in the swinging and heaving motion, which his slight substance communicates to them; but he is not the loquacious bird whose voice still comes, eager and busy, from his hidden whereabout. Insects are fluttering about. The cheerful, sunny hum of flies is altogether summer-like, and so gladsome that you pardon them their intrusiveness and impertinence, which continually impels them to fly against your face, to alight upon your hands, and to buzz in your very ear, as if they wished to get into your head, among your most secret thoughts. In fact, a fly is the most impertinent and indelicate thing in creation,--the very type and moral of human spirits whom one occasionally meets with, and who perhaps, after an existence troublesome and vexatious to all with whom they come in contact, have been doomed to reappear in this congenial shape. Here is one intent upon alighting on my nose. In a room, now,--in a human habitation,--I could find in my conscience to put him to death; but here we have intruded upon his own domain, which he holds in common with all the children of earth and air, and we have no right to slay him on his own ground. Now we look about us more minutely, and observe that the acorn-cups of last year are strewn plentifully on the bank and on the path; there is always pleasure in examining an acorn-cup, perhaps associated with fairy banquets, where they are said to compose the table-service. Here, too, are those balls which grow as excrescences on the leaves of the oak, aud which young kittens love so well to play with, rolling them on the carpet. We see mosses, likewise, growing on the banks, in as great variety as the trees of the wood. And how strange is the gradual process with which we detect objects that are right before the eyes! Here now are whortleberries, ripe and black, growing actually within reach of my hand, yet unseen till this moment. Were we to sit here all day, a week, a month, and doubtless a lifetime, objects would thus still be presenting themselves as new, though there would seem to be no reason why we should not have detected them at the first moment.

Now a catbird is mewing at no great distance. Then the shadow of a bird flitted across a sunny spot: there is a peculiar impressiveness in this mode of being made acquainted with the flight of a bird; it affects the mind more than if the eye had actually seen it. As we look round to catch a glimpse of the winged creature, we behold the living blue of the sky, and the brilliant disc of the sun, broken and made tolerable to the eye by the intervening foliage. Now, when you are not thinking of it, the fragrance of the white pines is suddenly wafted to you by an almost imperceptible breeze, which has begun to stir. Now the breeze is the gentlest sigh imaginable, yet with a spiritual potency, insomuch that it seems to penetrate, with its mild, ethereal coolness, through the outward clay, and breathe upon the spirit itself, which shivers with gentle delight. Now the breeze strengthens, so much as to shake all the leaves, making them rustle sharply; but it has lost its most ethereal power. And now, again, the shadows of the boughs lie as motionless as if they were painted on the pathway. Now, in the stillness, is heard the long, melancholy note of a bird, complaining alone. of some wrong or sorrow that man, or her own kind, or the immitigable doom of mortal affairs, has inflicted upon her, the complaining but unresisting sufferer. And now, all of a sudden, we hear the sharp, shrill chirrup of a red squirrel, angry, it seems, with somebody, perhaps with ourselves, for having intruded into what he is pleased to consider his own domain. And, hark terrible to the ear, here is the minute but intense hum of the mosquito! Instinct prevails over all the nonsense of sentiment; we crush him at once, and there is his grim and grisly corpse, the ugliest object in nature. This incident has disturbed our tranquillity. In truth, the whole insect tribe, so far as we can judge, are made more for themselves, and less for man, than any other portion of creation. With such reflections we look at a swarm of them, peopling, indeed, the whole air, but only visible when they flash into the sunshine, and annihilated out of visible existence when they dart into a region of shadow; to be again reproduced as suddenly. Now we hear the striking of the village clock, distant, but yet so near that each stroke is impressed distinctly upon the air. This is a sound that does not disturb the repose of the scene: it does not break our sabbath; for like a sabbath seems this place, and the more so on account of the cornfield rustling at our feet. It tells of human labor, but, being so solitary now, it seems as if it were on account of the sacredness of the sabbath. Yet it is not so, for we hear at a distance mowers whetting their scythes; but these sounds of labor, when at a proper remoteness, do but increase the quiet of one who lies at his ease, all in a mist of his own musings. There is the tinkling of a cow-bell, a noise how peevishly dissonant if close at hand, but even musical now. But, hark there is the whistle of the locomotive,--the long shriek, harsh above all other harshness, for the space of a mile cannot mollify it into harmony. It tells a story of busy men, citizens, from the hot street, who have come to spend a day in a country village,--men of business,--in short, of all unquietness; and no wonder that it gives such a startling shriek, since it brings the noisy world into the midst of our slumbrous peace. As our thoughts repose again, after this interruption, we find ourselves gazing up at the leaves, and comparing their different aspect, the beautiful diversity of green, as the sun is diffused through them as a medium, or reflected from their glossy surface. You see, too, here and there, dead and leafless branches, which you had no more been aware of before, than if they had assumed this old and dry decay since you sat down upon the bank. Look at our feet, and here likewise are objects as good as new. There are two little round white fungi, which probably sprang from the ground in the course of last night, curious productions of the mushroom tribe, and which, by and by, will be those little things with smoke in them, which children call puff-balls. Is there nothing else? Yes, here is a whole colony of little ant-hills, a real village of them; they are small round hillocks, framed of minute particles of gravel, with an entrance in the centre; and through some of them blades of grass or small shrubs have sprouted up, producing an effect not unlike that of trees overshadowing a homestead. Here is a type of domestic industry,--perhaps, too, something of municipal institutions,--perhaps, likewise, (who knows?) the very model of a community, which Fourierites and others are stumbling in pursuit of. Possibly the student of such philosophies should go to the ant, and find that nature has given him his lesson there. Meantime, like a malevolent genius, I drop a few grains of sand into the entrance of one of their dwellings, and thus quite obliterate it. And, behold! here comes one of the inhabitants, who has been abroad upon some public or private business, or perhaps to enjoy a fantastic walk,--and cannot any longer find his own door What surprise, what hurry, what confusion of mind, are expressed in his movement! How inexplicable to him must be the agency which has effected this mischief! The incident will probably be long remembered in the annals of the ant colony, and be talked of in the winter days, when they are making merry over their hoarded provisions.

But come, it is time to move. The sun has shifted his position, and has found a vacant space through the branches, by means of which he levels his rays full upon our heads. Yet now, as we arise, a cloud has come across him, and makes everything gently sombre in an instant. Many clouds, voluminous and heavy, are scattered about the sky, like the shattered ruins of a dreamer's Utopia. But we will not send our thoughts thitherward now, nor take one of them into our present observations. The clouds of any one day are material enough, of themselves, for the observation of either an idle man or a philosopher.

And now, how narrow, scanty, and meagre is this record of observation, compared with the immensity that was to be observed, within the bounds that we prescribed ourselves! How shallow and small a stream of thought, too,--of distinct and expressed thought,--compared with the broad tide of dim emotions, ideas, associations, which were flowing through the haunted regions of imagination, intellect, and sentiment; sometimes excited by what was around us; sometimes with no perceptible connection with them. When we see how little we can express, it is a wonder that any one ever takes up a pen a second time.

VOLUME 2
CHAPTER 1 - FIRST MONTHS IN ENGLAND

WE ARE TOLD, truly enough, that goodness does not always command good fortune in this world, that just hopes are often deferred until it is too late to enjoy their realization, fame and honor only discover a man after he has ceased to value them; and a large and respectable portion of modern fiction is occupied in impressing these sober lessons upon us. It is pleasant, nevertheless, to believe that sometimes fate condescends not to be so unmitigable, and that a cloudy and gusty morning does occasionally brighten into a sunny and genial afternoon. Too long a course of apparently perverse and unreasonable accidents bewilders the mind, and the few and fleeting gleams of compensation seem a mockery. One source of the perennial charm of Goldsmith's "Vicar of Wakefield" is, I think, that in it the dividing line between the good and the bad fortune is so distinctly drawn. Just when man has done his utmost, and all seems lost, Providence steps in, brings aid from the most unexpected quarter, and kindles everything into brighter and ever brighter prosperity. The action and reaction are positive and complete, and we arise refreshed and comforted from the experience.

It was somewhat thus with Hawthorne, though the picture of his career is to be painted in a lower and more delicate tone than that of Goldsmith's brilliant little canvas. Up to the time of the publication of "The Scarlet Letter," his external circumstances had certainly been growing more and more unpromising; though, on the other hand, his inner domestic life had been full of the most vital and tender satisfactions. But the date of his first popular success in literature also marks the commencement of a worldly prosperity which, though never by any means splendid (as we shall presently see), at any rate sufficed to allay the immediate anxiety about to-morrow's bread-and-butter, from which he had not hitherto been free. The three American novels were written and published in rapid succession, and were reprinted in England,--the first two being pirated; but for the last, "The Blithedale Romance," two hundred pounds was obtained from Messrs. Chapman and Hall for advance sheets. There is every reason to believe that during the ensuing years other romances would have been written; and perhaps they would have been as good as, or better than, those that went before. But it is vain to speculate as to what might have been. What actually happened was, that Hawthorne was appointed United States Consul to Liverpool; and for six years to come his literary exercises were confined to his consular despatches and to the six or eight manuscript volumes of his English, French, and Italian Journals. It was a long abstinence; possibly it was a beneficent one. The production of such books as "The Scarlet Letter" and "The House of the Seven Gables" cannot go on indefinitely; though they seem to be easily written when they are written, they represent a great deal of the writer's spiritual existence. At all events, it is better to write too little than too much.

This outlet to Europe was for both Hawthorne and his wife the unlooked-for realization of the dreams of a lifetime. Few Americans ever journeyed thither better equipped than they for appreciating and enjoying what lay before them. They might have said of England or Italy what Tennyson's Prince says of the Princess,--"Ere seen I loved, and loved thee seen." What can be more agreeable than to be born with tastes which cannot be fully gratified in the land of your birth, and then, when the bustle and struggle of life are over, and your faculties and judgment are ripened, to find yourself all at once in actual contact with the things, the scenes, and the people that have so long constituted the substance of your meditations? Such enjoyment repays much waiting; indeed, it can hardly exist save on that condition. And yet, I suppose, the best part of the enjoyment was the immediate anticipation of it. If for no other reason than that the climate of England is depressing, and that of Italy treacherous, those countries fail quite to fulfil the best that one has expected of them.

On the other side, a number of people who had made his acquaintance through his books, as the phrase is, were looking forward with hospitable pleasure to Hawthorne's arrival. Four or five months before the date fixed for sailing, Mrs. Hawthorne in a letter to her father quotes the following passage from a letter written by Miss De Quincey:--

"We lately received a letter written to a friend by one of De Quincey's daughters, who expresses herself very warmly about Mr. Hawthorne. This is what she says: 'Your mention of Mr. Hawthorne puts me in mind to tell you what rabid admirers we are of his. I am sure it was worth while saving his manuscripts from the flames, if his only reward was gaining one family, not millions, of such adorers as ourselves. There is no prose writer of the present day in whom I have half the interest that I have in him. His style is in my mind so beautifully refined, and there is such exquisite pathos and quaint humor, and such an *awfully* deep knowledge of human nature,-- not that hard, unloving, detestable, and (as it is purely one-sided or wrong-sided) false reading of it that one finds in Thackeray. He reminds me in many things of Charles Lamb, and of heaps of our rare old English humorists, with their deep, pathetic, natures. And one faculty he possesses beyond any writer I remember (not dramatic, for then I could certainly remember Shakspeare),--namely, that of exciting you to the highest pitch without ever, as I am aware of, making you feel by his catastrophe ashamed of having been so excited. What I mean is, if you have ever read it, such a case as occurs in the "Mysteries of Udolpho," where your disgust is beyond all expression at finding that all your fright about the ghostly creature that has haunted you throughout the volume has been caused by a pitiful wax image! I merely give this as an exaggerated case of what I feel in reading most books where any great passion is meant to be worked upon. And no author does work upon them more, apparently with no effort to himself. But it may be only his consummate art to succeed so effectually. I cannot satisfy myself as to whether I like his sort of essays contained in the "Twice-Told Tales" best, or his more finished works, such as "The Blithedale Romance." Every touch he adds to any character gives a higher interest to it, so that I *should* like the longer ones best; but there is a concentration of excellence in the shorter things, and passages that strike in force like daggers in their beauty and truth, so I generally end by liking that best which I have read last. Will you tell him how much we love and admire his gracious nature? There are other stars in your firmament, all of whom we admire, some *greatly;* but he outshines them all by infinite degrees.'"

--"This is very pleasant," adds Mrs. Hawthorne, and it is certainly as appreciative as one could wish, and, like most such eulogies, throws more light upon the eulogist than the eulogized.

A year or two later, when we were settled in England, this same Miss De Quincey wrote to Mr Hawthorne from Ireland, enclosing a note from her married sister, Mrs.

Craig, at whose house she was staying. Although at the sacrifice of chronological order, I subjoin the letters here. So far as I am aware, Mr. Hawthorne never happened to meet either De Quincey himself or any of his family.

PEGSBORO, TIPPERARY, 1RELAND, Nov. 13, 1854.

MY DEAR MR. HAWTHORNE,--I received a letter to-day to forward to my father, with the Liverpool postmark, and "N. H." on the seal. Partly hoping and partly fearing it may be from you, I write to explain to you why it is not already answered, and why it may *not* be answered for some time longer. Papa retired early this summer to the wilds of an Edinburgh lodging-house, in order to be nearer his publishers, and to be rid of the interruptions to which he was liable at home; and my youngest sister and I have taken advantage of his absence to shut up our house for a month or two, and to come over here to visit my eldest sister, and to worship our first niece, a very lovely little atom not yet two months old. Papa's letters are sent to me here to be forwarded to him, which will account for your letter not yet being answered; and should it still continue unanswered, this too will be accounted for, should you have heard anything of papa's shortcomings in the way of letter-writing, and of letter-reading too, as he very often does not open his letters unless he knows he has one of us at hand to answer them. We are all very much afraid your letter may be to offer a visit while we are from home, which we have been looking forward to so long. Should this be the case, I can at least give you papa's address in Edinburgh, that he may not miss the pleasure of seeing you, which--as I shall feel particularly savage at our own misfortune in doing so--is a stretch of generous consideration that I hope you and he will recognize. I feel as if we knew you, or rather as if you knew us, so intimately and so tenderly in your works, that I cannot finish my letter but as

Your affectionate friend,
FLORENCE DE QUINCEY.

--Here is the enclosure:--

MY DEAR MR. HAWTHORNE,--Though I have given up my claim to be "Miss De Quincey," I hope 1 have not given up the chance of becoming acquainted with you. I was included in the promise of introduction to you; and if I, then my husband too, for we are "one flesh." Mr. Craig desires me to say how heartily he joins me in hoping we may have the pleasure of welcoming such guests in our Irish home. I have a private reason of my own for wishing it too. You are a *baby-fancier*, and I want to compare notes with you about our little "Puck" as we call her; being made by nature as nearly like a little angel as anything I ever saw, she chooses to make herself, when we want to show her off to any one, like Puck and those gargoyle faces on the g outside of churches,--all to put her poor parents in confusion. But I suppose I had better stop this subject. So with our kindest regards to you all, I beg to remain, dear sir,

Faithfully yours,
M. CRAIG.

--Mr. Hawthorne always enjoyed De Quincey's writings. I remember his reading the brown-covered volumes of Ticknor's American edition, as they came out one after another; and he often recurred to them afterwards. The music of the style pleased him, and the smoothness and finish of the thought. After the return of the family to Concord, in 1860, he gave his son a passage from the essay on "The Caesars" to learn for his first school-declamation. It was a very eloquent piece of writing; but there is no record of its having produced a deep impression on the school. On another occasion Mrs. Hawthorne, who shared her husband's fondness for the author, read aloud to her children the whole of the story, or historical sketch, entitled "Klosterheim." It was good reading,--I do not know when I have listened to better; and it fixed the tale forever in the memory of the auditors. Both Mr. and Mrs. Hawthorne seem to have been born good readers; there were music, variety, and expression in every tone, and the charm of feeling that the reader was in sympathy with the reading. While we were in England, Mr. Hawthorne read to us Spenser's "Faerie Queene;" and his children were knights-errant and princesses for years afterwards. Again, two or three years before his death, he read aloud the whole of Walter Scott's novels, taking up the volumes night after night, until all were completed. That, too, was something to remember. All the characters seemed to live and move visibly before us. The expression of his face changed, as he read, in harmony with the speech or the passage. It was very pleasant to see him sitting with a book, he would settle himself comfortably in his chair, and hold the book open in his left hand, his fingers clasping it over the top; and as he read (whether aloud or to himself), there was a constantly recurrent forward movement of his head, which seemed somehow to give distinctness and significance to the sentences and paragraphs, and indicated the constant living rapport between him and the author. These movements were very slight and unobtrusive, but they were among the things which conveyed to the beholder that impression of unfailing spiritual vitality and intellectual comprehensiveness which always characterized Hawthorne.

What De Quincey thought of Hawthorne's writings, or whether he ever read them, we have no record. De Quincey's own countrymen do not seem, as a rule to have cared as much for him as his American admirers did. Mr. Henry Bright writes: "In 1854 I had written a review of De Quincey in the 'Westminster,' and Mr. Hawthorne wrote to me, quite indignant that I had not praised De Quincey more warmly." At this time, however, there was, I believe, no complete English edition of the man's writings, they were scattered through various reviews, and of course lost much of their collective effect.

But this is a digression. In February, 1853, Mrs. Hawthorne had more news of expectant English admirers to tell her father:--

"Mr. Hawthorne received the other day from Sheffield a very thick letter, and it contained one of his sketches, 'The White Old Maid,' rendered into verse; and with the poem, a letter from the poet, in which he expresses the greatest admiration and delight in his works. It is signed 'Henry Cecil.' He begins the letter 'My dear Brother;' and he says he attempted this poetical version because of a dispute that the spell of the tale could not be retained in rhyme. Lately Mr. Hawthorne also had a letter from Bennett, an English poet,--a very loving and admiring letter; and at the end he says his 'Baby May' bids him 'send Mr. Hawthorne a kiss for his promise of a Wonder Book, and her love to Una and Julian and little Rose-bud as she is. I am ordered too by Mrs. Bennett to be sure and tell you what an admirer you have in her.'"

--Hawthorne met both of these gentlemen after his arrival in England. I do not remember what became of Mr. Henry Cecil, and have found no letters of his, but Mr. Bennett became, and remained to the last, among the most cordial and agreeable friends of the American author.

The months preceding departure were occupied in preparations, whereof there seemed never to be an end. And yet Hawthorne did not anticipate so prolonged an absence as proved to be before him; and it was moreover intended to "run home" occasionally, and so break the spell of exile. But an ocean voyage is even now something of an undertaking, and was still more so then. Besides, Time is fertile in deceptions; he never gives us a fourth part as much leisure as he promises us. Furthermore, Atlantic journeys cost money, and the Liverpool Consulate turned out to be very much less of a gold-mine than it was thought to be. In a certain sense, too, all partings in this world are final: we never find on our return the same thing or person that we left; at any rate, we never bring the same person back. Certainly the Concord of 1860 was a very different place, to Hawthorne, from the Concord of 1853. But fortunately we perceive this sober truth only in the retrospect; the outlook forward is much more agreeable, as may be judged from this letter to Dr. Peabody from his daughter, written in May,--six weeks before sailing:--

"...I very much hope you are more glad than sorry at the turning up of our wheel of Fortune. I hope to come back from England and make you a visit before our final return to America, and show you the children before they are grown too big. Ericsson's caloric ships will soon be crossing the Atlantic; and they will as safe as a parlor, you know, and so people can make calls across the ocean with composure of mind. The two older children are filled with delighted wonder and hope; as to Rosebud, what matters it to her whether she stand on one hemisphere or the other, so long as Papa, Mamma, Oona, and Dulan are within sight? I do not intend to bid any one farewell. There is really no distance now. I do not feel as if Liverpool were far off. I can write to you by every steamer, and you will know exactly about us, as if you were in Newton and we in Concord. And soon the telegraph will take news by lightning between the Old and the New Worlds, and we can be well advised of one another.

"We receive the pleasantest and most cordial assurances from all quarters upon this Consulate. It was a very noble act of General Pierce; for the office is second in dignity only to the Embassy in London, and is more sought for than any other, and is nearly the most lucrative, and General Pierce might have made great political capital out of it if that were his way. But he acts from the highest and not lowest motives, and would make any sacrifice to the right. Mr. Charles Sumner sent a note written in the Senate Chamber at the moment of confirmation, that fairly shouted as with a silver trumpet, it was so cordial and stron, in joy. So from all sides. Mr. Hawthorne seems chosen by acclamation, as General Pierce was.

"Mr. Hawthorne got back from Washington last Thursday. He says he should have seen and learned much that was desirable for him to know and see it he had stayed three weeks longer; but he was tired out with even so much of it, being lionized to a painful degree everywhere he went. He received fifty letters while there, I forget how many telegraphic despatches, and a vast number of cards, and was introduced to everybody of any note. He had the satisfaction of accomplishing a good deal for others, and it proved a most fortunate moment for himself to be there. Many things he told me that teach me a great deal about the difficulty and delicacy of judging men in high positions, with wide responsibilities, *justly*.

"Mr. Hawthorne says he was very glad to look at the country from a central point. I can conceive how much he could gain from the right point, with his harvesting eye, generalizing and concentrating, all things. When he had once turned homeward, he came as fast as steam could bring him, though he had intended to remain in New York and then in Boston. This strong tendency towards home saved him from that terrific accident on Friday,--which he escaped so narrowly that it makes me shiver to think of it, though, to be sure, I cannot believe in chances. He arrived at noon. Julian was out of doors. Mary Herne, our cook, was sewing under the pine shrubbery. Julian rushed past her with a face of red fire, shouting 'Father! Papa!' with such a tremendous emphasis that everybody in and out of the house heard him at once. The stage drove up. Baby was asleep; and when she waked, she was dressed and put into the room, and unexpectedly saw Papa. It was too much for her. Her eyes twinkled and closed exactly as if a dazzling sun had blazed upon her; and when her father moved towards her, she burst into tears and clung to me and hid her face. It took a good while to tranquillize her; but finally, when she could manage her emotions, she shook hands with him, and then got up in his lap with an expression of the utmost satisfaction--

"*Monday Morning.* .--I was interrupted yesterday by Mr. Alcott coming, and he stayed to tea; so I send my letter this morning as it is."

--On a hot July morning Hawthorne, with his wife and children, left Concord and went by train to Boston, where they embarked on the Cunard steamer "Niagara," which was commanded by Captain Leitch. The captain was a very charming personage, as the children soon found out; he was rather below the medium height, slender, with a handsome countenance, bushy black whiskers, and very quiet and courteous manners. It so happened that he commanded the vessel on which, seven years later, Hawthorne made the return trip to Boston. That vessel, however, was not the "Niagara:" the latter was chartered by the British Government, during the Crimean war, to convey soldiers to the Black Sea; and Hawthorne took his son down to the Liverpool wharves to see her depart on that occasion, loaded down with red-coated heroes,--very few of whom, by the by, ever saw Liverpool again. The "Niagara" was, of course, a paddle-wheel steamer, and must have been something less than three hundred feet in length, though her beam was scarcely less than that of the great screw-propellers of the present day. She was a palace of wonder and delight to the young people; and she carried, as part of her crew, an amiable cow and a brood of clucking hens. The weather, at starting; was very fine; we passed several ships becalmed, outside Boston Harbor, their crews lounging over the bulwarks and giving us a parting cheer as we steamed seaward. Some of us were in high spirits, and longed to see the last headland of America vanish beneath the horizon; but Hawthorne, standing on the deck with his hands behind him, rebuked this unsentimental mood, and intimated that we should view with regret the disappearance of the land that we might never see again. After we were fairly at sea, however, his gravity lightened, and he gave himself up to the free enjoyment of the ocean he so dearly loved. Though his forefathers followed the sea, and he himself had scarce ever lived out of sight of blue water, this was the first extended voyage that Hawthorne had ever made, and he found the fullest satisfaction in it and was sorry when it was over. He never enjoyed such good health as when he was afloat, was never sea-sick, spent all his days on deck, and was never weary of watching the dance and rush of the waves and the changing hues and the lights and shadows of sea and sky. The voyage was, comparatively, an uneventful one; with the exception of one sharp squall, a few days before reaching Liverpool, it was fine weather nearly all the way. The only journalizing done during the voyage is comprised in a brief passage in Mrs. Hawthorne's note-book, which I subjoin.

"STEAMER NIAGARA, *July 8*, 1853.--This morning at one o'clock we left Halifax; and we are now careering on to England on a lovely summer sea, with summer air. Yesterday it was very cold. We entered the harbor of Halifax at eleven last night, and Mr. Hawthorne and Mr. Ticknor and I remained on deck to see all we could by the light of stars and lamps. The blue lights that were burned on the prow and on shore kindled up the rigging and fine ropes in the forepart of the vessel, and against the black-blue sky they looked like spun glass, glittering and white and wholly defined. The most brilliant stars, with a fine sharp twinkle, penetrated the dark; and the many faces, appearing and disappearing as the torchlight waved to and fro, were very picturesque. The salute of four cannon greeted the Queen's dominions, and Mr. Ticknor said that two were for my husband. There was no fog, which is very uncommon, for the fogs usually delay the steamers both in entering and leaving the harbor. Out of our smoke-stack poured a column of steam like a procession of snowy plumes waving off into the distance; relieved against the deep-toned sky, it was wonderfully beautiful. I wished to go towards the gangway of the steamer, in and out of which many people were passing (for we landed fourteen and received seventeen, I believe); and, behold my husband pressed on to the pier and on and on up into the streets of Halifax, till I was quite alarmed, and feared we should not get back. But I have really been to Halifax now! Her Majesty's subjects stood about the streets and on the pier. Then we went to our state-rooms; but I did not sleep till nearly morning, and heard the parting salute. I was very sorry not to see Halifax by day, or at least by moonlight, though it was very picturesque by starlight and torchlight. This morning it is milder weather, and there is a fair breeze. We have lost the British Minister Plenipotentiary, who landed at Halifax; and I do not see our unknown friend yet this morning, though I thought he was going to England. I miss the fine presence of Mr. Crampton, the Ambassador, very much; and I liked much to talk with him. This deep blue circle of sea is untiringly beautiful and satisfactory. We still... [illegible]...the motion makes it not possible to write."

--On the 18th of July, or thereabouts, the "Niagara" came to anchor in the Mersey, and it was a rainy day. Our first resting-place on English soil was at a hotel in one of the lower streets of the city,--gloomy, muddy, and grimy, but with the charm that belongs to the first experience of a foreign land. The most interesting objects to the children were, however, two or three gigantic turtles lying half immersed in a large tank in the basement of the hotel; it did not seem credible that such creatures could be made into soup, which we were assured was their destiny. They were very different from the little creatures with variegated carapaces which we used to find in the Concord ditches at home. A few days later we left the hotel, and went to Mrs. Blodgett's boarding-house, in Duke Street,--unquestionably the most comfortable, reasonable, hospitable, and delightful boarding-house that ever existed before or since; nor has nature been able to afford such another boarding-house keeper as Mrs. Blodgett,--so kind, so hearty, so generous, so unobtrusive, so friendly, so motherly. Never, certainly, has the present writer consumed so much food (in proportion to his weight and size) or of better quality than it was his good fortune to do during his sojourn beneath this excellent lady's roof. She was stout and rotund of figure, rosy and smiling of countenance, with brown curls on each side of her face, a clean white cap, a black dress, and (for the most part) a white apron. She also wore spectacles. Her cuisine was superb; her servants perfectly disciplined, everything went with the regularity and certainty of the solar system; she loved all her boarders, and they all loved her. Her house was the rallying-point of the better class of American captains who made voyages to Liverpool; and to her care some good friend of Hawthorne recommended him. We stayed there only a month on this first occasion; but afterwards, when Mrs. Hawthorne and her daughters visited Portugal and Madeira, Hawthorne returned to Mrs. Blodgett's with his son; and they lived there, in great comfort and plenty, the better part of a year.

Meanwhile he had made acquaintance with the Consulate, and with his duties there, which are sufficiently described in "Our Old Home." The windows of the Consul's office were on the left as you entered the room; the large double desk-table was placed against the wall between them; and Hawthorne sat facing the door. The opposite side of the desk was unoccupied, except when (as occasionally happened) the Consul had taken his son to the office with him. On those days a couple of volumes of Congressional Proceedings were placed in the seat of the chair, and the boy mounted upon them, thus bringing his head at an elevation above the table sufficient to admit of his using paper and pencil, scrawling letters to his relatives in America, staring out of the window at the cotton bales going up the sides of the opposite warehouse on long ropes,--an unfailing resource from ennui,--and pestering his father with questions. The latter generally had a book with him; and often it was a book-catalogue, a species of literature which he was very fond of reading. He had been elected a member of the Liverpool Book Society, to which Roscoe and g Sheppard had once belonged, and which circulated all its books among its members. Sometimes he would take paper and write, driving the pen rapidly, with brief intermittent pauses, and making corrections by smearing out the wrong word with his finger. At other times he would pace to and fro across the little room, with his head bent forward and his hands behind him; or, still with his hands behind him, he would stand in front of the fireplace, his feet apart, now swaying forward slightly on the front part of his feet and back again, now giving his body a sidewise movement. This had always been a habit of his, and is connected with his son's earliest memories of him. It was before the fireplace that he usually stood when receiving a deputation of sailors or captains. One day a captain--a dark, short, thickset man--came in to make a complaint against a sailor who had assaulted him with a marlin-spike, or some such nautical weapon. He brought with him the hat he had worn on the occasion,-- a dilapidated "stove-pipe," with a hole crushed through the crown. "First," said he, "there's my hat!" Hawthorne glanced at it and said, "H'm!" "Next," continued the captain, "there's my head!" and stooping forward he parted aside his hair with his hands, and exhibited a bloody wound on the scalp. "H'm!" said Hawthorne; but instead of looking at the wound he turned his face quite away, and kept it averted until the captain, satisfied that he had been sufficiently inspected, regained his perpendicular. The boy (who did see the head) never forgot the incident, because it was for many years incomprehensible to him how his father could have had the self-denial voluntarily to abstain from examining a wound in a man's scalp.

But there were other and more agreeable visitors; most welcome among whom was Mr. Henry Bright, who had been introduced to Hawthorne in Concord, by

Emerson, in the autumn of 1802, and who came to be perhaps the most intimate of his English friends. "Bright," says Hawthorne, in the "Consular Experiences," playing upon his friend's name,--"Bright was the illumination of my dusky little apartment as often as he made his appearance there." Mr. Bright seldom used to sit down, but stood erect on the hearth-rug; tall, slender, good-humored, laughing, voluble; with his English eyeglass, his English speech, and his English prejudices; arguing, remonstrating, asserting, contradicting,--certainly one of the most delightful, and delightfully English, Englishmen that ever lived. And Hawthorne would launch at him such appalling and unsparing home truths of democracy and republicanism as would utterly have choked and smothered any other subject of her Majesty; but they only served to make Mr. Bright laugh, and declare that it was impossible anybody should seriously entertain such opinions. I doubt if the American Consul ever expressed himself to any one else so forcibly, explicitly, and fluently as he did to this English friend; and the consequence of it all was, that they never could see enough of each other.

At one o'clock Hawthorne would sometimes put on his hat and take his son through one or two narrow back-streets to a certain baker's shop, where there was a lunch-counter at which one could stand and eat excellent bread and butter and cheese. Or, if the day were fine, and there were nothing going on at the office, they would go to the museum, or the Zoological Gardens, or to some other place of amusement; or take the ferry-boat and steam over to New Brighton, and stroll about on the beach. The last incident of the official day would be the entrance into the little office of old Mr. Pearce or young Mr. Wilding, with a paper full of coin, the proceeds of the day's labor. The gold and the silver Hawthorne would put in his pocket; but if there were any coppers, he would hand them over to the little boy, who used to wish that copper had been the only current coinage of the realm. Then they would walk home to Duke Street; or, after the final change of residence, go down to the steamboat landing, and get into the "Bee" or the "Wasp," and be steam-paddled over to Rock Ferry, about two miles up the muddy river. On Sundays Mrs. Hawthorne, with the two elder children, would go to the Unitarian Chapel in Renshaw Street, and listen to eloquent sermons from the Rev. W. H. Channing, the American; but Hawthorne himself never attended church, that I remember.

Rock Ferry was a pretty, green, quiet be-villa'd little suburb, consisting of one large hotel and a number of small private residences. Hawthorne first moved to the hotel; but on the 1st of September he took up his permanent abode in a villa in "Rock Park," a house (writes Mrs. Hawthorne in her journal) "in castellated form, of stone, with large pleasant rooms, a pretty, trim garden, and tolerably furnished." But it is time to insert the following batch of letters. The first is from Henry Bright.

CONISTON, Sept. 1, 1853.

MY DEAR SIR,--You see I am taking you at your word, and am about to inflict a letter upon you. However, should your patience fail before getting to the end of it, why, then consign it to the river Mersey as you recross in the evening to Rock Ferry, and exonerate me from my promise. We are delighted with our quarters here,--a most comfortable hotel, with the calm, clear lake in front of us, and such a grand, weather-worn old mountain behind. Nothing could be better, if only--a sadly too important "if"--it would stop raining. With the exception of Monday, it's rained for a blessed week, and we are boxed up, the whole day and the whole family, in one hotel parlor.

This is not the most exhilarating existence in the world, as you may imagine. Our chief amusements are letter-writing and oat-cake eating; my sisters sketch out of window, and I read up for an article I'm contemplating on De Quincey for the "Westminster." Post-time is of course particularly welcome,--I need hardly say how welcome, were you some day to spare me some few lines, if only to say how you all are, and how the mayoral hospitalities went off, and whether you have yet found a house. By the way, I heard from one of my American friends the other day,--Charles Morton; he gives a very poor account of his father's health, I am sorry to say. The Professor must now, I suppose, be an old man; but still it grieves one to hear of the increasing weakness of one whose writings we English Unitarians (at least) hold in such esteem, and for whose character we have so great respect.

Among the drawbacks of this wretched weather is that I have not yet been able to get to Ambleside to see Miss Martineau. When she has dined with us, or been at all to Liverpool, I have always missed her by being at Cambridge; and I own myself a little curious to hear from her, *viva voce,* some of her experiences. Her latest "craze" (to use a word of De Quincey's) is the establishment of a shop in London for the sale of--in plain English--infidel literature. She complained most bitterly the other day to my brother-in-law that whenever her book on "Man's Nature and Development" is inquired for, the shopman pulls it stealthily out from under the counter, as if ashamed of selling it, and fearful lest some bystander be scandalized; so that there's to be a shop in a central situation full of Miss Martineau and Auguste Comte, and Froude, who wrote the "Nemesis of Faith," and Frank Newman, who wrote "Phases of Faith;" and (as Clough said) the world is to receive the unbiassed truth "that there's no God, and Harriet is his prophet."

William Gray is also at the lakes; he is busily occupied in an article on "Madame de Stael" for (I think) the "North British;" and another on the "New Reform Bill" for the "Edinburgh," which is to feel the public's pulse on the question, for the Government's guidance.

The only author--and she is now all but forgotten--who ever dwelt at Coniston was a Miss Elizabeth Smith, friend of Hannah More, and mentioned in all books about British authoresses or the English Lakes, as the female Mezzofanti of her time, "a living polyglot." She only wrote translations of Job and such like, and is known chiefly through the kind offices of others, and their fond memory of her as a *woman.* Tennyson, however, sometimes visits Coniston, staying with a Mr. Marshall who owns a beautiful place at the head of the lake. The Marshalls are now from home; so last evening we strolled through their grounds (last evening having actually three rainless hours of its own). These grounds are nearly perfect; the park with its fine park trees is backed by hills covered with larch wood, and topped by mountains of bare gray crag, with some few purple patches of heather coloring them every here and there. As we came back from our walk, about eight o'clock, we found a party of miners from the coppermines above, rowing along in front of the hotel, and playing on some half-dozen wind instruments in most capital time and tune; and whenever they stopped for a moment, the "Old Man" mountain sent back upon the lake the most jubilant of echoes, repeating and vying with the music of the horns. But now I spare you any more,--indeed, I've but little more to tell, for I could not, "an I would," describe the spot which we visited on Monday, and which is immortalized in "Christabel." It is a gloriously wild fell!--and *since* Monday we have done nothing.

Pray remember me most kindly to Mrs. Hawthorne, and tell the children that they are not to forget me.

Believe me, dear sir, yours very faithfully,

HENRY A. BRIGHT.

Is the English edition of "Tanglewood Tales" out yet?

--The next extracts are from Mrs. Hawthorne to her father.

MY DEAREST FATHER,--I was afraid I should not have time to write to you by the "Canada" and Mr. Ticknor; but accidentally he has not arrived from Chester so early as I expected, so I have time to say a few words. We were all to go to Chester together to-day; but the weather was so threatening that the rest of us stayed behind, and only Mr. Hawthorne and Mr. Ticknor went. On Wednesday Mr. Henry Bright came over to dine. He visited Miss Martineau at Ambleside, and found her very entertaining, and a very singular state of doctrine,--for she now professes to believe and declare that there is no God and no future life! He says it is wholly impossible to argue with her, because she is so opinionated and dogmatical, and has such a peculiar advantage in putting down her ear-trumpet when she does not choose to hear any reply to her assertions. She has been making some beautiful designs for the windows of her brother's church in Liverpool, which are accepted and to be painted thereupon; but she is at enmity with her brother, and has no intercourse with him. Tennyson often visites Coniston, but was not to be seen at that time, and seldom is to be seen at any time, being "vox et praeterea nihil." Mr. Bright says that he and his family were imprisoned a great deal in the hotel by rain, but yet enjoyed themselves; and his sisters sketched out of window. Mr. Ticknor has been to see Mr. De Quincey, and says he is a noble old man and eloquent, and wins hearts in personal intercourse. His three daughters, Margaret, Florence, and Emily, are also very attractive and cultivated, and they are all most impatient to see Mr. Hawthorne.

We feel pretty much in order now in our house. My dinner-party on Wednesday went off quite elegantly. When the gentlemen joined me in the drawing-room, I had some tea ready for them, and Una requested to be the Hebe of the banquet. Mr. Bright thought it was lovely to have such an attendant.

He told us all about the gayeties of Liverpool,--the splendid balls and concerts. There is one ball given by the Roman Catholic nobility and gentry, which is a dazzling display of old family diamonds. So I can go there and see a galaxy of stars, as well as if I went to the prorogation of Parliarment. He says the old dowagers blaze with jewels. But there is something more interesting than balls and jewels to be told of England now. The nation seems awakened to the importance of reform in several important matters. One is the state of the gaols, which is frightful. The torture and cruelty are lately discovered to be awful, and the governors and minor officers are brought for trial before the courts. The revelations are appalling; and as light breaks in upon the diabolical practices, they must be put an end to. The "Times" also is now full of the extortion of hotelkeepers, and hundreds of letters from private individuals are printed to show how dishonest the charges are and have been. The pent-up wrath and indignation of all the victims of this high rate of charge seem to burst forth at this first chance, and it will not cease till there is a change. The customs and railroads are also under a keen inspection, for many accidents on railroads happen here also,--loss of life from carelessness; and the shareholders complain much that though the receipts are enormous, they get no dividends, and want to know where the money is.

A great many new and old abuses seem to be undergoing repairs on a sudden. The Queen's visit to Ireland is considered of great moment. Ireland is reviving from various causes; and one cause is the potato-blight itself! The immense immigration has thinned the population, and the Irish in America have sent really vast sums of money to their friends; and this Mr. Dargon rises up all at once like a savior to the land. It will be deeply interesting to watch on the spot all these progressive movements; and the "Times" is an extraordinary organ of expression for all good things. It is very just generally, I think (it is not of much importance what I think, however), and seems full of humanity and wisdom.

Last week Mr. Hawthorne was invited to dine with the magistrate in West Derby, and he met there a gentleman who wishes to introduce him to the two sons of Burns, and to-morrow evening is the time appointed. I expect another dinner-party this evening, and must now go and dress. Mr. Ticknor came from London rich in gifts: to Julian, a superb book, called "The Country Year Book," with a hundred and forty fine engravings; to Una, a green and gold morocco portfolio with "Una" in gilt letters impressed upon it, and quires of note paper and envelopes; to Rosebud, a real waxen doll; to Mr. Hawthorne, a pair of superfine razors, made to order in Sheffield, with ivory handles, and "N. Hawthorne" finely marked in the steel of the blades; and to me, a case of scissors made for me in Sheffield, with my name on the blade of each, and a very superb book of Flowers...

SOPHIA.

"...It takes a great while every day to keep so large a house as this of ours in proper order. The children dine and sup at separate hours from ours. They have their supper after our dinner; so the table has to be laid four times. Mr. Hawthorne eats a biscuit in his consulate office at noon, and I eat a morsel of bread at the children's dinner. But oh, no, dear father, we do not 'live in grand style,' neither do we intend to have much company. We could not afford it; for, though so many persons at home, who might be supposed to know, account the consular income here to be so great, and the arrival of ships so abundant, they are sadly mistaken. Elizabeth wrote me last week that the number of ships that arrived from the United States to Liverpool was nearly ten thousand, from each one of which Mr. Hawthorne must receive four dollars, making at once forty thousand dollars a year. So far is this from the truth, that it is really funny and melancholy at the same time. Instead of ten thousand ships, not quite seven hundred arrive yearly from the United States here; and so, instead of the income from the vessels being forty thousand dollars, it is not quite twenty-eight hundred dollars. Most of the income comes from the invoices of the great steamers. Ten and twelve thousand dollars has been hitherto the amount of the *whole* yearly income from whatever source,--about a quarter part of the estimate made of it. It is hoped that the business may increase; but perhaps it will be too late for us. And Mr. Hawthorne must lay aside a good part of this income, or we shall return ruined, not benefited, by this office; for he cannot write, and all that would remain for us would be the 'Wayside,' which would be a home, but not bread and butter and clothes and means of educating the children. Living is much more expensive here than at home: meat never below fourteen cents, and some kinds twenty cents; potatoes thirty cents a peck; no tea below a dollar a pound; grapes are a penny apiece, and the fruit here is not good. England cannot grow fruit, with a sun crying its eyes out every day.

"We gain one thing here, and that is an open fireplace. Coal is comparatively cheap, and it blazes delightfully, and we can really sit round a glowing hearth. Mr. Hawthorne truly enjoys it. It is what he always wanted. It is certainly a gloomy custom to bury the fire in tombstones, and then set up the graves on our very hearths. Over our marble mantelpiece hangs Mr. John Campbell, the former occupant of this house, now dead. He was Scotch, and perhaps of the family of the noble Campbells. He was a gentleman of fortune. He is not a very lovely looking person, but yet angelic compared to his brother, who hangs opposite him, and who looks as if he would keep his mother on very short allowance. In the recesses on each side the fireplace are pictures,--one a Magdalene in an oval frame, and the other an Italian scene in a hexagon frame. Opposite the two tall windows, which open to the floor, hang two fruit pieces and a landscape with figures. Not one of any of these pictures is good. Beneath Mr. William Campbell is the sideboard, upon which stands a pretty tea urn, which you may one day see, as we shall take it home. I am writing at a great central table, at which we dine. It is as heavy as a small planet; for in England things are made solid, not half pine. The chairs are also solid, and cost much pain to lift. Two or three lounging-chairs, a light mahogany stand for the dinner-tray, and a very rich Brussels carpet of dark blue, brown, and rose colors complete the furnishing of the dining-room. There are full blue and orange damask curtains to the windows, hanging from a broad gilded cornice with a valance and fringe, which set off the room very well. There are, besides, an alabaster vase beneath Mr. John Campbell's picture, a bronze vase in which is always a rose, two bronze candlesticks, and just now our new Taylor's moderator lamp, which is as tall as Bunker Hill Monument, and looks like a lighthouse."

--It takes some time to get accustomed to the rain and clouds in England; and as to the people, Hawthorne's acquaintance with them was not as yet extensive; he had seen them for the most part only superficially. He wandered about Liverpool streets, and saw the shops and the public buildings, the well-to-do population and the poor; he ate dinners with the mayor, and made speeches; he visited hospitals and asylums in the interests of American seamen (genuine or spurious); and once in a while he went on little excursions with Henry Bright, or spent a night at the latter's house (Sandheys), or at Norris Green, the residence of the Heywoods, relatives of Mr. Bright. But he did not like Liverpool, and he had not as yet made up his mind whether or not to like the English people. Speaking of Grace Greenwood's departure for America, after a year spent in England, he says: "Her health seemed not good, nor her spirits buoyant. This doubtless is partly due to her regret in leaving England, where she has met with great kindness, and the manners and institutions of which she likes rather better, I suspect, than an American ought. She speaks rapturously of the English hospitality and warmth of heart. I likewise have already experienced something of this, and apparently have a good deal more of it at my option. I wonder how far it is genuine, and in what degree it is better than the superficial good-feeling with which Yankees receive foreigners,--a feeling not calculated for endurance, but a good deal like a brushwood fire. We shall see!"

One gloomy winter's day, Mr. Francis Bennoch (who tells the story) called on Hawthorne at Rock Park, and found him in a chair before the fire in the sitting-room, prodding the black coals in a disheartened fashion with the poker. "Give me the poker, my dear sir!" exclaimed Mr. Bennoch, "and I'll give you a lesson." He seized the implement from Hawthorne s hand, and delivered two or three vigorous and well-aimed thrusts straight to the centre of the dark smouldering mass, which straightway sent forth a rustling luxuriance of brilliant flame. "That's the way to get the warmth out of an English fire," cried Mr. Bennoch, "and that's the way to get the warmth out of an English heart too! Treat us like that, my dear sir, and you 'll find us all good fellows!" Hereupon Hawthorne brightened up as jovially as the fire, and (Mr. Bennoch thinks) thought better of England ever after.

Mr. Bright and Mr. Bennoch were, at all events, the men of all others to bring him acquainted with the brighter and more genial aspects of the Old Country; they were overflowing with activity and energy, and insisted upon making Hawthorne do things which he would never have undertaken of his own accord, but which, being done, he was very glad to have accomplished, On one occasion he dined in company with the two sons of the poet Burns "Late in the evening," he writes, "Mr. Aikin and most of the gentlemen retired to the smoking-room, where we found brandy, whiskey, and some good cigars. The sons of the poet showed, I think, an hereditary appreciation of good liquor, both at the dinner-table (where they neglected neither sherry, port, hock, champagne, nor claret) and here in the smoking-room. Both of them, however, drank brandy, instead of the liquor which their father has immortalized. The Colonel smoked cigars; the Major filled and refilled a German pipe. Neither of them (nor, in fact, anybody else) was at all the worse for liquor; but I thought I saw a little of the coarser side of Burns in the rapturous approbation with which the Major responded to a very good, but rather indecorous story from one of the gentlemen. But I liked them both, and they liked me." And, in general, his conclusion was that the worst of an Englishman is his outside, and that to know him better is to like him better too.

Of course, the chief ostensible bonds of sympathy between him and his English friends were wrought from his literary achievements; they were never tired of telling him how much they admired his books. "I have to-day received," writes Mary Russell Mitford, "a copy of another of those charming books by which, in addition to that walk of prose poetry which is so peculiarly your own and which reproduces in so exquisite a manner the history, you have contrived to blend your own name with some of those lovely classical fables which are among the most valuable bequests of the Greek poets. How many thousands will think of you as the name of some glorious old classical legend comes across them! It is a fine thing, to make a holiday book of that which to schoolboys has too often been a dry lesson; and the popularity which is sure to follow it was never more richly earned.... Very little of me is now available, except the head and the heart; but I hope next spring, if not before, to have the great pleasure of making the personal acquaintance of one whom I can never think of except as a friend."

There were many similar assurances of good feeling continually coming in from all sides; and Hawthorne was far from being insensible to such kindness. He even seems to have desired to bring some of his own countrymen into similar pleasant relations with the British public. "I send you," he writes to Henry Bright, "an American book, 'Up-Country Letters,' which I beg you to read, and hope you will like. It would gratify me much if you would talk about it or write about it, and get it into some degree of notice in this country. England, within two or three years past, has read and praised a hundred American books that do not deserve it half so well;

but I somewhat question whether the English mind is not rather too bluff and beefy to appreciate the peculiar charm of these letters. Yet we have produced nothing more original nor more genuine."

I will conclude this chapter with extracts from Mrs. Hawthorne's letters to her father.

JANUARY 19.

Yesterday and to-day summer has made us in England a flying visit. There was lovely sunshine this afternoon, and this morning the birds were in full chorus. In two weeks we shall have snowdrops and crocuses; and to-day we found in the garden a fullblown pansy! An English lady, who called here, said it was "very close" out of doors, as if it were a dog-day; but yet it was agreeable to me to sit by the fire. One might imagine that the angry Czar had sent his snow and cold as Christmas presents to the rest of Europe, however. To-day has come the news of his rejection of the note, and therefore it is War; and we shall probably be witnesses of the greatest revolution that has ever yet convulsed the world. The English seem to be in some puzzle how to man their ships of war, and how to contrive to have commanding officers to rule them, who are of fit age and prowess. But I suppose Parliament will arrange all the difficulties. The Emperor Nicholas has spies all over Europe,--noble ladies as well as men in every society, in every court, who sow any kind of rumor and listen to everything. I never heard of such extraordinary espionage. The ladies accept his diamonds in return for being eavesdroppers and tools; but I suspect his vast network of gold and jewels will be early rent asunder. Somehow or other, I could never feel that the Czar was potent or fearful. He is a great north wind,--a northeast wind for Europe,--but a wind is emptiness when bravely met. Russia always seemed to me mere brute force. I have read lately such appalling accounts of the suffering and oppression of the people, that I think it Is probably the hour for God to send his judgments down. It is anomalous, I hear, for a Russian to speak the truth, and a matter of course for him to cheat and deceive.

Julian returned with papa from Liverpool the other day with four masks, with which we made merry. One was the face of a simpleton; and that was very funny upon papa,--such a transformation! Mary Herne frightened Emily (cook) nearly out of her wits, by putting one on one morning in the early dusk and sitting down quietly in the kitchen. Emily came along with her candle, and stumbled upon this glaring face of forlornness. "Oh, I'm dead!" said Emily.

Mr. Henry Bright entertained us with an account of a magnificent fancy ball which came off at Liverpool last Friday. He himself personated his ancestor, Sir Kenelm Digby, and nearly died beneath a heavy, long, curled black wig, and a hat upon the top of it; heated besides as he was by dancing nineteen times. His sword tore a lady's dress and assailed various persons while standing out straight in the whirling waltz. He had a distracting headache, and did not get home till five o'clock in the mowing. People were powdered and rouged and patched so as to be quite disguised. He said he had not the slightest idea who the Earl of Sefton's son was, even when he spoke to him, though he knows him very well indeed. One of the Ladies Mainwaring was there, blazing with diamonds, and Nebuchadnezzar, and Sardanapalus, and all kinds of past worthies and dignitaries. He said his aunt Heywood, of Norris, was to have another fancy ball at her house to-morrow, and she wanted us to go to it. But 1 cannot leave home, and Mr. Hawtllorne will not rig himself up in any strange finery. Mrs. Heywood is a very warm admirer of Mr. Hawthorne's books, and though her law is that no one shall enter her drawing-rooms that night except in fancy dress, she said Mr. Hawthorne should go just as he liked, in a black coat if he preferred it. But he will not.

CHAPTER 2 - FROM THE LAKES TO LONDON

EARLY in 1854 Hawthorne met a gentleman who was at that period somewhat distinguished in literature; and he gave the following account of him:--

"Dined with Mr. Bramley Moore, to meet Mr. Warren, author of 'Ten Thousand a Year.' There were eight or ten gentlemen at dinner, principally lawyers now attending the assizes, and of no great interest. Mr. Warren is a man (on his own authority) of forty-six; not tall nor large, with a pale, rather thin, and intelligent face,--American more than English in its aspect, except that his nose is more prominent than ordinary American noses, as most English noses are. He is Recorder of Hull, an office which he says brings him but little; nor does he get much practice as a barrister on account of the ill-will of the attorneys, who consider themselves aggrieved by his depictures of Quick, Gammon, and Snap.

"On the whole, the dinner was not a very agreeable one. I led in Mrs. Bramley Moore (the only lady present). The family are violent tories, fanatics for the Established Church, and followers of Dr. McMill, who is the present Low-Church pope of Liverpool. I could see little to distinguish her from a rigidly orthodox and Calvinistic woman of New England; for they acquire the same characteristics from their enmity to the Puseyite movement and Roman Catholic tendencies of the present day. The eatables and the drinkables were very praiseworthy; and Mr. Bramley Moore circulated his wines more briskly than is customary at gentlemen's tables. He seems to be rich, has property in the Brazils (where he was at one time resident), has been Mayor of Liverpool, an unsuccessful candidate for Parliament, and now lives at a very pretty place. But he alludes to the cost of wines and of other things that he possesses,--a frailty which I have not observed in any other Englishman of good station. He is a moderately bulky and rather round-shouldered man, with a kindly face enough, and seems to be a passably good man; but I hope, on the whole, that be will not ask me to dinner any more,--though his dinners are certainly very good.

"Mr. Warren, nevertheless, turned out agreeably; he sat opposite to me, and I observed that he took champagne very freely, not waiting till Mr. Bramley Moore should suggest it, or till the servants should periodically offer it, but inviting his neighbors to a glass of wine. Neither did be refuse hock, nor anything else that came round. He was talkative, and mostly about himself and his writings,--which I have no objection to in a writer, knowing that if he talks little of himself, he perhaps thinks the more. It is a trait of simplicity that ought not to be so scouted as it generally is. Mr. Warren said nothing very brilliant; but yet there was occasionally a champagny frothiness of his spirits, that enlivened us more than anything else at table. He told a laughable story about an American who had seen a portrait of Warren's father, which was prefixed to an American edition of his works as his own, and was perplexed at the dissimilarity between this effigy of an old be-wigged clergyman and the dapper, youthful personage before him. He appears to feel very kindly towards the Americans, and says somebody has sent him some of the Catawba champagne. Warren has a talent of mimicry, and gave us some touches of Sergeant Wilkins whom I met, several months ago, at the Mayor's dinner.

"After Mrs. Bramley Moore had retired, Warren began an informal little talk to Mr. Bramley Moore, who sat between him and me, on my merits as a man and an author. Mr. Bramley Moore urged him to speak up, and give the company the privilege of hearing his remarks; and though I remonstrated, it gradually grew into almost a regular dinner-table speech, the audience crying,--in rather a gentle tone, however,--'Hear! hear!' I have forgotten what he said, and also what I responded; but we were very laudatory on both sides, and shook hands in most brotherly fashion across the table. Anon, after a good while at table, Mrs. Bramley Moore sent to announce coffee and tea; and adjourning to the drawing-room we looked. among other pretty things, at some specimens of bright autumnal leaves which Mr. Bramley Moore had brought with him from his recent visit to America. Warren admired them greatly. His vanity (which those who know him speak of as a very prominent characteristic) kept peeping out in everything he said."

--A Yankee boy who feels uneasy in his mind or finds his surroundings irksome is apt to pick up the first stick of wood he comes across, and try upon it how sharp his jack-knife is; and men like Hawthorne, when they become sensible of a deficiency of sympathy in their companions, are apt to turn upon the latter the sharp edge of their observation and criticism. Hawthorne was always very tender of the feelings of others; and though he could not help perceiving the oddities and frailties of those about him, the perception implied no uncharitableness on his part, and was recorded only for his private satisfaction. He apprehended the queer traits of his friends quite as keenly as those of indifferent persons. He once remarked of Mr. George Bradford, for instance,--than whom no man had a larger share of his respect and affection,--that "his conscientiousness seems to be a kind of itch, keeping him always uneasy and inclined to scratch!"

The author of "Ten Thousand a Year" afterwards wrote him the following note:-
INNER TEMPLE, LONDON, 7th April, 1854.

MY DEAR MR. HAWTHORNE.--By this post I send you a copy of "The Intellectual and Moral Development of the Present Age," with divers manuscript corrections by myself. I hope you will like the book; for though small in bulk, it contains the results of many a long year's reflection. It gave me very great pleasure to meet, the other day, so distinguished an American brother in literature as yourself. I heartily wish you health and prosperity. I have an old--a very old--friend at Liverpool in Mr. Commissioner Perry, who lives at New Brighton. He occupies a highly honorable legal post, and is an amiable man, and also --*gives charming little dinners!* I have assured him that, if he called, you would like to see him. I hope this little book will reach you safely. Believe me, dear Mr. Hawthorne,

Yours very faithfully,
SAMUEL WARREN.

This day my gifted friend--that was--Professor Wilson, is buried, with public honors.

--As the spring advanced, Hawthorne, who was always a great walker, fell into the habit of taking occasional tramps about the country in the neighborhood of Rock Ferry and Liverpool, sometimes taking his son with him. On these expeditions he often talked quite freely, adapting his conversation, of course, to the calibre of his interlocutor. Among other matters which were discussed with animation, were the amazing adventures of a certain General Quattlebum,--a contemporary and rival of Baron Munchausen. and conversant with even greater marvels than came within the experience of that eminent nobleman. He was, in fact, a magician and enchanter of the first rank; and there was a kind of lofty and chivalrous hostility and emulation between him and Hawthorne, who was also a mighty wizard, and who in the constant trials of skill and power that took place between them generally contrived to gain the advantage. Some of these combats were more than Homeric; the struggles of Jupiter and the Titans were child's play in comparison. Unfortunately, none of the exploits of these two heroes were ever reduced to writing; and the particulars of their achievements have, in the course of thirty years, faded from the memory of him who heard them related. The recollection of one slight incident has, however, survived the general obliteration, and I will give. it here. Hawthorne and Quattlebum had intrenched themselves on opposite sides of a deep valley, about a mile in width, and all was ready for the bombardment to begin,--the cannon loaded and primed, and the aim taken. But the heroes, like two accomplished duellists about to engage with the small-sword, could not begin the conflict without having exchanged those graceful courtesies which should always accompany a truly heroic antagonism. Accordingly each mounted upon his largest cannon, and, standing at the very extremity of the muzzle, touched off the piece with the slow-match held in the left hand. As the missile left the gun, each leaped lightly upon it, and was borne through the air with the speed of lightning. In a few moments they met, just over the centre of the valley. Each lifted his hat, and made the other a grave salute, at the same instant springing off his own ball and alighting upon that of his adversary, which swiftly bore him back to the place whence he started. Hawthorne returned without mishap; but General Quattlebum had not paid sufficient attention to his centre of gravity: he fell from a vast height to the bottom of the valley, and his mighty carcass dammed up a river which flowed through it, so that before he could extricate himself the valley became a lake, which is known as Lake Quattlebum to this day.

There was an indescribable charm about the telling of these stories, which never can be reproduced in the written narration,--an archness, an emphasis, an atmosphere of awe and mystery, and exhaustless imaginative resources. Nor was General Quattlebum a mere figure of the past; he was even now alive and active, although, by the power of his enchantments, he rendered himself invisible to all eyes save Hawthorne's. If any unaccountable or absurd mishap occurred, it always turned out that the General was at the bottom of it. Even in the walks above mentioned, the younger pedestrian would occasionally feel the light stroke of a cane across his back ; looking round, no one would be there, and his father was walking at his side apparently in deep abstraction. "Father, somebody hit me with a stick." "Ah! it must have been Quattlebum!" And though the person thus attacked was sometimes inclined to suspect that Quattlebum had contrived to incarnate himself in Mr. Hawthorne's form,--for the latter also carried a cane,--he was never able to surprise him *flagrante delictu.*

In April, John O'Sullivan, his wife, and his mother made Hawthorne a visit at Rock Park; they were on their way to Lisbon, to which place O'Sullivan had been appointed American Minister. Their presence stimulated Hawthorne to somewhat more than his usual social activity; people were invited to meet them, and they were invited to meet people. Hawthorne's circle of English acquaintances was expanding in all directions. All who had read a book of his, or written one of their own, were ready to open relations with him. It was at about this period, I think, that a work appeared, and attracted attention in England, entitled "Land, Labor, and Gold," by Mr. William Howitt. It was descriptive of the state of things at the Australian gold-diggings, which had lately been discovered, and whither Mr. Howitt had betaken himself. Hawthorne, read the book, and was interested in it; and several little conspiring circumstances brought about an exchange of civilities between him and Mrs. Howitt. including this pleasant little letter:--

THE HERMITAGE, HIGHGATE RISE, May 14, 1854.

DEAR SIR,-- I thank you for sending the little package for me to Mr. Miller's. I have written to him about it) and I shall hope soon to receive it. If I were to meet you face to face, I should not say a word to you about the great pleasure we have derived from your works; but on paper may I not do so without offence? Of course you know the delight you have given to thousands, But you do not know how exquisite to our taste is all your minute detail,--your working out a character by Pre-Raphaelian touches, as it were,--if you understand my phrase; your delicate touch upon touch, which produces such a finished whole, so different from the slap-dash style of writing so common nowadays. Yes, I assure you that independently of the intrinsic interest with which we read your books at first, we now refer again and again to them as exquisite works of art, the elaborate finish and detail of which are never exhausted. When I say *we*, I mean myself and my husband--now an antipode--and my daughter. In September--please God--I hope for the great happiness of seeing my dear husband once more in England. Then I hope you will be coming to London, if not before. And if you will give us an opportunity of shaking hands with you, I promise you that we will not bore you about your books, nor will we lionize or torture you in any way; only be right glad to see you, as we would he to see any other good man.

I am, dear sir, yours sincerely,

MARY HOWITT.

--Hawthorne met Mr. Howitt in London a few months later, and seems not to have found him quite so genial as his books. Mention of him will be found in the "English Note-Books."

In July it was determined that Mrs. Hawthorne and the children should spend a fortnight at the Isle of Man, a small rock-bound spot midway between Liverpool and Dublin, in the Irish Channel. Hawthorne accompanied them thither on the Saturday, and spent the following Sunday, and came again the Sunday after that. The Isle of Man has the name of being a very rainy place; but during all the two weeks of our sojourn there, the sky was cloudless and the temperature delightful, though it did rain dismally both on the day of our arrival and on that of our departure. The island itself is a most picturesque and charming spot; the sea around it deep and clear, the cliffs abrupt and dark, and rendered additionally romantic by the ruined castles which surmount its tallest acclivities. A few hundred yards from shore, directly opposite the hotel, was a tiny islet, on which stood the ruin of a small tower, as if for the especial benefit of persons disposed to sketching. On the first Sunday a conveyance was hired, and the whole party drove about the island, which is of such limited extent that nearly all of it can be thus inspected in a single day. It turned out that the tradition that Manx cats have no tails is no more than the truth; and it was also discovered that Manx horses drink ale,--a bucketful of this beverage being furnished them at each halting-place. The pastures are grazed by great numbers of partly wild cattle, a drove of which, infuriated by the sight of a red shawl worn by one of the party, charged down upon us twenty strong, and had nearly swept us from the island before the offending garment could be stripped off and put out of sight. The most imposing ruin was Peel Castle, which also had a historic reputation for being haunted; one tradition being to the effect that a huge black demon in the shape of a dog infested the premises, and that a soldier of the garrison, who had undertaken to confront it, was found by his companions next morning in a speechless state, and died without having spoken a word.

Many of the remains on the island are of unknown antiquity,--as old as the Druids, or older; and the place has quite as distinct a character of its own (as regards its inhabitants, their speech and manners) as Jersey and Guernsey in the English Channel. Hawthorne was very much captivated by it; but he never had an opportunity of jotting down his impressions, except the short description of Kirk Madden in the Note-Books. On the second Sunday we embarked on board a small steamer, and completely circumnavigated the island; it was a calm, sunny day, and the changing aspects of the coast were like a prophetic vision of Doré. So quaint, unique, and lovable a little region as the Isle of Man seldom rewards the industry of travellers. But this was thirty years ago, and it may have become less primitive in the interim.

Hawthorne returned to Liverpool the next day, and on his arrival wrote the following letter to Mrs. Hawthorne. The Mr. Cecil alluded to therein is the same Mr. Henry Cecil whose brotherly overtures to the author of 'The White Old Maid,' have already been mentioned. It would seem that he had held out hopes of a personal renewal of fraternities.

LIVERPOOL, July 26, 1854.

DEAREST WIFE,-- We had the pleasantest passage, yesterday, that can be conceived of. How strange that the best weather I have ever known should have come to us on these English coasts

I enclose some letters from the O'Sullivans, whereby you will see that they have come to a true appreciation of Mr. Cecil's merits. They say nothing of his departure, but I shall live in daily terror of his arrival.

I hardly think it worth while for me to return to the Isle of Man this summer,-- that is, unless you conclude to stay longer than a week from this time. Do so, by all means, if you think the residence will benefit either yourself or the children's. Or it would be easy to return thither, should it seem desirable, or to go somewhere else. Tell me what day you fix upon for leaving, and I will either await you in person at the landing-place or send Henry. Do not start unless the weather promises to be favorable, even though you should be ready to go on board.

I think you should give something to the servants,--those of them, at least, who have taken any particular pains with you. Michael asked me for something, but I told him that I should probably he back again; so you must pay him my debts, and your own too.

It is very lonesome at Rock Ferry, and I long to have you all back again. Give my love to the children.

THINE OWNEST.

--Much to the regret of the younger members of the party,--a regret scarcely modified by the steady down-pour of rain,--we bade farewell to the Isle of Man on the last day of the week, and reached Rock Park the same evening. There Mrs.

Hawthorne found a letter from her father,--the last, I believe, that he wrote; for he died soon afterwards.

AMHERST, Friday, July 14, 1854.

DEAR SOPHIA,-- I did not receive your letter of June 22 till last Wednesday, the 12th. I had given up hearing from you by the last steamer, and feared you might be too sick to write. Nat delayed sending it. I was very glad to receive it, and was entertained with your account of the splendid palaces you described. I hope when you write again to hear that your cough is going off. What a sad time you have had with your servants! I received a letter from Elizabeth, who expected to be in Brattleboro this week. She has been everywhere. I had a very pleasant interview with Mr. Hawthorne last night, after I had gone to sleep. He was on here from Liverpool, and appeared very well. Thank Una for her letter, and Julian for his nice letter. There is nothing to communicate from here. Horace Mann junior is very fond of chemistry, and makes gunpowder, and got his eyebrows and eyelashes burnt off and his face burnt by its igniting accidentally,--a good lesson for all the boys. We had a very quiet time on the Fourth of July, only a few straggling guns fired, and a few crackers. I keep along as usual, but the hot weather operates upon me very sensibly. I have nothing here to stimulate my mind. I have a good appetite, however. To revert to your descriptions of the splendid places you mentioned in your last, how do you remember to describe them so minutely? It seems you must take notes as you go along.

Your uncle is building a new house. He is going to sell his present house and a large part of his land. I wish I had something interesting to write, but I have no genius and imagination to supply anything of the kind. So, with my love to you all, I subscribe myself as ever

Your affectionate father, N. P.

Don't let Rose forget me.

--The "cough" above spoken of was an attack of whooping-cough, which had seized upon the entire family several weeks before. and partly to promote convalescence from which it was that the visit to the Isle of Man had been projected. Mrs. Hawthorne had been afflicted with bronchial troubles soon after her arrival in England, and was never free from them so long as she remained there; and they led to her making a prolonged visit to Lisbon and Madeira during part of the two following years; taking her two daughters with her, and leaving the boy with his father.

The next month (August) Hawthorne and his wife saw the cricket-match of Liverpool vs. Derbyshire, and Mrs. Hawthorne wrote to her father the following amusing description of it. No doubt cricket must seem a very abstruse game to those who behold it for the first time.

"The last thing that happened was Mr. Hawthorne's and my going to see a cricket match between Liverpool and Derbyshire. We sat in the carriage, and looked out upon a perfectly level plain of eight or nine acres,--a smooth, sunny, velvet lawn. In the midst of it the two wickets were erected at the distance apart of twenty or thirty feet, each composed of three sticks, with another stick laid transversely. The cricketers were all dressed in pale buff wash-leather or felt doublet and hose, with boots of duck and buff leather in strips over the instep; and those who stood before each wicket with a bat in hand were guarded from the severe blows of the ball by a peculiar coat-of-mail reaching from the ankles above the knee. This shin-guard was made of buff leather) very much like a child's sun-bonnet; but instead of pasteboard sewed in, it is thickly padded with wool, and I do not know but a thin wooden board or whale-bone besides,--making the limb look very clumsy. At each wicket stood, therefore, a well-padded man with a bat. Behind him and each wicket stood another man who threw the ball and tried to knock down the wicket, which the man with the bat was studious to prevent. In a vast circle from these four stood, I believe, eight men,--at exact distances from one another, who were to catch the ball when a bat sent it off from either wicket. If the man with the bat was so fortunate as to drive it to a great distance, he and the other batman ran from one wicket to another; and just as many times as they could exchange places, so much the better for them, f-or each time counts one in the game. We alighted from the carriage, and went into the plain, and finally sat down under a tent, where were some ladies and gentlemen, or, more properly, respectable men and women; for in England there is great discrimination used in this nomenclature. If a batman hits the ball before it reaches the ground, and strikes it into the air, and it is caught by one of the outsiders, there is a loss. Once a young man who had been a bat-man and had failed to defend his wicket exclaimed near me, as an outstander caught the ball from the clouds, "Ah, what a shame,--and one of our own men too!" So it seemed that this man was obliged to play against himself in such circumstances. I was astonished, all the time, to see the want of animation in the players. They lounged along after the ball upon the ground, as if they were taking an evening stroll, with a sort of Oriental languor."

--Here is another passage which should gratify English people, though it may be surmised that few of them could lay their hands upon their hearts and swear that Mrs. Hawthorne bad not been exceptionally fortunate in her experience of the native English orthoepy.

". . .I am constantly struck here with the *correct English* which persons talk who are below the first rank, and even below the second rank. I very seldom hear a slang expression, and every word is well pronounced, well articulated and accented. It is only the very *first* circle with us who ever speak so well, and even with them one sometimes hears the wrong word or bad contractions. I do not believe that on English ground you would hear a person say "ain't" in any rank of life. "Had n't ought" is also an enormity never dreamed of in this island. I was always exceedingly annoyed by any incorrectness of language; but I never realized, till I lived in the mother country, what careless ways the daughter had contracted, what perpetual cold-blooded murders are perpetrated hourly on the Queen's English in the United States, by writers as well as talkers. I understand now why the English make so much account of Mr. Hawthorne's *language,* as being the only faultless English written by an American. Miss Wetherell, Mrs. Stowe, Grace Greenwood, all write slang a great deal. They ought all to be put upon a strict diet of old English prose-writers before they are allowed to use the pen any more.". . .

--The rest of the summer was spent in little excursions of a day or so each,--once to Conway, in Wales, with Henry Bright; and once to Eaton Hall, near Chester, when Hawthorne was accompanied by his wife and George Bradford. These expeditions are fully described in the Note-Books. About the middle of September lodgings were taken at Rhyl, a small town on the Welsh coast; and the family remained there for six or eight weeks, making occasional visits to places in the neighborhood. Hawthorne had previously made the acquaintance of Lord Houghton (at that time Mr. Richard Monckton Milnes), and had met with very appreciative treatment at his hands. A few years ago, the present writer saw Lord Houghton in London, when that nobleman remarked, somewhat regretfully, that Hawthorne had never liked him. So far as I am aware, there was no ground for this impression. With one or two exceptions, Hawthorne liked all the Englishmen with whom he had more than passing intercourse. He was not a gushing man, but he was a uniformly genial and kindly one. He was reserved: and Englishmen do not seem to understand reserve in any one except themselves. But English reserve is not like the reserve of such a man as Hawthorne. The former is an external matter, connected with caste and conventionality; the latter is innate. One is factitious; the other genuine.

Mr. Milnes used to write courteous little notes, like the following:--
CREWE HALL, CREWE, Nov. 7 1854.

DEAR MR. HAWTHORNE,-- I must have the pleasure of showing you this place before I go to Yorkshire. Lord Crewe begs me to say that he will be very happy if you can come here on Monday for a day or two ; or if you are too busy to absent yourself from Liverpool on a week day, from Saturday to Monday. Do just which is most convenient for you. The rail brings you to the Crewe station in an hour and a half, and we will send to meet you there. You will probably find us all sole alone in either case; but as I am lately returned from Scot-land and am soon to go away again, I do not like to lose this opportunity of seeing you. With Mrs. Milnes' best compliments, I remain

Yours very truly,
RICHARD MONCKTON MILNES.

--No doubt Hawthorne seldom accepted such invitations; but he was fully sensible of their kind intention, and never failed to make a suitable acknowledgment.

Rhyl is a region of illimitable sands, which at low tide are left bare beyond anticipation. Hawthorne enjoyed walking upon them, and gazing out upon the expanse, though they were very different from the hard white beaches to which he had been accustomed in New England; hut there was always the horizon, and he preferred the long sweep of meeting sea and sky to most kinds of prospects. One night, during a gale, a vessel came ashore opposite the town, and lay careened over on her beam ends, a fell mile distant from the Parade. The crew, with one exception, were rescued and brought ashore,--a forlorn and bedraggled group. The next day there was a thin stream of visitors going and coming between the wreck and the shore. Hawthorne did not go; but as he walked along the coast with his son that afternoon, he spoke of other wrecks that he had seen, and suggested the awful possibility of our coming upon the corpse of the drowned sailor in some inlet of the sands.

After a visit to Conway Castle, where Mrs. Hawthorne came near being lost forever in the secret passages of the walls, which are of indefinite extent and perfectly dark, the family returned to Rock Park for the winter. Winter in this part of England is a dreary and depressing affair, and it did no good to Mrs. Hawthorne's cough. The only episode that broke the monotony was a brief visit from Miss Sarah Clarke, sister of James Freeman Clarke and an old friend of Mrs. Hawthorne. She was on her way to Rome, and was the occasion of the following communication from Mr. Russell Sturgis, who had known Mrs. Hawthorne before her marriage:--

LONDON, Dec. 19, 1854.

MY DEAR MRS. HAWTHORNE,-- The Pope will not let us prepay letters to Rome, as be prefers to collect there; but we shall tell your friend Miss Sarah Clarke, that we credit her postage account with two shillings received from you, and she will get the benefit of your thoughtful regularity. "Rock Park" I take to be the pretty place where I saw you; but to be *sure*, I direct my letter to Liverpool. When we were running about in the rain, trying to find your whereabouts, the commander of the little steamboat could tell us nothing of *"Hawthorne;"* but the dignity of the "American Consul" had made its full impression, and he knew well where *he* lived. So much for fame, you see I did not know when I saw you that your boy had the same name as mine. Where did you get it? With regards to Mr. Hawthorne,

Yours very truly and affectionately,

RUSSELL STURGIS.

--Early in the summer of the following year (1855) was held in Liverpool a meeting of the "Provincial Assembly of Lancashire and Cheshire." This assembly was a relic of the Presbyterian organization established by the Parliament of 1647; but, like other Presbyterian institutions, it had become entirely Unitarian. To the meeting in question Hawthorne was invited; and the letter he wrote, declining the invitation, has more than ordinary interest, owing to the reference it contains to religious matters:--

LIVERPOOL, June 15, 1855.

GENTLEMEN,-- I regret that a long-contemplated and unavoidable absence from town will deprive me of the great pleasure of being present on the interesting occasion in the enjoyment of which you kindly invite me to participate. Few things have been more delightful to me, during my residence in England, than to find here the descendants (spiritually at least, and in many instances, I believe, the descendants by lineage and name) of that revered brotherhood a part of whose mission it was to plant the seeds of liberal Christianity in America. Some of that brotherhood sought freedom of worship on the other side of the Atlantic, while others reserved themselves to the perhaps more difficult task of keeping their religious faith pure and full of genial life beneath the shadow of English churches and cathedrals. And it seems to me a noble and beautiful testimony to the truth of our religious convictions, that after so long a period, coming down from the past with an ocean between us, the liberal churches of England and America should nevertheless have arrived at the same results; that an American, an offspring of Puritan sires, still finds himself in brotherly relations with the posterity of those free-minded men who exchanged a parting pressure of the hand with his forefathers more than two centuries ago; and that we can all unite in one tone of religious sentiment, whether uttered by the lips of the friend whom you have summoned from my native land (Rev. W. H. Channing), or by the lips of your honored guests whose faith has ripened in the mother country. With great respect,

Sincerely yours,

NATH. HAWTHORNE

--This letter expressed the writer's genuine sentiments, as far as it went; but it was in some sense a public document (it was, I believe, published in the Liverpool newspapers of that date), and it has somewhat of the formality and style of a speech. No doubt his speech, had he been present to make one, would have been on the lines of the letter. Meanwhile it need not be forgotten that he was not a frequenter of his friend Mr. Channing's church; and it may be surmised that the above expression of his views was none the less cordial because it was written with the consciousness that circumstances would prevent him from delivering it in person.

On the 18th of June the "long-contemplated" departure from Rock Park took place. The journey was in the first place to Leamington. "Leamington," he writes,

"seems to be made chiefly of lodging-houses, and to be built with a view to a continually shifting population. It is a very beautiful town, with regular streets of stone or stuccoed houses, very broad pavements, and much shade of noble trees, in many parts of the town; parks and gardens, too, of delicious verdure; and throughout all, an aspect of freshness and cleanness that I despaired of ever seeing in England. The town seems to be almost entirely new. The principal street has elegant shops; and the scene is very lively, with throngs of people more gayly dressed than one is accustomed to see in this country; soldiers, too, lounging at the corners, and officers, who appear less shy of showing themselves in their regimentals than it is the fashion to be elsewhere.

"In the forenoon we took a walk through what looked like a park, but seemed to be a sort of semi-public tract on the outskirts of the town,--hill and glade, with a fair gravel-path through it, and most stately and beautiful trees overshadowing it. Here and there benches were set beneath the trees. These old, vigorous, much-nurtured trees are fine beyond description, and in this leafy month of June they certainly surpass my recollections of American trees,--so tall, and with such an aspect of age-long life. But the fact that these English trees are traditional, and connected with the fortunes of old families,--such moral considerations inevitably enter into physical admiration of them. They are individuals,--which few American trees have the happiness to be. Julian compared an oak, which we saw on our journey, to a cauliflower; and its shape--its regular, compact rotundity--makes it very like one: there is a certain John-Bullism about it. I have never anywhere enjoyed weather so delightful as such a day as yesterday; so warm and genial, and yet not oppressive,--the sun a very little too warm while walking beneath it, but only enough too warm to assure us that it was warm enough. And, after all, there was an unconquered freshness in the atmosphere, which each little motion of the air made evident to us. I suppose there is still latent in us Americans (even of two centuries' date and more, like myself) an adaptation to the English climate, which makes it like native soil and air to us."

--About a month was spent in Leamington on this first visit; but Hawthorne returned there more than once, and seemed to conceive for it a more homelike feeling than for almost any other place in England. The environs, easily accessible, were indeed more interesting than Leamington itself; and Hawthorne never walked so much or with so much pleasure, while in England, as during his various sojournings at this pretty town.

One of the last days of June was spent in an excursion to Stratford-on-Avon, described in "Our Old Home;" and after a run up to Liverpool, and a visit to Lichfield and Uttoxeter, the family set forth, in the early part of July, for a fortnight among the English Lakes. Just before that event, however, the law had been passed by Congress, reducing the emoluments of the Consulate by a serious amount. Mr. Wilding had written to Hawthorne, under date of June 29, that it would be "put in force on Monday. What war-vessels," he adds, "are now in, must of course come under the old law. Under the Attorney-General's construction, I think the Consuls--here, at all events--may manage to make their expenses." Of course this put an end to all possibility of laying up any considerable sum of money against the future. With economy, there would be enough to get through with, and no more. It took away from the Consulate the only feature that could render it tolerable, and Hawthorne began to grow restive in the traces. He wrote under date of July 5:--

DEAR MR. BRIGHT, I have come back (only for a day or two) to this black and miserable hole.

Truly yours,

NATH. HAWTHORNE.

P.S. I don't mean to apply the above two disparaging adjectives merely to my Consulate, but to all Liverpool and its environs,--except Sandheys and Norris Green [these places being the residences, respectively, of Mr. Bright and Mr. Heywood].

--But the vacation among the Lakes compensated for a great deal of Liverpool. The weather was, for the most part, favorable, and the scenery wore its loveliest aspect. Our headquarters were made at the Newby Bridge Hotel, on Lake Windermere, whence every part of the Lake district lies within the limits of a comfortable excursion. The combination of mountain, water, and forest with reminiscences of Wordsworth, Coleridge, Southey, and the others of that conclave, was peculiarly grateful to the American man of letters; possibly, indeed, he more enjoyed the calm imaginative delight of this spiritual communion with the spots which their memory made famous, than he would have cared for their concrete living companionship. It is among the most valuable qualities of places associated with famous names, that you find therein more of what you wish to find of the personages in question, and have it more at your leisure and according to your humor, than they themselves could ever furnish you withal. Wordsworth's grave had--what the poet himself did not always have--a charm worthy of his poetry; and the cataract of Lodore gave to our conception of Southey a freshness and beauty which might have failed to discover themselves in the man. But the tour has been amply treated of in the Note-Books and need not be further commented upon here.

For a time Hawthorne entertained some idea of handing in his resignation as Consul, and, after a short visit to Italy, returning to America. There were several arguments in favor of such a step. He had been in England long enough to obtain a distinct impression of it; and he could, in the course of a month or two, visit such places of especial interest in the island as he had not already seen. A longer tenure of office would not materially increase his pecuniary resources; and, finally, his wife's health made it necessary that she, at any rate, should not pass another winter in the English climate. He seems to have spoken of this intention to persons outside his immediate circle; for I find the poet William Allingham writing to him from Ireland

"That Liverpool should be distasteful to you seems no marvel, and you are doubtless right to leave it. Men make much of their misery by what they call 'sticking to business,'--becoming human limpets. In England, at least, we are over-adhesive in our habits. Myself, I still laud (though relapsed) the virtue of Official Resignation; and I wish I could afford to practise it in my humble way."

But before the project could take definite shape, something occurred to materially modify it. John O'Sullivan was now United States Minister to the Court of Lisbon; and be wrote to propose that Mrs. Hawthorne should, with her children, spend the ensuing winter there. This would not only give her the advantage of the kind of climate most favorable to her complaint, but would effect some saving in expense. Hawthorne might then finish his term at the Consulate, and the visit to Italy would be only postponed, not abandoned. This plan, upon due consideration, appeared to combine so many advantages that it could not easily be put aside. The main objection to it was, of course, that it involved a separation which would certainly be prolonged, and might--having in view the uncertainties of life--be final. The husband and wife had never, since their marriage, been apart from each other more than a few weeks at a time, and the prospect of so grave an interruption of their companionship was hard to contemplate. It was at length decided that Mrs. Hawthorne should proceed to Lisbon in the autumn, taking with her her two daughters; while the son should remain in England with his father.

Hawthorne returned to Liverpool about the end of July, and took rooms at the Rock Ferry Hotel, whither his family followed him a few days later, and where they remained during the mouth of August. In the first week of that month Henry Bright took his friend to witness the launch of the "Royal Charter," which is described in detail in the Journal. This large and superb vessel was afterwards wrecked disastrously, with great loss of life, off the coast of Anglesea. The only other event of importance, of this date, was the visit to Smithell's Hall, which was made in fulfilment of an old engagement. It is to this Hall that the legend of the Bloody Footstep belongs, which haunted Hawthorne ever afterwards. I am inclined to think that the legend was more of a nuisance than a pleasure to him, after all. From a literary point of view, the idea is one of those which seem very alluring at first sight, but, when one comes to deal with them, prove strangely difficult and impracticable. Having once made up his mind to use the incident, in some form, in a romance, Hawthorne would not easily forego his purpose and nothing can be more interesting and instructive to would-be romancers than the repeated efforts he made to lick the incident into shape and harmony. But it is too fantastic to be made impressive,--at least, when incorporated in a narrative of any length. The symbol of the Scarlet Letter will be memorable and fearful while our literature lasts; but the Bloody Footstep is a comparatively crude and shallow idea,--not fine and subtle enough to be properly assimilated by a genius so pure and profound as Hawthorne's.

He dined at Smithell's Hall, and made one or two reflections not given in the Note-Books. "Mrs. Ainsworth," he says,

"talked rather copiously, but not particularly well. She seems to have pretensions to a knowledge of literature, and to take an interest in literary people; but her talk is quite superficial, and I must say I think her a silly woman. One anecdote which she told was very characteristic, not of the hero of it, but of herself and of the English people generally, as showing what their tone and feeling is respecting Americans. Mr. Bancroft, while minister here, was telling somebody about the effect of the London atmosphere on his wife's health. 'She is now very delicate,' said he, 'whereas, when she lived in New York, she was one of the most indelicate women in the city!' And Mrs. Ainsworth had the face to tell this foolish story for truth, and as indicating the mistakes into which Americans are liable to fall in the use of the English language. In other instances I have heard stories equally ridiculous about our diplomatic people, whom the English seem determined to make butts of, reason or none. It is very queer, the resolute quizzing of our manners, when we are really and truly much better figures, and with much better capacity of polish, for drawing-room or dining-room, than they themselves are. I bad been struck, on my arrival at Smithell's Hall, by the very rough aspect of these John Bulls in morning-garb,--their coarse frock coats, gray hats, checked trousers, and stout shoes. At dinner-table it was not at first easy to recognize the same individuals, in their white waistcoats, muslin cravats, thin black coats, with silk facings perhaps, as old Squire Ainsworth himself had. But after a while you see the same rough figure through all the finery, and become sensible that John Bull cannot make himself fine, whatever he may put on. He is a rough animal, and his female is well adapted to him."

--That is a frank and explicit bit of criticism, well calculated to augment the cordial understanding between the two countries. I have the more pleasure in quoting it, because the English have less to amend in their attitude towards our countrymen than was the case thirty years ago; and on the other hand, Mr. Lowell does, I believe, speak English with tolerable accuracy.

Leaving Liverpool on the 1st of September, Hawthorne took his family to London (pausing on the way at Shrewsbury), and hired lodgings at No. 24 George Street, Hanover Square. And now ensued a month of as great enjoyment as Hawthorne had hitherto known in England. No American better qualified than he to appreciate its sights, its historic and literary associations, its antiquities and its immensity had ever before lost himself in its streets. lie rejoiced in the human ocean that flooded its thorough-fares and eddied through its squares and courts; be greeted as old friends its cathedrals, its river, its bridges, its Tower, its inns, its Temple, its alleys and chop-houses,--so strange were they, and yet so familiar; so old, and so full of novelty. He cast himself adrift upon the great city, and cruised whithersoever the current took him; and when he could keep his feet no longer, he would hail a hansom and trundle homeward in happy weariness, to begin his exertions afresh the next morning. His appetite for London, which had been growing during his lifetime, was almost as big as London itself; he could not gratify it enough. He enjoyed the vague and irresponsible wandering even more than the deliberate and premeditated sight-seeing; but he was always ready for either. London seemed to fulfil his expectations better than any other city,--better than Paris, or even Rome.

His son accompanied him in many of his other-wise solitary rambles, and noticed a marked difference between his demeanor then and in their country walks. On the latter occasions his expression was generally meditative and introspective, and therefore grave; but in the London streets his glance struck outward, gathering in all external impressions, and his face wore a look of subdued pleasure. Sometimes he would pause in front of some famous edifice or momument, and gaze up at it,--seldom for longer than a minute or so, yet with an inspection so comprehensive and searching that one felt sure he carried the complete image of it away with him, In a few words he would tell his companion the event or the association that made the place memorable; but in a way so simple and yet vivid, that the latter would not have felt surprised to meet the burly form of Dr. Johnson rolling along beneath Temple Bar, or to behold Addison and Steele chatting in the famous coffee-house.

The month passed away very quickly; and in the second week of October we started for Southampton whence the steamer which was to convey Mrs. Hawthorne and her daughters to Lisbon was to sail. The night was spent at the Castle Hotel, not far from the steamship landing. By noon of the next day we were all on board. "My wife behaved heroically," Hawthorne wrote;

"Una was cheerful, and Rosebud seemed only anxious to get off. Poor Fanny, our nurse, was altogether cast down, and shed tears, either from regret at leaving her native land, or dread of sickness, or general despondency,--being a person of no hope, or spring of spirits. Julian bore the separation from his mother well, but took occasion to remind me that he had now no one hut myself to depend upon, and therefore suggested that I should be very kind to him. There is more tenderness in his own manner towards me than ordinary, since the great event. For my own part, I was not depressed (trusting in God's mercy that we shall all meet again); but yet the thought was not without a good deal of pain, that we were to be so long separated,--so long a gap in life, during which Una will quite have passed out of her childhood, and Rosebud out of her babyhood; for I shall not find them exactly such as I leave them, even if we are apart only two or three months. This will be a kind of era in their lives. My wife, I hope and pray, will meet me in better health and strength than for two years past."

The vessel steamed away; and the two who were left behind walked to the railway station, and took the train for Worcester. Spending the next night there, they proceeded to Liverpool the following day, where they were met by a driving rain-storm, complicated by rejoicings for the surrender of Sebastopol. It was comforting to get at last to Mrs. Blodgett's, and sit down, at nine o'clock, to a hearty supper.

CHAPTER 3 - MRS. BLODGETT'S, LISBON, AND LONDON

THE company at Mrs. Blodgett's, though not consisting of the most cultivated persons imaginable, was very hearty and genuine; and Hawthorne was as well content with it, for every-day purposes, as with any in England. He had, indeed, an hereditary sympathy with Yankee sea-captains, and found satisfaction in the downright simplicity and sagacity of their talk. "Captain Johnson," he writes, "assigned as a reason for not boarding at this house, that the conversation made him sea-sick; and, indeed, the smell of tar and bilge-water is somewhat strongly perceptible in it. Indisputably these men are alive, and to an extent to which the Englishman never seems conscious of life. It would do John Bull good to come and sit at our table, and adjourn with us to our smoking-room; but he would be apt to go away a little crestfallen."

The smoking-room was an apartment barely twenty feet square, though of a fair height; but the captains smoked a great deal, and by nine o'clock sat enveloped in a blue cloud. They played euchre with a jovial persistence that seems wonderful in the retrospect, especially as there was no gambling. The small boys in the house (there were two or three) soon succeeded in mastering the mysteries of the game, and occasionally took a hand with the captains. Hawthorne was always ready to play, and used to laugh a great deal at the turns of fortune. He rather enjoyed card-playing, and was a very good hand at whist; and knew, besides, a number of other games, many of which are now out of fashion, but which he, I suppose, had learned in his college days. Be the diversion or the conversation what it might, he was never lacking in geniality and good-fellowship; and sparkles of wit and good humor continually came brightening out of his mouth, making the stalwart captains haw-haw prodigiously, and wonder, perhaps, where his romances came from. Nevertheless, in his official capacity, he sometimes made things (in their own phrase) rather lively for them; and it is a tribute to his unfailing good sense and justice, that his enforcement of the law never made him unpopular.

The talk was not entirely of ships and things maritime; one might hear there, at first hand, tales of all parts of the world, and anecdotes of all persons, from royalty downwards. "The Doctor," writes Hawthorne, "told a story of the manner in which the young Queen intimated to Prince Albert that she had bestowed her heart on him. All the eligible young princes in Europe had been invited to England to visit the Queen,--trotted out, as it were, for inspection; and all were suffered to take their leave, in due time,--all but Prince Albert. When he came to pay his parting compliments, the Queen said to him, 'It depends on yourself whether you go!' This is rather pretty." He adds: "The Doctor avers that Prince Albert's immediate attendants speak contemptuously ('lightly' was his precise word) of him, as a slow, commonplace man."

Here is a passage on a more homely topic:

"Last evening two or three young men called in fortuitously to see some young ladies of our household, and chatted in parlor, hall, and smoking-room, just as they might have done in America. They stayed to tea with us. In our party of perhaps half a dozen married women and virgins, there are two or three who may fairly be called pretty,--an immense proportion compared with what one finds among the women of England, where, indeed, I could almost say I have found none. The aspect of my countrywomen, to be sure, seems to me somewhat peculiarly delicate, thin, pale, after becoming accustomed to the beefy rotundity and coarse complexions of the full-fed English dames; but, slight as they look, they always prove themselves sufficient for the whole purpose of life. Then the lightness, the dance, the ebullition of their minds, is so much pleasanter than the English propriety! I have not heard such a babble of feminine voices, on this side of the water, as I heard last night from these ladies, sitting round the table in the parlor,--all busy, all putting in their word, all ready with their laugh."

Christmas day was observed with much heartiness at Mrs. Blodgett's; branches of mistletoe were hung up everywhere, and it was dangerous to pass beneath them. The Yankee captains were extremely gallant to the ladies of the household on this occasion; and something like a plot was organized to inveigle the American Consul into paying due observance to the ceremony. The cook and the maid-servants, especially (who were allowed exceptional privileges at this celebration), openly threatened to catch this grand-looking gentleman and kiss him; and the captains, and even Mrs. Blodgett herself, were prepared to assist them in their design. The Consul, nevertheless, managed to escape; but there was a great deal of uproar and merriment, and it was a standing joke among some of Hawthorne's English friends, long afterwards, that he had, in truth, succumbed. Henry Bright, in particular, wrote a poem containing a reference to this matter, which has fortunately been preserved. "Hiawatha" had lately been published in England, and had attracted a great deal of attention and comment, not always of a respectful or appreciative kind. Henry Chorley had a review of it in the "Athenaeum," written in a highly unreceptive spirit. Mr. Bright employed the metre of "Hiawatha" in his verses, which run as follows:--

SONG OF CONSUL HAWTHORNE.

Should you ask me, "Who is Hawthorne?
Who this Hawthorne that you mention?"
I should answer, I should tell you,
"He's a Yankee, who has written
Many books you must have heard of;
For he wrote 'The Scarlet Letter'
And 'The House of Seven Gables,'
Wrote, too, 'Rappacini's Daughter,'
And a lot of other stories;--
Some are long, and some are shorter;
Some are good, and some are better.
And this Hawthorne is a Consul,
Sitting in a dismal office,--
Dark and dirty, dingy office,
Full of mates, and full of captains,
Full of sailors and of niggers,--
And he lords it over Yankees."
But you ask me, "Where the dwelling,
Where the mansion, of this Hawthorne?"
And I answer, and I tell you,
"'T is a house in upper Duke Street,--

'T is a red brick house in Duke Street.
Should you ask me further, saying,
"Where this house in upper Duke Street?"
I should answer, I should tell you,
"'T is the house of Missis Todgers,--
House of good old widow Todgers,
Where the noble Yankee captains
Meet, and throng, and spend their evening,
Hairy all, and all dyspeptic,
All of them with nasal voices,
Speaking all through nasal organs,
All of them with pig tobacco,
All of them with Colt's revolvers."
Should you ask me what they do there,--
What the manners and the customs
Of this house of widow Todgers,--
I should tell you that at Christmas
Mistletoe hangs in the parlors,
Mistletoe on hall and staircase,
Mistletoe in every chamber;
And the maids at widow Todgers',
Slyly laughing, softly stealing,
Whisper, "Kiss me, Yankee Captain,--
Kiss or shilling, Yankee Captain!"
Slyly laughing, softly saying,
Kiss from you too, Consul Hawthorne!
Kiss or shilling, Consul Hawthorne!" --
I should tell you how, at midnight
Of the last day in December,
Yankee Captain, Consul Hawthorne,
Open wide the mansion's front door,--
Door that opens into Duke Street,--
Wait to see the hoary Old Year
Pass into the frosty starlight,--
Wait to see the jocund New Year
Come with all its hopes and pleasures,
Come into the gas and firelight.
Do you ask me, "Tell me further
Of this Consul, of this Hawthorne"?
I would say, he is a sinner,--
Reprobate and churchless sinner,--
Never goes inside a chapel,
Only sees outsides of chapels,
Says his prayers without a chapel!
I would say that he is lazy,
Very lazy, good-for-nothing;
Hardly ever goes to dinners,

>Never goes to balls or soirées
>Thinks one friend worth twenty friendly;
>Cares for love, but not for liking;
>Hardly knows a dozen people,--
>Knows old Baucis, and Philemon,
>Knows a Besk, and knows a Parson,
>Knows a sucking, scribbling merchant,
>Hardly knows a soul worth knowing,--
>Lazy, good-for-nothing fellow!

This little *jeu d'esprit* pleased Hawthorne much; there are touches of true affection and discrimination hidden here and there in the doggerel. But before this date letters had been received from Mrs. Hawthorne in Lisbon.....

There are two letters from Hawthorne to his sister Elizabeth, and another to his daughter Una, which may come in here.

LIVERPOOL, Dec. 6, 1855.

DEAR B.,--I was glad to see your handwriting again in a letter to Una, and I don't think it would do you any harm to write oftener. I have received letters from Lisbon this morning. Sophia continues to receive benefit from the climate, and I see no reason to doubt that it will quite restore her. She is very pleasantly situated, and sees the King and all the grandees of the realm. I am getting tired of Liverpool, though not of England. It is not probable (though you need not mention this) that I shall remain here a great many mouths longer; for the consulate is not so profitable as it was, though it still yields a good income. But I have now got enough to live upon at home, with comfortable economy, and may besides reckon upon a considerable income from literature; so that it does not seem worth while to waste a great deal more time in this consular drudgery. I mean, however, to retain the office till next summer or autumn, and spend a good deal of the intervening time in travelling about England and Scotland. Then I propose two years on the Continent, after which there will be nothing for it but to return to America,--which does not look like a very agreeable prospect from this side of the water. I send some of the latest "Athenaeums," and am

Your affectionate brother,
NATH. HAWTHORNE.

LIVERPOOL, Feb. 16, 1856.

DEAR E.,--I send you some "Athenaeums," etc. Sophia and the two children have gone from Lisbon to Madeira, with Mr. O'Sullivan's family. Her health has very much improved, and I do not doubt that she will return to England perfectly restored, on the approach of summer. Julian is perfectly well. There is a good deal of talk of war between England and the United States; but I hardly think it will come to that There is no possibility of writing to such an impossible correspondent as you are.

Yours affectionately, N. H.

LIVERPOOL, March 19, 1856.

MY DEAREST UNA,--In answer to your crisscrossed note, I write you a very few words, and thank you very much for your kind and agreeable correspondence. You write very nice letters, and Julian and I are always greatly interested in them. He cannot puzzle out the meaning of them by himself; and I always have the pleasure of reading them over at least twice,--first to myself and afterwards to him. And when your letters contain nothing private, I likewise read them to Mrs. Blodgett and Miss Williams. Julian has lately got acquainted with a gentleman named Dr. Archer, and with some nice little daughters of his. Dr. Archer is very fond of natural history, and he has given Julian a good many shells, and a little book describing them; so that Julian is growing more learned than ever about shells. He means to spend all his money in purchasing them; and he has quite as much money as he ought, for I give him all the pence and half-pence that I get at the Consulate. Dr. Archer also shows him things through the microscope, and, among other things, the wing of a fly, which looked as big as the wing of a goose.

I have not yet been to hear Mr. Channing preach; but, to make amends, I send Julian every Sunday. There is always some lady or other who is glad to take charge of him and put herself under his protection. But, last Sunday, there happened to he no lady going to Mr. Channing's; so, rather than go to Mrs. Blodgett's church, Julian chose to go to our chapel all by himself. There he saw Dr. Archer, who invited him to dinner and to spend the day, and sent one of his daughters to ask my permission. Julian is very fond of society, and loses no opportunity of going abroad whenever he is asked. Sometimes Mrs. Warren asks him to her house; and I think he likes to go there better than anywhere else, for the sake of dancing with Mary. I often tell him that he will have to earn his living as a dancing-master; but he seems to think that that profession would he beneath the dignity of a Consul's son.

Tell Rosebud that I love her very much, and that I wrote her a letter a little while ago, and sent it to Uncle John, to be sent to her. She is the best little girl in the world, is she not? Does she ever get out of humor? Tell her that I wish very much to know whether she always behaves prettily, as a young lady ought. Is she kind to Nurse?

I am to dine at Sandheys this evening and going I suppose I shall see Annie Bright.

YOUR LOVING FATHER.

--It was in February of the New Year (1856) that Hawthorne made the visit to the workhouse which is recorded in his journal, and where the incident of the child's attaching itself to him occurred, that made so deep an impression on him. He was accompanied by Mr. Mansfield and Mrs. Heywood. In relation to the child, he says: "If it were within the limits of possibility,--if I could ever have done such wickedness as could have produced this child,--I should have certainly set down its affection to the score of blood-recognition; and I cannot conceive of any greater remorse than a parent must feel if he could see such a result of his illegitimate embraces. I wish I had not touched the imp; and yet I never should have forgiven myself if I had repelled its advances."

Hawthorne's spirits were very much depressed at this period; his loneliness weighed upon him, and he was in continual dread, as he says, "of ill-news from Lisbon that I may perhaps hear,--of black-sealed letters, or some such horrors." But it happened, fortunately no doubt, that he was more than usually involved in various forms of social activity. He lunched on board the "Princeton;" he visited the Mersey

Iron Foundry, and was delighted with the great vat full of boiling iron; he called on Mr. Dallas, the new ambassador, who "had risen in life by the lack of two powerful qualities and by a certain tact," and who "must be pronounced a humbug, yet almost or quite an innocent one." He went to London, stopping over night at Mr. Bowman's, in St. James Place; and called on Mr. Bennoch, at the latter's office, where they talked of the war, and of Jerdan, whom Mr. Bennoch characterized as "a very disreputable old fellow, who had spent all his life in dissipation, and has not left it off even now, in his old age. I do not see," adds Hawthorne, "how such a man has attained vogue in society, as he certainly has; for he had no remarkable gifts, more than scores of other literary men, and his manners had, to my taste, no charm. Yet he had contrived to live amongst and upon whatever is exquisite in society and in festivity." He and Bennoch visited Hampton Court, and dined at the "Star and Garter" on Richmond Hill; and the next day, still under Mr. Bennoch's guidance, he investigated Barber-Surgeon's Hall, and gives a minute description of the "Loving-cups" that he saw there, and of the ceremony in using them; and afterwards they took the rail to Greenwich, and mingled in the "Fair." The following evening he dined with Mr. Bennoch, meeting Mrs. Newton Crosland, who praised "The Scarlet Letter." "I would gladly have responded by praising her own works," he remarks;

"but although she sent me one of them, three or four years ago, I had quite forgotten its subject, and so could not say anything greatly to the purpose. Neither would it have been easy, at any rate, to respond in due measure; for Mrs. Crosland was unusually lavish in her admiration, preferring poor me to all the novelists of this age, or, I believe, any other; and she and Mr. Bennoch discussed, right across me, the uses to which I had better put my marvellous genius, as respects the mode of working up my English experiences!--I suppose this may be the tone of London literary society. But I really do not think that I like to be praised, *viva voce;* at least, I am glad when it is said and done with, though I will not say that my heart does not expand a little towards those who rightly appreciate my books. But I suspect that I am of somewhat sterner stuff than many romancers, and tougher of fibre; and the dark seclusion--the atmosphere without any oxygen of sympathy--in which I spent all the years of my youthful manhood, have enabled me to do almost as well without as with it."

Another day he strolled through the National Gallery, and remarks that his art culture had already advanced, so far that he was able to prefer some pictures to others; and he went to the British Museum, and wished, in his weariness, that the Elgin Marbles and the Frieze of the Parthenon were all burnt into lime. Then he got lost in the vicinity of Holborn, and "kept returning, in the strangest way, to the same point in Lincoln's Inn Fields; and I must say that I wished the Devil had London and them that built it, from King Lud's time downwards!" But he recovered sufficiently to go and see Kean play "Louis XI." the same evening, and liked him well. Mr. Bennoch now seized upon him once more, and whirled him off to Aldershott, where they sat down to a "splendid dinner" with the officers of an Irish regiment,--or, rather, the Irish officers of a regiment,--whom Hawthorne found capital company. Next morning they witnessed a shamfight, and saw fifteen thousand men pass in review before the Duke of Cambridge, who lifted his hat as each regiment went by.

"As he did so, there ensued a singular and half-ludicrous transformation. For the poor Duke had suffered a great deal in his Crimean warfare, and has grown bald and gray in consequence, although his beard and whiskers are still of a rich brown; so that, while his hat remained on his head, you saw a florid gentleman in his very prime, fringed about whith the brown beard of lusty manhood, but whenever the hat was lifted, behold an aged head, gray, bald, forlorn! It was the battle of Inkermann that did this mischief; for the Duke had been in a terrible excitement then, and, besides, Lord Raglan had treated him very severely for some of his conduct. The Duke had an awfully quick temper, which breaks out whenever he is in command and he blows up the officers right and left whenever anything happens not to suit him."

From Aldershott the two friends went, by previous invitation, to visit Mr. Martin Farquhar Tupper, the famous poet of the "Proverbial Philosophy;" and here follows an entertaining record of their experiences on that occasion.

APRIL 2, 1856.

We reached Albany somewhere about ten o'clock, and were met by a boy of twelve years, a son of Mr. Tupper, who had sent him to escort us. He was a forward, talkative, intelligent lad, and kept chattering profusely with Bennoch (whom he already knew). As we entered Albany, the boy exclaimed that there was his father. "Yes," said Bennoch, "as large as life !" "As small as life, you mean," said the boy; and, indeed, Mr. Martin Farquhar Tupper's size is best expressed so. He soon met us, and extended his arms with an affectionate greeting to Bennoch; and then, addressing me, "Oh, great Scarlet Letter!" he cried. I did not know what the Devil to say, unless it were "Oh, wondrous Man of Proverbs!" or "Oh, wiser than Solomon!" and as I was afraid to say either of these, I rather think I held my tongue. I felt in an instant that Mr. Tupper was a good soul, but a fussy little man, of a kind that always takes one entirely aback. He is a small man, with wonderfully short legs, fat (at least very round), and walks with a kind of waddle, not so much from corpulence of body as from brevity of leg. His hair is curly, and of an iron-gray hue; his features are good, even handsome, and his complexion very red. A person for whom I immediately felt a kindness, and instinctively knew to be a bore. He took me by the arm with vast cordiality, and led me towards his home; and before we reached the gate, if I mistake not, he had asked me whom I meant by Zenobia in the "Blithedale Romance," and whether I had drawn my own character in Miles Coverdale, and whether there really was a tombstone in Boston with the letter A upon it!--very posing queries, all of them. Tupper's house is a very delightful one, standing in the centre of the village, yet secluded from it by its own grounds, and encompassed by a wall. He says it has seven gables, and led me round it in order to count them; but I think we fairly made out eight or nine. It is a house of some antiquity, and its gables make it very picturesque in a quiet way; and Tupper, as his family increased, has made additions which are in good keeping with the original structure he inherited it from an uncle. Mrs. Tupper--a plain, pleasant, cordial, lady-like person--was now standing at the door with some of her children, and gave us a warm and kind welcome; and we entered the hall, which had old cabinets and pictures in it,--century-old portraits, which Tupper said he called ancestral, though really they were not so. The family had been waiting breakfast for us; so, though Bennoch and I had eaten two chops apiece at the camp, we all sat down to table, seven children inclusive, and I made another pretty fair meal. Tupper's three eldest children are girls, from eighteen downwards; and their cheeks were as red as roses, and they seemed to be nice, affectionate, well-behaved young people. Mr. Tupper has chiefly educated them himself; and to such good purpose that one of them already writes for the magazines. Tupper is really a good man, most domestic, most affectionate, most fussy; for it appeared as if he could hardly sit down, and even if he were sitting he still had the effect of bustling about. He has no dignity of character, no conception of what it is, nor perception of his deficiency. His son has an instinctive sense of this, and presumes upon it, and Tupper continually finds it necessary to repress him. "Martin, do not talk so much!" he cries,--for the boy really bubbles without a moment's intermission; "Martin, your father was born a day or two before you were!" and a thousand such half-pettish, half-kindly admonitions, none of which have the slightest effect. The girls, however, seem to respect him and love him.

In the dining-room are six fine lithographic portraits of the Queen's children, as large as life, and all taken at the same age, so that they would appear to have been littered at one birth, like kittens. They were presented by her Majesty, who is a great admirer of the "Proverbial Philosophy," and gives it to each of her children as they arrive at a proper age to comprehend the depths of its wisdom. Tupper is the man of all the world to be made supremely happy by such appreciation as this; for he is the vainest little man of all little men, and his vanity continually effervesces out of him as naturally as ginger-beer froths. Yet it is the least incommodious vanity I ever witnessed; he does not insist upon your expressing admiration; he does not even seem to wish it, nor hardly to know or care whether you admire him or not. He is so entirely satisfied with himself that he takes the admiration of all the world for granted,--the recognition of his supreme merit being inevitable. I liked him, and laughed in my sleeve at him, and was utterly weary of him; for, certainly, be is the ass of asses. Not but what he says sensible things, and even humorous ones; not but what be is a writer of strength and power,--for surely "The Crock of Gold" is a very powerful tale,--but, if it were not irreverent, I should say that his Creator, when He made Tupper, intended to show how easily He could turn a gifted, upright, warm hearted, and in many ways respectable person into a fool and laughing-stock even for persons much inferior to himself.

After breakfast we walked out to see a hunting-meet. The country is beautiful, swelling in long, high undulations, from the summit of one of which the diameter of the prospect is one hundred miles. There is a legend of saints connected with three of these Surrey hills, but I have forgotten it. On our way we saw here and there a red-coated horseman, hastening to the rendezvous. We heard now and then the sound of a horn and the voice of a huntsman; and by and by appeared the pack, nosing along the ground and scenting into the underbrush of furze to discover if any fox were there. The hunt followed (perhaps a score of huntsmen, some of them in red coats, and two or three ladies amongst them). Before we left the hill-top Tupper showed us some yew-trees of unknown antiquity, Druidical perhaps; their trunks were of immense size, upwards of twenty feet in girth. On our way home we passed through Albany Park, the seat of Mr. Drummond; within the park, and at no great distance from each other, stood two churches, a new one and an ancient, venerable one. The interior of the new church, which belongs to the Irvingites, is of Roman Catholic aspect, but very pleasant and soothing, with its stained windows, lamp, and holy symbols. The old church, though no longer used, is in excellent repair; and, gray and time-worn though it is, it might have answered its original purpose for centuries longer. Mr. Drummond's house is a modern structure, but in the Elizabethan style, and looking antique enough to be in keeping with the rest of the scene.

The Tupper burial-place for generations past was here; and the graves of three of his children were covered with a garden blooming with flowers, and evidently constantly aiid carefully cultivated and weeded. Tupper looked earnestly at it, and was quiet for a moment; and seemed pleased to see the flowers growing so finely, and said, "Ah, we must tell mamma of this." Then we looked into the church window, and saw the monunient of Mr. Drummond's three sons,--all the male posterity the rich man had. Tupper told us a story on this subject which might easily enough be worked up into a dark, impressive legend. Mr. Drummond had intended to pull down the old church, and level the stones in the graveyard. He was vehemently opposed, especially by Tupper, who said that if he persisted in his purpose of desecration, he might suffer the curse of Joshua on whomsoever should rebuild Jericho,--that his first-born and youngest sons should perish. The man holding to his purpose, all his three sons did die, one after another; and the bells of the old church, which he had transferred to the new steeple, tolled the funeral knell of his last son, who had died just as they were about to celebrate his coming of age. They had all been healthy and strong before. The old church was left untouched, and became the mausoleum of his children. It is queer to think of little Tupper being the prophet of such a doom as this!

Reaching Tupper's house, he took us up into his study, which is a large room, with plenty of books, a great many of which are editions of his own beloved works. The most remarkable object is a beautiful marble figure of a child, asleep on a cushion; a little girl two or three years old, very delicately sculptured, enjoying a sweet repose. It is the statue of his dead child, whose grave we had seen in the old churchyard. Tupper looked at it with evident delight, as he might have done at his child alive; and it almost seemed as if, so far as his feelings were concerned, it were the real presence of his living child. He spoke about it without any reserve, and showed me the different points of view; but for my part, though it was a very sweet little creature, I could not say much of it, feeling that a stranger tongue has no right to infringe upon the delicacy and sanctity of such a subject. But Tupper probably felt nothing of the kind, and the presence of the little marble girl seemed to soothe and comfort him, and he is just as merry, when the mood serves, as if she was not there. Besides the tender marble, he showed me some certificates of honorary membership of certain American literary societies, glazed and framed and hanging against the wall. I never heard before of any of the learned bodies. Likewise he opened one of the bookcases, and showed it packed quite full of the American editions of his works, all splendidly bound and gilt,--talking with evidently intense satisfaction of his American fame.

We dined early, the whole brood of children sitting down to table with us, and the patriarchal Tupper chatting away during the meal. A very small man seems rather out of place at the head of a large family; the dignity of the situation is not in keeping with his figure and demonstrations. We had quite a good plain dinner, in such abundance as the large appetites of seven small people rendered necessary. I sat next to Mrs. Tupper, and, talking with her about her home and her husband, she observed that they two had played together on the spot, and gathered the nuts beneath the trees, in earliest childhood; "for we were cousins," she said. . . . It is wonderful what a sadness this one great misery threw over my whole contemplation of Tupper's life and character. I had already made a remark to him about the means of happiness he had around him, and had noticed, with some surprise, that he did not respond with any heartiness. There was, for that only time, a marked reserve in his manner, a something repining in his tone. . . . After dinner we set out for Wooton, Tupper bestriding a horse. He breeds his own horses, and is very proud of them, though they are by no means remarkably good. One very commonplace pony he calls "Wonder," and has other fine names for all the rest. He rides pretty well; but his wife kept calling out to him to be careful, to go slowly down steep hills, and divers other affectionate admonitions,--for she is a truly good woman, and admires her husband just as much as if he were bigger and wiser. They are very kind people, all of them, and I heartily wish them well.

--Recommencing their travels, the pilgrims next went, *via* Tunbridge Wells, to Battle Abbey; the interior of which, Hawthorne says, "of all domestic things that I have seen in England, satisfied me most." From there they drove to Hastings, and called on Theodore Martin and his wife (*née* Helen Faucit), and, having lunched there, took the train back to London. But the gayeties were not yet over; for, the next day, Hawthorne was taken to dine at the Milton Club, where he met several distinguished persons, among them Mr. Tupper, Dr. Mackay, Tom Taylor, William Howitt, and Mr. Sidney Carter Hall, concerning which gentleman Hawthorne appears to have suffered considerable mental disquietude. He says:--

". . . While I was waiting for Bennoch at the Milton Club, a tall, fine-looking gentleman with white hair entered, and was presently introduced to me by Mr. Tupper. Mr. S. C. Hall--for it was no less a personage--immediately began, in a tone audible to the whole room, to express his admiration for me as 'the first--yes, it was really so--the very first writer of the age.' He said that he had written fifty thousand (I think that was the number) criticisms of books, but that, in all his vocation as a critic, he had never felt such delight as in recording his judgment of my merits. In short, I cannot possibly over-state what he said, and, for very shame, prefer not to record it any further; and it was all said in the most fluent, irrepressible, and yet quiet way, with a volubility of fine phrases, and with a calm benignity of face. I have never met so smooth an Englishman as Mr. S. C. Hall. He likewise presented me with a flower--a perfectly beautiful camellia--which his wife had sent me; for, it seems, her admiration is of the same intensity as her husband's. Good Heavens! what is a man to do in a case like this? By and by Bennoch entered, and, taking me by the arm, led the way to the dining-room. I besought him most earnestly to give me any other neighbor rather than Mr. S. C. Hall, for that I could not stand his incense. He put Mr. Charles Mackay (author of 'The Good Time Coming') between me and Mr. Hall; notwithstanding which the latter besmeared me with a great deal more butter and treacle before the dinner was over. God forbid that I should be other than grateful for true appreciation; but was this true? Did he speak because the fulness of his heart compelled him? Could be have said less if he had tried to restrain himself? for, if he could, he was utterly unpardonable for saying what he did. I verily believe that he had it all on his tongue and nowhere else. I ought to say that Bennoch strenuously affirms that he is a good and honest man, though with some absurdities of manner; and be says that he has positively known both Hall and his wife to make greater personal sacrifices for the welfare of art and literature than be has known any other persons to make. Douglas Jerrold, on the other hand, and Dr. Mackay think him an arrant humbug; and I believe there is no doubt of his having been the original of Dickens's Mr. Pecksniff."

On rising from the dinner-table at eleven o'clock, Mr. Dallas--"lest I should starve before morning"--took him to supper at his house in Park Lane, where he was presented to Mrs. Dallas, formerly Miss Glyn. "Our party broke up soon after midnight, and Mr. and Mrs. Dallas made me promise to come again on Saturday to meet Mr. Charles Reade." Meanwhile, on the Thursday, he dined with Dr. Mackay at the Reform Club, meeting Douglas Jerrold; and it was here that the little misunderstanding with the latter occurred, which was afterwards so amicably made up. Friday was a day of rest; but on Saturday the supper-party at Mr. Dallas's came off. Hawthorne does not seem to have been particularly impressed by Charles Reade; though I have heard him, since then, express great liking for some of his books, and I remember his reading "Griffith Gaunt" with much interest when it was appearing serially in the "Atlantic Monthly." "A tall man," be calls him, "more than thirty, fairhaired, in good flesh, and not of especially intellectual aspect, but of agreeable talk and demeanor."

"Miss Glyn," he proceeds,

"was not there when I arrived, but soon came in, hot and wearied, from the stage; and when she shook hands with me, her own was moist, and gave me a strong idea of how exhausting stage exertions are. She is not pretty at all, either in face or figure, being broad and full, with a short neck; but I can conceive that she may have a great deal of power in her acting. She is more haunted by the trick, tone, and glance of the actress, than either of the other distinguished ladies whom I have met. I should say that she still retains a native goodness and simplicity. I sat next her at supper; and she alluded to the statement she had made to me a few evenings ago, that she had read 'The House of Seven Gables' thirteen years since, and inquired if she had not made a little mistake. I said that she had, but that I felt much flattered by it, because it could only have arisen from the book having made itself so much a part of the permanent furniture of her mind that she could not tell when she first became acquainted with it. She laughed, and seemed a little confused, as well she might."

On the 6th of April this indefatigable man of society went with Bennoch and Mackay to Woking, to dine and spend the evening. Mrs. Hall was "a dame of ripe age, midway beyond fifty, but still an agreeable object to look at, and must once have possessed beauty. Her husband loves beautiful things, and chose his wife, no doubt, on the same principle--in part at least--that guides him in other matters. She is tall and large and rotund, but not too rotund, and was dressed in black, and is a good figure of a woman. As for Mr. Hall, be has his ridiculous side, and I cannot exactly judge what the depth of his heart may be; it may possibly be all surface, but still I do not think him insincere, even if he be all surface." At dinner Mr. Hall was delivered of a long tribute to Hawthorne's genius; and the latter replied in a short speech, of which he says "one half was in all probability very foolish, and the other half (God forgive me!) false." Dr. Mackay next proposed the health of Mrs. Hall; whereupon "her husband returned thanks in another very long speech, enlarging upon her merits, giving an account of their courtship and engagement and early marriage and subsequent happiness, and incidentally treating of the excellences of Mrs. Hall's mother, who had lived with them upwards of thirty years and was only recently deceased. If there were any good in him, he said, he owed it to those two women;--and there certainly is good, mixed up with a vast deal of nonsense and flummery."

Escaping thence, Hawthorne next fell into the clutches of the Lord Mayor, but was more than repaid for any inconvenience he may have been subjected to, by the spectacle of the beautiful Jewess who sat opposite him, and whose aspect he has immortalized in the Miriam of "The Marble Faun." Then to the House of Commons, where be saw Disraeli--" a very unwholesome-looking person"--and Lord Palmerston, and listened to a debate. In the Refectory they saw Disraeli again. "He don't look as if he had a healthy appetite. Bennoch says that he makes himself up with great care, and spends a long time picking the white hairs from his sable locks. He is said to be poor; and though he had property with his wife, it is all gone."

From the House they repaired to Albert Smith's "Mont Blanc" lecture. Mr. Albert Smith was " a gentleman of about forty, of the Dickens school, a little flashy and rowdy, but a good-hearted man and an agreeable companion. We went to Evans's supper-rooms, where I was introduced to the musical critic of the "Times," and to Mr. Lawrence, author of the "Life of Fielding." But the queerest introduction was that of the superintendent of the rooms, a Mr. Green, who expressed himself in tbe highest degree honored by my presence, and said if he could only have Emerson likewise, and Channing (the deceased Doctor, I presume), and Longfellow, the dream of his life would be fulfilled! It is a good place to see London life in, and I mean, sometime or other, to go there again,--perhaps with Longfellow."

Next day he dined with Henry Stevens, an American gentleman connected with the Library department of the British Museum, and again met Tom Taylor, whom he considered to be sensible and active-minded, with "a humorous way of showing up men and matters, but without originality or much imagination or dance of fancy." After dinner there was a reception in the drawing-room, where Hawthorne was introduced to a great many ladies and gentlemen who, "so far as I could judge, had all been invited there to see me." "It is ungracious, even hoggish," he continues (to quote a passage already printed from the Note-Books), "not to be gratified with the interest they expressed in me; but then it is really a bore, and one does not know what to do or say. I felt like the hippopotamus, or--to use a more modest illustration--like some strange insect imprisoned under a tumbler, with a dozen eyes watching whatever I did."

This, however, was his final trial. The next evening a telegram arrived at Mrs. Blodgett's, announcing his intended arrival; and his son, sharp-set from a three weeks' abstinence from the paternal society, rushed off the following morning to the Waterloo hotel, and found him seated at one of the small tables in the breakfast-room, looking much less depressed and heavy than before his excursion. I remember that day, just twenty-eight years ago, very well. It struck me then, perhaps for the first time, that he was the finest-looking man in the world.

In May, Hawthorne took another trip, this time to Scotland and the North of England, stopping at Abbotsford, and, on his way home, inspecting York Minster. He went over the same ground in 1857, in company with Mrs. Hawthorne and Julian. A few days after his return, he dined with Bennoch in Manchester, meeting Mr. Ireland, editor of the "Manchester Examiner;" Mr. Watson, a merchant; and the poet Swain. The latter impressed Hawthorne pleasantly; he says that he had simplicity, feeling, "no great energy, good sense, of which latter quality he makes perhaps but little use in his own behalf. Not that I take him for one of those literary men who make their very moderate talent an excuse for immoderate self-indulgence. I think him an irreproachable man, but probably a very inefficient one. He is an engraver, I believe, by profession; and as to his poetry, I had the volume, but I do not well recollect the contents. Mr. Ireland saw Mr. Emerson on his first visit to Europe, and directed him how to find Carlyle. When Emerson was again here, he spent some time as Ireland's guest. Ireland is one of the few men who have read Thoreau's books; and he spoke of Margaret Fuller, and of the 'Dial.' But, on the whole, I think the English Conservatives are the men best worth knowing. The Liberals, with all their zeal for novelty, originate nothing; and one feels a little disgusted to find them setting forth their poor little views of progress, especially if one happens to have been a Brook-Farmer! The best thing a man born in this island can do is, to eat his beef and mutton and drink his porter, and take things as they are; and think thoughts that shall be so beefish, muttonish, portish, and porterish, that they shall be matters rather material than intellectual. In this way an Englishman is natural, wholesome, and good; a being fit for the present time and circumstances, and entitled to let the future alone!"

He wandered about Manchester the next day, and saw, among other things, "the new picture by Millais, the distinguished Pre-Raphaelite artist," of "The Huguenots." He then returned to Liverpool, and there remained until, on the 9th of June, he received a telegram announcing the welcome news that Mrs. Hawthorne and their two daughters had arrived safely, from Lisbon, at Southampton. The next day he and his son set forth on the journey southwards.

CHAPTER 4 - EIGHTEEN MONTHS BEFORE ROME

IT was very hot weather. We spent the first night at Birmingham, and, resuming our journey the next morning passed through Leamington and Oxford, at each of which places we spent an hour or two. We reached Southampton in the dusk of the summer evening, and there, at the Castle Hotel, we found the travellers from Lisbon and Madeira, whom we had so longed to see.

Our plan was to spend two or three weeks at a country boarding-house near Southampton, and then to go up to London. The house in question was not officially a boarding-house; it was a young ladies' seminary, kept by a Mrs. Hume. This being vacation time, the young ladies, with the exception of two or three permanent boarders, had gone home, leaving plenty of accommodation. Mrs. Hume called upon us at the hotel; she was a small, agreeable, well-looking lady, and it seemed probable that our stay in her abode--Clifton Villa, it was called--would be very pleasant. So, after a week or so at the Castle Hotel, and a day at Salisbury and Stonehenge, we transferred ourselves thither. "We reached the house," writes Hawthorne,

"between six and seven o'clock. Looking a little more closely at the lady, I do not feel quite sure that the scheme of boarding with her for some weeks will be acted out. She seems to be a good and well-meaning little woman, with spirit, energy, and self-dependence and, being at the head of a respectable school for young ladies, it would be natural to suppose her cultivated and refined. But (at this stage of our acquaintance) I should pronounce her underbred, shallow, affected,--not through a natural lack of simplicity, but because her position impels her to pretend to qualities which she does not possess,--and, on the whole, a wearisome and unintentionally annoying sort of person. As mistress of a school, her faculties must be administrative rather than instructive. If she fed us better, I suppose I might be more lenient in my judgments; but eight months at Mrs. Blodgett's table have not been a very good preparation for the schoolgirl's bread and butter, morning and night, and the simple joint of mutton at two o'clock, which the good lady sets before us."

The simple truth was, that Mrs. Hume starved us, and afforded us nothing, in an aesthetic or intellectual direction, to compensate for the lack of substantial nourishment.

A visit was made to Gloucester; and after inspecting the cathedral, we went to an inn, and ordered a solid repast of meat and ale,--" a very satisfactory and by no means needless refreshment," Hawthorne remarks, "after such short commons as Mrs. Hume had kept us upon." And then he goes on to free his mind as follows:

"I never was more tired of a house than of Clifton Villa; and for Mrs. Hume's sake, I shall forever retain a detestation of thin slices of bread and butter. She is an awfully thrifty woman, and nobody can sit at her table without feeling that she both numbers and measures every mouthful that you eat; and the consequence is, that your appetite is discouraged and deadened, without ever being satisfied. She brews her own beer, and it is inexpressibly small, and is served out (only to the more favored guests) in one very little tumbler, with no offer or hint of a further supply. There is water in the milk, and she puts soda into the teapot, thereby to give the tea a color without adding to its strength. Human life gets cold and meagre under such a system; and I must say that I cordially hate Mrs. Hume, a little, bright, shallow, sharp, capable, self-relying, good woman enough. She seems to have a conscience; for she charged only four pounds a week, whereas we had paid nearly twenty at the Castle Hotel. The fare, I suppose, is a fair sample of the way of living in English boarding-houses; or, possibly, in economical English families generally."

Escaping from this Libby Prison of middle-class English propriety, we went to the suburban dwelling of Mr. Bennoch, in Blackheath, within arm's reach of London. Here we spent a month, comprising, says Hawthorne, "some of the happiest hours that I have known since we left our American home." Mrs. Newton Crosland lived at Blackheath, and Hawthorne met at her house Mr. Bailey, the author of "Festus." Another day he visited the wine-vaults of the London Docks; and called on Mr. Durham, the sculptor, and examined his busts and other works. In the evening Dr. Simpson, a London physician, came to see Mrs. Hawthorne professionally.

"He is a physician eminent in diseases of the throat and lungs ; about forty years of age, a very pleasant, cultivated, quickly perceptive man, easy and genial-mannered. After a glass of excellent burgundy, he assumed his professional character, and gave hopeful opinions respecting Sophia's case, and ordered some allopathic medicines, which she has great scruples of conscience and judgment about taking; but for my part, I am inclined to put faith in what is tangible. After tea Bennoch, the Doctor, Julian, and I walked across the heath, and from one point we had a fine and dusky view of immense London, with St. Paul's in the midst, and the towers of the two houses of Parliament, four or five miles off. On a bright morning it must form a splendid picture. Coming home by Greenwich Park, we saw many groups and couples wandering about, or sitting on the benches beneath the old trees, and decorously enjoying themselves. Continuing our ramble, Bennoch brought us to some ancient harrows, beneath which are supposed to be buried the slain of a great battle that was fought in the plain below, two or three centuries after Christ. They are small mounds, ten or twelve feet in diameter, elevated on]y a few feet, and with a shallow depression on the summit; and it seems to be pretty certain that they are as much as sixteen hundred years old. When one of them was opened, not long ago, nothing was found but a tuft of hair and some small jewels--no bones, nor aught beside."

He met Jenny Lind, and, "on the whole, was not very much interested in her;" Sir Emerson Tennent, Samuel Lover, and Miss Jewsbury. At a dinner at Mrs. Heywood's, he saw again Mr. Monckton Mimes, and his wife, who was of noble blood, and reminded him of "the best-mannered American women." She spoke to him of Tennyson, and said that Mrs. Tennyson was "a wise and tender woman, such as ought to be intrusted with such a fragile affair as Tennyson's comfort and happiness." Tom Taylor was there, and Hawthorne "liked him very well this evening; but be is a gentleman of very questionable aspect,--un-English, tall, slender, colorless, with a great beard of soft black, and, methinks, green goggles over his eyes."

Again, he breakfasted with Mr. Milnes, and met such persons as Mr. Ticknor (the historian of Spanish Literature), the old Marquis of Lansdowne, Florence Nightingale, Robert Browning, and Elizabeth Barrett Browning, whom he liked very much, and with whom he talked of spiritualism and of Miss Delia Bacon's theory regarding Shakspeare; and at last he saw, sitting next the host, a man of large presence, portly, gray-haired, but scarcely as yet aged, with a face fit for a scholar, a man of the world, a cultivated intelligence, and became aware that it was Macaulay. Hawthorne writes: "I am informed that the respectable old Marquis of Lansdowne, as I innocently considered him, is a most disreputable character, and that he is the original of Thackeray's Lord Steyne. I thought that honor belonged to the Marquis of Hertford." His trust in appearances received another shock in the case of a gentleman who had shown him many courtesies, but who, it was said, "began life as a hairdresser; was afterwards an unprincipled adventurer, on the Continent, and had made money in most questionable ways; but, growing wealthy, he put on respectability, and was now an honest man. I never should have suspected this beforehand," says Hawthorne;

"yet, now that I know it, it reconciles itself well enough with what I have seen of him. There is a kind of ease and smartness in his manner which I have never seen in any English gentleman; there is a trimness in his aspect very sutable for a hairdresser; and he wears what must be a wig, yet, if so, such an artful and exquisite one that no unprofessional man could so well have suited himself. In the presence of Lady Waldegrave he behaved like a footman; in short, I accept the statement about him, except as regards his deficient honesty. Well, his morality may have been scanty and ragged once, and have been pieced and mended as he rose in life. An Englishman with such facility and adaptiveness, so ready, so neat in his action, so devoid of the national clumsiness, is a kind of monster to begin with. On the other hand, the English are possibly less tolerant than ourselves of men who attain wealth by any other than the ordinary and regular methods and may accuse them of dishonesty when they have only been dexterous and shifty. Our friend would be altogether more at home, and more in keeping with the society around him, in America than here. Come what may, I shall always feel him to be, at least, a kind and hospitable man; and, hairdresser or not, he was a gentleman to us."

A visit to Blenheim, made about this time, is recorded in "Our Old Home;" but one of the pleasantest excursions of the summer was to Oxford, where Hawthorne and his wife were very kindly received and entertained by Mr. Speirs, the ex-mayor of the town. They remained several days, and before departing, the whole party (including Mr. and Mrs. S. C. Hall) were photographed on Mr. Speirs's lawn. In this photograph Hawthorne stands on the extreme right, facing the spectator, with his feet apart and his hands behind him, and his black frock coat unbuttoned. So far as figure and pose go, it is an admirable likeness; but the photograph, as a photograph, is execrably bad, and the faces of none of the group are recognizable.

About the middle of September Hawthorne and his family left Mr. Bennoch's, and betook themselves to Southport, a sandy seaside town on the northern coast of England. Lodgings had previously been engaged--or, rather, a house had been rented--on the esplanade. Liverpool was only about twenty miles distant, and therefore easily attainable by train; and Hawthorne was able to go down to his office in the morning and return at night. The tide, as at Rhyl, retired to immeasurable distances at low water; the neighboring country was flat and uninteresting; and, the "season" being just over at the time of our arrival, the place was deserted. The original intention was to remain there only until December; but our stay there, altogether, extended over ten months, though Hawthorne and his wife and their son made a somewhat extended trip into Scotland, as well as to Boston and other places in England, during that period. Before entering upon this, however, I will insert two letters, dating back to before the time we left Blackheath.

MY DEAR MRS. HAWTHORNE, I write a hurried line to say that we shall be in town on Thursday--Friday, rather--for some two weeks or more, and shall trust to see yourself; Una, Julian, and Rose--some or all--at 22 Woburn Square, where we shall be on our first arrival. I am to preach on the 20th and perhaps also on the 27th, though I believe I am expected to preach at Essex St. on that day. Mrs. Channing will tell you, when she meets you, the deep regret with which she learned, the other day, when calling on a friend at Mrs. Blodgett's, that Mrs. Blodgett knew as little as we did of the reasons which led Julian to leave us. We supposed that he had received directions to return, or we should have been more urgent with him to stay. I fear, however, he was not very happy; and he is a boy of so much independence and decision that we felt little inclined to interfere with his free choice. A very marked character he has, and I doubt not will be a high-minded and energetic man. But I must close. So with warm and friendly wishes, and the hope of soon meeting,

Yours faithfully,
W. H. CHANNING.

LIVERPOOL, Aug. 16, 1856.

OLD BOY,--We have very good dinners at Mrs. Blodgett's, and I think you would like very much to be there. There are so many people that Charley sits at a side-table, and he lives upon the fat of the land; and so would you, if you sat at the side-table with him. Yesterday he ate roast-beef and Yorkshire pudding: but if he had preferred it, he might have had some chicken-pie, with nice paste; or some roast duck, which looked very good; or some tripe fried in batter; or some boiled chicken,--or a great many other delectable things. And we had two kinds of fish,--boiled salmon and fried soles. I myself ate salmon; but the soles seemed to be very nice too. And we had so many green peas that they were not half eaten, and string-beans besides,--oh, how nice! When the puddings, and tarts, and custards, and Banbury cakes, and cheese-cakes, and greengages, and that kind of stuff, was put on the table, I had hardly any appetite left; but I did manage to eat some currant pudding, and a Banbury cake, and a Victoria cake, and a slice of a beautiful Spanish musk-melon, and some plums. If you had been there, I think you would have had a very good dinner, and there would not have been nearly so many nice things left on the table. Tell mamma that, if she pleases, I have no objection to your taking riding-lessons along with Una. Mamma says you have been a very good boy. I am glad to hear it, and hope you will keep good till I come back.

Your loving father,
NATH. HAWTHORNE.

--At Southport the chief event of interest during the winter was a visit from Herman Melville, who turned up at Liverpool on his way to Constantinople, and whom Hawthorne brought out to spend a night or two with us.

"He looked much the same as he used to do; a little paler, perhaps, and a little sadder, and with his characteristic gravity and reserve of manner. I felt rather awkward at first, for this is the first time I have met him since my ineffectual attempt to get him a consular appointment from General Pierce. However, I failed only from real lack of power to serve him; so there was no reason to be ashamed, and we soon found ourselves on pretty much the former terms of sociability and confidence. Melville has not been well, of late; he has been affected with neuralgic complaints, and no doubt has suffered from too constant literary occupation, pursued without much success latterly; and his writings, for a long while past, have indicated a morbid state of mind. So he left his place in Pittsfield, and has come to the Old World. He informed me that he had "pretty much made up his mind to be annihilated;" but still he does not seem to rest in that anticipation, and I think will never rest until he gets hold of some definite belief. It is strange how he persists--and has persisted ever since I knew him, and probably long before--in wandering to and fro over these deserts, as dismal and monotonous as the sandhills amidst which we were sitting. He can neither believe, nor he comfortable in his unbelief; and he is too honest and courageous not to try to do one or the other. If he were a religious man, he would be one of the most truly religious and reverential; he has a very high and noble nature, and better worth immortality than most of us."

Melville made the rounds of Liverpool under the guidance of Henry Bright; and afterwards Hawthorne took him to Chester; and they parted the same evening,

"at a street corner, in the rainy evening. I saw him again on Monday, however. He said that he already felt much better than in America; but observed that he did not anticipate much pleasure in his rambles, for that the spirit of adventure is gone out of him. He certainly is much overshadowed since I saw him last; but I hope he will brighten as he goes onward. He sailed on Tuesday, leaving a trunk behind him, and taking only a carpetbag to hold all his travelling-gear. This is the next best thing to going naked; and as he wears his beard and mustache, and so needs no dressing-case,--nothing but a toothbrush,--I do not know a more independent personage. He learned his travelling habits by drifting about, all over the South Seas, with no other clothes or equipage than a red flannel shirt and a pair of duck trousers. Yet we seldom see men of less criticisable manners than he."

Among the curiosities of Southport was Mr. Scarisbrook, the landlord of the township.

"He is an eccentric man, and there seems to be an obscurity about the early part of his life; according to some reports, he kept a gambling-house in Paris before succeeding to the estate. Neither is it a settled point whether or no he has ever been married: some authorities utterly ignoring the point; others affirming that he has legitimate children, who are now being educated in Paris. He is a Catholic, but is bringing up his children, they say, in the Protestant faith. He is a very eccentric and nervous man, and spends all his time at the secluded Hall, which stands in the midst of mosses and marshes; and sees nobody, not even his steward. He might be an interesting person to know; but, after all, his character, as I have just sketched it, turns out to be one of the commonplaces of novels and romance."

Towards the end of February of the next year (1857) our house was entered by burglars, who had come up from Liverpool, probably with splendid anticipations of the booty they would get at the residence of the American Consul. They did not get much, being frightened away prematurely by a noise; but, on coming down the next morning, we found the house in quite a dishevelled condition. Hawthorne was much amused, and chuckled a good deal over the misadventure, though the thieves had carried off, among other things, his boots and his top-coat. The police earnestly undertook the case, and, contrary to all anticipation, and not a little to Hawthorne's regret, they captured the two scamps, and we all went down to the police court to "appear" against them. They were young fellows; and although their appearance was that of thorough rascality, they steadfastly maintained a demeanor of more than infantile innocence; and one of them was something of a wag into the bargain, so that, altogether, the affair seemed vastly entertaining to the younger members of the Consul's family. But the thieves got five and ten years' imprisonment, respectively, which was probably no joke to them; and by this time they are probably in another and better world. English thieves seldom live long; the climate as well as the laws are against them.

On the 10th of April Hawthorne left his two daughters in charge of their governess, Miss Brown, at Southport, and took his wife and son with him on a three or four days' trip to York and Manchester. Accounts of this journey, as well as of succeeding ones to Scotland and to Old Boston, are to be found both in the Note-Books and in Mrs. Hawthorne's "Notes in England and Italy."

Five days later, Hawthorne attended a banquet on the occasion of the laying of the corner-stone of Mr. Browne's free library at Liverpool. He met there Lord Stanley (the present Earl of Derby), then a young man; and seems to have taken a fancy to him, though he says, considered as one whose destiny it was to take a leading part in political life, he appeared to labor under certain natural or physical disadvantages. "I would not care to take his position," he says, "unless I could have considerably more than his strength."

The expedition to Old Boston now followed; and on the way back, a visit was made to Newstead Abbey, formerly the residence of Lord Byron, and at that time in possession of Colonel Wildman. Mrs. Hawthorne, in a letter written to her daughter Una, describes the abbey with much minuteness, and says that after they had returned to their hotel, the landlady came in and gave her many interesting particulars about the Byrons, with whom her mother and herself had had considerable intercourse, years before.

"She told me that when Lady Lovelace, two years before her death, went to Newstead, Lord Lovelace brought her here (to the hotel), and remained here during her visit to her father's house, not being willing to accompany her, She said the Lady Ada was not beautiful, and did not resemble her father at all; that she was extremely careless in her dress, not looking as well-appointed as her maid; and that she was very silent and gloomy. After her departure Colonel Wildman came to see Mrs. Browne (the landlady) and told her all about the visit. He did not invite Lady Lovelace to Newstead, he said, and was quite amazed to see her and to find she intended to stay. He presumed, however, she would make herself a pleasant guest, as he had heard of her accomplishments and learning; and bethought him of all his Latin and Greek and algebra, so as to be able to cope with her in conversation. But she appeared to be a perfect blank; her only response to all his efforts at talking with her were 'Yes' and 'No.' She kept her eyes cast down, and her thoughts and ideas to herself. So it went on for two days, till the kind Colonel lost patience; and when on the third morning she went down in the gardens, he followed her, and accosted her with resolute sociability. She then suddenly burst through her cloud of reserve, and confided to him her thoughts. She told him how sad and absorbed she had been at finding herself in her father's home, and that she was so oppressed she could not utter a word or respond in any way to his kindness, but that she regretted her apparent incivility, and would no longer hold herself aloof. So from that moment she was very communicative, and the Colonel told Mrs. Browne he had never before met with so agreeable and cultivated a lady. The unfortunate Lady Lovelace had two sons, both of whom were wild young men; and I remember that Lord Lovelace called on papa at the Consulate to inquire after one of them, who had disappeared, he did not know where, but supposed he had gone to sea. He thought papa might know whether he had gone to America. With all her accomplishments, Lady Lovelace had great failings, like Lord Byron, and lost forty thousand pounds by gambling, a short time before her last illness. And Mrs. Browne believed that this loss caused her death. The good landlady had also entertained Lord Byron's beloved sister, Mrs. Augusta Leigh. She said she was not beautiful, but had a very gentle and amiable countenance. But she also had a son who was dissipated, and made his mother wretched. This young Leigh came here a great deal, and talked very freely with Mrs. Browne; and one day he told her he was going to be married. She begged him not to do so, because he was too wild and thoughtless, and could not make a wife happy. But he replied that it was too late,--that he had settled it all. So he soon brought to the George the Fourth Inn a lovely little fairy, whom he introduced as his wife; and he cautioned Mrs. Browne not to whisper a word to her about his true character, for she was loving and content, and he was going to be quite sedate and good. And this was the last she ever saw or heard of either him or his child-wife. Every one connected with Lord Byron seemed doomed,--for even Mary Chaworth, his first love, became very unhappy in her marriage. Mrs. Browne talked a great deal about Colonel Wildman. He bought the estate six years before the poet's death, and Lord Byron was very glad that he should have it. On account of a mortgage, he bought it for only L80,000, and he has since spent many thousands of pounds in restoring and adorning it. He has also been at great expense in entertaining distinguished and even royal guests; the Duke of Sussex (with a train of lords and gentlemen) was very fond of going there, and nearly ruined the poor Colonel at every visit, especially as he had lost a large amount of money in the East Indies. So now he is not very rich, but still most generous and hospitable. He is easily excited; and she described very amusingly his terrible rage when he rushed into the hotel one day, and told her about Barnum's having offered him L500 for the tree on which Byron had carved his name."

This George the Fourth Hotel seems to have been a veritable Dionysius's Ear; and good Mrs. Browne would stand as the prototype of all the loquacious housekeepers, with prodigious memories, who work up the historical portion of the Mrs. Wood and Miss Braddon species of romances.

Now followed the Scottish expedition; but I can only add, to what has been already printed on the subject, this little passage,--they had spent the 9th of July in wandering all over Edinburgh, and had enjoyed themselves greatly. "As it was our wedding-day," says Hawthorne, "and as our union has turned out to the uttermost satisfaction of both parties, after fifteen years' trial, I gave mamma a gold-and-amethyst-bodied cairngorm beetle, with a ruby head."

On the 20th of July, we finally uprooted ourselves from Southport, and went to Manchester, where the Exhibition was in progress, and where we remained six weeks, in homely but not homelike lodgings at Chorlton Road. However, as we were most of the time at the Exhibition, that did not make so much difference. Hawthorne went diligently and repeatedly through all the galleries of pictures and sculptures, at first with weariness and distrust, but afterwards more cordially. The truth is, he did not enjoy pictures. The art seemed to him artifice; he wished the picture to be as good as nature in the first place, and then as much better as selection and arrangement could make it. He was inclined to ascribe great merit to the Dutch School, on account of the minute perfection of their technique; and he disapproved of them at the same time because they expended these pains on such undignified subjects. As for the "Raphaels, Correggios, and stuff," their failure was the reverse of this: they chose lofty subjects, but there was not enough illusion of reality. In the end he favored the latter class of painters rather than the former, and admired more than aught else the portrait of "Beatrice Cenci" (as it used to be called), the charm of which depends wholly on the expression and pose; the brushwork being inferior. Mrs. Hawthorne, on the other hand, enjoyed the Exhibition without limit; she had vastly more artistic faith than her husband, and much less of the arrogant, uneasy, Puritan conscience, which would not let him unrestrainedly enjoy a rose unless he could feel convinced that both the rose and he deserved it.

While wandering about the galleries one day, with his friend Ireland, he had some glimpses of Alfred Tennyson, who was also strolling about in company with the sculptor Woolner. Hawthorne had the highest appreciation of Tennyson's poetry, and had long been desirous of seeing the man. "Tennyson," he says,

"is the most picturesque figure, without affectation, that I ever saw; of middle size, rather slouching, dressed entirely in black, and with nothing white about him except the collar of his shirt, which, methought, might have been whiter the day before. He had on a black wide-awake hat, with round crown and wide, irregular brim, beneath which came down his long black hair, looking terribly tangled; he had a long pointed beard, too, a little browner than the hair, and not so abundant as to encumber any of the expression of his face. His frock coat was buttoned up across the breast, though the afternoon was warm. His face was very dark, and not exactly a smooth face, but worn, and expressing great sensitiveness, though not at that moment the pain and sorrow that is seen in his bust. His eyes were black; but I know little of them, as they did not rest on me, nor on anything but the pictures. He seemed as if he did not see the crowd, nor think of them, but as if he defended himself from them by ignoring them altogether; nor did anybody but myself cast a glance at him. Mr. Woolner was as unlike Tennyson as could well be imagined; a small, smug man, in a blue frock and brown pantaloons. They talked about the pictures, and passed pretty rapidly from one to another, Tennyson looking at them through a pair of spectacles which he held in his hand, and then standing a minute before those that interested him, with his hands folded behind his back. There was an entire absence of stiffness in his figure; no set-up in him at all; no nicety nor trimness; and if there had been, it would have spoilt his whole aspect.

"Knowing should be glad to smoke a cigar with him. Mr. Ireland says that, having heard he was to be at the Exhibition, and not finding him there, he conjectured that he must have gone into the Botanical Garden to smoke; and, sure enough, he found him there. He told me an anecdote about Tennyson while on a visit to Paris. He had a friend with him who could not speak very good French, any more than the poet himself. They were sitting at the fireside in the parlor of the hotel; and the friend proposed a walk about the city, and finally departed, leaving Tennyson at the fireside, and telling the waiter '*ne souffrez pas le faire sortir.*' By and by Tennyson also rose to go out; but the waiter opposed him with might and main, and called another waiter to his assistance; and when Tennyson's friend returned, he found him really almost fit for a strait-jacket. He might well enough pass for a madman at any time, there being a wildness in his aspect. which doubtless might readily pass from quietude to frenzy. He is exceedingly nervous."

Our residence in Manchester came to an end soon after this, and we next settled down in Lansdowne Circus, Leamington, where the months of September and October were passed. It was at this place that we were joined by Miss Ada Shepard, who acted as governess in the family during the ensuing two years, and who--if Steele's classic compliment to Lady Elizabeth Hastings was not quite applicable to her--was at all events a young lady of sound and varied accomplishments, which were yet less noticeable than her winning manners and pleasant aspect. This American girl of three-and-twenty added not a little to the pleasure of our Italian tour, and was invaluable as an interpreter of the various strange tongues one meets with on the Continent.

The weather at Lansdowne Circus was very pleasant, and the autumnal air was an invitation to walking, which was often accepted. Hawthorne's favorite direction was the immemorial village of Witnash, where the houses were of the Elizabethan period or earlier, with frameworks of oak filled in with plaster, and where, in front of the old church, stood the older yew-tree, with space for half a dozen persons to stand inside its hollow trunk. Another walk we often took was to Warwick, about two miles distant. I take the following acount of one of them from the journal:

"On Monday, a warm and bright afternoon, Julian and I took a walk together to Warwick. It appeared to me that the suburbs of Warwick now stretch further towards Leamington than they did at our last visit; there being still some pretty reaches of sylvan road, with bordering hedges and overshadowing trees, and here and there a bench for the wayfarer; but then begin the vulgar brick dwellings for the poorer classes, or the stuccoed Elizabethan imitation for those a step or two above them. Neither did I find in the town itself such an air of antiquity as I thought I remembered there, though the old archway looks as ancient as ever. But the Hospital close by it has certainly undergone some trausmogrification, the nature of which I cannot quite make out.

"We turned aside, before entering the heart of the town, and went to the stone bridge over the Avon, where such a fine view of the castle is to be obtained. I suppose I have described it already; but I am certain that there is nothing more beautiful in the world, in such a quiet, sunny summer afternoon, than these turrets and towers and high-windowed walls, gray softened with abundant foliage intermixed, and looking down upon the sleepy river, along which, between the bridge and the castle, the willows droop into the water. I stayed a good while on the bridge, and Julian mounted astride of the balustrade and jogged up and down like a postilion, thereby exciting a smile from some ladies who drove by in a barouche. We afterwards returned towards the town and, turning down a narrow lane, bordered with some old cottages and one or two ale-houses, we found that it led straight to the castle walls, and terminated beneath them. It seemed to be the stable entrance; and as two gentlemen and a groom were just riding away, I felt ashamed to stand there staring at the walls which I had no leave to look upon; so I turned back with Julian and went into the town. The precincts of the castle seem to he very extensive, and its high and massive outer wall shoulders up almost to the principal street. We rambled about, without any definite aim, and passed under the pillars that support the spire of St. Mary's Church; and thence into the market-place, where we found an omnibus just on the point of starting for Leamington. I have never yet seen--what those who have seen it call the finest spectacle in England--the interior of Warwick Castle; it being shown only on Saturdays. I do not blame the Earl; for I would hardly take his magnificent castle as a gift, burthened with the condition that the public should be free to enter it."

--I recollect a visit we made to Coventry about this time, because of a little incident that happened there, not much in itself; but which impressed at least one of those present in a manner not to be forgotten. Hawthorne, his wife, and son arrived in Coventry after dark, and took a cab, the driver of which was ordered to drive us to a hotel. Off we rattled accordingly, and presently pulled up at a place the outward aspect of which was not inviting. The cabby got down to open the cab door; but Hawthorne told him to bid the landlord step out to us. The landlord came out in his shirt-sleeves, and, putting his head into our window, filled the vehicle with the aroma of inferior brandy. Hawthorne felt indignant, but asked the man, courteously, whether he could furnish us with a private sitting-room. "I don't know, sir,"he replied; "I'll see what we can do for you'" "Driver, this won't do," said Hawthorne ; "take us somewhere else." We rattled along once more, and at length again halted, aud the driver came to the window. We were in a shabby and ill-lighted part of the town, and alongside of an iron railing, with a gate through it. " If you'll come with me, sir," said the cabby, "I'll show you a place--" But here Hawthorne interrupted him. "Why should I go with you?" he demanded, in a tone that made the unfortunate jehu start as if he had been kicked; and then, in a voice as terrible as the blast of a trumpet, "Why don't you drive us to the best hotel in town, as I told you to?" As he spoke, there was an expression in his eyes--a sudden flame of wrath--which, together with the voice, not only sobered the half-tipsy cabby and sent him flying back to his box as if he had been blown thither by an explosion, but so appalled the other two auditors that they scarcely recovered their breath until they were safely ensconced in a good suite of rooms in "the best hotel in town." Mrs. Hawthorne afterwards said, "That was the first time I ever heard papa raise his voice to a human being." But in the days before his marriage, when overseeing the perverse and conscience-less coal-shippers on the Boston wharves, Hawthorne had made his voice heard and his indignation felt as forcibly as now.

Leaving Leamington on the 10th of November, we went into lodgings at 24 Great Russell Street, nearly opposite the British Museum. We intended starting for the Continent before the end of the month; but all the children were taken with measles, and our departure was consequently delayed until the first of the New Year (1858). The physician who attended the invalids was Dr. J. J. Garth Wilkinson, the biographer of Swedenborg, and at that period somewhat involved in spiritism. Hawthorne went to a small evening reception at his house, when the Doctor showed him spirit poetry, and told him of marvels in the "materializing" line, and so forth. "Do I believe in these wonders?" Hawthorne asks himself in the Note-Books. "Of course; for how is it possible to doubt either the solemn word or the sober observation of a learned and sensible man like Dr. Wilkinson? But, again, do I really believe it? Of course not; for I cannot consent to have heaven and earth, this world and the next, beaten up together like the white and yolk of an egg, merely out of respect to Dr. Wilkinson's sanity and integrity. . . Meanwhile this matter of spiritualism is surely the strangest that ever was heard of; and yet I feel unaccountably little interest in it,--a sluggish disgust, and repugnance to meddle with it;"--a repugnance, we may venture to add, characteristic of a thoroughly healthy and well-balanced mind. Whether spiritism be true or false is of small moment; but it is eminently expedient not to meddle with it.

Dr. Wilkinson introduced Hawthorne to Coventry Patmore, the poet of "The Angel in the House,"--a poem which Hawthorne had been greatly pleased with, as be now was with its author. He was the last person whom it was pleasant to think of as a friend, that we met previous to our departure for France and Italy.

It only remains to append some letters and documents referring to official matters. Hawthorne had sent in his resignation as American Consul early in the summer. During his term of office he had striven vigorously to improve the condition of affairs that obtained between the seamen and the officers on board American vessels. Mr. Henry Bright strongly sympathized with his action, and supported it in every way open to him; and he has kindly forwarded to me the extracts which I here append, and which explain themselves.

"Mr. Hawthorne," writes Mr. Bright, "took a warm interest in putting down cruelty at sea, especially in American ships; and I have a long letter from him on the subject. But he did not wish to come forward publicly in the matter. The question had disturbed me a good deal, and at that time (1859) I was preparing a pamphlet, and hoped to get a letter from your father which I might quote; but he did not wish to be quoted, and all I could do was to allude to him and to the then Consul, Mr. Dudley. Now the evil is much abated. I enclose an extract from your father's letter (Rome, April, 1859)."

--The extract is as follows:

"It is a very horrible state of things; there is an immense amount of unpunishable cruelty: but the perpetrators of it, as well as the sufferers by it, are the victims of a vicious system. At the bottom of the whole lies the fact that there are no good seamen to be had; the next worst thing is the mode of shipping seamen, and the payment of advance wages; lastly, there is the infinite absurdity of allowing our ships to go to sea without arming the officers with any legal means of enforcing their authority."

--In "Our Old Home" ("Consular Experiences") Mr. Hawthorne further remarks:

"The newspapers all over England contained paragraphs inveighing against the cruelties of American shipmasters. The British Parliament took up the matter (for nobody is so humane as John Bull when his benevolent propensities are to be gratified by finding fault with his neighbor), and caused Lord John Russell to remonstrate with our Government on the outrages for which it was responsible before the world, and which it failed to prevent or punish. The American Secretary of State, old General Cass, responded, with perfectly astounding ignorance of the subject, to the effect that the statements of outrages had probably been exaggerated, that the present laws of the United States were quite adequate to deal with them, and that the interference of the British Minister was uncalled for. . . I once thought of writing a pamphlet on the subject, but quitted the Consulate before finding time to effect my purpose; and all that phase of my life immediately assumed so dreamlike a consistency that I despaired of making it seem solid or tangible to the public."

The "paragraphs in the newspapers" and General Cass's reply to them had reflected obliquely on Hawthorne's conduct in office, and drew from him the following very strong despatch to the Secretary of State:--

Despatch No. 90.
CONSULATE OF THE UNITED STATES,
LIVERPOOL, June 17, 1857.

SIR,--There has recently appeared, in most of the English newspapers, what purports to be a letter from the Secretary of State of the United States, to Lord Napier, British Minister at Washington, in response to a communication from his Lordship on the treatment of American seamen. In making some remarks upon that letter, it is hardly necessary to say that I do not presume to interfere in a discussion between the head of a department, in which I am a subordinate officer, and the minister of a foreign power. But as the above-mentioned letter has been made public property, there is as much propriety in my referring to it as to any other matter of public importance bearing especial reference to my official duties. I therefore take the liberty to address you, on the supposition that this document expresses the opinion and intimates the policy of our Government respecting a subject on which I have bestowed much thought, and with which I have had opportunities to become practically acquainted.

The sentiment is very decidedly expressed in the letter, that "the laws now in force on the subject of seamen employed on board the mercantile vessels of the United States are quite sufficient for their protection." I believe that no man, practically connected with our commercial navy, whether as owner, officer, or seaman, would affirm that the present marine laws of the United States are such as the present condition of our nautical affairs imperatively demands. These laws may have been wise, and effectual for the welfare of all concerned, at the period of their enactment. But they had in view a state of things which has entirely passed away; for they are based upon the supposition that the United States really possess a body of native-born seamen, and that our ships are chiefly manned by crews whose home is on our own shores. It is unfortunately the fact, however, that not one in ten of the seamen employed on board our vessels is a native-born or even a naturalized citizen, or has any connection with our country beyond his engagement for the voyage. So far as my observation extends, there is not even a class of seamen who ship exclusively in American vessels, or who habitually give them the preference to others. While the present voyage lasts, the sailor is an American; in the next, he is as likely to be sailing under any other flag as our own. And there is still another aspect of the subject causing a yet wider discrepancy between the state of things contemplated by the law and that actually existing. This lies in the fact that many of the men shipped on board our vessels, comprising much the larger portion of those who suffer ill-usage, are not seamen at all. Almost every ship, on her trip from New York to Liverpool, brings a number of returning emigrants, wholly unacquainted with the sea and incapable of performing the duties of seamen, but who have shipped for the purpose merely of accomplishing their homeward passage. On this latter class of men falls most of the cruelty and severity which have drawn public notice and reprobation on our mercantile marine. It is a result, not, as one would naturally suppose, of systematic tyranny on the part of the constituted authorities of the ship, but of a state of war between two classes who find themselves for a period inextricably opposed on shipboard. One of these classes is composed of the mates and actual seamen, who are adequate to the performance of their own duty, and demand a similar efficiency in others; the second class consists of men who know nothing of the sea, but who have imposed themselves or been imposed upon the ship, as capable of a seaman's duty.

This deception, as it increases the toil and hardship of the real sailor, draws his vengeance upon the unfortunate impostor. In the worst case investigated by me, it appeared that there was not one of the sailor class, from the second mate down to the youngest boy, who had not more or less maltreated the landsmen. In another case, the chief and second mate, during the illness of the master, so maltreated a landsman, who had shipped as sailor, that he afterwards died in a fit. In scarcely a single instance has been possible to implicate the master as taking a share in these unjustifiable proceedings. In both the cases above alluded to, the guilty escaped punishment; and in many similar ones it has been found that the sufferers are practically without protection or redress. A few remarks will make this fact obvious.

A consul, as I need not inform the Department, has no power (nor could he have unless by treaty with the Government in whose territory he resides) to inflict condign punishment for assaults and other outrages which may come under his official cognizance. The extent of his power--except in a contingency hereafter to be noticed--is to enable a complainant to seek justice in our own courts of law. If the United States really possessed any native seamen, this might be effectual so far as they were concerned; for such seamen would naturally gravitate homeward, and would there meet the persons who had outraged them under circumstances which would insure redress. But the foreigner can very seldom be prevailed upon to return for the mere purpose of prosecuting his officers; and with the returning emigrant, who has suffered so much for the sake of obtaining a homeward passage, it is out of the question. In such cases what is the consul to do? Before the complainants make their appeal to him, they have ceased to be under the jurisdiction of his country; and they refuse to return to it in quest of a revenge which they cannot be secure of obtaining, and which would benefit them little if obtained. The perpetrators of these outrages are not men who can be made pecuniarily responsible, being almost invariably, as I have said, the lower officers and able seamen of the ship. In cases of unjustifiably severe usage, if the master of the vessel be found implicated in the offence, the consul has it at his option to order the discharge of the sufferer with the payment of three months' extra wages. But the instances of cruel treatment which have come under my notice are not of the kind contemplated by the act of 1840; not being the effect of the tyranny or bad passions of the master, or of officers acting under his authority, but, as already stated, of the hostile interests of two classes of the crew. To prevent these disorders would require the authority and influence of abler men, and of a higher stamp, than American shipmasters are now found to be. In very difficult circumstances, and having a vast responsibility of life and property upon their hands, they appear to me to do their best, with such materials as are at their command. So far as they lay themselves open to the law, I have been ready to inflict it, but have found few opportunities. Thus a great mass of petty outrage, unjustifiable assaults, shameful indignities, and nameless cruelty, demoralizing alike to those who perpetrate and to those who suffer, falls into the ocean between the two countries, and can be punished in neither. Such a state of things, as it can be met by no law now in existence, would seem to reqnire new legislation.

I have not failed to draw the attention of the Government to this subject on several former occasions. Nor has it been denied by the last Administration that our laws in this regard were defective and required revision. But the extent of those acknowledged defects and of that necessary revision was alleged as a reason why no partial measures should be adopted. The importance of the matter, as embracing the whole condition of our mercantile marine, cannot be overestimated. It is not an exaggeration to say that the United States have no seamen. Even the officers, from the mate downward, are usually foreigners, and of a very poor class; being the rejected mates and other subordinates of the British commercial navy. Men who have failed to pass their examinations, or have been deprived of their certificates by reason of drunkenness or other ill conduct, attain, on board of our noble ships, the posts for which they are deemed unworthy in their own. On the deterioration of this class of men necessarily follows that of the masters, who are promoted from it. I deeply regret to say, that the character of American shipmasters has already descended, many degrees, from the high standard which it held in years past,--an effect partly due, as I have just hinted, to the constantly narrowing field of selection, and likewise, in a great degree, to the terrible life which a shipmaster is now forced to lead. Respectable men are anxious to quit a service which links them with such comrades, loads them with such responsibility, and necessitates such modes of meeting it. In making this communication to the Department, I have deemed it my duty to speak with all possible plainness, believing that you will agree with me that official ceremony is of little importance in view of such a national emergency as is here presented. If there be an interest which requires the intervention of Government with all its wisdom and all its power,--and with more promptitude than Governments usually display,--it is this. The only efficient remedy, it appears to me, must be found in the creation of a class of native seamen; but, in the years that must elapse before that can be effected, it is most desirable that Government should at least recognize the evils that exist, and do its utmost to alleviate them. No American statesman, being in the position which makes it his especial duty to comprehend and deal with this matter, can neglect it without peril to his fame. It is a subject which requires only to be adequately represented in order to attract the deepest interest on the part of the public; and the now wasted or destructive energy of our philanthropists might here be most beneficially employed.

In conclusion, I beg leave to say a few words on the personal bearing which the Secretary's supposed letter has upon my own official character. The letter expresses the opinion that the laws of the United States are adequate to the protection of our seamen, and adds that the execution of these laws devolves mostly on consuls; some of whom, it suggests, in British ports, may have been "delinquent in the discharge of their duty." Now it is undeniable that outrages on board of our ships have actually occurred; and it is equally well known, and I myself hereby testify, that the majority of these outrages pass without any punishment whatever. Most of them, moreover, in the trade between America and England, have come under my own consular supervision, and been fully investigated by me. If I have possessod the power to punish these offences, and, whether through sluggishness or fear or favor, have failed to exercise it, then I am guilty of a great crime, which ought to be visited with a severity and an ignominy commensurate with its evil consequences; and those, surely, would be nothing less than national. If I am innocent,--if I have done my utmost, as an executive officer, under a defective law, to the defects of which I have repeatedly called the attention of my superiors,--then, unquestionably, the Secretary has wronged me by a suggestion pointing so directly at myself. It trenches upon one of the few rights, as a citizen and as a man, which an office-holder might imagine himself to retain. I leave the matter with the Department. It is peculiarly unfortunate for me that my resignation is already in the hands of the President; for, going out of office under this stigma, I foresee that I shall be supposed to have committed official suicide, as the only mode of escaping some worse fate. Whether it is right that an honorable and conscientious discharge of duty should be rewarded by loss of character, I leave to the wisdom and justice of the Department to decide. I am, sir, most respectfully,

Your obedient servant,
NATH. HAWTHORNE.
GEN. LEWIS CASS,
SECRETARY OF STATE, WASHINGTON, D.C.

--The General's reply is given below:--
DEPARTMENT OF STATE, WASHINGTON,
Sept. 24, 1857.
NATHANIEL HAWTHORNE, Esq., Consul, Liverpool

SIR.- Your despatch, No. 90, of the 17th of June last, upon the maltreatment of seamen on board vessels of the United States, was duly received. The note to Lord Napier, which accompanied it, was correctly published in the English journals, but without the previous knowledge or consent of this Department. You seem to suppose that some of its expressions may have been intended to charge you with delinquency in your official duties towards seamen. No such intention, however, was entertained; and now that you are about to retire from your position, I am happy to bear testimony to the prudent and efficient manner in which you have discharged your duties. I owe it to myself, however, to add that I perceive nothing in the letter to Lord Napier which justifies the construction you have placed on it. On the contrary, while it admits that some delinquency, on the part of our Consuls, in executing the laws of the United States concerning seamen, is not absolutely impossible, it expressly disclaims all knowledge of such delinquency; and where offenders have escaped punishment, it attributes the escape to causes over which our Consuls could exercise no control. What you say with regard to the evils that afflict our commercial marine, it is not now necessary to consider; but you quite misapprehend my views if you suppose that I am insensible to the magnitude of these evils, or could have ever intended to deny their existence. I concur with you in opinion, however, that they are not so much chargeable to defective laws as to the want of that very class of persons whom the laws were made to protect. While, therefore, our statutes may be, and probably are, as well adapted to their objects as those of any other country, it is none the less true that our merchant service suffers constantly from the want of American seamen. How this want can be supplied, is a question to which, in my note to Lord Napier, it was not my purpose to reply. I am, sir,

Your obedient servant,
LEWIS CASS

--Of the same date is the subjoined communication, accepting Hawthorne's resignation:--

DEPARTMENT OF STATE, WASHINGTON,
Sept. 24, 1857.
NATHANIEL HAWTHORNE,
Esq., U. S. Consul, Liverpool.

SIR,--I have to acknowledge the receipt of your despatches to No. 95, inclusive, with their respective enclosures. In transmitting the enclosed communication, in which you are requested to deliver the Archives of the Consulate at Liverpool to Mr. Beverly Tucker, the gentleman appointed by the President to be your successor, it gives the Department pleasure, on your voluntary retirement, to express its acknowledgments for the valuable information and suggestions relative to our commercial interests, which you have, from time to time, communicated, and to assure you of its satisfaction with the manner in which you have discharged the laborious and responsible duties of the office.

I am, sir, your obedient servant,
LEWIS CASS.

--The next two letters are from Henry Wilding, the head clerk of the Consulate, and Hawthorne's faithful friend and assistant during his incumbency. They refer to details connected with the office, and incidentally illustrate the spirit in which such things were conducted by the Foreign Office of that day:

LIVERPOOL, May 5, 1858.

MY DEAR SIR,--It required a search through the books, to find the names of the persons for whom the unclaimed wages were paid, before I could answer your letter. I have been slow in doing it, as my health is still too precarious to admit of my working in the evening unless the need were very pressing. I now enclose a statement of the amount, and the names, which, should be signed by you and sent to the fifth Auditor when you pay the money to Barings, when receipt should also be forwarded. There have been two letters about the disbursement accounts, one informing you that you had overdrawn for some three dollars against the account to September, 1856. You may remember this was drawn for while I was away, and it was found that only one part of the account had been drawn for, and neither yourself nor Mr. Pearce nor Mr. Shaw could tell what exchange had been drawn at; we drew for the rest of the account, leaving the exchange unsettled. No doubt the three dollars is the difference of exchange. The other letter was to say that the accounts (disbursement to June 30, 1857) had been adjusted, and that the amount charged for loss of exchange had been suspended, as there was no proof of your having actually sustained the loss on selling your drafts. I have been in communication with Baring, who informed me that you did not sell them your drafts, but only sent them out for collection; but they have furnished me with a statement which I think must satisfy the very particular Comptroller. I will forward it from here to Washington. A letter also informs me that your draft for office-rent has been paid, but that the amount has been placed against you in the books of the Treasury "until you furnish vouchers." What will you do? I have obtained a voucher for what you actually paid, including rate, and enclose amended account for your signature, if you should determine to claim the amount, which I certainly should do. The amount drawn for was the full ten per cent, amounting to $583.56. Of the accounts for fees there is not a word. I hope their silence means assent. I should think if they are not satisfied about the protest money they would have written before this. However, I will write to you if I hear anything. There is a bill before the Senate to amend the Consular Law. I don't know the provisions, but I believe an attempt is being made to allow clerk-hire. Pity they can't make that retrospective. We have still the regular succession of complaints,--brutal officers and vicious sailors, suffering and misery before us all day, and not to be forgotten at night.

Yours truly,
H. WILDING.

U. S. CONSULATE, Nov. 14, 1861.

DEAR SIR,--The enclosed letter to you was received here three months since. While you were in Italy, letters were received informing you that the sums charged in your accounts for losses of exchange were disallowed for want of vouchers. On communicating with Barings, it appeared that you had not *sold* your drafts to them, but only left them with them for collection. I got such certificates from them as they were willing to sign, and wrote to the Comptroller, showing him that although you had not sustained such loss in a literal sense, you had practically in the shape of interest commissions, etc. I heard no more of it, and supposed the matter settled. From this letter of the 8th inst. it appears that the certificates and explanation were accepted as to part of the amount only; why they were not for the rest, I cannot imagine. At this distance of time it is difficult to get at the accounts and vouchers among the mass of dusty accumulations, and one's memory affords but little help. I am therefore unable to ascertain the nature of all the items making up the $189.41, but believe they were all losses by exchange. I have found the vouchers for the $5.80, copies of which were ordered sent with the accounts. If you send these to the Comptroller he will have that amount brought to your credit, but I fear you will have to submit to the loss of the remainder, unless you can attack the present Comptroller more successfully than I did the other. It is a manifest injustice, as of course you had to pay Baring's commissions for collecting the drafts, and interest on the money advanced to pay the accounts. . . I am still at the Consulate, battling with hard captains and sailors,--struggling to do right amid threats and discouragements, when the truth is hard to find.

With best wishes and affectionate regards to you all,
HENRY WILDING.

--The last letter received before leaving England was this cordial one from the Rev. W. H. Channing:--

7 MONTPELIER TERRACE, UPPER PARLIAMENT ST.,
Dec.29, 1857.

MY DEAR MRS. HAWTHORNE,-Your most welcome note reached me this morning; and I at once reply, to tell you how rejoiced we all are that the communication between as is again opened. For I have felt as if the cable had snapped in the salt seas, and no message more might pass. What had become of you all we could not discover, and so fancied you as enjoying yourselves amid the gay splendors of Paris and the sunny scenes of Florence and Rome. But last week, one day, I met Mr. Wilding,--having called before at the office when he was ill,--and then learned with astonishment and sorrow that you were still in England, and that you had all been suffering from measles. How very sad your experience had been, however, I had no conception till your note arrived. Thank Heaven, the worst seems past. Please let me know your future movements, and your direction for the ensuing months; for we must not let the cable break again if we can help it.

Since I saw you I have made three charming trips,--to Wales, Devonshire, and Yorkshire. The last was especially interesting, as I visited Haworth and Bolton Priory. The day was dreary in extreme, with gloomy fog half veiling the mysterious hills, which, resting on their folded arms, bowed solemnly as we swept by. Not a breath of wind was stirring; all was still, as if in sleep. As I stood on the doorstep of the parsonage, and gazed into the narrow garden enclosure, which separates the house from the desolate graveyard, with its green mounds and mossy monuments, it seemed to me that the black gnarled shrubbery, and the dank, brown flower-beds, where the wilted stalks hung heavy with the wet, wonderfully symbolized dear Charlotte Bronte's sorrows. And seeing the scene in its hour of desolation, it was easy to fancy the sunbursts and wild breezes from the heathery moorland, and the spotless, snowy moonlights. . . .

And so, with cordial and affectionate greetings to one and all of you, from each and all of us, I am

Yours faithfully,

W. H. CHANNING.

Happy New Year!

--On the eve of embarking, Hawthorne delivered his English journals into the keeping of his friend, Henry Bright, with the accompanying little note:--

DEAR MR. BRIGHT,--Here are these journals. If unreclaimed by myself, or by my heirs or assigns, I consent to your breaking the seals in the year 1900, -not a day sooner. By that time, probably, England will be a minor republic, under the protection of the United States. If my countrymen of that day partake in the least of my feelings, they will treat you generously.

Your friend,

NATH. HAWTHORNE

--On the 3d of January, a gloomy and wintry day, we took the train to Folkestone, and two days later arrived in Paris.

CHAPTER 5 - DONATI'S COMET

IT might be said, from one point of view, that Hawthorne was better satisfied with Italy than with England; the reason being that he cared for it and sympathized with it less. One is apt to be a more severe critic of one's blood relations than of strangers; and the characteristics or a remote antiquity touch our hearts less than those of a comparatively recent past, wherein, perhaps, inhere some roots of our own. Hawthorne's attitude towards England was that of a descendant jealous of his ancestor's honor; nothing in her less good than the best would satisfy him. Upon Italy, however, his eyes rested with no deeper sentiment than belongs to a respectful and intelligent curiosity. He had no personal stake in the matter; whatever faults or perfections Italy might possess, were merely phenomenal to him, not vital. The Italian genius had no affiliations with his own; it was objective to his mind,-- something to examine into and speculate about, not intuitively to apprehend. The Italian people might be what they chose and do as they liked; his equanimity would remain undisturbed. But he could not be equally tranquil in the contemplation of any English shortcomings or perversities.

In process of time, it is true, he conceived an affection for Italy, or, to speak more precisely, for Rome. But it was an entirely aesthetic affection, such as may be aroused by beautiful statues and pictures, by music, blue skies, and gentle atmosphere. It resembled the delight that one feels in poetry, in romance, in the aroma of a mighty and splendid civilization long since passed away. It was such an affection as gives pleasure, but is not profound enough to give pain; able to soothe the heart, but impotent to break it. Hawthorne has given full expression to his feeling for Italy in the romance the scene of which is laid there; and in his case the feeling happened to be deepened by the poignant anxiety and suffering which he underwent for many months, in Rome, by reason of the dangerous illness of his eldest daughter. This personal emotion, associated with the region in which it bad come upon him, engrafted upon his merely Roman thoughts a tenderer and more sacred sentiment. It inspired in him a sort of dread, and even hatred, of the Eternal City; yet, having said farewell to it, he looked back to it with something of the yearning which one feels for a beloved grave.

The "Italian Note-Books," and "The Romance of Monte-Beni"--which is perhaps the most widely read of all Hawthorne's works, owing to its extensive circulation in Rome in the Tauchnitz edition--have made the public better acquainted with this period of the author's life than with any other. It was, for the most part, a period of much quiet happiness. The annoyances and restrictions of office had been laid aside forever, and there was nothing to do but to contemplate and enjoy. Hawthorne had, from his youth, been deeply read in the ancient and mediaeval history of Italy; and shortly before leaving England, he had caused his children to study Grote and Gibbon, and to learn by heart Macaulay's "Lays of Ancient Rome." Mrs. Hawthorne possessed, in addition to this, no little practical knowledge of classic and Italian art, and an almost inexhaustible capacity for seeing and appreciating such masterpieces as Italy overflows with. So that, upon the whole, the party was fairly well prepared for what was before them. It was the first complete holiday that Hawthorne had yet had; he was, as he expressed it, no longer a servant but a sovereign, and looked down "even upon the President." The people whom he was destined to meet with during his Italian residence were almost all Americans of the better class, with two or three of whom he formed lasting friendships; and his mind, having thrown aside the rights and wrongs of American seamen, began to concentrate itself upon the idea of a romance, detached fragments of which had been floating in his brain almost ever since his arrival in England.

Starting early in January, the cold weather met us at Folkestone, and did not altogether retreat until the ensuing March. The means of getting warm were imperfect in France, and wholly deficient in Italy; and Hawthorne frequently alludes to the discomfort which this constant chilliness occasioned. "This morning," he writes (Jan. 10), "Paris looked as black as London, with clouds and rain; and when we issued forth, it seemed as if a cold, sullen agony were interposed between each separate atom of our bodies. In all my experience of bad atmospheres, methinks I never knew anything so atrocious as this. England has nothing to be compared with it." And again: "The wicked chill of the air, and the increasing rain, now compelled us to set out homeward on foot. We looked anxiously for a cab, but saw none; and called to passing omnibuses, but found them all full, or going in wrong directions. We invaded the little shop of a second-hand bookseller (a dirty hole, and of ill odor), and stayed there a considerable time, hoping for some means of escape; but finally had to plunge forth and paddle onward, through rain and mud, amid this old, ugly, and dirty quarter of Paris, till we reached the Arcade along the Rue Rivoli. There we were under shelter all the way to the Hotel."--The only warm recollections connected with this visit to Paris are of the great eider-down bedquilts in the hotel, a foot thick, covered with crimson silk and as light as a feather. Ten minutes beneath one of these would have produced a perspiration in Siberia.

Before leaving Paris, we had the pleasure of makmg the acquaintance of Miss Maria Mitchell, the astronomer, who accompanied us to Rome, and was our neighbor during the greater part of our stay there. There was a simplicity and a dry humor about this lady that made her company delightful and consoling; as if a bit of shrewd, primitive, kindly New England were walking and talking in the midst of the gray antiquity of Europe. Hawthorne also called upon Judge Mason, the American Minister of that epoch, who was just at the end of his official existence,--

" a fat-brained, good~hearted, sensible old man. I fear the poor gentleman is going back, with narrow means, to seek some poor office at home for his livelihood. The Secretary of Legation is a man of very different aspect and address from the Minister: about thirty years old, dark-complexioned, with a black mustache, handsome, with a courteous but decided air, like a man of society and the world. I should think the heavy old Judge would often need some spirit more alert than his own. On the whole, (though I am sorry for him) there is no good reason why Uncle Sam should pay Judge Mason seventeen thousand dollars a year for sleeping in the dignified post of Ambassador to France. The true ground of complaint is, that, whether he slept or waked, the result would be the same."

On the 12th of January we left Paris,--" a very chill morning, and the rain began to fall as we left the hotel,"--spent that night at the Hotel de Provence in Lyons, and late the following day arrived at bleak and windy Marseilles. Here two uncomfortable days were spent, and then we embarked on board the steamer "Calabrese" for Civita Vecchia. The sun shone during this voyage, and at night the stars were brilliant; but the temperature was more that of the North Sea than of the Mediterranean. We stopped at Genoa, and shivered through some of the palaces and churches there; and again at Leghorn, which was uninteresting as well as ungenial; and so reached Civita Vecchia, the forlornest spot of all.

The railroad was not at that time in existence, and we must travel by *vettura*. The road was reported to be infested by brigands; and as the journey had to be performed after dark, it acquired somthing of the character of an adventure. Fortunately perhaps for us, the mail-carriage started at the same time that we did, and the mail officials carried arms. But our wretched steeds were hard put to it to keep pace with the nimble horses of the Government; and finally they gave up the chase, though not until the more dangerous part of the road had been passed. Hawthorne had with him a large sum of money in napoleons; and soon after starting he proceeded to bestow this in various improbable hiding-places,--I remember the inside of an old umbrella was made the repository of a good deal of it. Hawthorne laughed and joked while making these arrangements; and the children imbibed the notion that the whole affair was a game, played for their entertainment, and that the brigands were as mythical as the giants and enchanters of Spenser's "Faerie Queene." But, once, the figures of two men, in conical hats, and each with a long gun in his hand, appeared outlined against the evening sky on a high bank beneath which we drove. They did not attempt to stop us, however, and we reached the gates of Rome, without casualties, somewhere near midnight, in a cold, sleety rain-storm. The hotel that received us was only a degree less chilly and dreary than the street; and none of the party became really warm for a month or more. Hawthorne suffered the most, having caught a cold before leaving Paris, which had developed into a virulent influenza. He sat by the windy and wintry cavern called a fireplace, muffled up in rugs and great-coats, and seldom ventured outdoors when he could help it. He was too much benumbed even to write his journal, although, as he remarks, his impressions during the first fortnight would have shown modern Rome in an aspect in which it has never yet been depicted. A suite of rooms was rented in No. 37 Palazzo Larazani, Via Porta Pinciana; and there we waited for Italy to appear, for this did not seem at all like Italy. "Old Rome," said Hawthorne, "lies like a dead and mostly decayed corpse, retaining here and there a trace of the noble shape it was, but with a sort of fungous growth upon it, and no life but of the worms that creep in and out."

A few sallies were made, during this arctic interval, to acquire some idea of what was to be seen hereafter; but without very promising results. Even the St. Petersburg atmosphere could not diminish the grandeur of the Coliseum; but St. Peter's was, at first, a disappointment to Hawthorne. The fountains in the Piazza were frozen on our first visit, and boys were sliding on the ice. Of the church he says: "It disappointed me terribly by its want of effect, and the little justice it does to its real magnitude, externally; but the interior blazed upon me with altogether unexpected magnificence, so brilliant is it, with pictures, gilding, variegated and polished marbles, and all that splendor which I tried in vain to describe in the churches of Genoa. I had expected something vast and dim, like the great English cathedrals, only more vast and dim and gray; but there is as much difference as between noonday and twilight. I never saw or imagined so bright and splendid an interior as that of this immense church; but I am not sure that it would not be more grand and majestic if it were less magnificent, though I should be sorry to see the experiment tried." The narrow and dirty streets, with their uneven pavements, did not encourage pedestrianism. "Along these lanes, or gullies, a chill wind blows; down into their depths the sun never falls; they are bestrewn with the filth of the adjacent houses, which rise on each side to the height of five or six stories, generally plastered and whitewashed, and looking neither old nor new. Probably these houses have the brick and stone of old Rome in them,--of the Coliseum, and many another stately structure,--but they themselves look like magnified hovels. The lower regions of palaces come to strange uses in Rome: a cobbler or a tinker perhaps exercises his craft under the archway; a cook-shop may be established in one of the apartments;" and similar miscegenations.

It was towards St. Peter's, however, that Hawthorne most often bent his steps in these days, partly, no doubt, because its temperature had none of the malignancy of the outer air, or even of other buildings; and partly, and chiefly, because the superb incarnation of religious faith which it presented powwerfully fascinated him,--none the less because such an incarnation was so totally opposed to every religious tradition and association in which he had been educated. He has given expression to his thoughts on the matter in the description of Hilda's experience with the confessional; but it may be worth while to repeat his own words, untinged by the imaginative element.--"Saint Peter's," he says,

"offers itself as a place of worship and religious comfort for the whole human race; and in one of the transepts I found a range of confessionals, where the penitent might tell his sins in the tongue of his own country, whether French, German, Polish, English, or what not. If I had had a murder on my conscience, or any other great sin, I think I should have been inclined to kneel down there, and pour it into the safe secrecy of the confessional. What an institution that is man needs it so, that it seems as if God must have ordained it. The popish religion certainly does apply itself most closely and comfortably to human occasions; and I cannot but think that a great many people find their spiritual advantage in it, who would find none at all in our formless mode of worship. You cannot think it all a farce when you see peasant, citizen, and soldier coming into the church, each on his own hook, and kneeling for moments or for hours, directing his silent devotions to some particular shrine; too humble to approach his God directly, and therefore seeking the mediation of some saint who stands beside the Infinite Presence."

With February came the Carnival, which Hawthorne conscientiously inspected, and accepted its liberties, so far as they affected himself, with great good humor; but he would scarcely have seen so much of it as he did, but for the obligation imposed upon him by his children, who, of course, thought it the most glorious frolic that had ever been devised. He used to stroll along the streets, with a linen duster over his black coat, looking at everything, and laughing whenever the *confetti* struck him,-- occasionally, too, doing vigorous battle himself for a minute or two; and if the weather had not been so discouraging, he might have entered into the affair with more zeal, but as it was, he did not enjoy it much. "The festival," he says,

"seems to have sunk from the upper classes to the lower ones and probably it is only kept alive by tradition, and the curiosity which impels foreigners to join in it. The balconies were mostly filled with ladies, some of whom sat nearly on a level with the passers-by, in full dress, with deep-colored Italian faces, ready to encounter whatever the chances of the Carnival might bring them. The upper balconies (and there was sometimes a third, if not a fourth tier) were occupied, I think, chiefly by English or Americans; nor, I fancy, do the Roman ladies of rank and respectablity generally display themselves at this time. The confetti are very nasty things, resembling sugar-plums as the apples of Sodom do better fruit, being really made up of lime--or bad flour at best--with oats or worthless seeds as a nucleus; and they readily crumble and turn to dirty dust, making the hair irreverently hoary, and giving a miller-like aspect to hat and clothes. The bouquets were composed of the most ordinary flowers, and were miserably wilted, as if they had served two or three carnival-days already; they were muddy, too, as having been picked up from the pavement. Such were the flowery favors--the bunches of sentiment--that flew to and fro along the Corso, from lady to knight and back again; and I suppose they aptly enough symbolized the poor, battered, wilted, stained hearts, that had flown from one hand to another, along the muddy pathway of life, instead of being treasured in one faithful bosom. Really, it was great nonsense. There were some queer shapes and faces,--clowns, harlequins, apes' snouts, young men in feminine guise, and *vice versa*, and several samples of Italian costume; but either the masques were not very funny, or I was not in a funny mood,--there was little or nothing to laugh at. Upon my honor, I never in my life knew a shallower joke than the Carnival at Rome; and such a rainy and muddy day, too! Greenwich Fair was worth a hundred of it. I could not make it out to be the Roman's festival, or anybody's festival. It was curious, however, to see how safely the Corso was guarded; a strong patrol of the Papal Dragoons, in steel helmets and white cloaks, were stationed at the street corners, and rode up and down the thoroughfare singly or in a body. Detachments of the French troops stood by their stacked muskets in the Piazza del Popolo, and at the other end of the Corso; and if the chained tiger-cat (meaning thereby the Roman populace) had but shown the tips of its claws, the bullets would have been flying along the street. But the tiger-cat is a harmless brute."

--Hawthorne has drawn upon these notes in the description of the Carnival which appears in "The Marble Faun;" but he also does fuller justice, there, to the attractive features of the spectacle.

One of the first calls that Hawthorne made in Rome was upon William Story, whom he had met, as a young man, in America, and who now contributed not a little towards bringing him acquainted with what was worth seeing and knowing in Rome, and towards his general enjoyment. Hawthorne often talked and walked with him, and admired cordially the sculptor's own work,--the statue of "Cleopatra" had been just begun; and I remember Story's speaking to Hawthorne about another classic subject he had in contemplation, a figure of the Emperor Nero, as he lies in hiding, listening for the steps of his approaching executioners, and trying to screw up his courage to cut his own throat. It was Story, I think, who introduced Hawthorne to Miss Lander, who wished to make a bust of him. He gave her sittings, accordingly; and took her portrait while she took his. "Miss Lander," he says,

"is from my own native town, and appears to have genuine talent, and spirit and independence enough to give it fair play. She is living here quite alone, in delightful freedom, and has sculptured two or three things that may make her favorably known. 'Virginia Dare' is certainly very beautiful. During the sitting I talked a good deal with Miss Lander, being a little inclined to take a similar freedom with her moral likeness to that which she was taking with my physical one. There are very available points about her and her position: a young woman, living in almost perfect independence, thousands of miles from her New England home, going fearlessly about these mysterious streets, by night as well as by day; with no household ties, nor rule or law but that within her; yet acting with quietness and simplicity, and keeping, after all, within a homely line of right. In her studio she wears a sort of pea-jacket, buttoned across her breast, and a little foraging-cap, just covering the top of her head. She has become strongly attached to Rome, and says that when she dreams of home, it is merely of paying a short visit, and coming back before her trunk is unpacked."

--The bust, which was a tolerable likeness in the clay, was put into marble in due course. But while it was undergoing this process, a mishap befell it. A gentleman--I will not mention his name, but he was an American and a person of culture--happened to be in Rome at the time the marble work was proceeding (of course under the hands of the regular workmen employed by sculptors for that purpose, and whose only business it is to reproduce accurately the model placed before them). Hawthorne and Miss Lander were both absent from Rome; and this critic, visiting the studio, noticed what he thought were some errors in the modelling of the lower part of the face, and directed the marble-cutters to make certain alterations, for which he accepted the responsibility. The result was, as might have been expected, that the likeness was destroyed; and the bust, in its present state, looks like a combination of Daniel Webster and George Washington,--as any one may see who pays a visit to the Concord Library, of which institution it is an appurtenance.

It was during the early spring that Hawthorne and his wife, straying one morning into the church of the Capuchins, saw the dead monk which figures so impressively in "The Marble Faun." Hawthorne himself was evidently much impressed by the spectacle, and dwells upon it at some length. "He had been a somewhat short and punchy personage," he says,

"this poor monk, and had perhaps died of apoplexy; for his face did not look pale, but had almost, or quite, the natural flush of life, though the feet were of such a yellow, waxy hue. His gray eyebrows were very thick, and my wife had a fancy that she saw him contort them. A good many people were standing round the bier; and one woman knelt and kissed the dead monk's beads. By and by, as we moved round from chapel to chapel, still with our eyes turning often to the dead monk, we saw some blood oozing from his nostrils! Perhaps his murderer--or his doctor--had just then come into the church and drawn nigh the bier; at all events, it was about as queer a thing as I ever witnessed. We soon came away, and left him lying there,--a sight which I shall never forget."

The weather moderated somewhat as March drew near, and Hawthorne made his first visits to many of the chief objects of interest in Rome. He saw "Beatrice Cenci," the sculptures of the Capitol, and of the Vatican, the Forum, the Pantheon, and numerous churches and picture-galleries. Hawthorne was inclined to prefer sculptures to paintings,--especially the paintings of sacred subjects. "There is a terrible lack of variety in them," he says.

"A quarter part of the Borghese collection, I should think, consists of Virgins and Infant Christs, repeated over and over again, in pretty much the same spirit, and often with no more mixture of the divine in the picture than just enough to spoil it as a representation of maternity, with which everybody's heart has something to do. Then half of all the rest of the pictures are crucifixions, subjects from the Old Testament, or scenes in the lives of the saints; and the remainder are mythological. These old painters seldom treated their subjects in a homely way; they are above life, or on one side of it. Raphael, and other great painters, have done wonders with sacred subjects; but the greatest wonder is, how they could paint them at all; and always they paint them from the outside, and not from within."

--He relented somewhat from the severity of this opinion afterwards; but his Puritan conscience, more than his aesthetic sympathies, was, I think, responsible for much of his acquaintance with ancient pictorial art.

Slowly the Roman sun began to make its power felt; and its warmth inspired Hawthorne with a greater degree both of physical and of mental activity. Every day some fresh expedition was made; and the conceptions of a new romance were slowly assuming shape in the author's mind. The Faun of Praxiteles was to be the central figure of the story, which, as first imagined, was to have been brief and lightly touched. The description of the statue, in the romance, is an almost word-for-word reproduction of that in the Note-Books, even to the reproduction of a slight error respecting the position of the left arm. By degrees the original idea grew and developed, until, in its final form, it became the most elaborate and the longest tale that Hawthorne has written. The latter attribute is, however, mainly due to the number of descriptions of Roman and Florentine scenes, which, as he remarks, he had not the heart to cancel; and he might have added, that, in addition to their intrinsic beauty, they afford a grateful relief to the terrible and darksome events which make up the tissue of the story.

Among the most intimate of our Roman acquaintances were the family of Mr. C. G. Thompson, the artist, who had painted Hawthorne's portrait just previous to the latter's leaving America. They had been resident in Rome for several years, and the children--a girl and two boys--were valuable acquisitious in the way of companions to the younger members of Hawthorne's household. Under the guidance of Edmund and Hubert, the present writer, at all events, became more familiar with Rome and its environs than he ever was with his native city. They are a very kind and agreeable family," Hawthorne writes,--

"both grown people and children. During an evening that we spent with them, Mr. Ropes and his wife came in, he being an American landscape-painter, from my own old town indeed and likewise another American artist, with his wife. I suppose there is a class feeling among the artists who reside here, and they create a sort of atmosphere among themselves, which they do not find anywhere else, and which is comfortable for them to live in. Nevertheless they are not generous nor gracious critics of one another; and I hardly remember any full-breathed and whole-souled praise from sculptor to sculptor or from painter to painter. They dread one another's ill-word, and scrupulously exchange little attentions, for fear of giving offence; they pine, I suspect, at the sight of another's success, and would willingly keep a rich stranger from the door of any studio save their own. Their public is so much more limited than that of literary men that they have the better excuse for these petty jealousies. I do not mean to include Mr. Thompson in the above remarks; for I believe him to be an excellent man, and know him to be most friendly towards me, and, as an artist, earnestly aiming at beautiful things and achieving them. In the course of our visit he produced several rich portfolios, one containing some sketches from nature by an eminent German landscape-painter, long resident in Rome, and now deceased; another contained the contributions of many artists, his friends,--little pencil drawings and watercolor sketches, bits of landscapes, likenesses,--in short, an artistic album; another was a most curious collection of sketches, many of them very old, and by celebrated painters, which he had partly picked up at the shops of dealers in such things, but had bought the greater part in a lump for about two dollars. He conjectures that they were part of the collection of some old Cardinal, at whose death the servants had stolen them, and sold them for what they would fetch. Here were pen-and-pencil sketches and pencil-drawings, on coarse and yellow paper of centuries ago, often very bold and striking; the 'motives,' as artists say, or first hints and rude designs of pictures which were afterwards painted, and very probably were never equal to these original conceptions. Some of the sketches were so rough and hasty that the eye could hardly follow the design; yet, when you caught it, it proved to he full of fire and spirit. Others were exceedingly careful and accurate, yet seemed hardly the less spirited for that; and in almost all cases, whether rough or elaborate, they gave one a higher idea of the imaginative scope and toil of artists than I generally get from the finished pictures."

--It was evidently upon this "sketch" that Hawthorne based his picture of the studio of Miriam, with her portfolios of drawings.

Mrs. Jameson, author of " Lives of the Painters," was likewise among the friends of this period; and it was impossible not to like and respect the venerable old lady, although, in her role of prophetess of Italian culture, it was not always easy for Hawthorne to keep pace with her. Bryant was in Rome, too; and somewhat detailed mention of him is made in the Note-Books, though his name, as well as that of Sumner, of whom he spoke to Hawthorne, is generally omitted from the published passages. Miss Bremer and Miss Harriet Hosmer also appeared, and left pleasant memories behind them. But the malarious season in Rome was now at hand; and after having made an engagement (not without much chaffering) with a *vetturino* to transport us to Florence, all expenses included, for the sum of one hundred scudi, more or less, we set forth on the morning of the 24th of May, after a residence of little more than four months, and in the midst of an avalanche of curses from the servant whom we had employed during our sojourn, and her mother, prompted by Hawthorne's refusal to present them with a week's extra wages, in addition to the fortnight's warning which they had had. But the weather was superb, and the ten days' journey was accomplished without either death by apoplexy or any other misfortune. The railroad has taken the place of the carriage-road since those days, and I suppose the charms of the latter are unknown to the majority of visitors to Italy. But nothing could be more novel or delightful. The scenery is at no point other than beautiful or striking, apart from the historical interest of the scenes; the early summer air is both soft and inspiriting; and ever and anon we arrive at strange, mountainous villages, remote and lonely, and looking as if they were but natural modifications of the gray rock on which they are built. The fare provided was always ample and good, and all the labor of attending to that and other minor details is taken off the traveller's hands by the *vetturino*. Whenever there was a hill to climb,--and that happened often,--Hawthorne would alight, and, accompanied by his son, walk on in advance, every step bringing us farther into the heart of the matchless Italian landscape. At night we had sound and comfortable sleep in some grotesque old inn, perched aloft, perhaps, upon some naked hill-top, or nestling beside some famous lake or stream in the narrow valleys. The only drawback to enjoyment was the beggars, of whom the entire population of most of the towns on the route was composed. But after a while custom gives them a sort of semi-invisibility, and they scarcely interfere with one's appreciation of the sights and scenes amidst which they swarm, more than so many flies or mosquitoes. One cannot help wondering what has become of these innumerable mendicants, now that there are steam-engines to take foreigners out of the way.

"This journey from Rome," says Hawthorne, has been one of the brightest and most uncareful interludes of my life." And the same may be said of the entire Florentine experience. The chilliness of Rome at first, and the languor of spring afterwards, robbed his residence there of much of its charm. But the five or six months now to come had in them nothing that was not delightful. There was a lovely ardor about the Florentine summer that is not met with elsewhere; and the city itself so overflowed with beauty that nothing mere could have been desired. Such friends as Hiram Powers and Mr. and Mrs. Browning afforded all that nature and art could not supply; and the freedom from all present labor and all anxiety for the morrow gave an inward pleasantness to every moment. I believe this to have been, upon the whole, the happiest period of Hawthorne's life. To every life, probably, some such season comes; and six months is perhaps as long a draught of it as any mortal has a right to expect. The illness of his daughter cast a dark shadow over the remainder of Hawthorne's Italian experience; and after that, his gradually failing health made existence not seem so sweet that he could feel much regret to have done with it.

The Casa Bella, a floor of which we occupied from the date of our arrival until the 1st of August, was a fresh and bright-looking edifice, handsomely furnished and fitted, built round a court full of flowers, trees, and turf. A terrace, protected from the sun by a rustic roof built over it, extended along one side of the interior, and low windows or glass doors opened upon it. The house was all light and grace, and well deserved its title: a room, giving upon the garden, was used by Hawthorne as his study; and there, when not wandering about the genial, broad-flagged streets or in the galleries and churches and public gardens, he used to sit and sketch out his romance,--the English romance, I think, not the Italian one. He did not write very much as yet, however; the weather would have made it difficult to stay indoors in the daytime, even had the other attractions to go forth not been so alluring; and in the evenings, Powers or some other friend was apt to come in, or he visited Powers's studio, or went to Casa Guidi, near by, where the Brownings were. The lazy luxury of Italian life made itself strongly felt. Looking from the street windows of our apartment, I used often to watch with envy a young ostler, appertaining to a stable on the opposite corner, who was in the habit of lounging out, naked to the waist, with a broom in his hand, and spend an hour or two dawdling about the pavement and chatting with his acquaintances. His torso was statuesque, and his skin as smooth as a woman's, and he looked exceedingly comfortable and contented. In Powers's studio, across the way, were the statues which the world knows, and some which few, perhaps, have seen; and Powers himself, tall and strong, with his paper cap, his white apron, his immense black eyes, and his pleasant smile. But there also, within a five minutes' stroll, were the Duomo, most beautiful of Italian churches, and the Campanile, and all the noble charm of the Palazzo Vecchio and the Piazza del Gran Duca; and the Pitti and Uffizzi galleries, and the Boboli Gardens. And it was hard to linger even here, when one thought of the Ponte Vecchio, with its strange incrustation of old houses; and the Lung' Arno, and the Casino; and the sunny hills outside the walls, with their fragrant plantations òf olive and vine. When mankind returns to the Golden Age, such cities as Florence will be the rule, instead of the exception.

Hawthorne began once more his study of pictures, with somewhat better success than heretofore. He appreciated Raphael more, and found some other painters losing their hold upon him. The "Madonna della Seggiola" seemed to him, at this time, "the most beautiful picture in the world;" and he speaks harshly of Titian's "Magdalen,"--but from the moral not the artistic, point of view. In fact, he had not got so far in his pictorial training as to analyze the composition of a picture; he observed the workmanship, whether it were finished or rough, and the colors, whether they were brilliant or dull; but, for the rest, he accepted the work as it was, and either liked it or not, as if it were a pleasant or a disagreeable person. Of technicalities,--difficulties overcome, harmony of lines, and so forth,--he had no explicit knowledge; they produced their effect upon him, of course, but without his recognizing the manner of it. All that concerned him was the sentiment which the artist had meant to express; the means and method were comparatively unimportant. He accepted and respected the Dutch masters because they came into direct rivalry with concrete nature, and he could test the accuracy of their rendering by his own observation; but in the higher spheres of the art he continually found the beauty of the idea obstructed by the imperfection of the materials, and could not be quite happy about it. He wished that the "Transfiguration" might have combined Raphael's breadth with Gerard Douw's minuteness; the more strongly his imagination was appealed to, the more conscious was he of the discrepancy of execution. This discrepancy does not exist in the writer's art; there, the refinement and purity of the texture keeps pace with the beauty or grandeur of the conception; so that Hawthorne could not reason from the one to the other. I fancy, moreover, that he unloaded a good deal of his responsibility in this matter upon the shoulders of his wife, who rejoiced in pictures, not only for what they expressed but for what they were, and could take up his appreciation where it came to an end, and carry it on with enthusiasm. There is, in a letter of hers, written at this period, a description of the "Deposition" by Perugino, which may appositely be quoted here.

"It is a large picture, with perhaps twelve figures. The body of Christ, with Joseph of Arimathea at the feet, makes the base of a pyramidal group. At the head, tenderly holding it with both hands,--one low down at the back of the hair, and one at the brow,--kneels one of the Marys, looking earnestly at the dead face before her. The Virgin Mother kneels beside her Son, seizing the left arm, and gazing at him with lips apart, and deep eyes nearly quenched with tears,--an expression of boundless love; her grief communicates itself to all who see her, for it is a real and not a painted grief. Above the Madonna stands another Mary, looking down at the body with uplifted hands, with more passion in her attitude than the others; and she forms the apex of the pyramid. On the left kneels the third Mary, with folded bands, beautiful and absorbed, looking at Christ as if musing on the spectacle. These six make a perfect group, all with eyes fixed on the dead form. Behind Jesus kneels Saint Peter, a grand figure and head, support mg the body with both hands beneath the arms, but turning away, as unable to bear the sight. Above Peter is the fourth Mary, with clasped hands and bowed head and falling tears,--and she, I think, is Mary Magdalene. At her side is one of the disciples, united with the rest by his expression of unutterable sadness.

Above Joseph of Arimathea stands Saint John, perhaps the greatest triumph of genius of all. He does not look at Christ; his hands are locked, in desolation of spirit; his arms straight down, like iron, and his fingers strained and hard-pressed. But in his beautiful face is the marvel and the power. There is a strong passion of sorrow. He seems to gaze out of the picture, but his eyes do not meet your eyes. There is a bewilderment, an abandonment of grief, that causes a blank in his thoughts; also the calmness of that deepest emotion that cannot show itself by ordinary modes. He has gone into his own soul to mourn, finding nothing left for him without. A lovely landscape lies beyond,--the sun just gone down, even as the Sun of Righteousness has set. No one else need attempt to paint the 'Deposition.' Raphael's magnificent 'Entombment' does not equal this picture in sentiment, though in beauty and execution nothing could surpass it. Noble master! Noble pupil--also master! What immense magnetic force proceeds from a work like this, over which the artist lived and breathed for months or years,in devout, religious worship! Such pictures ought to be made eternal, for the benefit and culture of the nations."

Hawthorne's success with sculpture was always better, the conditions upon which to base a judgment being more sure and simple. He saw as much in the "Venus de' Medici" as any one, not a sculptor, has seen; and the "Lorenzo di' Medici," of Michael Angelo, was, in his opinion, a miracle in marble. "To take a block of marble and convert it wholly into thought! . . . Its naturalness is as if it came out of the marble of its own accord, with all its grandeur hanging heavily about it, and sat down there beneath its weight." And not less deep and creative was his insight into the bronze statue of Pope Julius III., in the market-place of Perugia; and of Marcus Aurelius, on the Capitoline Hill,--"the most majestic representation of the kingly character that ever the world has seen." He had many long talks on the subject of sculpture with Hiram Powers, who had the venial infirmity of believing that "no other man besides himself was worthy to touch marble," but whose ideas were "square, solid, and tangible, and therefore readily grasped and retained; . . . but when you have his ultimate thought and perception, you feel inclined to think and see a little further for yourself." The substance of many of these talks is given in the Note-Books; and it is entertaining to note how Hawthorne would eliminate from Powers's assertions the personal element, and then submit what remained to an analysis which, though perfectly unassuming, and deferential to the artist's superior knowledge, is always keen and often very destructive. In truth, Powers, in comparison with Michael Angelo and the great Greek sculptors, had learned only the alphabet of his art; he ended where they began, but was us bold and fertile in criticism as such incipient knowledge generally is.

The only external event that occurred during this month was the Feast of St. John,--in effect, a sort of carnival with the masks and the confetti omitted. Its only interest for Hawthorne and his wife was the opportunity it afforded them of having a glimpse of the Grand Duke and his court, who occupied the loggia of a house opposite our balcony, and who were resplendent in gold embroidery and diamonds, which last Mrs. Hawthorne described as "an indescribable fineness of fierceness,--so ethereal and so real,--like the crossing of wit in angels!" But the Grand Duke himself was not beautiful,--he "looked like a monkey with an evil disposition," and had "that frightful, coarse, protruding under-lip, peculiar to the Imperial race of Austria. It is worth while," adds Mrs. Hawthorne, "to extinguish the race for the sake of expunging that lip, and all it signifies."--I quote from her printed Journal.

The white sunshine, falling straight downwards upon the flat pavements of the Florentine streets, or striking against the stuccoed walls of the houses, and reflected thence upon the inhabitants, wrought a fervency of heat that was almost too much even for Hawthorne, tropic-loving though he was. But on the summit of the hill of Bellosguardo, a mile beyond the Porta Romana, there was an ancient castle or villa, belonging to the noble family of Montauto. The Count, the then bearer of the name and title, being, like so many of his peers, less rich in gold than in ancestors, was willing to rent his castle for what appeared to foreigners the unreasonably reasonable sum of forty scudi a month; the castle itself containing upwards of forty large rooms, besides a *podere,* or plantation of grapes and figs, a dozen acres in extent. There was, moreover, a historic tower, said to be haunted, and commanding a vast prospect of the valley of the Arno, hemmed in by distant hills; and whatever breath of air happened to be stirring was sure to find its way up to this height. Near at hand, across the gray groves of olives, was the tower to which Mrs. Browning had attached her poem of "Aurora Leigh;" and Galileo's tower was also visible from our battlements. Each member of the family had three or four rooms for his or her private use, and more than twenty were still left for our joint occupation. The podere was in charge of the contadini belonging to the estate, who were always ready to provide us with as many figs and grapes as we wanted. Each day after sunset the mighty and brilliant comet of Donati stretched itself across the valley in a great fiery arch, and remained in view till near morning. In addition to the ghost, the tower was tenanted by a couple of owls, who at dusk hovered forth on noiseless wings beneath the battlements with strange, melancholy hootings. It was the custom of Hawthorne and his family to ascend every evening to the summit of the tower, and sit or recline there till bedtime, looking at the comet and the stars, or watching the progress of the distant thunder-storms on the hills. Meanwhile the distance to the city was so inconsiderable that almost daily expeditions were made thither; and if the hill sometimes seemed steep on the way home, every step upward was into a fresher and more invigorating atmosphere. Hawthorne used to regret the lack of water in the view; but the constantly varying phenomena of clouds and sunshine, storm and calm, which the breadth of the valley made visible, atoned for this defect. The villa of Montauto was, as readers of Hawthorne know, the prototype of that of Monte Beni; though the latter is placed in another region, and the blue lakes and gleaming river, which were wanting to the former prospect, are supplied in the latter.

It was in this mountain stronghold that Hawthorne wrote the first sketch of "The Marble Faun," which he afterwards rewrote and elaborated in Redcar, on the northeastern coast of England. He had temporarily laid aside the idea of the English romance, which afterwards assumed at least three distinct shapes, but which he did not live to complete. His mind at this period was as fertile in imaginative conceptions as it had ever been in his life; and could he have spent four or five years in Montauto, instead of a couple of months, he might have written as many romances again as now bear his name. Probably he would have remained, had it not been for his children. But he wished his daughters to grow up in their own country, and his son to have an American education; nor could he free himself from a restless longing to see again the land of his birth. An exile commonly ascribes to his native country the best of the attractions of foreign lands and the attraction of home, besides. Hawthorne, however, looked forward to a return to Europe at some undefined date; and when be bade it farewell, he did not know it was forever.

About the beginning of October we set out on our return to Rome. It was Hawthorne's intention to finish his romance there, and then, passing rapidly through Switzerland and France, to stop in England only long enough to obtain his English copyright, and sail for America in June or July of 1859. But all these plans were upset by his daughter Una's illness. He wrote nothing while in Rome, and on reaching England decided to rewrite the book there; so that our return home was postponed one year. We did not follow the same route in returning to Rome that we had taken in leaving it. There was a railroad between Florence and Siena, to which town the train took us in about three hours. William Story and his family were living in a country-seat--the Villa Belvedere--outside the walls, and their presence made the strange old place familiar and pleasant to us. Siena seemed to Hawthorne the most picturesque town that he had seen in Italy, with the exception of Perugia, and he fancied that be would prefer it to Florence as a residence: "A thoughtful, shy man might settle down here with the view of making the place a home, and spend many years in a sombre kind of happiness." Mrs. Hawthorne was delighted with the frescos of Sodoma. Ten days were spent in Siena, though Hawthorne would scarcely bave stayed so long but for Story's company and conversation.

"We spoke," he writes, "of the idea, which has been realized in my own experience, that a piece of good fortune is apt to be attended by an equivalent misfortune, as its shadow or black twin. There seems to be a vein of melancholy in William Story which I was not aware of in my previous acquaintance with him. He acknowledged that for three years past he had lived in dread that some sorrow would come to counterbalance the prosperity of his present life. I hope not; for I like him particularly well, and indeed it is very hard if we cannot enjoy a little sunshine in this short and hard life without a deadly shadow gliding close behind. Old age, and death in its due time, will surely come; let those suffice. The notion, however, is a comfortable one or otherwise, according to your point of view. If the misfortune comes first, it is consolatory to think of the good that is soon to follow; in the other category, it is exceedingly disagreeable."

From Siena we pursued our way to Rome by vettura,--a five-days' journey, much the same in general character as the former one, though the weather, of course, was cooler, and the first bloom of novelty was wanting to the experience. But the journey was enlivened by the magnificent aspect, rapid and skilful driving, and genial disposition of our vetturino, Constantino Bacci by name,--a massive, stately fellow, with black eyes almost or quite as large as those of Powers, and with a gentler expression. The children and the "Emperor," as Mrs. Hawthorne called him, became greatly attached to one another during their sojourn together, and were more than sorry when the hour of parting came. We met with no more favorable specimens of Italians during our residence in the country than our two vetturinos,--Gaetano and Constantino. The "Emperor," then, drove us to the door of the house No. 68 Piazza Poli, which Mr. Thompson the artist had engaged for us; and the last six months of our Roman residence began.

CHAPTER 6 - ROME TO ENGLAND

THE Piazza Poli house was comfortable in itself,--though, of course, on an indefinitely compacter scale than the vast caravanserai to which we had accustomed ourselves in Florence,--stood in a convenient place, nearly at the centre of Rome. At night we could hear the murmurous plash of the Fountain of Trevi, which was accessible from our piazza by a short alley; and in Carnival-time the more tumultuous roar of the maskers and merry-makers was plainly audible, surging up and down the narrow channel of the Corso, on our right. And the Piazza del Popolo, the Roman Forum, the Pincian, the Pantheon,--all were at short radii from our starting-point. Looking out of our front windows, we beheld an oblong space of perhaps two acres of cobblestones, with a palace on the right hand and another on the left; and overhead the intensely blue Roman sky. Our short absence from the city led us to regard it in the peculiar light of a home in a foreign land,--a kind of home-feeling which has an element of the adventurous mixed up in it, and which carries with it no burden of responsibility. We were in a better mood than before, too, to understand and enjoy Rome on her own terms. We had become accustomed to the Italian sentiment of things, and we knew where to go and how to observe. Altogether, therefore, the prospect was highly agreeable, and we anticipated a great deal of happiness in our snug little lodgings. Mr. Thompson the artist, who had engaged the house for us, accompamed us on our first visit to it; and I remember the miraculous way in which the door opened in response to our ring. The latch lifted, and the door swung inwards; but no human hand or form appeared. We mounted the dark and narrow stairs, and were greeted above by the elderly lady who acted in the capacity of servant during our sojourn; and found the solution of the mystery in a sort of bell-rope depending from the wall, which was attached to a system of wires that acted upon the latch.

The old lady aforesaid comprised within her own person the total retinue of domestics that we employed or required; for there was no kitchen-work done in the house: we had our meals brought from a neighboring restaurant. They came in a large tin box on a man's head; and very good meals they were, in the French style,--three courses and a dessert at dinner; and if the *brisée* beef appeared rather often, it was always very nicely cooked and flavored. In the evenings, which were long for everybody was indoors by six o'clock, Roman air not being considered quite salubrious after that hour--it got to be the custom to play cards, all the family taking a hand first or last. We played whist and euchre and old maid, and had great fun. Hawthorne was an incomparable companion at such times; he made the life and jollity of the amusement. Everybody wanted to be his partner, not because he always won, for he did not, but because either good or evil fortune was delightful in alliance with him. He was charming in victory; but I am not sure that he was not more charming in defeat. The true nature of a person is sure to discover itself in a long series of games of cards. He entered heartily and unreservedly into the spirit of the contest. When he was beaten he defrauded his opponents of none of their legitimate triumph by affecting indifference; and when he captured the odd trick he made no pretence of not caring. It was a genuine struggle all the way through, and refreshing, however it turned out. Perhaps there are few men of fifty-four years who have enough of boyish freshness left in them to sit down with their family, night after night, and laugh and exult through an hour or two's play, in which the only stakes were the honor of victory. It never occurred to me to think it remarkable then; but now it seems different. He never seemed old to us, however, even to the last. There was a primitive freshness in him, that was always arching his eyebrow and twitching the corners of his mouth.

I remember this the better on account of what occurred afterwards. The Roman malaria was not supposed to be dangerous after October; nevertheless, in order to be on the safe side, our rule, as has been already observed, was to be in at six. But Hawthorne's eldest daughter, Una, was much devoted to sketching, and showed some talent for it; and was therein aided and abetted by Miss Ada Shepard, our young American governess. Roman ruins are tempting material; and one evening she and Una overstayed their time a little at the Palace of the Caesars, in order to finish a drawing. A few days afterwards, Una showed symptoms of chills and fever, and the attacks returned intermittently. It was evident that she had caught the Roman fever, but for a time the attack seemed to be slight. Dr. Franco, the most prominent homeopathic physician in Rome, was in attendance; and the youth of the patient and the unimpaired vigor of her constitution were in her favor. The disease held on, however, gradually becoming more severe, and undermining her strength. After a month or two she was no longer able to leave her bed in the intervals of her attacks as formerly; and the matter began to look serious. Mrs. Hawthorne was, from the first, constantly beside her daughter, and a better nurse--more self-possessed, cheerful, tender, and exact--could not probably have been found in Europe. She was also unweariable so long as there was any need for nursing; and it would be difficult to say how little sleep she had during the four months that Una's illness was critical. It became very critical at length; and one morning Dr. Franco came out of the room looking unusually serious, and spoke privately to Mr. and Mrs. Hawthorne. After he had gone, we knew that Una was not only ill, but that the chances were now against her recovery.

Mrs. Hawthorne said afterwards that Hawthorne had never taken a hopeful view of the case. The grief he felt at the idea that perhaps his daughter might die was so keen that he could not endure the alternations of hope and fear, and therefore had settled with himself not to hope at all. Indeed, he was at no period of his life of a sanguine temperament; and whether from philosophic determination or by force of nature, he uniformly chose to anticipate the darker alternative of whatever event was developing. But when the physician was obliged to admit that his skill had done all it could, and that the rest must be left to fate, the shock found Hawthorne scarcely prepared. He had been grave before, but now a positive darkness seemed to gather over his face. He said nothing, emotion never found verbal expression with him; but no one who looked in his eyes would have felt that there was any need of speech.

All this time, the card playing had been going on, evening after evening, just as usual. At the accustomed hour we would take our places at the table, even Mrs. Hawthorne and Una occasionally taking hands, before the latter was wholly confined to her bed; and Hawthorne always sat in his chair at the head. The rest of us laughed and enjoyed ourselves pretty much as before, and scarcely noticed how seldom Hawthorne contrived to smile. We thought that, so long as he could play cards, there was no danger of an evil issue of the fever. And this, of course, was precisely his object in continuing the practice. Until concealment was no longer of use, he was resolved to keep us from suspecting any danger. At what cost to his own nerves and patience he had persevered in this daily infliction, one can imagine now, but we had no suspicion of it then. And so it went on, until Dr. Franco made the communication above mentioned. We did not expect to have any game that evening; but at seven o'clock Hawthorne produced the cards, and we sat down. The game was whist, and certainly it was silent enough to satisfy the most exacting disciple. One hand was played; and then Hawthorne put down his cards. He had gone to the limit of his possibility. "We won't play any more," said he. And neither at that nor at any future time was that rubber of whist decided.

Gloomy days followed, without and within. The winter was peculiarly dark and depressing, and there was nothing to lighten it in the sick-chamber. Mrs. Hawthorne, who, at the other extreme from her husband, never gave up hope until there was absolutely nothing left to hope for, had gathered herself up after the blow, and gone back to her patient with unfaltering strength and energy. Franco afterwards said that the girl would undoubtedly have died under any other hands than her mother's. There is a sympathy that does by intuition what no medical skill can advise. Mrs. Hawthorne had at least her duties to support her, but Hawthorne had nothing; there was no distraction for his thoughts, from day to day. At length the crisis in the disease came. Unless Una's fever abated before morning, she would die.

With this sentence in her ears, the mother confronted her night's work. She had not slept for eight-and-forty hours, and had lain down but for a few minutes at a time. As she thought of what might be to come, she was conscious of a strong rebellion in her heart. She could not resign herself to losing her daughter. Una was the first-born, and on many accounts perhaps the dearest of the children. She had the finest mind of any, the most complex and beautiful character, and in various ways most strongly resembled her father. She was just emerging from childhood, and becoming a young woman. The struggle had been so prolonged that it seemed impossible to surrender now. And yet death or life lay in the beating of a pulse. For the first time in her life, the mother found herself at odds with Providence.

Una had been wandering in her mind for several days, and was continually talking in a vague unintelligible murmur, and recognized no one. If she were now to die, there could be no farewell,--no comprehension on her part of the end. As the night deepened, and the hour drew near which was to decide all, she ceased her mutterings, and lay quite still. Her mother was alone in the room with her. Hawthorne, whether awake or not, was lying on his bed in an adjoining chamber. Mrs. Hawthorne went to the window and looked out on the piazza. It was dark and silent; no one was abroad. The sky, too, was heavy with clouds. She looked up at the clouds, and said to herself that she could not bear this loss.

All at once, however, her feeling changed. It was one of those apparently miraculous transformations that sometimes come over faithful and loving hearts. "Why should I doubt the goodness of God?" she asked herself. "Let Him take her, if He sees best. I can give her to Him. I will not fight against Him any more."

Her spirits were lighter than at any time since the illness began; she had made the sacrifice, and found herself not sadder but happier. She went back to the bedside, and put her hand on Una's forehead; it was cool and moist. Her pulse was slow and regular, and she was sleeping naturally. The crisis had passed, favorably. One can imagine the wife going to the husband, and telling him "She will live!" Such a moment would atone for many months of suffering.

The convalescence was long and tedious, but it proceeded without relapse. Roman fever is a disease from which one seldom recovers unequivocally, and the present case was perhaps no exception to the rule; though the ill effects of the large doses of quinine that had been taken were probably quite as lasting and injurious as those of the fever itself. But it was enough, for the present, that the peril to life was passed. Soon after the favorable change had set in, General Pierce, whose presidential term had lately concluded, came to Rome, and he and Hawthorne saw a great deal of each other. "I found all my early friend in him," the latter said. I recollect the first evening that Pierce came to our house, and sat in the little parlor, in the dusk, listening to the story of Una's illness. "Poor child! poor child!" he said occasionally, in a low voice. His sympathy was like something palpable,--strong, warm, and comforting. He said very little, but it was impossible not to feel how much he cared. He knew of his own experience what it was to lose children: He stayed in Rome several weeks, and he and Hawthorne talked over all their former years and adventures, since they were boys in college together. There are some interesting observations on the ex-President's character in the Note-Books. "I do not love him one whit the less for having been President," says Hawthorne, "nor for having done me the greatest good in his power. If he only had been the benefactor or, perhaps I might not have borne it so well; but each did his best for the other, as friend for friend."

The Carnival came again, and this time Hawthorne seems to have entered more freely than before into the spirit of the festivaL Indeed, it fell in with a private festival of his own, for his daughter was often able to take part in the frolic. We had a carriage, and drove up and down, amidst bouquets and confetti, in the endless procession of the Corso; and Hawthorne flung his ammunition as zealously as any one. While he was actually engaged, he fell cordially enough into the humor of the sport; but as he became merely a spectator, he could perceive only the absurdity of it all. Absurd or not, and whether or no he contemplated making use of the Carnival in a romance, he studied it pretty thoroughly on the two opportunities that were afforded him.

As the spring advanced, he resumed his walks about Rome, sometimes alone and sometimes with a companion. On one occasion we were trudging along a road that skirted the outside of the walls, from one gate to the other, and the companion, who was always on the lookout for snail-shells and lizards, had fallen a couple of hundred yards in the rear. Hawthorne had disappeared round a bend of the road; and on catching sight of him again, his son saw that he was engaged in conversation with a dingy-looking personage, who had evidently just asked him what time it was. Hawthorne was not very fluent in conversational Italian, whereas his son, in his daily excursions about the city with his friends Edmund and Hubert Thompson, had picked up what he thought was a sufficiently practical knowledge of the language. Prompted, therefore, by a charitable desire to render his attainments useful, he shouted out to his father to wait till he came up, and he would translate the hour into the inquirer's native tongue; and at the same time. he set out towards them at top speed. But the stranger immediately left Hawthorne, and continued on his way; and it appeared that the former had made shift to give him the desired information. On reaching home, however, Hawthorne told the anecdote to his wife, and remarked that he had every reason to think that the man had intended to rob him. For, as he produced his watch, the man's hand had crept to the handle of a knife in his belt, and his countenance had assumed an ominous expression; but the sudden shout in the distance, and the apparition of a figure of indeterminate dimensions making all haste towards the scene of operations, had altered his intention; he had muttered, "Grazie, signor," and walked off Within a few weeks there had been five or six highway robberies outside the walls of Rome. The moral of this story seems to be that a disinterested wish to air one's Italian may result in averting the blow of a stiletto.

Hawthorne appears to have enjoyed the last month or two of his Roman sojourn. His spirits had rebounded after the heavy depression of the winter, and had not yet settled to their normal level; nor was he as yet aware how fatally that period of anguish had told upon him. The weather was warm and sunny, and pleasant friends were around him. He saw a good deal of William Story, and it was in his company that he visited the farm on which the new statue of Venus had just been excavated,--that which was thought to be the original from which the Medicean Venus was copied. Then there were farewell visits to be made to all. the familiar places of interest; and there is always a peculiar charm in a farewell visit, even if it be a melancholy one. Hawthorne was glad to leave Rome, and yet he was sensible of a strong affection for it. It endeared itself to him even by the suffering it had inflicted; and had his daughter died there, it is doubtful if he would have found it possible ever to return to America. As it was, however, he hastened to be gone.

We left Rome on the 26th of May, Hawthorne having taken an early walk that morning to the Pincian, and through the Borghese gardens, and to Saint Peter's; and "methought," he says, "they never looked so beautiful, nor the sky so bright and blue." The railroad to Civita Vecchia had been completed a few months before, and it was by that route that we departed. "We had great pother and difficulty in getting ourselves and our mountain of luggage taken to the station in season," Hawthorne wrote,

"and I know not that we should have succeeded in leaving Rome, but for the good offices of Dr. Appleton, who took as much as possible of the rough and tumble of the matter upon himself, out of mere kindness of heart. On getting to our destination, we had further trouble in getting our luggage transported from the railway to the water-side; for the people of Civita Vecchia are absolute harpies of luggage, and cannot be hindered from laying their unclean hands upon it by any efforts of the owner. I think they are really the most pertinacious rogues in Italy, and the most exorbitant; and my remnant of Roman silver (with which I had expected to be burthened in Leghorn and further onward) melted away as if it were coined of snow. After shouldering our way through this difficulty, a new one sprung up; for on applying at the ticket-office of the steamer, we were told that we could not be received, because my passport had not the visa of the French Embassy in Rome. This signature had not been obtained, because we meant to go in the first instance, only to Leghorn; but as I had taken a through-ticket to Marseilles, with liberty of stopping at the intermediate places, the steamer agent declared it impossible to take us without the French visé. Here was great horror and despair on my part; for I do think life would scarcely be worth having at the expense of spending one night at Civita Vecchia; and besides, in these crowded times, there was some doubt whether we could have obtained a shelter. However, the agent (who had at first put on an immitigable face--to frighten us the more, I suppose) finally intimated that the signature of the French consul at Civita Vecchia might be sufficient, if there were time to obtain it; so I sent off a commissionaire forthwith, and the passport soon came back duly viséd. I must do the steamer-people and the commissionaire the justice to say that they seemed to be honest men, and not only asked for no undue fees, but returned (it was the commissionaire who did this unheard-of act) a slight overcharge which he had made. Having got on board, the female part of us were assigned a state-room to themselves, and Julian and I were put into a room with six berths in it, most of which were occupied; a hot place, too, down almost to the water's edge, and aired and lighted only by a small round hole. We shortly left the port (which appears to be entirely an artificial harbor, built all round with stone), and I rejoiced from the bottom of my soul to see this hateful place sinking under the horizon. Dinner was served soon after our departure, but I think only Julian, Una, and I, of our party, profited much by it; and we had a beautiful sunset, and clear, calm evening till bedtime."

These details of travel were always a great bugbear to Hawthorne, the rather since he was obliged to conduct his negotiations through an interpreter; and it seems a pity that he could not have been relieved of all such discomfort by the services of a good courier.

It had been our intention to spend a week or two (on Una's account) at Leghorn; but as she seemed benefited instead of fatigued by the voyage, and in order to avoid the inconvenience of having "all Tophet let loose upon us, in the shape of custom-house officers, gendarmes, commissionaires, luggage-harpies, and beggars," we decided to keep on to Marseilles. So, after spending the night on board the steamer in the harbor, we sailed next morning for Genoa, and thence proceeded without incident to Marseilles, "which was really," says Hawthorne, "like passing from death into life."

Our next objective point was Geneva, to which we travelled by way of Avignon, remaining several days at the latter town. On arriving there,

"an omnibus took us to the Hotel d'Europe, where, on driving into the courtyard, we were received by an elderly lady in black, of brisk and kindly manners. She assigned us a suite of rooms, extending along a gallery that looks down into the court; a saloon and, I believe, four bedrooms, which number we have since diminished to save expense, and because our hostess cannot conveniently let us have so many, in view of some races which will bring her a great crowd of guests in a day or two. We dine at the table d'hote at five o'clock with very little company; most of the guests dining at seven. It was a very good dinner; some claret, which appeared very tolerable to me after my experience of the sour old wines of Italy, was placed on the table in liberal quantity. The whole thing is far better managed than at the table d'hote of an American hotel; and though the viands here were not half so good or so numerous, it was much easier to get a comfortable dinner."

The characteristics of Avignon are dwelt upon at some length in the Note-Books, and nothing need be added here.

"We left on the 7th of June for Geneva, stopping on the way at Lyons, where, after a good deal of search, I found my way to the Consul's. Here it was my misfortune to encounter, instead of the Consul, two American ladies, with whom I stayed talking for above an hour, I should think,--to our mutual weariness, no doubt.

By and by, however, the Consul came in, a Mr. White, an elderly, frank, agreeable gentleman, who received me with great courtesy when he knew my name. After all, I needed no assistance from him, my passport having been viséd for Switzerland by the Consul at Marseilles; and this little republic makes everybody welcome. Returning to our hotel, I spent as much as an hour and a half in arranging to send four trunks to await us at Macon, instead of taking them with us on our journey. The same business would not have required five minutes on an American railway."

In alluding to the scenery between Lyons and Geneva, which was very beautiful, Hawthorne observes:

"I have come to see the nonsense of attempting to describe fine scenery. There is no such possibility. If scenery could be adequately reproduced in words, there would have been no need of God's making it in reality. And I have no heart any longer, as I have said a dozen times already, for journalizing. Had it been otherwise, there is enough of picturesque and peculiar in Geneva to fill a good many of these pages; but really I lack energy to seek objects of interest, curiosity even so much as to glance at them, heart to enjoy them, intellect to profit by them. I deem it a grace of Providence when I have a decent excuse to my wife and to my own conscience for not seeing even those things that have helped to tempt me abroad. It may be disease; it may be age; it may be the effect of the lassitudinous Roman atmosphere but such is the fact."

It was a fact to a certain extent; but much of the vigor of expression with which it is stated is due to the circumstance that Hawthorne was in the habit of journalizing in the evenings, when he, fatigued by the labors of the day, and was thus liable to import into the recollection of what he had been seeing the weariness and distaste of the moment of writing. But there is no doubt that the springs of external enjoyment were beginning to run dry for him.

After a day or two at Geneva, we took the boat down the lake to Villeneuve, and put up at the Hotel de Byron. Here again Hawthorne was stimulated to describe much and effectively; though, once more, looking back upon it all, he insists that he has not "any spirit to write, as of yore. I flag terribly: scenes and things make but dim reflections in my inward mirror; and if ever I have a thought, words do not come aptly to clothe it." Nevertheless, the whole of "The Marble Faun" was written after this date. But the Continental journal now comes to an end, and not more than twenty or thirty pages are added of the final English and the American experiences. Returning at the end of a week to Geneva, we went to Paris, and thence to London, and so found ourselves again in the Old Home, after a residence on the other side of the Channel of about eighteen months.

Hawthorne now decided to remain another year in England, in order to prepare the new romance for the English market; being the more moved thereto because he had unadvisedly made a loan to a friend of a large sum of money, which was never repaid, and the loss of which necessitated his insuring an English copyright. The English atmosphere--moral, if not physical--revived him somewhat. He appreciated England the better for his absence from it. On the Continent he had neither felt nor known anything of the national social life. Always inclined even in his own country to be rather a spectator of society than an active participant in it, he had been more so than ever in England, while in Italy his estrangement had been absolute; and consequently he had been forced to confine himself almost exclusively to the companionship of art and archaeology. Such association is, no doubt, educative and refining in moderate doses, taken in connection with social intercourse or in the way of relaxation therefrom. But to expect a man like Hawthorne to put up contentedly with nothing else, was too much. He was already a highly cultivated man, but his culture had proceeded in the direction of humanity and nature rather than of art. In studying works of art, he had been subjected to an inevitable disappointment. Understanding nothing of technique,--of the difficulties to be overcome, and the means adopted to overcome them,--he could only feel that the results were not commensurate with his expectations. The sky of the painter was not so bright as that of nature; the statue lacked movement and variety. He looked for the achievement of the impossible, and, not finding it, failed to give due credit to what was actually accomplished. Had his refinement been less, he would have been ignorantly pleased; had his technical knowledge and perception of relativity been greater, he could have felt conscientiously satisfied. A great part of specific art culture consists in learning the limitations of art, and judging, not absolutely, but comparatively. Hawthorne had never had opportunity for this; and the ideal notions of art which his noble imagination had engendered in his mind, and which had been nourished by the report of art-lovers, were bound to be discomfited. He succeeded best with architecture, because that is the most spontaneous and least artificial form that art assumes. His appreciation of the famous buildings and ruins of Europe was profound and cordial; yet even here he is continually finding the beauty enhanced by its connection with humanity and antiquity,--a connection, of course, not intrinsic, but created by the observer's imagination. During his residence abroad, he labored strenuously to attain a more complacent point of view: he succeeded in no small degree; but, as he constantly refused to say he was satisfied until he felt that he was so, and could explain why, his Note-Books rather understate his progress than the contrary. All the while, he was hungering (perhaps without knowing it) for human beings,--for a society which he understood and was congenitally in sympathy with. Such a society could exist, for him, only in New England. There only could he feel, without need of practically demonstrating it, that he was essentially at one with those around him. Elsewhere he would be anxious about the differences; there he could be confident of the similarities. He had felt the differences sensibly enough during his first residence in England; but the social comparison between England and the Continent was so much in favor of the former as almost to make him feel, on his return thither, that he was actually at home again. Here, at all events, were English friends whom he knew and loved; and friendly regards encompassed him wherever he went. For several weeks previous to retiring to Redcar to write, he stayed in London, and was half surprised to find himself meeting a good many people and enjoying it.

    Henry Bright was in Cambridge at the time of Hawthorne's arrival in London, and lost no time in inviting him to come down and see that seat of classical learning. "It is settled," he writes, "that you must stay with me till Monday at Cambridge. Rooms are engaged in college, and you are engaged to dinner on Friday, Saturday and Sunday. Had you been at S----'s last night, you would have met a charming madman who favored us with his company. Are you at the 'Derby' to-day?" Hawthorne, however, was unable to leave London, and presently received another communication beginning,

"Consul Hawthorne, you're a sinner—
Make engagements--do *not* keep 'em!

What am I to say to S-----? However, I find I can stay at Cambridge some time longer; so you must stay too. Can I see you here to-morrow at twelve?" Hawthorne could not go; and not many days later Bright came up to London, where, he writes to me,

I saw much of your father. On July 8 we went together to the House of Commons, where Mr. Whitbread, the member for Bedford, got us places. We came in for a debate on the navy estimates, and heard Lord John Russell, Lord Palmerston, and Mr. Disraeli. On the 9th we all dined at Richmond; and I remember how amused Hawthorne was at a lady in a curiously antique costume who passed us in the street: she reminded him, he said, of a maid of honor of Queen Anne's time. On the 10th we dined at the Heywoods', at Connaught Place. On the 12th we went to call on Charles Sumner, though Hawthorne said, 'As we're neither of us the Lord Chancellor, he won't care about us!' Mr. Sumner had been very kind to me in America. We afterwards went to see Dr. Williams's library, then in Red Cross Street,--an out-of-the-way sight, but very curious for its pictures of Puritan divines and its manuscripts of Baxter. On the 13th we went for an hour to the Workingmen's College, where Tom Hughes had asked us. A number of men were sitting round the table, and Hughes read to them Tennyson's 'The Grandmother's Apology,' which had just come out. We also breakfasted with Monckton Milnes (Lord Houghton), but I forget the date."

It was about this time, also, that Hawthorne first met Henry Chorley, who claimed the merit of having "discovered" him so long ago as the epoch of the "Twice-Told Tales." Mr. Chorley was the literary critic of the "Athenaeum," which was then, I believe, edited by Hepworth Dixon. He admired Hawthorne's genius, and had written cordial things of the three American novels. Personally he was an agreeable and brilliant little man, and he gave Mr. and Mrs. Hawthorne a charming dinner at his tiny, but delightful house in London. I find this characteristic note from him, alluding to the occasion :--

DEAR MR. HAWTHORNE,--Put a card in the post, to say (as I hope) that you are no worse for having come to me. I cannot say *how* pleased I was to receive your letter. Surely, though one cannot believe in *spirits,* must one not in sympathies? Pray, recollect my readiness to do you both any pleasure; and also, that *if* I can't, I shall say I can't: so you cannot be strange with

Very gratefully and respectfully yours,
HENRY CHORLEY.
13 EATON PLACE, WEST.

--We shall see Mr. Chorley again after "The Marble Faun" has been published. Meanwhile Hawthorne and his family left London, and went first to Whitby, on the Yorkshire coast, in search of the seclusion necessary for writing the romance, which was at this time in pieces, as it were, ready to be remodelled and put together. Whitby was a moderately agreeable watering-place, with a high cliff on which were the remains of an abbey built in past ages by Saint Hilda. The names of the personages in the new book were in their usual unsettled condition; and I recollect that this abbey, with its tradition, suggested to Hawthorne the appellation which he bestowed upon the New England girl in the story. Hilda has, I believe, been supposed to have been based upon the character of Miss Ada Shepard, the young American governess before mentioned, who had returned to the United States before we recrossed the Channel. The hypothesis is more than usually infelicitous. Hilda--whose fault, if she have any, as a creation, is that she is too much of an abstraction--has in her some traits of Mrs. Hawthorne, though the latter, and perhaps Hawthorne himself, were not aware of it. Mrs. Hawthorne's was much the larger and broader nature of the two, and was remarkable for a gentle humor and sunniness of disposition, in which Hilda is conspicuously deficient. Nevertheless, Sophia Hawthorne, with her more winning and humane characteristics omitted, would have furnished ample materials for a Hilda; but of Miss Shepard the latter shows no trace.

Hawthorne did not remain long at Whitby; it does not seem to have suited him as a place to compose in. It was too much of a seaside resort, perhaps, and it did not possess any special facilities for undisturbed walks. The cliffs were neither of rock nor of chalk, but of a dirty kind of clay; interesting to geologists from the quantity of ammonites and other fossil remains contained in them, but not otherwise attractive. It was finally decided to go to Redcar, which was not far distant, but greatly more secluded. Here the broad brown sands stretched for miles, with the sombre German ocean breaking over them; and inland there were long wastes of lonely country, with small, remote villages here and there. The place was little known then; and certainly it offered the strongest possible contrast to the scenes amidst which the Romance was laid, and therefore gave these the stronger relief in the writer's memory and imagination.

Owing, in great measure, to the exertions of Mr. Bright, who wrote a pamphlet on the subject, and talked with various personages in authority, an agitation was set on foot at this period relative to the old matter of the ill-treatment of sailors on board of American vessels. Hawthorne himself intended publishing something on the subject, but, with the exception of some letters to private individuals and his despatches to Congress, never found opportunity to carry out his purpose. The evil, in time, abated itself, chiefly owing to the decay of the commerce that had given rise to it. But the subject was discussed in the House, on the motion of Lord Houghton, as may be seen in the subjoined letter from Bright to Hawthorne:--

WEST DERBY, LIVERPOOL, July 29, 1859.

MY DEAR MR. HAWTHORNE,--A letter is waiting for you at Whitby, where I supposed you were. Monckton Milnes is bringing on the ship-cruelty question in the House on the 2d August, and he wishes you very much to send him a few lines relative to the matter. Do please write to him at 16 Upper Brook Street, and tell him, if you will kindly do so, that the evils are very real, and the law quite inoperative. Mr. Ticknor, Mr. Jay, and Charles Morton are going to try what your Congress can do; and on this side, Mr. Milnes will move an address to the Queen, "praying her to enter into negotiations with the Government of the United States for the purpose of preventing the gross cruelties practised on merchant seamen engaged in the traffic between this country and the United States, and for bringing the offenders to justice." To this I hope no objection can be raised, either on this side or on yours. Please do not lose a post in writing to Milnes, or it may be too late. Tuesday is the day.

I am already longing to be with you all again, and must certainly come to see you if you will let me.

Ever yours,
H. A. BRIGHT.

--At Redcar, Hawthorne used to write during the morning until dinner-time, which was at half-past one; and after dinner, except when it rained too heavily, he would take his son out to walk with him. We generally went northward along the sands; and at a certain point of the coast, where there was a sort of inlet, Hawthorne would seat himself, and allow the boy to go in swimming. Then they would resume their walk, and generally strike inland, and return by a roundabout way to Redcar. The dark mass of the little town, with the red sunset sky behind it, presented quite a picturesque effect, of the solemn and dreary order. Hawthorne's health improved during his residence here; and upon the whole he seems rather to have gained than lost from this last year in England.

We remained between three and four months in Redcar, and, so far as I can recollect, we had the place entirely to ourselves. It was not the "season; and even Henry Bright did not succeed in getting out to see us, although, as appears from the following letter, he had partly formed some such project in his mind:--

WEST DERBY, Sept. 8, 1859.

MY DEAR HAWTHORNE,--How are you all, and how is the novel, and how is the Faun? Do write me a line, and tell me about your doings and beings and thinkings. I send Mrs. Hawthorne an American paper with an article in it on Mr. Horace Mann. Thank you most heartily for writing to Monckton Milnes on the cruelty question. You no doubt saw the papers of the 4th August with an account of the debate in them, and how Mr. Milnes quoted us both. I do hope your people (I mean the people who *were* yours,--you are an Englishman now) will help our Government in getting something done.

I have been staying with Mr. Milnes for a week at his place in Yorkshire. It was the pleasantest time I ever spent, and I have to parody Tom Appleton's *mot* and say, "If I 'm *very* good in this world, I shall go to 'Frystone' in the next." A beautiful park and gardens; a library--such a library, with tempting *readable* books, books You always wanted to see, just the by-paths of literature which lead nowhere in particular, but are leafy and flowery and fruity all the same; and then a large and pleasant party of people, each one of whom was interesting; and a good cook (!) and excursions; and, best of all, the kindest of hostesses, and a host who *is* a host,--a host in himself. There, does n't your mouth water? It ought to.

I saw Mrs. Gaskell the other day. She too is writing a novel, and the scene is to be somewhere near Redcar; so I think it is probable she may pay you a visit, and in that case the double magnet will draw me too. Would n't it be glorious? Only I'm afraid the two novels might suffer; *still*, it would be so jolly,--*almost* as good as Frystone. I can't say more than that. By the way, how perverse you novelists are! Mrs. Gaskell is going to "smash" her hero's face, which she says is quite a new idea, and he is to be horrible to look upon, and then a young lady is to love him. It 's as bad as your Faun committing murder. But it's no good arguing with you; as somebody says in one of Scott's novels, "a wilfu' and obstinate mon [or woman] will hae his [her] ain way!"

Dr. Lothrop was over here the other day. I did n't like him quite so well as I fancied I remembered liking him. He is--well, never mind what he is; I don't like being censorious on paper, and he has certainly been very kind to me, and his daughter is certainly very beautiful. I have been showing my chirography to a woman who pretends to tell character from handwriting, and she has just sent such an account of me that I feel absolutely vain to think what opportunities I have of making my own acquaintance, and what pleasure it must be to my tailor to make clothes for so eminent an individual. Who now will venture to say anything uncivil of my pothooks and hangers? Shall we hand up your handwriting and see what comes of that?

Yours ever,
H. A. BRIGHT.

--In October we left Redcar, which was becoming somewhat too inclement for comfort, and made another visit to Leamington, which had become a comparatively familiar place to us. The house we occupied, however, was no longer in Lansdowne Circus, at the upper extremity of the town, but in the midst of the town itself, on the other side of the bridge. Here, with the exception of one or two brief excursions to London, Hawthorne remained until March of 1860, and finished the romance. Every day he walked out, visiting the towns in the neighborhood,--Lillington, Warwick, and Witnash. It was on one of these expeditions that we discovered the grave of John Treeo, close beneath the wall of Lillington Church, as described in the Note-Books. Another day, at Warwick, "it was market-day: in tbe sort of colonnade of the town-house, or whatever they call it, there were people selling small wares, apples, vegetables, etc., and all through the market-place there was a little scattered trade of the same kind going forward; pigs, too, and sheep, alive or dead. All was very quiet and dull. We went into the museum, among the most interesting objects in which were some small portions of the auburn hair and beard of King Edward IV." Again, he went to Coventry, where his friend Bennoch was staying, and was entertained there by a retired manufacturer, Mr. Bill. "His house," writes Hawthorne, "is a very good and unpretending one, and Mr. Bill seems to live a most quiet and comfortable life, without coach-house or man-servant, though Mr. Bennoch says he has an income of three thousand pounds ($15,000), besides retaining an interest in his former business."

The weather, however, was very unpropitious, and Hawthorne cannot forbear referring to it. "I think" he says,

"I never felt how dreary and tedious winter can be, till this present English winter, though I have spent four or five in England before. But always heretofore it has been necessary for me to venture out and look the dark weather in the face; whereas, this winter, I have chiefly moped by the fireside, and at most have ventured out but an hour or two in the day. It has been inconceivably depressing: such fog; such dark mornings, that sulked onwards till nightfall; such damp and rain; such sullen and penetrating chills; such mud and mire; surely, the bright serenity of a New England winter can never be so bad as this. I have not really emerged into life through the whole season."

On one of his trips to London, to arrange the details of the publication of his book, he called again on Leigh Hunt, accompanied by his wife and Una. They found the old gentleman as cordial and agreeable as on the former occasion; and, Mrs. Hawthorne having accidentally left her cloak behind her, Hunt sent it back the next day, with this little note:--

DEAR MR. AND MRS. HAWTHORNE (for " The Scarlet Letter" and " The Indicator" will warrant me, I trust, in thus addressing you, to say nothing of gratitude for your visit),--Had there been any reason in time, weather, or any other contingency, for allowing me to expect the return of any one of you for the accompanying cloak, I would have kept it accordingly in that "look-out;" but as this is out of the question, I send it you by parcels' delivery, trusting that it will at all events be in time for you before your departure. I guess it belongs to the young lady, the look of whose face upon the old man (with the others') I shall not easily forget.

Your obliged visitee,
LEIGH HUNT.

The "Romance of Monte Beni" was finished early in the spring of 1860; but I will close this chapter with the following letters from Mr. Samuel Lucas, the editor of "Once a Week," to which periodical George Meredith was at that time, I believe, contributing one of his remarkable novels. The journal was finely illustrated, and, though it had only lately come into existence, was taking a high place among the magazines of the day. Hawthorne entertained some thoughts of publishing his projected English novel in its pages; but the design was never fulfilled.

"ONCE A WEEK" OFFICE, No. 11 BOUVERIE ST.,
FLEET ST., LONDON, Nov. 5, 1859.

DEAR SIR,--Will you excuse the liberty which, as editor of "Once a Week," I take of addressing you without waiting for an introduction from any common friend, and will you permit me to trouble you, without preamble, on a matter of business?

It would give me the *greatest* satisfaction if you are at liberty to entertain a proposal to write a tale for "Once a Week," and I am confident that Bradbury and Evans would meet your views in a pecuniary sense, should that desideratum be attainable. For myself I may claim better opportunities than most of appreciating the profound truthfulness of the descriptions in "The Scarlet Letter" and "The House of the Seven Gables;" for at one time I took a keen interest in cognate subjects, and must have gone over much of your ground to write, for example, papers like that in the Edinburgh Review, three or four years ago, on "The Fathers of New England." I mention these circumstances by way of excusing myself for breaking in upon you thus abruptly. Hoping for your favorable consideration of my proposal, I remain,

Respectfully yours,
SAMUEL LUCAS.

--Mr. Hawthorne replied with a doubtful and contingent affirmative, and Mr. Lucas promptly rejoined as follows

11 BOUVERIE ST., Nov. 17, 1859.

MY DEAR SIR,--I am both gratified and obliged by your answer to my letter. Moreover, it is quite as satisfactory as I could have expected, as it leaves me the hope that hereafter you may be induced to comply with our very earnest wishes. I agree with you that the Puritan chord is monotonous, and would indeed *prefer* any other theme. I know with what power you can touch other themes, for I have just read "The Blithedale Romance." And perhaps, having lived so long in England as I am glad to hear you have, and enjoyed your sojourn, you may have acquired such an interest in some phases of English life that you may be prompted to weave these into a story. In this respect you seem to have an advantage possessed by none of your inventive compatriots whom I can recall, except Washington Irving, and I sincerely believe it is open to you, by striking into this track, to achieve as thoroughly an English and European reputation as he has. Highly honored as you are in England, in my opinion your name has not acquired here, as yet, nearly as much prestige as should fairly belong to it; and I do think your association with us would materially help towards this, in the first place, because of our great and increasing circulation, and in the next, because I can put at your disposal for illustrative purposes the best artistic resources in this country. In this respect we are aiming at something unique. I may add that it will equally suit us if we could make arrangements with yourself for some time hence, say even towards the close of 1860. I shall be greatly pleased if you will give me a further warranty to discuss the matter with Bradbury and Evans, who are quite prepared to meet you on your own terms in a pecuniary sense.

Believe me yours sincerely,
SAM. LUCAS.

--The new romance was placed in the hands of the printers in February, and was published in three volumes by Messrs. Smith and Elder at the end of that month, under the title of "Transformation,"

CHAPTER 7 - THE MARBLE FAUN

IT was before leaving Leamington, I think, that Hawthorne accompanied his friend Henry Bright to Rugby, where the latter had been at school when a boy, and was introduced to Dr. Temple, the head master, since made Bishop of Exeter. Bright then took him over to Bilton Hall, across the fields, where Addison had lived; and be was much interested in some of the pictures there.

He met Bright again on coming to London, and (says the latter)

"we spent several hours wandering about and chatting. I told him I had heard that his Miriam (it was Arthur Penrhyn Stanley's idea) was Mdlle. de Luzzy, the governess of the Duc de Praslyn. He was much amused. 'Well, I dare say she was,' he said. 'I knew I had some *dim* recollection of some crime, but I didn't know what.' He added, 'As regards the last chapter of "Transformation" in the second edition, don't read it; it's good for nothing. The story isn't meant to be explained; it's cloudland.' We went together to the National Gallery, and looked for a faun among the Bacchanalian pictures; but no faun we could see had furry ears. The satyrs all had. We had a great deal of fun about this."

Hawthorne went in March to Bath, and remained there six or seven weeks. "I have no longer any impulse to describe what I see," he writes, "and cannot overcome my reluctance to take up the pen." A brief but comprehensive description of Bath will, however, be found in the Note-Books. He found the air preferable to that of Leamington, "yet heavy enough, in the lack of any object of interest which I at present have, to make me feverish and miserable. Perhaps," he adds, "I will describe the Pump-Room some time; and no matter if I don't!" He appends to his journal two or three notes for use in possible stories,--the last notes of the kind he ever made.

"At the shop-window of a carpenter and undertaker, the other day, I saw two or three rows of books, of all sizes, from folio to duodecimo, and mostly wearing an antique aspect. There was the old folio of Fox's 'Book of Martyrs,' and volumes of old sermons, and histories, looking like books that had long been the household literature of families, and which the present owner had got possession of, probably, when he went to measure the dead man for his coffin, and perform the other funeral rites,-- taking these volumes, perhaps, in part payment of his services."

"Imagine a ghost, just passed into the other state of being, looking back into this mortal world, and shocked by many things that were delightful just before,--more shocked than the living are at the ghostly world."

"A pretty young girl, so small and lustrous that you would like to set her in a brooch and wear her in your bosom."

--The first English reviews of "Transformation" appeared early in March, 1860. The book was received with eagerness; but general disappointment was felt at what was considered to be its inconclusive conclusion. Most of the reviewers, and many of Hawthorne's personal acquaintances, shared in this feeling. The most shining exception to the rule was John Lothrop Motley, who wrote the author an admirable letter about the romance, which, since it has been quoted in another place (together with Hawthorne's reply), I will not give here. The book was the first that Hawthorne had written which had not been cordially welcomed, and no doubt the change was a disappointment to him. He was always too ready to think slightly of his own work, and, in his then condition of mind, he found little spirits to make head against what seemed the popular verdict. He used to read the letters and the reviews with a smile, and sometimes with a laugh, but sadly, too. "The thing is a failure," he used to say. He meant, perhaps, that he had failed in making his audience take his point of view towards the story. Certainly, he had taken most of them out of their depth. There was a general demand for an "explanation" of the mysteries of the tale; and at last Hawthorne, in a half-ironic mood, wrote the short chapter now appended to the book. Nothing, of course, is explained; it was impossible to explain to the reader his own stupidity. It was not till many years afterwards, when Hawthorne was in his grave, that a more intelligent criticism began to perceive that the story had been told after all.

One of the first letters received was from Henry Bright.

". . . I 'm in the middle of 'Monte Beni' (why did Smith and Elder transform it into 'Transformation'?--they are rather given to playing these pranks with author's titles), and I am delighted with it. I am glad that sulky 'Athenaeum' was so civil; for they are equally powerful and unprincipled, and a bad word there would have done harm. I think your descriptions of scenery and places most admirable; and as for statues and pictures, I think they never were so described before,--you seem to enter into their (or their artists') very soul, and lay it bare before us. As I 've not read more than a volume yet, I can say nothing about the plot, except that it interests and excites me. Donatello I hardly quite like and understand as yet; a being half man, half child, half animal, puzzles me; to me there seems a something a little--just a little-- *wanting,* and that gives me an uncomfortable feeling of half development, half idiocy, which is of course unpleasant. But as I know him better I may like him more. Harriet says you 've stolen the description of Miriam from *her* Jewess--as she calls the extract you gave her--and intends to accuse you of plagiarism if not of theft. In Hilda it seems to me you had a thought of Una. My acquaintance with Kenyon is as yet too slight. You have not, I trust, forgotten about the precious manuscript which is to be the gem, the Koh-i-noor, of my autographs. . . .

"I 've finished *the* book, and am, I think, more angry at your tantalizing cruelty than either 'Athenaeum' or 'Saturday Review.' I want to know a hundred things you do not tell me,--who Miriam was, what was the crime in which she was concerned and of which all Europe knew, what was in the packet, what became of Hilda, whether Miriam married Donatello, whether Donatello got his head cut off, etc. Of course you'll say I ought to *guess;* well, if I do guess, it is but a guess, and I want to *know.* Yesterday I wrote a review of you in the 'Examiner,' and in spite of my natural indignation, I hope you will not altogether dislike what I have said. In other respects I admire 'Monte Beni' more than I can tell you; and I suppose no one now will visit Rome without a copy of it in his band. Nowhere are descriptions to be found so beautiful, so true, and so pathetic. And there are little bits of *you* in the book which are best of all, -half moralizing, half thinking aloud. There is a bit about *women sewing* which Harriet raves about. There are bits about Catholicism and love and sin, which are marvellously thought and gloriously written." .

To the first instalment of this letter Hawthorne wrote the following reply:

DEAR MR. BRIGHT,--I thank you very much for your letter, and am glad you like the romance so far and so well. I shall be really gratified if you review it. Very likely you are right about Donatello; for, though the idea in my mind was an agreeable and beautiful one, it was not easy to present it to the reader.

Smith and Elder certainly do take strange liberties with the titles of books. I wanted to call it "The Marble Faun," but they insisted upon "Transformation," which will lead the reader to anticipate a sort of pantomime. They wrote me some days ago that the edition was nearly all sold, and that they are going to print another; to which I mean to append a few pages, in the shape of a conversation between Kenyon, Hilda, and the author, throwing some further light on matters which seem to have been left too much in the dark. For my own part, however, I should prefer the book as it now stands.

It so happened that, at the very time you were writing, Una was making up a parcel of the manuscript to send to you. There is a further portion, now in the hands of Smith and Elder, which I will procure when I go to London,--that is, if you do not consider this immense mass more than enough.

I begin to be restless (and so do we all) with the anticipation of our approaching departure, and, almost for the first time, I long to be at home. Nothing more can be done or enjoyed till we have breathed our native air again. I do not even care for London now, though I mean to spend a few weeks there before taking our final leave; not that I mean to think it a last leave-taking, either. In three or four more years or less, my longings will no doubt be transferred from that side of the water to this; and perhaps I shall write another book, and come over to get it published.

We are rather at a loss for a suitable place to stay at during the interval between this and the middle of June, when we mean to sail. Liverpool is to be avoided, on Mrs. Hawthorne's account, till the last moment; and I am afraid there is no air in England fit for her to breathe. We have some idea of going to Bath, but more probably we shall establish ourselves for a month or two in the neighborhood of London. But, as I said before, we shall enjoy little or nothing, wherever we may be. Our roots are pulled up, and we cannot really live till we stick them into the ground again. There will be pleasure, indeed, in greeting you again at Liverpool (the most disagreeable city in England, nevertheless), but a sharp pain in bidding you farewell. The sooner it is all over, the better. What an uneasy kind of world we live in! With this very original remark, I remain

Most sincerely your friend,
NATH. HAWTHORNE
--Mr. Bright answered as follows--
MY DEAR MR. HAWTHORNE,--Thank you most heartily for your kind letter, and for the manuscript of " Transformation," which has this morning reached me. Please get the missing pages from Smith and Elder. I am going to bind the book up in three gorgeous volumes; there always seems to me to be a peculiar *color* about every story you write, and my binding will depend on what I think when I have finished the book. What binding do you think would be most appropriate? I must really try to be in London again in May, that I may meet you in that most heavenly place,--that we may again dine together at the Club, and see strange, out-of-the-way nooks, and watch the carriages in the Park, Please let me know where you are to be found. If before going to London you are looking for a pleasant place to spend a month, why not Malvern? I do so want you to see it and love it as I do.

Ever most truly yours,
H. A. BRIGHT.

--Concerning the bound volumes of the manuscript, Mr. Bright writes to me : "It is beautifully written, and I remember that he spoke of the few corrections with some pride. Kenyon's name was originally Grayson, and is altered throughout."

Among other letters, there was this from Monckton Milnes--

MY DEAR SIR,--I would not return you my thanks for the gift of your book till I could return thanks for the delight of reading it. I enjoyed it as a true Anglo-Roman; it took me back twenty years, and gave me a true sentimental journey round all my old haunts and impressions. Your moral is bold and most true,--

Man cannot stand,--he must advance, or fall,

And sometimes, falling, makes most way of all

Had you any real "Tale of Horrors" in your mind, as the solution of your enigma? Where are you? Shall we meet ?

Yours very truly,

RICHD. MONCKTON MILNES.

--Mr. Henry Bright's review of "Transformation" followed generally the lines of his letter, though the grumbling was toned down to a mild remonstrance. But I will append extracts from the "Athenaeum's" (Mr. Chorley's) notice, and from that in the "Saturday Review," which is amusingly characteristic.

"To Mr. Hawthorne truth always seems to arrive through the medium of the imagination.... His hero, the Count of Monte Beni, would never have lived had not the Faun of Praxiteles stirred the author's admiration.... The other characters, Mr. Hawthorne must bear to be told, are not new to a tale of his. Miriam, the mysterious, with her hideous tormentor, was indicated in the Zenobia of 'The Blithedale Romance,'--Hilda, the pure and innocent, is own cousin to Phoebe in 'The House of the Seven Gables,'--Kenyon, the sculptor, though carefully wrought out, is a stone image, with little that appeals to our experience of men."--Of the plot the writer says: "We know of little in romance more inconclusive and hazy than the manner in which the tale is brought to a close. Hints will not suffice to satisfy interest which has been excited to voracity.... Hilda and Kenyon marry, as it was to be seen they would do on the first page; but the secret of Miriam's agony and unrest, the manner of final extrication from it, for herself and the gay Faun, who shed blood to defend her, then grew sad and human under the consciousness of the stain, are all left too vaporously involved in suggestion to satisfy any one whose blood has turned back at the admirable, clear, and forcible last scenes of 'The Scarlet Letter.'"

--This was the best Mr. Chorley could do, under his sense of disappointment; and no doubt he might have done worse. But Mrs. Hawthorne, who had formed a high idea of the clever little critic's ability, was not satisfied to let his exceptions pass without a protest. It was a part of her creed that agreeable people would always take just views of things if they were afforded a proper opportunity; and she had found Mr. Chorley very agreeable. So she sat down and wrote him the following letter, which, were he conscious of error, might, one would fancy, have consoled him for having fallen into it. Whether or not he made amends, there is nothing to show; his answer, if he wrote one, not having been preserved.

MY DEAR MR. CHORLEY,--Why do you run with your fine lance directly into the face of Hilda? You were so fierce and wrathful at being shut out from the mysteries (for which we are all disappointed), that you struck in your spurs and plunged with your visor down. For, in deed and in truth, Hilda is not Phoebe, no more than a wild rose is a calm lily. They are alike only in purity and innocence; and I am sure you will see this whenever you read the romance a second time. I am very much grieved that *Mr. Chorley* should seem not to be nicely discriminating; for what are we to do in that case? The artistic, pensive, reserved, contemplative, delicately appreciative Hilda can in no wise be related to the enchanting little housewife, whose energy, radiance, and eglantine sweetness fill her daily homely duties with joy, animation, and fragrance. Tell me, then, is it not so? I utterly protest against being supposed partial because I am Mrs. Hawthorne. But it is so very naughty of you to demolish this new growth in such a hurry, that I cannot help a disclaimer; and I am so sure of your friendliness and largeness, that I am not in the least afraid. You took all the fright out of me by that exquisite, gemlike, aesthetic dinner and tea which you gave us at the fairest of houses last summer. It was a prettier and more *mignonne* thing than I thought could happen in London; so safe and so quiet, and so very satisfactory, with the light of thought playing all about. I have a good deal of fight left in me still about Kenyon, and the "of course" union of Kenyon and Hilda; but I will not say more, except that Mr. Hawthorne had no idea that they were destined for each other. Mr. Hawthorne is driven by his muse, but does not drive her; and I have known him to be in an inextricable doubt, in the midst of a book or sketch, as to its probable issue, waiting upon the muse for the rounding in of the sphere which every true work of art is. I am surprised to find that Mr. Hawthorne was so absorbed in Italy that he had no idea that the story, as such, was interesting! and therefore is somewhat absolved for having "excited our interest to voracity.". . . I dare say you are laughing (gently) at my explosion of small muskets. But I feel more comfortable now I have discharged a little of my opposition. With sincere regard I am, dear Mr. Chorley,

 Yours,
SOPHIA HAWTHORNE.

On the blank page Mr. Hawthorne added the following--

DEAR MR. CHORLEY,--You see how fortunate I am in having a critic close at hand, whose favorable verdict consoles me for any lack of appreciation in other quarters. Really, I think you were wrong in assaulting the individuality of my poor Hilda. If her portrait bears any resemblance to that of Phoebe, it must be the fault of my mannerism as a painter. But I thank you for the kind spirit of your notice; and if you had found ten times as much fault, you are amply entitled to do so by the quantity of generous praise heretofore bestowed.

 Sincerely yours,
NATH. HAWTHORNE

Hawthorne had sent a copy of the book to Mr. and Mrs. S. C. Hall, who had received it as coming from the publishers, and Mr. Hall reviewed it in the art periodical of which he was at that time the editor, but made no communication to Hawthorne on the subject. Subsequently, however, the fact of the book's having been an "author's copy" came out, and Mrs. Hall wrote:--

I wish I could prevail on you to come to us on the 30th. I will write and ask dear Mrs. Hawthorne to give you her sanction--for *one day more*, if she will but do so. It is sad to think we cannot have you together, that one evening; but, if to have *both* is impossible, do please come yourself. Mr. Bennoch wrote me that you were so kind and gracious as to send me your book. I only heard that on Saturday. Mr. Hall thought it came as usual from the publishers,--with the line written by them "from the author,"--and he reviewed it in the "Art Journal." I took up my pen more than once to thank you most gratefully for the *intense enjoyment* the book gave us,--eloquent and poetic and thoughtful as it is,--such a glory of a book--but I imagined again you might think it presumptuous, and so I restrained myself; little thinking the book was mine from its gifted author Please, when you dine with us on the 30th, you must write my name in it. Mr. Hall would call on you if you would graciously fix an hour to receive him.

My dear sir, with great admiration, sincerely yours
ANNA M. HALL.

--This was as flattering as the most exacting romancer could desire; and Mr. Hall took pains to express his enthusiasm over the romance in no less measured terms, and gave it to be understood that his review of it had been the deliberate concentration of his spoken delight The review itself, however, was not produced, for some unexplained reason, and Hawthorne never saw it. Twenty years afterwards the present writer met Mr. Hall in London, when the latter, in the course of conversation, recurred to the above episode, and gave a glowing reminiscence of the criticism in the "Art Journal." It so happened, however, that I was shortly afterwards in the house of a friend, in whose library I found a complete edition of the volumes of the "Art Journal;" and it occurred to me to look up the famous review of" Transformation." It was a brief notice, and began as follows:--

"We are not to accept this book as a story; in that respect it is grievously deficient. The characters are utterly untrue to nature and to fact; they speak, all and always, the sentiments of the author; their words also are his; there is no one of them for which the world has furnished a model."

--The reviewer then goes on to commend some of the descriptions of scenery, and so concludes. No doubt the "review" expressed Mr. Hall's genuine opinion; but it is perplexing that he should so promptly have forgotten what that opinion was, and even have imagined it to be quite the opposite of what is here recorded. But the incident is so characteristic of Mr. Hall that no one who has had the pleasure of knowing him will be surprised at it. His temperamental tendency to paint the lily of truth is beyond his control and even beyond his consciousness. I recollect his having related, before a company of gentlemen at dinner, an anecdote of "myself and my friend Hawthorne," which was accurate enough in all particulars, except that the "myself" in question happened to have been, not Mr. Hall, but another gentleman, there present, and occupying the next chair to my own.

The "Saturday Review" notice appeared on the same day as that in the "Athenaeum," and is worth recalling as another thoroughly English effort to deal with an abstruse problem. We are told that

"a mystery is set before us to unriddle, and at the end the author turns round and asks us what is the good of solving it. That the impression of emptiness and unmeaningness thus produced is in itself a blemish to the work, no one can deny. Mr. Hawthorne really trades upon the honesty of other writers. We feel a sort of interest in the story, slightly and sketchily as it is told, because our experience of other novels leads us to assume that, when an author pretends to have a plot, he has one."

The reviewer goes on to say that, in regard to Donatello,

"Mr. Hawthorne does not refrain from giving the loosest rein to his fancy;" while as for "Miriani" (as the name is printed throughout the article), "the lady for whom this unhappy animal conceives a passionate love," she "belongs scarcely less to the region of pure fancy. She first presents herself as an artist; and it appears to be accepted as an axiom in every description of artist life that a man or woman who paints pictures or moulds clay is released from all the ties and burdens of life,-- that it is impertinent to inquire whence they came or how they live, or with whom or on what." "Hilda" is "the type of high-souled innocence, purity, and virgin modesty. She also is an artist; and we are therefore supposed not to feel surprise at finding that she lives, without any one to protect her, at the top of a high tower in the centre of Rome, where she feeds a brood of milky doves, and keeps a lamp burning in honor of the Virgin. . . . A lover is assigned her, both that his successful love may mitigate the blackness of the story, and also because, as he is a sculptor, Mr. Hawthorne has the pleasure of describing the real works of American sculptors at Rome under the fiction that they were the creations of the imaginary artist." The reviewer goes on to remark that "Mr. Hawthorne seems to have been greatly attracted by Catholicism. . . . No one could fall more entirely than Mr. Hawthorne into the modern fashion of asking, not whether a religion is true, but whether it is suitable to a particular individual . . As it happens, however, the same sensibility that attracts him to Catholicism also repels him from it; and when he ceases to reason he is as little able to make allowances where they are due as to discover faults where they exist. It is the priests and the Papal Government that seem to have scared Mr. Hawthorne from the Romish Church. They are such poor, mean creatures, and the Papal Government produced so much misery, poverty, and dirt, that, as the clean citizen of a State accustomed to make its own way in the world he would not mix himself up with what he so thoroughly despised. His Protestantism seems to have been greatly indebted to the theory in which he finally rested,--that the Papal system is dying out." But, although feeling constrained thus to condemn the characters, plot, and sentiment of the romance, the reviewer awards it high praise as "a tourist's sketch," and "we may add that the style is singularly beautiful, the writing most careful, and the justness and felicity of the epithets used to convey the effect of scenery unusually great. The Americans may be proud that they have produced a writer who, in his own special walk of English, has few rivals or equals in the mother country, and they may perhaps allow this excellence to atone for the sincere contempt with which he evidently regards the large majority of his countrymen who show themselves on this side of the Atlantic."

--This must suffice as an exposition of the English attitude towards "Transformation" at the time of its first appearance; for the following poetic tribute to the writer, though emanating from the pen of a born Londoner, Mr. William Bennett, can hardly be considered English in its tone. Mr. Bennett, it will be remembered, had always been among the most sincere of Hawthorne's admirers, and he did not fail now to avouch that admiration in the heartiest terms at his command. As a poem, the writing may perhaps be open to criticism; but as an honest and cordial effort at appreciation and friendly sympathy, it is well worth preserving.

I.

O mightiest name of Death,--O awful Rome,--
How has he writ, in marble, on thy hills
His presence Death thy stony valleys fills

> There, with the ghostly past, he makes his home;
> Yet, in the shadow of thy mighty dome,
> What life eternal lives--a breath that stills
> His boasts to dumbness, and thy conqueror kills.
> Who breathe thy air, deathless henceforth become;
> For ears that hear, thy lips have mystic lore;
> To those who question thee, in the weird might
> Of genius, lo, thy thousand tongues restore
> The spells that scare oblivion to flight
> Greatness is in thy touch. Lo, here once more
> To one thou givest thy glory as his right.
>
> II.
>
> Here is the life of Rome ;--the air of death,
> Silence and solitude and awe, are here,
> Spectres of grandeur, at whose bygone breath
> Earth stilled and trembled, from these leaves appear;
> From these weird words steal wonder and strange fear,
> An awful past, which he who listeneth
> In solemn awe, with trembling heart, may hear,
> Hearing what from her stones the bygone saith.
> Here is the double life that haunts Rome's hills,
> Power spelt in ruins, art that wreathes all time,
> Beauty eternal that the rapt air fills
> With reverence from fit souls from every clime.
> Hawthorne, henceforth, here, with life's joys and ills,
> Rome's thoughts are with me, and her dreams sublime.
>
> III.
>
> "From evils, goods,--from sin and sorrow, peace,
> A holier future, and a loftier faith,"--
> This to the soul thy mystic volume saith,
> Hawthorne, and bids doubt's spectral night to cease,
> Offering from its dread gloom what bless'd release!
> If any say, "Evil accuses Him
> From whom is all, of evil," here, in dim,
> Wan characters is writ, "Good hath increase
> Even from the stifling ill with which it strives;
> God's wisdom is not ours. From blackest ill
> Souls, sorrow-deepened, have won whitest lives;
> Bless Him for all things all things are His will.
> His stroke the granite of our hearts but rives,
> That light may enter and His ends fulfil."

W. BENNETT.

Early in May, Hawthorne wrote the following letter to Henry Bright:

18 CHARLES STEEET, BATH, May 5, 1860.

DEAR MR. BRIGHT,--Here is Mr. Lemprière Hammond's very kind note. Under your auspices, I think I may venture to accept his hospitality, and I should be delighted to spend one night within the walls of Trinity. Is Mr. Hammond a descendant of Lemprière's Classical Dictionary?--or perchance a mythical personage? Do not let him hear of this foolish query; for people are as touchy about their names as a cat about her tail.

I mean to go to London either the latter part of next week or the first of the succeeding one. Part of the time I shall be at the house of Mr. Motley (the Dutch historian), 31 Hertford Street. It is not my purpose to return to Bath till after our visit to Cambridge.

You will not find any photograph nor (so far as I am aware) any engraving of the Faun of Praxiteles. There are photographs, stereoscopic and otherwise, of another Faun, which is almost identical with the hero of my romance, though only an inferior repetition of it. My Faun is in the Capitol; the other, in the Vatican. The genuine statue has never been photographed, on account, I suppose, of its standing in a bad light. The photograph of the Vatican Faun supplies its place very well, except as to the face, which is very inferior.

I think your club is the Oxford and Cambridge. When I come to London, I shall send or call there unless I otherwise hear of you.

Truly yours, NATH. HAWTHORNE.

--Soon after his arrival (on the 16th), they took breakfast with Monckton Milnes, meeting Lady Galway, Thiriwall (Bishop of Saint David's), and one or two more; and, on the 19th, went to Mayal, the photographer, where Hawthorne sat for his photograph (the same that has been etched for this work). In regard to this photograph, by the by, an erroneous story has gone abroad, which it may be as well to correct. I know not by whom it was originally invented; but I find it quoted from the "Salem Gazette" as follows:

"J. Lothrop Motley, who well knew Hawthorne's aversion to photographic processes, set a trap for his friend in this wise. He invited him to walk one day in London; and as they were passing the studio of a well-known photographer, Motley asked Hawthorne to step in and make a selection from some pictures of himself, which were ready, he supposed, for examination. They entered, chatting pleasantly together, Hawthorne at the time being in the best of spirits. Dropping into a chair, which Motley placed for him, he looked brightly after his friend disappearing behind a screen in quest of the proofs. At this moment, and with this look of animation upon his face, the photograph referred to was taken, the artist having made all necessary preparations to capture a likeness from the unsuspecting sitter. Motley's proofs were produced and examined, and Hawthorne was never told that he had been taken. This was shortly before the family returned home. One of the children, it seems,--I think it was the ethereal Una,--had seen the surreptitious picture at Motley's or at Bennoch's, and on the homeward voyage she referred to it, and said it was a beautiful likeness, far better than she had ever seen before. Hawthorne, of course, was incredulous, and assured his wife that the child must be mistaken. After her husband's death, Mrs. Hawthorne became acquainted with the facts as above narrated, and at her earnest entreaty the photograph was sent to her."

This story is a real curiosity in fabrication. There is not one syllable of truth in it from beginning to end; but the ingenious and elaborate manner in which it is worked up from point to point is remarkable, showing as it does that the writer was in no respect laboring under a misapprehension, or suffering from a defective memory or incomplete information, but that he was consciously inventing all the way through, and enjoying his invention. The real facts are as follows,--I will quote the entire passage from a recent letter from Henry Bright to me:

"The account of the photograph being taken for Mr. Motley is quite wrong. I went with Hawthorne to the photographer (Mayal), as he had promised me a photograph of himself. He gave his name, and Mayal came up in a great state of excitement. Hawthorne got very shy, and grasped his umbrella as if it were the last friend left him. This, of course, was taken away from him by the photographer, and a table with a book on it was put in its place. 'Now, sir,' said Mayal, 'please to look *intense!*' He was afterwards told to look smiling (at the portrait of a lady!). I chose the 'intense' one, and afterwards had a copy taken of it for a friend of Hawthorne. I am amused to find (in the current anecdote) that Mr. Motley attracted Hawthorne's attention 'at the critical moment.' This is quite imaginative; for Mayal insisted on my going behind a screen, where your father could not see me. After your father's death the photograph was engraved, and I sent other copies to your mother, Mr. Longfellow, and one or two more. The original (there was only one taken at the time) hangs in my own room."

--It may be worth noting, for those who are interested in coincidences, that the 19th of May, four years afterwards, was the date of Hawthorne's death. The note which Bright had sent to Hawthorne the previous day, reminding him of his appointment, runs thus--

THURSDAY, May 18, 1860.

MY DEAR MR. HAWTHORNE,--*If* to-morrow is sunshiny enough to photograph you, and *if* you are not otherwise engaged, well, let us get it done! I shall be here (Oxford and Cambridge Club) at twelve, and again at four, if you will look in at either time. Milnes says I am to bring you punctually at ten on Saturday; so I will call for you five minutes before. It is no party; and Mrs. Milnes, who has just come. will be there. I was very glad indeed to see Mr. Motley last night.

Ever yours, H. A. BRIGHT

--On the following evening Hawthorne was at the Cosmopolitan Club, where he and Mr. Layard found a great deal to say to each other; and on the 25th of May he left London for Cambridge, by previous appointment with Bright, who was to receive his master's degree there. Mr. Bright says

"My old friend, Lemprière Hammond (well known at Cambridge), got rooms for him in the oldest part of the old Court of Trinity. I remember how amused Hawthorne was to find that the room had been so dark that he had lost his umbrella--the precious umbrella--in it for two days! He was much delighted with Cambridge, and saw everything, including Cromwell's picture in Sydney College, and 'Byron's Pool.' He also visited the Union. Our best friends there were Hammond, and that most accomplished of Cambridge men (whose too early death was a real loss to the University), W. G. Clark, the public orator, and afterwards vice-master of Trinity."

--Hawthorne has himself given some impressions of this excursion in a letter to his daughter. The "Uncle John" referred to is John O'Sullivan.

TRINITY COLLEGE, CAMBRIDGE, May 25, 1860.

DEAR UNA,--I am established here in an ancient set of college rooms, which happen to be temporarily vacated by the rightful possessor. I arrived yesterday evening, and am pretty well wearied by a day of sightseeing,--as you may suppose,

Mr. Bright being the cicerone. I snatch just this moment to write, before going to dine with one of the fellows of the college. You ask about Uncle John. I have very little to say on that subject, except that I called at his hotel some days ago, and found him not there; and shortly after received a note, informing me that be had left for the Continent. I think you had better intermit writing to him till we hear more. I shall return to London on Monday morning, go to Canterbury the same day, return to Bennoch's the next day (Tuesday), and probably stay there till Thursday morning, when I am resolved to come home. I have received an invitation to dine with Smith and Elder, and meet the contributors to the "Cornhill Magazine;" but I declined it, being tired to death of dinners, and longing to see you all again; and this dinner would detain me another weary day. You had better direct your next letter to the care of Bennoch, unless there should be urgent need of communicating with me between now and Monday, in which case you might direct to the care of Lemprieère Hammond, Esq., Trinity College, Cambridge. But I trust there will be no necessity for this. I long to see you all again, for it seems ages since I went away. I heard a nightingale--two or three, indeed--last night! Give my best love to mamma, and very warm love to Julian, Rosebud, and yourself. Affectionately yours,

NATH. HAWTHORNE.

--He returned to Bath about the 1st June, and we shortly afterwards set out for Liverpool, whence, after a brief sojourn at Mrs. Blodgett's, we embarked for Boston, under the captaincy of our old friend Leitch, After a pleasant voyage of ten days, we were safely landed at our destination.

CHAPTER 8 - THE WAYSIDE AND THE WAR

IT was a hot day towards the close of June, 1860, when Hawthorne alighted from the train at Concord station, and drove up in the railway wagon to the Wayside. The fields looked brown, the trees were dusty, and the sun white and brilliant. At certain seasons in Concord the heat in summer stagnates and simmers, until it seems as if nothing but a grasshopper could live. The water in the river is so warm that to bathe in it is merely to exchange one kind of heat for another. The very shadow of the trees is torrid; and I have known the thermometer to touch 112 degrees in the shade. No breeze stirs throughout the long, sultry day; and the feverish nights bring mosquitoes, but no relief. To come from the salt freshness of the Atlantic into this living oven is a startling change, especially when one has his memory full of green England. Such was America's first greeting to Hawthorne, on his return from a seven years' absence; it was to this that he had looked forward so lovingly and so long. As be passed one little wooden house after another, with their white clapboards and their green blinds, perhaps be found his thoughts not quite so cloudless as the sky. It is dangerous to have a home; too much is required of it.

The Wayside, however, was not white; it was painted a dingy buff color. The larches and Norway pines, several hundred of which had been sent out from England, were planted along the paths, and were for the most part doing well. The well-remembered hillside, with its rude terraces, shadowed by apple-trees, and its summit green with pines, rose behind the house; and in front, on the other side of the highway, extended a broad meadow of seven acres, bounded by a brook, above which hung drooping willows. It was, upon the whole, as pleasant a place as any in the village, and much might be done to enhance its beauty. It had been occupied, during our absence, by a brother of Mrs. Hawthorne; and the house itself was in excellent order, and looked just the same as in our last memory of it. A good many alterations have been made since then; another story was added to the western wing, the tower was built up behind, and two other rooms were put on in the rear. These changes, together with some modifications about the place, such as the opening up of paths, the cutting down of some trees, and the planting of others, were among the last things that engaged Hawthorne's attention in this life.

The John Brown episode had just taken place, and Mr. Frank Sanborn, a citizen of Concord, and the principal of a private school there, had taken a prominent part in connection with it. It was to this school that Hawthorne sent his son, being specially moved thereto by the following letter from Ellery Channing:

CONCORD, Sept. 3, 1860.

MY DEAR HAWTHORNE,--In numbering over the things that had been added to the town, t' other day, I left out the first and best, which is, the school for girls and boys, under the charge of Mr. Sanborn. No words that I could use on this occasion could do justice to his happy influence on the characters of those confided to him, and more especially of the girls. He has supplied a want long felt here, and, by having a school for young children, leaves nothing to be desired. His scholars are from desirable families, and many of them are very attractive and pleasing persons. The mere fact of associating with him and those he has drawn about him I should regard as a matter of first importance. I have never heard of a school before where there was so much to please and so little to offend, and in this country, to every one who purposes to take the least part in any social affairs, the value of a good school is unquestioned. Our school-days are the days of our life; it is then we learn all we ever know, and without these mimic contests, these services, sports, and petty grievances, what were all the after days! If you were as intimate with Mr. Sanborn as I have the good fortune to be, I think nothing would give you so much satisfaction as to have such nice girls as yours seem to be directly under his charge. Nothing seems to me more unfortunate in this land of activity than to bring up children in seclusion, without the invaluable discipline that a good school presents. Forgive me for dwelling a little on this, out of regard to Mr. Sanborn, who deserves to be sustained. I was greatly pleased with the success of your last book, "The Marble Faun." It seemed to me at first, until I got well a-going, a little difficult to seize the thread; hut when I once found it, I went rapidly forward unto the end. I always consider the rapidity with which I can read a story the test of its merit, at least for me. Many others have spoken to me of its effect on them. I greatly enjoyed the Italian criticism. As a matter of art, there is possibly always a certain danger in combining didactic and dramatic situations; but if any field is open to this, it should be Italy. "Corinne," I think, deals in character rather than criticism. I should be ashamed to tell you how often I have read "The Marble Faun," or "The Blithedale Romance." The latter is, I think, of all your pieces the one I like the best. No book was ever printed containing better effects for illustration. I also have often read over the sorrows of Aunt Hepzibah.

I am a little late in welcoming you back to the stern and simple fields of this ancient Puritan land; but a traveller is like coffee, and needs to be well settled.

With regards to Mrs. Hawthorne, believe me

Ever faithfully yours,

W. ELLERY CHANNING.

--Hawthorne and his wife had themselves borne the chief part in the instruction of their children hitherto. The former had grounded his son carefully in Latin, and had introduced him to Greek, his own acquaintance with these languages being sound, if not critical. French and Italian had been added by Mrs. Hawthorne and Miss Shepard; and during his mother's absence in Lisbon, the boy had received the benefit of training in drawing from an eminent artist in Liverpool. He also took many "quarters'" lessons in the small-sword from a certain Corporal Blair, of the Fourth Dragoon Guards, the most amiable and unexceptionable of British soldiers, gently imperturbable of manner, courteous of speech, six feet in height, erect as a mast, and with the chest and shoulders of a Greek athlete. I also cherish tender recollections of an old Peninsula veteran, Major Johnstone, who trained me in the use of the broadsword, and who, during the pauses of the encounter, used to regale us with anecdotes of Spain, Waterloo, and Wellington. The thorough education of his children was, in short, Hawthorne's one extravagance; he spared neither pains nor money to that end. His own patience and conscientiousness as a teacher seem more and more wonderful to me, as time goes on: nothing escaped him; he shirked nothing, nor did he ever speak a harsh word, no matter how trying the circumstances,--and they must often have been very trying! Were all instructors like him, the world would soon be wise.

He did not fall in with his friend Channing's opinion as to the expediency of sending his daughters to the school; which, however, it may be remarked in passing, fully bore out Mr. Channing's recommendation. But Rose was still very young, and Una was delicate and, besides, Hawthorne was always very chary of his daughters.

But the school was not more excellent as a school than in its social aspects; every week there was a school-dance, and, twice or thrice a year, a grand picnic, not to mention other jollifications; and in these Hawthorne's girls took part. Mr. Emerson's house was also a centre of polite and intellectual amenities; and another unfailing spring of hospitable entertainment was always to be found at the Alcotts', our next-door neighbors. Altogether, it may be surmised that there never was and never will be such a genial Concord--for young people at least--as that which existed from 1859 to 1865, or thereabouts; and several marriages were among the happy results of the experience.

Hawthorne, meanwhile, was taking counsel with Mr. Wetherbee and Mr. Watts, the Concord carpenters, as to the best way of augmenting the Wayside's commodiousness; the estimates were made out, and the work was begun. For many months thereafter the sound of hammering and sawing was heard every day; boards were piled up on the lawn, and the barn was full of shavings and sawdust. Hawthorne had always wanted a tower to write in. There was a tower at Montauto; but unfortunately it contained accommodations only for a couple of owls and a ghostly monk. The present tower was a less picturesque and gloomy affair, built of American deal boards, and haunted by nothing but the smell of new wood. A staircase, narrow and steep, ascends through the floor, the opening being covered by a sort of gabled structure, to one end of which a standing-desk was affixed; a desk-table was placed against the side. The room was about twenty feet square, with four gables; and the ceiling, instead of being flat, was a four-sided vault, following the conformation of the roof. There were five windows, the southern and eastern ones opening upon a flat tin roof upon which one might walk or sit in suitable weather. The walls were papered with paper of a pale golden hue, without figures. There was a closet for books on each side of the northern window, which looked out upon the hill. A small fireplace, to which a stove was attached, was placed between the two southern windows. The room was pleasant in autumn and spring; but in winter the stove rendered the air stifling, and in summer the heat of the sun was scarcely endurable. Hawthorne, however, spent several hours of each day in his study, and it was here that the "Old Home" was written, and "Septimius Felton," and "Dr. Grimshawe," and the Dolliver fragment. But in the afternoon he was in the habit of strolling about the grounds with his wife; and about sunset he generally ascended the hill alone, and paced to and fro along its summit, wearing a narrow path between the huckleberry and sweet-fern bushes and beneath the pines, of which some traces, I believe, still remain. In the evenings he sat in the library,--the room in the western wing, which had formerly been the study; and here he either read to himself or aloud to the assembled family. Messrs. Ticknor and Fields published a complete edition of Walter Scott's works about this time, and sent him a handsomely bound copy; and, beginning at the beginning, he read all those admirable romances to his children and wife. There was no conceivable entertainment which they would not have postponed in favor of this presentation of Scott through the medium of Hawthorne. I have never since ventured to open the Waverley Novels.

He took few or no long walks after his return to America: Walden Pond (about two miles distant) was the limit of his excursions; and he generally confined himself to his own grounds, except on Sundays, when we all strolled together about the neighboring fields and wood-paths. His physical energy was on the wane, and he lost flesh rapidly. The first winter, with its drifting snows, imprisoned him much in the house, and the ensuing spring found him languid and lacking in enterprise. Meantime the war had broken out; and he, in common with the rest of his countrymen, perused the bulletins with great diligence.

Among his son's earliest recollections are the lessons of vigorous patriotism which Hawthorne used to inculcate upon him. He told him the story of the Revolution until it was the most vivid and familiar part of the boy's life, and the latter went to England almost with the idea of carrying fire and sword into a hostile country. There was an innate love of battle and of warlike emprise in Hawthorne's nature; and except when he took pains to make his reason supersede his instinct, his expressions of enthusiasm against the Southern pretensions were as rousing and hearty as any utterances of the time. "I hope," he used to say, "that we shall give them a terrible thrashing, and then kick them out." He did not hope for the preservation of the Union; because, if it came peacefully, it would sooner or later involve the extension of slavery over the Northern States, and if by war, it seemed to him it would be only superficial and temporary. The essence of all true union being mutual good-will, it would follow that compulsion could effect nothing worth having. At the same time the prospect of the dissolution of that mighty nation which had embodied the best hopes of mankind was a deep pain to him; it seemed likely to be the death of that old spirit of patriotism which had come down to us from the Revolution. A civil war, in the Republic of the Future, was a sorry thing, no matter what the pretext for it; nor was it easy to discover what the real pretext was In wars between countries foreign to each other, there is seldom either opportunity or desire to investigate the moral attitude of the opposing party; but it was otherwise in our civil war. It was impossible not to hear the arguments of the other side, or not to understand that those arguments might seem unanswerable to the men whose geographical and traditional accidents had brought them under their influence. The conflict, in short, appeared to be less moral than irrepressible,--the result of spontaneous and inevitable natural tendencies; and, if this were so, then so much the less hope was there that it would fail to destroy whatever was most imposing and majestic in our national life. As for abolition, considered as a motive for battle, Hawthorne rejected all belief in it. He regarded slavery as an evil, and would have made any personal sacrifice to be rid of it, as an element in the national existence; but to maintain that we were ready to imperil our life merely out of regard for the liberation of the negroes was, in his opinion, to utter sentimental nonsense. The best reason that he could give himself for going to war was, that the arrogance of the slave-holders would otherwise reach such a pitch that the Republic would in effect be transformed into an oligarchy, or possibly something worse. There must be a limit to Northern concession, and, "if compelled to choose," he said, "I go for the North." But the choice was between two evils,-not between an undoubted good and its opposite.

Thus his deeper feeling could not but be one of depression and misgiving. Let us fight the South and conquer her, since so it must be, but let us not rejoice too much at our victory; for victory will cost us almost as much as defeat. As the war continued, however, and luck went uniformly against us, he postponed more and more all speculations as to the ultimate result, and allowed the grim spirit of battle to take possession of him. Had we conquered the South more easily, Hawthorne would never have found it in his heart to feel so hardly towards her, and would have advocated all possible leniency. As it was, the utmost restraint his conscience could impose upon him was to abstain from stimulating and inflaming, by any public utterance, the public hatred against our fellow-countrymen, which was already more than enough aroused. In what little he has written having reference to the struggle, he has adopted a colder and more dispassionate tone than he actually felt, lest, by yielding to the animosity of the moment, he should be found to have swerved from the permanent truth. This course brought upon him some local odium at the time; but he was of course then, as always, utterly unmoved by anything of that kind.

For more than a year after the outbreak of hostilities, however, he made no serious attempt to resume the habit of imaginative composition. Every morning brought fresh news, of hope or of disaster, from the seat of war, and there was no escape therefrom into calm regions of meditation. As he wrote in the preface of "Our Old Home:"

"The Present, the Immediate, the Actual, has proved too potent for me. It takes away not only my scanty faculty, but even my desire for imaginative composition, and leaves me sadly content to scatter a thousand peaceful fantasies upon the hurricane that is sweeping us all along with it, possibly, into a limbo where our nation and its polity may be as literally the fragments of a shattered dream as my unwritten romance."

He could not sit calmly inventing stories, while the fate of his country was in suspense; he must wait either until war had become our second nature, or until the issue was beyond doubt. And though he struggled hard to overcome this disinclination, indeed, his circumstances could ill afford that he should be idle,--the effort was too much for him. The seclusion of his tower was not secluded enough. Among other of Hawthorne's correspondents at this period was a young poet, possessing his full share of the suspicious sensitiveness of the poetic fraternity, though not, perhaps, overburdened with genius. The two following specimens of his epistolary style will be found entertaining:--

GREENFIELD, April 4, 1S61.
NATH'L HAWTHORNE, Esq.

DEAR SIR,--I have just sent to your address, through my sister now in Rome, a little volume of poems (the same that you will find herewith), supposing that you were still abroad. Please accept it as an acknowledgment of deep indebtedness for very great pleasure and instruction that I have received from your writings; indeed, so great that it has run into my blood and bones, and perhaps out of my fingers' ends. I had the pleasure not long since of sending to Alfred Tennyson (whom I knew in England) your "Mosses," as he wanted to see more New England poetry from the pen of the author of "The Scarlet Letter." But it seems almost irreverent to speak passingly of your works, or in terms of compliment; and I beg you will pardon my having spoken of them at all, but will accept this little volume as a very slight return of what I cannot in any way repay. With the hope that you may find something that will reward perusal, and that you will pardon what may seem a liberty in a stranger,

I remain with great respect, yours,
F. G. TUCKERMAN.

N. B. Will you permit me to ask, before sending the book, whether it will be acceptable? As in one instance such an act has received no acknowledgment from the recipient.

--Hawthorne replied to the young poet, whose faith in human nature had been so cruelly betrayed, in terms as encouraging as the circumstances admitted, and got this answer:--

GREENFIELD, April 10, 1861.

MY DEAR SIR,--Your kind note has just reached me, and I hasten to avail myself of your permission to send my little volume. If I had only waited one day more, I should have had no occasion for insisting upon a manifestation of willingness from yourself, for the acknowledgment, and a graceful one, came at last. For the book, which I offer with a certain tremor to yourself, I claim little, but that it is New Englandy (I hope), was not written to please anybody, and is addressed to those only who understand it,--and this latter clause, because the other day I had a line from a clerical critic who, after reading the "Sonnets," gravely accuses the author of "idolatry," and then goes on to remark that "Margites" would have been much better employed in some work of Christian usefulness. Pardon this, and let me hope that you will find something that may deserve your favorable opinion, which I shall be proud to know of. My hope is to have the book published in England (if it seem worthy), as here I fancy it would be but coldly received, even with that proviso. Thank you for receiving so pleasantly what I said about yourself, or rather what I did not say; only your own audience know the value of your benefactions, hardly to be communicated; and many a time have I laid down your volume with the conviction "that only silence suiteth best." Still I cannot promise, should we ever meet, to be always so discreet. Please pardon a few corrections and emendations that I have made in the margin of my book, and many that I should, but have not, made; and believe me, dear sir,

Both warmly and gratefully yours,

F. G. TUCKERMAN.

--There were various inducements to social activity held out to him by his friends in Boston at this time; especially the meetings of the famous club of which Emerson Holmes, Lowell, Whittier, and others were members; but he uniformly declined the invitations. He had tried the experiment of such things pretty thoroughly on the other side of the Atlantic, and was doubtful of his ability either to give or to receive much benefit from them. Besides, he was not in the physical or mental humor for general social intercourse; and probably wished to avoid the political discussions which would be apt to arise, and in which he might be compelled to oppose the views of those with whom his friendly relations were most agreeable. He reserved the expression of his opinions on those matters for his letters to Bright and Bennoch in England, and to Horatio Bridge in this country. The following, written to the latter not long after the outbreak of hostilities, has, I think, already found its way into print, but should be preserved here as a part of the history of his thoughts at this juncture:-

CONCORD, May 26, 1861.

MY DEAR BRIDGE,--. . . The war, strange to say, has had a beneficial effect upon my spirits, which were flagging wofully before it broke out. But it was delightful to share in the heroic sentiment of the time, and to feel that I had a country,--a consciousness which seemed to make me young again. One thing as regards this matter I regret, and one thing I am glad of. The regrettable thing is that I am too old to shoulder a musket myself and the joyful thing is that Julian is too young. He drills constantly with a company of lads, and means to enlist as soon as he reaches the minimum age. But I trust we shall either be victorious or vanquished before that time. Meantime, though I approve the war as much as any man, I don't quite understand what we are fighting for, or what definite result can be expected. If we pummel the South ever so hard, they will love us none the better for it; and even if we subjugate them, our next step should be to cut them adrift. If we are fighting for the annihilation of slavery, to be sure it may be a wise object, and offer a tangible result, and the only one which is consistent with a future union between North and South. A continuance of the war would soon make this plain to us, and we should see the expediency of preparing our black brethren for future citizenship by allowing them to fight for their own liberties, and educating them through heroic influences. Whatever happens next, I must say that I rejoice that the old Union is smashed. We never were one people, and never really had a country since the Constitution was formed. .

NATH. HAWTHORNE.

--Two letters from Henry Bright, though written a couple of years apart, may be placed together here, as there is nothing in them of especially chronological importance. The second one refers to the renowned passage about Englishwomen in "Our Old Home," which retains to this day a ludicrous power to make the great nation gnash its teeth with resentment.

. . . I went to the opening of the Exhibition. It was a dull sight, and rather a sad one: the ghost of the poor Prince would *not* be laid! and then, too, one thought of the Exhibition of 1851, with its charmmg gayety; its freshness, its beauty, and the dream of lasting peace and good-will among men, which lingered about it, and half hallowed it. *Now*, that dream could not come again; and the Exhibition seems but some big bazaar,--and the friendship of nations is only the buying and selling of luxuries,--and everywhere there seems to be a spirit of self-seeking and greed and hollow pretence of lofty purpose. Beautiful things of course there are in all the courts, but they are beautiful in detail, not as parts of one grand whole. *Most* beautiful are the pictures) though even here I for one remember the art-galleries of Manchester still more pleasantly, and would readily give up French galleries and Belgian galleries for that head of Fra Angelico, the Murillo, the Rubens Rainbow, and others, which you will at once call up again.--Then, some of the sculpture here is good. First and best is Story's "Cleopatra," which *you* it was, who told us of. It is a noble statue, and every one admires it,--every one thinks it the finest statue there. How good your description is (I read it over again yesterday) ; and how wise you were to recognize the power of Story's work. It is curious that both in 1851 and now America should carry off the palm of Phidias. As for Gibson's "Venus," I hate and despise her. So meretricious a lady should not venture into decent company. How *cruel* too she looks,--with that blue, stony eye, with no particle of light to give it life. She is a goddess of Corinth in the worst days,--or the Venus of the Tannhaueser!

I saw a good deal of Milnes. He is more *Northern* in his sympathies than any one I met except Hughes (I suspect Tom Brown wishes to avenge the death of his kinsman "Old John"), and the editor of "Macmillan's Magazine." I spent one pleasant evening at the "Cosmopolitan;"--Milnes was there, Sir John Simeon, Captain Bruce, and one or two others whom you will remember. I had also a pleasant talk with Millais, Woolner the sculptor, and Hughes. Another night I was at a soirée at Milnes's,--such a den of lions! Du Chaillu, the gorilla; Jules Gérard, the lion-slayer;

Rupell of the "Times;" Theodore Martin; an exiled Prince; certain grandees, and certain unknown characters. Milnes is really the kindest, most lovable man, and is a perfectly fearless Daniel in the midst of it all. Synge you certainly remember. I went to Thackeray's new house, where he was staying, to bid him good-by. . . .

MY DEAR MR. HAWTHORNE,--Thank you most warmly, most heartily, for all your kindness,--for sending me your book,--and for the too generous words of friendship in which you speak of me. It is one of the best things of my life to have made a friend of you. With this I send a review of mine, in the "Examiner," of "Our Old Home." Don't think me very ungrateful for my abuse of your abuse of English ladies. You see I positively could not help it. An inevitable lance had to be broken, both for the fun of it and the truth of it. It really was too bad, some of the things you say. You talk like a cannibal. Mrs. Heywood says to my mother, "I really believe you and I were the only ladies he knew in Liverpool, and we are not like beefsteaks." So all the ladies are furious. Within the last day or two I also have become more intolerant, for I am the happy father of a little girl who promises to be a typical Englishwoman; and were I again to write a review, my lance, for her sake, must needs be sharper, and my thrust more vigorous!

I will not write politics to you, for I have nothing new to say. "Fraternization or death" is no doubt a good and eminently logical cry, and no doubt the result will prove its admirable expediency. When all the men are killed, the women and children will be left, and "fraternization," or more intimate relationship, will of course be possible. I 'm glad you 're not to fight us about these "rams;" but perhaps Jeff Davis will: it is so very difficult to please every one. I went over one of the "rams" the other day. It looks formidable enough: two revolving turrets, immense iron plates, huge battering-prow. One is sorry for the intending punchatees,--so nearly ready as she was--and now the "broad arrow" is upon her, and she must not stir. Mr. Ward Beecher has been lecturing here. I regret to say that some one was unmannerly enough to placard the walls with "sensation" placards in black and red, quoting from a speech of his (Ward Beecher's) on the Trent affair, in which he was pleased to remark that "the best blood of England must flow" in consequence. I 'm afraid that Mr. Beecher found a portion of his audience inattentive, and given to groans and stamps; however, there was no *regular* row; and Mr. Beecher's audacity in lecturing at all had a touch of sublimity in it. Mr. Channing has also been lecturing in Leeds and elsewhere. I am very sorry to have seen so little of him, but I am afraid he has not a strictly philosophic mind, and would resent any expression of opinion adverse to his own.

Your affectionate friend,
H. A. BRIGHT.

--During the summer the "beneficial effect" of the war upon Hawthorne's spirits sensibly diminished, and the severe heat contributed to render him uncomfortable. Still, he was not actually ill, and was very far from admitting any need of change of scene. That was a medicine which he had tried (he thought) more than enough. His wife, however, was very anxious to get him off to the seaside; but it was vain to urge him to take any such step on his own account. As good luck would have it, his son Julian was enabled to become the *deus ex machina* of the predicament. In swimming across Concord River under water (during a competitive contest with his school-fellows) he had contrived to produce a congestion of blood to the brain, which laid him up for several days with a smart illness, and made it possible for his mother to insist upon his being immediately taken to the seaside by his father, to obtain the necessary rest and refreshment. This was in July, 1861, and is alluded to by Hawthorne in a letter to Lowell. "I am to start, in two or three days," he says, "on an excursion with Julian, who has something the matter with him, and seems to need sea-air and change. If I alone were concerned, I would most gladly put off my trip till after your dinner; but, as the case stands, I am compelled to decline. Speaking of dinner, last evening's news [of the first battle of Bull Run] will dull the edge of many a Northern appetite; but if it puts all of us into the same grim and bloody humor that it does me, the South had better have suffered ten defeats than won this victory."

We started, accordingly, on the morning of Saturday, July 25th, and proceeded to an out-of-the-way place called Pride's Crossing, some miles out of Salem. The following letter from Mrs. Hawthorne gives a good picture of the domestic situation at the time:--

SATURDAY EVENING, July 25, 1861.

MY DEAREST HUSBAND,--My babies are a-bed, and I must write down my day to you, or it will not be rounded in. I do not know how to impress you with adequate force concerning the absolutely inspiring effect of thy absence! I have been weighed to the earth by my sense of your depressed energies and spirits, in a way from which I tried in vain to rally. I could not sit down in the house and think about it, and so I kept out as much as possible, at work. For in the house a millstone weighed on my heart and head, and I had to struggle to keep off the bed, where I only fell into a half--a stupid and an unrefreshing sleep. Of all the trials, this is the heaviest to me,--to see you so apathetic, so indifferent, so hopeless, so unstrung. Rome has no sin to answer for so unpardonable as this of wrenching off your wings and hanging lead upon your arrowy feet. Rome--and all Rome caused to you. What a mixed cup is this to drink! My heart's desire has been, ever since the warm days, to get you to the sea under pleasant auspices, in a free and unencumbered way,--the sea only, and no people. I saw no way, until this plan of taking Julian occurred to you; and devoutly I blessed God for it, and do now bless Him. I felt so sure that Julian would be only a comfort and a pleasure to you, and am easier to have him with you. It is good for him to be out of the fret of common routine, and it is good for you to have a change from river-damps and sand-heats to ocean fogs and cool sands,--and also from the usual days. You especially need *change* of scene and air. I can flourish like purslain anywhere if my heart is at peace. I cannot flourish anywhere if it be not at peace,--not in any imaginable Paradise. Well, beloved, you were no sooner fairly gone,-- it was no sooner half-past eight o'clock,--than a great thick cloud rose off my heart and head. I had a thousand things which I meant to do in the house; but Rose wanted me to weed the paths with her while she weeded the beds. So I took advantage of the shaded sun and went out. First she took a small basket and I took a big one, and we went down into the garden to get potatoes and squashes. I gathered four squashes, and she got a basket nearly full of potatoes. Then we weeded. At ten, Mary Ellen Bull came to draw, and I set her to work, and continued to weed the paths, feeling better than I had for months,--feeling an endless energy and a new joy quite intoxicating. I went on weeding till after twelve! Rose and Joanna wheeling off wheelbarrows full of my spoils, and leaving such delightful order as would rejoice your eyes to see. Una went down for the mail, and thereby caught a history lesson from Aunt Lizzie Peabody. She brought a letter from London for you, from Miss Adelaide Procter, probably the lovely daughter of Barry Cornwall. I shall send you the letter to amuse you, for I hope it will not bore you to receive such a request. If it do, I shall wish the Society Victoria Regia abolished. "Hawthorne, Nathaniel" need only say that he cannot write now, but will in some future time,--unless he choose to send an extract from his journals. After dinner, instead of being *obliged* to lie down, as usual, I felt a new lease of life and awakeness. Una became a "blue being" and sat to sew, and Rose and I returned to our muttons,--that is, weeds. Presently the Blue Being came out to nail up vines, and Rose cut her thumb with the sickle, and had to leave off work. . . .

--Pride's Crossing, as I remember it in those days, consisted of a farm-house standing near the railway, and surrounded by woods. We ate and slept in the farm-house, and tramped through the woods, which, traversed in an easterly direction, led to the sea-shore, where there was an agreeable alternation of sands and rocks. We used to spend most of our days on the beach, and in the evenings Hawthorne would generally go in swimming. Fishing, likewise, was our daily diversion, and we caught every day sea-perch and bass enough to serve for our supper. The people at the farm-house were quiet and uninquisitive; but newspapers found their way there, as they did to every other place in the States at that epoch, and we were obliged to remember that the civil war was still going on. Hawthorne, however, merely glanced at the "Latest News" column, and let the rest go; and in the course of a week or so he had recovered somewhat of his elasticity. Our conversation had little relation to war-matters; but be had been familiar with this part of the coast in his boyhood and youth. and used to tell tales of those early days, and recall various old local traditions of the neighborhood. He had begun to show himself to me as a friend, as well as a father, and sometimes spoke to me about my possible future,--my approaching college days, and what was to come after. "I suppose, when you are grown up, you will do so and so," he would say,--usually suggesting something so preposterous or distasteful as to stimulate me to define an alternative, which he would then criticise. But he always carefully avoided forcing upon his companion any wishes or expectations of his own; he would suggest, and then observe and perhaps modify the effect of his suggestions.

Before the end of the week, Mrs. Hawthorne wrote again :--

JULY 30, 1861.

. . While Rose drew, I read aloud to her the "Miraculous Pitcher." It is the divinest exposition of hospitality that ever was written or thought. It is altogether perfect in every way. You only can use language, or have adequate ideas to clothe with it. This is my multum-in-parvo criticism upon your works. After dinner we made a settlement with chairs and a table and crickets out by the acacia path, in a delicious shade on thick grass, hard by the tomato-bed. It was delightful out there, and the air nectar; and we all thought how you and Julian were enjoying the fine weather. We had early tea, and soon after--it being Wednesday, our reception-day--a stream of ladies appeared from the Alcott path,--the larch path,--which gradually was resolved into Mrs. Emerson, Mrs. Brown, and Elizabeth. They made a long call, and then Mrs. Emerson and Mrs. Brown left, and E. P. P. remained. At seven she said, "Why, do you have no tea?" and I exclaimed we had finished tea an hour and a half ago! But we ran and found some bread and butter and cheese, and she ate a sorry supper. All I can boast of in the way of Baucis is, that she was saved from water-porridge and unleavened bread. When she had gone, Rose and I went on a sentimental journey up the acacia path to the hill-top, and to your winding foot-track; and we sat down under your tree, and I rejoiced that you were not there! I had no need of sleep to-day again, so restored am I by your absence. We saw the sunset glory, and then descended. Upon dressing at the glass this morning, I was really attracted by the immense change in my own face, such a relief, such a serenity, such a health! and Una remarked the entire difference of my look: it seemed miraculous. So you perceive that the only way to restore *me* is for you to remain at the sea, having thrown care into Walden Pond as you steamed away. You will surely stay as long as possible *for my sake*. Do not grudge money for it. It is better to spend money so than to give it to doctors,--and I shall have to go to Dr. Esterbrook if you come back pretty soon. Yours and Julian's shirts and collars can be washed by the divine Mrs. Pierce when they fail; but stay--stay--stay, at Pride's Crossing, or somewhere where there is sea, with a happy and easy mind; and we shall all be better in health for it. It is far better than if I went to the sea, or to anywhere. It restores my life to have you breathing in the salt. I hope you will have sea-bathing as well as Julian, and do always have towels to rub dry the skin. So now good~night, and God bless thee ever.

--Hawthorne had written, a day or two before, to his daughter Una (whom he called "Onion," for love). The "Aunt Lizzie" mentioned was Miss Elizabeth Hawthorne, whose abode was but two or three miles from our farm-house.

WEST BEACH (or somewhere else), July 28, 1861.

DEAR ONION,--We arrived duly, yesterday after-noon, and find it a tolerably comfortable place. Indeed, Julian seems to like it exceedingly, and I am not much more discontented than with many other spots in this weary world. It is a little, black, old house, on the edge of the railroad, and close by a wood which intervenes between it and the sea, and in which Julian finds high-bush blueberries, and blackberries half ripened. The host and hostess are two uncouth specimens of New England yeomanry, very unobtrusive, however, and as attentive as they know how to be. Julian was delighted with flie supper-table, inasmuch as it afforded him a pie made of dried apples, and some tarts of barberry stewed in molasses; and he seemed to think it princely fare. In the way of literature, we have half a dozen religious books, such as "The Life of Christ, with a Portrait" (from an original photograph, I suppose), "Solomon's Proverbs, illustrated," "Pearls of Grace from the Depths of Divine Love," and several others of the same stamp. We have abundant accommodations of every kind,--one bowl and pitcher between us, there being no other in the house, and everything on a similar scale. Nevertheless, if the weather is favorable, we shall have little to do with the inside of this house, but shall haunt the woods and the sea-shore. I shall thank Heaven when we get back. Aunt Lizzie came to see us yesterday after tea.

I don't know what is the direction of this place, but am of opinion that a letter sent to "West Beach, Beverly," would reach the nearest post-office. Julian is redundantly well.

Love to all. N. H.

P.S. *Monday Morning*. We went yesterday afternoon to see Aunt Lizzie, and had a very pleasant ramble through the woods, gathering berries all the way. Julian enjoys himself very much, and I do not think we shall come home so soon as Saturday, as I at first intended. I forgot to mention that I was recognized in some inscrutable way by a gentleman in the train, who brought us to the door in his carriage, and put his house, his beach, and everything else, at our disposal. O ye Heavens! How absurd that a man should spend the best of his years in getting a little mite of reputation, and then immediiately find the annoyance of it more than the profit. I hope you keep mamma in good order, and do not let her do anything imprudent. Aunt Lizzie wants Rosebud to come and stay with her.

N.H.

West Beach, Beverly Farms, I think.

--We remained another week, and then Hawthorne wrote, "I suppose we shall come home Saturday. I am very well, which is a wonder, considering how I am daily fried in the sun. I do really sizzle, sometimes; but I guzzle more than I sizzle!"

Some correspondence, chiefly about war-matters, took place between Hawthorne and his friends Bright and Bennoch, during the ensuing months. Hawthorne's letter has already appeared in a newspaper; the letters of the two Englishmen are worth preserving, as voicing the attitude of a very large and intelligent part of the British nation during the time of our greatest need.

MY DEAR BENNOCH,--. . . We also have gone to war, and we seem to have little, or at least a very misty idea of what we are fighting for. It depends upon the speaker; and that, again, depends upon the section of the country in which his sympathies are enlisted. The Southern man will say, "We fight for State rights, liberty, and independence." The Middle Western man will avow that he fights for the Union; while our Northern and Eastern man will swear that from the beginning his only idea was liberty to the blacks and the annihilation of slavery. All are thoroughly in earnest, and all pray for the blessing of Heaven to rest upon the enterprise. The appeals are so numerous, fervent, and yet so contradictory, that the Great Arbiter to whom they so piously and solemnly appeal must be sorely puzzled how to decide. One thing is indisputable,--the spirit of our young men is thoroughly aroused. Their enthusiasm is boundless, and the smiles of our fragile and delicate women cheer them on. When I hear their drums beating, and see their colors flying, and witness their steady marching, I declare, were it not for certain silvery monitors hanging by my temples, suggesting prudence, I feel as if I could catch the infection, shoulder a musket, and be off to the war myself! Meditating on these matters, I begin to think our custom as to war is a mistake. Why draw from our young men in the bloom and heyday of their youth the soldiers who are to fight our battles? Had I my way, no man should go to war under fifty years of age, such men having already had their natural share of worldly pleasures and life's enjoyments. And I don't see how they could make a more creditable or more honorable exit from the world's stage than by becoming food for powder, and gloriously dying in defence of their home and country. Then I would add a premium in favor of recruits of threescore years and upward, as, virtually with one foot in the grave, they would not be likely to run away. I apprehend that no people ever built up the skeleton of a warlike history so rapidly as we are doing. What a fine theme for the poet! If you were not a born Britisher, from whose country we expect no help and little sympathy, I would ask you for a martial strain,--a song to be sung by our camp-fires, to soothe the feelings and rouse the energies of our troops, inspiring them to meet like men the great conflict that awaits them, resolved to conquer or die--if dying, still to conquer. Ten thousand poetasters have tried, and tried in vain, to give us a rousing "Scots wha hae wi' Wallace bled." If we fight no better than we sing, may the Lord have mercy upon us and upon the nation!

NATH. HAWTHORNE.

LONDON, Aug. 1, 1861.

MY DEAR HAWTHORNE,--. . . It would be easy to write a thrilling trumpet-blast which should rouse almost the dead to action. But I cannot feel savage enough or indignant enough with these Southerners. Whenever I attempt it, some blatant folly (such as was published at Paris by your precious foreign representatives, among whom was Burlingame, who ought to have known better) on the part of the North rushes into our system, and condenses what was becoming patriotic steam into a few drops of tainted water; and so I, and millions more, remain quiescent, almost impassive, being unable to find out from any speech or statement what the principle involved really is.

The President argues in favor of secession, and permits it, if he does not treacherously encourage it; the succeeding President ignores it, pooh-poohs it, and then fights it. If the second is right, the first should be arraigned for treason against the State, and be treated *according to law*. The obnoxious members of your body politic wish to slough off and be independent. The stigma of the North, and the scandal of the world, wishes to be amputated, and leave the Northern system a purer and more healthy constitution. The North rebels against the rebels, and so they get to fisticuffs. Europe, and especially England, is warned against intermeddling; she has no wish to intermeddle, and warns her subjects against having anything to do with the quarrel. Then she is accused of lukewarmness, and of being untrue to her principles of abolition of slavery, which is the real aim of the North! We don't believe a bit of it. We don't think that the Northerners desire to liberate the slave by the violence now in action. We feel that this was merely a ruse to excite fury and rouse the passions, while it wins the support of genuine Northern abolitionists. Altogether, the absence of a distinct, well-defined object to be settled by the fight bewilders not only our public men, but also our public writers. To me, it has been partly plain that, first, the Union must, by peace or war, by cajoling, coercion, or imagination, be held unbroken. Next, how keep the South, or how let them go? If held, must slavery be extended, or the slave emancipated? If the former, what becomes of the principle so loudly proclaimed? and if the latter, is it to be done piratically, or honorably, by giving compensation to the owners? Altogether, your statesmen, at first, did not believe in war, but by considerable ingenuity excited the South to strike (see Lincoln's message), and then "cry havoc and let slip," etc. Having begun, I have failed to discover the precise grounds on which or principles for which they are fighting. The money voted for the war, which is not one fourth of the loss sustained by the people, would have bought every slave and set him free. We are persuaded that the end is near, and we believe that the South will attain *all* they wanted,--extension and security to slavery; while the North will give up all for which it has vaunted it was fighting. If so, an everlasting stigma will remain on the names of your present rulers, while the hated South will rise with the consciousness of triumph. My dear Hawthorne, I may be mistaken in all this. I almost hope I am; it has humbled us all greatly; to think that our high-spirited and highly moral friends and dear cousins should have exhibited such a desire to imitate the blood-spilling propensities of despots, has touched our conceit not a little.

What a terrible catastrophe that is that has befallen poor Longfellow! I wish he would come to us for a few weeks. Try and persuade him to do so. Love to all.

I am ever yours, F. BENNOCH.

--The allusion to Longfellow recalls the tragical death of his wife, which occurred this year.

The next two extracts are from Henry Bright's letters; the omitted portions being charming descriptions of his new-married life,--too intimate and lovable to be published.

. . . Your thoughts no doubt are all taken up with your own country; and so indeed are many of our thoughts too. What is to. come of it all? Here in England, among those who have known and loved America best (and I *have* loved America, though you and I used to break a lance or two in not unfriendly tilt!), there is but one feeling,--of great sadness and great regret. We do not know whose is the fault,--whose the crime, --but we *do* feel that we cannot endure this dreadful civil war, and that any separation would be better. Still, we can understand how you, who are on the spot, may be carried away by the hot tide of battle, and we don't blame or reproach you; we only do regret most deeply the saddest event which has taken place this half-century.

What are you writing now? Is Longfellow writing anything? Don't let him forget me. Have you seen Norton lately, or Mr. Ticknor? Can you tell me anything about a Mr. Holland, who has written a poem called" Bitter-Sweet"? It is very clever. Mimes admires it immensely. The excitement of this year's London season is a countryman of yonrs,--Mr. Paul du Chaillu.

H. A. BRIGHT

SEPTEMBER 10, 1861.

I don't know what you are thinking about this most frightful war; I can only hope that somehow or other it will soon be ended. *Here,* we cannot but feel that the end is inevitable. The South must and will be independent of the Union,-- as the United States would be independent of this country. Why, then, this cruel waste of blood and treasure? In your last letter, I remember you said, "We shall be better off without the South,--better and nobler than hitherto,--without them." Is not this still true? Let them go; they will suffer for it. You cannot hold them as conquered provinces. You cannot compel them to become sister States again. A fraternity brought about by the cry of "Fraternity or death," will not be *very*cordiaL But perhaps you will think all this indifferent and heartless. Indeed, indeed it is not. It is because I feel so very strongly every horror of this civil war,--because I know men on both sides,--that I have said these few words. My personal feelings must of course always be with dear old Massachusetts; but my reason and conscience are clear as to the wrong and uselessness of this most dreadful struggle You will forgive me, if you disagree with me.

--All this goes to confirm the old saying that, in politics as in other things, it is not safe to prophesy unless you know. A calmer, more sympathetic, and more penetrating view of the situation is contained in the following letter from another Englishman, Henry Wilding, Hawthorne's former clerk at the Liverpool Consulate, and at this time holding the rank of vice--consul:--

MY DEAR SIR,--. . . I often think of you, and wonder what your feelings are with regard to the fearful events now happening. On this side, "the American Civil War" is the prevailing topic, and the commercial and manufacturing classes, at all events, are decidedly Southern in their sympathies, and I believe a great majority of the leading men in politics also are. It is not easy to see why this is so, after what appeared to be the feeling in England against slavery. The anti-slavery people profess to believe that slavery has nothing to do with the struggle; that the Federal Government are no more contending for the abolition of slavery than are the Confederates. They *won't* see that the contest is for the abolition of slavery in the only way that reasonable men in America have ever supposed it possible, by confining It to its present limits; and that the South, rather than submit to that, will, if they can, destroy the Union. There are many reasons for this feeling in England. In the first place, I believe Englishmen instinctively sympathize with rebels--if the rebellion be not against England. A great many also desire to see the American Union divided, supposing that it will be less powerful, and less threatening to England. All the enemies of popular government--and there are plenty even in England--rejoice to see what they suppose to be the failure of Republican institutions. The ship-owning community dislike the United States on account of the coasting navigation laws, and believe the Southern profession of free trade. Merchants and manufacturers want cotton, and are mad with the United States because she won't make peace on any terms so as to let cotton come. Then there is the multitude who are habitually led by the "Times," and the "Times" has been Secession all along. There is no doubt great suffering will be felt among the working classes of England this winter on account of the war. I feel that if the North be in earnest, and the leaders honest, she will succeed; and I hope success may come soon. Thinking men are in great perplexity, and watch with intense interest this struggle of popular liberty with its old enemy, oligarchy,--the government of the few. If it emerge successful, and its own master,-- well for free institutions in Europe! If unsuccessful, or under the yoke of military despotism; then woe for them They will be in the dust, but not subdued. Passing events will indeed depress one, but--for the hope in Christ of a peaceful hereafter, when the selfish and unchristian passions of men will no more have place. . .

Ever yours, H. WILDING.

--I will bring this chapter, and the year 1861, to a close, with this note from an old friend of Hawthorne. It would appear, from the mention of "gray-head spiders," that Hawthorne had begun to turn his thoughts in the direction of Dr. Grimshawe.

OLD SALT HOUSE, LONG WHARF, BOSTON,

Monday, Oct. 28, 1861.

MY DEAR SIR,--I took the liberty of sending you this morning a paper containing a view of the exterior of my old store, but forgot to tell you that I have been on Long Wharf forty years!--thirty-one of which have I been an occupant of the old store. There are old gray-head spiders still here with whom I have been acquainted for nearly twenty years, and you can well understand that we have become well acquainted with each other. Pray drop in and see the old fellows. I doubt not they will recognize you as an old friend.

Always sincerely yours,

JAMES OAKES.

NATH. HAWTHORNE, Esq.

CHAPTER 9 - THE BEGINNING OF THE END

THE following winter was a wearisome one for Hawthorne, who was not fond of cold weather, and was not in the humor to warm himself by vigorous exercise in the open air. In the "Old Manse" days he had been in the habit of walking and skating,--according to his wife, he was a graceful skater,--and of sawing and splitting the wood for the family hearth. But now he devolved these offices on his son, and himself remained for the most part within-doors. He had begun to struggle with his new romance the previous autumn, and wrote the first study for "Septimius," which has never been published; though, as a study, it is more interesting than the second (published) version, and covers more paper. It did not satisfy him, and the failure increased his depression, by confirming the notion he had acquired that he was no longer up to the writing mark. In order to get the "Septimius" matter off his mind, however, he rewrote it rapidly to a conclusion, though the latter part of it at least was, I think, composed in a spirit of irony towards himself. "The whole thing is nonsense," he seems to say; "let us see what it looks like." He could not bring himself into sympathy with Septimius's infatuation, and yet he had not wished to write a commonplace satire. That a studious and intelligent young man, even a hundred years ago, should solemnly persuade himself that he could brew a drink that would confer immortal life, was found, upon examination, to he too improbable to be entertained. The young man must be a fool; and Hawthorne finally decides that he is a fool, and makes him appear so. The fault of the story was, that the idea had not been presented in the right way. The idea in itself was good: a spiritual moral was to be deduced from it; but it must not be deliberately and consciously evolved, by the chief actor in the drama. Moreover, the Bloody Footstep episode did not assimilate kindly with the Immortality part of the plot. The main interest should be concentrated upon the latter, and therefore the former became supererogatory; though this, too, would be available enough by itself.

In fact, he next began to consider whether it might not be advisable to make the Bloody Footstep the central thread of his English romance, and to postpone, for the present at any rater all reference to the theme of immortality. He had already, while in Florence, jotted down some notes for such a story, and he now proceeded to reinvestigate the matter. The first result was a partially complete sketch, in which the American portion of the tale is dismissed in a dozen pages or so, and the hero is brought to England and carried through his adventures there, ending with the discovery of the imprisoned ancestor in the secret chamber. In the manuscript as written the story continually breaks off, and the author plunges into a conversation with himself (as it were) upon this or that obstinate feature of the plot or characters; and, having arrived at a temporary and approximate solution thereof, goes on with the thread of the narrative, until another hitch occurs, which is again canvassed as before. By the time he got to the end, Hawthorne had perceived the expediency of introducing certain modifications into the plot, and in particular of giving more space and minuteness to the American scenes. He consequently turned back, and began the book again, importing new scenes and characters, and continuing until the hero is fairly landed in England, and has come into relations with the English personages of the tale. Here the revised first part overlaps the first, and connects itself with it, the last sentence of the former being identical with a corresponding one in the latter. In printing the story under the title of "Dr. Grimshawe's Secret," I ignored so much of the original as is covered by the revise, and omitted the intercalary studies, some parts of which were afterwards printed in a New York magazine. Of course, the author would have rewritten and remodelled the whole, before publishing it.

But he seems to have come to the conclusion to abandon the whole thing,--whether from lack of physical strength to carry it out to his satisfaction, or from distrust of the value of the story itself. By this time also he had got new light upon the other theme,--that of immortality. Instead of taking as his hero a youth who should brew the elixir of malice prepense, he would have an aged and simpleminded man, just on the brink of the grave, who, half inadvertently, should dose himself from time to time with a few drops of a certain mysterious cordial, which was among the legacies of a deceased predecessor. By this treatment he should gradually become younger; yet the change was to be so gradual that the reader, as well as the old gentleman himself, might be in doubt whether it were real or imaginary. By this means the technical difficulties and incongruities of the "Septimius" version would be avoided, or, at all events, so softened and moulded as not to interfere with the essential power and beauty of the conception. And it was upon these lines, accordingly, that "The Dolliver Romance" was begun; which, so far as it goes, is the most exquisite specimen of the mere charm of narration that ever came from Hawthorne's pen.

But I am anticipating a little. After giving up "Grimshawe," Hawthorne--not entirely to lose the labor of his English journalizing--composed from his Note-Books, from time to time, the series of essays on English subjects which were printed in the "Atlantic Monthly," and afterwards collected in a volume under the title of "Our Old Home." They were paid for at the rate (I believe) of two hundred dollars each in the magazine. Hawthorne himself took little interest in the completed work. It was, in one sense, the record of a failure,--a failure to use the material to better purpose. The book would probably have been different had it been intended, from the first, to write a book of that kind. The key, however, such as it is, having been once struck, is perfectly kept throughout, and no more beautiful example of English composition could well be produced: and yet the changes from the original version in the journals are apparently very slight. But they are just the right changes; and a certain magical translucence is given to the style that is inimitable and indescribable. The book--much to the distress and consternation of its publisher--was dedicated to Franklin Pierce. "I find," Hawthorne wrote,

"that it would be a piece of poltroonery in me to withdraw either the dedication or the dedicatory letter. . . . If Pierce is so exceedingly unpopular that his name is enough to sink the volume, there is so much the more need that an old friend should stand by him. I cannot, merely on account of pecuniary profit or literary reputation, go back from what I have deliberately felt and thought it right to do. . . . As for the literary public, it must accept my book precisely as I see fit to give it, or let it alone."

The volume was accepted very cordially, at least in this country, and Hawthorne expressed his pleasure at the appreciation, though remarking that he felt "rather gloomy" about the book himself. In England, as will be remembered, it aroused a good deal of what the English themselves called indignation. We should probably describe the feeling by another name. Here are two letters,--one from Fanny Aikin Kortright, whose *nom de plume* was Berkeley Aikin, the author of some very able novels; the other from Francis Bennoch. The latter's defence of English fruit is not, as might be supposed, a jest, but is made in all sadness and sincerity. I have myself heard highly educated and intelligent Englishmen express the same sentiments; and it is also a fact that they prefer--at any rate, they say that they prefer--their oysters to ours! If they really do so, it would seem almost too kind a dispensation of Providence.

DEAR MR. HAWTHORNE,--... I believe and am sure that "The Scarlet Letter" will endure as long as the language in which it is written; and should that language become dead, the wonderful work will be translated. Mr. S. C. Hall says I am to tell you that your works will live when marble crumbles into dust. I can well understand that even genius stands breathless in silence, watching events ; still, master, you must send us forth soma fresh enchantment ere-long, though you have done so much. Forgive my freedom, dear Mr. Hawthorne, and imagine me the reader you speak of in the preface to "Transformation." Forgive me also if I ask you a question. What is the event you refer to in that romance, which, you say, must be fresh in the memories of men as having happened some years before the work was written?. . . .

Alas, my dear Sir, what have you been doing to the English ladies? You might almost as well have sent circular letters to them asking their ages, as have reflected on their personal appearance! I have not seen your new book, but on every hand I hear, "Mr. Hawthorne has written such a book! He says the English ladies are all like--like--beef!" I cannot make out even from literary folks that you have said anything else; but this bovine matter will not easily be forgiven, to even so great a favorite as yourself. Oh, pray do write another romance to wipe out this crime! Let us have a new Donatello or something else very beautiful, such as you alone--I really believe--can produce; how much pleasanter it will be reading that than running to the looking-glass to see if one really is like--like--beef! . . . . I hope you will accept my best good-wishes for yourself and all yours, and believe me, despite the bovine question, as much as ever

Your very admiring and faithful
B. AIKIN.

MY DEAR HAWTHORNE,--The "Atlantic" Magazine brings you prominently forward. If all your notes are calculated to cast such poetical halos round ordinary places as those you have wreathed round one old cottage in Blackheath Park, I fear the owners and neighbors will hardly know their own homes. It is of course to us a marvellous evidence of power. Had every incident been photographed, the descriptions could not have been more vivid. Let me, however, set you right on two points. You refer to some wretched fruit-trees fastened to a dingy wall, and wonder if anybody ever tasted good fruit in England. Now it so happens that the only fruit-trees so impaled were one or two morella cherries, not meant to be eaten until they have had a month's soaking in good brandy, and *that* cherry-brandy is tipple for the goddesses. We won't be put down as to the quality of our fruit, but challenge all creation. I should like to know whether all America could equal our straw-berries, cherries, grapes, Ribston pippins, pineapples, etc., etc.; and as for pears my teeth water when I think of them. A friend of mine who was in America last year declares on his honor that, with one or two exceptions, he never tasted throughout America an apple better than a crab-apple in England. They were so sour that he has never been able to look pleasant since.

"Kiss in the Ring," too, you misdescribe, and make what is really a very pretty game of forfeits when played with pretty people, to appear absolutely loathsome. The game is this: boys and girls alternately take hands and form a ring. A youth armed with a handkerchief paces round the ring and drops it at the feet of the girl he admires. He then slips under the festooned hands, escapes from the ring and runs, not to escape but to be overtaken; when, being caught, he gallantly conducts the damsel back into the centre of the ring, where, lifting his hat, he kisses the cheek of the fair one, takes the place where she had stood, completes the ring, and the beauty drops her handkerchief at the feet of some eager swain, and off she flies like a deer pursued by the swift-footed buck. At the first she runs rapidly, but, somehow, she always slackens her pace in time, and willingly becomes a captive; and so the game goes on. Here, too, you take the opportunity of having a fling at English beauty, contrasting it unfavorably with that fragile and most delicate fabric of American womanhood. This won't do! For either grace or loveliness, good bearing or refined gentleness, I'll back England's daughters against the world; unless it be our new princess, who is a very charming piece of humanity.

I have neither time nor inclination to talk politics, so I won't begin. I should only irritate you, although I must congratulate you on personally belonging to the rising and what must be the controlling party soon. When are we to have your new romance?

With all best wishes from me and mine to you and yours, I am

Your attached

F. BENNOCH.

--In the spring of 1862 Hawthorne took a trip to Washington and to the outskirts of the seat of war, chiefly for the benefit of his health. The journey proved to be an agreeable one; and its literary result was an article, "Chiefly about War Matters," contributed to the "Atlantic Monthly." While in Washington he met Leutze, the artist and consented to sit to him for a portrait. I do not know what has become of this portrait; but it is said to have been successful. In the sitter's opinion, it would be "the best ever painted of the same unworthy subject." He was also photographed twice or thrice, with only indifferent results. "My hair is not really so white. . . The sun seems to take an infernal pleasure in making me venerable--as if I were as old as himself." He saw the President, and also General McClellan, whose aspect and bearing pleased him greatly; and he came into close enough contact with the Confederates to be conscious of a passing shadow of peril. Altogether, the experience was of some benefit to him. He sent the following letter to his daughter:--

WASHINGTON, Sunday, March 16, 1862.

DEAR UNA,--I have never a moment's time to write, for I move about all day, and am engaged all the evening; and if ever there is a vacant space, I want to employ it in writing my journal, which keeps terribly behindhand. But I suppose mamma and the rest of you sometimes remember there is such a person, and wish to know what I am about. I went up yesterday to Harper's Ferry (a distance of eighty miles from Washington) by invitation of the directors of a railroad; so that I made the whole journey without expense, and partook of two cold collations besides. To be sure, I paid my expenses with a speech; but it was a very short one. I shall not describe what I saw, because very likely I shall print it in the "Atlantic Monthly;" but I made acquaintance with some rebel prisoners, and liked them very much. It rained horribly all day, and the mud was such as nobody in New England can conceive of. I have shaken hands with Uncle Abe, and have seen various notabilities, and am infested by people who want to exhibit me as a lion. I have seen a camp, and am going in a few days to Manassas, if the mud of the Sacred Soil will permit. Tell mamma that the outcry opened against General McClellan, since the enemy's retreat from Manassas, is really terrible, and almost universal; because it is found that we might have taken their fortifications with perfect ease six months ago, they being defended chiefly by wooden guns. Unless he achieves something wonderful within a week, he will be removed from command, and perhaps shot,--at least I hope so; I never did more than half believe in him. By a message from the State Department, I have reason to think that there is money enough due me from the Government to pay the expenses of my journey. I think the public buildings are as fine if not finer than anything we saw in Europe. I am very well. I have no doubt that Julian well supplies my place as the head of the family. I hope the masquerade passed off to the satisfaction of all concerned. I send my love to everybody (within our own circle, I mean), and remain

Your dutiful father, N. H.

I forget the date of mamma's last letter; but two days have intervened since I received it. I shall set out on my return within a day or two after I have been to Manassas; but the weather is so uncertain, and the road so difficult, that I scarcely hope to go thither much before the end of this week. I have really so little time to write, that you may very probably see me again before hearing from me; but not, at soonest, till the early part of next week.

Thank Bab for her note. Neither you nor Julian can claim any thanks on that score; and as for mamma, her letters are beyond thanks,

--The article above mentioned was published in July, 1862. It was written with great frankness, insomuch that the editor of the magazine was somewhat apprehensive of the consequences; but Hawthorne would abate nothing of his utterances. He, however, ironically appended annotations to the more hazardous portions, purporting to be the horror-stricken comments of the editor upon the writer's want of patriotism. Intentionally absurd though these "comments" were, they seem to have possessed verisimilitude enough to deceive most readers; and I remember that one person, who felt the indignation which they pretended to express, declared, when apprised of their true authorship, "Then I have no respect for a man who runs with the hare, and hunts with the hounds!" But our sense of humor in New England was, at this period, not seldom exanimated by our insatiable political conscientiousness Another gentleman, whose letter is subjoined, takes an equally serious view in the opposite direction.

EDGEWOOD, NEW HAVEN, July 5, 1862.

MY DEAR SIR,--I am glad to see your mark in the "Atlantic;" but should be ready to swear--if I swore--at the marginal impertinences. Pray, is Governor Andrew editor ? A man's opinions can take no catholic or philosophic range nowadays, but they call out some shrewish accusation of disloyalty. It is to me one of the most humiliating things about our present national status, that no talk can be tolerated which is not narrowed to the humor of our tyrannic *majority*. I can recognize the enormity of basing a new nationality, in our day, upon slavery; but why should this blind me to all other enormities? I have no hope for the country, as a unit, in our generation; and I hope your personal relations (if you have any) with General Butler will excuse my saying that he is the best representative of barbarism in our epoch. It is quite in keeping that "Harpers' Journal of Civilization" should eulogize him.

I remain very truly yours,
DONALD G. MITCHELL.
NATH. HAWTHORNE, Esq.

--In the course of the article Hawthorne made an allusion to the recent action between the "Cumberland" and the "Merrimac," in which the former was sunk by the Confederate ironclad. Longfellow has immortalized the same incident in one of his most stirring lyrics, beginning,

"At anchor in Hampton Roads we lay,
On board of the 'Cumberland,' sloop-of-war."

The "Cumberland" was commanded by a gallant young officer, George U. Morris--

"'Strike your flag' the rebel cries,
In his arrogant, old-plantation strain;
'Never! our gallant Morris replies,--
'It is better to sink than to yield !'—
And the whole air pealed
With the cheers of our men."

Among the letters left by Hawthorne I found one from "our gallant Morris" himself; written in a round, schoolboy hand, but well worth reproducing here.

U.S. GUNBOAT "PORT ROYAL," APPALACHICOLA, FLA.,
March 20, 1863.
MR. N. HAWTHORNE,

DEAR SIR,--I received to-day from a friend the July, 1862, number of the "Atlantic Monthly." Please accept my heartfelt thanks for the flattering manner in which you mentioned my having performed my duty faithfully. As you almost predicted, the Government has not promoted me; though it did Worden; but you must remember he was successful, and without loss,--I unsuccessful, and with a very heavy loss. But, sir, even had I been "honored by Government and other authorities," I assure you it could not have caused me more pleasure than I felt when reading your remarks concerning the fight between the "Merrimac" and "Cumberland." It was a proud and high honor to receive for having tried to sustain unspotted the honor of our Flag, which my father had so well sustained before me. Believe me

Respectfully and gratefully yours,
GEORGE U. MORRIS,
Lieut. Com'g U.S. N.

--Hawthorne returned to Concord about the end of March, 1862, but did little literary work besides finishing his article, and writing a short narrative for the "Weal Reaf;"--a small sheet published at a fair at the Essex Institute, in aid of some patriotic purpose. It described a boyish reminiscence of a legend connected with an old house in the neighborhood, called "Browne's Folly." In sending the narrative to his sister, he wrote:--

DEAR ELIZABETH,--It seemed to me most convenient to write this article in the form of a letter, and it may be published just as it stands. I wish you to correct the proof-sheets, and to be very careful about it. The Essex Institute certainly ought to be grateful to me, for I could get $100 for such an article.

N.H.

--In the following July he made another excursion to the seaside with his son, this time to West Gouldsboro', Maine, on the mainland opposite Mt. Desert. The journey thither was made by boat, rail, stage, turn and turn about, and made an impression of adventure upon the younger of the two travelers; from whose journal I will make a few extracts:--

"Our boat was to start at seven in the evening; and after eating some ice-cream in a restaurant, we drove down to the wharf. The boat is described as 'The New and Splendid Steamship, Eastern Queen;' but it could not have been new less than twenty years ago, and all the splendor consisted in a gandily painted paddle-box. We were already hungry when we got on board, but were then informed, to our surprise and consternation, that nothing to eat was ever provided on these steamers. It was a long time before we could get a stateroom, and then it was only six feet square, with no window to let in the air. We turned in supperless. During the night there was a big thunderstorm, and the waves were pretty high. Next morning there was a thick fog, but it gradually cleared away, and showed the rocky banks of the river.

"At last we stopped at a small place called Bath, and papa said he would go on shore and get something to eat. I went with him, and we had just drunk a glass of cider, and were bargaining for half a dozen biscuits, when there was an alarm of the boat starting. We ran back just in time to get on board by a desperate leap. Continuing on up the river, with occasional short stoppages, we finally reached our destination, Hallowell, and immediately boarded an old stagecoach, with 'Hallowell House' written on it. The town was in great commotion at the departure of its volunteers, who were just going off in the train. It was then about eleven: our train was to start at four. The most interesting thing we did in Hallowell was to eat our dinner, which consisted chiefly of thin soup and a very tough beefsteak. When the train came, it was so crowded that we could hardly find seats; and tired as we were already, we had a three-hours' hot ride before us. The road lay through tangled pine-woods, and clearings covered with the stumps of trees, and over bridges with rocky streams tumbling underneath, and then into another wild wood, and so on. It was dusk when we reached Bangor. We got into an old stage, and drove to the 'Penobscot Exchange.'

"This morning we took a walk round the town. It is large, with well-built brick houses and broad streets. There are a great many churches, and stables, and stove-shops, and a great dearth of bookstores for so large a town. Enlisting is going on here very fast; crowds of men are collected all about, talking it over.

"We left Bangor at night by stage-coach, and drove all night over rough roads, up hill and down, for thirty miles. Papa rode inside, and I outside. There were more than twenty passengers on board, and a great deal of luggage. I sat on the box with the driver, and a returned invalid soldier from the Peninsula, who drank out of a bottle, and sang songs, and told stories, all the way. The driver, on being offered whiskey, refused, saying, 'I never drank a drop in my life,--no, sir! nary!' There was beautiful moonlight, but it was very cold. We drove among high hills, with now and then a lake between them, reflecting the moon. Most of the hills were covered with loose boulders of rock. We had four horses. The men here are fine fellows, better than our Massachusetts folk; they are mostly six-footers or seven-footers. Mr. Sanborn would be thought nothing of here.

"We have just met Mr. George Bradford, who says West Gouldsboro' is a delightful place, with beautiful scenery, entire seclusion, plenty of fishing, and a boat to row. Papa enjoys the prospect very much. The only drawback is, that it is rather rainy.

". . . .We are living in a small farm-house close by the beach. Our landlord, Mr. Hill, is tall and broad-shouldered, with a high head, aquiline nose, and large chin. He is over sixty, but looks strong and hearty. At such an age a man's head is generally partly bald; but though his hair is perfectly white, it covers his head all over, and is cropped short. When in doubt or perplexity, he scratches it. He is sensible on politics, and is not (like his daughter) an abolitionist, but can hear and understand two sides of a thing. He eats with his knife; but so does everybody here. He blows his nose every day at dinner, once, and very hard. When one answers a question of his, he always says, 'Oh, yes!' as if he was reminded of something he had forgotten. His daughter does the same. She is about thirty, very deaf; square and broad-shouldered, with a strong-minded sort of face. When she is talking, she keeps her hand to her right ear, to catch the answer. She says she has an ear-trumpet, but she does not use it. Every evening papa has political discussions with Mr. Hill and Miss Charlotte. He addresses himself chiefly to Mr. Hill, but since the daughter is always sitting by, papa has to talk loud so that she may hear; but the old man is not deaf, and does not need to be shouted at. Altogether it is rather awkward."

Hawthorne himself made some brief entries in the journal. Speaking of the volunteers, he says:

"The bounties offered by the General and State Governments, and largely increased by the towns, make a very strong inducement to young men who have never seen, or would be likely to see, so much money together as is now within their reach, --between two and three hundred dollars in some cases; and no doubt Yankee thrift combines with love of adventure and love of country, to urge them on. It is remarkable how many stalwart men cannot pass the medical examination, on account of some unsuspected and unapparent defect. One third, at least, seem to fall within this class.

"The people of Maine, I think, are very much ruder of aspect than those of Massachusetts, but quite as intelligent, and as comprehensive of the affairs of the time. Indeed, intelligence might well be more general than with us, because high and low sit down together in bar-rooms, and intermix freely in talk. At one hotel in Ellsworth there was a Colonel Burnham, home on furlough from the Army of the Potomac,--quite a distinguished officer, I believe, and in my judgment a very reliable man, fit to lead men in perils and difficulties. He is a middle-aged man, or little more; a dark, intelligent, rather kindly-looking man, with black hair curling on his head, and a black beard and mustache, and wearing a black national wide-awake,--giving him an air something between a soldier and a bandit,--his shoulder-straps having two stars on them, in token of his rank. He was smoking a German pipe, and talked in a quick, good-humored, familiar way about his adventures, answering the questions of all and sundry familiarly, not repelling the humblest, but yet with a kind of natural dignity that would not be presumed upon. He had been in all McClellan's six days' battles, and in how many more I know not; and without volunteering any account of his perils and achievements, was quite willing to talk of them, in an unaffected way, when asked. He had been in the lumber business, and had doubtless met with adventures, and been thrown into positions, as a captain of logging men, that gave him some experience such as a military man might need; at least, he had led a hardy life, and so was not to be abashed by the roughness of war. Another officer, an elderly man, who had likewise been with the Army of the Potomac, came to see him, and eke out his camp and battle reminiscences; and there was a young lieutenant from Port Royal, a handsome youth, who had returned in very ill health, but now seemed in a hopeful state of convalescence. There were likewise in the group some of the notables of the town: the lawyer, probably, and the editor of the village newspaper; and besides these, some private soldiers of the Colonel's own and other regiments. These latter made him the proper military salute; after which he conversed affably with them, and one or two of them hesitated not to put in their remarks among those of the other interlocutors, the Colonel not shunning their familiarities, yet neither he nor they forgetting their relative positions. It was curious to see how all parties could so freely dispense with ceremony and formalities, and yet not transgress any nice respect that ought to be observed. There was no condescension on the Colonel's part, nor aspiration on the other side, and yet they met in a very natural and agreeable way. By and by the Colonel (who was quite the lion of the day) drove off with a friend in a one-horse wagon, and the company (after discussing him for a while, with a laudatory summing-up, and somebody remarking that the Colonel was making more money now than in the lumber business) dispersed."

--This is an American Van Ostade, painted with the careless ease of a master.

We lived at Mr. Hill's in peace and plenty for two weeks or more. We went out rowing every day in the boat, and fished for flounders in the bay, and landed on the islands, and went in swimming. There was a society of young girls and fellows in the neighborhood, and one day we went on a picnic with them,--about twenty of us, and cooked a chowder on the beach, which we ate with clam-shell spoons; and afterwards danced in a barn, while Miss Charlotte played on the fiddle. Every day we took walks through the pastures and along the coast, eating great quantities of blueberries, blackberries, raspberries, and gooseberries, and pelting each other with green elderberries on the way home. Sometimes we would sit for hours beneath the shadow of a rock, with a lovely scene spread out before us, while Hawthorne smoked a cigar, and his son wished he might do likewise. At length Hawthorne wrote home that "it will be impossible for us to stay longer than till a week from to-morrow, because Julian's breeches are in such terrible disrepair, what with bushes, briers, swamps, rocks, beach, mud, sea-water, and various hard usage and mischances. Neither could I keep myself decent a great many days longer. I struggle hard to prevent him from spoiling his light trousers, because if he spoils them, he will inevitably be compelled to stay in bed all summer." So we bade farewell to our host and hostess about the 1st of September, and got back to Concord two days later. We hoped to go back again next year; but this was the last excursion we ever were to make together.

During the autumn there was a good deal of social gayety in Concord, in spite of the war, and although several of our schoolboys had enlisted and gone to the front; we had one or two little parties at our own house; and several times Mr. Alcott's daughters came over to play cards. The "Nonsense Verses" were coming into vogue at this epoch, and everybody was trying his own hand at producing them; and

Hawthorne once took a piece of paper and scratched off the following bit of doggerel, which I am sure the revered subject of it will not object to see in print:

"There dwelt a Sage at Apple-Slump,
Whose dinner never made him plump;
Give him carrots, potatoes, squash, parsnips, and peas,
And some boiled macaroni, without any cheese,
And a plate of raw apples, to hold on his knees,
And a glass of sweet cider, to wash down all these,--
And he 'd prate of the Spirit as long as you 'd please,--
This airy Sage of Apple-Slump!"

Another ballad, on another subject, ran as follows:--

"There was an old Boy, with a new coat and breeches,
Who jumped over fences, and tumbled in ditches,
While the mud and the mire
Spattered higher and higher,
Till he went to the fire,
And, as he grew drier,
Burnt great holes in his new coat and breeches!"

And here is still another:--

"There was an Old Lady of Guessme
Whose talking did greatly distress me;
She talked of the nigger,
And still she grew bigger,
This tiresome Old Lady of Guessme!"

The winter had always been Hawthorne's best time for work; and after completing his volume of English sketches, he applied himself to the "Dolliver Romance." Contrary to his usual custom, he permitted his publisher to begin the serial issue of the story in a magazine, but he never expected to furnish the monthly instalments regularly; and it was against his better judgment that any of it saw the light until the whole was finished. It was hoped, however, that when he had once made a beginning, he would be stimulated to continue. But, "there is something preternatural," he writes,

"in my reluctance to begin. I linger at the threshold, and have a perception of very disagreeable phantoms to be encountered if I enter. . . . I don't see much probability of my having the first chapter of the Romance ready as soon as you want it. There are two or three chapters ready to be written, but I am not robust enough to begin, and I feel as if I should never carry it through." And again: "I am not quite up to writing yet, but shall make an effort as soon as I see any hope of success. You ought to be thankful that (like most other broken-down authors) I do not pester you with decrepit pages, and insist upon your accepting them as full of the old spirit and vigor. That trouble, perhaps, still awaits you, after I shall have reached a further stage of decay. Seriously, my mind has, for the present, lost its temper and its fine edge, and I have an instinct that I had better keep quiet. Perhaps I shall have a new spirit of vigor, if I wait quietly for it; perhaps not."

His untoward condition was made worse by the illness of his daughter Una, caused chiefly by the after effects of the quinine she had taken in Rome. The least mischance to Una wrung her father's heart; and it seemed, for a time, as if her ailment might turn out very seriously. Her aunt, Miss Elizabeth Hawthorne, who was also extremely fond of her, wrote inviting her to visit Beverly, near Salem, for change of air and scene, and Una went. In the course of her letter Miss Hawthorne says in reference to "Our Old Home:"--

"I do not, as you suppose I do, like to see the English abused; but your papa is never abusive, only appreciative, which I think nobody ever was before, and only an American ever can be; for the mind of a cultivated American must necessarily be fed upon the best that other nations can supply, and so is likely to share in the qualities of all, --sufficiently, at least, to discover their real nature. As for the English, there were no eyes, at least no earthly eyes, to survey them before they came under your papa's observation; and as for any supervision from on high, they seem to live in the most heathenish unconsciousness of it, and, indeed, of the existence of anything above themselves. Their supreme praise is, that a thing is English; and their censure, when bestowed upon any person of another nation is, that an Englishman would not have done or said so and so. There is no right and wrong,--only English and un-English. What time is to develop in them, of course, cannot be foretold; hut if they were to perish now, to be turned into stone, for instance, becoming motionless in whatever movement was in progress, would they not save their life by losing it? And should you not revisit England with more interest than you could feel to see them in their present transition state? There are symptoms of weakness apparent in their condition which I am half sorry for. Lord Palmerston is always assuring the public that 'the most perfect concord subsists between the cabinets of France and England,' that 'no steps will be taken without the concurrence of France;' and now the 'London Times' asserts that when the Emperor has conquered Mexico he will oblige the Americans to make peace! A threat ominous of evil to England, who thus lets '"I dare not" wait upon "I would,"' and relies upon France for what is beyond her own power, though within her desires."

--This secluded old lady was always observant of politics, and her opinions are often both shrewd and profound, and are expressed in a very entertaining manner.

While Una was at Beverly, her mother wrote to her as follows:--

CONCORD, Dec. 11, 1862.

MY DEAREST UNA,--Great events seem thickening here. Louisa Alcott has had her summons to the Washington Hospitals; and Abby came to ask me about some indelible ink she had, and I offered to do anything I could for Louisa. She said if I could mark her clothes it would assist very much. So I went over, in the divine afternoon, and marked till dusk, and finished all she had. Mrs. Alcott says she shall feel helpless without Louisa, and Mr. Alcott says he sends his only son. Louisa is determined to make the soldiers jolly, and takes all of Dickens that she has, and games. At supper-time Julian came in with the portentous news that the battle has at last begun, and Fredericksburg is on fire from our guns. So Louisa goes into the very mouth of the war. Now, to-day, is the Bible Fair. I carried to Mrs. Alcott early this morning some maizena blancmange which Ann made for papa, and turned out of the sheaf-mould very nicely. A letter has been received from Sergeant-Major How, who reported dirty, ill-ordered barracks, drunken hotels, and general discomfort. He is at Long Island, and may stay five or six weeks there.

Papa has not a good appetite, and eats no dinners except a little potato. But he is trying to write, and locks himself into the library and pulls down the blinds.

General Hitchcock has sent me a catalogue of his Hermetic Library. Good-night. Your most affectionate MAMMA.

--The visit to Beverly was of decided benefit to Una and after her return home her aunt wrote her frequent letters, full of sense and dry humor. I append a few extracts:

"...Concord seems a good place for you, but it must be dull for your father, who as far as I could observe, has no society at all out of his own family. But there is pleasure now in reading the newspapers. I heard a man say yesterday that our people are doing 'a handsome piece of business.' It is said that every eighth man in Marblehead is in either the army or the navy. And I have heard that it was the Salem Zouaves who charged upon the redoubtable Obadiah Jennings Wise and his followers, and put them to flight. I suppose Mrs. Dike will send me the Salem papers containing the achievements of the regiment from Essex County, and I mean to send them to your papa.

"I am glad you were all well when you wrote, 'including the cats,' whom I always like to hear from. Palmetto, the Secessionist, has become an exemplary Union animal. She is as fierce as ever, and scratches *me* to show how she would treat any rebel she could get at. I only wish we had an army actuated by her spirit . . . I congratulate you upon the pleasure you must have felt in hearing your papa read Scott's novels. I have read the 'Gray Champion' lately with renewed delight. I wish he would write something in the same spirit now, for the 'Atlantic Monthly. It is certainly time for the 'Gray Champion' to walk once more. Ask him to think of it. I am glad Julian is no older than he is, otherwise I should expect to hear he was gone to the wars. I am very sorry that your papa has not been well. I wish you were not settled at Concord. The air of the place is not invigorating. People born near the sea require its breezes. . . .

"There is a Secession lady here, who has two daughters married to South Carolina planters. She knows Mr. Yancey and other leading men, and admires Yancey excessively. I am quite in luck, for I have longed to see a Secessionist.

"I agree with your mamma as to who upholds the 'Atlantic,' which was certainly dull before your papa contributed to it, and I wish he would publish something more from his Euglish journal. Is he aware that he has 'earned the undying enmity of all Englishmen, by his remarks upon Englishwomen'? I never doubted that the English were as sensitive as other people, if you could only hit them in the right place. But it may be some compensation to know that the Emperor of Brazil is a warm admirer of both his writings and his photograph,--having been made acquainted with both by some Baptist minister, and singling out your papa's likeness, of his own accord, from a book full of portraits of eminent men. I wish your papa would read, or at least look at, Napier's 'History of tlie Peninsular War.' I have read it with much satisfaction, finding that other nations blunder, when they are in difficulties, as badly as we do; and that the British Government (according to Napier) did nothing but blunder. Do not forget to speak about the 'Gray Champion.' I should like to know whether it seems so wonderful a thing to you as it does to me. It should be read at war-meetings. Men would enlist after hearing it. It would be well to have it printed in the form of a tract, and distributed to the soldiers. I know of nothing written in America so effective."

--There was no improvement in Hawthorne's condition during the spring and summer of 1863. He seemed to have no definite disease, but he grew thinner, paler, and more languid day by day; he sat indoors most of the time, or, when he went out, would walk slowly and feebly, or stand gazing across the fields, with his hands in the side-pockets of his coat,--a wistful, grave look. Early in the summer he had an attack of nose-bleeding, which lasted without intermission for more than twenty-four hours; and though he joked about it, and took it lightly, he was distinctly feebler from that time, and his death occurred within the twelvemonth. He no longer, indeed, seemed to find any sufficient interest in life; and he had always dreaded surviving his own ability to take care of himself; and thus becoming (as he supposed) a burden upon others. The breaking-down of his romance was another weight upon his shoulders. It was at this period, I think, that his friend Richard Henry Stoddard sent him a poem, "The King's Bell," embodying a profound and sombre moral. Hawthorne, in acknowledging the receipt of the poem, gives a glimpse of his state of mind. "I sincerely thank you for your beautiful poem," he says, "which I have read with a great deal of pleasure. It is such as the public have a right to expect, from what you have given us in years gone by; only I wish the idea had not been so sad. I think Felix might have rung the bell once in his lifetime, and once again at the moment of death. Yet you may be right. I have been a happy man, and yet I do not remember any one moment of such happy conspiring circumstances that I could have rung a joy-bell at it." Hawthorne had a high regard for Stoddard, both as an author and as a man, and would have been glad had circumstances enabled him to see and know more of him.

Hawthorne's son was to undergo the autumn examinations for admission to the class of '67 this year; and his father felt more interest in the matter than he, at the time, permitted to appear. He was not ambitious of high rank in scholarship for the boy,--and this was well, for the boy was never out of arm's reach of the bottom of the class,--but he ascribed great importance to the general and incidental instruction that college life brings, and to its social aspects. When Julian left home to meet his trial at Cambridge, his father shook hands with him, and said, smiling, "Mind you get in; but I don't expect you will!" The saving clause was, of course, to soften my own mortification in the event of failure. Happily, I succeeded after a fashion; but only afterwards learned that he would have been much cast down had my fate been different. I remember the happy expression with which he greeted the new-fledged collegian's return home.

In September Hawthorne made a short visit to the seaside with Una; and I find a letter to the latter from her mother:--

SEPTEMBER 10, 1863.

MY DARLING UNA,--. . . I hoped to hear about papa's visit to Rockport, and "all sorts," as dear Mrs. Browning used to say. But I know it is very difficult to write when a guest. When I was writing in that gay sort of way, yesterday, I was very ill myself; and determined you should not know it. I bad a most terrific cold, and coughed my very worst, so that I thought all my blood-vessels would literally burst. I was really alarmed. I even coughed all night, which generally I do not. Oh, I was so thankful that Papa could not hear me I was all praise just for that. When Rose had gone to school, I coughed in real peace, because nobody was hurt. Yesterday morning I lamented over the rain for you, but by driving-time it was all clear and lovely, much to my joy. Last evening Aunt E. P. P. and Miss Eliza Clapp came. You know that I like Miss Clapp very much indeed, and I was therefore glad to see her. Aunt Lizzie looked infinitely delightful, just like a mighty Peace and Union. Rose looked angelic in white muslin, with low neck and short sleeves, and blue sash, and blue bows on her shoulders. She had a sort of pearl~and-rose look that was exquisite. Miss Clapp talked very enchantingly, and I consider her a rare and remarkable person.

--During the winter Hawthorne's state became, for the first time, somewhat alarming. A chief difficulty about him was, that he was extremely reluctant to be thought ill, and to receive the care which illness requires. He wished to do everything for himself. Mrs. Hawthorne, of course, was his nurse, and her tact and discretion achieved what nothing else could have accomplished ; she contrived, too, to maintain her cheerfulness in his presence, but her heart was full. In her letters to her daughter, also, she assumes a hopeful tone, in order that Una might not be deprived of the pleasure of her holidays by home anxieties; but the anguish cannot be entirely hidden. I will close the present chapter with two extracts referring to this period:--

CONCORD, Dec. 17, 1863.

MY DEAREST UNA,--I have a moment to write before Rose goes to the mail. Papa grew better towards last evening, so that he read in one of his huge books of the English State Trials. He had been lying down on the couch and sitting up alternately all day; and at noon he wrapped up and walked out for ten minutes. He slept quietly all night, and went up to bathe feeling quite well. When he came down, after a long time, he looked very ill, and said he had felt very sick in the too hot room; and, as far as I could understand. he had been faint. He is better now, and asleep on the couch. Rose is admirable. . . . My darling, I meant to write you a long letter, but no time is left. I love you with an infinite love, Enjoy yourself heartily; we are doing well here.

Your most loving MAMMA.

I am perfectly well.

DECEMBER 19.

DEAREST UNA,--Papa is comfortable to-day, but very thin and pale and weak. I give him oysters now. Hitherto he has had only toasted crackers and lamb and beef tea. I am very impatient that he should see Dr. Vandersende, but he wants to go to him himself; and he cannot go till it be good weather. How forever I shall bless the old German doctor if he can give papa again the zest of life he used to have! It is long since he had it,-- four or five years, I think. I am amazed that such a fortress as his digestion should give way. But his brain has been battering it for a long time,--his brain and his heart. The splendor and pride of strength in him have succumbed; hut they can be restored, I am sure. Meantime he is very nervous and delicate; he cannot bear anything, and he must he handled like the airiest Venetian glass. . . . The earth is gorgeous now with diamonds. Every twig and blade are incrusted with crystal, and the sun makes a glory that must be seen to be known. But our trees are sadly broken by such a weight of icy splendor. I love you with a mighty love, my darling.

Your own MAMMA.

CHAPTER 10 - CONCLUSION

IT is not probable that Hawthorne deceived himself as to the gravity of his condition; and when the New Year of 1864 came, he must have felt that it was his last year in this world. He did not, however, give way to despair, or even to dejection. On the contrary, there was a more than usual cheerfulness in his manner. The vein of arch playfulness, never long out of sight in him, appeared now with a touching and beautiful quality superadded; he seemed to admit his feebleness and physical decay, and to make a gentle sport of it. He bowed to the inevitable, not with a groan but with a smile. His face was pale and wasted, so that his great eyes, with their dark overhanging brows, looked like caverns with a gleam of blue in them; his figure had become much attenuated, and his once firm and strong stride was slow and uncertain. But his mind was awake, composed, and clear; and whenever he spoke,--in a voice that had now become very low,--it was to utter some pleasant and gracious thing. He professed to take a hopeful view of everything, and perhaps succeeded in concealing the extent of his illness from every one except his wife. I remember reading to him, some time during this winter, a passage from Longfellow's "Evangeline,"--where she, after long wandering, at last finds her lover on his death-bed, and holds him in her arms while his spirit passes. My father listened silently and intently; and, as I read the last verses, a feeling came upon me that there was something in the occasion more memorable than I had thought of, so that I could hardly conclude without a faltering of the voice. That was my fore-glimpse of the truth; but afterwards I persuaded myself that he must, after all, be well again.

In January, 1864, Una wrote to Hawthorne's sister that he seemed very unwell, and received the following in reply:--

MY DEAR UNA,--I was very glad to see your handwriting again; I was beginning to be a little anxious, because you said that your papa was not particularly well; and now, in your last letter, you say that General Pierce had heard of it, and came to see for himself. I want to know as much as General Pierce does, and you must tell me if he is seriously indisposed. But I infer that it is no more than a cold, and perhaps the influence of the weather, which has been unusually gloomy this winter. And there is no society in Concord that suits him. I enjoy winter more now than when young, because never could imagine the pleasure of skating, and sliding down hill, and amusing myself in the way other children did; and all I want is to sit quietly and read. If I am disposed to talk, it must be to myself,--to whom I do sometimes talk; indeed, it has become so much a habit with me, that when I go to meeting, in Salem, I am afraid to forget for an instant where I am, lest I should speak out loud. Think how terrible it would he if I did. So you see I am deprived of the benefit of my own meditations, and even of my own being, in such a situation. Fortunately it does not often happen that I am obliged so to stultify myself. My last visit to Salem was not very long. I came home Christmas day, bringing a cold with me, imbibed in that close atmosphere. I have been reading Bayard Taylor's "Hannah Thurston," and could not help saying, "Friend, how camest thou in hither, not having on a wedding garment?" The characters are people gathered from the highways and hedges of the outer world, but in no way fit for fiction; indeed, there is no atmosphere of fiction in the book, which is as dreary as actual life.

E. M. H.

In March it was decided that Hawthorne should make another journey southward with his faithful friend and publisher, W. D. Ticknor. The limits of the trip were not defined; they were to move or to pause, as the humor and occasion suited. Miss Hawthorne was apprised of this plan, and wrote in reply:--

". . . I feel very badly about your father being unwell, especially because his health has been so uniformly good. I am afraid I am hard-hearted towards confirmed invalids, but for a well person to become ill is a pity. I wish he could be prevailed upon to wear more clothes, an abundance of which are necessary to comfort in this climate. We hardly feel the changes if we are dressed warmly; but cold benumbs all the vital powers, and the stomach especially suffers. But perhaps he has not eaten animal food enough; he ate none when I was in Concord. You know the stomach needs to be exercised, else it will lose its vigor. I think people should habitually eat a good deal, and that a variety of food is good. He never had a great appetite, and perhaps now it needs to be tempted with delicacies. He ought to eat fruit, which is always wholesome. I am glad he is going away for a little while. When he went with Mr. Ticknor to Washington a year or two ago, I believe he enjoyed his journey and was benefited by it; and not only he, but the public, for then he wrote the best article that has ever appeared in the Atlantic Monthly,--'Chiefly about War Matters.' It is amusing to see how little time seems to mollify the wrath of the English, who continue to quote his description of the fat dowager, and would make a war matter of that, I think, if they dared. I have read 'The Marble Faun' again, lately, with even more interest than at first. . ."

--On the 27th or 28th of March Hawthorne went to Boston, and while there saw Dr. O. W. Holmes, who was to endeavor, without Hawthorne's suspecting it, to get an idea of his condition. His opinion, as reported afterwards, was unfavorable. He was startled at the change in Hawthorne's appearance, who seemed to him to be suffering from a gradual wasting or consumption of the bodily organs. There was not much to be hoped from the pharmacopoeia; a journey, with change of scene, and a succession of minor incidents, sufficient to keep the spirits awake, was about as good a prescription as could be made. And it was not thought at this time that all hope need be abandoned. Hawthorne was a man so peculiarly constituted--his mind and his body were so finely interwoven, as it were as almost to make it seem that he might live if he would firmly resolve to do so. But it is characteristic of a high organization not to cling strongly to life,--at any rate, to life under mortal conditions. The spirit uses the body, and uses it thoroughly, but never comes to look upon it as other than a hindrance to the full realization of its aims. Hawthorne could not "resolve to live" in this world, because he inevitably desired, and felt the need of, the greater scope and freedom of a life emancipated from material conditions. Nevertheless, for the sake of those he loved, and who loved him, he was willing to co-operate in whatever measures they saw fit to adopt for the improvement of his condition. He would have preferred, perhaps, to await the end quietly; but be would not let his friends have the pain of supposing, after he was dead, that any thing had been left undone that they could do. So he started on his journey with Ticknor, determined that it should not be his fault if it did not do him all the good that was anticipated from it. Mr. Ticknor was an admirable companion for such an emergency,--active, cheerful, careful and sagacious, and full of affectionate regard for his charge. Whatever a man can do for his friend, he was ready and eager to do for Hawthorne.

They left Boston on the evening of the 28th, and arrived the next morning in New York. They put up at the Astor House, and remained there nearly a week, being imprisoned most of the time by rainy and inclement weather. Ticknor wrote repeatedly to Mrs. Hawthorne, describing Hawthorne's condition from day to day, and noting a slight but steady improvement. I subjoin these bulletins, the last of which was dated at Philadelphia,--the limit which destiny put to their travels together.

ASTOR HOUSE, NEW YORK, March 30, 1864.

MY DEAR MRS. HAWTHORNE,--I regret that I am too late for the afternoon mail, but that can't be helped now. A worse than a northeaster has prevailed here to-day. I have hardly been out of the house; Mr. Hawthorne not at all. But we have been very comfortable within. He needed the rest, and the storm seemed to say that both he and I must be content, and we have not complained. I do not think that Mr. Hawthorne suffered any inconvenience from the journey, but, on the contrary, I think he is better to-day than when we started. He is looking better, and says he feels very well. It will take a few days to see what effect this change will have upon him; but I can't but hope that it will prove the right medicine. I shall remain here two or three days, and perhaps more. The storm has prevented my doing what I intended to-day, and of course I cannot at once decide what shall be best to do. I can only say that I hope the trip may accomplish what we all desire; and I have great faith. I will keep you advised.

Sincerely yours,
W. D. TICKNOR.

MARCH 31, 1864.

DEAR MRS. HAWTHORNE,--The storm of yesterday continues, but not as violent. Mr. Hawthorne is improving, I trust The weather makes everything very gloomy; notwithstanding, we took a short walk this morning. I hope the sun will appear to-morrow, so that we may see something of New York. Mr. Hawthorne left me, saying that he proposed to sleep an hour before dinner. He seems afraid that he shall eat too much, as he says his appetite is good. I assure him he is very prudent, and there is no fear of his eating too much. He slept well last night, and is evidently gaining strength. But it will take time to restore him.

Truly yours,
W. D. T.

P. S. Mr. Hawthorne said this morning that he thought he must write home to-day; but I hardly think he will do so.

ASTOR HOUSE, NEW YORK, April 3,1864.
12 o'clock, noon.

MY DEAR MRS. HAWTHORNE,--Your letter has just arrived. The mail was very late. I handed it to our "King," and he read it with interest and delight, and is now writing an answer. I assure you he is much improved, but he is yet very weak. The weather has been as bad as possible, and of course we have not been out much. I intended to have left New York yesterday, but I thought it not best to leave in a driving storm. We took quite a long walk this morning, and Mr. Hawthorne does not seem fatigued. I cannot now say where we go next, as I shall be governed by what shall seem best for him. We shall float along for a while. Probably to Philadelphia to-morrow. I will keep you posted, though at this time I do not feel like laying out any definite plan. I shall be much disappointed if our friend does not return in much better health than when he left Boston. We have been very quiet here, and this, I am satisfied, was the right thing at first. He slept well last night. I write this short note now, as you will have from him his own account.

Sincerely and truly yours,
W. D. TICKNOR.

ASTOR HOUSE, NEW YORK, April 4, 1864. 7 A. M.
MY DEAR MRS. HAWTHORNE,--I wrote you a short note yesterday upon the receipt of your letter. I have not much to add. The fact that we have a bright sun to greet us this morning is most cheering. Yesterday afternoon we went to Central Park, in spite of the weather. Mr. Hawthorne seemed to enjoy the drive, and was not much fatigued on our return. We had a good cheerful evening in his room. He retired as usual at nine, and I hope to find him bright this morning. He is gaining strength, but very slow]y. I think we may go to Philadelphia to-day, but am not certain. We could n't have had more unpleasant weather; but I tell him we will make it up by staying so much longer. Hearing from home did him much good. He reads the papers, moderately to be sure, but at first he declined entirely. His appetite is very good, but he eats very moderately. Perhaps it is as well, at present.

Sincerely yours,
W. D. TICKNOR.

PHILADELPHIA, April 7, 1864.
DEAR MRS. HAWTHORNE,--You will be glad to hear that our patient continues to improve. He wrote to you yesterday. He reads the papers, and sleeps well. The first real sunshine since we left Boston came upon us yesterday. On Tuesday it rained and blew furiously. Mr. Hawthorne did not go out; I only for an hour--by his permission; but was glad to return and keep within doors. It was too blue a day even to write. I hardly know how we got through the day. The bright sun of yesterday was a relief. We improved it. Made calls on some of the publishers, then on Mr. John Grigg, a retired *rich* bookseller. After dinner a gentleman called and invited us to drive. We had a pleasant drive to Fairmount, Girard College, etc. Mr. Hawthorne seemed somewhat fatigued. Retired before nine. This morning he is bright, and said at breakfast he was feeling much better. Now, I don't know exactly what next, but, if he is inclined, I shall go to Baltimore. But it is not best to lay out a business plan, or feel that so much must be done in a given time. I tell him we will float along and see what "turns up." One thing is certain, it has been altogether too stormy to try the sea.

Sincerely and truly yours,
W. D. TICKNOR.

--Matters were looking thus far favorable, when, without warning, the fair prospect was made dark by Ticknor's sudden death. Such a calamity would have been a poignant shock to Hawthorne at the best of times, but it smote the very roots of his life now. From the patient, assisted and guided in every movement, he was all at once compelled to become responsible and executive; to make and to carry out all arrangements, and this among strangers, and when weighed down not only by physical weakness, but by heavy grief for the loss of his friend. A more untoward event--one more fatal in its consequences upon him--could scarcely have occurred. He found strength to perform the duties that had devolved upon him, but it was the last strength he had. He telegraphed home the news, had the body prepared for transportation, and after its departure in charge of a son of Mr. Ticknor, who had come on for the purpose, he returned to Boston,--a melancholy and grievous journey. When, at last, he reached home, his wife was appalled at his aspect. He showed the traces of terrible agitation; his bodily substance seemed to have evaporated. He appeared to feel that there had been a ghastly mistake,--that he, and not Ticknor, should have died. There was pain in his glance, and heart-breaking recollections. He brooded over what had passed, and could not rouse himself. The image of death that he had witnessed would not be banished.

After Ticknor's funeral it speedily became evident that Hawthorne must not remain in Concord, or he would sink into the grave at once. Nothing, indeed, could have saved him now; but we could only feel that nothing must be left untried. Pierce immediately arranged with him for an excursion through Northern New England. No man was better fitted than Pierce to be of use to him. Of widely different natures, and of not less divergent tastes, pursuits, and experience, these two men had been life-long friends. They loved, understood, and believed in each other. They could afford each other, in the fullest sense, companionship; they could converse without words. The quiet, masculine charm of Pierce's manner, his knowledge of men and the world, his strength, and his tenderness were, moreover, precious qualities in such nursing as was needed now. There was no man with whom Hawthorne would more willingly have passed the last hours of his life; and perhaps it was for this reason that he consented to go with him. He must have known that the journey was to be his final one, and that the farewell to his wife was probably the last farewell of all. And though to say good-by to the beloved woman who for more than twenty years had been nearest and dearest to him of anything in the world, must have been the worst pang of death, he could bear it, in the conviction he felt that he was thereby saving her from the lingering anguish of seeing him fade out of existence before her eyes. It was better for her that the blow should be dealt suddenly; that she should not know he was going, but only that he had gone. He had always dreaded the slow parting scenes that precede death, and had often expressed the hope that he might die in his sleep, and unawares. And it was according to his wish that the end came to him.

A few days before he and Pierce set forth, I came up to Concord from Cambridge to make some request of him. I remained only an hour, having to take the afternoon train back to the college. He was sitting in the bedroom upstairs; my mother and my two sisters were there also. It was a pleasant morning in early May. I made my request (whatever it was), and, after listening to the ins and outs of the whole matter, he acceded to it. I had half anticipated refusal, and was the more gratified. I said good-by, and went to the door, where I stood a moment, looking back into the room. He was standing at the foot of the bed, leaning against it, and looking at me with a smile. He had on his old dark coat; his hair was almost wholly white, and he was very pale. But the expression of his face was full of beautiful kindness,--the gladness of having given his son a pleasure, and perhaps something more, that I did not then know of. His aspect at that moment, and the sun-shine in the little room, are vivid in my memory. I never saw my father again.

The friends started about the middle of May, and, travelling leisurely, reached Plymouth, New Hampshire, on the 18th of the month. There is a little memorandum book, in which are jotted down, in a small and almost illegible handwriting, a few words as to the results of each day's journey; but there is no entry after the 17th. They put up at the Pemigewasset House, and Hawthorne went to bed early. Pierce's room communicated with Hawthorne's; the door was open between, and once or twice during the night Pierce went in to see whether his friend were resting easily. Hawthorne breathed quietly, and lay in a natural position, on his right side. Some time after midnight Pierce, who had been disturbed by the persistent howling of a dog in the courtyard of the hotel, went to Hawthorne's bedside again. He still lay in precisely the same position as when he first fell asleep; but no breathing was now perceptible. Pierce quickly laid his hand on the sleeper's heart, and found that it had stopped beating.

By noon of that day the news of Hawthorne's death was known to his family and immediate friends. On the 20th I met General Pierce in Boston, and heard from him the details of the event. In the afternoon I took the train to Concord, and found my mother and sisters at the Wayside. The next day Hawthorne's body arrived. It was taken to the Unitarian Church, and the coffin was there decorated with flowers by Mrs. Hawthorne and her daughters. They showed that exalted kind of composure which is created by a grief too tender and profound for tears. But, indeed, he did not seem dead; we could only feel that a great change had come to pass, in the depths of which was a peace too sacred to be invaded by the common shows of mourning.

The funeral took place on the 23d, and was conducted by the Rev. James Freeman Clarke, who had performed Hawthorne's marriage service two-and-twenty years before. The church was filled with a great crowd of people, most of them personal strangers to us, though not to Hawthorne's name. It was a mild, sunny afternoon,--"The one bright day in the long week of rain," as Longfellow has said; and the cemetery at Sleepy Hollow was full of the fragrance and freshness of May. The grave was dug at the top of the little hill, beneath a group of tall pines, where Hawthorne and his wife had often sat in days gone by, and planned their pleasure-house. When the rites at the grave were over, the crowd moved away, and at last the carriage containing Mrs. Hawthorne followed. But at the gates of the cemetery stood, on either side of the path, Longfellow, Holmes, Whittier, Lowell, Pierce, Emerson, and half a dozen more; and as the carriage passed between them, they uncovered their honored heads in honor of Hawthorne's widow.

Miss Hawthorne had written as follows on receipt of the news of her brother's death:--

MY DEAR UNA,--Rebecca is going to write to you to tell you that I cannot come. I do not think you will be surprised. The shock was so terrible that I am too ill to make the necessary preparations. Happy are those who die, and can be at rest When I look forward, I can anticipate nothing but sorrow; few people are so completely left alone as I am,--all have gone before me. It is sad to hear, as we sometimes do, of whole families being swept away by disease; but it is far sadder to be the only survivor. I cannot tell you how much I feel for you all. I suppose you were no better prepared for what has happened than I am. I have been anxious all the week to hear about Dr. Holmes's opinion, but I hoped everything from travelling. Perhaps it would have been an effectual remedy if poor Mr. Ticknor's unfortunate death had not occurred. But now your father will never know old age and infirmity. I shall always think of him as I saw him in Concord, when he seemed to be in the prime of manhood. It is not desirable to live to be old. Dear Una, do let me know, as soon as you feel as if you could write, whatever there is to tell.

Your aunt,

E. M. HAWTHORNE.

--When the news reached England, Henry Bright wrote to Longfellow, asking particulars, and received this answer. The "lines" referred to are, of course, the well-known ones which Longfellow wrote soon after the funeral.

NAHANT, July 16, 1864.

MY DEAR MR. BRIGHT,--I have had the pleasure of receiving your very friendly letter, and make all haste to answer your affectionate inquiries about Hawthorne's illness. I first heard of it in the winter. He suddenly withdrew from the publisher the introductory chapter of the "The Dolliver Romance," saying he was too unwell to go on with it. Later, he came to town, much worn and wasted, and discouraged about himself. Soon after came his journey to Philadelphia with Mr. Ticknor, who suddenly died there, as you have read in the papers, doubtless; and then his last journey with General Pierce to the White Mountains, from which he came no more back. This you will find, more in detail, in the July number of the "Atlantic" magazine; and in the August number some lines by me on the funeral, which I will send you if I can get a copy in season.

Mrs. Hawthorne still remains in Concord, and people begin to find out what a loss they have suffered. I am glad to know how deeply you feel this loss; for I know, having heard it from his own lips, that he liked you more than any man in England. He always spoke of you with great warmth of friendship. I like very much your remarks in the "Examiner," and shall send them to Mrs. Hawthorne.

With kindest regards, yours truly,

H. W. LONGFELLOW.

--Mr. Bright himself wrote to me within the past year:--

"...Your father's death was a great shock to me. I had hoped that our friendship might continue for years to come. I have beautiful letters from your mother and Una, but they are too sacred to publish. I need hardly say with what a feeling of affection I always regarded your father. He was almost the *best* man I ever knew,--and quite the most interesting. Nothing annoys me more than the 'morbid' as applied to him,--he was the *least* morbid of men, with a singularly sweet temper, and a very far-reaching charity; he was reserved and (in a sense) a proud man, who did not care to be worried or bored by people he was not fond of. But he was, I am sure, a singularly happy man,--happy in all his domestic relations, happy in his own wonderful imaginative faculty, and in the fame which he had achieved. He was full of a quiet common-sense, which contrasted strangely with the weird nature of his 'genius.' He had a strong sense of fun, too, and it was delightful when anything called out the low chuckle of his laughter. And then again I always felt with your father as Lord Carlisle once said he felt with Dr. Channing,--'that you were in a presence in which nothing that was impure, base, or selfish could breathe at ease.'

"Justice has never yet been done to your mother. Of course she was overshadowed by *him*,--but she was a singularly accomplished woman, with a great gift of expression, and a most sympathetic nature; she was, too, an artist of no mean quality. Her 'Notes in England and Italy' contain much that is valuable, and much that is beautifully written. Dear Una, too, you will no doubt speak of her. Her memory must ever he very dear to all who knew her.

"You will (but you will know all this) find various allusions to my friendship with your father in various of his writings,--in the first chapter of ' Our Old Home,' twice within the last pages of the 'French and Italian Note-Books,' and often in the 'English Note-Books.' Here there may be some confusion: another Mr. B. (Mr. Bennoch, I think), also a third Mr. B. (Mr. Barber of Poulton), also a fourth Mr. B. (of the American Chamber of Commerce), are there mentioned. . ."

--The present writer does not feel disposed to make a final summing-up of his subject's character, such as customarily closes a biography; but will append here a passage from a letter of Mrs. Hawthorne, which contains all that the occasion calls for. It was written soon after Hawthorne's death.

". . . Everything noble, beautiful, and generous in his action Mr. Hawthorne hid from himself, even more cunningly than he hid himself from others. He positively never contemplated the best thing he could do as in the slightest degree a personal matter; but somehow as a small concordance with God's order,--a matter of course. It was almost impossible to utter to him a word of commendation. He made praise show absurd and out of place, and the praiser a mean blunderer; so perfectly did everything take its true place before him. The flame of his eyes consumed compliment, cant, sham, and falsehood, while the most wretched sinners--so many of whom came to confess to him--met in his glance a pity and sympathy so infinite, that they ceased to be afraid oo God, and began to return to Him. In his eyes, as Tennyson sings, 'God and Nature met in Light.' So that he could hardly be quarrelled with for veiling himself from others, since he veiled himself from himself. His own soul was behind the wings of the cherubim,--sacred, like all souls which have not been desecrated by the world. I never dared to gaze at him, even I, unless his lids were down. It seemed an invasion into a holy place. To the last, he was in a measure to me a divine mystery; for he was so to himself. I have an eternity, thank God, in which to know him more and more, or I should die in despair. Even now I progress in knowledge of him, for he informs me constantly."

--Hawthorne's family remained at the Wayside until the autumn of 1868, when it was decided to go to Germany. We went first to New York, and after a week's stay there, sailed on a Bremen steamer on the 20th of October. We remained in Dresden until the summer of 1869, when I went back to America for a visit, leaving my mother and sisters in Dresden, whither I purposed to return again before winter. Circumstances, however, prevented this; and soon after, the outbreak of the Franco-German war constrained Mrs. Hawthorne to take her daughters to London. Here they dwelt, amid a circle of pleasant friends, for two years.

Before leaving America Mrs. Hawthorne had suffered from a severe attack of typhoid pneumonia, which came near proving fatal; and during the winter of 1870-71, in London, she had a return of the disease, and this time she did not recover. Her daughter Una, who tended her throughout, has left an account of this last illness, which may be quoted here:--

"On Saturday, the 11th of February, Mr. Channing was to lecture at the Royal Institution rooms, and mamma and I agreed to meet there at the appointed time. It proved to be the last thing I ever did with her. I arrived first. She was quite late, but at last I saw the darling little black figure at the door, her face looking very pale and tired; but it lighted up when she saw me, and she said, 'Oh, there you are, my darling! I have been waiting for you downstairs.' The lecture was somewhat of a disappointment to us, and the next day mamma felt very tired. But she had an invitation to take tea with Mr. and Mrs. Tom Hughes, and looked forward to it with so much pleasure that she made an effort to go. She came downstairs looking lovely, as she always did when dressed to go out, with delicate black lace on her white hair, and fastened under her chin, and a jet coronet; and she said, as always, 'Do you like my looks?' with her radiant, caressing smile. She came home very early, and could hardly wait to get upstairs before she exclaimed, 'Whom do you think I have seen? whom do you think?--Mr. Browning!' Then she gave us a glowing account of how delightedly he came forward to meet her; how he said he had been most anxious to see her, and was only waiting to hear we were settled in order to call; and how charming her talk with him was altogether. He was the only other guest; and Mrs. Hughes made tea on the parlor hob, and called their pretty children down for mamma to see; and Mr. Hughes was beaming, and she felt so glad she had not stayed at home.

"On Monday she felt very weary again; but Mr. Channing was to lecture once more, and she said she felt she ought to go, because so few people went, and he must feel so discouraged; so she dragged herself there, and afterwards to call on Lady Amberly by appointment. The next day, Tuesday, a man came who was to finish hanging the pictures under mamma's directions, and do various other little jobs; and she wanted to oversee everything herself, and got dreadfully tired. As I was bidding her good-night, she said, 'I have a sort of defenceless feeling, as if I had no refuge.' It struck a chill to my heart; for they were the exact words she used the night before she was stricken with her dreadful illness in America. She did not, and indeed hardly could, look more pale and tired than she had often done during the last month or more; but she would never spare herself, and was always going beyond her strength, and I had been feeling very anxious about her, without seeing any possible way to make a change.

"The next morning when Louisa, the servant, brought my warm water, she said, 'I think your mamma seems very poorly, Miss.' It seems she had had nausea during the night, and when I went down she was looking wretchedly,--very feverish, lying with closed eyes, and other symptoms I knew too well. I wrote at once to the doctor; but then, fearing the note would be delayed, I sent Louisa in a cab with another note, and the doctor came. This was Wednesday, February 15, and during the following week she constantly spit blood. The nausea was almost unabated, and she had severe headache and much fever. The left lung was congested until the last three or four days, when it began to clear, and pleurisy came on. The tongue and lips were parched, so that speech was difficult, and her words hard to catch, and her breathing was very short and hard, and terribly fatiguing; so that she often said, 'Oh, if I could rest from this a little while!' I made my bed on the couch every night, but there was little to do except to give her medicine every hour. Her continued sickness made her loathe food, and she would take only a little milk and water. At first the doctor was not anxious about her; and having inquired particularly about her former illness, and learned that it was worse, he said he could feel no doubt of her getting well. But when her strength decreased day by day, I saw that his anxiety was growing; and I, seeing how a few days had brought mamma where it took several weeks to bring her before, began to feel most terribly anxious indeed. She was very unwilling to yield to her weakness, and at first she would say, 'Now you can go to sleep, dear, and put the watch near me, and the medicine to take.' But she made no rejoinder when I would not consent.

"One day I had left Rose with her for a little while, and when I came back was utterly astonished to see her sitting up almost straight; and then I first realized how ill she looked. She said she wanted to ease her head. Of course she soon sank back, for she would not let me hold her, having a strange dislike of being touched in this illness. She wandered slightly, though she always answered a question clearly; but she would sometimes think she was in the rush and noise of Piccadilly, or doing some wearisome and difficult thing. At other times the spheres of people she knew would seem to haunt her. Once she said, speaking of a friend of ours in Dresden,--Edward Hosmer,--'I think he was a good, true man,--kind-hearted.'

"A letter came from her old Boston friend, Mrs. Augustus Hemmenway, which gave her much pleasure, though she was only able to hear from me the chief news in it. Then one came from Fanny Cammann, with a photograph of herself. Mamma was very anxious to see the photograph, and I gave it to her with a large magnifying-glass, and she held them for a long time, opening her eyes to look every now and then. At last she dropped them, and said, 'I can't see much, but it is very handsome.' Another letter came from Annie Bright, enclosing some snowdrops, which I put in water and they opened out beautifully; and I held them up to mamma and told her about them, and she was much pleased.

"The least noise was most distressing to her, and we had the door-knocker taken off; and sent away every hand-organ in the vicinity. There was a persistent church-bell which rang a long time, twice a day, and annoyed mamma excessively. I sent several times to ask them to ring only a few minutes; but they made scarcely any change.

"She liked the doctor, and his visits were always a pleasure to her. The only time she opened her eyes with her own starry smile was at one of his visits; and another time she held out both her bands. 'My good, cold doctor!' she called him, for his bands were always cool, and she liked to have him put them on her head. He had a soothing influence upon her. He was much touched by her regard, and by her always inquiring after his wife and children.

The least start or emotion was so liable to make her cough, that I seldom ventured to talk to her; and it was a day or two after a long letter from Julian came, that I told her of it. She smiled brightly, but did not speak till a good while after. She then said, 'Julian.' So then I gave her a sketch of the letter, and told her about Julian's arrangements in New York, and of his love for her. She was very happy in his marriage.

"On Monday, the 20th, she was very ill, and I began to feel as if the responsibility and care were wearing out my strength; and yet I did not know which way to turn for just the help I needed, when Mrs. Bennoch's Ellen walked in, and said, if I would let her, she would be most glad to stay with me. I felt at once she was the only person I should be glad to have; mamma also was fond of her, and now needed all we could both do. Ellen had so many nice little ways, and was so tender. The next two days mamma seemed a little better; we could lift her from one side of the bed to the other, which was a great refreshment. It was sweet to me always to notice how conscious mamma was of my presence, through her closed eyes. She was glad to have Ellen relieve me, but she wanted me to be there just the same. Once Ellen and Louisa were lifting her and she said, 'What is Una doing?' 'Oh, I am moving the pillows, mamma.' And then she smiled.

"We had a rubber hot-water bottle which was a great comfort to her; but once, in the middle of the night, when we wanted it very much, the stopper would not unscrew. Ellen, Louisa, and I all tried in vain. At last, as I was sitting before the fire, hopelessly turning it, it suddenly came off. We did not know mamma was aware of what was going on; but when we put it in the bed, she said, 'Who got the stopper out at last?' 'I did, mamma.' And though she did not say anything, I knew she was glad I did it. I sent for an air-pillow, which was a great rest to her. She asked, 'Oh, who thought of this?' I told her that I did, and she said, 'Just like my darling. She always thinks of the best things. There is nobody like her in the world!' I told her how many people came to inquire after her, and how dearly everybody loved her; and the sweet, deprecating look showed faintly on her face again.

"On one of these two comparatively happy days, when mamma was looking a little brighter, Lady Hardy sent up a loving message to her, and a request that I might go for a half-hour's drive with her. Mamma was delighted to have me go, and I shall never forget how sweet Lady Hardy was. She took me in Kensington Gardens, by the water and it was one of those exquisite, prophetic days, when all spring seems in the sunny air and the returning birds; and she watched the freshening of my face, and my enjoyment of it, with a sympathy that went to my heart. And I did feel, for a little while, as if my fears might be lightened after all.

"But the shadow came down again when I entered that hushed room, and mamma looked so much more ill in contrast with the bright air and the singing birds. I had hitherto worn a black dress, which I thought mamma liked; and at night I was robed in a blue dressing-gown. To my surprise, mamma now said, 'I wish you would n't wear that old thing: why don't you wear the purple one I bought for you?' I said I would; and, thinking her dear eyes might enjoy brightness of color, I wore in the day time a purple merino, prettily made, and purple ribbons in my hair. The first time, I said, 'See, mamma, I have put on my nicest gown, and made myself look as pretty as I could.' It took several openings of her eyes to examine me all over, and then she said, 'Yes, that is very nice; you do look very pretty.' And I noticed the first time I came to her in the night, she looked to see if I had on the right dressing-gown.

"Until the 23d, I had always sent Ellen to bed about ten, having myself taken a sleep before; and I did the night nursing myself. But that night (Thursday) Ellen begged me to go regularly to bed in my own room; and mamma seemed quiet, and Ellen felt quite able to take care of her. So I went, rather unwillingly; but when I fairly got to bed, the first time for nine nights, I remember nothing more, until Ellen's voice roused me, to ask about a lotion; for she said mamma had a pain in her chest, and wanted it. If I had not been so heavy with sleep, I should have gone down at once; but I hardly knew where I was for a moment, and mechanically gave Ellen the direction. It seemed but a moment after that Ellen came again, and said, 'You must come, please, Miss Una. Your mamma thinks nobody else can do anything for her.'

"I was wide awake in a second, then, and flew downstairs in an agony to think I had ever consented to leave her; but, indeed, I could not have foreseen the dreadful pain in which I found her. I think I must understand something of the agony of love with which a mother would rush to her child, for our positions seemed reversed; and I saw that Ellen's unwillingness to wake me had made her try things herself, when what mamma really wanted was to have me.

"'Oh,' she said, 'Ellen is so kind; but she doesn't know what I wanted. I have such a terrible pain, it seems as if I could n't bear it; and I 'm sure the lotion will make it better.' It seems she had felt this pain beginning before I went upstairs, but had not said anything about it, because she thought nothing could be done for it. I put the lotion on her chest, but after a few moments she said it did not burn at all; and then, that her chest suddenly felt terribly cold. I heated some of the lotion almost boiling hot, and put it on again, and even laid the bottle of boiling water over it, without the slightest effect. The pain became so excruciating that every breath was a cry; and Ellen and I, after trying every conceivable thing, were at our wit's end indeed; and I was most seriously alarmed, for the pain was in an entirely new place, and the doctor had told me the congestion was clearing which had encouraged me very much. I think in this world I can never pass such awful hours again. Mamma, I am sure, thought she was dying, and once in a while she gasped, 'Oh, how long can this last! Oh, I cannot draw another breath!' And then every breath began to be a rattle in her throat, and tossed her about the bed; and I, knowing what her weakness really was, expected almost every moment would be the last. It was awful to think of her dying in such an agony; but I did pray from my heart that this might be the last time she would ever suffer so. And so the night wore away like weary years, and I hung over her broken-hearted, thinking, 'O Lord, how long, how long!' About six o'clock she became quiet, but hardly had strength to draw her breath; and I did nothing but listen for the doctor.

"The moment he saw her his face fell, and he said, 'Oh, what has happened!' and he was quite overcome for a moment. She smiled faintly as he took her hand, and said, 'Oh, such a bad night!' He stayed a long time, rubbing her chest with oil, soothing her head, giving her brandy, and ordering various comforting things. When I followed him out of the room, he said he was very much alarmed about her, the exhaustion was so complete, and the disease had taken a turn for which he was not in the least prepared; and he said he would come again very soon, with another physician. Then the cold certainty came over me that hope was really gone; and when the door closed on him I sat down in the dining-mom and shed a few bitter tears. Louisa came up to me, and, crying herself, said, 'Don't give way, Miss Una; while there's life there's hope.' I went back, quiet and cheerful again, and the hours seemed to pass very slowly till the doctors came.

"After talking together awhile they came into mamma's room, and our doctor said, bending over her, 'I have brought a friend of mine to see you, Mrs. Hawthorne.' She made a slight, consenting motion witli her head, and opened her eyes to look at the new face. It was a kind, careful face; and he was quite an elderly man. He examined and questioned her very closely, and I interpreted the faint answers that no one else could understand. At last he bent over her, and said gently, 'You are very, very ill; but I see cause for some encouragement, and, please God, I hope you will get well.' Again she moved her head, and said, 'Yes.' After a long talk in another room they called me, and I saw by Dr. Wyld's agitated face that he, at least. had little hope. The other doctor was spokesman, and told me that it was typhoid pneumonia, complicated with some other congestion; but still there were encouraging symptoms, if mamma could only rally from her excessive prostration; but this, he felt, was very doubtful. Still, I must not lose hope. If she could be kept from the least cough or disturbance, and with constant stimulants and nourishment, she might get through.

"When I went back, mamma asked me what they thought, and I said, 'They think you are dangerously ill, mamma, but you have so much vitality there is a hope still.' She said, 'I know the other doctor did not think I would live.' This I disclaimed, and talked to her cheerfully. She was very quiet all the afternoon, and who can tell how breathlessly Ellen and I watched her! And there was now the consolation of having little things to do for her constantly, and seeing her take nourishment in tiny quantities. She hated the taste of the brandy, and always made a face at it. When the doctor came in the evening, he stayed for several hours, going into her room two or three times to see how she got on. The last time, he said, 'Mrs. Hawthorne, I have now come to see how you feel, and to say good-night.' After he had gone, mamma said, 'I know the doctor thinks I am very ill.' 'Yes, mamma,' I said, 'he is very anxious, but we have great hope still.'

"Ellen would not consent to leave me, and after a while mamma noticed we were both there, and said, 'I don't see why you are both sitting up; I think one would do.' I said, 'Well, I am going to lie down by you now, mamma.' So I made Ellen lie down on the sofa, and placed myself on one side of mamma's broad bed, with the medicines and other things within my reach. And so the night passed peacefully; and on the next day (Saturday) I felt hope reviving again.

". . . In the course of the afternoon she said suddenly, 'Have you telegraphed to Julian?'--'Why, no, mamma, I never thought of it.' She said reproachfully, 'Oh, you should have telegraphed.' '--But you know, mamma, we hope you will get better.' I felt great sorrow that she should have thought of this, yet I could not but think it would have been a great mistake, and unnecessary pain to Julian.

"Mamma had been very fond of our kitten, which was a remarkably bright and pretty one, and used to come and lie on her bed, and cuddle up under her chin in the mornings. But the day she was taken ill kitty had disappeared, and we never saw her again. On this afternoon I happened to say, 'We have lost kitty, mamma;' and she said, 'Oh, I have wondered where she was, and why she did not come to see me. I know if she would lie on my chest it would make it warm.'

"It was near eleven o'clock that night, as Ellen and I were preparing to lie down, and were feeling quite cheerful, that mamma suddenly cried out, 'Send for the doctor!' I glanced at her face, on which there was a deathly change, and I flew downstairs to call Louisa. She ran out of her room, and seized my hands, sobbing, and exclaiming, 'Oh, Miss Una, I could not go to bed, for I knew you'd want to send!' In a moment she was gone, with orders to drive at utmost speed; and she was no sooner gone, than I remembered, with perfect misery, that I had directed her to the doctor's house, instead of to the place he told me. This occasioned some delay, though it was not more than an hour before he arrived. But poor mamma kept saying,

'Why does n't he come? Why does n't he come?.' She complained of most deathly faintness and sinking; 'Oh, I never felt anything like this before!' and she eagerly took brandy, and asked for ammonia to smell, and said, 'I know when these things are needed. I never needed them before.' She said, 'There was silence in heaven for the space of half an hour. I know now how long half an hour can be!' I had told Rose, and she sat on the stairs till after the doctor came, and then she came into mamma's room, and did not go out again. She had been hysterical and frightened, but now she was perfectly calm and sweet. I was kneeling by the bed, and holding up mamma in my arms, when the doctor came in; and there was no need of words between us. He gave stronger stimulants than I had dared to use,--even spoonfuls of ammonia, with scarcely any water; but with hardly perceptible effect. After that mamma said 'I pinned my faith on the ammonia; now I know nothing can be done.' Her breathing became very labored, and she said, 'Oh, can't you give me something to make me sleep?' Dr. Wyld took me aside, and said it could only be a question of a few hours, that there was absolutely no hope; but that if he gave her chloroform, it might hasten the end. It was very hard for me to say yes; but suddenly mamma said, 'Why do you wait? Can't you give me anything?' And I said, 'Yes, anything to give her a moment's ease.' So the chloroform was sent for; but even that only rendered her partially unconscious, and the deathlike rattle in her throat came all the time.

"Then I had the relief, for a little while, of passionate tears, down on the floor beside her, sobbing, and calling for Julian--Julian! It seemed as if I could not bear to have him away. And yet almost at once the revulsion came, 'Oh, I am so glad this agony is spared him! He could be of no use to her.' But oh, how I longed for him, to feel I had some one to do more than I! There was the bitter sense that mamma would never need my self-control or tender care again.

"Then I went out and sat by the doctor, and he told me that he did not think anything could have been done to save her, and, at the best, it could have been but for a very little while. She was too delicate, and unable to bear the slightest shock. Otherwise, she would not have failed so rapidly, for the actual conplaint she began with was not sufficient to account for it.

"After a while the doctor went home to sleep; Rose and Ellen also lay down. I never expected to hear mamma's voice again, and it was as if she spoke after death, when she suddenly exclaimed that she wanted more air. Again the agony of losing her woke up fully in my heart, and also a wild hope that, if she could rally so wonderfully, she might get over it after alL We kindled the fire up brightly, and then opened the window wide, and the cold air from the starless night rushed in. We raised mamma upon pillows. She said she hoped Rose had gone to bed, and told Ellen to lie down; and then she said, 'Una, come here!' I got on the outside of the bed, and crept close up behind her, as she lay on her side; and so the rest of the night passed in a sort of dream, that was not rest nor sleep, but more a conscious holding of one's breath to hear the end.

"When the gray dawn came, she said she was very cold. We heated flannel and bottles, and put cotton wool all about her face and neck. The upper part of her face looked already exquisite in its pale peace; but there was an expression of intense pain and laboring for breath about her mouth. She frequently opened her eyes partially, and seemed to take a yearning, fading look, that became more and more dim. We offered some nourishment, but she shook her' head. 'No--no more--that is past!' And then I knew it was only a question of how long her unaided strength would flicker to the end. She had been very sensitive to touch throughout the illness; but now I sat down close by the bed, where she could see me whenever she opened her eyes, and laid my hand close beside hers. In a few moments she grasped it, and held it with so tight a grasp, that, for hours after her death, I felt as if her hand were still in mine. Then I knew I was beginning the last precious office I could do for her on earth,--to make her conscious of my love and strength while she trod with her own sweet patience through the valley of the shadow of death.

"With my other hand I fanned her all the time with a slow, regular motion, hour after hour, hoping--praying that my strength might last while she lived. When her eyes were closed, the tears would pour over my face, and Ellen or Rose would wipe them away. They wanted me to let them take my place, but, if I had known I should die, I would not have left it. I felt as if my hand spoke to her all the words of cheer and comfort that I could not say, and to which doubtless she could not have listened. I was not sure she could see me, but whenever her eyes were partly open, I could smile brightly at her; and I answered a good many things that I knew she might be thinking about, if she could think at all, as I do not doubt she did. Once she said, very slowly, 'I am tired--too tired--I am--glad to go--I only--wanted to live--for you--and Rose.' Another time she said, 'Flowers--flowers--,' and I told them to bring an exquisite white hyacinth; and she smiled. Rose had brought in a little yellow crocus, early in the morning, the first that had come up; and I told her about it, and it was laid on the bed beside her. The sweet church-bells sounded, and the sun shone brightly. 'It is Sunday morning, mamma, and a very lovely day.' Towards noon, I saw that the little crocus had opened wide upon the quilt,--a perfect sun. Presently Mrs. Bennoch came in, and knelt down at the head of the bed. The doctor came in, and mamma seemed to know it, and, with a great effort, stretched out her other hand, and he knelt down, and hid his face upon it. I rose up, still holding her precious hand, and Rose came and stood behind me. Some one at the foot of the bed was sobbing; but I did not want to cry, then. I did not look at her face any more when I heard the last struggle for breath, but held her hand tighter. Then a breathless stillness and silence. I laid her hand gently down, still without looking, and Rose and I went upstairs together....

"The next day we drove out and got flowers, the whitest and most fragrant, and put them around her on the bed, and they were kept there, fresh and fragrant, until the next Friday; and we would come in, from the sad business we were obliged to attend to, and gather peace and strength. Her face looked more and more like an angel's; a delicate color stayed upon the cheeks, a lovely smile upon the slightly parted lips; her beautiful white hair was brushed a little back from her face, under a pretty cap, and her waxen hands lay softly folded against each other upon her breast; the last day we took off her wedding ring and I wore it. The Friday was my birthday, and I sat beside her a long time, and her presence seemed to bless me, as she had always done upon my birth-day.

"On Saturday we followed her to Kensal Green, and she was laid there on a sunny hillside looking towards the east. We had a head and foot stone of white marble, with a place for flowers between, and Rose and I planted some ivy there that I had brought from America, and a periwinkle from papa's grave. The inscription is,--*Sophia, wife of Nathaniel Hawthorne;* and on the foot-stone, 'I am the Resurrection and the Life.'"

--Sophia Hawthorne had been loved by every one who knew her. She had given happiness and emancipation to one of the foremost men of his time. Apart from her blessed influence, he could never have become the man he was. Greater humility, tenderness, enlightenment, and strength have not been combined in a woman. She lived for her husband; and when he died, her love of life died also; but her children remained, and she stayed in this world for their sake. Their love and support was the very breath of her existence had these failed, or had she felt that they no longer needed her, she would have vanished at once. Her every act and thought had reference to them; it was almost appalling to be the object of such limitless devotion and affection.

During these closing years of her life she had occupied much of her time in transcribing her husband's journals for publication. This work was a great pleasure to her, for much of the material she had never till then read, and much of it recalled scenes and events in which they had participated; so that it seemed as if they were still conversing together. Indeed, from a short time after his departure until the hour came for her to rejoin him, she always had a feeling that he was near her,--that their separation was of the senses only, not spiritual. After the journals were published, she turned to the posthumous novels and had begun the transcription of "Grimshawe" when her earthly career ceased. Afterwards, her daughter Una, assisted by Robert Browning, deciphered the manuscript of "Septimius," and it was published in the "Atlantic Monthly," and then in book form in England and America. Meanwhile "Grimshawe" was lost sight of, and only came to light again recently.

The preceding transcript from Una's journal has a double interest,--in respect of its subject, and in respect of the light it throws upon the writer's character. The first-born child of Hawthorne and his wife was in every way worthy of her parents. Whatever they had hoped and prayed for was fulfilled in her character. Her short life was acquainted with more than enough of sadness; but no occasion for the manifestation of truth, charity, generosity, self-sacrifice ever found her wanting. After her mother's death she lived in London, and devoted herself for several years to the care of orphan and destitute children. Her great heart longed to love and benefit all poor and unhappy persons, and she brought succor and happiness to many. Her intellect was active and capacious, and at one period of her life took a radical turn, questioning and testing all things with a boldness and penetration, combined with a sound impartiality, rare in the feminine mind. But at length the lofty religious bias of her nature triumphed over all doubts, and she was confirmed in the Church of England. After leaving London, she lived for a time with her brother in Dresden; and then made a visit to her married sister in New York, where she became acquainted with Albert Webster, a young writer who bade fair to do great things for American literature. When I moved to London, she rejoined me there; and Webster wrote, offering her marriage. She accepted him. His health was delicate, and, in order to strengthen it, he started on a voyage to the Sandwich Islands. He died on the passage; and a friend wrote to Una, announcing the news. The letter came one afternoon, as we were all sitting in our little library. She began to read, but after a moment quickly turned over the page and glanced on the other side. "Ah--yes!" she said slowly, with a slight sigh. She made no complaint, nor gave way to any passion of grief; but she seemed to become spiritualized,--to relinquish the world along with her hopes of happiness in it. She made no change in her daily life and occupations.

She was a "district visitor" in the church, and she continued to make her regular rounds as usual. But before the end of the year her dark auburn hair had become gray, and her vital functions and organs were quite (as the physician afterwards told me) those of an old woman. In the summer of 1877 I went to Hastings with my family; but Una preferred to pay a visit to some friends of hers in a sort of Protestant convent at the little town of Clewer, near Windsor. We had no suspicion--nor, I think, had she--that her health was even precarious. But ten days after our parting I received a telegram from Clewer stating that Una was dangerously ill. Leaving Hastings immediately, I arrived at Clewer at midnight. The lady who met me at the railway-station said, "You are too late." We drove to the convent, and there, in the little cell-like room, on a narrow bed, she lay. She had died within an hour after the telegram was sent. We laid her in Kensal Green Cemetery, close beside her mother.

Hawthorne's nature was so large, vigorous, and in many respects unprecedented, and his objective activity was at the same time so disproportionately small, that it would be impossible to give his portrait relief and solidity without the aid of such reflections and partial reproductions of himself as were presented in those nearest and dearest to him. They serve to humanize and define what would else seem vague and obscure. He was a man who easily and indeed inevitably produced an impression upon the observer, but whom it was very difficult to know. Superficial men are readily described and understood; but men like Hawthorne can never he touched and dissected, because the essence of their character is never concretely manifested. They must be studied more in their effects than in themselves; and, at last, the true revelation will be made only to those who have in themselves somewhat of the same mystery they seek to fathom.

APPENDIX

SINCE the Biography was in print, the author has received from Mrs. Horace Mann the three following letters, written by Hawthorne to her husband at the time of his ejection from the Custom House. While they do not add anything of importance to our knowledge of the situation, they are interesting as defining his attitude in his own words, and as incidental evidence of the independence of his personal character,

SALEM, June 26, 1849.

MY DEAR SIR,--I have just received your note, in which you kindly offer me your interest towards reinstating me in the office of Surveyor.

I was perfectly in earnest in what I told Elizabeth, and should still be unwilling to have you enter into treaty with Mr. King, Mr. Upham, or other members of the local party, in my behalf. But, on returning here, I found a state of things rather different from what I expected; the general feeling being strongly in my favor, and a disposition to make a compromise, advantageous to me, on the part of some, at least, of those who had acted against me. The "Essex Register" of yesterday speaks of an intention to offer me some better office than that of which I have been deprived. Now I do not think that I can, preserving my self-respect, accept of any compromise. No otber office can be offered me, that will not have been made vacant by the removal of a Democrat; and even if there were such an office, still, as charges have been made against me, complete justice can be done only by placing me exactly where I was before. This also would be the easiest thing for the Administration to do, as they still hold my successor's commission suspended. A compromise might indeed be made, not with me, but with Captain Putnam, by giving him a place in this Custom House,--which would be of greater emolument than my office; and I have reason to believe that the Collector would accede to such an arrangement. Perhaps this idea might do something towards inducing Mr. Meredith to make the reinstatement.

I did not intend to involve you in this business, nor, indeed, have I desired any friend to take up my cause; but if, in view of the whole matter, you should see fit to do as Mr. Mills advises, I shall feel truly obliged. Of course, after consenting that you should use your influence in my behalf, I should feel myself bound to accept the reinstatement, if offered. I beg you to believe, also, that I would not allow you to say a word for me if I did not know that I have within my power a complete refutation of any charges of official misconduct that have been or may be brought against me.

Sophia and the children are well. The managers of the Lyceum desire to know if you will deliver two lectures for them, before the Session of Congress.

Very truly yours,

NATH. HAWTHORNE.

Hon. HORACE MANN, West Newton.

SALEM, July 2, 1849.

MY DEAR SIR,--I am inclined to think, from various suspicious indications that I have noticed or heard of, between the Whigs and one or two of my subordinate officers, that they are concocting, or have already concocted, a new set of charges against me. Would it not be a judicious measure for you to write to the Department, requesting a copy of these charges, that I may have an opportunity of answering them? There can be nothing (setting aside the most direct false testimony, if even that) which I shall not have it in my power either to explain, defend, or disprove. I had some idea of calling for these charges through the newspapers; but it would bring on a controversy which might be interminable, and could only, however clearly I should prove my innocence, make my reinstatement the more difficult; so that I judge it best to meet the charges in this way,--always provided that there are any. It grieves me to give you so much trouble; but you must recollect that it was your own voluntary kindness, and not my importunity, that involved you in it.

Very truly yours,
NATH. HAWTHORNE.

SALEM, Aug. 8, 1849.

MY DEAR SIR,--My case is so simple, and the necessary evidence comes from so few sources and is so direct in its application, that I think I cannot mistake my way through it; nor do I see how it can be prejudiced by my remaining quiet for the present. I will sketch it to you as briefly as possible.

Mr. Upham accuses me of suspending one or more Inspectors, for refusing to pay party-subscriptions, and avers that I sent them a letter of suspension by a messenger, whom he names, and that--I suppose after the payment of the subscriptions--I withdrew the suspension. I shall prove that a question was referred to me, as chief executive officer of the Custom House, from the Collector's office, as to what action should be taken on a letter from the Treasury Department requiring the dismissal of our temporary Inspectors. We had two officers in that position. They were Democrats, men with large families and no resources, and irreproachable as officers; and for these reasons I was unwilling that they should lose their situations. In order, therefore, to comply with the spirit of the Treasury order, without removing these two men, I projected a plan of suspending them from office during the inactive season of the year, but without removing them, and in such a manner that they might return to duty when the state of business should justify it I wrote an order (which I still hold in my possession) covering these objects, which, however, was not intended to be acted on immediately, but for previous consultation with the Deputy Collector and the head clerk. On consulting the latter gentleman, he was of opinion, for various reasons, which he cited, that the two Inspectors might be allowed to remain undisturbed until further orders from the Treasury, to which, as the responsibility was entirely with the Collector's department, I made no objection. And here, so far as I had any knowledge or concern, the matter ended.

But it is said that I notified the Inspectors of their suspension by a certain person, who is named. I have required an explanation of this person; and he at once avowed that, being aware of this contemplated movement, and being in friendly relations with these two men, he thought it his duty to inform them of it; but he most distinctly states that he did it without my authority or knowledge, and that he will testify to this effect whenever I shall call upon him so to do. I did not inquire what communication he had with the two Inspectors, or with either of them; for I look upon his evidence as clearing me, whatever may have passed between him and them. But my idea is (I may be mistaken, but it is founded on some observation of the manoeuvres of small politicians, and knowing the rigid discipline of Custom Houses as to party-subscriptions) that there really was an operation to squeeze an assessment out of the recusant Inspectors, under the terror of an impending removal or suspension; that one of the Inspectors turned traitor, and was impelled, by the threats and promises of Mr. Upham and his coadjutors, to bring his evidence to a pretty direct point on me; and that Mr. Upham, in his memorial to the Treasury Department, defined and completed the lie in such shape as I have given it above. But I do not see how it can stand, for a moment, against my defence.

The head clerk (the same Mr. Burchmore whose letter I transmitted to you) was turned out a week ago, and will gladly give his evidence at any moment, proving the grounds on which I acted. The other person, who is said to have acted as messenger, is still in office, as Weigher and Gauger, at a salary of fifteen hundred dollars per annum. He is a poor man, having been in office but two years, and expended all his income in paying debts for which he was an indorser; and he now wishes to get a few hundred dollars to carry him to California, or give him some other start in life. Still he will come forward if I call upon him, but of course would rather wait for his removal, which will doubtless take place before the session of Congress. Meantime I have no object to attain, worth purchasing at the sacrifice he must make. My Surveyorship is lost; and I have no expectation, nor any desire, of regaining it. My purpose is simply to make such a defence to the Senate as will insure the rejection of my successor, and thus satisfy the public that I was removed on false or insufficient grounds. Then, if Mr. Upham should give me occasion--or perhaps if he should not--I shall do my best to kill and scalp him in the public prints; and I think I shall succeed. . . .

[Here a dozen lines or so have been cut out by Mrs. Mann, to satisfy the rapacity of some autograph-fiend, who, should this meet his eye, is requested to forward a copy of the passage to the publishers.]

I mean soon to comply with your kind invitation to come and see you, not on the above business, but because I think of writing a school-book, or, at any rate, a book for the young,--and should highly prize your advice as to what is wanted, and how it should be achieved. I mean as soon as possible--that is to say, as soon as I can find a cheap, pleasant, and healthy residence--to remove into the country, and bid farewell forever to this abominable city; for, now that my mother is gone, I have no longer anything to keep me here.--Sophia and the children are pretty well. With my best regards to Mrs. Mann, I am

Very truly yours,
NATH. HAWTHORNE.

P.S. Do pardon me for troubling you with this long letter; but I am glad to put you in possession of the facts, in case of accidents.

--The order of suspension above referred to (with the day of the month left blank) is given below.

NOTICE.

SURVEYOR'S OFFICE, SALEM, Nov. --, 1847.

The services of temporary officers being seldom required at this season of the year, Messrs. Millet and Laidsey will consider themselves relieved from duty, after the discharge of the vessels on which they may be at present engaged, unless when the permanent Inspectors are all employed.

NATH. HAWTHORNE, *Surveyor.*

www.ingramcontent.com/pod-product-compliance
Lightning Source LLC
Chambersburg PA
CBHW051412090426
42737CB00014B/2629